SIMON BALL studied at Braseno[...] College, Cambridge. He teaches hist[...]

For automatic updates on Simon Ball visit harperperennial.co.uk and register for AuthorTracker.

From the reviews of *The Guardsmen*:

'Scholarly, readable and perceptive ... [Ball's] shrewd and even-handed narrative combines the grand sweep with juicy morsels'
TLS

'This is a highly enjoyable book, chiefly because of the quality of its anecdotage. The drolleries of the ruling class transcend parody ... Its author shows himself to be a substantial writer'
MAX HASTINGS, *Sunday Telegraph*

'*The Guardsmen* is good reading because political warfare is at its centre, and Ball skilfully evokes that inter-war world ... [A] stylish book'
Daily Telegraph

'*The Guardsmen* is an accomplished work ... Simon Ball has command of his subject matter and demonstrates an assured touch with primary material that has not appeared in previous biographies and memoirs'
Literary Review

'Excellent ... Simon Ball illuminates [the story] with an enormous amount of new material gleaned from original sources ... [He] writes far better than most academic historians and he enriches his text with delightful anecdotes'
The Oldie

THE
GUARDSMEN

Harold Macmillan, Three Friends,
and the World They Made

SIMON BALL

HARPER PERENNIAL
London, New York, Toronto and Sydney

While every effort has been made to trace the owners of copyright material reproduced herein, the publishers would like to apologise for any omissions and will be pleased to incorporate missing acknowledgements in any future editions

Harper Perennial
An imprint of HarperCollins*Publishers*
77–85 Fulham Palace Road
Hammersmith
London w6 8jb

www.harperperennial.co.uk

This edition published by Harper Perennial 2005
1

First published by HarperCollins*Publishers* 2004

A catalogue record for this book
is available from the British Library

ISBN 0 00 653163 6

Set in PostScript Linotype Minion with Janson and Castellar display by
Rowland Phototypesetting Ltd, Bury St Edmunds, Suffolk

Printed and bound in Great Britain by
Clays Limited, St Ives plc

To Helen

CONTENTS

ILLUSTRATIONS

SOURCES AND ACKNOWLEDGEMENTS

Until recently, a book of this kind could not have been written. It is only in the past decade that the archival materials to make it possible have entered the public domain. We now have a critical mass of papers, produced by the four principals of this story, allowing us to understand their thoughts and actions in detail.

Harold Macmillan wrote prolifically on his own life. He also inspired a number of biographies, culminating in Alistair Horne's official two-volume life completed in 1989. Underlying both Macmillan's autobiography and Horne's biography were Macmillan's voluminous diaries. These diaries are now open for inspection at the Bodleian Library, Oxford. There are two versions of the diary: the original hand-written volumes and an edited and typed copy Macmillan subsequently had made up. Both versions are used in this book. Also in the Bodleian is a collection of letters Macmillan wrote to his friend Ava Waverley, which, in some cases, served as first drafts for his memoirs. The diaries are a magnificent historical source. Indeed they will, when published, endure as Macmillan's best and most important contribution to literature. They must nevertheless be treated with some caution. Macmillan did not keep a diary simply for his own amusement. His diaries were always meant to be read by others. In the first instance he wrote diary letters to his mother and later to his wife. These diaries were shown around the family and the Macmillan circle, including political acquaintances. By the time Macmillan started his continuous 'political diary' in 1951, he was a very self-aware recorder of events. The later diaries were kept with the sensibility of memoirist. Macmillan's explanation of events, and in particular of his own motivations, was thus both an immediate reaction and a footnote for the future. Such self-conscious writing loses nothing in value yet needs to be read for what it is –

self-justification rather than justification of the self. Horne's fine biography, which I have used extensively, can be criticized for taking Macmillan a little too much at his own valuation.

Potentially as important a part of the Macmillan collection at the Bodleian is his political correspondence. This book draws on the Stockton constituency correspondence written between 1924 and 1945. Much of this correspondence is ephemera. There are, however, letters which reflect on wider political events. Those letters dealing with the minutiae of politics are much less self-conscious than the diaries and have the value of immediacy. Of value for the same reason are the diaries of Cuthbert Headlam, which have been published in an expertly edited two-volume edition by Stuart Ball. Headlam's diary is a goldmine, for he not only knew Macmillan well, but also Crookshank and Lyttelton. In 1915 Headlam and Lyttelton served together as aides-de-camp to Lord Cavan. After the First World War Headlam entered Parliament at the same election as Macmillan and Crookshank in 1924. Headlam's seat, Barnard Castle, abutted Macmillan's in Stockton. They were political allies in the 1920s. Along with the constituency letters, Headlam's diary allows one to reconstruct Macmillan's early political trajectory from contemporary sources rather than relying solely on his own memoirs.

Oliver Lyttelton ranks second to Macmillan as a memoirist in volume of output. He published volumes of autobiography in 1962 and 1968. During the same period he was involved with the foundation of Churchill College, Cambridge, as a memorial to his leader and friend, Winston Churchill. He left his papers, and those of his mother and father, to the college as the Chandos Papers. The collection is thus particularly rich for Lyttelton's early life – to the point when he left the army in 1918. These early letters formed the basis for his own 1968 volume, *From Peace to War*. He published most of the letters he wrote to his mother during the First World War, lightly edited, in that volume. When Lyttelton decided to remain in public life after 1945, he started a collection of political papers. The papers relating to the intervening period are exiguous. This gap has had to be filled using papers from other sources. Most obviously, Lyttelton's official papers relating to his ministerial offices – President of the

Board of Trade, Minister Resident in Cairo, Minister of Production and colonial secretary – are to be found in the Public Record Office, Kew. In the inter-war years, however, Lyttelton was businessman rather than public servant. With the indispensable help of Mr Andrew Green, company secretary of the Amalgamated Metal Corporation, the company Lyttelton founded in 1929, I tracked down Lyttleton's business archive. Now part of AMC's non-current archive, the papers were housed in a storage warehouse in Docklands. As a result of Mr Green's kindness I was able to extract these papers and examine them. As Lyttelton became a prominent business leader in the 1930s, he starts to appear also in the official papers of the Board of Trade. There are also papers relating to Lyttelton's post-war business career in the archives of GEC, the company that took over Lyttelton's AEI in 1967.

In contrast to Lyttelton and Macmillan, Harry Crookshank published no memoirs and next to nothing has been written about his life. The only extended appreciation in print was published by Lyttelton in the *Dictionary of National Biography*. In fact Crookshank, like Macmillan, was a formidable diarist. By the time the Macmillan papers arrived at the Bodleian, the library had long since bought Crookshank's diaries, covering the years 1934 to 1961, at auction. These diaries have over the years been read by a small number of historians interested in the political events upon which they touch. They receive only passing references in most secondary literature. There is a very good reason for this. Unlike his closest friend, Macmillan, Crookshank was a true diarist. He kept his diaries for himself rather than for posterity. They are thus concerned largely with the mundane and the quotidian. If one wished to understand Lincolnshire weather patterns in the age of appeasement, Crookshank's diaries are the place to look. The diaries have thus proved a grave disappointment to political historians. This may be one of the reasons why so few have a good word for their author. They are even so a treasure trove of information for anyone interested in Harry Crookshank himself.

Indeed, Crookshank's concern for recording the events of his life went even further than his diaries. He, his mother and his sister maintained massive scrapbooks of cuttings regarding his life and career, starting with items pertaining to the Crookshank family going back into the nineteenth century. These books have found their way into Lincolnshire Record Office. The coverage of Crookshank's life in these two sources is fairly complete. A search of the archives of the Grenadier Guards, greatly assisted by the staff of Royal Headquarters, Wellington Barracks, then yielded a missing segment of the Crookshank diary. As well as the later political and personal diary, Crookshank kept a very full war diary covering his military service on the Western Front and in the Balkans between 1915 and 1917. In contravention to all regulations, he wrote up regular entries in his pocketbook when he was on active service. Whenever he returned to London he wrote out these pocketbook diaries, adding detail, into desk diaries. At some later stage, probably in the 1920s, he interpolated typed recollections into the desk diaries. Crookshank also wrote an account of his diplomatic career in long letters to his friend and fellow diplomat Paul Emrys-Evans, whose papers are held by the British Library.

At the start of this project it appeared that the most difficult of its subjects in archival terms would be Bobbety Cranborne – or Lord Salisbury, as he became in 1947. Papers related to his leadership and shadow leadership of the House of Lords between 1941 and 1957 are held by the House of Lords Record Office. The papers of his uncle and early mentor, Lord Cecil of Chelwood, were deposited in the British Library. Lord Salisbury was a prominent member of Anthony Eden's circle. His correspondence thus appears frequently in the papers of Anthony Eden himself, deposited by Lady Avon in the archives of Birmingham University Library. He carried on a regular correspondence with Jim Thomas, and Thomas, by then Lord Cilcennin, left his papers in Carmarthenshire Record Office. There was also a correspondence with Paul Emrys-Evans, who, having become an MP, had become a prominent Edenite backbencher. Emrys-Evans was also secretary of James, 4th Marquess of Salisbury's Watching Committee and Bobbety Cranborne's under-secretary at the Dominions Office. Their long association continued after the war. When Emrys-Evans lost his seat in 1945, he went into business,

rising to be chairman of Cecil Rhodes's chartered British South Africa
Company. The chartered company was much involved in the politics
of southern Africa in the late 1950s and Lord Salisbury joined its
board on his resignation from the Cabinet in 1957.

It was my great good fortune to use an even better source. Lord
Salisbury had left an extensive collection of political and other papers
in his archive at Hatfield, but these were not open to the public.
They had been reorganized by his former secretary in the early 1980s,
but were not formally catalogued. Through the good offices of the
Tudor historian Professor A. G. R. Smith and Hatfield House's librarian, Robin Harcourt Williams, the late Lord Salisbury was made
aware of my project. Not only did he grant me access to his father's
hitherto closed papers, but he also talked to me about his father and
his circle. Lord Salisbury's generosity was of immeasurable assistance.

In addition to those mentioned above, I have received assistance
from many other individuals and institutions. For their consent to
quote from papers to which they hold copyright, I wish to thank the
Amalgamated Metal Corporation plc, Lady Avon, the Carmarthenshire Archives Service, Lord Chandos, the Trustees of the Chatsworth
Settlement, the Grenadier Guards, Mrs Rachel Fraser, Lincolnshire
Archives, the Trustees of the Harold Macmillan Book Trust, Lord
Salisbury, the Master and Fellows of Trinity College, Cambridge, Sir
Charles Willink. If I have infringed upon the copyright of any persons or institutions I hope they will forgive the oversight and inform
me, so that the error may be corrected in any future edition of this
book.

The University of Glasgow gave me leave from my teaching duties
in order to research and write this book. That leave was extended
by a grant from the Arts and Humanities Research Board. The British
Academy awarded me a grant to defray the costs of travelling to
archives. All Souls College provided me with rooms in Oxford. The
John Robertson Bequest gave me a grant towards the cost of photo-
graphs from the Imperial War Museum. I am most grateful to the
trustees and administrators of these bodies for showing such confidence in my work when this book was little more than an idea. For
similar confidence on a more personal level I would like to thank Hew

Strachan, formerly Professor of Modern History at the University of Glasgow, and David Bates, formerly Edwards Professor of Medieval History at the University of Glasgow. Without their encouragement writing this book would have been a more difficult and less enjoyable task. The book would not have been written at all if Tony Morris had not suggested that it had commercial potential, if Robyn Airlie had not introduced me to the late Giles Gordon and if Giles had not been enthused enough to place me in the capable hands of Arabella Pike. I am extremely thankful to them all for their help, advice and support.

During the course of the research for this book I visited many archives and libraries around Britain. I was met with unfailing courtesy and helpfulness. Without these institutions historical research would be impossible; with them it is most pleasant. I would like to thank the staff of the Modern Papers Reading Room, Bodleian Library, Oxford; Rhodes House Library, Oxford; the British Library; the Public Record Office, Kew; the House of Lords Record Office; the Archives Centre, Churchill College, Cambridge; Carmarthen Record Office; Lincoln Record Office; Lincoln Cathedral; Royal Headquarters, Grenadier Guards, Wellington Barracks; the Imperial War Museum; Rio Tinto Zinc plc Archives, London; GEC-Marconi plc Archives, Chelmsford; AMC; Hatfield House; Chatsworth Archives; the National Library of Scotland, Edinburgh and the London Library.

I have benefited enormously from the help of a number of scholars of British history. I would like to thank, in particular, Dr Stuart Ball of the University of Leicester for discussing his work on Cuthbert Headlam and claryifying details of the Headlam-Lyttelton relationship, Dr Philip Murphy of the University of Reading for discussing his work on Lyttelton, Alan Lennox-Boyd and Sir Roy Welensky, Dr Nicholas Crowson of the University of Birmingham for sharing his ideas about the anti-appeasers; and Dr Ronald Hyam of Magdalene College, Cambridge for acting as my mentor in imperial history. Each took time away from their own scholarly research to guide me in fields in which they are expert and I was not. Professor David Reynolds of Christ's College, Cambridge, Dr Richard Aldous of University College, Dublin and Robin Harcourt

Williams, Librarian to the Marquess of Salisbury, undertook the lengthy task of reading my manuscript in full and providing a detailed commentary on what I had written. The improvements in style and content they introduced were many and various. I thank them for taking such care with my work. Since Richard Aldous and I have talked endlessly about our books since we were at Cambridge together, some of the work he was correcting was probably originally his in any case.

One of the chief joys of writing a book is sharing it with one's family. I count myself fortunate that my family are bibliophiles. My parents, Eric and Sheila, have encouraged me to write from an early age. My father read the manuscript of this book as he has those of my previous books. I have incorporated many of his suggestions and dropped those passages that did not meet paternal approval. My wife, Helen, has read every draft of this book as it left my pen. If I had listened to her advice more often I would have finished quicker and written better. I dedicate this book to her, with love.

PREFACE

Harold Macmillan, Oliver Lyttelton, Bobbety Cranborne and Harry Crookshank all arrived at Eton in 1906, all served in the Great War in the same battalion of the Grenadier Guards and all entered the Cabinet under Winston Churchill during the Second World War. They helped Churchill to seize back power from the socialists in 1951 and once more joined his Cabinet, now as senior figures. Macmillan rose to be prime minister in 1957. This quartet thus socialized with each other, argued with each other, fought together and climbed the political ladder together for over forty years. 'From the playing fields of Eton, to the horrors of the Western Front, to the pinnacle of political power,' was not the blurb of a Jeffrey Archer novel but the reality of these men's lives.

A friend of Crookshank and Cranborne's, Paul Emrys-Evans defined their generation as those, born between Queen Victoria's Golden Jubilee in 1888 and the turn of the century, who fought in the Great War. Subsequent studies have confirmed that this was indeed the group that bore the brunt of the front-line fighting and thus the heaviest casualties. Few Englishmen, on the other hand, have ever defined themselves solely as 'old soldiers'. In any subsequent career, including politics, individuals cooperated with those both older and younger than themselves. In political life they might well have been drawn to those with similar life experiences, but this attraction seldom provided the main explanation for political action. It is hard to understand later events without a knowledge of generations, but unwise to expect an understanding of relationships within a generation to explain everything. Bearing this in mind, the present work is only in part a collective biography of four contemporaries. It certainly tries to evoke what living and working cheek by jowl with the acquaintances of childhood and the friends of wartime was like for Conservative politicians in the 1920s, 1930s, 1940s and 1950s. This evocation, however, merely sets the scene for the action.

As much as a collective biography this book is a comparative biography. It is concerned with those moments when its subjects interacted with each other but also with those situations where their actions might be contrasted. From early childhood Macmillan, Lyttelton, Cranborne and Crookshank were brought up with the notion that they were in competition with their contemporaries for the glittering prizes, the marks of honour accorded to men in public life. Although they were each under pressure to surpass the achievements of earlier generations of their own families, the main competition had to be against their own cohort. To use a sporting simile, an athlete can only race on the same track with those who reach their peak at the same age as himself. These four men came to the starting-line at the same time, and thus their performances can legitimately be measured against one another. The theme of this book is a race, a competition, willingly entered into, for power and glory. It seeks to explain why some men fell by the wayside while others prospered. 'It's not a flat race, it's a steeplechase,' as Winston Churchill once told Harold Macmillan.

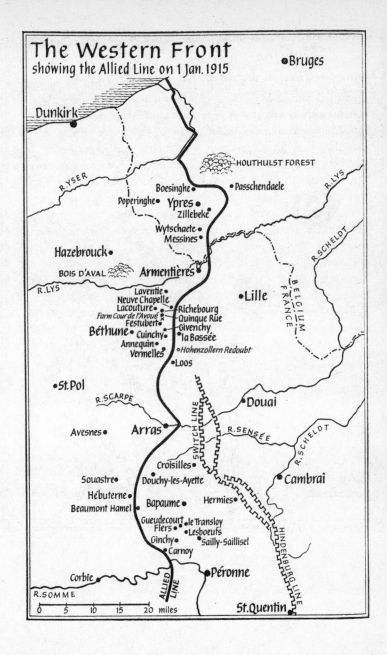

The Western Front
showing the Allied Line on 1 Jan. 1915

Bruges

Dunkirk

HOUTHULST FOREST

R. YSER

Boesinghe

Passchendaele

R. LYS

Poperinghe

Ypres

Zillebeke

Wytschaete

Messines

R. SCHELDT

Hazebrouck

BOIS D'AVAL

Armentières

R. LYS

Laventie

Neuve Chapelle

Lacouture

Richebourg

Lille

Farm Cour de l'Avoué

Quinque Rue

Festubert

Givenchy

Béthune

Cuinchy

la Bassée

Annequin

Vermelles

Hohenzollern Redoubt

Loos

B E L G I U M

F R A N C E

St. Pol

R. SCARPE

Douai

Avesnes

Arras

R. SENSÉE

SWITCH LINE

R. SCHELDT

Croisilles

Souastre

Douchy-les-Ayette

Cambrai

Hébuterne

Bapaume

Hermies

Beaumont Hamel

Gueudecourt

le Transloy

Flers

Lesboeufs

Ginchy

Sailly-Saillisel

Carnoy

Corbie

ALLIED LINE

Péronne

HINDENBURG LINE

R. SOMME

0   5   10   15   20 miles

St. Quentin

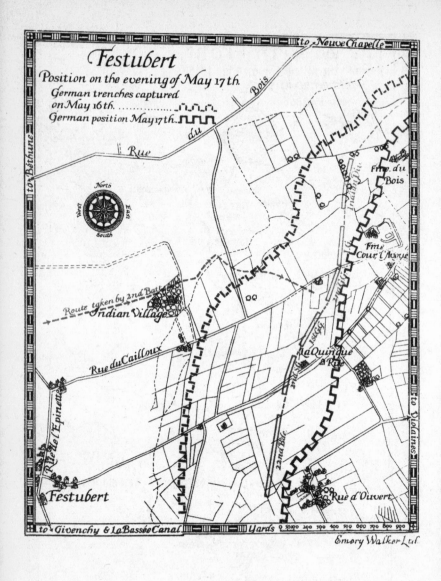

Festubert

Position on the evening of May 17th.
German trenches captured
on May 16th. ....
German position May 17th.

to Neuve Chapelle

Bois

du

Rue

to Béthune

North
East
West
South

Frie du
Bois

Infantry Ruc

Frie
Cour l'Avoué

Route taken by 2nd Batt

Indian Village

1st G.G.

Rue du Cailloux

La Quinque
à Rue

2nd B.G.

Rue de l'Epinette

2nd G.G.

to Violaines

22nd B.G.

Festubert

Rue d'Ouvert

to Givenchy & La Bassée Canal   Yards 0 50 100 200 300 400 500 600 700 800 900

Emery Walker Ltd.

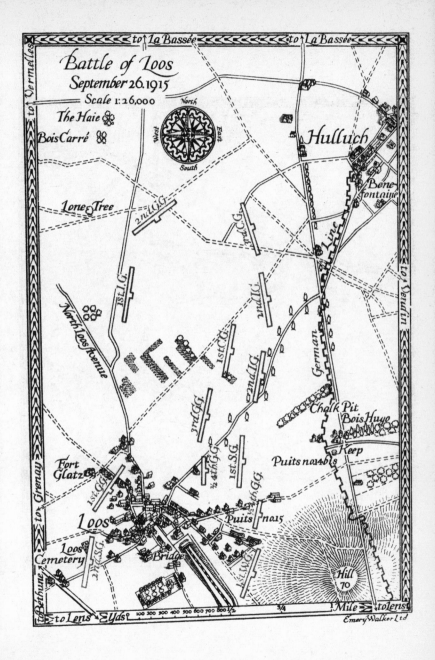

Battle of Loos
September 26.1915
Scale 1:26,000

The Haie
Bois Carré

to La Bassée
to La Bassée

to Vermelles

North
West East
South

Hulluch

Béne
fontaine

Lone Tree

2nd G.G.

3rd G.G.

1st I.G.

2nd I.G.

German Line

North Loos Avenue

1st G.G.

2nd I.G.

3rd G.G.

Chalk Pit
Bois Hugo

German

Keep

Puits no.14 bis

Fort
Glatz

1st G.G.

4th G.G.

1st S.G.

5th G.G.

Loos

Puits no.15

Loos
Cemetery

2nd G.S.G.

Bridge

1st W.G.

Hill
70

to Béthune
to Lens

to Lens

to Grenay

to Verdun

Yds. 100 200 300 400 500 600 700 800 1/2   3/4   1.Mile

Emery Walker Ltd

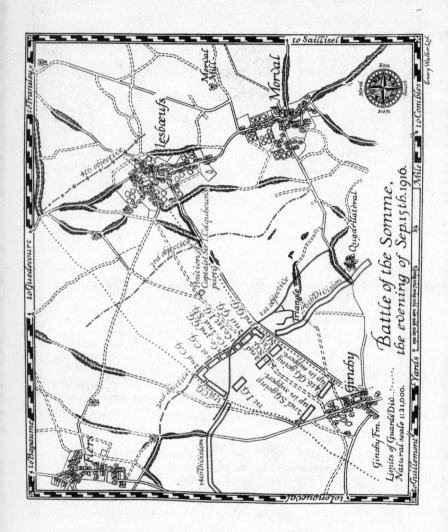

Battle of the Somme,
the evening of Sep.15th.1916.

Limits of Guards Div. ....
Natural scale 1:21.000.

Yards 100 0 100 200 300 400 500 600 700 800 900 1000 | 1⁄4 | 1⁄2 | 1 Mile

Emery Walker Ltd.

1

Sons

Harold Macmillan, Bobbety Cranborne, Oliver Lyttelton and Harry Crookshank were members of a remarkable group. The four were born within a year of one another, Bobbety Cranborne, Oliver Lyttelton and Harry Crookshank in 1893, Harold Macmillan, the youngest of the quartet, in February 1894. As Lyttelton himself wrote, 'Harold Macmillan went to Eton as a Scholar at the beginning of the school year of 1906. Strangely amongst his exact contemporaries at Eton were three boys, Cranborne, Crookshank and Lyttelton, all – like he – destined to be officers in the Grenadier Guards, all destined to survive ... and all to be members of Mr Churchill's governments in war and peace.'[1]

In the carefully cadenced world of Edwardian society, the four had started out not as a quartet but as two distinct pairs. Cranborne and Lyttelton were patricians, Macmillan and Crookshank 'new men'. Eton was the clasp, a link sought quite consciously by the Macmillan and Crookshank families, that bound patrician and plebeian together. In the event this link was annealed by the Grenadier Guards.

The Lytteltons and the Cecils were aristocratic families who enjoyed a warm friendship. Not only was Oliver Lyttelton's father, Alfred, close to Bobbety's father, Jim Salisbury, but Oliver's mother, Didi Lyttelton, and Bobbety's mother, Alice Salisbury, were firm friends.[2] In 1875 Jim Salisbury's cousin, the future prime minister Arthur Balfour, fancied himself in love with Alfred's sister, May. AJB was disconsolate at her early death from diphtheria, placing an emerald ring in her coffin. Naturally his friends rallied round. They rallied round once more in 1886 to console Alfred in his grief after the death of his wife, Laura, in childbirth just eleven months after their marriage. Alfred Lyttelton subsequently found solace in the love of a young beauty they had adopted into their circle, Didi Balfour. Her physical similarity to Laura was, some of his friends and relations thought, unnerving. Alfred and Didi married in 1892: Oliver was born within eleven months.

Oliver 'had a hero worship of my father but stood in some awe of him'. It was hardly surprising. Alfred Lyttelton was the beau ideal of the muscular Christian. He was strikingly handsome, clever and well-liked. Beyond that, he was a true sporting celebrity, a natural at any game to which he turned his hand. These included both 'aristocratic' and 'popular' pursuits. He was a dominant figure at Eton fives, racquets and real tennis. He played football for England. He was best known as a 'gentleman' cricketer, second only to W. G. Grace in the England team, in which he played as a hard-charging batsman and as wicket-keeper. In middle age he took up golf with a passion that dominated Oliver's childhood landscape. In 1899 he bought land near Muirfield and called in Edwin Lutyens to build him a splendid golfing lodge, High Walls at Gullane.[3] It was a burden Oliver had to carry as he grew into manhood that, although he was big and tall, he could never approach his father in sporting prowess.

Oliver was, however, doted on by his beautiful but highly strung mother. She was much given to 'premonitions'. She later became, somewhat to his embarrassment, one of the leading figures in the British spiritualist movement. She forced Alfred to give up High Walls because she could not bear the separations his golfing forays involved. Instead she found a new country home at Wittersham near Rye, where Alfred and Oliver could golf under her watchful eye. At an early age Mrs Lyttelton's worries affected Oliver's schooling. He was not sent to prep school as a boarder but instead attended Mr Bull's in Baker Street with his cousin Gil Talbot, later a close Oxford friend of Harold Macmillan who was killed fighting on the Western Front in 1915.[4] At one stage Alfred Lyttelton even wavered in his intention to send Oliver to Eton, where his family had been outstanding figures for generations, considering instead the merits of Westminster, where he would be a day-boy within easy walking distance of home.[5]

Alfred Lyttelton entered politics in his late thirties soon after his second marriage and the birth of his son. Like his Cecil friends Arthur Balfour and Jim Salisbury, he was a staunch Tory. After a relatively brief apprenticeship he was catapulted straight into the Cabinet by Balfour, who had himself succeeded his uncle, Lord Salisbury, as prime minister the previous year. Although many would feel jealous about such rapid advancement on the 'Bob's your uncle' principle, Alfred in fact entered high office at a difficult moment. The Conservative government was on the ebb tide that would lead to its crushing defeat in the 1906 election. Lyttelton himself, as colonial secretary, was soon embroiled in the unedifying aftermath of the Boer War and in particular the issue of 'Chinese Slavery' in South Africa. Lyttelton was excoriated by sections of the press on the issue. He was used to adulation rather than criticism and reacted badly. After hearing him speak in the Commons, Lord Balcarres, a Conservative whip, observed that his speech was 'able in its way but marred by a certain asperity of voice which is not borne out by his smiling countenance. The result is that the newspaper men think his remarks virulent and acrimonious, whereas members in the House itself (to whom he addresses himself exclusively), see by his face that he does not mean to be disagreeable. Hence the divergence of criticism between MPs and journalists.'[6]

Neither did Alfred Lyttelton have much taste for opposition. Party managers found the tendency of ex-ministers, of whom Lyttelton was one, to follow the example of Balfour, who lost Manchester and was returned for City of London, to gravitate towards town in search of safe seats comfortably near their homes 'indefensible'.[7] Lyttelton had bought 16 Great College Street, Westminster, in 1895 when he had become an MP; now he bought No. 18 next door and had Lutyens create a substantial house. Defeated at Warwick and Leamington, he was found the excellent seat of St George's, Hanover Square. This 'selfishness' as far as the party in the country was concerned was compounded by 'indolence' in the House itself. He was accounted 'tame and ineffectual' in the Commons.[8]

British politics were moving into an exceptionally bitter phase as the Liberals, or 'Radicals' as the Conservatives preferred to call them, attempted to push through their ambitious social, financial and constitutional programme. It seemed to some Conservatives that they were engaged in a class war with enemies such as the Welsh Liberal politician Lloyd George and the socialists of the Independent Labour Party. Yet in the Lyttelton household the political creed of the latter was a suitable subject for humour: 'I went to the Mission [in the East End of London],' Oliver told his mother in 1908, 'but I am still not yet a socialist. The "staff" are particularly nice as is only natural considering they are Old Etonians.'⁹ Alfred seemed 'opposed to any actions except quiescence' and was not in favour of the House of Lords wrecking Liberal legislation. He and his friends, 'comfortable in rich metropolitan seats', did not seem to register the depth of the crisis: if the Tories did not resist with all their might and main 'we should look upon ourselves as a dejected indeed a defeated party'.¹⁰

The unpleasantness of politics communicated itself to Oliver: 'I hope,' he wrote to his mother from Eton in 1909, the year of Lloyd George's 'People's Budget', 'we are very full for Christmas, I don't mind sleeping on the floor, even if everybody is over thirty. I do hope there won't be any ghastly election or any other political absurdity this time.'¹¹ Unfortunately the political absurdity was unstoppable. In November Lloyd George described the peers as a useless group randomly chosen from among the unemployed and the House of Lords threw out his budget. That Christmas was ruined by an election in January 1910. The next Christmas was ruined by an election in December 1910. The elections solved nothing. The Liberals were weakened, indeed reliant on Irish nationalists for their parliamentary majority, but still in power. In front stretched the crisis of the 1911 Parliament Act, which was designed to cripple the power of the peers. Electoral failure in 1910 also brought about the fall of Balfour and the advent of the Scottish 'hard man' Andrew Bonar Law as Conservative leader. Alfred had tried to persuade his party to avoid conflict. Although he had supported Law for the leadership, once it was clear that Balfour had no stomach for the fight, politics could no longer be an adventure shared by friends.

If the political crisis of 1909 onwards dispirited the Lyttelton family, it reinvigorated the Cecils. Bobbety – 'a ridiculous name but the one by which I am known to my friends' – Cranborne grew up in a house full of 'die-hards' fighting the good fight for their family and class.[12] The dominating figure of his early years was his grandfather, the 3rd Marquess. By his exertions Lord Salisbury had lifted the Cecils of Hatfield from centuries spent as political ciphers back to the heights of power they had enjoyed at the turn of the sixteenth century. He was in all ways an awe-inspiring figure, luxuriantly bearded, of huge stature, lapidary judgement and, in the outside world, prime minister until his retirement in 1902, when Bobbety was nine years old. The Cecils were by then the nearest Britain possessed to an imperial family.

Although Lord Salisbury himself had had to struggle hard and rise through his talents, once he reached the pinnacle he buttressed his rule by employing members of his own family. Although he had to look to his sister's son Balfour as a political lieutenant and eventual successor, three of Salisbury's five sons also entered politics: the eldest and his heir, Jim (or Jem), Bobbety's father, and two younger brothers, Lord Robert and Lord Hugh, known as Linkie. It was said of the Cecil boys that 'their ability varies inversely with their age'. Jim was thus regarded as the least talented, Hugh as the most. By the time Bobbety was old enough to take an interest in the public lives of his father and uncles, the rolling political salons that were Hatfield and Salisbury House in Arlington Street had become his homes. Yet the memory of the great 3rd Marquess still cast a long shadow. Not only did outsiders persistently compare him to his sons, to their perpetual disadvantage, but they themselves were prey to deep feelings of inadequacy. Since 1883 Jim Salisbury had suffered from periodic bouts of depression brought on by 'these festering feelings of failure'.[13]

If Oliver Lyttelton grew up in awe of his father, Bobbety grew up in a household of men in awe of his grandfather's dominating presence. This perhaps contributed to the family traits of fierce pride in the gens, intractability and odd diffidence. On the other hand, the dominant figure in his early life was not his father but his mother,

Alice, the daughter of an Irish peer, whom James Cranborne had married in 1887. Although not a public figure as her friend Didi Lyttelton became after her husband's death, Alice Salisbury was the undisputed chatelaine of Hatfield. She had no compunction about dabbling in politics: she made herself instrumental in the downfall of the Viceroy of India, George Curzon, by acting as the 'back channel' between his enemies and Balfour. More than her secret interest in political affairs, however, she provided the social flair and taste for entertaining on a magnificent scale from which her husband shied. She was to prove, behind the scenes, the mainstay of both her husband and her son.[14]

Lack of appreciable talent did not stop Lord Salisbury raising his son to ministerial rank as under-secretary of state for foreign affairs in 1900. Quips about Cecil nepotism struck and stuck because they were so obviously true. To nobody's surprise, least of all his own one suspects, Jim Cranborne was not a success in his performance as a Foreign Office minister. He was not impressive in the House of Commons, never having got over his nervousness at speaking. He was thus 'forbidden to give answers to supplementary questions' in case he said something damaging. Unfortunately, since he did not have the parliamentary skill of avoiding a question by saying nothing at length, he simply refused to respond to any inquiry that had not been properly notified in advance and for which he had no clear brief. This procedure caused ire and mirth in the House in equal measure. There was soon in existence 'a universal belief in Jim Cranborne's complete and invincible incompetence'.[15]

In the short term, matters did not seem set to improve. In 1903 Lord Salisbury died and Jim Cranborne succeeded him, becoming the 4th Marquess. His translation to the Upper House was a blessed relief. He felt more at home among men who were literally his peers; he was accorded the respect to which his position in society entitled him, with none of the rowdyism of the demotic Commons. His cousin Balfour brought him into the Cabinet as Lord Privy Seal at the same time as Alfred Lyttelton became colonial secretary in October 1903.

As Jim Salisbury was entering into his inheritance, the Conservative party started to tear itself to pieces over the issue of Tariff Reform, the campaign launched by Joseph Chamberlain in May 1903 to convert the party from laissez-faire to protectionism. Chamberlain hit on a sore point. The party had nearly destroyed itself over the issue of Free Trade in the 1840s, had condemned itself to a generation of political impotence and had only fully re-established itself as the natural party of government under Jim's father. The Cecils were avowed Free Traders, yet the manner in which they prosecuted their campaign did not initially enhance their reputation.

Immediately after the crushing election defeat of 1906, Salisbury circularized all Unionist MPs in order to identify them as Free Traders or Tariff Reformers, or 'food taxers' as he called them. The move did not receive a warm response. 'I am bound to say,' wrote Lord Balcarres, 'that I resent this catechism from one whose incompetence has been a contributory cause to our disaster. Good fellow as [Jim] is, his tact is not generally visible: and it would not be unfair to reply that the taxation of food has doubtless injured the Party – though we have suffered largely from nepotism, sacerdotalism, and inefficiency.'[16] Lord Robert and Lord Hugh were on the wilder fringes of the party, locked into spiteful conflict with their constituency parties.[17]

Like Alfred Lyttelton, Jim Salisbury found the inevitable squabbling in a party forced humiliatingly into opposition after years of rule disheartening. Unlike Lyttelton, he subsequently found a great cause and a method of prosecuting it to call his own. The cause was the House of Lords and the method was obstructionism. The method, it is true, predated the cause. In 1908 one of his colleagues recorded that 'Jem wanted a guerrilla war with the House of Commons'.[18] Jim Salisbury had little talent for constructive political achievement, but he found himself to have a genius for saying no. In 1910, for the first time, he became one of the most important men in the party. It was he who convened the meeting of party grandees at Hatfield in December that forced on Balfour far-reaching changes to party organization. He found willing allies in his brothers. It was Lord Hugh Cecil who led his 'Hughligans', a band of about thirty MPs dedicated to howling down Asquith and the Liberal leaders and disrupting the House of Commons. George Wyndham, Oliver Lyttelton's favourite among his father's circle, drew the memorable distinction between 'Ditchers', 'those who would die in the last ditch', and 'Hedgers', who were 'liable to trimming'.[19] Lord Salisbury found life much more comfortable once he became a committed Ditcher. In 1905, on the grounds that one should not let mere politics interfere with civilized life, he had had Asquith to dine at Hatfield within twenty-four hours of his cousin and chief Balfour's resignation as prime minister. In July 1911, the same month in which his brother decided to shout Asquith down in the House of Commons, 'Lord and Lady Salisbury refused the invitation of the Asquiths to dine at the party given to the King and Queen'. Even Salisbury's fiercest detractors in the party approved: 'Asquith and his colleagues are out for blood. He has poured insult and contumely on the peers: why break bread or uncork champagne at his table?'[20]

The passing of the 1911 Parliament Act by the Liberals under the threat that the new king, George V, would be obliged to swamp the Lords with new peers, was a crushing blow. 'Politics are beastly', was Salisbury's comment. Yet the Act guaranteed the House very considerable powers of delay while Liberal dependence on the Irish nationalists gave the peers a much greater excuse for using those powers than they had had for wrecking Liberal social legislation. Many peers were demoralized by their defeat, but Jim Salisbury was suffused in a glow of moral righteousness. Thereafter he never entirely lost his reputation as the keeper of the true flame of Conservatism. This made him a powerful man, though he was not always comfortable with the role. After the war he confided to his son that he found continual calls to save the Conservative party tiresome. One should remember, he told Bobbety, that parties came and went: principles and family were much more durable.

Bobbety Cranborne and Oliver Lyttelton were brought up at the apex of English social and political life. Politics was the constant backdrop to their childhood. To have Cabinet ministers, even prime ministers, in the house was a regular occurrence. From an early age they were aware of the fascination of politics, but also became youthfully cynical about it. Harry Crookshank and Harold Macmillan did not have such easy access to the political élite. Whereas Cranborne and Lyttelton could see the casualties of ambition – the burnt-out drunks like George Wyndham – ambition for the Crookshank and Macmillan families was entirely positive. It was also more impersonal and structured than for the aristocrats. From the start the course was clear: a forcing prep school, leading to a scholarship at Eton, leading in turn to the best colleges at Oxford. The perfectly respectable schools and colleges attended by their fathers simply would not do.

Although the Macmillan and Crookshank *pères* followed quite different professions, they had arrived at a remarkably similar social location by the time their sons were born. Harry Maule Crookshank was a doctor who had taken advantage of the expansion of the Empire in the last quarter of the nineteenth century to become an imperial administrator. He came from an old Ulster Protestant family of some distinction. The Crookshanks had arrived in Ulster as part of the seventeenth-century plantation of Scottish Protestants. The family took great pride in their most famous ancestor, William Crookshank, who had been one of the thirteen men who shut the gates of Derry in 1688. Since then the family could boast a brace of Ulster MPs. By the nineteenth century, however, Harry Maule Crookshank's father and grandfather were making their way through soldiering. Both served as officers in line infantry regiments. Before the Cardwell reforms of the 1870s, officers in the British army purchased their rank. The Crookshanks thus had some funds behind them but could not rise to great heights. Harry Maule's grandfather finished his career as a colonel. His father was a captain at the time of his early death while serving in India. While overseas Harry Maule was to send his son, Harry Comfort, for his initial education in Europe. This seems to have been part of a family pattern, for he himself received his early education in Boulogne before proceeding to a minor public school in Cheltenham. He was not destined for the army but instead studied medicine at University College Hospital, London. Although Crookshank had not joined the British army, he maintained his family's military tradition. At the age of twenty-one he joined a Red Cross ambulance unit serving in the Franco-Prussian War of 1870–71. He repeated the experience later in the decade, joining a similar unit in the Russo-Turkish War of 1877–8. Crookshank's contact with the Ottoman Empire brought about a fundamental change in his life. In 1882 British forces invaded Egypt to secure the recently completed Suez Canal. Following in the wake of the troops were British officials dedicated to the reform of the corrupt and ineffectual Egyptian state. Between 1883 and 1914 the real power in Egypt lay with the British, led by Lord Cromer.

Harry Maule Crookshank found himself an important cog in Cromer's machine as director-general of the Egyptian Prisons Administration. Coming from an undistinguished background he was, at the age of thirty-four, relatively young for his responsibilities. In 1883 Crookshank faced a difficult situation. The British regarded the Egyptian prisons they found as utterly barbarous and in urgent need of reform. 'No report,' wrote the author of the initial survey of the system, 'can convey the feeblest impression of the helpless misery of the prisoners, who live for months like wild beasts, without change of clothing, half-starved, ignorant of the fate of their families and bewailing their own.' The problem of the prisons was part of a wider malaise in a justice system dominated 'by venality, tyranny and personal vindictiveness'.[21] Yet British officials were being somewhat disingenuous in their criticism of the existing Egyptian prison system. The first concern for Cromer's new administration was not reforming the prisons but bringing Egypt under its own firm control. To this end the 1880s were marked by a system akin to martial law. 'Brigandage commissions' ensured that as many potential troublemakers as possible were imprisoned. The combination of Egyptian inefficiency and British efficiency meant that there was massive overcrowding in the prisons: the gaols were at four times their nominal capacity.[22]

Crookshank's eventual reform programme followed four main lines: old prisons were improved and made sanitary, new prisons were built, prisoners were provided with proper food and clothing and a separate system of reformatories for young offenders was created. The work was long, arduous and not always rewarding. Since the criminal justice system formed the keystone of 'indirect' rule, its conduct was the matter of much debate, even conflict, among the

British themselves. Crookshank became involved on the side of those pragmatists who believed that as much use as possible should be made of the existing Egyptian system, already reformed on French lines before the occupation. His chief opponent was Sir Benson Maxwell, a naturally disputatious man who served as first *procureur-général* and believed the system should be purged of any intermediary foreign taint and thoroughly anglicized on the colonial model. Money was always tight. As Lord Cromer recorded in 1907, the year Crookshank left Egypt, 'These reforms took time: Even now the prison accommodation can scarcely be said to be adequate to meet all the requirements of the country.' Crookshank's successor as director-general, Charles Coles, who took over in 1897, had a police rather than a medical background. He implied that his predecessor had been too soft. It was arguable, Coles felt, 'that prison life is not sufficiently deterrent, and that the swing of the pendulum has carried the Administration too far in the direction of humanity, if not of luxury'.

There is no record of how the Crookshanks felt when Cromer gave credit to Coles rather than Harry Maule as the man 'to whom the credit of reforming this branch of the Public Service is mainly due'. It was not in Harry Maule's nature to push himself forward. Indeed, Coles felt that Crookshank had been unnecessarily diffident in his dealings with Cromer.[23] It would seem even so that Crookshank's performance in fourteen years of overseeing the prisons was rated highly enough for him to be given another important and far more agreeable job within the administration. In 1897 he was made controller of the Daira Sanieh Administration. The Daira estates were lands that the former ruler of Egypt, Ismail Pasha, had 'contrived, generally by illicit and arbitrary methods, to accumulate in his own hands'. By the time the British arrived they amounted to over half a million acres. They were, however, very heavily mortgaged. When the profligate Ismail had got into severe financial difficulties he had borrowed £9.5 million on the security of the properties.

Under the Cromer regime the estates were run in the manner that became standard practice: giving the appearance of authority to Egyptians but severely trammelling their power. The putative administrator of the lands was an Egyptian director-general, but he was joined on a board of directors by two controllers, one British, the post Crookshank took on, and one French. The controllers 'had ample powers of supervision and inspection. They alone were the legal representatives of the bondholders.' Cromer regarded Crookshank's performance as British controller as admirable. The main problem for the board was that the estates were so heavily indebted that expenditure on loan repayments always outran revenue. The first step, taken before Crookshank's time, was to extract higher revenues from the estates.

From 1892 onwards, the properties started to yield a profit, though there was a brief crisis in 1895 not long before Crookshank's arrival. By Crookshank's last years in office, revenue was very healthy indeed, amounting to over £800,000 in 1904–5. Under Crookshank, however, a new policy was instituted. Cromer had close relations with the banker Ernest Cassel. Cassel thought that a great deal of money could be made from the estates. In 1898 the estates were made over to a new company charged with selling them off in lots. By the time Crookshank demitted office, all the lots had been sold, yielding a net profit for the government of over £3.25 million.[24] Crookshank was leaving at a good time. When Cromer retired, the speculation in Egyptian land and shares in which Crookshank had been a pivotal figure rebounded into a financial crisis. Cromer's successor, Eldon Gorst, concluded that the relationship between financiers and Cromer's apparat had been rather too close for comfort. Profit had not necessarily walked hand in hand with good governance.[25] Crookshank slipped into comfortable retirement in the wake of his master. He had been a faithful and discreet servant.

In later life Harry Crookshank was proud of and interested in his father's official career. He too was to serve as an official in what was by then the former Ottoman Empire. He planned to make Egypt and Turkey his areas of particular expertise when he first entered the House of Commons, though these plans went awry. In many ways it was the position that Harry Maule's achievements gave him in society that shaped Harry Comfort's world. In 1890, at the mid-point of his term in the prison administration, Harry Crookshank was accorded the honorific 'Pasha'. It was as Crookshank Pasha that he was known there-after. Although his job had not changed, the oriental glamour of his new status helped him to woo a young Vassar-educated American visitor to Egypt, Emma Walraven Comfort.

Crookshank's marriage to Emma Comfort in 1891 was wholly advantageous. Her father, Samuel Comfort, was one of the founders of Standard Oil, the company created by his contemporary John D. Rockefeller in 1870. By the end the 1870s Standard Oil had come to control the entire American oil market. In 1882 its owners created the 'Trust': at the time Crookshank met Emma the conflict between Standard and the 'trustbusters' was one of the most important struggles in American political life. Samuel Comfort was a 'robber baron' of the 'Gilded Age'.[26] He was rich and Emma was his only daughter. When Harry Comfort Crookshank was born in 1893, his way of life had already been determined. He would never have to work for a living. Money would continue to flow in from the most 'blue chip' stocks and shares imaginable, given to or inherited by his mother.

One of Crookshank Pasha's enthusiasms had a profound effect on his son's life. In his *annus mirabilis* of 1891, Harry Maule Crookshank was installed in the Grecia Lodge in Cairo. The lodge's best-known member was Kitchener, who became master the year after Crookshank joined.[27] Like his father Harry Comfort was to be a passionate Freemason. He joined the Apollo Lodge as soon as he arrived in Oxford in 1912, the earliest possible opportunity. His attachment to Freemasonry thus predated his political ambitions. He would pursue his Masonic career with as much enthusiasm and ambition as he embraced Parliament.

Crookshank spent his early childhood in Cairo, but in 1903 he was sent to school in Lausanne.[28] In May 1904 he arrived at Summer Fields, a prep school at Oxford, to find Harold Macmillan already installed. Macmillan's road to Summer Fields had been much less exotic. His father, Maurice, had after a few years schoolmastering joined the family publishing firm. On a trip to Paris he met a young American widow, Nellie Hill. Nellie was the daughter of a Methodist preacher in Indiana. At the age of eighteen she had married into a well-to-do family in Indianapolis. Her husband survived only five months of marriage. Using the money he left her, Nellie decamped for Europe in the late 1870s. She had no fondness for the American Midwest and was happy to move to England with Maurice when they married in 1884. Unlike his new friend Harry Crookshank, Harold was a late child, born ten years later when his mother was forty. By then the family was firmly established in a tall, narrow house in Cadogan Place, the connecting link 'between the aristocratic pavements of Belgrave Square and the barbarism of Chelsea'. There was also a substantial if inelegant country house in Sussex, Birch Grove.

In contrast to the Crookshanks, where the mother's wealth was paramount, it was Maurice Macmillan who financed the family's lifestyle. Yet there was no doubt that the 'master of the house' was the dominant figure of Nellie Macmillan. Mrs Macmillan threw herself with gusto into the public life of her adopted country. Her milieu was the societies of rich and well-connected ladies devoted to some public cause. Her main efforts were expended on the Victoria League, a body of imperial enthusiasts founded in memory of the recently deceased Queen-Empress, of which, for many years, she was honorary treasurer. She became acquainted with her fellow American imperial enthusiast Emma Crookshank.

For both the Macmillans and the Crookshanks to send a son to Summer Fields was a clear declaration of intent. The establishment had been created so that its pupils could compete for scholarships to the major public schools. Between 1897 and 1916 the school averaged more than five Eton scholarships a year. By the time Macmillan and Crookshank reached College, one in three of their fellow scholars had been to Summer Fields.[29] As Henry Willink, who scraped into the same election at Eton as Macmillan and Crookshank, recalled: 'I had not been skilfully prepared for the Scholarship examination as ... boys at Summer Fields were prepared.'[30] 'If,' as the school history puts it, 'the boys were not force-fed they were certainly stuffed.' Summer Fields, where Macmillan and Crookshank became close friends, duly delivered on its promises. Both boys were placed on the list of seventeen that made up the Eton election of 1906.

Eton in 1906 was undoubtedly the most famous and prestigious school in England.[31] It was also in many ways the perfect microcosm of the social universe represented by Macmillan and Crookshank on the one hand and Lyttelton and Cranborne on the other. Eton was divided into two unequal parts. In College there were a total of seventy scholars, 'Collegers', or 'Tugs'. Entrance was by the fiercely competitive examination Macmillan and Crookshank had just sat. As a result College was dominated by boys just like them: from families dedicated to the late Victorian cult of achievement through hard work.

There were a much larger number of boys in School, the Oppidans. The year 1906 was a bumper one for School, with 224 new boys, of whom Cranborne and Lyttelton were two. School was of distinctly mixed ability, entrance being governed by family tradition and contacts. As Oliver Lyttelton observed, the masters 'were inclined to be slightly snobbish . . . they conceived their role in the State to be that of training and teaching those who were likely to shape its future [and thus] . . . wanted to have pupils from the great families. The sons of those families would have a start in the race.'[32] Initially the Collegers and Oppidans, further divided into their boarding houses, were kept fairly separate. As they progressed through the school there would be more mixing, particularly as they shared the pupil rooms of the Classical Tutors. Lyttelton and Cranborne were members of Henry Bowlby's house and mixed with Macmillan and Crookshank in his pupil room. It was exactly this mixing that attracted ambitious families to Eton.

The Eton the four boys attended was, on the surface, in a process of dynamic expansion. The school was nevertheless plagued with troubling undercurrents. In 1905 the long headmastership of Dr Warre came to an end. Warre had instituted an extensive building programme completed while the boys were at Eton: the gymnasium was opened in 1907, the hall in 1908 and the library in 1910. Although the fruit of previous expenditure was in the process of realization, the school was thus in a period of financial retrenchment. Warre's departure also opened the way for a power struggle between his presumed successor, A. C. Benson, a brilliant but depressive homosexual, and the leader of the younger 'Classics', the acerbic A. B. Ramsay, known as 'the Ram'. The most powerful voice on the selection panel, Lord Cobham, was able to usher in his kinsman, Edward Lyttelton, as a compromise candidate.

Oliver Lyttelton was thus faced with every schoolboy's nightmare – a close relative as headmaster. He was frequently mortified by his uncle's tendency to trumpet the moral superiority of the Lytteltons – which he later described as 'washing clean linen in public'. Lyttelton's embarrassment was accentuated by Uncle Edward's undoubted peculiarities. No one doubted that he was a perfect Christian gentleman and a fine sportsman, but he was an indifferent classicist and soon became the butt of Collegers whose grasp of Latin far exceeded his own. He was also a health faddist, following a vegetarian diet and lauding the virtues of outdoor living. His healthy tan earned him the nickname 'the Brown Man' in an age that valued alabaster complexions. The headmaster's attempts to keep in check the tendency of Etonians to lord it over the neighbouring population won him few friends in the school and met with limited success. Lyttelton failed to persuade the Master and Fellows to broaden the curriculum at the expense of an unleavened diet of literary classics. The boys, as so often, were dyed-in-the-wool reactionaries when it came to such matters. Macmillan angrily noted: 'I am rather annoyed at the nonsense that people are talking and writing about "Education" ... we are all to learn, it seems, about stocks and shares. Instead of humanities we are to dissect frogs and make horrible smells in expensive laboratories ... I do not see that an ignorance of chemistry is any better than an ignorance of Classics.'[33] Edward Lyttelton's career at Eton was ended during the war by a brave if – given the temper of the times – unwise speech proposing that Britain should cede Gibraltar to Germany in return for peace.

Each of the boys had a rather different experience of Eton. Of the four Lyttelton's is by far the best recorded. The main challenge he faced was the long shadow cast by his father's glittering reputation at Eton. His solid school career was always found wanting when set next to that of Alfred. He worked hard at everything, becoming house captain of Lubbock's and achieving entrance to the Classical

First where the best scholars, whether Colleger or Oppidan, were taught together. Success had its drawbacks: 'Everything is rather an ordeal at present,' he reported home, 'I mean I am always finding myself in solitary positions of responsibility; either I am leading sixth form into chapel or I am making a speech or I am commanding the company in the Corps or I am president of the debate but I am getting used to them all.'[34] Of some importance for the future, he did plenty of soldiering.[35] His housemaster, Samuel Lubbock, who had taken the house over from Bowlby when the latter left to become headmaster of Lancing, noticed his efforts with pleasure: 'He deserves the best report I can give him,' he wrote to Alfred, 'certainly the house will never have a better captain . . . His work has improved to a far greater [extent] than a year ago I thought probable and his marks in trials are quite encouraging.'[36] Lubbock also made the rather rash prediction that 'with really hard work he might just be up to a First at Cambridge': he subsequently had to admit that his enthusiasm for Oliver's personality had led him to overestimate his scholarly abilities.

Most pleasing of all, Oliver was finally elected to Eton's self-selecting élite of senior boys, the Eton Society or 'Pop', of which, inevitably, his father had been president, in his final half. It had been a struggle to ingratiate himself. His election, Lubbock reported, 'does credit to Pop: for great and sound as his merits are, he is rather too clever and too old [for] many average boys: as I have said before he jests rather too frequently and they don't quite understand all his jokes . . . and boys are very self-conscious creatures. But he is quick at seeing things and I think he has seen this clearly enough.'[37] Unfortunately Lubbock was rather too sanguine on the last point. Three years later Raymond Asquith reported from the trenches that 'his chief defect to my mind is one inherited from Alfred – telling rather long and moderately good stories and laughing hysterically long before he comes to the point'.[38] Fifty-two years later, a former Cabinet colleague wrote that Lyttelton's sense of humour 'varied from classical to Rabelaisian or even third form . . . The only difficulty was that an immediate appreciation of the humorous aspects of any question was inclined to limit the expression of the arguments in mundane terms.'[39]

It was towards the end of their time at Eton that Oliver and Bobbety became close friends. For many Oppidans there was no presumption that they would go on to university; many drifted away to join the army or to travel on the Continent as a means of finishing their education. Lyttelton bemoaned the fact that by 1910 'all my particular pals will be gone except Cranborne'.[40] From then on the two started messing together.[41]

Fifty years on Osbert Sitwell reminded Bobbety 'that you were a studious small boy'.[42] Yet if his scholarly performance was anything to go by, the school inspectors who visited Eton in 1910 might have been thinking of Cranborne when they wrote in their report: 'we do not forget that Eton's highest service to the nation is that she educates boys whose circumstances make it difficult or impossible for the school work to be as important in their eyes as it is in the eyes of less fortunate schoolboys'. The main strength of the Eton education was languages and Cranborne left School in 1911 with no firm grasp of any, whether classical or modern.

In College meanwhile Crookshank made good progress. His main problem was a complete lack of sporting prowess. Even Macmillan, a self-confessed duffer at games, was picked for the College team that played the Oppidans at the uniquely Etonian form of football known as the Wall Game. Crookshank was no more than an ardent admirer of those who could play. The *Daily Graphic* printed a picture of him among the crowd carrying the Collegers' wall keeper in triumph after College had defeated the School. 'It is dreadful,' he lamented in 1917, while serving in Salonika, 'this is the first Wall Match I have missed since I first went to Eton in 1906. I suppose it had to come some time, but it is rather a bitter blow.'[43] Apart from his deficiency in games he excelled in most other areas. He was good at his work, was a fine debater, edited the school magazine and was elected to Pop with rather more ease than Lyttelton. In their final year these two found themselves thrown together quite regularly. They studied classics together, with Crookshank consistently near the top of the class, Lyttelton consistently near the bottom.[44] At their final speech day in June 1912, Lyttelton gave a reading from the essay 'On Murder Considered as One of the Fine Arts' by de Quincey,

Crookshank from Lincoln's second inaugural. They performed together in a sketch adapted from the *Pickwick Papers*: Crookshank taking the part of Mr Phunky, Lyttelton of Sam Weller.[45]

By the time Cranborne, Lyttelton and Crookshank were forming their mature friendships at school, they were no longer boys but young men. The notable absentee was, of course, Macmillan, who was the only one who crashed at Eton. Macmillan and Crookshank had maintained their Summer Fields friendship. Whereas Crookshank flowered at Eton, Macmillan struggled. He was withdrawn by his mother in 1909. Macmillan was tight-lipped about his failure. He devoted a page in his memoirs to Eton as compared to a full chapter in Lyttelton's. By his own account: 'During my first half at Eton I had a serious attack of pneumonia, which I only just survived. Some years later, I suffered from growing too fast, and a bad state of the heart was diagnosed. This led to my leaving Eton prematurely and spending many months in bed or as an invalid.'[46] Many years later J. B. S. Haldane spread the rumour that Macmillan had, in fact, been expelled for egregious homosexuality. Eton, like all public schools, lived in fear of the nameless vice. One of Edward Lyttelton's first acts as headmaster was to break a house whose captain had an appetite for buggery. Haldane was certainly in a position to know the cause of Macmillan's departure. 'Of course I remember him very well,' Macmillan acknowledged when he was prime minister. 'He was in the election above me at College, as well as a pupil of Henry Bowlby. I used to see him after the first war but have not seen him for many years.'[47] Haldane was, in all likelihood, motivated by malice. Macmillan himself was certainly malicious about Haldane's family. Enjoying the discomfiture of Gilbert Mitchison in the House of Commons, his mind was thrown back to Eton. 'He was Captain of Oppidans in my time and was a silly, pompous and conceited ass even then. As a punishment he married Naomi Haldane, and is now more or less insane.'[48] Whatever the truth about Macmillan's departure from Eton, it certainly denied him the opportunity to mix with boys of his own age at the very time when he was maturing into manhood. This was to presage an unfortunate pattern. His time at Oxford was also cut short, as was his time in the army. Throughout his life Macmillan was to have difficulties in his relations with male contemporaries. The one relationship in which there was never awkwardness was that with Harry Crookshank. That they had been friends even before they reached Eton was significant.

Macmillan returned home from Eton to an even more pressurized environment. A. B. Ramsay, the fearsome Classic, called regularly to give him lessons. He seemed to Macmillan 'a man of the world, elegant, refined and a most perfect gentleman', much superior to Dr Lyttelton.[49] His mother's other choices of tutor were somewhat stranger. The first to arrive was a Dilly Knox, friend of Harold's brother, Daniel. On the face of it, the Knox connection seemed safe enough. Knox *père* was the fiercely evangelical Bishop of Manchester, known as 'Hard Knox' for his no-nonsense approach to educating the young.[50] Dilly Knox, on the other hand, was one of those young masters who took the lead in ragging Edward Lyttelton. Knox was a formidable classical scholar but was found too 'austere' for Harold. He was replaced by his younger brother Ronnie. Dilly was eleven years older than Harold, whereas Ronnie was only six years his senior. Harold was seventeen, Ronnie twenty-two: they were close enough in age to become intimate friends. Too intimate, in the view of Nellie Macmillan. She ordered Ronnie from the house in 1910. They had already argued about his pay, but this was '7000 times more important'. Mrs Macmillan had accused Ronnie of infecting Harold with 'papism'. The situation was fraught with emotion: 'I am extremely (and not unreturnedly) fond of the boy,' Ronnie told his sister, 'and it's been a horrid wrench to go without saying a word to him of what I wanted to say.'[51] Whatever its dangers, Harold's high-priced and exceptional tuition did pay off in one sense: he won an Exhibition to Balliol and was thus able to arrive at university at the same time as his Eton contemporaries.

Just as Eton was not just another public school, so the colleges the boys attended at Oxford and Cambridge were notable for their wealth, size and social prestige. Lyttelton and Cranborne could simply follow in family tradition, Lyttelton to Trinity College, Cambridge, Cranborne to Christ Church, Oxford. Family tradition meant nothing to the new men. Crookshank went up to Magdalen College, Oxford,

Macmillan followed his brother to the worldly Balliol College, Oxford, rather than his father to the more ascetic Christ's College, Cambridge.

The traditional patterns established at Eton persisted at university. Lyttelton and Cranborne gravitated to the aristocratic beau monde, giving little thought to their studies. Macmillan and Crookshank were exceptionally serious. Lyttelton quickly discovered the joy of girls. In the Easter vacation of his first year he found himself staying at Lympne Castle, not far from Wittersham, with 'Dinah'. He regaled his mother with their adventures: 'Dinah and I . . . set off to walk to Lympne. After half an hour Dinah fell into a ditch and got wet and being anxious to see me in the same state made a compact with me that we wouldn't go round any canal. Soon we *swam* a broad canal having thrown most of our clothes over the other side and we ended up swimming the military canal.'[52] He drew a discreet veil over the denouement of their unclothed adventures in the Royal Military Canal. He also abjured his parents' distaste for horse racing. Lyttelton's passion for gambling led to inevitable conflicts, unconvincing excuses and anguished reconciliations when he had to borrow money from his parents to settle his debts:

> I am so terribly sorry that you should have thought I was ungrateful or anything, that I don't know what to do. But for the last three days I have been ill, I eat [sic] something that has poisoned me, and I have been bad and very sick but am better today. I am clearing up my accounts and will write you tomorrow at the latest. Darling Mother, for God's sake don't think me ungrateful for I simply can't stand it. I have done ill enough without this: but that you should think me ungrateful or callous is too awful. You can't realize how I feel towards you both or you couldn't think such a thing for a minute. So please understand, I am sure you do really.[53]

Bobbety Cranborne had no such money worries. His set at Oxford consisted of aristocrats, both English and foreign, as well as royalty. He roomed with the Russian prince Serge Obolensky, whom Lyttelton found 'rather nice and very good looking'.[54] Unlike Obolensky, who was a fanatical polo player, Cranborne was not particularly horsy. This did not prevent him living a 'hearty' lifestyle. He was a member of the Loders Club, where a requirement for membership was that one was 'a gentleman, a sportsman, and a jolly good fellow'. Established in 1814 as a debating club, it had long since degenerated into a group that dedicated each Sunday in term to hard drinking. In a mockery of the Oxford–Cambridge polo match, in which Obolensky was playing 'at some unearthly inappropriate hour', Bobbety and Prince Paul of Yugoslavia 'got bicycles and awakened the echoes by playing polo in the street'. When they were arrested, a drunken Cranborne declared that he needed no lawyer and would defend in person the right of freeborn Englishmen to play bicycle polo. In court he 'said he did not think they had annoyed any of the residents, but had merely entertained them'. For all his pains, they were fined a crown each and costs.[55]

Cranborne's academic performance was abject. In his first year he failed in his attempts to avoid his matriculation examination.[56] In 1913 he failed his Mods completely, drawing 'sympathy . . . qualified by remonstrance and admonition' from his tutor.[57] He decided that he would not bother to try again. In any case, of much more long-term moment than a failure to grapple with the classical authors was his burgeoning interest in international affairs.[58] He became close friends with Timothy Eden, 'a shy, retiring, soft-featured young man' who was the heir to a baronetcy.[59] Eden was part of the more 'worthy' side of Cranborne's Oxford life.[60] He ran a 'Round Table' devoted to public affairs. He made contact with serious-minded young men like Frank Walters, who later became an official and champion of the League of Nations.[61] Through his uncles, both outspoken champions of Anglo-Catholicism, Cranborne also got to know Macmillan's mentor Ronnie Knox whom he invited to his eponymous country seat, Cranborne in Dorset, during the Easter vacation of 1914.

In 1912 Cranborne's father decided that he should be sent to South Africa with his prospective brother-in-law, a precocious if pompous MP in his twenties, Billy Ormsby-Gore.[62] The choice was important for the future. Most undergraduates tended to travel to France or Germany in the summers to improve their languages.

Macmillan went on a reading party to Austria in 1913, Lyttelton 'studied French in a small house in Fontainebleau, where the food did not live up to French standards'. Crookshank was in Germany with four friends during the summer of 1914 and barely escaped internment: the certificate of British nationality that enabled him to flee was stamped by the British consul in Hanover as late as 31 July. Indeed, Cranborne had intended to go to Germany himself in 1913 with Jock Balfour, an Eton friend, but cried off because of ill-health.[63] It was a lucky escape. Both Jock Balfour and Timothy Eden returned to Germany the following summer and spent the war in internment. By choice as well as chance Cranborne was caught up by the glamour of the Empire. His trip with Ormsby-Gore, including a return journey up the east coast of Africa and through the Suez Canal, imbued him with an abiding interest in the continent and a love of southern Africa.[64]

Crookshank and Macmillan took their time at Oxford much more seriously. Crookshank devoted himself to work and Freemasonry. It was thus 'simply sickening' when he 'only *just* missed' his First in Mods.[65] The problem was fairly plain: he was a good Latinist but much weaker at Greek. Macmillan's superb tuition enabled him to overtake his friend: he 'just managed to scrape a First with some difficulty'.[66] Macmillan had other strings to his bow. His renewed relationship with Ronnie Knox brought with it a friendship with Knox's other acolyte, the Wykehamist Guy Lawrence, and gave his life emotional intensity. 'It is hard to give a definition or even a description of them,' Ronnie wrote of the pair in 1917, 'except perhaps to say that in a rather varied experience I have never met conversation so brilliant – with the brilliance of humour not wit.' Macmillan and Lawrence 'had already adopted what I heard (and shuddered to hear) described as "Ronnie's religion"'. Indeed, serving Ronnie at Mass was a regular element of Macmillan's Oxford experience.

Knox is often described as leading Lawrence and Macmillan towards Rome. Although Knox had decided by 1915 that the Church of England was illegitimate, he did not become a Roman Catholic until 1917. In fact it was Guy Lawrence who jumped first. 'God made it clear to me and I went straight to [the Jesuits at] Farm Street ... Come and be happy,' Lawrence urged Knox. Lawrence believed that

'Harold will, I think, follow very soon'. Harold did no such thing. He told Knox that he was 'not going to "Pope" until after the war (if I'm still alive)'. This strange response suggests that Macmillan had little real feeling for the religious issues as Knox and Lawrence felt them. If one came to the realization that Anglican rites and orders, however modified, were a 'sham jewel', one risked the immortal soul by dying in error. It seems likely that Macmillan was more excited by the cell's mixture of incense and intimacy than theology *per se*. In Trinity term 1914 he was poised between another overseas reading party organized by the don, 'Sligger' Urquhart, and Knox and Lawrence's planned retreat in rural Gloucestershire for the summer vacation. Both promised an intimate atmosphere.

Conversion in any case threatened an irreparable breach with his mother, a dyed-in-the-wool anti-Catholic bigot, exclusion from Macmillan money and thus an end to worldly ambition. Macmillan had the sort of open ambition that is displayed by running for office in the Union. In May 1913 he made 'the best speech we have heard this year from a Freshman'. Returning at the beginning of the next academic year, he made 'an exceedingly brilliant speech, witty, powerful and at moments eloquent'. He was elected secretary in 1913 and treasurer in 1914. Having held the two junior posts in the triumvirate at the head of the Union, he would still have had time to run for president before the end of his undergraduate career. It is perhaps revealing that his star-struck younger friend Bimbo Tennant believed he *had* been president of the Union.[67]

Whereas Macmillan's second year at university was filled with excitement and expanding horizons, that of Lyttelton and Crookshank was blighted by the deaths of their fathers in July 1913 and March 1914 respectively. While the Crookshanks' grief was private, the Lytteltons' was all too public. The golden good fortune that had always followed Alfred Lyttelton was brought to an abrupt end at a time when he seemed to have hit a good seam in politics. At least one knowledgeable observer noted that the kind of business coming before the House in 1913 suited his style. On plans to disestablish the Church of Wales and attempts to hold government ministers to account for their corrupt personal involvement in the 'Marconi scandal' 'he had lately made some good speeches. His extreme moderation gave extra effect to any attack that did come from him.'[68] As Oliver put it, 'I feel the political situation is improving for Dada.'[69]

The best gentleman cricketer of his generation was felled by a ball bowled by a professional fast bowler in a charity match. Incompetently treated, he died from acute peritonitis a few days later. The prime minister, Asquith, delivered his encomium in the House of Commons. 'I hardly trust myself to speak,' he told the House, 'for, apart from ties of relationship, there had subsisted between us thirty-three years of close friendship and affection.' Asquith's oratory rose to the occasion as he famously memorialized his friend as the one who 'perhaps of all men of this generation, came nearest to the mould and ideal of manhood, which every English father would like to see his son aspire to, and if possible attain'. Thus another heavy burden was laid on Oliver: to be the son of the man who was the perfect son. Fifty years later he would still feel 'acutely how far short of the example which I was set' he had fallen. Even in an age of numberless tragedies, those that struck some individuals most grievously were coeval to the war but entirely unrelated to it.

If the celebrity accorded their fathers differed, so too did the private circumstances of Crookshank and Lyttelton. The removal of Crookshank Pasha made no material difference to his family since it was from his wife that his wealth stemmed. There was now created the ménage that would sustain Crookshank for most of the rest of his life. His sister and his mother ministered to his every need, cared for him physically and sustained him emotionally until their deaths in 1948 and 1954 respectively. The Crookshanks' initial London base was in Queen Anne's Mansions, a fourteen-storey apartment block that had just been built, 'without any external decoration . . . for real ugliness unsurpassed by any other great building in all London'. In 1937 they moved to 51 Pont Street. Visiting them there just after the outbreak of the Second World War, the politician Cuthbert Headlam found 'the Crookshanks *mère fils et fille* exactly the same as ever – the women garrulous, Harry as self centred'.[70] 'As you entered through the heavily leaded glass door,' Harold Macmillan's brother-in-law remembered, 'the catacomb like gloom was relieved only by one small weak electric bulb, like the light on the tabernacle "dimly burning".' The house was a shrine to the Crookshanks' life in the 1890s: 'Eastern *objets d'art* and uncomfortable Victorian furniture.'[71]

For Lyttelton the death of his father changed a great deal in his life. Alfred Lyttelton had been a rich man, but his wealth derived mainly from the income he earned not capital he had accumulated. On his deathbed Alfred Lyttelton had commended Oliver to the care of his friend Arthur Balfour. This was a choice based on sentiment or ignorance given Balfour's spectacular mismanagement of the fortune that he had inherited. It was quite clear that Oliver would have to make his own way in the world. The most obvious way forward was to follow his father into the law: by 1914 he was eating dinners at the Inns of Court and clerking for judges on the circuit.[72]

Although by the summer of 1914 the future was beginning to be limned, – Lyttelton would be a lawyer, Cranborne would be a lord, Macmillan would be a gentleman publisher – the four were still little more than interested observers of the scene. Their hopes and interests reflected very accurately their position in society. They did not lack talent but none of them was outstanding. If the example of others, grandfathers, fathers and brothers, brought this home to them they nevertheless had a high opinion of themselves. They had a fund of impressions and sometimes inchoate opinions. They were, in a word, undergraduates, and typical of the breed. As Lyttelton himself later put it: 'At the University I merely became social and an educated *flâneur*. It was the camp and the Army that turned me into a case-hardened man.'[73] The fact that one in four of those who were at Oxford and Cambridge at the same time as this quartet were to be killed in the Great War should not lead us to over-dramatize their pre-war experience. They had not 'grown up in a society which was half in love with death'. They would have been surprised to have been told that 'they were afflicted with the romantic fatalism that characterized that apocalyptic age'.[74] The picture of a golden but doomed generation is an *ex post facto* invention.

2

Grenadiers

To serve in the Guards was to have a very specific experience of the war. They were socially élitist, officered by aristocrats or by those who aspired to be like aristocrats. They were also a combat élite. Robert Graves reported the view that the British army in France was divided into three equal parts: units that were always reliable, units that were usually reliable and unreliable units.[1] The Guards were on his 'always reliable' list. They were introverted, especially so once an entire Guards division was created in 1915. A junior officer would rarely ever come into contact with a senior officer who was himself not a Guardsman. They had an unshakeable *esprit de corps*. They were envied by other units. James Stuart, Cranborne and Macmillan's brother-in-law, who served with the Royal Scots, remembered that 'the Guards were always regarded by the Regiments of the Line as spoilt darlings'.[2]

All this mattered. Although the experience of war was one of terrifying loneliness, to succeed one had to be part of a successful team. Seen from a distance, the industrialized slaughter of the Great War seemed to submerge the individual in the mass. Yet this was not the experience of the young officers. The mass was very distant: the platoon, the company, the battalion and especially the battalion officers were the points of reference that mattered. Combatants faced the terror of 'men against fire': caught in an artillery barrage or enfiladed by machine-guns, it did not matter whether a man was the best or worst soldier – survival was purely a matter of luck. Yet on other occasions success in close-quarters fighting rested on skill, strength and the will to prevail.

It mattered what one did and with whom. It also mattered when one joined the army. Those undergraduates who volunteered in 1914 reached the front in 1915. Although they were part of the process by which the army transformed itself from a small professional force into a 'people's army', those in the Guards were inoculated against this experience. Many 'hostilities only' officers entered the Guards regiments, but 'dilution' was strictly limited: the Grenadier Guards had doubled in size from two to four battalions by 1915, but the process went no further for the rest of the war. The new Guards officers were, however, not insulated from the battles of 1915 and 1916. It was in these battles that the army grappled with the problem of how to fight a modern war. It was a bitter experience. Casualties were very high. Nearly 15 per cent of those officers who fought in the battles of 1915 died, nearly one quarter were wounded. Well over one quarter of those who had joined up from Oxford and Cambridge at the start of the war died.[3] This cohort's career as regimental infantry officers was effectively over by the end of the battle of the Somme in 1916.

The horrors of the Western Front were not, as it happened, at the forefront of the minds of four patriotic undergraduates in the first months of the war. Their anxieties were more about their social position in the struggle. Cranborne and Lyttelton had, as usual, a head start because of their connections. Cranborne's father had a proprietary interest in the 4th Battalion of the Bedfordshire Regiment, which he himself had taken to South Africa to fight in the Boer War. Salisbury had promised Alfred Lyttelton on his deathbed that he would watch out for Oliver's interests. He promised to fix commissions for his son and his ward as soon as possible. Little over a week after the outbreak of the war, Lyttelton and Cranborne handed in their applications for a commission.[4] Cranborne invited Lyttelton and another friend, Arthur Penn, to Hatfield to await their call-up.[5] They whiled away their time with shotguns. The juxtaposition of a shooting party as the preliminary to a war later caused them some grim amusement. Penn, invalided home, having been shot in both legs, wrote up his own game book as, 'BEAT – Cour de l'Avoué: BAG – Self'.[6]

Despite Lord Salisbury's patronage, the trio remained fearful that they would become trapped in the wrong part of the military machine. 'We are having trouble about our commissions,' Lyttelton wrote anxiously. 'The War Office, gazetted six officers, all complete outsiders, yesterday to the Regiment and none of us. The Regiment is furious because they loathe having outsiders naturally, we are angry because it seems possible that we may be gazetted to K[itchener]'s army.' Salisbury made a personal visit to the War Office and 'raised hell'.[7] The wait was made even more maddening for Lyttelton and Penn by Cranborne's new-found enthusiasm for playing the mouth organ.[8]

Salisbury was able to secure commissions for his son and his son's friends. They joined their regiment at Harwich. It seems the trio had originally intended to stay with the Bedfordshires: Salisbury had hoped that the battalion would be sent overseas as a garrison or to France as a second-echelon formation. This plan was abandoned as soon as it became clear that reserve formations like the Bedfordshire militia would be cannibalized to provide manpower for fighting formations. Cranborne and Lyttelton had ambivalent feelings about not being posted to a line infantry battalion. 'I am sorry because I must fight,' Lyttelton wrote, 'and I am glad ... because I should rather dislike going into a regiment – probably a bad one – in which I know no one.'[9] On 12 November 1914 their chances of going to France as part of a battalion disappeared: 'it was the most tragic sight,' in Lyttelton's view, 'seeing three hundred of our best men leaving for the front ... without a single officer of their own'.[10] Rumours flew around the camp that the battalion would become little more than a training establishment. Lyttelton and Cranborne felt that any obligation they had had to stay with their regiment had been removed. Lord Salisbury had always kept up close links with the Guards, recruiting time-expired NCOs to provide the backbone of his own regiment. With this kind of backing it was relatively easy to effect a transfer. In December 1914 they were commissioned into the Grenadier Guards.

Although they were a little slower off the mark, Crookshank and Macmillan had similar experiences. Crookshank initially obtained a commission with the Hampshire Regiment.[11] Then a 'course of instruction at Chelsea' gave him 'furiously to think, and made me decide for a transfer into the Grenadier Guards, in spite of arguments on the part of the 12 Hants and offer of a captaincy'.[12] While Lyttelton and Cranborne were at Harwich, Macmillan was at Southend with the King's Royal Rifle Corps. He too saw that his battalion would be used as a training establishment. His later recollection tallies so closely with Lyttelton's experience that it has the ring of truth. He hung on, but 'after Christmas [1914] was over and my twenty-first birthday approaching, I began to lose heart'. As Lyttelton and Cranborne had turned to Lord Salisbury to use his influence, so Macmillan 'naturally' turned to his mother: 'I was sent for and interviewed by . . . Sir Henry Streatfeild [the officer commanding the Grenadiers' reserve battalion in London],' Macmillan recalled. 'It was all done by influence.'[13] Sir Henry had become an old hand at dispensing these 'favours'. It must have seemed that virtually every English family with social influence and a son of military age was beating a path to his door.[14]

There were, however, few more decisive ways in which to emerge from the protective carapace of family influence than to join a front-line combat unit on the Western Front. The superior connections of Lyttelton and Cranborne gave them the first crack of the whip. They crossed to France together on 21 February 1915 and joined the 2nd Battalion, Grenadier Guards, on duty as part of the 4th Guards Brigade in northern France. They were immediately thrown into the classic pattern of battalion life: alternations between the trenches and billets behind the front line. The trenches they found themselves in were also typical of a quiet but active sector. Each side was using snipers and grenade throwers to harass the other and artillery shelled the positions intermittently.[15]

Beyond the physical dangers of trench warfare the most striking feature of their new world was the regimental 'characters'. These were the regular officers who had joined the Guards in the late 1890s. Their years of peacetime soldiering had inculcated them with the proper Grenadier 'attitude'. Promotion in peace had been glacially slow. At the time when the new arrivals encountered them they were still only captains or majors, the war being their chance for advancement. By the end of it those that survived were generals. They were attractive monsters, the ideals to which a new boy must aspire.

The second-in-command of the 2nd Battalion was 'Ma' Jeffreys, named for a popular madam of his subaltern days. A huge corvine presence, Jeffreys was known for his utter dedication to doing things the Grenadier way. He was a reactionary who regretted that the parvenu Irish and Welsh Guards were allowed to be members of the Brigade of Guards. It should be Star, Thistle and Grenade only in his view.[16] E. R. M. Fryer, another Old Etonian, described by Lyttelton as the 'imperturbable Fryer', who joined the 2nd Battalion in May 1915, regretted that 'Guardsmen aren't made in a day and I was one of a very small number who joined the Regiment in France direct from another regiment without passing through the very necessary moulding process at Chelsea barracks'. He found himself being given special, and not particularly enjoyable, lessons by Jeffreys on how to be a Grenadier.'[17] Jeffreys was considered to be 'one of the greatest regimental soldiers'.[18]

Many years after the fact, Lyttelton admired Jeffreys as an example of insouciant courage. A runner was missing and Jeffreys, accompanied by his orderly 'in full view of the enemy and in broad daylight, strode out to find him, and did find him. By some chance, or probably because the enemy had started to cook their breakfasts, he was not shot at. Such actions are not readily forgotten by officers or men, and the very same second-in-command, who had without any question risked his life ... would have of course damned a young officer into heaps for halting his platoon on the wrong foot on the parade ground.'[19] While he was serving with him, however, he admired him as a courageous realist: 'He is exceedingly careful of his own safety,' he noted in June 1915, 'where precautions are possible, but where they are not courageous. Any risk where necessary, none where not.' When his commanding officer was killed at Festubert, he showed no emotion: 'after seven months in the closest intimacy with a man whom he liked, you might have thought that that man's death by a bullet which passed through his own coat would have shaken him. Not at all.'[20]

'Boy' Brooke, who was brigade-major of the 4th Guards Brigade and later CO of the 3rd Battalion Grenadier Guards, never spoke before luncheon. He treated his subordinates to 'intimidating silences, when the most that could be expected was a curt order delivered between clenched teeth, derived from a slow acting digestion, which clothed the world in a bilious haze until the first glass of port brought a ray of sunshine'. After luncheon he was 'charming, helpful and humorous'.[21] Boy could take a dislike to a junior officer. One such, who was 'rather over-refined and a fearful snob', 'should not', he believed, 'have found his way into the regiment'. Arriving at the end of a five-hour march, Brooke could not find his billeting party. Eventually the officer 'emerged from an *estaminet*, and gave some impression of wiping drops of beer from his moustache. He came up and saluted, and not a Grenadier salute at that. His jacket was flecked with white at the back' from sitting against the wall of the pub, '"Ay regret to inform you, Sir, that the accommodation in this village is quite inadequate".' To which Brooke replied, '"Is that any reason you should be covered with bird-shit?"' and had him transferred.[22]

Lord Henry 'Copper' (he was red-haired and blue-eyed) Seymour and 'Crawley' de Crespigny, a family friend of the Cecils, were 2nd Battalion company commanders in 1915. Lord Henry had had to take leave of absence from the regiment because of his gambling debts. As a result he had been wounded early in the war while leading 'native levies' in Africa. He evaded a medical board and found his way to France. His wounds had not healed and needed to be dressed regularly by his subalterns. He was a notorious disciplinarian.

De Crespigny was also a fierce disciplinarian on duty but notoriously lax off duty with those he liked. He had been a well-known gentleman jockey, feared for having horse-whipped a punter who suggested he had thrown a race. Since his best friend was Lord Henry, he was known to treat officers with gambling debts lightly while damning anyone who reported any of them as a bounder. He suffered greatly with his stomach as a result of the alcoholic excess of his early years.[23] 'Hunting, steeplechasing, gambling and fighting were "Crawley's" chief if not only interests', remembered Harold Macmillan. Macmillan 'never saw him read a book, or even refer to one. To all intents and purposes, he was illiterate.' Even when ordered to desist, because they made him too visible, 'Crawley' always wore gold spurs.[24]

Whatever private thoughts Lyttelton and Cranborne had about their new life, they kept up a joking façade for their families back in England: 'The worst of it is that the hotel is very bad,' Lyttelton reported to Cranborne's mother, 'if (as Bobbety and I have hoped) we come to explore the fields of battle after the war with our respective families en masse we shall have to look elsewhere for lodging. By Jove how we shall "old soldier" you.'[25] A ten-day stay in Béthune, punctuated by light-hearted 'regimentals', boxing matches and concert parties, was merely a prelude to more serious business.

On 10 March 1915 the 4th Guards Brigade marched north to take part in an attack around Neuve Chapelle. The attack proved to be a bloody disaster. Luckily for the new officers they did not take part. Twice the battalion prepared to go over the top but twice was ordered to stand down. Within their first three weeks at the front, Cranborne and Lyttelton experienced manning the front line, the off-duty regimental routine and the nightmarish possibilities of the offensive. The horrors of war were all too apparent. The battalion returned to trenches near Givenchy that were neither deep enough nor bulletproof. The experience was nerve-jangling. German artillery and mortar fire was effective against these trenches. On one occasion such fire was induced for frivolous reasons: the Prince of Wales visited the battalion and 'tried his hand at sniping, and ... there was an immediate retaliation'. The threat of mines was constant: 'everyone was always listening for any sound'. In May the first reports of German gas attacks further north at Ypres arrived and there were desperate attempts to rig up makeshift respirators. The visible landscape was grim. 'The village was a complete ruin, the farms were burnt, the remains of wagons and farm implements were scattered on each side of the road. This part of the country had been taken and re-taken several times, and many hundreds of British, Indian, French and German troops were buried here.'[26]

Givenchy was also their first sight of 'war crimes' or 'Hun beastliness'. Anyone wounded in trench raids was hard to recover. The Germans fired at the stretcher bearers who tried to reach them. Cases occurred 'of men being left out wounded and without food or drink four or five days, conscious all the time that if they moved the Germans would shoot or throw bombs at them. At night the German raiding parties would be sent out to bayonet any of the wounded still living.' It is unclear whether the 'beastliness' was solely on the German side. Certainly by 1916 there were clear instances of the British refusing to take prisoners on the grounds that 'a live Boche is no use to us or to the world in general'.[27] Indeed, a memoir written by a private in the Scots Guards about his experiences later in the war was at the centre of German counter-charges in the 1920s about British 'war crimes'. The private, Stephen Graham, reported that the 'opinion cultivated in the army regarding the Germans was that they were a sort of vermin like plague-rats and had to be exterminated'. He provided an anecdote set near Festubert, where both Lyttelton and Cranborne fought: 'the idea of taking prisoners had become very unpopular. A good soldier was one who would not take a prisoner.'[28] Even leaving aside 'war crimes', the fighting was desperate and personal. Armar Corry, an Eton contemporary of Lyttelton and Cranborne, led a wire-cutting party that ran into a German patrol. Corry shot one of the Germans, as did his sergeant. His private threw a grenade. The German officer leading the patrol drew his pistol and shot Corry's sergeant, corporal and private. With his entire party dead, Corry fled for his life.[29]

Whatever the extent of the brutalization Lyttelton and Cranborne were undergoing, they were certainly becoming cynical about their senior commanders. In March a printed order of the day arrived over the name of Sir Douglas Haig, who was immediately pronounced an 'infernal bounder'. There was 'much angry comment' from the junior officers about Haig's 'bombastic nonsense'. Looking out from his trench, Lyttelton commented: 'the attacks on Givenchy had failed . . . I know the position from which these attempts were launched and a more criminal piece of generalship you cannot imagine.'[30] Five days after the launch of the Festubert offensive in May, Lyttelton wrote: 'There is some depression among the officers at the great offensive . . . We are rather asking ourselves: if we can't advance after that cannonade how are we to get through?'[31]

Their anger at and fear of the incompetence of the army commander was mitigated, however, by a continued belief in the superiority of the Guards. The Indian troops and the Camerons alongside whom they fought may have 'showed the utmost gallantry in the attack, but their ways are not ours at other times. When it comes to bayonet work they are as courageous as we are, but they haven't got the method, the care or the discipline to make good their gains, or show the same steadiness as the Brigade.'[32] Lyttelton and Cranborne were also buoyed up by each other's company. 'I had a very amusing talk with Bobbety yesterday,' Oliver wrote in April, 'we nearly always have a good crack now and great fun it is. The more I see of him the more I like him.' The two young men found themselves convulsed by laughter at the thought that the pictures on the date boxes they received in their food parcels looked exactly like the paintings of an 'artistic' acquaintance of theirs, Lady Wenlock.[33]

Although the Guards Brigade had seen plenty of action since Lyttelton and Cranborne joined their unit in February, it had been used as a support formation rather than an assault unit. The 2nd Battalion Grenadier Guards was finally committed to lead an attack on 17 May 1915, eight days after the beginning of the battle of Festubert. Lyttelton and Cranborne had the chance of a brief conversation before the battle began. They were, Lyttelton wrote, 'pretty cheerful as it was clear that we were in the course of wiping the eye of the rest of the army and justifying the German name of "the Iron Division"'.[34] They began moving up at 3.30 in the morning in extremely difficult conditions. The Germans were shelling all the roads leading towards the trenches so the battalion had to move at snail's pace in dispersed 'artillery formation' over open ground. Confusion reigned. 'When it reached the supports of the front line, it was by no means easy to ascertain precisely what line the Battalion was expected to occupy. Units had become mixed as the . . . result of the previous attack, and it was impossible to say for certain what battalion occupied a trench, or to locate the exact front.'

It was not until late afternoon that the battalion started to move towards the actual front line. The route was clogged in mud and it was dark before they reached the front trenches. 'The men had stumbled over obstacles of every sort, wrecked trenches and shell holes, and had finally wriggled themselves into the front line.' The German trenches captured on the previous day which they passed over 'were a mass of dead men, both German and British, with heads, legs and other gruesome objects lying about amid bits of wire obstacles and remains of accoutrements'.[35] 'It was a night,' Lyttelton recalled a week later, 'I shall never forget.' The encounter with such carnage sickened him but 'only turned me up for about ten minutes. After that,' he admitted, 'you cease to feel that you are dealing with what were once men . . . We were trying to drag a body out – it had no head – and I found by flashing a light that one of my fellows was standing on its legs. So I said, "Get off. How can we get it out if you stand on it, show some sense." Then I flashed my light behind me and I found I had both feet on a German's chest who had [been] nearly trodden right in.'[36]

The advance had been so difficult that the commanding officer, Wilfred Smith, decided that he could not launch his attack on the position known as 'La Quinque Rue' as he had been ordered. He decided instead to wait until dawn. Ma Jeffreys was put in charge of the front line, commanding 2 and 3 Companies. Cranborne was commanding a platoon in 2 Company with Percy Clive, a Conservative MP serving as a 'hostilities only' officer, as his company commander. Held in reserve were 1 and 4 Companies. Lyttelton was thus further back with his platoon in 4 Company, commanded by 'Crawley' de Crespigny.

The 18th of May dawned misty and wet. Visibility was so bad that the attack was postponed once more. They lay in their waterlogged scrapes all day. Suddenly at 3.45 in the afternoon a peremptory order arrived to attack at 4.30 p.m. Jeffreys had to make hurried preparations. He decided to launch the assault using 3 Company, with one platoon of 2 Company under Cranborne in support. Haste proved fatal. The attacking force was decimated. A short artillery bombardment failed to knock out the German machine-guns. As a result 'the men never had any real chance of reaching the German trenches . . . the first platoon was mown down before it had covered a hundred yards, the second melted before it reached even as far, and the third shared the same fate'. Armar Corry was the only officer in the company to survive.[37]

Cranborne, however, cheated death. He did not lead his platoon forward into this maelstrom. Indeed, he was rendered unfit to do anything by the noise of the battle. Accounts differ about what rendered him *hors de combat*. The regimental history records that he was 'completely deafened by the shells which burst incessantly round his platoon during the attack'.[38] His own medical report, based on a doctor's examination on 26 May, states: 'Near Festubert on 18 May 1915, he became deaf from the noise of rifle fire close to his left ear. He also had "ringing" noises in that ear.'[39] Near the stunned Cranborne a fierce argument raged between the remaining officers of the battalion. Percy Clive, Cranborne's company commander, had realized that the attack was a senseless massacre. When Ma Jeffreys ordered him to lead 2 Company forward once more, Clive refused to obey on the grounds that to advance was plainly suicidal. As a result the battalion stayed put. As the casualties, including Cranborne, were evacuated, the brigade major, 'Fat Boy' Gort, came up to investigate. Gort, 'the bravest of the brave', who finished the war bedecked with medals including the Victoria Cross, agreed with Clive. Lord Cavan, the Grenadier commander of the 4th Guards Brigade, ordered the battalion to dig in where it lay – they had advanced about 300 yards and come up short of their objective by about 200 yards.[40]

That night Lyttelton moved up with 4 Company to relieve the shattered remnants of 3 Company: 'it was pitch dark, raining and cold'. He and another officer went out to try and recover some of the wounded. 'It was a bad job. Some of these fellows had crawled into shell-holes about twenty feet deep and getting them out was a critical business.' 'The whole place,' wrote Lyttelton as he tried to piece together his experiences afterwards, 'was a sea of mud, and the scene still remains incoherent in my memory, plunging about for overworked stretcher bearers, falling into shell-holes, losing our way, wet and tired, we felt all the time rather impotent.'[41] Opinion among the surviving battalion officers was that the whole affair had been mismanaged. The generals had bungled in ordering them to attack on the afternoon of the 18th with so little warning.[42]

The battle of Festubert convinced the relatives who had been instrumental in getting men into the Guards that service with a combat infantry battalion on the Western Front was not necessarily a good idea. When Cranborne was shipped home, it was discovered that his injuries were not serious and that he would soon be able to rejoin his regiment. 'The ear,' his medical board was told, 'has been examined by a specialist and has been diagnosed as a course of labyrinthine deafness; prognosis good.'[43] He was granted three weeks' leave. While he was on leave the Cecils' family doctor diagnosed him with appendicitis. His friends regarded this as an amazing stroke of luck,[44] as was clear from the letters of commiseration he received. It must be sore having a bad ear and a bad gut: 'But,' one friend serving with a line infantry regiment in France, added, 'I wonder if you are sorry. For goodness' sake don't come out here again.'[45] Lyttelton cheerfully chipped in, 'There is a great deal of satisfaction in hearing from someone whom you have just seen in Flanders, at Park Lane.'[46] Another friend, also recuperating from wounds, wrote, 'I think we are both well out of it for a bit, Bobbety, don't you agree with me. It was the most unpleasant two months I've ever spent and I don't think you cared for it much – did you?'[47]

Cranborne attended regular medical boards. On each occasion his leave was extended. There seemed to be enough time to attend to his own affairs. He proposed marriage to Betty Cavendish, the daughter of Lord Richard Cavendish, the younger brother of the Duke of Devonshire. It was an entirely suitable match between two of the great aristocratic families of England, though Bobbety's father wryly noted that his son's choice had let him in for some difficult dowry negotiations: Dick Cavendish was notorious for pleading poverty.[48] Lord Richard, however, did his new son-in-law a good turn by intervening with the War Office to have his leave of absence extended to the end of the year.[49]

Families were caught between a desire to see their sons removed from danger and their sons' desire not to be seen pulling strings to escape the front line. Another junior officer in the Grenadier Guards, Raymond Asquith, son of the prime minister, angrily told his wife that: 'The PM in disregard of a perfectly explicit order from me to take no steps in that direction without my express permission has tipped the wink to Haig ... no one will believe that this [staff] job has been arranged without my knowledge ... So in mere self-defence I shall have to try to get back to the Regiment when the fighting season starts.'[50] He was right to suspect that people were keeping a spiteful eye on these things. When Asquith himself was killed, one of his father's Cabinet colleagues wrote to a newspaper editor, 'As for Lloyd George himself, he risks very little. His sons are well sheltered.'[51]

Someone was looking out for Oliver Lyttelton. Soon after meeting his mother in Brussels, he was offered a post as ADC to Lord Cavan. Cavan needed an ADC because he was to give up the 4th Guards Brigade and take command of a line division. 'I feel very weepy reading of your meeting with Oliver and the news of Cavan's offer,' wrote Lyttelton's uncle to his mother. 'I do hope to heavens there will not be a hitch in Oliver's appointment and that nobody will put any obstacles in the way or, which is just as important, [he] feel[s] that he oughtn't to take it.' If strings had been pulled, that was no cause for shame. 'After all the boy has had his grilling in the trenches, gone out ... and done the brave thing and if some general does *choose* to pick him out one can only be thankful ... Of course there are plenty of risks still but it must be *much* safer than a platoon leader.'[52] His friends agreed that his removal from the front line was a matter for celebration.[53]

In fact intervention by figures considerably more eminent even than the Lyttelton clan was to change the pattern of the war for both Lyttelton and Macmillan. As Lyttelton took up his post, Lord Cavan was preparing himself to meet King George at Windsor. Cavan had gone home to visit his wife, who was sick with diphtheria. Calling in at Chelsea barracks, he was shocked when Streatfeild told him that not only would a fourth battalion of Grenadiers be formed, but that it would be sent to France as part of a Guards division. Two days later His Majesty graciously informed Cavan that he would command the new formation. As far as Cavan could tell, the idea had been put to the king by Lord Kitchener. It seemed that his lordship was keen to curry favour by giving the Prince of Wales, who was attached to the Grenadiers, a bigger stage on which to perform. Cavan did not believe that the division had any military logic. He was horrified to discover that the four battalions of Grenadiers were to be formed into a single Grenadier brigade within the division. This, no doubt, seemed a glorious idea in Windsor and Whitehall, but it struck the Grenadier Cavan as disastrous. As he explained to Kitchener, 'if they went into action we might lose at one blow more officers than we could replace all belonging to one Regiment'. Although Cavan could do little about the *fait accompli* of a Guards division, he at least averted the potential destruction of the Grenadier Guards by insisting that all brigades contain a mixture of battalions from each Guards regiment.[54]

Because of the creation of the Guards Division Lyttelton did not leave the Guards for a line division: he became a junior staff officer in the Guards Division. As Lyttelton left the 2nd Battalion, Crookshank joined it, having missed Festubert cooling his heels in a base camp near Le Havre. They were eventually able to meet up for tea and bridge when Lyttelton came back to visit his old unit.[55] Macmillan was also affected by the reorganization. Gazetted into the Grenadiers in March, he was assigned to the new 4th Battalion in July 1915. It was almost as if the old Eton pattern remained in place. The two Oppidans had used their influence to be first in and first out. Now the scholars had arrived. If Festubert was the baptism of fire for Cranborne and Lyttelton, Loos was to be Crookshank and Macmillan's battle.

The first to arrive, Crookshank, had a hot welcome. Three days after he reached the 2nd Battalion they were sent into a set of notorious trenches known as the 'Valley of Death'. Ten days later they moved to better trenches only to face the threat of a new, and lethally effective, German trench mortar – the *Minenwerfer*. Even when they retired to billets in Béthune, their luck did not improve. The Germans shelled the town, rendering their rest period 'a farce'.[56] It was in the trenches near Givenchy, however, that Crookshank made his name in the regiment. The battle of Festubert had proved to the satisfaction of both British and Germans that charging enemy machine-gun emplacements was suicidal. The obvious alternative was to approach the enemy underground. Both sides had initiated a large number of tunnelling operations to set mines. The Germans in the Givenchy sector were particularly keen on these operations and had seized the upper hand: they made the Guards' life both dangerous and miserable through a combination of mines and mortar bombs lobbed into the craters they created. 'The casualties from mining and bombing in addition to those from rifle fire and shells were very heavy,' noted the regimental history.

Digging deeper trenches and counter-mines became an unpleasant necessity for the Guards. Percy Clive and Crookshank were leading a digging party into an orchard near the trenches when they were caught in a German mine explosion. By the greatest good fortune they were just short of the mine when it went off. The whole ground moved up in one great convulsion, and when it settled down several men were completely buried. Clive was shot straight up in the air by the blast and came down so doubled up that he nearly knocked his teeth out with his knees. Crookshank, on the other hand, was buried by the earth thrown up in the explosion. It was a perilous situation. He was trapped in an earthen tomb, quite unable to move. No one on the surface could see where he was. If no one came to his rescue he would suffocate. If Clive had rescued Cranborne's platoon from certain death by disobeying Jeffreys's order to advance, his quick thinking saved Crookshank also. Although cut, bruised and groggy himself, he had enough presence of mind to work out where Crookshank had been standing just before the mine went off. Clive directed his men to dig hard.[57] A brother officer estimated that Crookshank had been buried for twenty minutes before the rescue party dug him out. He was in a state of shock but otherwise unhurt. He 'won his name' by his insouciant reaction to his experience. By evening he had returned to duty with the company. 'He didn't seem to worry at all at his misfortune,' in the recollection of an officer in 3 Company, 'and carried on duty as soon as he had been disinterred, minus, however, his cap, and the one he borrowed from a private soldier didn't fit, and this was his only trouble!'[58] Crookshank's own account of the incident was suitably laconic: 'I was ... buried for a long time, but rescued in the end.'[59]

Of any of the quartet Macmillan adapted least well to army life. In his memoirs he famously drew the distinctions between 'gownsmen' and 'swordsmen', characterizing himself as one of the former who had by force of circumstances become one of the latter.[60] Lyttelton and Crookshank threw themselves into the role of regimental officer with enthusiasm, whereas Macmillan tried to re-create an intimate bookish coterie in the trenches. 'My library is indeed very wide and Liberal,' he noted with satisfaction, already thinking of posterity. 'I shall try to send back some which I have read and should like to preserve. I have written inside "France Sept. 1915."' 'I have a friend who was said to have read the *Iliad* "to make him fierce",' he told his mother. 'I confess that I prefer to do so to keep myself civilized. For the more I live in these warlike surroundings, the more thankful I am for all the traditions of the classic culture compared to which these which journalists would have us call "the realities of life" are little but extravagant visions of a fleeting nightmare, lacking true value or permanency.'[61] Macmillan and his friend Bimbo Tennant were delighted, for instance, when they rode over for dinner with a friend at the 1st Battalion to find most of the officers, 'snorting Generals and Majors', absent. 'We had,' Tennant told his mother, 'a delightful evening *à trois* and had one good laugh after another, being all blessed with the same sense of humour, and unhampered by any shadow of militarism.'[62] Lyttelton's letters too were full of pleas for books, but he wanted 'shockers' rather than Homer or Theocritus. He even enjoyed *Greenmantle* by his mother's friend John Buchan, despite the fact that 'he hasn't been within a hundred yards of the truth yet'.[63]

It was with heartfelt relief that the Guards left Givenchy and marched south. Now that the Guards Division had assembled, Lyttelton, Crookshank and Macmillan were all present. Lyttelton was mounted at Cavan's side, Crookshank was marching with the 2nd Battalion, Macmillan with the newly arrived 4th Battalion. They all met up at the end of August. To mark the combination of all four Grenadier battalions in one Guards formation, the regiment held a formal dinner to celebrate the occasion. It was, as Macmillan reported, 'a most unique dinner party. All the officers of the Regiment who are in France – (that) is in the four battalions or on the Staff . . . There were 96 of us in all.'[64] Even the newest and most temporary Grenadier officer was made to feel part of an exclusive club as well as a great and glorious enterprise. 'I saw many old friends,' wrote Harold's fellow 4th Battalion new boy, Bimbo Tennant, 'and was very happy.'[65] Just as important as the *élan* of the Guards Division was a sense of a more scientific approach to the new warfare. The battalions carried out practice attacks on mock-ups of trenches under the watchful eyes of Jeffreys and Seymour. The army had realized that rifle and bayonet were not necessarily the most effective tools for trench warfare. Weapons that could give infantry more 'bang for their shilling', such as grenades, machine-guns and mortars, were coming into vogue. Macmillan was nominated as a bombing officer and spent his time training troops in his battalion in grenade techniques.[66]

The *esprit de corps* of the young officers did little to avert disaster at their next engagement, the battle of Loos. It is doubtful whether the Guards Division's attack at Loos ever had a chance: 'it had to start from old German trenches, the range of which the German artillery knew to an inch, while the effect of our own original bombardment had died away'.[67] Crookshank and the 2nd Battalion arrived on the battlefield on 26 September 1915. During the 27th they slowly worked their way into the old German trenches, Crookshank in the rearguard. Despite their proximity to the battle, however, the order never came to attack.[68] The 4th Battalion, however, bore the brunt of it. It was Macmillan who was to experience the full force of the battle.

Owing to incompetent staff work, the 4th Battalion had spent the 26th uncomfortably sitting on a muddy road while a cavalry corps passed by.[69] Next day the battalion officers were gathered together by their commanding officer, Claud Hamilton, and told they were to attack Hill 70 just to the east of Loos. Macmillan's company commander, Aubrey Fletcher, was sent forward to discover the best route into Loos.[70] Macmillan himself did 'not feel frightened yet, only rather bewildered'.[71] At 2.30 p.m. on the 27th the battalion advanced down the road into Loos in dispersed formation. They were immediately and heavily shelled by German artillery. To make matters worse, they were enfiladed from the right by a German machine-gun. As they approached Loos, Aubrey Fletcher led them running down a slope into an old German communications trench. Unfortunately he had taken them the wrong way. The brigade commander came galloping down the road and ordered the battalion not to enter the trench but follow him in an entirely different direction. The result was chaos, with the battalion split in half. In the confusion, neither half of the battalion could find the other. The main body of the Grenadiers attacked Hill 70 with the Welsh Guards. Macmillan was lucky to miss this assault. The Guards swept forward taking heavy casualties, but reached the crest of Hill 70. In the heat of battle, however, the Grenadiers advanced too far over the crest and exposed themselves to fire from the next German line. All who took part in this attack were killed.[72]

Meanwhile the remainder of the battalion, including Macmillan, under the leadership of Captain Jummie Morrison, had no orders whatsoever. They decided to attach themselves to the 2nd Guards Brigade and attack Puits 14, a German strongpoint to the north. This attack too was a disaster. Unbeknown to the Grenadiers, the 2nd Guards Brigade had withdrawn without them: they thus 'found themselves completely isolated'.[73] They had to try and escape by crawling away from the German line. Jummie Morrison was too fat to be a good crawler. As he and Macmillan tried to take their turn, Macmillan was shot in the head. He was incredibly lucky – it was a glancing blow. He was, however, concussed and no longer capable of taking an active part in proceedings.[74] As the small, lost and bewildered force tried to make themselves safer by digging in, Macmillan was shot again, this time in the right hand. The bullet fractured his third metacarpus bone. With his right arm crippled and in excruciating pain, he was ordered by Morrison to go back and find a clearing station. The hand wound proved to be much more serious than the head wound: Macmillan was troubled by his right arm for the rest of his life. Within a few days he found himself in hospital at Rouen, 'more frightened than hurt'.

The Guards Division's attack on Loos was hardly a triumph of the military art, the 4th Battalion Grenadier Guards alone having lost eleven officers and 342 men – 'it has been', Macmillan recorded, 'rather awful – most of our officers are hit'. Nevertheless the Guards exculpated themselves from all blame. 'The Guards Division,' Macmillan proudly proclaimed, 'has won undying glory, and *I was long enough there to see the lost Hill 70 recaptured.*'[75] Indeed Jummie Morrison's sad remnant had been sent to dig in on the hill that night, although in truth the Guards had only captured the western slopes, leaving the Germans in possession of the redoubt. From both Macmillan's perspective as a platoon officer and from Lyttelton's rather more elevated position at divisional HQ, it seemed that the Guards élite had been let down by Kitchener's army. 'Some of the New Army Divisions are rather shaky,' Macmillan wrote the day before the Guards went into action, 'my chief feeling at present is one of thankfulness that I am in the Brigade of Guards. All the way up on the road we were greeted with delight by the wounded and all other troops. And it is so much easier to command men who seem to obey orders with engrained [*sic*] and well disciplined alacrity as soon as they are given.'

'That the 21st and the 24th divisions,' Lyttelton confirmed, 'completely spoilt the show is I fear true.' Like Macmillan he felt that, as a Guards officer, he was in a position to patronize the line infantry. 'I'm afraid,' he observed with all the assurance of a man of twenty-two, 'that the New Army is trained too much with the idea: Oh we don't need discipline. These are not recruits driven into the ranks by hunger, they are patriots, it's ridiculous to ask a well-educated man of forty to salute an officer of twenty, and so on. The alpha and omega of soldiering and training is discipline and drill.' 'However,' he charitably conceded, 'those divisions of the New Army who have been blooded did quite creditably, the ninth and the fifteenth. The Territorials, who have some tradition if no discipline, attacked with great gallantry if not very efficiently.' Alternative accounts circulating in London drew his derision: 'As to the Guards Division being three hours late it is simply *pour rire* and goes to prove how very little people know of the war.'[76]

It was not only the Guards that used the 'Kitchener' divisions as scapegoats for the failure of the Loos offensive. Haig also laid the blame at the door of their tactical inadequacies. GHQ's post-mortem on Loos called for an increase in offensive raids and enhanced training for and use of grenades.[77] Thus the Guards found themselves thrust back into low-level but high-intensity warfare in the trenches just north of Loos. The post-Loos battle lines meant that in some places the British and German trenches were only thirty yards apart. There were continuous bombing and sniping duels. For the first time 2nd Battalion snipers were issued with telescopic sights, making the duels even more deadly. Crookshank was an early victim.[78] On 23 October his company commander took advantage of vision-obscuring mist to send him out at the head of a wiring party. He led his men out and back safely. As they gathered more wire to go out again, a German sniper shot him in the left leg. The bullet seems to have been a ricochet, for although it ended the 1915 campaigning season for him, it did no permanent damage. The next day he was safely ensconced on a hospital train heading back to the coast, 'very comfortable and everything to eat and drink that we wanted'.[79] Comfort levels improved even further when he reached England: he was sent to the officers' nursing home housed in Arlington Street, next door to Cranborne's London home.

Crookshank's wound meant that he missed the arrival of a national celebrity to serve with the 2nd Battalion. Winston Churchill, ejected from the Cabinet in disgrace after the failure of the Dardanelles expedition, was assigned to a reluctant Jeffreys to 'learn the ropes' before taking command of his own unit. Lyttelton, visiting the battalion dugout of his old unit, was surprised when the 'well-known domed head and stocky figure' emerged out of the darkness. It was their first proper meeting: Churchill, following his defection from the Tory party to the Liberals in 1904, had been *persona non grata* in the Lyttelton circle during Oliver's school and university days. That night at dinner Churchill held the floor. 'We listened – we had to,' Lyttelton remembered, as Churchill expounded his idea that the 'land battleship' or 'tank' would break the deadlock on the Western Front.[80] Churchill went on to describe to his sceptical audience the first trials of the new weapon that had taken place at Hatfield House. Later he was to present Lord Salisbury with the first tank as a memento to stand in the grounds.

In his letters home Churchill gave a vivid picture of the brutal war fought by the Grenadiers in the winter of 1915. 'Ten grenadiers under a kid went across by night to the German Trench which they found largely deserted or waterlogged,' he informed his wife, instructing her for obvious reasons to keep this account to herself.

> They fell upon a picket of Germans, beat the brains out of two of them with clubs & dragged a third home triumphantly as a prisoner. The young officer by accident let off his pistol & shot one of his own Grenadiers dead: but the others kept this secret and pretended it was done by the enemy – do likewise. The scene in the little dugout when the prisoner was brought in surrounded by these terrific warriors, in jerkins and steel helmets with their bloody clubs in hand – looking pictures of ruthless war – was one to stay in the memory. *C'est tres bon.*[81]

So many regular Guards officers were killed at Loos that 'even old-fashioned Guardsmen became convinced' that the 'patriots' would have to be used to fill junior command positions: 'from this time onwards', noted the official history, 'the battalions of the Guards Division were officered to a large extent by officers of the Special Reserve with very short training behind them'.[82] Lyttelton was one of the first 'beneficiaries' of this policy.[83] He had never really become comfortable as Cavan's ADC. Cavan's other ADC was his brother-in-law, Cuthbert Headlam, who was a good deal older than Lyttelton. Lyttelton was thus very much the youngest and most junior member of the divisional team.[84] There was 'nothing very much to do but fuss about horses and motor cars'. He was thus sanguine when it became clear that his position on the staff was untenable. When the adjutant of the 3rd Battalion went sick with varicose veins in the middle of the battle for Loos, Lyttelton was offered the chance to take his place. 'It was,' he admitted, 'rather unpleasant leaving our comfortable chateau especially as I knew that we were for the trenches and probably for a push . . . it was certainly not cheering.'[85] The offer was, however, too good an opportunity to miss, since he 'should anyway [have] *had* to return to duty with the Grenadiers as their losses have been so severe as to amount almost to irreparable'. He consoled his mother with the thought that 'an Adjutant is *far* safer than a company officer'.[86]

To become adjutant of a Guards battalion was quite a promotion. The adjutant was the senior captain in the battalion and in charge of its day-to-day organization. He acted as the staff officer to the commanding officer and was third-in-command in battle. The opportunities for promotion opened up both by casualties and the winnowing out of less forceful officers piqued the ambition of the army's 'thrusters'. Although this was really a game for regulars who could aspire to higher command positions, Lyttelton caught the bug. From late 1915 onwards his letters are as much about his ambitions and disappointments concerning further promotion as they are about the routine of trench warfare. He was turning into a first-class 'thruster'.

The importance of being a 'thruster' was brought home to Lyttelton when he arrived at the 3rd Battalion. This was a world away from Jeffreys's élite 2nd Battalion in which Lyttelton had been schooled. 'I never realized till that day,' he wrote after a month with his new unit, 'how good the 2nd Battalion were.'[87] Like the 4th Battalion, the 3rd had been badly mauled at Loos. Only six officers had survived the battle and Lyttelton did not find them an impressive group: 'I knew some of them but was not writing home about them.' 'They were all in a state of "Isn't it awful" and doing very little to make it less so.'[88] As one of those officers later confirmed, 'I think we felt a bit dazed and were glad enough when we were relieved [in the front line].' The situation was no better among the other ranks. The battalion had been severely weakened in the summer of 1915 when it had been 'skinned' of some of its best NCOs to create the 4th Battalion. After Loos most of the remaining experienced NCOs and nearly 400 men were dead and had been replaced by new drafts.[89]

The worst problem by far, it so happened, was the commanding officer. Lieutenant-Colonel Noel 'Porkie' Corry was the senior battalion commander in the brigade. He had specifically requested Lyttelton's assignment to his battalion. Corry's son, Armar, had not only been at Eton with Lyttelton but had also served with him in the 2nd Battalion, where he gained the reputation of an audacious trench raider, finally falling victim to a severe face wound during the pre-Loos skirmishing of August 1915. He was to lose his life at the Somme in 1916. Corry *père* was another matter entirely. Behind the lines he cut quite a dash.[90] The trenches, however, had broken his nerve. He was an incompetent, a coward and a drunkard.[91] Even worse for Lyttelton, he was desperately trying to deny his inadequacies both to himself and to his superiors by blaming others for the shortcomings of his unit. The situation was excruciatingly dangerous. Like the 2nd Battalion, the 3rd was expected to undertake aggressive skirmishing. Such operations were potentially deadly enough when carried out by brilliant young 'thrusters' under the command of equally brilliant officers like Jeffreys; they were doubly so when run by incompetents. Just before Lyttelton arrived, the battalion had been surprised by a German attack as they ham-fistedly tried to change over forward companies. 'The Germans had got possession of the whole battalion's front' and had to be ejected by the Coldstream Guards.[92]

As the 3rd Battalion moved back into the trenches near Loos Lyttelton's heart sank. The manoeuvre was carried out in a farcical manner. Porkie was 'rather like a monkey on hot bricks and one could see he was no good'. He didn't seem to know what his battalion was doing and blamed everybody else for the confusion. He fastened on to the problem of sandbags. 'It was so simple,' noted a frustrated Lyttelton, 'send a party for sandbags with an officer and let them follow us up the trench. Meanwhile let us go on. But he would have it that the whole battalion should go off and get the sandbags ... come back and go on.' Lyttelton was forced to stand in a trench arguing with his commanding officer. His arguments prevailed but they wasted precious time, moving neither forwards nor backwards, until the Germans started to shell their communications trench. As

Lyttelton noted viciously: 'this bit of shelling put the wind up Porkie' and all talk of sandbags was abandoned in the rush to a safer position.[93]

Things became even worse when the battalion was given the chance to 'recover its name' by carrying out a bombing attack on 'Little Willie', on one of the flanks of the formidable German strong-point known as the Hohenzollern Redoubt. Before the attack could go in, the battalion was ordered to dig a trench over to the Cold-streams to ensure that grenades could be moved up quickly and safely enough to keep the attack going. Lyttelton soon realized that Corry was in no hurry to push on with work on the trench since once it was completed the battalion would have to go 'over the top' on its raid. Lyttelton decided that 'if anything was to be done I should have to command the Battalion'. Although he was 'enjoying myself beyond measure' at the taste of command, he could not persuade his fellow officers to speed up the sapping by taking the risk of climbing out of the trench and digging over ground at night. 'This was awful,' he realized, 'because Porkie has got a poorish repu-tation for ability and is supposed to be likely to cart you.' He had taken responsibility and now risked being made a scapegoat for failure. Since the trench was not finished in time the Coldstreams had to step in once more and carry out the operation for the Grenadiers. Lyttelton 'could have cried with chagrin and disappointment'. He had never been 'so bitterly despondent as I was that morning'. It was more 'loss of name to the battalion'.[94] The post-mortem was equally depressing. The captain who had been digging the trench had in fact 'carted' Corry to John Ponsonby, the commander of the 2nd Guards Brigade, before Corry could blame anyone else. Corry 'looked grey and hopelessly rattled and walked up and down swear-ing, accusing, excusing, asking me questions no-one could answer like a child. "Do you think the Brigadier thinks" . . . "It's all the fault of the Coldstreams, they didn't help".' Then the word came down the line that the brigadier was not particularly worried by the trench-digging fiasco, 'which restored Porkie's morale at once'.[95] At the next opportunity he got 'very tight, and began to talk the most awful rot'.[96]

The wake-up call of the failed bombing operation did nothing to make Corry change his ways. He always seemed to find routes to avoid action. All he did was waste time by looking through a periscope, claiming 'he can see Germans everywhere'. His boasting was incessant: 'if he goes up alone, which is rare', Lyttelton complained, 'he always comes back having had the narrowest shave and having behaved with the utmost coolness'. The drinking continued to get worse, often leaving him incapable by the afternoon. He claimed credit for work done by his subordinate officers. To add insult to injury, Lyttelton noticed with the eye of an experienced gambler, he even cheated at poker.[97]

The commanding officer and adjutant of an infantry battalion perforce had an intimate relationship. Pressed daily into close contact with Corry, Lyttelton came to loathe him. While enjoying the increased responsibility thrust on his shoulders, he was placed in a dilemma. 'I wish to heaven he would be sent home but all the time I have to work to keep him on the job and not let him flout.' He began to despair that his superiors had not noticed Corry's incompetence clearly enough to relieve him of his command. By December he had made up his mind that he would 'cart' Corry as soon as he made a mistake that was clear and important enough to be laid at his door.[98] He rightly suspected that Corry was not the only one being blamed for the battalion's plight. Many of the other junior officers in the battalion thought he himself was 'too casual and conceited'.[99] He was, they charged, a 'bully and a toady'.[100] What he thought of as a difficult balancing act they saw as sucking up. A badly run unit was corrosive of relationships on all levels.

Fortunately for Lyttelton's reputation, the standards of the Brigade of Guards had not in fact slipped as much as he was coming to believe. Even without his dropping his commanding officer in the soup, senior officers had noticed that Corry was not up to the job. He was an old comrade of many of them, but he had to go. At the turn of the year, as Lyttelton was settling in to bear the same yoke he had carried through the autumn and winter of 1915, suddenly Corry was gone and Lyttelton found himself in temporary command of the battalion. Within days Ma Jeffreys arrived in a black temper.

He had been confidently expecting promotion and command of a Guards brigade.[101] 'I hate,' he confided to his diary, 'going to yet *another* temporary job, but I am told that it is in the best interests of the Regiment and I am expected to "pull the battalion through".'[102] A brisk tour of inspection suggested that the situation was not as black as had been thought. Corry really had been the main problem. After parading each company and talking to every officer, Jeffreys came to the conclusion that 'there is nothing much wrong except inexperience and that they are a bit "down on their luck"'. He was particularly complimentary about Lyttelton. His former subaltern had, he noted, 'the qualities to make a good' adjutant. In particular he had ensured that 'the system of the Regiment is being carried out and all want to do their best'.[103] The warmth was reciprocated. 'Ma was wonderful,' wrote a relieved and delighted Lyttelton. 'As soon as he found there was nothing very wrong he cheered up enormously.'[104] In fact Jeffreys found that after his initial pep-up the battalion did not need the special attention of a senior officer and he turned the unit over to Boy Brooke. After some difficult months, Lyttelton now found himself once more in an élite formation.

Lyttelton was becoming a valuable asset to the army. All too few of those volunteer officers who had gained experience in 1915 were still at their posts at the beginning of 1916. As the 1916 campaigning season approached, the army therefore started to comb through its sick lists to identify officers fit enough to be sent back to France. Cranborne, Crookshank and Macmillan were each examined by medical boards, though with somewhat different results. While Macmillan, with his hand wound, and Crookshank, with his leg wound, were declared fit for service on the Western Front, Cranborne was passed as fit only for light duties.[105] His services as an ADC had already been requested by the commander of the reserve centre in Southern Command.[106] Although he was refused this dignity by a tetchy personnel officer in the War Office, he was allowed to join the general as an unpaid orderly.[107] Thus Cranborne departed for Swanage while Macmillan and Crookshank headed back to the 2nd Battalion in the Ypres salient.

Crookshank was delayed at Le Havre. Like Macmillan the year

before, he was caught up in the growing technological sophistication of the British Army. Whereas Macmillan was a bombing officer, Crookshank now became a Lewis gun officer. The Lewis gun was a relatively portable machine-gun designed by an American for the Belgians and brought from there to Birmingham in 1914. By the start of 1916 large numbers were being issued to infantry companies.[108] The Lewis gun went some way to compensating for the decline in musketry standards which affected the whole army as long-service professionals were replaced by volunteers and finally by conscripts.[109] Crookshank was even so less than delighted with his new role. After his Lewis gun course he 'knew as little at the end as at the beginning'.[110] He found it hard to drop into the role of the 'old soldier'. He was 'getting rather bored with some of our more stupid brother officers'.[111] Giving a series of lectures on the trench attack to new arrivals, he felt a complete fraud, 'knowing nothing about it'.[112] He even managed to miss duties with badly blistered feet caused by wearing natty but insubstantial pure silk socks.[113]

Macmillan would have been glad to stay on the coast with Crookshank. He looked forward to their new posting with dread.[114] Indeed, Macmillan's rebaptism of fire was brutal. Under the command of Crawley de Crespigny, Macmillan's new battalion was still taking a robust view of its aggressive role in the trenches. On Good Friday 1916 he found himself in charge of a platoon, in an exposed trench near Ypres, completely cut off from other British forces. He could reach neither the unit on his left nor right. The communications trench to his rear was too dangerous to use in daylight, so he could not even contact the rest of his company. His only solace was reading the Passion in Luke's Gospel. He was cold, lonely and frightened and 'already calculating the days till my first leave'.[115]

By early 1916 Lyttelton had sloughed off any hint of boyishness. He was an experienced soldier who had had responsibility beyond his years thrust upon him. His letters home were detailed, hard-edged and often cynically funny. Macmillan, on the other hand, retained a certain pompous innocence: he didn't 'know why I write such solemn stuff' but write it he did. The army possessed that 'indomitable and patient determination, which has saved England over and over again'. It was 'prepared to fight for another 50 years if necessary until the final object is attained'. The war was not just a war, it was 'a Crusade': 'I never see a man killed but think of him as a martyr.'[116] He found the words of the French high command at Verdun – resist to the last man, no retreat, sacrifice is the key to victory – so stirring that he copied them into his field pocketbook. Whereas Lyttelton had felt the prick of ambition, Macmillan had to deflect his mother's demands that he should get on. His ambition was to survive and 'get command of a company some day', though he disparaged his mother's wish that he should get out of the front line to 'join the much abused staff'.[117]

Macmillan and Crookshank were finally united in mid June near Ypres. Crookshank had slowly made his way to the battalion in an 'odd kind of procession', braving the danger of inadequate messing facilities, 'perfectly abominable . . . a disgrace to the Brigade'.[118] Each was delighted to see the other. If they had to be in this awful place, it was at least some solace to tackle the task ahead with your closest friend. They immediately became tent-mates.[119] Crookshank was assigned to his old platoon: 'rather like going to school after the holidays seeing so many of the old faces after the long absence'.[120] Crookshank believed he had done rather well in the battalion the previous year and was much less self-deprecating than Macmillan about his chances of promotion. He was thus 'very annoyed and disappointed' when both of them were transferred into 3 Company under the command of another subaltern, Nils Beaumont-Nesbitt.[121] In early July they went into the 'Irish Farm', 'one of the worst positions [the battalion] had been in'. It offered 1,300 yards of 'trenches' that were 'mainly shell holes full of water with no connecting saps, constant casualties and back-breaking work.'[122] Raymond Asquith described it as 'the most accursed, unholy and abominable place I have ever seen, the ugliest, filthiest most fetid and most desolate – craters swimming in blood, dirt, rotting and swelling bodies and rats like shadows . . . limbs . . . resting in the hedges'. The aspect that disturbed him most was 'the supernaturally shocking scent of death and corruption [so] that the place simply stank of sin and all Floris could not have made it sweet'.[123]

Crookshank escaped the worst by being sent on a Lewis gun course at Étaples, 'mechanism cleaning and stripping (I did but very slowly)', although he encountered another mess that was the 'absolute limit – had some words with the CO on the subject of servants, went to dine at the Continental'.[124] Crookshank was a fusspot. He liked things just so. His doting mother made sure that he was never short of funds to make himself comfortable. As a result his girth was beginning to swell. He was lucky to have in such close attendance Macmillan, who always appreciated the waspish humour with which he leavened his perpetual moaning. Although Crookshank's undoubted bravery won him friends, he could be an irritating companion in those trying circumstances.

Macmillan himself, on the other hand, having had little opportunity to shine during his last spell at the front, 'made his name' from the battalion's unpromising position. On 19 July he led two men on a scouting patrol in no man's land. They managed to get quite near the German line, but then ran into some German soldiers digging a sap. A German threw a grenade, the explosion from which wounded Macmillan in the face. One of his men was also wounded and they struggled back to the British lines.[125] Macmillan's wound was serious enough for him to have left the battalion, but he refused to do so out of a mixture of bravado and opportunism piqued by Crookshank's more militant attitude to promotion. 'My first duty is to the Regiment which I have the honour to serve,' he decided, 'and not only are we very short of officers of any experience just now ... but I was told confidentially by the Adjutant the other day that the commanding officer would probably give me command of the next company vacant, when I had had a little more experience of trench work.' Macmillan was mentioned in dispatches for his bravery, but more immediately he basked in the good opinion of de Crespigny, who 'was pleased with me for staying'.[126]

They all nevertheless knew that these skirmishes in Flanders were a mere sideshow, overshadowed by 'der Tag – the first day of the great Fourth Army and French push' on the Somme, leagues away to the south.[127] As far as they could tell, 'the Somme seems to be progressing favourably, if slowly and methodically'. They were all too aware that 'the casualties have been very heavy'.[128] In fact the first and indeed subsequent days of the Somme offensive were a bloody disaster. As the Guards Division was sent marching south, GHQ acknowledged that the loss of men was unsustainable. The Fourth Army would revert to a 'wearing out' battle until the 'last reserves', of which the Guards were part, could be thrown into a renewed 'decisive' attack in mid September.[129] News of these disasters soon filtered down to the junior officers and undermined their initial optimism.[130] One subaltern in their company was court-martialled for sending an 'indiscreet' letter, opened by the censors, criticizing the staff. It was rumoured that this letter was the reason why King George had not inspected the battalion when he visited the Guards at the beginning of August. It was noted that the Prince of Wales, so obvious a presence the previous year, was no longer anywhere to be seen near the battalion.[131]

On the road Crookshank and Macmillan 'were having very amusing conversations'. The northern part of the Somme battlefield was even 'quite a nice change after Ypres'. There was a 'wonderful view all round especially of the Thiepval plateau', which they observed for hours. The trenches were very good. Crookshank and Macmillan were even allocated their own dugout, although it proved to be less than a blessing, located at 'the end of a communications trench junction and well shelled'. They abandoned it after only one night.[132] Indeed, it was at night that they had time to mull over the grimness of their situation. Sitting in their shared tent, they were 'frightfully depressed' by the fact that their 'most intimate circle [had been] killed in the push, it's enough to make anybody feel very sad'. Crookshank was particularly upset by the death of his 'great friend' at Magdalen, Pat Harding. Harding, a 'great Oxford friend' of Macmillan as well, had already risen to rank of major in a Scottish regiment before he was killed. Not only was the war cruel, it was insidious. Arthur Mackworth, for instance, a young classics tutor who had taught Crookshank at Magdalen, and who escaped the front after being transferred from the Rifle Brigade to the War Office Intelligence Department because of a heart condition, was so tormented by insomnia that he shot himself dead.

They had little time to dwell on these tragedies: they were soon in the midst of a major training programme that continued throughout August and into September to prepare the Fourth Army for its second great push on the Somme. Something of the kind had been tried before Loos, but this was on a much bigger scale. The Fourth Army tried to learn the lessons of the first phase of the offensive and inculcate its troops with the best ways of carrying out trench attacks and of using their equipment.[133] One change of doctrine in the summer of 1916 affected Macmillan. Initial operations on the Somme led to a reversal of Haig's post-Loos enthusiasm for the grenade and a return to the doctrine that 'the rifle and the bayonet is the main infantry weapon'. Supposedly, 'when attacking troops are reduced to bombing down a trench, the attack is as good as over'.[134] The Guards nevertheless still put considerable emphasis on grenade training, and as their attack at Ginchy was to show, front-line troops would remain deeply attached to their grenades whatever the official prognostications. Macmillan, however, was not called on to resume the role of bombing officer, which he had managed to abandon just before the beginning of the march south. Crookshank's Lewis guns remained in vogue. Ma Jeffreys descended on a tour of inspection and told him in no uncertain terms that the machine-guns would play an important role and he would be leading the gun team.[135]

At the beginning of September the whole tempo of preparations stepped up.[136] Crookshank's impression, after he and Macmillan had walked the ground together, was that the Loos battle they had taken part in during the previous September 'didn't start to be compared with this'.[137] They were in 'a glorified camp and depot for every kind of stores', he recorded in an unsent letter. 'One can hardly see a square yard of grass, it is absolutely thick and swarming with men, tents and horses ... as for the guns they are past counting battery after battery of big ones ... with mountains of ammunition and a light railway to supply it. It certainly was a revelation,' he concluded, 'and shows that we really have begun fighting now.'[138]

The Guards Division was deployed as part of Cavan's XIV Corps on the south of the Somme front. Its mission was to move forward from the village of Ginchy, just to the south of Delville Wood, which still contained Germans, to the village of Lesboeufs to the north-east. On 11 September the detailed attack orders arrived.[139] Crookshank held a Lewis gun parade 'to tell off the different teams'. His own team consisted of a sergeant, four corporals and twenty-four men servicing four Lewis guns.[140] On 12 September the 3rd Battalion moved up into the line, so that Lyttelton was posted only a few hundred yards to the right of Macmillan and Crookshank.[141]

It was Macmillan who went into action first. German machine-gunners were positioned in an orchard on the northern edge of Ginchy. It was clear the moment the Guards started to advance they would be machine-gunned in the flank. On the night of 13 September de Crespigny ordered 4 Company, supported by two platoons of 3 Company, commanded by Macmillan, to clear the Germans out of the orchard.[142] The attack took place in bright moonlight and in the face of heavy German fire; 'it was very expensive, as they found better trenches and more Germans than expected'.

The next day, the 14th, 'was terrible'. The 2nd Battalion's trenches suffered a direct hit from a twenty-eight inch bomb. Many were buried alive and a company commander had to be relieved because of shell shock.[143] 'That day,' wrote Lyttelton, 'dawdled away.' Towards evening the word came down that H-hour was 6.20 a.m. the next day. 'Action,' Lyttelton recorded. 'Changed into thick clothes, filled everything with cigarettes. Put on webbing equipment. Drank a good whack of port. Looked to the revolver ammunition.' They moved into position that night. It was bitterly cold. They looked 'out into the moonlight beyond into the most extraordinary desolation you can imagine'. 'The ground,' Lyttelton wrote, 'is like a rough sea, there is not a blade of grass, not a feature left on that diseased face. Just the rubble of two villages and the black smoke of shells to show that the enemy did not like losing them ... the steely light of the dawn is just beginning to show at 5.30.'

This moonscape, devoid of landmarks, was to prove a terrible problem. Officers had their objectives clearly and neatly drawn in on the maps: first the Green Line, then the Brown Line, on to the Blue Line and finally crossing the Red Line to victory. Yet it was impossible to tell where these map lines fell on the real terrain. This sense of dislocation was made worse for the 3rd Battalion because of a tactical manoeuvre. Boy Brooke deployed his men too far to the right, intending that the Germans, expecting an attack in a straight line, would miss with their initial artillery strike. At 6 a.m. the British artillery opened up, the German guns replying within seconds. To the great satisfaction of Brooke and Lyttelton, the shells rained down on their former position, missing their new position completely. The disadvantage of the move, however, was that the 3rd Battalion had to make a dog-leg to the left once the attack had started. At 6.20 a.m. they went over the top.[144]

The advance was chaotic. Because the front was so narrow, both the 2nd Battalion and their next-door neighbours, the 3rd Battalion, were supposed to follow battalions of the Coldstream Guards into the attack. Within yards they had both lost all sense of direction. The three battalions of Coldstream Guards lurched off to the left. It was thus very difficult for the Grenadiers to fix their own position. They then discovered that the Germans had created an undetected forward skirmish line that, although it was completely outnumbered, 'fought with the utmost bravery'. The 2nd Battalion found themselves caught in a 'German barrage of huge shells bursting at the appalling rate of one a second, [they] were shooting up showers of mud in every direction and the noise was deafening. All this in addition to fierce rifle fire, which came from the right rear.'[145] The German skirmishers succeeded in slowing down and breaking up the British formation before they were overwhelmed. Lyttelton and Brooke 'flushed two or three Huns from a shell hole, who ran back. They did not get far.' 'I have,' wrote Lyttelton after the battle, 'only a blurred image of slaughter. I saw about ten Germans writhing like trout in a creel at the bottom of a shell hole and our fellows firing at them from the hip. One or two red bayonets.'

Macmillan was wounded in the knee as they tried to clear these lines. He kept going. Although the battalion passed through the barrage, it immediately 'came under machine-gun fire from the left front and rifle fire from the right rear. Instead of finding itself . . . in rear of Coldstream, it was suddenly confronted by a trench full of enemy. This was the first objective, which the men naturally imagined had been taken by the Coldstream.' They were deployed in artillery formation instead of in line, marching forward under the impression that two battalions of Coldstream Guards were in front of them. To approach the trench with any prospect of success, 'it was necessary to deploy into line, and in doing this they lost very heavily'. During this manoeuvre Macmillan was shot in the left buttock.[146] It was a severe wound: he rolled into a shell hole and dosed himself with morphine.

Crookshank was equally unlucky. His Lewis guns were doing good work.[147] At about 7 a.m. he was just getting up to push forward once more when a high-explosive shell burst about eight yards in front of him. 'I felt,' he later remembered, 'a great knock in the stomach and saw a stream of blood and gently subsided into a shell hole.' He was in a perilous position: the shallow shell hole did not provide good cover. If any more shells landed near by he would be sure to be killed. He was saved by his orderly, who crawled to another shell hole and found a corporal, wounded in the head but fit enough to help. Between them the orderly and the corporal managed to carry Crookshank to a better hole, 'where there were rather fewer shells dropping'. Like Macmillan Crookshank dosed himself with morphine and he and the corporal lay in their waterproof sheets. His orderly went back towards the British lines for help. They lay there for about an hour before the stretcher bearers arrived to evacuate them. Crookshank was conscious but mutilated: the shell had castrated him. Eventually he was taken back towards Ginchy. It was a nightmarish journey.[148] Macmillan's evacuation had been equally nightmarish. He crawled until he was rescued and had no medical attention for hours. Even when he was picked up by medical orderlies, heavy shelling forced him to abandon his stretcher and scuttle back towards safety.[149] Although they had each escaped death by a fraction and reached field hospitals without being hit again, both were horribly wounded.

Although it was no longer of much interest to either Macmillan or Crookshank, the whole Guards Division was also in deep trouble. On its right the 6th Division had made no progress whatsoever. The tanks over which Churchill had rhapsodized to a sceptical Lyttelton a year before made no impression on their first day of battle. As a result the Guards' right flank was exposed to a German strongpoint called 'the Quadrilateral' that poured fire into it. Their own formation was breaking up under a combination of German fire and the lack of any clear features in the terrain. There were no longer Grenadiers, Coldstreamers, Scots or Irish; they were mixed up together. Small units of men led by charismatic leaders were engaged increasingly in freelance actions. Lyttelton was one such freelancer. Spotting that a gap was opening up between the Coldstream Guards, who were veering to the left, and the Grenadiers, who were trying to shore up the right, he led about a hundred men forward to try and plug their front. His party of Grenadiers caught up with the Coldstreamers, but instead of repairing the front they were simply dragged along by the Scottish regiment, losing contact with their own battalion.

Then Lyttelton 'heard behind me the unmistakable sound of a hunting horn'. It was the commanding officer of the Coldstream Guards, Colonel John Campbell whose use of the horn to urge on his men was remembered by most participants in the battle. By the time he came across Lyttelton, Campbell was in a frenzy. He was 'yelling "Stop!" and using some pretty expressive language to give it "tone"'.

> So we stopped, [Lyttelton reported], and I went back to talk to him. 'This is great fun I must say,' was all the report I could give. 'Fun be damned,' Campbell shouted. 'We have taken everything in sight but, you blasted idiot, if you go on you will be in to your own barrage. Don't you know this is the second objective? Dig! Where's my map? Where's my adjutant? Damn, he's been killed ... where are those pigeons? Oliver, give me your map.' I expressed the opinion [Lyttelton recalled] that it was the first objective, owing to the contours.

Campbell laughed at this, pointing at Ginchy, 'which did', Lyttelton conceded, 'certainly look the hell of a way off'. Lyttelton's navigation was, in fact, superior. They had reached the first line of German trenches, the Green Line rather than the Brown. Wherever they were, it was clear that plenty of Germans were there too. Campbell ordered Lyttelton to take his Grenadiers and some Irish Guards and clear the trench using grenades. Lyttelton set off but had hardly begun when a mass of Germans, pursued by another group of Grenadiers, came running down the trench, holding up their hands in surrender.[150]

This jumble of small units was untrammelled by the usual chains of command. It was clear to the divisional commander, provided with the results of aerial intelligence, that the Guards could not go on. To do so would be to invite a devastating counter-attack on their exposed right flank. This was in no way clear to the young bloods in the middle of the line. After hours of confused and bloody fighting they had secured the German front line. They could finally see something. Ahead of them they could discern the village of Lesboeufs, which represented, in their minds' eyes, a blue pencil line on their maps, the third objective. Lyttelton ran into Sir Ian Colquhoun, already leading his twenty Scots Guards forward. Colquhoun was a fearsome trench fighter, 'credited with having killed a large number of Germans in personal combat' and known as 'Luss of the Bloody Club'. Colquhoun and Lyttelton decided to pool their tiny forces and advance towards Lesboeufs. Before doing so they managed to find three Irish Guards officers willing to join them, including Harold Alexander, the future field marshal.

They had no orders: an officer could, with perfect honour, wait in the trench for the brigades to re-form or he could make a personal decision to go on. The five officers advanced with about 115 men. After travelling for 800 yards or so without opposition they dropped into an unoccupied trench running along the bottom of a little gully. To the front their vision was obscured by a line of tall crops. They were alone. There was no sign of any other British troops advancing. The Germans were out there somewhere, but were not to be seen. All realized the precariousness of their position. If any German force appeared it could attack them in the flank or cut them off from the rest of the British army with ease. After a hurried conference they decided to send back about twenty men to look for the Brigade HQ and ask for support. The messengers were to ask each officer they met on the way to come and reinforce them. Meanwhile the remaining men settled down in the trench to wait. They posted a Lewis gun at each end to give themselves some chance should Germans appear from the left or the right. It was 1 p.m. They sat in the trench and waited: 2 p.m., 3 p.m., 4 p.m. passed with no sign of any other British troops joining them. Just after 5 p.m., they realized they were no longer alone – they could see a whole battalion of German infantry advancing towards them. To their distress it soon became clear that the Germans knew they were there. Methodically the German troops worked round to the right and left of their position. Neither side fired, but the men in the trench could see they would soon be surrounded. Nervously looking to their flanks and rear, they took their eyes off the front. At 6 p.m. 250 Germans burst out of the standing crops and into the trench. The British party were in a hopeless position. Their shelter was now a death trap, but instead of surrendering they tried to fight their way out. The very violence of their response bought them a few seconds. Lyttelton fired off the six shots in his revolver, but rifle-armed German soldiers surrounded him. In utter desperation he hurled the empty pistol at them. Thinking it was a grenade, they shied away and he scrambled out of the back of the trench and ran.

Lyttelton and the others should have been dead men. If the Germans had simply used their rifles to pick off the fleeing British it would have been a massacre. But, with adrenaline pumping, they continued their charge. Eight hundred yards was twice the distance a man can sprint. To run the distance over rough ground was lung-bursting. Their salvation was the lack of artillery fire. Vision was not obscured, as it usually was, by smoke. As the remnant of Colquhoun and Lyttelton's forlorn hope fled towards the British line, the Guards in the front trenches could see their plight: they opened up concerted fire on the pursuing Germans, who either died or fled. Even so over forty of the sally were either killed or wounded – although observers considered these casualties 'astonishingly low' given the circumstances.[151]

If it is possible to talk of a day changing men's lives then 15 September 1916 was that day for Lyttelton, Macmillan and Crookshank. As night fell, Macmillan and Crookshank were cripples, Lyttelton was a hero.[152] In retrospect, to dare such things and survive appeared to him the very acme of pleasure. 'The 15th was the most wonderful day of my life,' he wrote. 'I drank every emotion to the dregs and was drunk. It was superbly exhilarating.' 'About 2 a.m.' on 16 September 'I was sent for by Brigade HQ to report on the situation. Unfortunately the orderly lost his way – very naturally, it being as black as your hat – and did not get there until about 4.30 or 5. I was given a whisky and soda and went to sleep on my feet. The brigadier kept me at his HQ until the relief so I do not know much more.' He could bask in his 'name' – he was awarded the DSO for his conduct in the battle. It had been a 'wonderful show'.[153]

These, however, were the sentiments of one who had miraculously emerged unscathed. Macmillan, by contrast, would never recover sufficiently to play an active role in the army. During his brief military career, he had been shot in the head, the face, the hand, the knee and in the back. He barely survived the last wound. His right arm and left leg never worked properly again. Over the same short period, Crookshank had been buried alive, shot in the leg and blown up. It was horrifyingly apparent that he would never father children; it took him a year to recuperate, and even then he had to wear a surgical truss for the rest of his life. As in 1915, therefore, Lyttelton alone was left at the front.

Lyttelton had experienced an intense emotional high at the Somme, though in reality the life of discomfort and danger was beginning to pall for all the officers in the division. When during the spring of 1917 Lyttelton revisited the trench he and his band had reached on 15 September, he was much less sanguine: 'this country stinks of corruption', he noted in disgust. 'As far as the eye can reach is that brown and torn sea of desolation and every yard there is a grave, some marked with rifles, others with crosses, some with white skulls, some with beckoning hands. But everything is dead: the trees, the fields, the corn, the church, even the prayers of those that went there in their Sunday clothes with their sweaty pennies for the plate: it is all dead and God has forsaken it.'[154]

The 3rd Battalion was not used again at the Somme because it had lost over three quarters of its officers and had ceased to function as a serious fighting force. The survivors were sent back to Paris to enjoy the high life. The Parisian hoteliers were doing their bit for the war effort while maintaining the social exclusivity of their clientele. 'At present I am wallowing in the luxury of this place,' Lyttelton wrote from the Ritz. 'Everything is done wonderfully well . . . all for 10 francs because we are officers in the Brigade.' After the Ritz the life of the front-line infantry officer held few attractions.[155] 'I think I should quite like a change,' Lyttelton, back at the front, told his mother, 'when I wake up in the morning and see a vignette of the Somme battlefield communications through the bellying flaps of my tent and mud, mud, mud.'[156] His former boss and current corps commander, Lord Cavan, agreed with him. At the beginning of November 1916 he 'mutinied' and refused to send his men into the attack once more. 'No one who has not visited the trenches,' Cavan said in a swipe against chateaux-bound staff officers, 'can really know the state of exhaustion to which the men are reduced. The conditions are far worse than the first battle of Ypres, all my General officers and staff officers agree that they are the worse they have seen, owing to the enormous distance of the carry of all munitions – such as food, water and ammunition.'[157] At the same time as the Somme offensive ground to a stop in the winter mud of northern France, Oliver Lyttelton was applying for a job as a staff captain.

For much of their lives Lyttelton, Crookshank, Macmillan and Cranborne had marched in close step. At Christmas 1916, however, they were operating on entirely different time-scales. Crookshank and Macmillan, lying in London hospital beds under the watchful eyes of their mothers, could barely think about more than one day at a time. For them survival was victory. Crookshank's wound was horrible, but Macmillan's was more life threatening. He had received inadequate initial treatment: the wound became infected and the bullet was still lodged in his body. Crookshank was declared fit for 'very light duty' six months after the Somme at a time when Macmillan's recovery was still in doubt.[158]

Cranborne, on the other hand, was looking forward to the bright horizon. His wife had just given birth to a son, thus securing the Cecil succession for another generation.[159] Acquaintances urged him to take up his rightful position in national life. 'God knows,' one star-struck admirer wrote, 'there will be need of all straight men who have no axe to grind after this war is over ... the country has need of you and your obligation to its service did not begin and will not end with the War.'[160] He was starting to put out feelers about opportunities in the two civilian careers he was eventually to follow – the City and politics.[161]

Lyttelton was looking ahead a few months. He knew 'the one job I really would like, which is staff captain of one of the three Guards brigades' and was manoeuvring to achieve it.[162] To get a good post outside the regiment, one had to attract the attention of a senior officer, either through connections or by personal conduct. When Lyttelton stumbled into the headquarters of 2nd Guards Brigade to report on the events of 15 September he was taken under the wing of Brigadier John Ponsonby, an officer who 'broke most of the rules and refused to take life too seriously'.[163] Although Ponsonby was a Coldstreamer he was another character like the Grenadiers Jeffreys, Brooke and de Crespigny. He had a very bad speech impediment that set for his staff a challenging task of translation, and he refused to wear any head protection, favouring a pith helmet instead. Ponsonby and Lyttelton were to become firm friends. Both had a taste for the high life in the Ritz and the casinos of Paris.[164] Ponsonby certainly had no objection to Lyttelton parading his new mistress – 'a French lady married to an American officer in the flying corps ... [who] belonged to the substantial (and I don't mean fat) type' – in either venue.[165]

Lyttelton returned to Flanders in April 1917 to prepare for the battle of Passchendaele as a fully fledged brigade staff officer. His duties were mainly involved with the organization of logistics. The work was important but routine. His most exciting moment came when he had to take a mule train up to resupply the 3rd Battalion Grenadiers under heavy shell fire. His former comrades subjected him to much ribbing about a member of the 'gilded staff' being reduced to a humble muleteer.[166] Once again the experience of the Guards differed from other parts of the army. Used as an assault force, the Guards Division achieved a brilliant tactical success in crossing the Yser canal and seizing most of its objectives east of Boesinghe at the beginning of the battle on 31 July 1917. Their attempts to learn from the Somme through intensive training on mock attacks thus paid off before Passchendaele degenerated into 'an almost impassable quagmire' and 'pursued its dreary and exhausting course' to eventual failure. Before the offensive, Lyttelton had dared to hope that the Germans were cracking – it was 'not all we take in the way of ground or even of prisoners, but it is they allow them to be taken . . . if in two months the submarine campaign is no better for them, they will chuck it'.[167] The vision of endless mud and seemingly endless war was a crushing disappointment even for those like Lyttelton who believed in the 'battle of attrition' – 'the Hun when we have a few young Somme offensives going in the spring hasn't an earthly'.[168] Yet although Lyttelton's hopes of victory were dashed, his interest in soldiering was sustained by his continued hopes for promotion.

As Lyttelton returned to England to further his ambitions with a staff course, Crookshank set out to the wars once more. He too had caught the eye of a Grenadier general, 'Corky' Corkran, who had been appointed as the British military liaison officer to the Serb army. In a private arrangement with the War Office Political Department Crookshank was appointed as Corkran's ADC.[169] Whereas Lyttelton strained at the bit for promotion, however, Crookshank no longer had any such thoughts. Crookshank's preparatory meetings with the Political Department suggested that they did not view Corkran's mission as entirely serious.[170] Corkran himself viewed his trip to Greece as little more than a well-deserved jaunt. The Corkran party's journey to Salonika was a golden opportunity for tourism. They travelled via Paris, Rome and Taranto. Once in Greece there was plenty of time to indulge in classical sightseeing at Delphi and the Vale of Tempe. They arrived in Salonika ten days after they left London. A week later they addressed the main point of their mission – to visit and report on the state of Serb forces. In mid October they set out in a Vauxhall staff car along the Via Ignatia from Greece into Macedonia. At the headquarters of the Serb army they conducted a brief tour of the lines and were able to view the Austrian army at a distance through binoculars. The staff car then whisked them back to the comfort of Salonika. The whole tour of inspection had taken three days.[171]

With Corkran's primary mission completed, Crookshank turned to his own primary mission of finding them somewhere elegant and comfortable to live in Salonika. In a city overflowing with troops doing little fighting, accommodation was at a premium. House hunting was considerably more challenging than military liaison – it took three weeks to get them installed in a house.[172] Their main task in Salonika was to try and estimate the actual number of troops the Serbs had under arms – a question to which it proved impossible to get a straight answer. In reality the bulk of Crookshank's time was taken up with eating, drinking and sightseeing. The general was happily engaged in shooting geese and learning French from a pretty Greek lady.

To Crookshank's delight, Salonika was full of the flotsam and jetsam of war. He took tea with Flora Sandys, the cross-dressing Englishwoman whose service with the Serbian army had made her a minor celebrity in Britain.[173] He found Sandys rather dull. More to his taste was the Reverend R. G. D. Laffan, who had left Eton the year Crookshank arrived and was 'funnily enough' the chaplain to the Serb First Army and seemed 'a complete favourite naturally'. At dinner Crookshank and Laffan 'had a tremendous talk partly Eton shop and partly on religion and High Church both being rather unusual subjects up here I think'.[174] On the other hand, with his Guards trained eye, Crookshank did not think much of the British forces in Salonika and the pretensions they gave themselves. 'The main marble step entrance of the new GHQ,' he noted, for example, 'is reserved entirely for Brigadiers and Generals and upwards: this is a typical order of the British Salonika forces.'

Lyttelton, in contrast, was spending another miserable winter on the Western Front. He also was beginning to take a somewhat jaundiced view of the higher directors of the war in the 'seats of the mighty at Versailles'. 'Walter Dalkeith,' his Eton and Grenadier contemporary, he complained, 'is in a Louis Quatorze house with five bathrooms and unlimited motor cars. I think if I finish five years continuously out here I must get a job as a [staff officer] there!'[175] In fact his eyes were still firmly fixed on achieving the brigade majorship of a Guards brigade. When he finally achieved his ambition at the beginning of 1918, it was something of a mixed blessing. To make their manpower go further, the army had begun to reduce the number of battalions in each brigade. As a general rule infantry battalions were broken up and used as reinforcements for the remaining battalions of the regiments to which they belonged.[176] The three 'spare' Guards battalions, on the other hand, were put together to form a new 4th Guards Brigade under the command of Lord Ardee, a very inexperienced officer, with Lyttelton as his brigade major. But instead of staying with the Guards Division the new brigade 'departed very sorrowfully to a line division', the 31st.[177] They did not stray too far, however, the 31st and the Guards Division being deployed next door to each other in the Arras sector of the Third Army. Nevertheless Lyttelton had transferred from one of the best divisions in the British army to what was usually regarded as the poorest, the 'thirty-worst'.

Lyttelton seems to have had a genius for finding the action. A little over a month after he took up his new job the massive German March offensive hit the British line. In many ways the battles of March and April 1918 showed the British army at its least impressive. Loos, the Somme and Passchendaele had been static battles. The British attacked from a firm line. Now the army was on the back foot, fighting a battle of manoeuvre in which the positions of enemy and Allied troops were unclear, the battle lines confused and lines of command often disrupted. Regrettably, not only did these battles show up a lack of competence, they also revealed a tendency to panic, a 'funk' that almost amounted to cowardice in the face of the enemy.

Expelled from the protective cocoon of the Guards Division, the 4th Guards Brigade experienced these problems in full. Even before the Germans attacked there was a worrying feeling of uncertainty. Rumours abounded that while the Fifth Army would retreat if attacked, the Third Army, of which both the Guards Division and Guards Brigade were part, would attempt to stand its ground: 'everyone to the private soldiers knew the troops on their flank would retire, so that rumours of these divergent policies weakened the junction of the Third and Fifth Armies'. A junior officer in the Gordon Highlanders in the same corps as Lyttelton reported that commanders had the 'wind up' from bombing and shelling of back areas. They deluged formations with paperwork about resisting tank and aerial attack and so undermined morale.[178]

Lyttelton shared these worries. Within a few days of joining 31st Division he had an 'unpleasant feeling that the professional standards were different from our own'.[179] He was even less impressed with the command of VI Corps, to which the division was assigned once the German attack began. The commanding officer of the 31st Division bitterly accused the corps staff of running away – they 'upped it and left us in the soup'.[180] Lyttelton agreed that the commander of VI Corps, Sir Aylmer Haldane, had abandoned his post. Lyttelton accompanied his boss Ardee to see Haldane on 22 March. 'We were,' he recalled, 'neither of us particularly reassured by the atmosphere at Corps HQ, which was busy packing up, and we had the uncomfortable feeling that something near a rout had taken place, and that the General no longer had any control over the battle . . . the spectacle of a general clearing out in some disorder is never very encouraging.'[181]

These fears were borne out when the brigade moved into the line. The 40th Division on the left of the 31st Division began to cave in. Rumours buzzed along the line that the Germans had broken through. When the brigade pushed forward a battalion to try and find out what was happening, they discovered that troops of the 40th Division were paralysed with fear and refused to help them. The line infantry had become a 'rabble'. Lyttelton arrested an officer who tried to flee through the Guards.[182] To make matters worse, the Guards were shelled by British artillery and no one could be found to tell them to stop.[183] On 24 March the brigade moved back to try and form a new defensive line, but along with their surrounding formations they had to retreat again on each of the next two days.

Lyttelton had already lost all confidence in the chain of command when he found himself a player in the so-called Hébuterne incident of 26 March 1918. When Ardee was gassed Lyttelton rode over to the Guards Division and tried to place the brigade back under its command. He was reassured to find the divisional staff officer, Ned Grigg, who had joined the second battalion with him as a subaltern in 1915, playing badminton. He greeted the re-establishment of communications with 31st Division and the resumption of the proper chain of command with deep regret. This regret was deepened even further when the brigade received a message from the division that the Germans had broken through to the south of their position.[184] Then communications went dead. Lyttelton and many others feared the worst – a complete collapse of the British line. Other units of the division abandoned their positions and tried to retreat. The next day the Guards Brigade found itself defending the whole divisional front against a German attack. Not only had the original signal been false, but it also turned out that the loss of communications was caused by the incompetence of a staff officer who had felled a tree on to the telephone lines while trying to build a defensive position.[185]

When Lyttelton's brigade was withdrawn from the line on 31 March it had lost 14 officers and 372 men. 'We had,' Lyttelton wrote, 'emerged from the battle with little confidence in the command and still less the staff of our new Division.' As usual, however, the Guards were proud of their own performance. They were soon in 'good trim' under a new commanding officer, Brigadier Butler. 'That's that,' was Lyttelton's feeling.[186] Unfortunately the Germans had merely shifted the attack further north. On 9 April they carefully picked a weak point in the line held by Portuguese troops and drove straight through them deep into the British line.

Instead of being able to lick its wounds, the Guards Brigade was thrown back into the fighting in a desperate defence. In the words of Rudyard Kipling, the Guards were sent to 'discover and fill the nearest or widest gap . . . to get in touch with the Divisions on their left and right, whose present whereabouts were rather doubtful'. Lyttelton thus found himself back where he had begun his military career near Festubert. As brigade major, he was supposed to be at the hub of information coming into brigade headquarters and orders being issued from it. But he had little information and that which he did receive was nearly always wrong. On 12 April the brigade was ordered to advance in search of friendly troops. As soon as they moved off they were caught in a vicious crossfire from enemy troops waiting for them with rifles, machine-guns, mortars and field guns operating at close range. At 4.30 p.m. the Germans attacked in force. Desperately, the Guards fought them off. Butler and Lyttelton signalled the division that they could not hold another attack on such a wide front. They believed they had been informed that another division would send troops to take over part of their line. But no troops arrived.

When the Germans came on again at 6.30 the next morning it was war to the knife – German troops masqueraded as Grenadiers so as to get close to the British lines before opening fire. Lyttelton later called this a 'soldier's battle,' but the reality was much grimmer.[187] The Guards were isolated and being wiped out piecemeal. Companies were cut off from each other in their own pockets and fighting the best they could. At 3.30 p.m. the commander of the Grenadier company on the far left flank managed to get a message through that he was surrounded. Brigade HQ ordered the Irish Guards to send a company to try and rescue him: only one NCO and six men survived the ensuing massacre. The Grenadiers fought and died where they stood. Lyttelton later said that when their leader, Captain Pryce, who was awarded a posthumous VC, had less than ten men left he charged the enemy. By the time the Guards were rescued by Australian troops late in the afternoon, the brigade had been shattered. In two days of fighting it had lost 39 officers and 1,244 men. The butcher's bill was worse than the Somme.[188]

It was perhaps ironic that, having survived this maelstrom intact, Lyttelton was gassed a few days later while sitting at his table writing. A shell-burst spattered him with liquid mustard gas. His scrotum, penis and thighs were severely burned, his lungs were damaged and he was blinded.[189] Like Macmillan and Crookshank before him, he returned to his mother and a private hospital.[190] He made, however, a near-miraculous recovery.[191] There was no long-term damage and he was even able to return to the Guards Division in time for the final advance and the occupation of Germany.

As Lyttelton was shipped home to England, Cranborne was finally making his way back to France. He went out as ADC to an old comrade-in-arms of his father, General Sir Walter Congreve, who had won a VC in the Boer War.[192] General Congreve had unfortunately not shown up too well in the March débâcle. He was described as 'absolutely down and out and incapable of any clear thinking'.

His chief of staff, another VC, with whom Cranborne was supposed to work, was, in the words of an old friend, 'a monstrous appointment' who had 'failed to pass into the Army through any orthodox channel . . . with a minimum of intellect . . . cool and collected, but had not the slightest idea of what was going on'.[193] Since they were likely to be *dégommé, limogé, stellenbosched* – the army had any number of loan words for sacked – Cranborne moved rapidly on, ending up as ADC to the GOC XXII Corps, Alix Godley.[194] There had been plenty of other options. Lord Derby was willing to take him to Paris; Douglas Haig wanted him at GHQ.[195] He discovered, as he told Macmillan, that the war could even be 'pleasant'.[196]

Cranborne's war ended in October 1918 when a bout of sickness forced him to give up his staff job and return to London.[197] Crookshank's war ended in June 1918, his Balkan mission completed, standing on Victoria station in the rain.[198] At the time of the Armistice Macmillan was still in hospital. Only Lyttelton saw it through to the bitter end. He finished the war in France as Boy Brooke's brigade major in the 2nd Guards Brigade.[199] Each of the quartet had experienced 'the pity of war distilled'. The war had not, however, changed either their personalities or their world view. In each the effect of being a combatant was rather to magnify existing personality traits.

The war touched Cranborne least. He saw the least service, he made a conventional marriage, he fathered a son during the war. Two factors were now to play a major role in his future. The first was the family project. This was unaltered by the war. His grandfather had intended to found a dynasty that would add political power to its wealth and social status. His father, though by temperament ill-equipped to further this project, had nevertheless tried his best to do so. His uncles and his mother were even keener that it should continue. Neither before nor after the war did Cranborne show any sign of kicking against the traces. He embraced his destiny as an ineluctable duty, though in this he suffered a severe impediment. He had inherited his father's weak constitution. The war exacerbated his medical problems. His health first broke down in 1915 after a few weeks' service on the Western Front. He then spent most of the war on sick leave or light duties. He even had to return home from his staff duties in 1918 because of a renewed bout of illness. Yet these chronic illnesses would have affected him whether or not he had fought. Crookshank and Macmillan had serious health problems for the rest of their lives as a direct result of their war wounds. Cranborne's most debilitating post-war illness was the polio that struck him some years after the end of the war in the 1920s.[200]

Despite the handicap of a lack of any sporting prowess, Crookshank had turned himself into a highly professional infantry officer. His rapid return to duty after his entombment in 1915 was regarded by his acquaintances as particularly heroic. Nevertheless he had been humiliated by his loss of manhood. Although his physical wounds had healed surprisingly smoothly, he would never be entirely whole. He had always been a serious young man, working hard at Summer Fields, Eton, Oxford, in the Masons and in the Grenadiers. His early diaries reveal a habit of tart comment on the shortcomings of others. At home he was used to things being organized just as he liked them. Trifles such as badly cooked food or inattentive servants drew from him torrents of complaint. And far from lessening his own fine conceit of himself, his suffering increased it. He now found it even harder to admire the efforts of others. He became even more dismissive of anything that did not meet his own needs. His family had always treated him with adulation. Crookshank's terrible wound thrust him back even further towards them. Deprived by the war of the normal reason, marriage, to leave home, he never did. At home he was never exposed to any hint of criticism. He always seemed to find it hard to understand why others did not afford him the same unstinting admiration as he received from his family. He returned from the war dissatisfied, embittered and convinced the world was unjustly determined to do him down.

Macmillan too was forced back into the bosom of his family. At Oxford he had been torn between smothering intimacies, whether of Sligger Urquhart or Ronnie Knox, and the wider society of the university. This wider world was beginning to win out by 1914 – he was becoming, albeit slowly, less of a cosseted 'mummy's boy', less pompous, more worldly. His successes in the Union indicated a gift for public speaking and an ability to charm voters. His wounds, on the other hand, drastically retarded the emergence of his maturing personality. He once again became entirely dependent on his mother, immersed in his books and lacking the company of men and women his own age. As a result for the next quarter of a century he was regarded, by both friends and enemies, as impossibly pompous, self-obsessed and utterly lacking in charm. This reputation only began to change during the Second World War, six years after his mother's death.

The contrast with Lyttelton is striking. He also had a mother to whom he remained exceptionally close. Four years of active service had, however, made Lyttelton entirely his own man. For the first time he had achieved something in a field that his father had not effortlessly dominated before him. His contact with the Guards 'characters' had convinced him that he too was a 'character'. He was, for the rest of his life, self-confident and self-assured. If anything he was too convinced of his own opinion and too proud to conceal it from those he considered his inferiors – a disadvantage in a political system so full of egos that the ability to dissemble the extent of one's own ego could be vital.

3

Bottle-washers

The end of the war came as a shock to many young men. As Lyttelton told his mother, 'with youth the war is tolerable even enjoyable'.[1] Peace did not appear at all enticing. All the plans and hopes entertained in 1914 had had to be put to one side. Now, quite suddenly it seemed to them, they needed to take stock of their situation.

Macmillan, confined to a hospital bed in Belgrave Square, had the most time to think. His prospects seemed bleak. One operation had removed half the bullet lodged in his back but he needed another. He had little to do except read and look forward to visitors. With the most exciting event in his life being a trip to see Thomas Beecham conduct Mendelssohn, he envied Cranborne his sojourn in France. 'France' was, in his imagination, 'wonderful'. England, in contrast, seemed suburban, bourgeois and corrupt. Macmillan responded enthusiastically to Cranborne's tongue-in-cheek idea that 'after the war, we really must start a League of Individuals'. 'We will *refuse* to do things . . . and all go to Italy,' Macmillan enthused, 'and live in a villa in Fiesole, with Cypresses . . . and dear Italian wines with their ravishing names. How wonderful it would be! Let George and Beaverbrook and the rest of them reconstruct to their hearts' content, as long as we are not obliged to live in their monstrous edifice.'[2]

Many men of a poetic temperament – one thinks of Robert Graves and his retreat to Majorca – put these principles into practice. Pragmatists like the Guardsmen did not let this reverie last for long. Before the war they had been committed to seeking conventional worldly success. Within weeks of the end of the war they were again embracing this goal. Even Macmillan found, once he was released from hospital, that maudlin thoughts of inaction or exile dissipated. 'To a young man of twenty-four, scarred but not disfigured,' he recalled, 'with all the quick mental and moral recovery of which youth is capable, life at the end of 1918 seemed to offer an attractive, not to say exciting prospect.'[3]

The door that the war had opened to the military career unconsidered by any of them in 1914 was rapidly closed. The fact that none of them remained a soldier was not of their own choosing. As early as 1916 Lyttelton had applied for a permanent commission in the Grenadier Guards.[4] Crookshank too explored the possibility at the end of the war. In 1918 they both applied to remain in the regiment. They were both men in good odour with dominant figures in the Guards. But the Guards traditionalists were determined to get back to normal, purge their ranks of 'patriots' and guarantee the careers of regular officers.[5] By the time they reconsidered this policy, it was too late. Lyttelton and Crookshank were launched on other careers. Even Ma Jeffreys couldn't get them back.[6]

The war also ended Lyttelton's ambition to enter the law – his contacts, so good at the time his father died, had gone stale. Not that this altered the central fact that he had to do something that made plenty of money. Even if his father's experience of politics had not soured him on Parliament, his father's example had shown the necessity of securing financial security before considering other avenues. In the months after the Armistice he courted Lady Moira Osborne, the daughter of the Duke of Leeds. His Grace disapproved of his daughter's suitor on grounds of his poverty. Their engagement was made possible by Didi Lyttelton making 'a kind of financial *hara-kiri*' to provide her son with a respectable establishment. Retreating to visit Cranborne, he considered his good fortune: 'Perfect Hatfield though baddish morning with the thermometer at 90 degrees in the shade. Phew but happy.'[7] Oliver and Moira Osborne were married a few months later at St Margaret's, Westminster.[8]

For a young man in need of cash the City was the obvious place to be. Many of Lyttelton's Etonian contemporaries had already gravitated towards it. At least his army career exempted him from the jibe of his friend Geoffrey Madan, 'Attractive Etonians who go straight on to the Stock Exchange ... the raw material of the *great* bores.'[9] In 1919 Lyttelton joined the firm of Brown, Shipley & Co. 'The change,' he remembered wryly, 'from being a guardsman and a brigade major, under whose eye every knee stiffened, to being a clerk in the postal department was marked.'

Within a few months of his marriage Lyttelton's career prospects looked up: he was recruited to work for a new concern, the British Metal Corporation run by Sir Cecil Budd, one of the leading figures in the metals trade.[10] When Lyttelton first crossed the threshold of BMC's new offices in Abchurch Yard he was, however, taking a risk. It was not at all clear that BMC would have a secure future. In 1920 the metals market suffered a 'universal collapse'. Out of the blue a relatively stable market was affected by a massive drop in prices: a ton of tin fell from £423 to £195. 'The trade has, in fact,' BMC's chairman lamented, 'passed through a succession of crises of great magnitude.' The future looked shaky.[11] Fortunately for Lyttelton, the very newness of BMC acted as a hedge against these problems. Most of its assets were still liquid.

Lyttelton soon mastered the mechanics of dealing under the guidance of Budd's principal dealer, Henry Arthur Buck, whose methods some in the City regarded as hovering on the edges of sharp practice.[12] Just as significantly, Budd himself was exhausted by the efforts he had had to put into dealing with the crisis of 1920. He decided that he needed help in the form of a joint managing director and one of the existing directors was appointed to this position. Lyttelton himself moved up to the post of general manager.[13]

As a result of his rapid promotion, Lyttelton soon got his first real taste of being a 'tycoon'. Having weathered the storms of the immediate post-war period, the corporation adopted an aggressive programme of acquisitions. Among them was the National Smelting Company.[14] National Smelting was a group mainly concerned with zinc put together during the war by a flamboyant company promoter named Richard Tilden Smith, financed by the British government and Lloyds Bank.[15] In 1916 Tilden Smith had persuaded the government that he should build facilities to process zinc concentrates formerly shipped to Germany. He signally failed to live up to his promises: not one ounce of zinc had been processed before the end of the war and in 1922 the government wrote off its loans and refused any further subsidy.[16] The jewel in the crown of National Smelting was, however, not its zinc-processing business but its controlling interest in the Burma Corporation, 'the great zinc-lead mine east of Mandalay'. Burma Corporation was of great strategic importance, but it was also undercapitalized and unprofitable. BMC believed they could turn the business around. As one of the company's negotiators, Lyttelton was given his first chance to shine. This, his first big deal, was 'stamped for ever on my memory'. He was thirty: facing him across the table was Sir Robert Horne, a former Chancellor of the Exchequer. 'We had,' Lyttelton remembered, 'rivals; their offer was on the point of being accepted; we had put in a counter bid . . . We waited tensely. After some pregnant minutes Sir Robert said our terms were reasonable . . . I had been sitting with both hands on the table and, when I got up, I could see their damp imprint on the shiny mahogany. It is quite wrong to suppose that business is not sometimes very exciting.'[17]

Lyttelton's career choice had been dictated by his need to earn serious money if he was not to find himself living off his mother's rapidly diminishing capital. Marrying the daughter of a duke brought social obligations. By contrast, his friends, untrammelled by the prick of financial necessity, could afford to abjure remunerative employment, at least for a time. Macmillan, as he hobbled out of hospital at the beginning of 1919, 'was not anxious to go immediately into business, although my father and his partners had invited me to do so'. 'I fully expected,' he later recalled, 'to spend the rest of my life at an office desk, and shrank from starting unnecessarily soon.' He, Crookshank and Cranborne were more concerned with seeing the world.

Cranborne and Crookshank made a conventional career choice in deciding to become diplomats in a Foreign Office dominated by Etonians.[18] At the beginning of 1919 they presented themselves on the same day to sit the diplomatic services entrance examination. In a reflection of the Foreign Office's changing culture, however, the selection board accepted Crookshank, the Etonian scholar, the son of a surgeon, and rejected the grandson of the great Lord Salisbury. The decision was made purely on merit. Although Cranborne had prepared hard for the exam, his utter lack of academic distinction at Eton and Oxford did not stand him in good stead. In addition, though good French was traditionally an aristocratic accomplishment, Crookshank's childhood in Francophone Egypt and his service in France, Belgium and Serbia had given him excellent spoken French, whereas Cranborne's was mediocre.*

Cranborne's diplomatic career was nevertheless rapidly resurrected by his family. Lord Salisbury crossed over to Paris to see his brother Robert, who was acting as one of Britain's principal negotiators at the Peace Conference. They agreed that Cranborne would come to Paris to act as his uncle's secretary. The current incumbent was unceremoniously sacked and within three weeks of failing the Foreign Office exam Cranborne was at Lord Robert Cecil's side in Paris – a literal case of 'Bob's your Uncle'.[19] He was thus able to observe the conduct of high policy at close quarters while Crookshank and the other successful entrants remained back in London learning how to write a proper minute.[20]

There was drudgery in London and in Paris the high life. The British delegation housed in the Hôtel Majestic on the Avenue Kléber

* Foreign Office Examination, 4 February 1919, Crookshank Papers

	Arithmetic	Essay Examiner 1	Essay Examiner 2	Précis	English	General Knowledge
Crookshank	A+	A	A	B–	B+	A+
Cranborne	A+	B+	B+	B	B	B+

	French Translation	French Composition	French Dictation	French Oral
Crookshank	A	B+	B+	A+
Cranborne	B+	B	B	B

was always busy and exciting. 'All the world is here,' wrote the editor of *The Times*. 'It's like a gigantic cinema-show of eminent persons.' 'A vast caravanserai,' thought Lord Milner, 'not uncomfortable, but much too full of all and sundry, too much of a "circus" for my taste.'[21] For all the people that there were milling around, very few seemed to be doing any useful work.[22] Betty Cranborne joined her husband. Bobbety's sister was already there with her husband, Eddie Hartington, who was working for Lord Derby, the British ambassador in Paris. Paris may have been a jamboree, but Cranborne saw some serious work and some serious high politics. His uncle was at the pinnacle of his influence. 'President Wilson says,' recorded James Headlam-Morley in January 1919, 'that Lord Robert Cecil is the greatest man in Europe – the greatest man he has ever met.'[23] Indeed on the very evening that Jim and Robert Cecil agreed that Cranborne should come out to Paris, Lloyd George was telling his dinner companions that Cecil was one of his most formidable rivals.[24]

When Cranborne arrived in Paris the conference was entering its second phase.[25] Most of the work on the creation of the League of Nations, which made Cecil's name as its architect, was finished. Considering his main work done the President of the United States, Woodrow Wilson, had sailed for America. The fact that his and Cecil's handiwork would be rejected by the US Congress was still not apparent to those left behind in Paris.[26] The great issue to them was whether the Allies should impose a 'Carthaginian peace' on Germany. As chairman of the Supreme Economic Council, Cecil was immediately swept up into the bitter arguments about whether to feed Germany. With the threat of revolution in Germany and actual revolution in Hungary the situation seemed bleak.[27] Unlike many of his colleagues in 1919, Cecil saw that it was Britain's relationship with the United States rather than its relationship to its European allies that was the key factor.[28] Lord Robert believed that if the Americans were to be involved in an overall settlement, the Europeans had to be lenient to the Germans. In the run-up to the crucial meetings of the British Empire delegation at the end of May and the beginning of June 1919, Cecil tried hard to persuade Lloyd George to follow the path of moderation. The French were deeply suspicious of his influence. Clemenceau accused Lloyd George of being beguiled by Cecil 'to open his arms to the Germans'.[29]

Although Cranborne's position was in the ante-rooms of the great rather than in the conference hall, Lord Robert's method of proceeding gave him a particularly close acquaintance with events since Cecil chose to act in those ante-rooms rather than in council. In his efforts to convince Lloyd George to stand up to the French, Cecil relied on the impact of carefully drafted and reasoned written argument. On a range of issues, whether territorial, such as the Saarland or Poland, or financial, above all reparations, he contended that the proposed settlement was 'out of harmony with the spirit, if not the letter, of the professed war aims'. The terms were not 'suitable for a lasting pacification of Europe' and in the inter-allied negoti-ations that had produced them 'our moral prestige had greatly suf-fered'. He even went so far as to point to the 'moral bankruptcy of the Entente'.[30] Cecil was cogent and persuasive, but having made his point he chose not press the issue in public.[31] 'You do no good,' he noted, 'by jogging a man's elbow. If you can't manage a thing in the way you think right, it is better to leave someone else to do it altogether rather than, by making pushes for this or that change, reduce the whole scheme to incoherence, without curing its injus-tice.'[32] It was an early lesson in the possibilities and limitations of indirect influence for Cranborne.

Cecil himself soon came to regret the fact that he had not jogged Lloyd George's arm more forcefully. Before he left Paris, Cecil had told a meeting that, 'There is not a single person in this room who is not disappointed with the terms we have drafted . . . Our disappointment is an excellent symptom; let us perpetuate it.' Six months later when he had read John Maynard Keynes's indictment of Versailles, *The Economic Consequences of the Peace*, Cecil no longer thought disappointment an excellent symptom: 'I am quite clear that we shall have to begin a campaign for the revision of the Treaty as soon as possible,' he announced. It was Lord Robert's emergence as a crusader that attracted young men to the Cecil banner.[33] His mix-ture of 'the crusading instinct strongly developed' with 'an amiable touch of vanity' appealed to those repelled by Lloyd George's perceived cynicism. As Macmillan commented in a letter congratulating Cranborne on his role in Paris, 'I suppose our nasty little Prime Minister is not really popular any more, except with the International Jew.' Cecil's League of Nations campaign gave Cranborne the opportunity to cut his teeth on political oratory. As someone who knew the inside story of the Peace Conference as the nephew and confidant of its hero he was in considerable demand as a speaker. Few seemed to mind that he spoke with a pronounced lisp that caused him to pronounce his 'r' as 'w'. Lord Robert was encouraging. He told his friends that his nephew had become a 'very good speaker' through all his experience with the League of Nations Union.[34] In truth Cranborne was not particularly attracted to Lord Robert's new revivalist brand of politics. Although it was politic to be associated with his uncle's liberal conservatism in public, in private he had more sympathy with his father's die-hard version. The 1919 League of Nations campaign was, however, the start of his apprenticeship.[35] Most important was the fact that on his return from Paris not only his uncle but his father began to take him into their political counsels.[36]

If Cranborne witnessed the first act of the post-war peace settlement at close quarters, then Crookshank saw its final act from an even closer and much more uncomfortable vantage. He had some regrets about his decision to join the Foreign Office and still hankered after the Guards. He was on first-name terms with the Guards generals who had been company commanders in 1915. The Foreign Office seemed in contrast rigidly hierarchical. Its dominant figure, the foreign secretary, Lord Curzon, was capable of great charm and kindness. An old friend of Alfred Lyttelton, he treated Oliver 'like a nephew, almost like a son'. Junior clerks such as Crookshank, however, encountered him only at the risk of fierce rebuke.[37] Nevertheless Crookshank found that the Foreign Office did have some of the same appeal as the Guards, such as an insistence on the 'proper' way of doing things, rituals that clearly marked off insiders from outsiders. If the work was tedious, there was at least the prospect of better things to come. Before the war the Foreign Office and the Diplomatic Service had been different entities – men who joined the former spent most of their careers in London, those who entered the latter served mainly in embassies overseas. In the year Crookshank joined, the two services were merged and the more modern system of rotation was introduced: a new group of generalists, of whom he was one, would be expected to split their time between Whitehall and the embassies. Thus, in 1921, Crookshank was posted to the British High Commission in Constantinople. It was a plum appointment.

Not only was Constantinople one of the great embassies of the 'old diplomacy', but when Crookshank arrived it was overseeing one of the most important tests of the new world order. As a result of his experiences in 1917 and 1918, Crookshank himself did not think much of the Greek contribution to Allied victory in the Great War. 'In ancient times the Greeks at Thermopylae fought to the death and one man came back to tell the story; now one man is killed and they all come back to Salonika to tell the story,' he was fond of saying.[38] The Greek government did nevertheless expect to profit from its titular alliance with the victorious powers at the expense of the Turks. As part of the Versailles process, the Allies had forced the Ottoman government to cede territory to the Greeks under the terms of the treaty of Sèvres, signed in August 1920. By that time the Sultan's government was little more than a cipher. The Turkish war hero Mustapha Kemal had set up in Ankara a rival regime committed to the indivisibility of Anatolia and eastern Turkey. In March 1920, Britain, France and Italy had responded by occupying Constantinople. The High Commission that Crookshank joined thus had, as well as its diplomatic duties, executive responsibility for the administration of the city. The British were, however, in a precarious position. In March 1921 the Greek army attacked the Kemalists and were soundly beaten. Britain's French and Italian allies, to say nothing of the Russian Bolsheviks, were keen to cut a deal with the martial nationalists.

When Crookshank arrived, Constantinople was in turmoil. The two most important Britons in the city, charged with navigating through the crisis, were his boss, the High Commissioner, Sir Horace Rumbold, and the commander of British troops, General Tim Harington. As late as March 1921 Crookshank had been continuing his efforts to leave the Foreign Office for the Grenadier Guards.[39]

Constantinople confirmed his view about the relative merits of soldiers and diplomats. 'Tim Harington ... is quite excellent and a
tower of strength whereas Horace is only a mountain of flesh.' He
consistently found himself agreeing with Harington's HQ rather than
his own High Commission. He came to believe that Rumbold was
a buffoon and that his number two, Nevile Henderson, was a snake.
The diplomats did not compare well with the army officers in Turkey,
such as 'Alex' Alexander, who had been part of Oliver Lyttelton's
party at the Somme and was now commanding a battalion of Irish
Guards. Crookshank laid three main charges at Rumbold's door.
First, he seemed more interested in going on leave than doing his
job; secondly, he was unnecessarily anti-French; and thirdly he was
a yes-man who told London only what it wanted to hear. In
Crookshank's view he was entirely culpable when the Chanak crisis
broke around the High Commission's heads in September 1922.

It was certainly true that Rumbold liked his leave. In May 1921,
when the capital was rife with rumours of a nationalist attack, he asked
the Foreign Office for two months off. Even Rumbold was aware that
his superiors would find it rather odd that he wanted to leave his post
at such a critical juncture. He pleaded sleeplessness, high blood pressure and general tiredness and argued, 'I should work better after I
had a bit of a rest.' In the summer of 1922 he was at it again. He
knew a crisis was brewing and agreed to take a holiday on the Turkish
coast so that he could immediately return to the capital, but in the
end he could not resist leaving for London. In his absence the Greeks
threatened to attack Constantinople and had to be faced down by Harington and Henderson. Rumbold only arrived back for the denouement of the crisis at the end of July 1922. Having returned, however,
he then impressed everyone with his sang-froid. 'Horace *groans* and
wishes he had stopped for a week in Switzerland!' his wife wrote. 'He
remains most annoyingly calm! I believe if the last trump sounded he
would gaze unperturbed through his eye glass and wish there were
not so many damned foreigners about.'[40] Even Crookshank had to
concede that it was an impressive display. '"Horatio" returned with
great gusto on the very day that the excitement was boiling up about
the proposed Greek advance on Constantinople,' he wrote in an

account to his friend Paul Evans, 'when asked to call a special meeting at once on arrival his only remark was that he must have lunch and a bath first.'[41]

Rumbold did engage in constant disputes with the French. He distrusted his French opposite number, General Pellé, profoundly and considered, rightly, that he would always conspire with the Kemalists behind his back whenever the opportunity arose. The French were in his words 'dreadful Allies' and might well force Britain to 'have to eat dirt to an unlimited extent'. They were 'always "playing the dirty" on us'. Henderson seconded his chief's views in spades: the French were 'cads and apes', 'in the grip of the international financier or Jew who cares for French financial interests and nothing else'.[42] When Rumbold returned from leave, he clashed with Harington over the latter's attempt to cooperate with the French in taking a more hostile line to the Greeks and recognizing that the Ankara regime formed the true government of Turkey. On 8 August 1922 he vetoed plans to act against Greek shipping, deprecating 'the interesting spectacle of Pellé ... slobbering over Harington, telling him what a fine fellow he was'. Rumbold was very aware that Lloyd George had publicly expressed pro-Greek views. Although intellectually he acknowledged that it was 'useless to regard Mustapha Kemal any longer as a brigand chief', and that the treaty of Sèvres was a dead letter, he could not rid himself of a visceral dislike of the Turks. 'I have never dealt with people who have so little political sagacity,' he noted, and did not mind 'confessing privately that I should be rather glad to see the Greeks give the Nationalists one big knock before hostilities come to an end'.[43] Once more his boss's echo, Henderson, called the Turks 'misguided barbarians'.[44]

Any hopes that Rumbold may have had of a stalemate in the Graeco-Turkish War were soon dashed. At the end of August 1922 the Kemalists opened their major offensive and routed the Greeks. By the second week in September they had captured the port of Smyrna. Not only did this pave the way to horrific ethnic cleansing, it also meant that nationalist forces directly threatened the straits zone held by the Allies. True to form, Pellé slipped out of Constantinople to negotiate directly with Kemal; on 20 September the French and Italians abandoned the British garrisoning Chanak on the Dardanelles. Three days later British and Turkish troops came into contact for the first time.

On 26 September Harington cabled Lord Cavan, now Chief of the Imperial General Staff, 'Losing a lot of lives in hanging on is what I want to guard against. Why not start at once and give Turkey Constantinople and [Eastern Thrace] . . . Remember Turks are within sight of their goal and are naturally elated.' On the same day Crookshank wrote his private appreciation of the situation: 'We have got into a nice mess here haven't we!' He placed the blame for his predicament squarely on the shoulders of his senior colleagues.

> I consider [Rumbold] a good deal to blame for the situation having arisen. He often I fancy sends telegrams which he thinks will please [Curzon] or [Lloyd George] rather than containing his own views. The last four or five months can be summed up as a world wide wrangle (short sighted) with France everywhere, owing to this very wicked anti-French feeling that has been brewing everywhere in the FO: as far as this part of the world is concerned it consisted in endless verbal quibbles in answering each others' notes – if HR had any views of his own, he should have pushed them forward and gone on arguing for an immediate Conference. Instead precious months were wasted, whose bad fruit we are now beginning to taste. You can hardly believe [he concluded maliciously] what an atmosphere of gloom surrounds [Rumbold] and Henderson. My lighthearted flippancy, I can assure you, is far from appreciated.[45]

It was at this point that Crookshank had, to his delight, his first brush with high policy. He and the military attaché, Colonel Baird, 'wrote an interesting and logical joint memorandum which was dished out with one of their meetings to Rumbold [and] the General . . . The General thought it wise and telegraphed the suggestions to the War Office . . . The suggestion was that in order to keep ourselves out of the war we should act with complete neutrality and allow the Turks to go to Thrace if they could. At present we are controlling the Marmora against them and so acting as a rearguard to the Greeks.'[46] In London Lloyd George's government was puffing itself up with righteous indignation to face down the Turks.[47] When the Cabinet met at 4 p.m. on 28 September they had before them Harington's dispatch of the Crookshank–Baird memorandum, which had arrived via the War Office. Rumbold had been too slow off the mark to register his dissent. His telegram did not reach London until 8.15 p.m. As a result the Cabinet believed that he in some way concurred with Harington. Curzon signalled a rebuke to them both. According to London the proposal

> would involved [sic] consequences which Harington has not fully foreseen . . . The liberty accorded to Kemal could not in logic or fairness be unilateral. If he were permitted to cross into Europe to fight the Greeks and anticipate the decision of peace conference establishing his rule in Eastern Thrace, Greek ships could not be prevented from using non-neutral waters of Marmora at same time, in order to resist his passage . . . In this way proposed plan might have consequence of not only re-opening war between Turkey and Greece but of transferring theatre of war to Europe with consequences that cannot be foreseen.[48]

Crookshank cared not one whit that his plan had been shot down in flames. He was simply delighted that 'Rumbold . . . got his fingers smacked for not having sent his comments at once' and that 'little Harry . . . [had] caused a Cabinet discussion and a slight flutter'.[49] In fact his memorandum was the high point of the crisis as far as Crookshank was concerned. Harington and Rumbold put aside their differences to thwart London's desire to provoke a shooting war with the Kemalists. As Crookshank was writing up his part in the proceedings, Harington left Constantinople to open direct negotiations with the Kemalists. Early on the morning of 11 October he signed the Mudania Convention: the British, French and Italians would remove Eastern Thrace from Greek control and in return the Turks would retire fifteen kilometres from the coast at Chanak.

The Chanak crisis was an exciting time for Crookshank at its epicentre. It also had profound reverberations for British politics. Indeed, the crisis did much to create the political arena which he and Macmillan subsequently entered. The Dominions had refused to support Britain in its potential war with the Turkish nationalists. The majority of Conservative MPs became convinced that they could no longer support a coalition led by Lloyd George. On 7 October the Conservative leader, Bonar Law, publicly criticized government policy in a letter to *The Times*. If the French were not willing to support Britain, the government had 'no alternative except to imitate the Government of the United States and to restrict our attention to the safeguarding of the more immediate interests of the Empire'.[50] No one stationed in Constantinople in the autumn of 1922 could hope for a sudden collapse of the British position – Crookshank feared 'an internal pro-Kemal and anti-foreign outbreak in [Constantinople] itself . . . we have very little strength to cope with that, and one day we may find ourselves like the Legation did at Peking in Boxer times . . . how ignominious it would be to be killed by a riotous mob, after all the battles one has been through.' Once the immediate threat of anarchy was averted at Mudania, however, Crookshank could not have agreed with Bonar Law more: 'I am quite convinced,' he wrote at the beginning of November, 'that having made a stand in October, having refused to be browbeaten and having been vindicated we should now wash our hands of the whole thing.'[51]

Chanak convinced Crookshank that politics rather than diplomacy was the career to be in. Junior diplomats did not get the opportunity to fight for great causes. One incident further finally soured him on a diplomatic career. He despised Nevile Henderson, who was left in charge of the Commission when Rumbold departed to act as Curzon's adviser at the conference convened at Lausanne to draw up a new peace treaty with Turkey. 'Henderson goes on, with his temper fraying more and his long-winded words in dispatches misapplied more than ever! Lately he talked about Zenophobic and also mentioned the "opaque chaos" of the country. He will not hear of corrections and I can't help thinking the Department must laugh a bit.' It was not so much Henderson's bad English that he found truly offensive as the fact that he was an egregious crawler. Any ambitious man in a hierarchical structure like the Foreign Office had to try and make a good impression on his superiors. What really stuck in Crookshank's throat was Henderson's willingness to chum up with any potentially powerful figure, however unacceptable.

In the autumn of 1922 the Labour politician Ramsay MacDonald visited Constantinople. He did not have nice things to say about the Allies in Constantinople. 'Away from the Galata Bridge,' he wrote in *The Nation*, 'the tunnel tramway leads up to the European quarter where the West, infected by the sensuous luxuriousness of the East, is iridescent with putrefaction, where the bookshops are piled with carnal filth, and where troops of coloured men in khaki can be seen in open daylight marching with officers at their head to where the brothels are.'[52] MacDonald's most famous moral stand was, however, not against pornography and prostitution but against war. He had been the most outspoken critic of the Great War from a pacifist standpoint. In February 1921 he tried to win the Woolwich by-election for the Labour party. It was a vicious campaign, his opponent being a former soldier who had won the VC at Cambrai. Placards on local trams asked, 'A Traitor for Parliament?' 'The Woolwich ex-serviceman,' MacDonald had retorted, 'knows that military decorations are no indication of political wisdom, and that a Parliament of gallant officers will be a Prussian Diet not a British House of Commons.'[53] In Constantinople Crookshank was certainly one gallant officer who agreed that MacDonald was a traitor. To Crookshank's fury, Henderson, 'with as always an eye on the main chance asked him to dine in the Mess which I was running at the time'. Crookshank kicked up a stink: 'I point blank refused to be there and went out to an hotel.' His valet, Page, a former guardsman, 'like master like man . . . refused to wait at table on the "traitor"'. The spat, although minor, was hardly private: one of Crookshank's friends heard about it while serving in the Sudan.[54] Within two years MacDonald was prime minister, within nine years he was a prime minister at the head of the Conservative administration. Crookshank had made a dangerous enemy.

By November 1922 he was 'fed up to the teeth' with Constantinople 'and everyone else and the preposterous Rumbold'.[55] By the next summer Crookshank was 'beginning to feel very desperate about this place'. The Turks having had their demands met by the great powers at Lausanne were cocky and unpleasant, 'constant instances of rough handling, maltreatment etc. happen'.[56] Even his hero Harington was beginning to irritate him: 'The Army went off, as Harington told us about forty million times, with "flag flying high" – but the Turks let themselves go at once in scurrilous abuse. You never read such filth as they wrote. They had a final ceremony, entirely inspired by Harington – three Allied guards of honour and one Turkish and everyone saluting each others flags and then the Allies marching off leaving the Turks *in situ*. This resulted in a lot of stuff about "the Allies have bowed themselves before our glorious flag" and have "proved the victory of Eastern over Western Civilisation". Ugh!'[57] Those left when the troops marched away knew that this was not peace with honour but a bloody nose.

Crookshank believed that the British Empire should dish out punishment rather than receive it. He thus found a political hero in the South African prime minister, Jan Christian Smuts, who visited London in October 1923. Smuts charmed his hosts by heaping obloquy on the French for their arrogance, failures, unreliability and stupidity. More importantly, the former Boer leader propounded a noble vision of empire: 'Here in a tumbling, falling world, here in a world where all the foundations are quaking,' he declared in an address at the Savoy, 'you have something solid and enduring. The greatest thing on earth, the greatest political [organization] of all times, it has passed through the awful blizzard and has emerged stronger than before ... It is because in this Empire we sincerely believe in and practise certain fundamental principles of human government, such as peace, freedom, self-development, self-government.' According to Smuts Irish independence, self-government in India, the end of the Protectorate in Egypt – which could all be read, like Chanak, as examples of British power buckling in the face of violent nationalism – in fact bore 'testimony to the political faith which holds us together and will continue to hold us together while the kingdoms and empires founded on force and constraint pass away'.[58] The sentiments were hardly original, but that they should be expressed so eloquently at that moment by a former enemy gave them huge impact. *The Times* reproduced the speech as a pamphlet. More immediately Smuts's words hummed down the wires to British missions around the world. Here was a political leader and a political creed worthy of admiration. Having read Smuts with 'daily increasing imagination', Crookshank concluded, 'there is a lure about politics, especially in their present Imperial aspect.'[59]

At exactly the same time as Crookshank's mind was turning to politics and Empire so was Harold Macmillan's. Macmillan, like Crookshank and Cranborne, was attracted to the idea of foreign climes.[60] Macmillan's contacts were perhaps not as highly placed as Cranborne's, but he was not without resources. His first port of call was George Lloyd, a former Conservative MP whom he had met through his Oxford Union activities. Lloyd was about to depart for India as Governor of Bombay and offered Macmillan a post as his ADC. It was not to be, since the Bombay climate was, as his doctors pointed out, hardly ideal for a man with still suppurating wounds. Macmillan wanted to be an ADC, however, and an imperial governor operating in a colder climate was desperate for his services.

Victor Cavendish, ninth Duke of Devonshire, had been shipped off to Canada for the duration in 1916. At times he felt himself sadly neglected – not least in the matter of ADCs. The kind of young men His Grace wanted were not to be had when there was a war on. Those he was sent were 'worse than useless'.[61] They were as keen to leave him as he was to be rid of them.[62] His wife, Evie, was dispatched to London on a desperate mission to recruit some new blood. Although Macmillan was not one of the young aristocrats Devonshire had in mind, Nellie Macmillan was an acquaintance of the Duchess of Devonshire from the pre-war charity circuit. Harold was laid in her path and snapped up with gratitude. When he stepped off the boat in Canada, he was greeted by a most eager employer. The bond was sealed by a game of golf. 'He plays quite well and is much better than I am,' noted Devonshire, for whom his own lack of prowess on the links was a constant lament. 'Macmillan is certainly a great acquisition,' the duke concluded.

On departing for Canada, Macmillan had planned to take a close interest in the North American political scene. The main interest of the Devonshire circle, as it turned out, was romance. The two Cavendish girls had been deprived of suitable male company for nearly three years and were more than a little excited by the arrival of so many eligible young bachelors. Lady Rachel Cavendish whisked the new ADCs straight off the boat to a dance. Within a month of their arrival Macmillan's fellow ADC, Harry Cator, 'a most attractive boy', had to be disentangled from an unsuitable romantic attachment.[63] Unlike his friend, Macmillan was no young blade, but within months he had shown an interest in the Devonshires' other daughter, Lady Dorothy. At the end of July the duke noticed that they had 'got up early to go to Mt Jacques to see the sun rise'.[64] Devonshire regarded Macmillan as a perfectly acceptable match for his daughter.[65] Lady Dorothy herself seemed much less sure. 'After tea,' one day at the beginning of December 1919, 'Harold proposed in a sort of way to Dorothy but although she did not refuse him definitely nothing was settled. She seemed to like him but not enough to accept and says she does not want to marry just yet.' Her father was glad to see that 'She seemed in excellent spirits. After dinner they went skating.'[66] Macmillan broke her down over Christmas. On Boxing Day 1919 'Dorothy and Harold settled to call themselves engaged'.[67] 'I do hope it is alright,' noted her father worriedly.[68] There was certainly something in the air that Canadian New Year which inclined the young to romance: two more of Harold's fellow ADCs also became engaged.

When Harold Macmillan married Dorothy Cavendish in April 1920 at St Margaret's, Westminster – the same church Oliver and Moira Lyttelton had used a few weeks previously – he committed himself to making money from publishing. At the same time he gained an entrée into high politics. Devonshire was very fond of his new son-in-law. Indeed, he saw something of his young self in him. He himself had been an enthusiastic professional politician, a 'painstaking' financial secretary to the Treasury. In many ways his elevation to a great dukedom – which he inherited from his uncle – had deprived him of a career.[69]

Devonshire gladly re-entered politics in October 1922 when the coalition disintegrated over Chanak. Victor Devonshire replaced Winston Churchill in the Cabinet as colonial secretary. While in Canada, Devonshire 'found', as Macmillan recalled, 'that I was interested in political problems, he would discuss them freely with me'.[70] In London this habit continued – but now with much more interesting issues to mull over.[71] Macmillan remembered calling on the duke during the course of the formation of Bonar Law's government. 'I found Lord Derby in conference with him. The Duke . . . pointed out the extreme weakness of the front bench in the House of Commons . . . "Ah," said Lord Derby, "you are too pessimistic. They have found a wonderful little man. One of those attorney fellows, you know. He will do all the work." "What's his name?" said the Duke. "Pig," said Lord Derby. Turning to me, the Duke replied, "Do you know Pig?" . . . It turned out to be Sir Douglas Hogg!'[72]

The most pressing policy issue that Victor Devonshire had to face at the Colonial Office was the need for some kind of new relationship with two British colonies in Africa: Rhodesia and Kenya. Both were examples of entrepreneurial colonies – initially exploited by chartered companies. Each had a group of European settlers keen to lay their hands on as much political power as possible. Yet in Kenya and Rhodesia the white settlers were only a small proportion of the total population, the majority being made up of indigenous Africans. The dream of Commonwealth came directly into collision with the duties of trusteeship. The Colonial Office's official view was that 'whether therefore we look to natives for whom we hold a trusteeship or [a] white community which is insufficiently strong politically and financially – the obstacles to early responsible government . . . appear prohibitive'. In each case the solution in the eyes of civil servants in London was to incorporate these small but troublesome outposts of empire into some wider whole. In the case of Rhodesia, union with South Africa seemed to beckon; in the case of Kenya, closer association across the Indian Ocean with India. Whitehall had, however, underestimated the contrary spirit of the settlers. In both countries the settlers spawned rebarbative political leaders quite willing to defy the mother country.

In Southern Rhodesia the opposition was led by Sir Charles Coghlan, an Irish Roman Catholic lawyer from Bulawayo. In London Smuts might be hailed as the great imperial statesman-visionary. In Salisbury he was seen as little more than the frontman for Boer imperialism. When he declared that 'the Union is going to be for the African continent what the United States has become for the American continent; Rhodesia is but another day's march on the high road of destiny', Rhodesian unionists took it as a signal that a republican South Africa might secede from the Empire. In November 1922 the settlers voted by 59.43 per cent to 40.57 per cent against union with South Africa.[73] Effectively they forced the British government to buy out the chartered South Africa Company and grant self-government. The negotiations created much ill-will. In July 1923 the Colonial Office gave the company two weeks to accept appropriation. Devonshire's under-secretary, Cranborne's brother-in-law and friend, Billy Ormsby-Gore, struck a deal that gave the company three and three-quarter million pounds and half the proceeds on government land sales until 1965.[74] The deal left a settler community confident in its own power to manipulate Britain and a disgruntled company that, all admitted, still dominated the economic life of its former domain.

Devonshire had even more problems with Kenya. 'Afraid we shall have a very difficult matter with Kenya. The white settlers really make everything very difficult,' he lamented.[75] The Kenyan settlers were led by the largest landowner and larger-than-life figure, Lord Delamere. In the summer of 1922 the Colonial Office and the India Office agreed that Indians should be able to settle freely in Kenya and should enjoy equal political rights to the European settlers. In January 1923 Devonshire ordered preparations to be made for a common voting role. The settlers' leaders formed a so-called 'Vigilance Committee' to organize political and military opposition – an armed militia was embodied and plans drawn up to seize key points and kidnap the governor if need be. The settlers' military organization was, in the context of East Africa, formidable and they were quite capable of carrying through a coup.[76] Faced with such extreme action, Devonshire invited both Delamere's faction and Indian representatives to London for a conference. Delamere acted in considerable style: he took a house in Grosvenor Place that acted as a hub for an intensive lobbying effort. Out of it spewed articles and communiqués; in came journalists and people of influence for lunches, dinners and interviews. When Devonshire met Delamere in April 1923, the race issue was presented to him in unvarnished fashion: 'If the Duke of Devonshire could see a typical row of Indian *dukas* in a Kenya township he would understand their feelings better,' the settlers told Macmillan's father-in-law. 'Dirt, smells, flies, disregard of sanitation.' Once more the key figure in the negotiations was Billy Ormsby-Gore. Gore was one of the champions of trusteeship who saw the settlers as an alien force getting in the way of what he believed would be a friendly and enduring paternal relationship between Britain and its native subjects. To the horror of many Kenyan settlers, the White Paper they received on 25 July 1923 – the same day as the Rhodesian settlement – met many of their political demands but firmly declared, 'Primarily, Kenya is an African territory ... [the] interests of the African natives must be paramount ... His Majesty's Government regard themselves as exercising a trust on behalf of the African population.' Threats of armed revolt were made. To stave off trouble Devonshire agreed at the eleventh hour to instruct the governor of Kenya to prevent Indian immigration.[77]

Macmillan had therefore seen at close quarters the reality of Britain's position in Africa. It left him with a healthy distrust of all the parties involved. To his mind the South Africans had demonstrated themselves to be tinpot imperialists. The chartered company was exposed as a rapacious exploiter. Worst of all, the white settlers were revealed as turbulent bigots and potential traitors. All three posed a threat to the good governance of the Empire. Unlike his friend Crookshank, operating on the fringes of British power, Macmillan, sitting at the centre, took Smuts's heady rhetoric with a large pinch of salt. Nevertheless his interest in politics was piqued quite as much. Billy Gore, a man only a few years older than himself, was very much the figure of the moment.

It was by now quite clear to Macmillan that if he wished to enter politics he would have do so under his own steam. Although Devonshire may have given him an outstanding insight into the workings of high policy, the duke was naturally much more concerned to bring forward his own son, Eddie Hartington, a mere year younger than Macmillan.[78] He was determined to nurse a seat for

Eddie and give him as much exposure to office as possible. Macmillan enjoyed regular conversations, but Hartington accompanied his father to the office each day to gain experience.[79] Macmillan was never going to be the Cavendishes' favoured son.

The Conservative party was, however, keen to recruit men like Macmillan. In 1923 he was adopted for the industrial seat of Stockton in north-east England. It was a world away from the kind of seats young aristocrats would be expected to fight. Macmillan faced an uphill struggle to win such a seat as a Conservative. The new leader of the Conservative party, Stanley Baldwin, favoured the introduction of protection – the levying of tariffs on foreign goods imported into Britain. He felt, however, that in order to requite previous promises he must call a general election before enacting such a policy. A year after Bonar Law had led the party to victory, Baldwin led it to defeat. Those contemporaries of Macmillan elected in 1923 tell the story: they were blue bloods in safe seats. Eddie Hartington entered Parliament much to his father's delight – 'a really very good, remarkable and satisfactory victory which he thoroughly deserves.'[80] Two Eton and Grenadier contemporaries also entered Parliament in 1923. One, Dick Briscoe, a particular friend of Crookshank, with whom he had been at Magdalen, was the scion of a wealthy Cambridgeshire gentry family. The other, Walter Dalkeith, a close friend of Cranborne, was the heir of the Duke of Buccleuch – the wealthiest of the great aristocratic landowners. It was a rather different story in marginal constituencies in the north of England. These were the very areas where Baldwin's embrace of tariff reform seemed like a vote for dear food. Although he made a good job of campaigning, Macmillan's bid for the Stockton seat was doomed to failure.

It was fortunate for Macmillan, and indeed Crookshank, that the immediate post-war years saw such frequent appeals to the country: there were general elections in 1918, 1922, 1923 and 1924. They would soon have another opportunity of getting elected. Macmillan was determined to give Stockton another try and Crookshank was sure that he wanted to try for Parliament at the next opportunity. This was despite the fact that he had been transferred from Constantinople to a another plum posting in Washington, with all the discomforts of Turkey left far behind. He had a beautiful apartment and, because many of his investments were in American stocks, was flush with dollars. Yet he felt little warmer to diplomacy. Whereas in Constantinople he had seen too much of Rumbold and Henderson, now he rarely saw the ambassador, Sir Esme Howard. To make matters worse, Howard had specifically requested the services of Crookshank's Eton contemporary Jock Balfour, for which 'I am sorry for I have no particular passion for JB'. Since Howard was the brother-in-law of Balfour's aunt and treated him 'as a member of the family' the omens did not look good.[81]

Although neither Crookshank nor Macmillan were favoured sons, they were exactly the kind of candidate the party was looking for to fight marginal but winnable seats. They were young, energetic, of good family, well-educated with good war records. Although Crookshank was not married, his sister Betty was devoted to him and willing to throw herself into constituency work. Of overriding importance for both Central Office and the local party, moreover, was their independent wealth. Both Macmillan and Crookshank could and did finance their own constituency organizations for both day-to-day running costs and campaigning. Such men needed no links with their constituencies – they could parachute in at short notice. As Crookshank said, 'I rather hate to think that one would have to be a real carpet-bagger but in these days it is apt to happen and after all [our] training ought to count for something.'[82] With a minority Labour government in power, both men felt their chance would come soon.

Thus in September 1924, when the prospective Conservative parliamentary candidate for Gainsborough in Lincolnshire fell ill, the party put the constituency in touch with Crookshank as a man who could fill in at very short notice. Within a fortnight of him having been adopted, it became clear that an election was imminent. To considerable irritation in Whitehall, Crookshank resigned from the foreign service with immediate effect. 'I burnt my boats,' he wrote a few days before the poll, 'so far as the FO was concerned "on spec".' What made the gamble worthwhile for both Macmillan and Crookshank was the changing nature of British politics. Although the Liberals were a declining force in national politics, they still maintained some of their strength at local level. Both Stockton and Gainsborough were three-way constituencies. The anti-Conservative vote was strong but split. It made 1924 the optimum year to run.[83]

Apart from this feature of psephological geography, the two constituencies were quite dissimilar. Indeed, the different nature of their constituencies did much to shape Macmillan and Crookshank's very different conduct in the 1924 Parliament. Stockton was in an industrial 'rustbelt', whereas Gainsborough was one of the most rural seats in England – even inhabitants of Lincoln regarded Gainsborough folk as a little yokelish. Neither candidate had much knowledge of local conditions. 'It is really comic,' Crookshank wrote soon after his election, 'when you come to think of it that I represent an agricultural area ... I shall never become an agricultural expert: I don't want to!'[84] He was lucky in as much as he did not have to. Although he had to face a powerful local farming lobby which was often dissatisfied with the Conservatives, the combination of his support for protectionism and strong constituency work enabled him to convince his constituents that he was doing his best for them.[85] The most important gains that won the Conservatives the 1924 election, however, had been in industrial areas. These seats had once more become winnable because Baldwin abandoned protection in the wake of the 1923 defeat. Early declarations in the north had foretold the overall result: Salford, Manchester, Wakefield and then Macmillan's Stockton, 'a very fine performance',[86] were the first seats to be announced, all swinging to the Conservatives.[87] The volatility of these seats was bound to make their MPs activists.

Both Macmillan and Crookshank knew that any institution had rules for getting on in life. As at school and university, there would always be competition from similarly equipped rivals. 'Four recent Foreign Office people all got in,' Crookshank noted, 'Bob Hudson, Duff Cooper, John Loder and I – I am also one of the twelve Magdalen men and one of the twelve Old Grenadiers!'[88] The trick was to find a good approach and stick to it. Both arrived at Westminster with well-thought-out strategies for advancement. Both had every chance of success.

Crookshank's plan was fairly conventional. He would establish himself as a noted speaker and expert. His impact would be such that the front bench would take notice and promotion would follow. As someone inspired by Smuts's rhetoric, it was natural that he should be drawn towards foreign affairs. Given his family background and his own more recent diplomatic experience, he believed that he was splendidly equipped to make a big impression. He felt he would be marching to the same tune as the party hierarchy. 'I have every confidence in Baldwin,' he told a friend, 'and I'm sure he is out for a big Imperial policy which is what we want.'[89] Even international events seemed to be moving in his favour. On 19 November 1924 Sir Lee Stack, the sirdar, or governor, of the Sudan had been murdered by an Egyptian nationalist in Cairo. As the new House of Commons assembled, the political world was abuzz with a new crisis in Anglo-Egyptian relations. Crookshank planned to use the opportunity of the debate on the address to make his maiden speech, creating what he hoped would be maximum exposure. Unfortunately for him, another Etonian, Grenadier diplomat had exactly the same idea. As Crookshank was working on *his* speech, Duff Cooper was at Hatfield working on a similar speech with the help of his friend Bobbety Cranborne.[90]

Three years senior to the quartet, Cooper had established himself in London before the outbreak of the war. He had caused a stir by obtaining an appointment to the Foreign Office: the son of a successful surgeon, Cooper was one of the first non-aristocrats to be recruited to the administrative grade. He had ostentatiously not volunteered for the army but had been conscripted into the Guards and won a DSO towards the end of the war. Cooper's greatest coup, however, was to marry Diana Manners, daughter of the Duke of Rutland and reputedly the most beautiful woman in England. The Rutland connection further enhanced Cooper's standing. The Rutlands' London home was next door to that of the Salisburys, for instance, and the two families were close. Cooper assiduously worked his connections – the Chancellor of the Exchequer, Winston Churchill, the whips, the Speaker, the press lord Max Beaverbrook – to make sure he was called.[91] His hard work was not in vain. Crookshank and other new MPs had to watch, consumed with jealousy, as Cooper was put on at a 'wonderfully fortunate moment'.

He rose at seven o'clock in the evening. 'Ministers and ex-Ministers hadn't left the House – Lloyd George was there throughout and so was Baldwin.' Austen Chamberlain came in and was heard to say to Baldwin, 'I hear he's very good.' Cooper began by twitting the recently defeated government about the Zinoviev letter, a document published by the *Daily Mail* which purported to show that the Soviet Union was trying to stir up revolution in Britain, which many Labour MPs believed had lost them the election. It did not matter whether or not the letter was a forgery, Cooper claimed, the Labour party and the electorate knew 'that Bolshevist propaganda was taking place in this country'. Moving on to the Egyptian situation, he mocked any suggestion that the League of Nations should become involved. 'When,' he asked, 'you have appointed this commission of broad-minded, broad-browed, learned Scandinavian professors, what are you going to do?' He lauded British rule to the skies. 'We restored an independence which Egypt had not enjoyed since some time before Alexander the Great.' He excoriated the idol of the Egyptian nationalists, Sa'ad Zaghloul, for having 'indirectly inspired the hand that held the revolver and threw the bomb'.[92]

The speech was a *tour de force*, as even his rivals had to admit. Crookshank could not contain his envy. 'Duff Cooper made a very good speech for his maiden effort on Egypt. Subject matter good and a fair delivery, though rather too like a saying lesson at school. It was frightfully advertised – he lives (like or because of his wife) in a press atmosphere.'[93] 'Duff Cooper,' noted Cuthbert Headlam, Lyttelton's fellow ADC in 1915, himself a new Tory MP in 1924, 'is now a marked man.'[94] Headlam was quite right. One well-timed and well-delivered speech could make a political career. The plaudits poured in on Cooper. 'I had,' he wrote to his wife the next day, 'a letter of congratulation from the Speaker which I gather is a rather unusual honour – and also one from Winston – all the evening people whom I didn't know were coming up to me and congratulating me. In other words, baby, it was a triumph.'[95]

The lead Cooper established over his contemporaries that night lasted for the rest of the decade. In 1929 William Bridgeman, a senior member of Baldwin's Cabinet who had been much concerned with party management, noted that after Cooper 'there did not seem to me anyone so markedly brilliant as to deserve immediate promotion from the back benches'.[96] Although Crookshank subsequently pursued his interest in eastern affairs, having missed his opportunity in December, it was to little effect. His first parliamentary question two months later on the subject of the ecumenical patriarch was hardly likely to set the heather on fire. His maiden speech was given not in the early evening of a great debate, as was Cooper's, but late at night to a thin house. It was not a *succès d'estime*. It did cover foreign policy, but was chiefly noted for the dictum that, 'The conduct of foreign affairs must be in the hands of the few,' which, stated in such an unvarnished fashion, led to unflattering comparisons with Jim Salisbury.[97] Crookshank, who had come into politics knowledgeable about and fascinated by imperial affairs, was never able to take an opportunity to become involved in them.

Crookshank was nevertheless an able and quick-witted parliamentary speaker, in contrast to Macmillan, who tended to the ponderous. But this only seemed to gain him a reputation for idiosyncrasy, one of the last attributes desirable in a ministerial careerist. He was not helped by two aspects of his physical appearance. One he could not help. Early hair loss revealed a large cranium. He looked like nothing other than the spitting image of William Shakespeare. No newspaper seemed able to mention his name without alluding to this resemblance. His dress, on the other hand, was entirely his own choice. Until the outbreak of the Second World War he insisted on wearing a shiny topper to the House. He looked like a shorter version of Sir Austen Chamberlain – which was probably worse than looking like the Bard. No newspaper seemed able to mention his name without alluding to this resemblance either. Physically equipped for quirkiness, he started to make his name as a backbencher rather than as a potential minister. When another well-known House of Commons character, Commander Kenworthy, drew up his list of new MPs to watch, he noted that 'the outstanding figure amongst the younger members is Mr Duff Cooper'. Crookshank was notable as one 'who has realized that one of the first essentials of success in Parliament is to be always in his place'.

Instead of Asiatic affairs, Crookshank was increasingly drawn to quixotic affairs. His first great parliamentary set piece came in 1926 when he tried to wreck a government bill obviating the need for MPs to seek re-election when they became ministers. He managed to insult a number of groups: the party's business managers, liberal Conservatives, Liberals who had become Conservatives. Labelling himself an 'ultra-conservative', he mocked, 'Debates ... extraordinarily busy with the question of safeguarding industries,' and suggested that the Commons should instead 'follow out the principle of safeguarding the present rights of the electorate'. He also had a dig at turncoats. In a considerable coup for the whips, two former Liberal Cabinet ministers had just defected to the Conservatives. Crookshank expressed the view that if such men, 'in crossing the floor, were quite sure of office, then I think it is important and absolutely essential that the present safeguard should be maintained'. Not only was Crookshank intemperate, he also got his parliamentary procedure wrong. His amendment to the bill inadvertently implied that a Cabinet minister moving to another post in the Cabinet would have to seek re-election to the House of Commons. 'It is the first time I have tried my hand at this kind of thing, and I am not a lawyer,' was Crookshank's somewhat lame excuse. His friend Charles Waterhouse, another of the 1924 intake, had to come to his aid, amending the amendment to make it coherent. To no one's surprise this stand for parliamentary precedence over the convenience of the government was defeated by a large margin. Crookshank was also associated with another parliamentary revolt against Baldwin over the Prayer Book. Given his own Irish background and the fact that his Gainsborough seat contained the highest proportion of non-conformists in England,[98] Crookshank had little choice but to line up behind the home secretary, 'Jix' Joynson-Hicks, who believed the Church of England's proposed new liturgy was papism by the back door. In this case he was part of the majority, but he had been dragged, this time reluctantly, into another quixotic fight.[99]

Macmillan's strategy for success was quite different from that of

Crookshank. In part it derived from the constituency he represented. Stockton was one of the seats won by Baldwin's abandonment of 'dear food'. Yet a change of national policy was certainly not enough to secure the seat for any length of time. The MPs for the newly won northern seats had to be seen actively lobbying for the interests of their constituents if they were to stand a chance of keeping their places. So although Macmillan was more interested in foreign than domestic affairs, he could not afford the luxury of following his natural inclination. Support for industrial protection and urban relief was almost inevitable. Yet the manner in which Macmillan chose to prosecute his agenda revealed a sophisticated grasp of tactics. Crookshank's stance as an independent member was positively Victorian, Macmillan's was exceptionally modern.

The experience of the previous decade had changed the House of Commons. Of the ten years between 1914 and 1924, seven, 1915 to 1922, saw coalition government. The two years following the fall of Lloyd George had demonstrated a high degree of political instability. Although the Conservatives secured a massive majority in 1924, the clock could not simply be put back to 1900. The lessons learnt by ambitious backbenchers submerged within an overwhelming parliamentary majority were just as applicable to single-party as to coalition rule. The years of coalition had produced new forms of back-bench action. As the veteran political journalist Sir Henry Lucy noted at the beginning of the coalition period: 'not since the days of Mr Gladstone's prime as leader of the House of Commons has there been such activity in the creation of what were known as Tea Room Cabals. Now they are called Ginger Committees, their avowed patriotic purpose being to keep the Government on the hop.'[100]

Some of these groups, such as the wartime Unionist Business Committee or the 1922 Committee, founded in 1923 as a form of self-help organization for new members, had over 100 members.[101] Others, the 'ginger groups' proper, were much smaller. They tended to be bound together by some policy positions and a determination to support each other in the House. In effect they were a claque. If one member was speaking in a debate, the others would be sure to attend to give him support. They would cheer him to the echo and shout down anyone who attempted to intervene. Some of these groups were for or contained ideologues. Most, however, were means to an end. Successful parliamentary performance helped by one's fellows, good publicity, the threat of limited acts of rebellion all helped to draw the attention of party managers to backbenchers. Soon members of the ginger group would find themselves asked to join the government as junior ministers. Careers would be launched and the claque would have served its purpose.

For an ambitious young liberal Conservative like Macmillan, the most notable group of this type was one launched in 1917, 'to lunch together once a week and try to act together', by a group of Tories interested in social reform.[102] The political careers of its leading lights certainly prospered. By 1924 Billy Ormsby-Gore, whose successes had so piqued Macmillan's ambition, was under-secretary at the Colonial Office, Top Wolmer, Bobbety Cranborne's cousin, was parliamentary secretary to the Board of Trade, Walter Guinness was financial secretary to the Treasury, Eddie Winterton was under-secretary of state for India, Philip Cunliffe-Lister was president of the Board of Trade. Of most interest to Macmillan, however, was the rapid progress of Edward Wood, recently president of the Board of Education and soon to embark on the viceroyalty of India. Wood had publicized the views of the group – support for housing and agricultural subsidies, voting equality for women, regional devolution, support for the League of Nations – in *The Great Opportunity*, a short book co-written with George Lloyd, whose ADC Macmillan was to have been in 1919.[103] Macmillan had a great advantage as a member of any ginger group: he was a publisher. He could guarantee a first-class vehicle for any publication – however trite or boring. The ability to give or withhold the right of publication often grated with those not so blessed. One of the first clashes between Macmillan and Rab Butler occurred over Macmillan's reluctance to publish propaganda for Butler's campaign on India.[104] From his first day in the House, Macmillan was determined to be part of a ginger group.[105]

It was entirely logical for Macmillan to concentrate his activities on ginger groups. What surprised many is how assiduously he stuck to the idea once it had become politically counter-productive. Indeed, until he finally entered the government in 1940 he displayed a positive passion for such cabals. For most of the 1924 to 1929 Parliament, however, the political strategy that had sent him down this road seemed to hold good. Macmillan rapidly became involved with two groups. One was the northern MPs: a regional alliance that was largely one of convenience – they would all sink or swim together. The other ginger group resembled more closely Wood's successful model. By the middle of 1925 they were already being given names like the EYM (Eager Young Men).[106] Like its predecessor, it was made up of men drawn from the same political generation and at much the same point in their careers. At its core were two young aristocrats, Oliver Stanley and John Loder, two Scottish MPs, Bob Boothby and Noel Skelton, and Macmillan himself.

The aim of a ginger group was to benefit all of its members. It was inevitable, however, that some would be left behind. As the party managers selected the cream of the crop, the group would dissolve. The problem for Macmillan was that most of his new-found allies had more obvious talents than himself. John Loder had charm – he could get away with admitting that he would have joined the Liberal party if it had still been a credible political organization. Noel Skelton flung out interesting ideas with 'reckless prodigality'. Oliver Stanley had impeccable political connections through his father, Lord Derby. He could afford to sow his political wild oats in the happy knowledge that the party leadership would view him with indulgence. Like Cooper's, his maiden speech was heavily trailed and widely hailed. It made the right noises about political harmony. Also like Cooper, Stanley used humour well.[107] Some people regarded Stanley as an empty suit. The perceptive Cuthbert Headlam had dinner with Stanley and Macmillan at the end of their first year in Parliament. Of 'the two rising hopes of the Conservative Party' he said, 'The latter strikes me as much the abler of the two, but of course the former has the greater backing'.[108] As a result it was Stanley who came to be regarded as a future liberal Conservative prime minister. Boothby was quite different. He was very young. Born in 1900, his war service had amounted to nothing more than training with the Scots Guards. There was something wild, even a little dangerous about Boothby.

Both Macmillan and Boothby were offensive about the opposition in their maiden speeches. Whereas Cooper and Stanley had got their digs in by using humour, and had been well received, many were offended by Boothby and Macmillan. The difference was that Boothby was offensive with brio and panache. Macmillan tried to savage his opponent by reading him an essay.[109]

Within two years, the eager young men of 1925 had acquired a more enduring sobriquet, the YMCA. It implied that they were keen but priggish, lecturing their elders on the best way to run things. Like all young, talented and ambitious men they aroused their share of animus. Yet they always kept on the right side of the party managers, claiming as their inspiration Baldwin himself. It suited the prime minister to be seen encouraging voices of progressive Conservatism. Part of his political strategy was to reach out to all non-socialists and form a grand union of the centre and the right.[110] The YMCA were a useful tool in pursuit of that goal. Macmillan was convinced that ministerial office was just round the corner.

Like his model, Edward Wood, he intended to make his mark with a short book publicizing the ginger group. His first trial balloon for the book was a letter to *The Times* co-written with Jack Hills, who had actually been a member of Wood's group.[111] As a publisher Macmillan knew how to organize and collate research. The book that became *Industry and the State* was not published until April 1927, though Macmillan had set the wheels in motion in the summer of 1926. Its putative authors were Macmillan, Stanley, Loder and Boothby. Macmillan, however, knew the value of a research team. He made great use of Herbert Williams, an MP known as the 'walking Blue Book', and sympathetic civil servants.[112]

The whole purpose of the ginger group seemed to be working. Macmillan was being talked about as a man who would soon achieve office. An anxious Cuthbert Headlam recorded in December 1926, 'Today a note appeared in *The Times* suggesting that I, Harold Macmillan, Oliver Stanley or Noel Skelton would admirably fill the vacant post at the Admiralty ... Macmillan ... is being backed heavily for an early appointment – he is considered so very able and knows how to make his way.'[113] The First Lord of the Admiralty, William

Bridgeman, took a close interest in the connection between industrial relations, social reform and electoral politics.[114] In the event, Bridgeman overlooked all the members of the YMCA and chose Headlam, part of the 1924 intake, a member of the northern group with a next-door constituency to Macmillan, but a much older man.

This was a setback for Macmillan, but Boothby landed a job as Churchill's parliamentary private secretary. Despite the principle that every time a friend succeeds something within one dies, this promotion at least suggested that the group was making the right kind of impact. Although the actual publication of *Industry and the State* caused a minor furore, the *Daily Mail* finding its vision of an 'economic general staff', nationalization of education and the police service, international intervention by states in the banking system, worker–employer partnerships and national wage boards across industry, nothing less than socialism in disguise, it hardly came as a surprise within the party. It succeeded in its purpose of drawing attention to its authors.

Indeed, for Macmillan it seemed that Boothby's good fortune might become his own. Boothby's new boss, Winston Churchill, was casting around for eye-catching ideas. Churchill was not a natural soulmate for the YMCA, but he was an exceptionally attractive potential patron. In the summer of 1927 he picked up an idea that Macmillan had floated two years previously: the re-rating of industry. As Churchill told the Cabinet, 'productive industry of every kind suffers an excessive and injurious oppression. The burden falls most severely upon the heavy producer. The more plant and real property he has to use for his business, and consequently the more labour he employs, the more he is penalized.'[115] In the words of Neville Chamberlain, Churchill had been 'looking around for some new thing to ornament and illuminate his next budget . . . he has a keen political nose and he saw the makings of a first class political sensation if this startling proposal landed upon an unsuspecting world next April'.[116]

This was Macmillan's big chance. Not only was Churchill willing to concede parenthood of the idea to him, but he needed details men to flesh out the concept into plausible legislation. To Macmillan's great joy, he was called into the Treasury to work as an unofficial adviser. He and Boothby were to sit down with the relevant papers and go through the scheme in detail, looking for potential holes.[117] They were heady days. He had the ear of one of the great and the chance to ingratiate himself further. 'I should . . . like you to know,' he wrote to Churchill after a Christmas abandoned to the joys of re-rating, 'how deeply I appreciate the favour of your confidence. You have always been most kind to those of us who are ordinarily classed merely as troublesome young men, and if I can be of any assistance to you at any time in this or similar matters, you have only to command me.'[118] His keenness seemed to pay immediate dividends: Churchill took the trouble to commend his work directly to the prime minister, even sending Macmillan's papers to Baldwin.[119] 'I considered your statement . . . so lucid and well-balanced,' he informed Macmillan, 'that I sent it to the PM. I thought it would interest you to know that he spoke to me about it . . . in extremely complimentary terms.'[120] Yet danger lurked for Macmillan. Churchill was only too aware that radical reform of the rates was a gamble – it would create a big bang in time for the next election, but the government as much as the opposition risked becoming victims. To share the credit was also to lay off the blame. As his private secretary, P. J. Grigg, told Churchill, 'Altogether the Dardanelles situation seems to be re-creating itself. Everybody loves the idea, everybody but you is frightened by its boldness and magnitude. Everybody therefore stands looking on idly, perfectly ready to be pleased if it succeeds and equally ready to say "I told you so" if it doesn't and try to kick you downstairs.'[121]

While Churchill knew the risk he was running, for Macmillan it was his first taste of power. By accepting the patronage of one powerful minister, he ran the risk of crossing an equally powerful figure in the party, Neville Chamberlain. Chamberlain believed that Churchill was poaching on territory that he had marked out for himself. He therefore bent his considerable powers of argument to belittling Churchill's scheme. Chamberlain had been one of those who had taken notice of *Industry and the State* and had had kind things to say to Macmillan about it. He too had been a potential patron.

Helped by Macmillan's brainstorming, Churchill won his argument with Chamberlain. As a result Chamberlain did not bother to talk to Macmillan for the rest of the Parliament.

Nevertheless Macmillan revelled in the triumph, allowing himself a degree of self-satisfaction that was hardly likely to recommend him to his colleagues. Cuthbert Headlam described him, with some asperity, as a 'little bottle-washer sloping about with an air of mystery'. Budget Day was indeed a triumph. Churchill was on his best commanding form. 'The House,' the prime minister informed the king, 'became intensely interested in watching a master in the art of oratory and of tantalizing the imagination unfold his ideas in a speech packed with detail, yet so simple and clear that there could be no possible misunderstanding ... almost the most remarkable achievement of Mr Churchill's career.'[122] Macmillan basked in the reflected glory, and then – nothing. Churchill had achieved his purpose, made his mark, won the plaudits. He did not have much further interest in the tedious details of the rates. The task of steering the complex legislation through Parliament was handed over to Neville Chamberlain, whom Macmillan had just alienated.

In Churchill's phrase, 'The dogs bark, the caravan passes.' The final year of the 1924 Parliament was thus rather a bleak affair for Macmillan. Turning to the man whom the disaffected usually regarded as their lost leader, who was also his parents' neighbour in Sussex, Lord Robert Cecil, Macmillan poured out his 'egotistical and disjointed sentiments'. 'It is,' he confided, 'a very difficult position for a private member, without position or influence; nor is anything more galling than to watch impotently a series of blunders.' His own rating scheme was, of course, 'admirable'. 'But we ought to have continued with it much more far reaching attempts to correct the balance between the *rentier* and the producer.' He ranted against the 'folly and lack of imagination of my leaders'. In his view they were 'fools'. 'I don't so much mind being thrown out,' he claimed disingenuously, 'but it is not a very inspiring thing to sit on the back benches.'[123] In the spring of 1928 everything had looked so promising; by the autumn he was facing not only lack of office but eviction from his own seat.

Macmillan's disappointment at his lack of progress was sharpened by Cranborne's appearance on the political scene.[124] In some ways the fact that Cranborne had not joined Macmillan and Crookshank in the 1924 Parliament, given the number of his contemporaries who were sons of great aristocrats entering politics – the Stanley brothers, Hartington and Dalkeith – was surprising. Cranborne had recovered his health after the war: in 1920 he was fit enough to take part in the national real tennis championships with some success. His family was at the highest point of its power since the great Lord Salisbury had retired a quarter of a century previously. Both his father and his uncle were in the Cabinet.[125]

The reason why Cranborne refused to commit himself to his family calling was simple: money. By the time of the 1923 and 1924 elections, Cranborne had committed himself instead to the City. It was an attempt to diversify the family fortune out of land because of the fear 'that under the present scale of Death Duties and taxation no Estate could survive unless it was supplemented by other resources'. In June 1922 he entered into an agreement to join the City bill-broking house of King & Foa. He would serve two years' probation, receiving 1 per cent of profits. On 1 July 1924 he would invest £50,000 in the firm and become a full partner, receiving 5 per cent of profits. So while Crookshank, secure in his private income, could throw in his diplomatic career at the drop of a hat and chase after Gainsborough, for Cranborne, overall much richer, to do so would risk losing a very great deal of money indeed. The losses might even, in the long term, put the Cranborne estate in danger.

Not that he was not sorely tempted. He had at least two seats on offer. The emotional pull came from the widow of Aubrey Herbert, the 'half blind and wholly eccentric' Tory eastern expert who seemed to have stepped out of the pages of John Buchan, who wanted him to replace her recently deceased husband.[126] He was also asked to become candidate for North Hackney – a good three-way marginal – 'nothing but the terror of dear food would have made it go wrong last November', the former incumbent assured him.[127]

These siren calls were so strong that his prospective business associates began to doubt that they should go ahead with his admission to full partnership on 1 July. He had to move to pacify them: 'My position is simple. Owing to my Father having made over to me some of his land I am now a fairly large landowner in Hertfordshire. This will no doubt involve obligations which it would not be right to ignore. It might even mean more County Council or even Parliamentary work, though I do not contemplate that at present or think it probable in the future. But I do not see in the least why these interests should conflict with my business . . . I mean to make not an occupation but a real profession of Bill Broking.'[128] Unfortunately his partners were right and he was wrong. Although he eschewed hopes of politics and became a bill broker, his heart was not really in it. In a City innocent of the looming crash of 1929, where there were fortunes to be made, Cranborne made nothing. He did so badly that the partnership lasted only a little over two years. 'I shall always rather feel,' wrote his associate Edward King, 'that you did not benefit much financially during your time in the City but I hope you made up for that by a making a few new friends and gaining some experience.'[129] His contacts were good enough to acquire a bank directorship. He was even accused of not being a gentleman, after discussing bank business at dinner, by his formidable mother-in-law. But five years in the City convinced him that he wanted to be a politician not a businessman.

Cranborne was only too glad to disentangle himself from the affairs of King & Foa. His hopes of greatly increasing rather than simply managing his personal fortune had come to nought. The entrepreneurial spirit did not beat in his breast. Exactly how little Cranborne was fitted to become a businessman was illustrated by Oliver Lyttelton's great success. Even as he had turned out to be a good soldier, so he turned out to be a good speculator. In 1925, BMC's joint managing director, Reginald Rucker, died unexpectedly.[130] It was Rucker's promotion to this post in 1921 that had opened up the position of general manager for Lyttelton. Now Lyttelton joined his patron Budd as joint managing director. As an extra fillip he was placed on the board of Burma. At the same time as Macmillan and Crookshank were making their maiden speeches in the House of Commons and Cranborne was elsewhere in the square mile struggling unsuccessfully with bill broking, Lyttelton had secured his finances and 'was beginning to emerge into a larger field'.

In contrast to the difficult days when he joined the corporation, the outlook was increasingly rosy.[131] Budd progressively handed over the reins of the company to Lyttelton. In March 1929 Sir Cecil formally retired and Lyttelton became the leader of a new triumvirate of managing directors with William Mure and Budd's son, Jack.[132] He failed to convince the board to invest in Rhodesian copper, which later proved hugely profitable. Three decades later Lyttelton still winced at missing 'by far the greatest opportunity in a century'. 'My feelings' on turning down the opportunity to invest in the Roan Antelope mine, Lyttelton wrote, 'were like those of the Duke of Marlborough ... when he was thwarted by the Stadtholders and Dutch Generals. I cannot even now bear to calculate what our holdings would have eventually have been worth ... our position would have been unrivalled.'[133] He did succeed in wooing Cecil Budd's greatest enemy. Budd had once tried to put Henry Gardner out of business.[134] Gardner, however, had enjoyed considerable success as a metals trader in the 1920s. In particular he had beaten BMC to important agencies in Canadian nickel. Although Lyttelton's relationship with Gardner was prickly, he believed he could do business with him.

In July 1929 Lyttelton and Gardner agreed to form a holding company, the Amalgamated Metal Corporation, that would purchase the entire share capital of BMC and Henry Gardner.[135] Lyttelton's cartel building made him plenty of enemies.[136] He earned the undying hatred of Cornish tin men, who labelled him the 'crypto-Bolivian', because he did not support the survival of a national industry.[137] Luckily for Lyttelton, those who vilified him and questioned his patriotism were dismissed by Whitehall as 'stupid and disagreeable' people who made 'infinite trouble'.[138] Lyttelton was regarded as neither stupid nor disagreeable by those who mattered.[139] Although the decrease in the consumption of non-ferrous metals brought about by the Wall Street crash and ensuing Great Depression almost immediately lowered AMC's value, it never lost the confidence of the City. Lyttelton was praised for competent crisis management and keeping the company solvent while continuing to pay a yearly dividend.[140] Investors were convinced that AMC's fortunes would improve whenever recovery started.[141]

As Lyttelton forged ahead in business, Cranborne embraced with relief and enthusiasm the political career he had reluctantly disavowed five years previously. Cranborne's first task was to find a good seat: an industrial marginal like Macmillan's was no good. In the spring of 1927, he started putting out feelers to constituencies in southern England.[142] There was little doubt that the Conservative party still preferred young aristocrats if they had some talent and were not unutterably odd. Eddie Hartington, Cranborne and Macmillan's brother-in-law, for instance, was perennially disappointed of office. But he did drink too much and had rather surprised his fellow diners at his club by announcing himself to be 'an enthusiast, even an apologist' for cock fighting.[143] Cranborne was articulate and sane. He was neither an oddball nor a drunk. By the beginning of 1928 he had found the perfect safe seat, South Dorset, close to his country seat at Cranborne.

The contrast between Cranborne and Macmillan in 1929 was stark. Although Macmillan, as the sitting MP, was senior to a mere prospective parliamentary candidate, in real terms this advantage meant little. With relatively little effort Cranborne acquired a plum seat – both in terms of convenience and political security – while Macmillan had spent five years tied to a difficult and inconvenient constituency. When Baldwin called the general election for May 1929, Cranborne won his seat with little difficulty while Macmillan lost his. As men like Cranborne slipped smoothly on to the benches he had just vacated, Macmillan could be forgiven for participating in the general bitterness that engulfed the party after its defeat. Certainly the wind had been knocked out of his sails. Cuthbert Headlam, who had also lost his seat, described him, rather cruelly, as the 'dejected statesman' and recorded that 'he does not know what to do about a seat'. Condolences, however genuine, could do little to alleviate the hurt. 'We nearly cried last night when the Stockton result came through,' Alice Salisbury, Cranborne's mother, wrote from Hatfield. Perhaps a little insensitively, since Cranborne and Macmillan had just gone in opposite directions through the revolving door, she added, 'You are so *young* and have done so well.'[144] 'Harold,' wrote Crookshank, who held Gainsborough, 'I am more than distressed that for one brief moment our lives should not be on parallel lines.'[145]

But old habits died hard. When an old Oxford friend, Terence O'Connor, suggested forming a Defeated Candidates Association to 'ginger up the leaders', Macmillan was torn. His strategy of the previous five years had hardly been an overwhelming success. He worried that an attempt to badger Baldwin would send him even further into the outer darkness.[146] Within days he was even so in the thick of organizing just such a body.[147] The ex-MPs lobbied Baldwin to grant them a formal role in the party.[148] Macmillan drafted the letter that was sent over the signature of John Moore-Brabazon to Baldwin detailing this demand.[149] Given his initial doubts, Macmillan could not have been surprised when the party leader brushed them off with a veiled threat – 'I beg you will not be in a hurry and put either yourselves or me in a difficult position' – and recommended that they all take a holiday.[150] Nevertheless Macmillan had the bit between his teeth once more. Even before Baldwin had had a chance to reply to the group, Macmillan had sent him a personal letter about party organization. Baldwin was perfectly civil, regretting that Macmillan had not come to a house party at Hatfield as expected so they could discuss his views. Even more surprisingly, Neville Chamberlain abandoned a two-year silence and invited him to lunch. Subsequently they spent a weekend at Hatfield discussing the formation of the Conservative Research Department.

Macmillan was not *persona non grata* with the party leadership. Neither was he unattractive to constituency parties. A young, energetic candidate with ample personal funds was exactly what many constituencies required. It was quite clear that Macmillan had not lost Stockton as a result of his own inadequacies. Discreet inquiries about his availability started to arrive within weeks of the election. He could even afford to be picky. 'The combination of business and politics is not possible except in a borough seat,' he wrote on being asked if he would like to be a candidate for Huntingdonshire. 'I shall either fight my old seat again, or else look out for another borough.

The only county seat I could manage would be one near my old home in Sussex.'[151] Macmillan was inflexible about his demands, even when the perfect seat fell straight into his lap. The MP for the safe seat of Hitchin, Guy Kindersley, planned to resign and Macmillan was offered the opportunity to get back into Parliament through a by-election. Hitchin in Hertfordshire had been Lord Robert Cecil's seat. Macmillan told friends that he had secured the offer 'oddly enough through ... the Liberal Chief Whip, who happens to be a friend of the Chairman of Hitchin Conservative Association'.[152] The seat was in fact widely known as a Cecil 'pocket borough'.[153] Lady Salisbury's condolences were not empty words. The Cecils were aiding Macmillan. They preferred him even to a close relation, the dashing young aviator Lord Knebworth, who also threw his hat into the ring.[154]

Knowing how much in demand he was, Macmillan negotiated hard with the Hitchin association, rejecting their request that he should buy a house in Hertfordshire.

I am unwilling [he told them] to start a new home in Hertfordshire ... my father and mother live in Sussex, and their house is to all intents and purposes a home for us and our children. Both my parents are old – my father is in his seventy-seventh, my mother in her seventy-sixth year. Their home will ultimately be mine, and indeed the property is already in my hands ... It would be a great blow to my parents, since it would probably reduce the amount of time our children could hope to be with them. And, in view not only of a sense of common filial duty, but of rather special circumstances involving more than ordinary devotion which binds me to my parents, I am afraid I must adhere to this decision which I have only reached after careful and prolonged thought.[155]

What the Hitchin Conservatives made of this rather emotional declaration is unclear. They did, however, accept his terms and pursued their suit.[156] At the time he accepted the Hitchin nomination, Macmillan had not risen as fast in politics as he had hoped, but neither was he any sort of failure. When Baldwin's ally William

Bridgeman made an assessment of the coming men in the party *after* the 1929 election, he picked out Anthony Eden, Oliver Stanley, Boothby and Macmillan.[157]

Macmillan's sudden attachment to hearth and home over political ambition was evidence of his deep personal unhappiness. His friend Bob Boothby and Dorothy Macmillan 'became lovers either very late in 1929 or early in 1930, and for the next five years virtually lived together publicly'.[158] It was his betrayal by his friend and his wife that made Macmillan a desperate man. His wife gloried in her affair with Boothby, taunting Macmillan that the daughter she bore in 1930 was not his child but Boothby's bastard. Everyone who mattered in his political and social circles knew about his humiliation and how badly it affected him. Cranborne's younger brother, David, witnessed him beating his head against the inside of a railway carriage window. Neither Dorothy nor Harold Macmillan were playing by the rules of the game. Others followed the long-standing aristocratic code, that since unmarried girls from their own class should not be subjected to anything more than flirtation, sexual relationships with married friends were legitimate.[159] If it was in bad taste to flaunt such liaisons, then it was bad form to fall out with old friends over them.[160]

Macmillan's political judgement became seriously erratic during the course of 1930. He had a mental breakdown in the early summer of 1931 and was shipped off by his mother to a Bavarian sanatorium. Some people regarded him as a details-obsessed bore during the 1920s, but he had been pursuing a sensible political course aimed at maximizing his advantages. In 1930 and subsequently he seemed to lose all sense of proportion, purveying his ideas as if they were holy writ, impatient of contradiction, seeming to believe that the more details he amassed, the more authorities he cited, the more convincing he would become. The sensible Macmillan of the 1920s became the obsessed Macmillan of the 1930s.

Macmillan's personal frangibility was matched by the extraordinary volatility in politics during 1930. In retrospect the 1929 election, coming just a few months before the onset of the Great Depression, seemed a good vote to have lost. In 1930, however, electoral defeat seemed merely a precursor to the suppuration of the Right's political sores. The Conservative party appeared to be caught in a pincer movement. From the right came the press lords, Rothermere and Beaverbrook, campaigning for protectionism, gunning for Baldwin and running parliamentary candidates against the Tories. From what then seemed like the left came a new star in the sky, Sir Oswald Mosley, ready to leave the Labour party and appeal to the YMCA and their ilk to join him in a new grouping to be called the New Party.

Tom Mosley was a fascinating character, not least because he was the one major politician who consistently enunciated in public the idea of the 'Great War generation'. Three years younger than the Guardsmen, he had seen combat both in the army and the Royal Flying Corps. Unlike other war veterans, however, he argued that their experiences gave them unique insights and rights. The Guardsmen were quite happy to use their reputation as 'gallant gentlemen' to influence constituency selection committees or to inspire confidence in the City: hence Captain Macmillan, Captain Crookshank and Captain Lyttelton. Yet these gallant gentlemen never pushed this point too far. A by-election held as long ago as 1917 had discouraged that course. In June of that year Oliver Stanley's older brother Eddie had stood for Parliament. Eddie Stanley was a Grenadier Guards officer of the same Eton vintage as the quartet. He was generally agreed to be a good sort, if rather dim. His father, Lord Derby, was the dominant political figure in Lancashire. It seemed only natural that Eddie should be put up for the Abercromby seat in Liverpool. His family and friends were shocked therefore when he was vigorously opposed by Frank Hughes, a one-legged former private standing on behalf of the Federation of Discharged and Demobilized Sailors and Soldiers. The federation had been organized by a radical MP, James Hogge, and was campaigning against government attempts to question discharges and so force men back into the army. Lord Derby, as Secretary of State for War, was regarded as the villain of the piece. Stanley won the election, but Hughes's campaign was a straw in the wind. Derby was concerned enough to warn the War Cabinet about the dangers of a citizen army prey to demagogues and to set about forming ex-servicemen's organizations that stressed class solidarity rather than class conflict. The trouble with a land fit for heroes was that the wrong heroes might prevail. A veterans' movement could so easily become radicalized. Conservative leaders were reluctant to use such a movement as a political vehicle lest they lost control of it.[161]

Such a loss of control rather appealed to Mosley. In the 1920s he had returned again and again to his theme that the experience of industrialized combat had created a generational gap. When Mosley lost his power struggle with old men of the Labour Cabinet and resigned from the government in May 1930, he lost no time in outlining a vision of youth on the march as a means of attracting supporters to his cause. They were modern men, and 'modern man', Mosley declared, was 'a hard realistic type, hammered into existence on the anvil of great ordeal. In mind and spirit he is much further away from the pre-war man than he is from an ancient Roman, or from any other product of ages which were dynamic like his own ... The men of the pre-war age are much "nicer" people than we are [but] I have always been painfully aware that our outlooks and methods ... were those of different planets.'[162] In February 1930 a cross-section of the YMCA and the defeated candidates, including Boothby, O'Connor and Moore-Brabazon, had dined with Mosley at Oliver Stanley's. Macmillan was not present since his cuckolder was. The company, in their cups, 'talked about the decay of democracy and of parliamentarism'. They discussed 'whether it would be well to have a fascist coup'. They said disrespectful things about all the party leaders.[163] Despite his absence from this party for personal reasons, it was Macmillan who gave Mosley public support. He wrote to *The Times* calling for his friends in Parliament to have 'the courage to applaud and support' Mosley.[164] Even if they would not say so publicly, many of his friends, even outside the YMCA, agreed. Cranborne, for instance, thought that Mosley cut an imposing figure. 'All the papers seem to agree with your account of the Moseley [*sic*] debate,' his mother-in-law wrote, 'and all agree with his speech and his manner being good – I thought him so right to leave and hope something good will come of it.'[165]

Even before his life had been cast adrift of its bearings by his wife's infidelity, Macmillan had asked himself 'whether it is better to stick with this party or chuck it'. He had concluded that 'the Tory Party is an enormously powerful instrument'.[166] The events of the summer of 1930 did not really alter that conclusion. With Baldwin spending his usual torpid summer in Aix-les-Bains, the party seemed moribund and Macmillan gave himself over to political speculation. He told Mosley's aide, Harold Nicolson, that 'the old party machines are worn out and that the modern electorate thinks more of personalities and programmes than of the pressure put upon them by an election agent'. 'He thinks,' Nicolson recorded, 'that the economic situation is so serious that it will lead to a breakdown of the whole party system. He foresees that the Tories may return with a majority of 20 and then be swept away on a snap vote. No other single party will form a Government and then there will be a Cabinet of young men.'[167] Macmillan became a regular visitor to the rolling political salon Mosley held in his house on Smith Square.[168] Conservative party managers marked Macmillan down as the most likely potential defector. 'Mosley's advance,' wrote William Bridgeman to J. C. C. Davidson, 'is rather disquieting and I think he will impose on young men of all parties and no party. Harold Macmillan probably will join him ere long.'[169] Mosley himself believed that if he formed his New Party, Macmillan and Oliver Stanley would be his likeliest Tory adherents.[170]

Yet what the YMCA were thinking of was not a 'New Party' but a more effective ginger group. At the beginning of the parliamentary session Mosley laid out his plans for the economic regeneration of an autarkic British empire. He was supported by a pre-arranged claque led by Oliver Stanley – Macmillan, lacking a seat, was merely a spectator – the classic ginger-group tactic. Mosley followed this parliamentary *démarche* with a published manifesto, again seeming to echo the YMCA's tactics with *Industry and the State*. Here Macmillan could play his part by once more writing to *The Times* in support. By then the Conservative party had rallied somewhat with a party meeting that had confirmed Baldwin as leader with 80 per cent support.

When Mosley went ahead with the formation of the New Party in February 1931 none of the YMCA joined him. They may have

'Tugs': Eton scholars, June 1907. Macmillan (on left) and Crookshank (centre) stare into the camera.

Left Oliver Lyttelton as an Etonian.

The 'Guards Club' near Festubert, July 1915.

Right Harold Macmillan in Grenadier uniform, 1915.

Below 2nd Battalion, Grenadier Guards marching through a French village, 1915.

Officers of the Second Battalion Grenadier Guards: Crookshank is third from the left on the back row.

Left The Somme: A wounded officer of the Grenadier Guards is carried away on a stretcher, near Ginchy, 14 September 1916. Macmillan and Crookshank suffered the same experience, in the same place, on the next day.

Left below The Enemy: German position near Lesboeufs, August 1916.

Below Captain Lyttelton, DSO in 1918.

The wedding of Harold Macmillan and Lady Dorothy Cavendish, St Margaret's, Westminster, April 1920.

Chatsworth, 1928: The Duke of Devonshire and his household. His sons-in-law, the MPs Harold Macmillan and James Stuart, are second and third from left on the back row.

Right Lord and Lady Cranborne, July 1933.

Churchill, Cranborne and James Stuart, 1936: Cranborne and Stuart were rising up the ranks of the Conservative Party, Cranborne as a Foreign Office minister, Stuart as a Whip. Churchill was at a low ebb.

STOP-IN STRIKE.

'Just about the least pleasant department', January 1936: Crookshank spent much of his time as Minister of Mines arbitrating between the militant miners and the truculent mine owners. He was delighted by David Low's cartoon in the *Evening Standard*.

Low's cartoon in the *Evening Standard* portrays Harry Crookshank cowering behind Chamberlain and Oliver Stanley, February 1938: Crookshank's attempts to increase state-control of the mining industry were bitterly opposed by the mine owners. The long parliamentary battle for the Coal Bill adversely affected Crookshank's relationship with both Chamberlain and Stanley.

ANTI-BOLSHEVIK RISING.

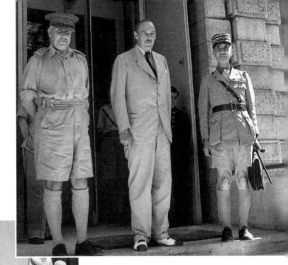

Above Monte Carlo strollers: General 'Jumbo' Wilson, Oliver Lyttelton and the Free French leader, Georges Catroux, make peace in Syria, August 1941.

Left Bottleneck: Lyttelton tells Sir Robert Haining to get the Egyptian docks working, 1941. Lyttelton believed that Haining's conduct was a major impediment to the war effort in North Africa.

Right 'I am subsequently rather *dégonflé*': Lady Diana Cooper, Duff Cooper, Lady Moira Lyttelton and Oliver Lyttelton in Iraq, February 1942. Cooper, a political star of the 1920s and 1930s, was heading for political oblivion. Lyttelton too feared that Churchill had lost faith in him, but this was not the case. On his return to London he was given a key position in the War Cabinet as Minister of Production.

Political reality, March 1942: Lord Beaverbrook, Lyttelton's short-lived predecessor as Minister of Production, had discovered that Ernest Bevin's position as the leader of organised labour made him too powerful to control. Lyttelton worked out a series of compromises with the Minister of Labour. The economist and writer Walter Layton, shown standing next to Churchill in Low's cartoon for the *Evening Standard*, was the architect of the Ministry of Production's organisation during Lyttelton's first months in office.

Military reality: Lyttelton and Churchill discuss the Churchill tank, April 1942. The shortcomings of British tanks, 'deathtraps' in the view of a vociferous group of MPs, were Lyttelton's bane throughout the war.

Success story: Lyttelton climbs out of a tank at the Chrysler Tank Arsenal in Detroit, watched by Averell Harriman – in charge of Lend-Lease – and K. T. Keller, Chrysler's President, June 1942. The smooth running of the programme that supplied Britain with American equipment was a triumph for Lyttelton.

been willing to join him in dreaming of themselves as 'men on horseback' over a port-soaked dinner, but they were certainly not going to appear in that guise on a public platform. As Bill Allen, the one Tory MP to defect to Mosley, later wrote, they were 'all the clever men who had been clever enough to keep out of the New Party'. There was a wide gap between a ginger group and a breakaway movement with uncertain prospects.[171] Running into Harold Nicolson on the train to Oxford, Macmillan took 'the usual young Tory view that his heart is entirely with the New Party but that he feels he can help us better by remaining in the Conservative ranks'.[172] Harry Crookshank had a much more cynical explanation. Thinking primarily of Oliver Stanley, he told Cuthbert Headlam 'that no one on our side really has any energy and that precious few have any ability – no one takes the trouble to harass the Government and any idea of forming a "Fourth Party" is out of the question because you could not get four parties with the requisite keenness to sit in the House continuously'.[173] If Macmillan had been an MP he would have had the necessary energy to make a stir. Yet in Macmillan's case his relationship with Mosley's New Party resembled his relationship with Ronnie Knox's Catholic Church. He enjoyed the cosseting, the feeling of intimate conspiracy, but in the end he was not willing to sacrifice any more of his established relationships when so many were already in tatters.

What he had sacrificed was the Conservative candidature for Hitchin. Instead of resigning, Guy Kindersley aligned himself with the anti-Baldwinites on the right of the Tory party, making a 'putrid' speech on their behalf at a party meeting. Both he and Macmillan were rebelling, but at polar opposites of the party. By the end of 1930 Macmillan was beginning to realize that Hitchin was a blind alley.[174] All of a sudden he had to scramble to get back into Stockton's good books. 'Nearly eighteen months have gone by,' he wrote in his letter of resignation from the Hitchin candidature. 'If I am not elected for Hitchin until a General Election . . . I am placed in the position of having misled my friends . . . I do not choose to suffer such an imputation. While everyone in the North appreciated my desire to return as soon as possible to the House of Commons, I am afraid they will judge differently of my action, if, in fact, I wait for the General Election.'[175]

This declaration was Macmillan's last political decision before his personal difficulties overwhelmed him and he beat his involuntary retreat to Germany. Just as he had been voted out of the House because of the Conservatives' national unpopularity, through no particular fault of his own, so he was voted back in the Conservative landslide of November 1931. In August 1931 Ramsay MacDonald split the Labour party and led his few supporters into coalition with the Conservatives in a 'National' government. As Cranborne observed, 'in practically every industrial constituency in England and Scotland a supporter of the National government returned'.[176] Macmillan won back Stockton through no particular virtue of his own other than his courage in dragging himself back from his Bavarian refuge to fight the election.

For Crookshank the early 1930s were much less uncertain and miserable than they were for his close friend Macmillan. Sitting for a relatively prosperous rural constituency, political activism was a personal choice rather than a political necessity. Nevertheless he still found politics hard going. Indeed, in some respects Opposition suited Crookshank. Perversely, his career would probably have prospered in inverse proportion to the Conservatives' electoral success. He had a rebarbative but controlled style of debating that was particularly effective in puncturing the pretensions of government ministers. For such a good parliamentary sniper it was most advantageous to pour down unrestrained fire on the opposition rather than be trammelled by the rules of constructive criticism in operation when one's own side was in office.

Baldwin recognized these qualities. Immediately the new House assembled he asked Crookshank to make Ramsay MacDonald's life as difficult as possible. Since Crookshank had an entirely genuine contempt for MacDonald, this was certainly no penance. MacDonald had acquired something of a taste for the finer things in life. Lacking any personal wealth, he had to rely on others to provide them. A gift of a chauffeur-driven limousine from a confectionery magnate led to the cry of 'Biscuits' every time he entered the chamber. Now

Crookshank twitted him for using an RAF military aeroplane to fly north for a political meeting. 'There is no lack of publicity – for that is MacDonaldism in its ultimate,' was Crookshank's view. Crookshank's sardonic eye fell on other targets too. In the autumn of 1929 he installed himself in the luxury of the Montreux Palace Hôtel in order to observe the goings on at the League of Nations Assembly at Geneva. He made every effort to publicize his contempt. When Macmillan lost his seat, the League of Nations Union sent him a letter of condolence thanking him 'for what you have done towards keeping the LNU non-party and keeping the Conservative Party true to the League'.[177] Crookshank thought he had been wasting his time. The real business of foreign policy was done at meetings of the great powers. The League had as much relevance to international peace as a Boy Scouts jamboree. 'September at Geneva,' he wrote, 'is *la grande saison*; so many little cocktail parties, and big dinners, and balls. Is it for that I in my generation suffered unmentionable hardships in the Great World War? Surely the "war to end war" and those who fought in it meant something more effective than this *Opera Bouffe* at Geneva? This *Opera Bouffe*, to which every politician in every country is forced to pay homage, to which every Mothers' Meeting and every ardent curate, belonging to the League of Nations Union, must give lip service.'[178]

Crookshank's withering salvos certainly raised his profile, but it is doubtful whether they did him much good.[179] Carrying on the role of His Majesty's Opposition to oppose was not something 'the Old Gang' of Conservative leaders, especially Baldwin, seemed to take too seriously. Like Macmillan, Crookshank was particularly galled by the favour that seemed to fall on Oliver Stanley despite his involvement with Mosley. He was both contemptuous and jealous of Stanley, 'who is at present the Party's blue-eyed boy . . . he is always given the opportunity of firing off a speech on a great occasion, but except on these occasions is never in the House'.[180]

The one senior Conservative politician who offered him patronage was Austen Chamberlain.[181] Even this was a two-edged sword. Chamberlain had been foreign secretary in the previous government and still carried many laurels, including the Nobel Peace Prize. He was, however, most unpopular in the party and had bad relations with Baldwin. The political crisis of August 1931 that led to MacDonald abandoning the Labour party to head a Conservative–Liberal coalition under the 'National Banner' was a disaster for both Chamberlain and his potential protégé, Crookshank. Chamberlain was deprived of a return to the Foreign Office.[182] Crookshank to his horror saw MacDonald, whom he had long hated and had attacked with venom, become his leader. He could do little more than watch his more emollient contemporaries waft past him. Not only was Oliver Stanley made parliamentary under-secretary to the Home Office, but his less talented brother, Eddie, was parliamentary under-secretary to the Admiralty. 'Harry,' noted his friend Cuthbert Headlam, 'is not in the swim – probably because he has brains and individuality. What a Party we are – and what folly and robbery and snobbery and foulness there are in politics.'[183]

It did a young aristocrat like Stanley, who was 'being pushed for all he is worth and has the ball at his feet', no harm to become 'rather too much the statesman'.[184] It was a lesson Cranborne took well to heart. He had no intention of becoming a rebel immediately he entered the House, even if this meant soft-peddling a Cecil crusade. One of the most controversial issues that split opinion in the Conservative party in the early 1930s was the reform of the government of India. The leadership of the Conservative party were willing to acquiesce to the Labour government's proposals to bring this about. Lord Salisbury was not. In 1930 he was instrumental in establishing the India Empire Society as an anti-reform campaigning body. This was soon followed by a committee of Conservative backbenchers concerned with Indian affairs.[185] Salisbury preferred to work behind the scenes. The other senior figure opposed to Indian reform, Winston Churchill, did not. 'Winston,' wrote Stanley Baldwin, 'has gone quite mad about India and has engaged the Free Trade Hall at Manchester in which to propound his views.'[186] By the end of 1930 the rift in the party was open for all to see. Cranborne agreed with his father and Churchill rather than the party leadership over India. Churchill later noted that, 'This India business has brought all the Cecils into line against the Government.'[187]

Yet Cranborne was a notable absentee from this family compact. From long experience the family knew how to nourish the early shoots of a political career. Lord Robert and Lord Hugh had injured their prospects by their own careers as violent controversialists. There was no need to repeat the mistake. So over India, while his father and uncles, 'though frail and seemingly at the point of death, continue[d] to exert themselves with unshakeable conviction', Cranborne kept his powder dry. He contented himself with small acts of rebellion that registered his opinion while causing no inconvenience to the National government. He, for instance, voted against Baldwin's close friend J. C. C. Davidson's membership of the Joint Select Committee of both Houses formed to consider drafts of the new constitution, but immediately apologized for having done so.[188] He was not part of parliamentary caucuses organized by his father to oppose that constitution. Instead, Cranborne played the 'statesman' card.

In contrast to Crookshank's voice of mockery, Cranborne adopted a tone of high seriousness. His chosen vehicle was the venerable Tory journal the *Quarterly Review*, not read by many but read by the right people. The *Quarterly* had been the outlet for much of his grandfather's political journalism and its editor fell over himself to have contributions bearing the Cecil name.[189] Yet whereas the great marquess's essays had been volcanic eruptions of ultra-Toryism, Cranborne's were carefully crafted paeans of praise for the idea of National government. In them he presented himself as a progressive young Tory on the liberal wing of the party. He even cited Macmillan's de-rating scheme as evidence that the Conservative party was not 'a very citadel of reaction, bolted and barred with privilege and prejudice'.[190] According to Cranborne, the election victory of November 1931 might 'be claimed as a victory for Constitutionalism, even as victory for abstract conservatism – but certainly not for the Conservative Party.' 'Indeed,' he concluded, 'it is very doubtful if the Conservative Party has made any appreciable gain in public esteem since 1929.' The election result instead reflected a change in British society. 'This country,' he wrote, 'has reached the stage of economic development where the great majority of those who vote have a stake in it. They own something. We have, in fact,' he continued, borrowing a phrase from the YMCA's lexicon, 'become a property-owning democracy.' The resonance of this phrase was somewhat decreased by a printing error which rendered it as a 'property-*owing* democracy'.

No matter. Cranborne's stance was clear. For the moment the alliance of great and small property was instinctive rather than deliberate. It was 'the most fundamentally important task before this and other Governments . . . to make conscious the forces of stability . . . to show the working-man that he is a member of a community, and not the slave of a system'. His method of doing this reflected the views of his uncle, Lord Robert. Britain needed an 'industrial constitution'. He left the details of such a constitution deliberately vague, since 'compulsion and standardization are out of the question', but it seemed to comprise a national council where industry, the City and labour could meet to share their views.[191] The ideas Cranborne propounded in the 1930s echoed those Stanley and Macmillan had outlined in the 1920s. Yet his essays contained none of the worrying praise of authoritarianism evident in Macmillan's writings.

In the House of Commons Cranborne also sedulously pursued his 'statesmanlike' course. He may have adopted some of the language of the YMCA, but he was firmly with the majority of Conservative MPs in calling for decreases in public spending. Public works were a nonsense. 'Nothing, for instance, can excuse the expenditure on roads during the last few years,' he claimed. Drastic economies in education were necessary. 'Carpentry and nature study' were, in Cranborne's view, 'pleasant and useful occupations. But the average man could go through life without them.' He hoped that the Geneva disarmament conference 'would in itself lead to an enormous saving in expenditure on national defence'. Nevertheless, Cranborne intervened decisively when such views started to embarrass the National government.

In June 1932, Sir Gervais Rentoul, the chairman of the 1922 Committee, suggested that the frustration felt by many Tory MPs that the government was not making deep cuts in expenditure should be channelled into an 'Economy Inquiry'. One hundred and forty-three MPs volunteered to help produce an avalanche of cost-cutting proposals. The report was political dynamite: it suggested that the benign face of the National government merely hid the cruel sneer of unreconstructed Toryism. Cranborne tried to bury the report, proposing it 'should neither be circulated nor published'.[192] When Rentoul ignored him, he had no hesitation in putting the entire blame for the report on Rentoul and dissociating the Conservative party from it. He scored a resounding success. The report was buried, its existence merely a one-day wonder in the press. The cost was Rentoul's career. Cranborne's friend 'Shakes' Morrison was successfully run against him as chairman. Rentoul's reputation was so badly shattered that he resigned his seat in Parliament.[193] Cranborne had thus done the government a considerable favour. He had averted a major political embarrassment.

In the chamber of the House itself Cranborne was a low-key presence. He rarely spoke except on matters of interest in Dorset. He did, however, know how to choose his moment. If his articles in the *Quarterly* showed off his qualities as a progressive but sound Tory, his performances in the House demonstrated that he had the same qualities when it came to foreign affairs. He expanded on his view that the best hope for British foreign policy was the search for international disarmament. Whereas Crookshank had returned from Geneva full of mockery, Cranborne, although he leavened his speeches with 'more than a touch of delightful humour', was all seriousness. 'War is a gamble,' he opined, 'and a gamble which in the modern world depends on immediate success. For if a war goes on for a long time, it is absolutely certain that every one concerned with it will be ruined. If you can take away from every nation the weapons which make immediate success possible, you greatly reduce the chances of war taking place, because even the most bellicose nation will not indulge in the gamble.'[194]

These may have seemed rather strange sentiments to express in December 1933, given that Germany had walked out of the disarmament conference in October 1933. Yet Cranborne's words were carefully calculated. He was defending the position of Sir John Simon, the foreign secretary, who a few days before had tried to revive disarmament negotiations with Hitler. Sir John's parliamentary

under-secretary, Cranborne's close friend, Anthony Eden, was wind-
ing up the debate. Sir John was also leader of the Liberal party in
the coalition and had recently indicated that he had his eye on the
young Tory aristocrat who, despite the die-hard and Free Trade
pedigree of his father, could write: 'the Liberal and Conservative
parties must work together. With every month that passes, moreover,
the bonds that join them are likely to become closer rather than
looser.' Sir John had just read Cranborne's articles of the previous
year and sent a personal note of 'warm congratulations'. They were
'not only extremely well written', Sir John wrote, 'but ... full of
perceptions and judgements which appeal to me very much'.[195] Cranborne's intervention was well, and one must assume deliberately,
timed. For well over a month there had been talk of appointing
Anthony Eden as overseer of League of Nations affairs. On 19
December 1933 Baldwin offered Eden the post of Lord Privy Seal.
When he took up the office on 1 January 1934, one of his first acts
was to appoint Cranborne as his parliamentary private secretary.

Cranborne had positioned himself as an intelligent loyalist and
had garnered the rewards. He was able to reinforce his reputation
for loyalty by one more piece of fire-fighting on the disarmament
issue. Cranborne's entry into public life had been through his uncle's
League of Nations Union. In 1932 he had been coopted on to its
council. By then, however, Lord Robert's Conservative credentials
were becoming increasingly threadbare. Having resigned from the
Cabinet in 1927, he rarely spared his former colleagues the lash of
his tongue when he thought they were not acting in the best interests
of the League of Nations. The League still enjoyed broad popular
support. Baldwin was concerned that if the Conservatives became
tarred with the anti-League brush, their electoral prospects could be
damaged. He persuaded the recently retired Austen Chamberlain to
join the League's Executive Committee to rein in Cecil's activities.[196]
Chamberlain was not impressed by his new colleagues. 'In addition
to including a first-class collection of cranks,' he told his sister, 'the
Committee contains some of the most churlish & ill-mannered
people I have ever had to work with.'[197]

Chamberlain found working with the 'cranks' most wearing. At the beginning of 1934, Lord Robert Cecil had hit on the idea of demonstrating the popularity of the League of Nations by organizing a national ballot in its support. In March 1934 he established the National Declaration Committee to oversee the process. In the eyes of most Conservatives, the 'Peace Ballot' was little more than a cranks' charter. 'Bob Cecil,' in the opinion of Chamberlain, 'is a fanatic who in the slang of the day is constantly "going off the deep end" & whose actions are on the verge of hysteria.' They were particularly offended by the enthusiasm with which LNU literature denounced the 'merchants of death' in the arms exports trade.[198] The matter came to a head in the summer of 1934.[199] Chamberlain asked Cranborne to don the hair shirt of acting as his representative to the LNU. Cranborne could hardly refuse. He was, however, placed in an uncomfortable position – acting as honest broker between his party and his uncle. The dispute boiled down to the issue of the briefing paper which was to be distributed with the ballot.

Cranborne laid the blame for the situation in which he found himself at the door of his uncle's confidant Philip Noel-Baker, a Labour MP who had been on Cecil's staff in Paris. 'I am really anxious about it,' he told Chamberlain. 'It is all very well for Philip to say light-heartedly that he never puts in arguments on the other side – that might be all right if this was an attempt by the Union to spread its own propaganda – but . . . it is not. I can see that it suits Philip very well – either the Conservative Party comes in, or he and his friends go about the Country saying that the Conservatives are against the Collective peace system.'[200] Cranborne's own proposal was that Chamberlain and his friends should write their own 'Blue paper' to offset the LNU's 'Green paper'. He thus let himself in for weeks of bitter wrangling and many a harangue about his own iniquities.[201] He believed that 'the Declaration Committee has been guilty of a great breach of faith with us'. It took him until November to wriggle out of the business. He persuaded Chamberlain not to resign from the LNU and to attend important meetings in person. In defusing the clash between Chamberlain and 'Uncle Bob', he took much of the blame for their 'misunderstandings' on to his own shoulders.[202] The 'rainbow papers' controversy was quietly allowed to fizzle out by both sides. It was with some relief that Cranborne made his way into the Foreign Office. International politics seemed less complex than family politics.

To Macmillan and Crookshank aristocrats like Oliver Stanley and Bobbety Cranborne seemed the living proof that good connections and a smooth manner were rather more important than brains. In the summer of 1933 Crookshank's friend Cuthbert Headlam had noticed that he was 'not making as much mark as I had expected – of course he has not many opportunities and I suppose he is going canny – it is no use antagonizing the powers that be when their position appears to be assured and their possible successors are impossible'. 'He is,' Headlam concluded, 'young enough and clever enough to bide his time.'[203] In the summer of 1934 he received the call to become parliamentary under-secretary at the Home Office. The fact that Oliver Stanley had already held the post and passed on to better things was both an irritation and a lure.

Macmillan too tried to reform himself. 'Harold,' Headlam noted soon after they had both returned to the Commons, 'has immensely improved . . . he is not nearly so superior as he used to be and does occasionally listen to what one says.' He was resentful that men he regarded as less talented than himself had been preferred, but 'he realizes well enough that he has played his cards badly'. It was, however, a hard struggle: 'He is clever and takes infinite pains to make himself well-informed – but . . . he bores people too quickly and has little or no sense of humour.' A couple of months further into the parliamentary term, Headlam observed wryly that, 'Harold . . . has adopted an entirely conciliatory line towards anything and everything that very wise man Mr Baldwin may do – let us hope this new attitude may bring him what he wants.' At Easter Headlam was invited to stay with Macmillan at Birch Grove. It was not a pleasant experience. 'The gloom of H. Macmillan is something terrible but he is a much disappointed man quite irrespective of anything else . . . he is not a cheering companion even for a weekend.'[204]

Although Macmillan was much chastened by his miserable private life and the seeming lack of any immediate hope of advancement, he nevertheless continued with his tactics of the 1920s, albeit in a modified form. He was stuck in a rut. The YMCA had in the end done nothing for him. Bob Boothby, whom he had found it most congenial to work with, was cuckolding him. Yet the YMCA had launched Oliver Stanley's political career, which was going from strength to strength. Macmillan still felt the need to surround himself with like-minded souls for high-minded discussions of 'high policy'. Having recruited Mosley's former aide Allan Young as his own research assistant, he continually republished and reified his ideas, each time adding more and more detail.

Those who knew him in those years doubted he was altogether stable. In the autumn of 1932, for instance, he took Young on a visit to the Soviet Union. This was hardly ground-breaking. The first Conservative MPs, including Boothby, had visited the USSR in 1926. The Astors had been there the previous year. Macmillan himself ran into a number of Conservative MPs in Moscow. A pilgrimage to Russia was, however, usually the mark of those with left-wing sympathies – Nye Bevan, John Strachey, the Webbs and Hugh Dalton all made nearly contemporaneous tours.[205] Macmillan and Young wrote *Reconstruction* on their return. *Reconstruction* was supposed to replace *Industry and the State* of six years earlier as the most advanced statement of progressive economic policy. As Macmillan himself admitted, he was giving something of a hostage to fortune since his policy would 'no doubt be described as "Socialism" by some elements on the right, and as "Fascism" by some elements on the left'. Indeed the *Observer* understood that Macmillan was an admirer of 'Signor Mussolini's "Corporate State"'. The proto-fascist *English Review*, edited by his Oxford contemporary Douglas Jerrold, accused him of being part of a Marxist-Zionist conspiracy dedicated to enslaving Britain to Communism. More tellingly, the neo-liberal LSE economists Friedrich Hayek and Lionel Robbins denounced Macmillan's plans as a blueprint for the destruction of liberty. 'Nothing but intellectual confusion can result,' they warned, 'from a failure to realize that Planning and Socialism are fundamentally the same.' It was as a catalyst to Hayek's masterwork *The Road to Serfdom* that Macmillan was eventually to make his greatest contribution to twentieth-century political thought.[206]

Macmillan still believed that his role as gadfly would endear him to the electors of Stockton. In the constituency Headlam heard him make 'a good little speech explaining what a sound MP he was – and explaining too, how free and independent he was – voting as he liked – and spurring on the government to plan and provide work – it all went down like hot cakes'. Headlam's advice was 'to go on pushing his ideas and developing them – but not to keep speaking and voting against the Government – and, above all else, to find a safer seat than Stockton'.[207] After this stern lecture he was a little surprised some months later when Macmillan laid out a new political strategy: 'He wants us to work together in the House of Commons to push his *Reconstruction* and to worry the government to be constructive!' Headlam had heard Macmillan talk in this fashion for the past decade. 'I fancy the one thing he is really hankering after is political success,' he noted cynically. 'I feel he would accept any job that was offered to him ... if he makes a nuisance of himself and can form a small and effective group to assist him in the job he may persuade "those in authority" to offer him a billet to silence his opposition.'[208] Macmillan, it seemed, was stuck recycling his tired old tactics.

Of the quartet who had set off into public life at the end of the war, Macmillan was the one who had prospered least. His isolation, if extreme, was not, however, atypical of his cohort. The period between the mid 1920s and the mid 1930s was the one in which school, university and regimental friends had the least to do with each other. Each year Harold Macmillan and Bobbety Cranborne invited one another to shoot. In late summer Macmillan would ask Cranborne to shoot at Birch Grove in late October. The shoot was usually a bachelor party including their mutual Grenadier friend Arthur Penn. In return Cranborne would invite Macmillan to shoot at Cranborne.[209] Macmillan and Cranborne were quite often members of larger, mixed parties that met at houses such as Bolton Abbey, their in-laws, the Devonshires' estate in Yorkshire.[210] Under the tutelage of their brother-in-law, Evan Baillie, Macmillan spent much time and effort shooting game in the 1920s. The country-house weekend served as a useful opportunity for keeping up old acquaintances. Lyttelton and Cranborne kept in touch in similar fashion. Friends who had known each other 'on and off' since Eton 'sometimes met at dinner parties or country house'.[211] Even Crookshank, to whom the Duke of Devonshire took a shine after meeting him through the Masons, shot at Chatsworth.[212]

Macmillan, Lyttelton, Cranborne and Crookshank all maintained family homes in the West End and thus naturally gravitated towards the London club circuit that provided another piece of the 'hidden wiring' of political life in the inter-war period. Each had a favourite club to suit their personality – Macmillan favoured the Beefsteak, which did not allow gambling, Lyttelton the hard-gambling St James's. For aspiring Tory politicians, however, the dominant establishment was Pratt's. An unprepossessing basement, its sweaty cramped dining room dominated by a large grill, the club opened at 7 p.m. and closed whenever the last member left – often when Parliament was sitting well after dawn had broken. Women were forbidden to telephone the club. Macmillan had an easy entrée to it through his Cavendish connection.[213] Crookshank was elected in February 1926. Even in Pratt's they could form an inner circle. When, to Crookshank's 'disgust', a Conservative minister whom he loathed was elected, 'as he didn't know any of the Brigade [of Guards] people there, he was out of it'.[214] Macmillan and Eddie Hartington retired to Pratt's to drown their sorrows and lick their wounds after they both lost their seats in the 1929 election.[215]

Yet the intimacies of club and hunting party, unlike those of school and regiment, were more apparent than real. 'Like so many of the friends of youth,' Macmillan said revealingly of his Eton and Oxford friend Geoffrey Madan, whom he put up for Pratt's in 1927, 'one could feel able with him to take up an unfinished conversation begun several years before exactly at the point it had been left off'.[216] 'Driven shooting,' writes its historian, providing a useful metaphor for their life in the 1920s, 'is not really a "social" sport at all. Unlike hunting where all participants combine in the common purpose of pursuing the quarry, the sporting element in shooting is the interplay between the individual hunter and the game. This was reflected in the shooting field; each gun would be placed some distance from his neighbour, cocooned by a small army of loaders, valets and cartridge boys.'[217] The network whose life had been artificially extended by the war tended to dissipate. Everyone had their own private concerns. Macmillan's life was all but swamped by his marital difficulties. Cranborne was stunned by the death of his son, Michael, from heart disease. Michael died suddenly at Eton when he was just sixteen. It was politics in the shadow of another war that forced a renewal of intimacy.

4

Anti-fascists

D uring the 1930s each of the Guardsmen in turn brushed up against the far right. Each of them was repelled by what they saw. The idea that the upper reaches of British politics and society were somehow tainted with crypto-fascism is impossible to sustain. The fellow-travellers of the Right were notable for their isolation. The quartet's Eton and Scots Guards contemporary, the Scottish Tory MP Archibald Maule Ramsay, ran a series of virulently anti-Semitic and pro-Nazi pressure groups in the 1930s. Yet Ramsay was a figure of no consequence in the party and very few MPs colluded with him.[1] Another Eton and Grenadier contemporary, Walter Dalkeith, was an outspoken champion of an Anglo-Nazi alliance. Dalkeith and Cranborne were, and remained, close friends. But Dalkeith retired from front-line politics in 1935 when he inherited the dukedom of Buccleuch. He remained a leading social figure within the Conservative party – but there is no evidence that he had any political influence over policy makers such as Cranborne.

Most notably of all, any charm Tom Mosley had once had for his contemporaries disappeared once he openly embraced fascism in 1934. Cranborne and Lyttelton remained friendly with his wife, and fellow fascist, Cimmie Curzon, until her early death, but once again this was merely a personal relationship that had no political implications. As Crookshank joined the Home Office, Mosley's Blackshirts were trying to convert the British people to fascism through a series of mass rallies. On 7 June 1934 the British Union of Fascists' most ambitious rally of over 13,000 people at Olympia saw fighting between fascists and communist protestors. An even bigger rally was planned for White City in August 1934. The commissioner of the Metropolitan Police, Lord Trenchard, was 'very fearful of the next few months'. Trenchard wanted the Home Office to give him legal powers to stop the rally. From within the government Crookshank was a keen supporter of Trenchard's robust approach. It was the home secretary, Jack Gilmour, a Scot in his late fifties, who dismissed the idea as an infringement of civil liberties.[2] Applauded all the way by Crookshank, Trenchard found a way around Gilmour's reluctance to act: he persuaded the White City Board to cancel the letting. Trenchard's action took a great deal of steam out of the Mosleyite movement. Its subsequent descent into violence rapidly alienated even libertarian Tories. Within two years of Mosley embracing fascism, the Conservative-dominated government passed legislation to hamstring the activities of his movement.

This is not to say that an unpleasant strain of anti-Semitism was not prevalent among politicians of the Great War generation. Most were casually prejudiced. Acquaintances of Macmillan and Cranborne's brother-in-law Eddie Hartington greeted the news that he was the secretary of the Jewish Committee in the House of Commons with incredulity.[3] More the norm was Cranborne, Crookshank and Macmillan's barely disguised distaste for their contemporary, the Jewish minister, Leslie Hore-Belisha. They called him Horeb. 'Offensive people said his name was Horeb Elisha and that he had changed it by deed poll,' remembered a Conservative parliamentary candidate who admired Belisha.[4] When Lewis Namier, the distinguished historian, tried to persuade Cranborne that German Jews were exiles in their own country, the minister was most unsympathetic: 'I was glad that no encouragement was given to Professor Namier,' he wrote in April 1936. 'He is a most tiresome person, and we know already he is not to be trusted. We cannot say enough to Jews of this type that people do not become refugees until they leave.'[5] Not that Cranborne was the minister least sympathetic to the sufferings of refugees. From his first days in the Foreign Office until his resignation he worked hard to set up an official League of Nations body for the care of refugees in the face of vigorous opposition from the Home

Office, who feared that such a body might 'pursue an idealistic and adventurous policy'.[6] Cranborne's approach throughout was based around proper procedure rather than freelance efforts to alleviate suffering. He did not believe there was anything Britain could do for German Jews, 'for these are really primarily German domestic affairs and however revolting we may think their behaviour they have, I suppose, the right to do what they will with their own nationals, and would certainly resent interference by us in their domestic sphere'.[7]

The exceptional figure in this context was Oliver Lyttelton. Unlike his politician friends with their, at best, fleeting impressions of foreign countries, he was a frequent visitor to Europe. Just as importantly, Lyttelton became friends with Richard Merton, a Jewish businessman whose family had once been denounced as a 'German Octopus' that was plotting to crush Britain by taking control of the world's trade in strategic minerals.

To understand how Lyttelton's views diverged so much from his contemporaries one had to know something of the anti-Semitic origins of the British Metal Corporation, the organization he headed. In 1914 the most successful metal-trading company in the City of London had been Henry R. Merton & Co., founded by three brothers, Henry, Emile and Zachary Merton, in 1860. Another brother, William Merton, emigrated to Germany, where he became the chairman and chief shareholder of an even more successful integrated metals group, Metallgesellschaft, based in Frankfurt. William Merton and his sons became German subjects at the turn of the century. Henry Merton himself died in 1873, and when his company became a limited corporation in 1898, its main shareholder was Metallgesellschaft, in which the directors of Henry Merton were themselves also shareholders. The Merton family described the father of Henry and William Merton, Ralph Merton, as a 'natural-born British subject'.[8] During the Great War the yellow press were less kind – 'their name, we believe, was originally Moses and ... they are German Jews'.[9] The relationship between Metallgesellschaft and Henry Merton gave the family enormous commercial strength. It was, however, deeply embarrassing once Britain and Germany were at war with one another. What might have been a private tragedy of a family split asunder rapidly became a public cause for concern. The Mertons were caught out by one of their pre-war successes. Germany dominated the trade in lead and zinc concentrates extracted from the great Broken Hill mines in New South Wales. The bulk of Australian concentrates went to German or German-controlled Belgian works for treatment.[10]

On 4 August 1914 Merton's were, as usual, acting on behalf of Metallgesellschaft for the transport of Australian concentrates to German refineries. A number of ships were caught in transit by the outbreak of war. 'In our ignorance,' as the company later put it, 'we presumed that with the Bills of Lading in our possession, and not having been paid by anyone for the goods, we had prior lien on them.' Accordingly Merton's diverted the shipments to warehouses in Britain. As a result they were found guilty in a British prize court of aiding and abetting the enemy. They had, the court found, 'made the payment in order to preserve the goods for the owners whom they knew to be enemies, and to gain some possible advantage for themselves or their principals or co-adventurers the *Metallgesellschaft* and in acting thus they appear not to have hesitated to engage in commercial intercourse with the enemies of this country'. To make matters much worse, the prosecuting counsel in the prize court was the Attorney-General himself, the Conservative politician F. E. Smith. 'F. E.' did not hesitate to make political capital from the case: it was he who coined the phrase 'the German octopus' to suggest a world-wide conspiracy of German-Jewish business interests out to destroy the British Empire. Merton's became the unlikely world HQ for this conspiracy. The case was taken up with enthusiasm by the right-wing press: 'No one on the face of it would suspect Messrs Henry R. Merton and Co., of 2, Metal Exchange-buildings, of being anything but an out-and-out British company,' ran an article entitled, 'All About the German Octopus: The Length and Grasp of the Tentacles; World-wide Ramifications; Messrs. H. R. Merton and the Teutonic "Tree".' 'Yet when you examine the Board of Directors you begin to realize the German influences.'[11]

Although dislike of the Mertons was fuelled by anti-Semitism, the company's intimate links with Germany were real enough. On

7 and 8 February 1916 representatives of the two branches of the family travelled to The Hague in neutral Holland. Although the meeting was sanctioned by the British government and was a genuine attempt to solve the problem of friends, relations and business partners separated by war, it could only add fuel to the fire of the conspiracy theorists. The meetings were 'cordial' and deliberately left out 'sentiment and war results'. At the end of the two days the two delegations agreed that an exchange of shares could take place, leaving a balance of £43,386 10s. 9d. owed by the British to the Germans. The two Merton firms would thereafter go separate ways.[12]

Henry Merton was reconstituted, purged of German interests, in July 1916. The controversy did not subside. The Australian government publicly branded the firm as an 'enemy concern'. What steps, demanded one senior Tory MP, had really been taken 'other than the change of their German surnames into English surnames by two shareholders who are naturalized aliens, and the use by a Swiss company of its French instead of its German name'. 'Unless this firm is wound up now,' declared another backbencher, 'as it is entirely under the Germans, they will rule our methods again exactly as before: there is no answer to that.' The importance of this hostility was greatly magnified by the fall of Asquith's government in December 1916. The new Lloyd George government, kept in power by the Conservatives, followed the advice of nationalistic MPs and sought ways of destroying Merton's. Cecil Budd, subsequently Oliver Lyttelton's business mentor, Merton's chief rival in the City, emerged as the new ministry's chief adviser on metals control.[13]

By the spring of 1917 the writing was on the wall for Merton's. Budd argued that the British government should persuade the Dominions governments to have their mineral resources marketed by an organization free of 'alien control' and encourage the creation of British-owned companies in foreign countries to supplement deficiencies in imperial supply. Budd proposed that the government should form a public–private partnership in the form of a corporation. This corporation should have not only capital of its own but good credit lines upon which to call. Its job would, on the face of it, be to purchase and sell minerals. Just as importantly, it would target mining operations in the Empire and British companies outside it for assistance, either by shared investment on a profit-sharing basis or by purchasing and selling their output. This was the origin of the British Metal Corporation.

The corollary of founding such a corporation, however, was the need to destroy the Merton organization. If that company had not been under anathema, it would, with its contacts and expertise, have been the obvious vehicle for overseeing the mineral resources of the empire. It would have been hard to persuade investors to support the new corporation if it was in direct competition with Merton's. The means by which the government planned to remove Merton's from the picture was the Non-Ferrous Metals Bill. The proposed law decreed that anyone involved in the trade would need an annually renewable licence issued by the Board of Trade. As a High Court judge later commented, the law was so obviously targeted at one company that it 'might very well be described as the Statute of Merton'. Non-ferrous metals hardly seemed an issue to stir the blood of all true patriots, but the fate of Merton's touched an unlovely nerve in some politicians and journalists. The bill would, in the opinion of the *Morning Post*, go so far as 'to reinstate the British born in a small part of his ancient birth-right'. 'May it not,' the paper continued, 'be the beginning of a return to the old and true conceptions of the rights of British subjects? There was a time in England when foreigners were on a distinct and inferior footing to natives.'[14] The measure became law, Merton's applied for a licence and were duly turned down. Robbed of its *raison d'être* the company went into voluntary liquidation.[15]

A decade after the destruction of Merton's, Oliver Lyttelton rose to the top of BMC, though he soon realized that the company was facing in the wrong direction. BMC had been created to prevent Germany re-establishing a monopoly position in strategic metals. Yet the threat in the 1920s came not from Europe but from the United States.[16] Lyttelton and his colleagues watched with concern the creation of the Copper Exporters Incorporated, an American-dominated cartel.[17] The market domination of the American cartel was so great that BMC was reluctantly forced to join.[18] Instead of being a market leader, organizing trade for the strategic benefit of the British Empire, it had been forced into the position of a bit player.[19]

Lyttelton had become convinced that the true commercial logic of the metals trade called for the creation of a much bigger combine. Since cooperation with the Americans as anything other than a junior partner was not on offer, the obvious way forward was consolidation in Britain and Europe. Lyttelton pressed ahead with this 'grand strategy'. In March 1930 he reached an agreement for an alliance with the Société Générale de Minéraux in Belgium, involving an exchange of shares. Lyttelton became a director of SGM.[20] In May 1930 he travelled to Frankfurt to negotiate a similar deal with the Metallgesellschaft.[21] Naturally, of particular concern was the risk of another war between Britain and Germany. BMC would be in exactly the same bind as Merton's had found itself at the time of the disastrous Hague conference. The solution was to exchange shares through a Swiss company. In the event of war, the Swiss would sell BMC shares back to the company, while buying BMC's Metallgesellschaft shareholding.[22] Lyttelton and Cecil Budd became directors of Metallgesellschaft, while a member of the Merton family became a director of AMC.[23] The new alliance was full of these ironies.[24] Although British commentators were reluctant to put it in such terms, Lyttelton had re-created Merton's – the very organization BMC had been established to destroy. The Germans themselves were less shy of calling a spade a spade. 'The English-German-Belgian group,' wrote the *Berliner Tageblatt* once the deal had been done, 'which now exists in the metal trade, comprises all the undertakings upon which was built the Merton Metallgesellschaft Group which existed before the war.'[25]

Yet not only did Lyttelton find he could he do business with the head of Metallgesellschaft, Richard Merton, but they also developed a relationship of genuine warmth. 'We became friends,' Lyttelton remembered. 'He was a man of great flexibility of mind, and of wide vision. His command of English and French only just fell short of being perfect, and his knowledge of the European metal trade w as unrivalled.'[26] In both business and personal terms, the Metallgesellschaft deal was a triumph for Lyttelton. It was unfortunately a short-lived triumph. After 1933 a close relationship with a Jewish-owned industrial combine that would be central to any process of German rearmament was hardly comfortable. His German business associates were predominantly Jews. He watched as their lives became harder and harder as they were progressively purged from businesses in Nazi Germany.[27] He was finally galvanized into action in 1938.

Lyttelton was making one of his frequent visits to Frankfurt on 10 November 1938, the date of *Kristallnacht*, the Nazis' direct and brutal attack on German Jewry. Frankfurt had a large Jewish community and was one of the major centres of the purge. In the dark of the early morning storm troopers fired the synagogue. By the light of day British observers in the city saw highly organized squads, each led by an SA or SS officer, 'consulting lists of names and addresses before proceeding to the next scene of destruction'. They were followed by less organized mobs who destroyed any Jewish property they could lay their hands on in 'scenes of indescribable, destructive sadism'. It was poor Jews, shopkeepers and the like who suffered first. Lyttelton was there to see 'a scene which can never be effaced from my memory'. 'It haunts me today,' he said in 1963. 'The shops were attacked by these thugs, who threw the stock from the shops into the gutter, and added to them all the small household possessions and household Gods of the owner.'[28] By evening, the organized vandals had worked their way to the west of the city, where Lyttelton's rich business contacts lived. That evening too the arrests began. Jews were herded into the international Exhibition Centre. There they were held for days without food and water. Individual Jews were brought out for ritual humiliation in front of the howling mob. A few days later pairs of SS troopers or Gestapo started entering houses and arresting more Jews on the grounds that they were planning to escape from Germany. It was clear that not only did the Nazis hate the Jews, but they were savagely choking off any means of escape. The state offices charged with 'cleansing' Germany by encouraging Jewish emigration were closed.[29]

The directors of Metallgesellschaft were not just business partners, they were Lyttelton's friends. He decided he had to help them. Helping Jews may not have been a particularly popular act in his class and generation; yet neither was it hard to help individual Jews, especially for a man with Lyttelton's contacts and resources. The Nazis were robbing German Jews of their money. For the Cabinet this was the 'crux of the whole question'. Britain would not accept large-scale emigration unless the Germans would allow the Jews to bring their resources with them. The Nazis, of course, were unwilling to do any such thing. On 21 November 1938 the home secretary, Sir Samuel Hoare, assured the House of Commons that any refugee who could maintain himself or who had friends who could guarantee to maintain him would 'almost invariably – I think I may say invariably' receive a visa.[30] Lyttelton needed no more invitation. 'I am glad to say,' he recalled, 'I was successful in smuggling three of my Jewish friends, including Richard Merton, out of Germany, and in seeing them safely settled in this country.'

Lyttelton was changed by the moment as so few of his English friends were. He himself recognized the difference. In 1951 he put up the philosopher Isaiah Berlin for membership of his favourite club, the St James's. Berlin was blackballed purely on grounds of race. Members were 'determined to have no one of Jewish extraction in the Club'.[31] The clubbishness that remained at the heart of Macmillan's life lost much of its allure for Lyttelton. It was not an altogether comfortable feeling – 'my hatred of the persecution of Jews, or discrimination against Jews is, in me,' he explained, 'obsessional rather than rational'.[32]

Lyttelton's views and actions appear in a much more favourable light than those of his friends. He was lucky to be a businessman rather than a politician. Yet it would be wrong to argue that the inability of the up and coming generation of Tories to shape British foreign policy was a result either of moral failing or a failure to understand the pernicious threat that faced them. Rather their failure lay in the inability of like-minded men of the same age and background to cooperate effectively with each other. They were still at the stage of their careers at which they were competing against each other for the glittering prizes. This made them relatively easy prey for older party leaders who had patronage to give or withhold. In the late 1930s, blind but wily older politicians ran rings round their perceptive but green younger colleagues.[33] Each of the three politician members of the quartet eventually was sucked into this 'low, dishonest' business. For most of the 1930s it was Cranborne who, as the result of his success, bore the brunt.

One of the best friends Cranborne had made as an undergraduate at Oxford was Timothy Eden.[34] Indeed, Cranborne and Timothy Eden remained friends for the rest of their lives. Their friendship was the first link in a chain that was completed when Cranborne's younger brother, David, became a close friend of Eden's younger brother, Anthony, at Oxford after the war.[35] As a result of this double connection, Cranborne and Anthony Eden became increasingly close friends in the 1920s. They made a glamorous pair, a 'dream team'.

Anthony Eden had good looks, oratorical flair, quick intelligence and an easy mastery of detail. He also had a brilliant war record with the Rifle Corps. Eden entered Parliament in 1923 for Alfred Lyttelton's former seat, Leamington, when he was just twenty-six. He was quickly spotted as a talent. Thereafter Eden's rise up the ranks of the Conservative party seemed effortless except, from the beginning, there were doubts about his staying power. He had the weaknesses of a younger son. He ached with ill-concealed ambition, was touchy of his honour and was quick to take offence at perceived slights. An elderly Conservative peer described him as 'fussing and fidgeting, very self-conscious and blushing with handsomeness – vain as a peacock and all the mannerisms of the *petit maître* – very studied costume, moustache curled inside out'.[36] Even a younger admirer observed that he 'has much of the artist in him; his reactions are incredibly quick, he is nervous and excitable and rather like a Prima Donna'.[37] There was a brittle quality to Eden, an inconsistency of temperament and policy that would always dog him. Cranborne therefore seemed to many the perfect foil for Eden. He had the virtues of an elder son. His was the easy charm of the socially impregnable. Men many years and offices his senior basked under his approbation. Since his boyhood he had been on intimate terms with kings, princes and cabinet ministers. Although his early career had not spoken of outstanding talents, he had not wasted his time in the courts of the mighty. He was well informed and well read on foreign affairs and political philosophy. He was a competent and effective speaker. What struck his intimates most forcibly, however, was his good judgement and common sense. Although quite capable of mouthing platitudes in public, he spoke his mind with clarity and force in private. He was not afraid to face the unpalatable consequences of a course of action that appeared to him right. Cranborne was ambitious: he had a great deal to live up to. Yet not only did he conceal that ambition well, but it was tempered by the position he already held as of right. Eden lusted after the premiership; Cranborne always knew that it was a greater thing to be Marquess of Salisbury.

Yet if Eden was brittle then so in his own way was Cranborne. His health was frail. He had recurring liver problems and suffered from the after-effects of polio. Any great exertion heralded a physical breakdown. As early as 1935, for instance, the combined stress of the Abyssinian crisis and the general election saw him suffering from scarlet fever, chills, flu, heart palpitations and serious oral abscesses. In November 1935, during the crisis that brought Anthony Eden the foreign secretaryship, he was forced to offer his resignation from the Foreign Office.[38] His ailments demanded extended bedrest and thus absence not only from his desk but from London itself at key moments. It was only the willingness of his colleagues and superiors repeatedly to cover his work that allowed his political career to go on.[39] Throughout his career much of his private correspondence was taken up by health bulletins and 'get well soon' messages. Even if Cranborne's ambitions had run towards holding the great offices of state, he must have known that his health would not have stood the prolonged stress they brought. His future was as a counsellor rather than a leader. Unfortunately political intimates who could rely on him to set a firm course could not always rely on him to be there to give counsel. At any moment he could disappear, rendered *hors de combat*, ineffective and ill-informed in enforced exile. If Cranborne provided the backbone that Eden sometimes lacked, that backbone was inclined to break.

Cranborne entered the arena of European diplomacy at what seemed a crucial moment. In October 1933 Hitler had announced to the world that Germany was resigning from the League of Nations. By

May 1934 the last rites had been read over the proposed disarmament convention that had been the centrepiece of British diplomacy for the previous five years. Yet European political alliances had not yet ossified into two camps. The Soviet Union reappeared as an active player on the international stage, Italy was as much a potential ally as a potential enemy. To many people in 1934 it still appeared that diplomacy might make a difference. After he had visited the major European capitals with Eden in 1934 and 1935, Cranborne began to doubt whether this was in fact so.

On the basis of two visits to Berlin with Eden he regretfully concluded that the Nazi 'ruling clique' wanted a war, or at any rate domination of Europe. Having just begun rearming Germany, however, the Nazis, Cranborne realized, would not be ready for this conflict for some years. In the meantime, he deduced, the purpose of German diplomacy was to drive a wedge between Britain and France.[40] Cranborne was less prey to the wishful thinking and self-delusion from which many British politicians, commentators and diplomats of this period suffered. 'The idea,' he wrote, 'that by beaming seductively on the present German government we shall persuade them to moderate their attitude is to my mind pure bunkum.' 'The visit to Berlin was,' he recorded in his diary in March 1935, 'to me at any rate both depressing and alarming ... German rearmament has gone too far for them to be reasonable. From their point of view the present policy of facing Europe with *faits accomplis* has, it must be confessed, been supremely successful'. 'Sooner or later,' he believed, 'we shall have to bring united pressure on Germany to call a halt. This can only be done by the threat of force, in some form or other, and every month that passes it will be more difficult ... There seems no other alternative.'[41]

Cranborne and Eden also visited Moscow in 1935. Eden was the first British government minister to visit Russia since the revolution. He was also the first to meet Stalin – the Soviet leader being notoriously unwilling to travel abroad. The uniqueness of his opportunity perhaps influenced Eden's judgement. Eden was struck by Stalin's 'quality of mind', his 'pragmatic approach', how 'well-informed' he was.[42] Once more left in the ante-room, Cranborne picked up a more accurate picture of the Soviet Union. While Eden was involved with high politics, Cranborne sought out one George Ardreachin, an acquaintance of Bob Boothby. Somewhat to Cranborne's disgust, Boothby had just become his brother-in-law, having married Betty Cranborne's younger sister, Diana, on 21 March 1935. Cranborne's search for Ardreachin proved fruitless. Each time he made inquiries he was told he had 'disappeared'. Ardreachin had either been shipped into a forced labour camp or murdered by the secret police. Fresh from his private search, Cranborne was not fooled by Soviet 'civilization': 'the thing that strikes one most', he wrote of Moscow, 'is the pall of horror and suspicion which hangs over the city . . . it is a grim place, and it gives one an indescribable feeling of horror and squalor'. In his view 'one thing . . . must be clear to anyone who has been there even for four days. The German idea of an imminent Russian military peril is pure myth.'[43] He was convinced that Russia was not a fit ally for Britain – combining as it did untrustworthiness with weakness.

Cranborne's next encounter with a world leader was equally depressing. On the way back from Europe the aeroplane in which Eden's party were travelling flew straight into a storm that hurled its passengers about with 'seismic violence'. By the time they made an emergency landing at Cologne, Eden was feeling desperately unwell. The party returned home by train and boat. Doctors advised Eden that he must take a six-week holiday to recover from his exertions. As a result Cranborne represented Eden at the Stresa Conference: a meeting with the Italian dictator, Benito Mussolini, and the French leaders, Pierre-Étienne Flandin and Pierre Laval. 'Mussolini at Stresa was superb,' according to Cranborne's word picture, 'strutting about with his nose in the air, never addressing a word to anyone while all the Italians shouted and cheered – *Il Duce.*' His observations at Stresa convinced him that the fascist dictator was a buffoon. 'I cannot say that I am at all optimistic,' he told his uncle. 'I am afraid the truth is that Mussolini is quite, quite mad.'[44]

On 7 June 1935 Ramsay MacDonald's resignation as prime minister at the advanced age of seventy-nine paved the way for a Cabinet reshuffle. He was replaced in Downing Street by Stanley Baldwin,

Anthony Eden's sometime patron. To the immense chagrin of Eden and Cranborne, it was not Eden but Sir Samuel Hoare who was appointed to replace Sir John Simon as foreign secretary. A career Tory politician, the fifty-five-year old Hoare had first entered politics as Alfred Lyttelton's secretary. For the previous four years he had been in charge of steering the government's plans for the reform of the government of India through Parliament in the face of a virulent Tory opposition led by Winston Churchill and Lord Salisbury. To Baldwin's cautious advisers, Eden's willingness to talk tough to dictators appeared a little too gung-ho. Hoare 'seemed just the man to carry through the long and patient negotiations required at that difficult moment'. Baldwin, however, tried to have his cake and eat it. Having disappointed Eden, he handed him the consolation prize of a newly created post as Minister for League of Nations Affairs with a place in the Cabinet. This was an obvious recipe for disaster: there could not be 'two kings of Brentford'.[45] For Cranborne, though, this spatchcocked arrangement had a silver lining. He had impressed many by his conduct while Eden was ill.[46] By special Act of Parliament he was promoted to under-secretary of state in the Foreign Office.

The chief business for the new Foreign Office team was the preparation of Sir Samuel Hoare's speech to the League of Nations on the Abyssinian crisis. 'For fascism,' Mussolini had decreed, 'the growth of empire, that is to say the expansion of the nation, is an essential manifestation of vitality, and its opposite a sign of decadence.' In 1896 liberal Italy's decadence had been exposed when its attempt to conquer Abyssinia had been halted in its tracks at the battle of Adowa. Mussolini's determination to expunge this humiliation for Italian arms and seize the independent east African kingdom threw British foreign policy into confusion. If Britain was to build an anti-German coalition in Europe, Italy would play a key role as the guarantor of Austrian independence. There was thus an argument for encouraging Mussolini's imperial ambitions in Africa. On the other hand, Mussolini's planned act of unprovoked aggression against an independent and peaceful country made a nonsense of the League of Nations and created an appalling precedent should the Germans choose to follow it.

Having bested Eden in the race for the Foreign Office, Hoare was not averse to stealing his ideas. Eden had sedulously identified himself with the concept of 'collective security' through the League of Nations. To do so had real political advantages. The Peace Ballot that had caused Cranborne such irritation the previous year was drawing to a close. Although the results were not published until July 1935, it was already clear that this great exercise would provide a ringing endorsement of the League from the 11 million Britons who took part. Through Lord Robert Cecil, Cranborne and Eden were well aware of this groundswell as it developed. They realized that they could turn it to their own advantage. Eden noted: 'Opinion here has grown steadily in support of the League during the recent difficult European situation, so that there is now an overwhelmingly powerful volume of opinion . . . in support of the League as the one means of maintaining peace.' Eden courted pro-League public opinion. 'My generation,' explained the historian John Wheeler-Bennett, 'looked upon him as typifying the generation who had survived the war to become the champion and defender of our pathetic belief in what proved to be the ephemeral shibboleths of "a war to end war" and "let us make the world safe for democracy".'

Samuel Hoare calculated that what was working for Eden could work for him. If the foreign secretary could deliver a foreign policy triumph on the eve of a general election it would help the government to victory and make him the darling of the Conservative party. Although in truth he was convinced that Britain should *not* take a lead in opposing Italy but leave the job to France, he was willing to go to Geneva and say exactly the opposite.[47] Cranborne thought this approach laughable – France had no desire to oppose Italy: the French leader, Laval, was, he pointed out, 'a proper twister'.[48] Yet Hoare was not to be diverted from his central purpose. Thus, in ringing tones whose insincerity amply justified his reputation as 'Slippery Sam', Hoare declared that Britain would back the League in steady and collective resistance to unprovoked aggression.

The speech placed Eden and Cranborne in a most uncomfortable position. Once Hoare had received the applause of the League of Nations and departed, it was they who were left in Geneva to work out how economic sanctions could be imposed on Italy. This was a hopeless task. Since the French government had no wish to cross the Italians, and since Hoare believed that Britain 'might get out by the failure of others to support us', they had been manoeuvred into an impossible position.[49] The Italian invasion of Abyssinia duly began on 3 October 1935. Safely back in London, Hoare blamed the débâcle on Eden.[50]

In October 1935 Eden and Cranborne were caught in a trap of their own making. Those who had lived by the League were dying by the League. Luckily for them, Sam Hoare had been too clever by half. He was caught in an even worse trap. Baldwin chose to capitalize on Hoare's 'success' and called a snap election at the end of October 1935. A short campaign followed and after the poll was taken on 14 November the government emerged with its massive majority virtually intact. The Conservatives' election success did not, however, alter the fact that Britain was faced with a major international crisis. Italian forces were crushing Abyssinia; Britain was committed to opposing Italian aggression; but the government had little idea about how to go about it. One solution was to cut a deal with Italy which would give Mussolini most of his demands while preserving some semblance of independence for the Abyssinians. This settlement could then be touted as a kind of success for the League and proof that British promises had been requited. The other way forward was actually to live up to the spirit of Hoare's speech and impose meaningful sanctions on Italy. Britain could try and cut off Italy's oil supply and block the passage of its ships through the Suez Canal. This second option found few friends in the Foreign Office. Less than a fortnight after the general election Eden agreed to the cession of large parts of Abyssinia to Italy. Britain, he suggested, could act as a broker in negotiations that would decide how extensive these 'large' territorial gains would be.[51]

With Eden conceding grudging support, Hoare departed for the Continent to meet Laval and conclude an agreement along these very lines. Unfortunately for Sir Samuel, Paris was not a safe place for diplomacy. Almost as soon as the ink was dry on the Hoare–Laval Pact, its details were leaked to the French press. They were soon winging their way over the channel into the British papers. What had seemed a sensible exercise in *realpolitik* to the British government seemed a massive exercise in hypocrisy to most other people.[52] 'It may be,' wrote Harold Macmillan in *The Times*, 'that we must face the failure or collapse of the League in its present form. That is no reason to undermine the very structure which a few weeks ago the nation authorized us to underpin. I have never attended the funeral of a murdered man; but I take it that at such a ceremony some distinction is made between the mourners and the assassin.'[53] Like Simon before him, Hoare proved to have few friends: from Baldwin down, the leaders of the government were determined that he should be a sacrificial lamb. On 17 December 1935 Samuel Hoare resigned and Anthony Eden was appointed in his place.

Eden's promotion brought Cranborne no increase in rank but an immeasurable increase in influence. The ridiculous position of League of Nations minister was abolished. Cranborne was now under-secretary to the Secretary of State for Foreign Affairs, the position his father had held nearly forty years previously. Eden and Cranborne's elevation to the top of the Foreign Office allowed the 'Edenite' circle to take on its mature form. Cranborne was Eden's closest adviser. Their inner council was joined by Eden's new Foreign Office private secretary, Oliver Harvey, who had shared rooms at Cambridge with Oliver Lyttelton in 1913, Roger Lumley, Eden's parliamentary private secretary, and Mark Patrick, Cranborne's PPS. It was an inbred group. They were all the same age – born between 1893 and 1897. Lumley had been Eden's contemporary at Eton, Patrick, Cranborne's at both Eton and Christ Church. Their strength was their mutual loyalty and support. Their weakness was also their mutual loyalty and support. Sporting the same ties, moustaches and accents, they were a self-contained unit. Outsiders and their ideas were not welcome. This was apparent even to foreigners. In identifying the importance of Eden's 'young entourage', Charles Corbin, the French ambassador in London, noted that they were 'imbued with theories but lacking practical knowledge'.[54] Most notably they had little time for the Foreign Office's senior civil servant, Sir Robert Vansittart, familiarly known as 'Van'. The brilliant Vansittart, with his network of friends throughout the highest reaches of the civil service, could have proved a powerful ally. Instead, Eden made the highly damaging mistake of siding with Neville Chamberlain against Van rather than with Van against Chamberlain.

Cranborne played a central role in this miscalculation. He had already crossed swords with Van. Cranborne's observations during the course of 1935 made him question whether Italy, Russia or France were fit allies for Britain. Vansittart believed that this was the height of naïvety. Such views, Van counselled Eden, 'might easily lead us into a situation in which we should not have a friend in Europe, and we should not have reached that situation before our own practical re-equipment is anything like far enough advanced'.[55] In particular Cranborne strongly objected to Van's view that, for Britain to rearm, it had to gain time by giving some of its colonial territories to Italy, Germany or both. During the struggle over Hoare's Geneva speech, Cranborne had vetoed 'a passage about the future of colonial territories' inserted by Vansittart, with the comment that 'he is always anxious to buy peace by giving away the British Empire – but if we once begin that the dictators will be down on us like a pack of wolves'.[56]

The Eden–Cranborne équipe believed that they had outwitted Simon and Hoare. This was hubris. Eden had not outmanoeuvred Simon, he had merely benefited from his universal unpopularity. Eden had not outmanoeuvred Hoare, Hoare had repeatedly outmanoeuvred Eden. Certainly Eden had wasted no time in kicking Hoare while he was down – literally down, having broken a bone ice-skating – but Hoare's demise had been providential. The ease with which Simon and Hoare had been overcome misled the Edenites. Not only did it give them an overrated opinion of their own political skills, but it left them facing the wrong enemy. Simon was still in the Cabinet, Hoare was to rejoin it later in 1936. They quite obviously hated Eden. Eden in turn was 'sarcastic about the war records of the senior members' of the Cabinet. He pointedly 'snubbed Hoare after the latter's comment at an Armistice Day celebration, "I wish we could put an end to all this rubbish"'.[57] The Edenites were always on the look-out for their plots. Their fascination with their vanquished foes, however, lulled them into a false sense of security. When faced with a truly formidable opponent in the shape of Neville Chamberlain, they were unprepared for the malevolence and the skill of the attacks with which they would be faced.

Eden and Cranborne had got what they wanted: now they had to do something with it. The dilemma for Cranborne was this. He was unsure whether diplomacy could achieve a great deal. He regarded the dictators as unbiddable, he believed that Britain's potential allies were weak and unreliable. This was not something that it was politic for a man hoping to make a success of running the nation's foreign policy to say. Instead, he had to help Eden differentiate himself from the previous regime.

One way in which Eden and Cranborne believed they could make an instant mark was to increase hostile action against Italy. They ran immediately into a serious problem. To make theirs a feasible policy it was necessary to believe that economic sanctions against Italy were effective and more sanctions would bring Italy to her knees. Yet officials monitoring the sanctions told a different story. 'I cannot agree,' wrote Cranborne in slapping down these officials, 'all the indications are that existing sanctions are more successful than could possibly have been expected. Indeed the chief argument against the oil sanction is that it is no longer necessary, as Italy is in any case finding it difficult to buy oil, so effective have been the embargo on loans and the refusal of League states to take Italian exports.'[58] Not only was Cranborne wrong, but given his views on French pusilla-nimity, he should have known that France would wreck any attempt to construct an effective sanctions regime.

In addition to their hostility to Italy, Eden and Cranborne also tried a more audacious gambit. They launched a set of new diplomatic overtures towards Germany. Visiting Berlin in 1935 Cranborne had formed 'one very definite impression': the Nazi leaders 'were delighted to see us'. 'Although they do not intend to be diverted in any way from the attainment of their policy of domination,' he argued, 'they hate being isolated.' He and Eden were soon bruiting the idea of a rapprochement with Germany through both the corridors of Whitehall and those of Westminster. At a meeting with Eden the newly elected National Labour MP Harold Nicolson found him 'very frank'. 'He says,' reported Nicolson, 'that his aim is to avert another German war. To do this he is prepared to make great concessions to German appetites'.[59] The first concession Eden and Cranborne had in mind was the surrender of the Rhineland, 'while such a surrender still has got a bargaining value'. Indeed, it was Cranborne's task to make the first formal approach to the Germans over this issue. On 15 February 1936 he held an interview with Prince Bismarck, the counsellor at the German embassy, who was an old acquaintance. Cranborne told the grandson of the Second Reich's founder that Eden's first priority was cordial relations with Germany. Amicable Anglo-German relations would be the foundation of future European peace and security. 'This interview,' commented Eden in complimenting Cranborne for his performance, 'should have a good effect.'[60] Regrettably, while Eden and Cranborne were showing themselves to be most energetic in the cause of appeasement, Hitler was showing himself to be even more energetic in the cause of aggrandizement. On 7 March 1936 German troops invaded the Rhineland.

Eden and Cranborne had come to office with two big ideas. Within two months those ideas had been shredded. Sanctions against Italy were ineffective and irrelevant. The Rhineland, the bargaining counter they had hoped to use in a carefully choreographed diplomatic *pas de deux* with Germany, had been seized by brute force. Not that their confidence was in the least affected. Cranborne's response was to retire to his study to pen a discursive 'whither now' paper. 'Like everyone else,' he began, 'I have been meditating not only on the immediate way out of the present crisis, but on the implications of it on British and European policy.' His overall conclusion was that they should carry on regardless. England must not seek a military alliance with France. Germany, on the other hand, should be treated with kid gloves. Germany had the Rhineland: that was a *fait accompli*. The Germans had even so spoken soft words about non-aggression pacts. To Cranborne, German offers seemed to offer a way out of the impasse. 'The essence of the German proposal is mutuality,' he observed. 'A permanent military alliance with France would destroy the whole idea of mutuality. Western

Europe would still be divided into pro-German and anti-German camps. On such a basis no permanent stability can be achieved'. Further than this: 'The great power of Central Europe must inevitably be Germany.' 'It seems to me therefore,' Cranborne concluded, 'that our main object must be to stabilize the situation in Western Europe, and give Germany a free hand . . . further east.' Reading the reports of British diplomats in Germany, he observed 'that Germany at the present moment cannot afford to slacken her production of armaments, for to do so would create such widespread unemployment and misery as would almost certainly bring about the collapse of the present regime. We want . . . a reduction . . . of German armaments . . . but we cannot achieve this unless we provide some outlet for the products of German civil industry. This might be done by giving her, economically, a free hand in Central Europe'.

It was surprising stuff from one who knew only too well the threat posed by the Nazis. Cranborne seemed to be accepting the views of the 'economic appeasers'. He was even ready to concede that 'colonial appeasement', which he had previously disparaged most vigorously, was now worth throwing into the melting pot. The Germans could do just about anything as long as they did not 'cross the frontiers of Belgium and France'.[61] The reason for his about-face only became clear in his peroration. The British government should be willing to discuss anything with the Germans. Details could be worked out. 'But the main thing is that these questions should be discussed freely and openly, on equal terms, round a table.' It was the central dilemma once more: Cranborne did not believe that diplomatic manoeuvres had much chance of success, but Eden needed to be seen making the grand gesture to secure his political position. The casualty rate in foreign secretaries was alarming. There were forces in the government who were willing to use the prospect of future rearmament as an excuse for current inaction.[62] If Eden did nothing in the diplomatic sphere, his enemies would portray him as either impotent or supine. He could not wait until the golden moment – as yet not fully defined – when Britain would be militarily strong enough to act. The foreign secretary had to meet the Rhineland crisis with the promise of a great diplomatic reconstruction. Eden thus followed Cranborne's prescription to the letter. Harold Nicolson reported Eden's reception in the House thus: 'Eden makes his statement . . . Very calm. Promises to help if France is attacked, otherwise negotiation. General mood of the House is one of fear. Anything to keep out of war.'[63]

Eden's ability to keep the House of Commons happy was especially important since his Abyssinian policy was about to end in embarrassing failure. He and Cranborne clung to it as long as they could. Indeed, Cranborne fought the corner harder than Eden himself. The lifting of sanctions would be an unmitigated disaster, he argued, 'bad, both for the future of the League and the government and of our Mediterranean position in the future'.[64] Yet long before he wrote this it was clear that Italy had already won the war.[65] There were people only too happy to take advantage of Eden's discomfiture. Sir Samuel Hoare was welcomed back into the Cabinet. His return was, in the words of press baron Lord Rothermere's political diarist, 'a distinct blow to the prestige of Eden, and surely heralds the abandonment of Sanctions policy. Hoare, although he inaugurated that policy, had the wit to see at an early stage that it might lead to war . . . he returns as a symbol [who] himself now realizes that the Eden insistence on a British might that no longer exists may bring the Empire to sudden and utter ruin.'[66] In fact Baldwin told Cranborne's father that sanctions against Italy had shown 'the people' that they were 'butting their heads against a brick wall'.[67] An even more serious challenge to Eden emerged on 11 June 1936 when Neville Chamberlain made a speech in which he called the continuation of sanctions 'the very midsummer of madness'. 'I did it deliberately,' Chamberlain confided in his diary, 'because I felt the Party and the country needed a lead.' The implication was that Eden's leadership was not satisfactory. The political capital that Eden had built up by holding out the hope that he could negotiate successfully with Hitler was thus very important when he had to announce to the House of Commons that the sanctions in which he and Cranborne had placed such faith had failed utterly.[68] In the event their embarrassment was for the moment forgotten. Soon political London's sole topic of conversation was Mrs Simpson and Abdication fever began to swell. The political vulnerability of Eden's position in the long term remained acute.

Cranborne had given Eden shrewd political advice. Unfortunately it hardly addressed the wider problem. Hitler had no interest in a great-power conference. The centrepiece of Cranborne's plan was thus unrealistic. Anti-Nazi alliances with Italy or Russia he regarded as outside the pale. He had ruled out an anti-Nazi alliance with France. He was if anything more anti-French than Eden himself. Dispatched to France in September 1936 to assess the situation in Paris in person as a new socialist-communist Popular Front government took power, he concluded, 'France must be written off as a force in international politics for some time to come.' French politics were dominated by two crises: the flight of capital as the rich put their money beyond the Left's reach and the 'Salengro case' – neo-fascists, incensed by the arrest of their leader, Charles Maurras, were smearing the Minister of the Interior with the charge that he had deserted from the army during the war. Cranborne quizzed the senior diplomats in the Paris embassy as to whether 'the German danger would not pull the various sections of opinion together', but they concluded 'that the general disorganization had gone too far'.[69] The gap between the British and French was wide and widening. His old friend Jean de Ribes, an aristocratic French diplomat, griped about the taxation of the rich under the Popular Front. 'A man could not even afford now to keep a mistress,' he groaned. He, de Ribes, 'had had a charming little opera girl'. How could his son 'afford that, he said with indignation'. 'This in a man of the highest respectability shows the difference between the British and French points of view,' Cranborne concluded.[70] It was an amusing conversation, but it held for him a profound truth – Britain and France were not natural allies.

Nevertheless Cranborne thought he saw a possible way out of their difficulties. In April 1937 he had a most important visitor at the Foreign Office. For once it was not a member of the European aristocracy in the service of a *déclassé* thug. This was Norman Davis, the ambassador-at-large sent to Europe by the President of the United States, Franklin Roosevelt. Davis brought with him a tantalizing message. Like Cranborne, Roosevelt had been at Versailles. Then he had been a champion of Wilsonian internationalism. In the early

1930s, however, he had seen quite clearly that such sentiments would deny him the presidency. Thus he became an internationalist in isolationist clothing. In November 1936, however, he had won his second presidential term. Ever so cautiously, Roosevelt began to peel back his isolationist carapace. His point man, Davis, 'was most anxious to find out whether we consider there was any way in which some negotiations for a settlement could be restarted.' 'President Roosevelt was passionately anxious,' in Davis's words, 'to take a hand in this, but was very reluctant to do so until the moment was opportune.'

As Cranborne sat in his office with Davis, he realized that Roosevelt's tentative expression of interest could be used to revivify Eden's stalled foreign policy. Eager to grasp this opportunity, Cranborne suggested to Davis 'that, in my opinion, the key to the whole lay in the hands of the United States themselves. If they were to make their views strongly felt, this would be of overwhelming importance.' Davis immediately backed away: 'he did not think that the United States would ever come into a political settlement, however desirable this may be'. Nevertheless Davis was not entirely negative. The United States could 'make an approach to Europe by way of some economic agreement'. It was hardly a proposal to set the pulse racing. Davis's concluding remarks were nevertheless, it seemed to Cranborne, full of future possibilities. Davis had 'said that one could get away with murder under the name of economic appeasement in the US today. It was for that reason that he was most particularly anxious for a trade agreement between Great Britain and the United States . . . the only method of drawing his country closer to Europe.'[71] Here was the basis of a long-term foreign policy. If Britain could edge closer to America, a true alliance of equals was possible; there would be no further need to toy with alliances of despair with the weak and the evil.

Unfortunately British and American politics were badly out of step. Within a month of Cranborne adumbrating a rational and morally sound way forward for British foreign policy, the domestic political landscape shifted decisively against such a hopeful outcome. In May 1937 Stanley Baldwin retired as prime minister. Baldwin had treated Eden with almost paternal care. Eden reciprocated this warmth. Cranborne had a more jaundiced view of Baldwin than his friend. Both Cranborne and Eden could agree, however, that their position within the government had changed very much for the worse as a result of Baldwin's departure. They viewed the new premier, Neville Chamberlain, with deep suspicion.

Chamberlain did not believe that there could be two arbiters of British foreign policy. There could only be one: himself. Eden, Chamberlain felt, was useful merely as an errand boy. Chamberlain made the short move from 11 to 10 Downing Street with three clear ideas in his mind. First, that Britain should ally itself with Italy.[72] Secondly, that any talk of an alliance with the Unites States was fatuous. In his view the possibility of such an alliance was not only tenuous but untenable: he saw the Americans as rivals forever scoring points off Britain in the economic and financial spheres. Thirdly, economic strength was the 'fourth arm' of defence. Rearmament had to be sustainable over the long-term: Britain should not, he believed, strain every nerve to rearm in a fashion that, if maintained for many years, would weaken the economy, on the assumption that war against Germany was inevitable within a finite span. Skilful diplomacy combined with a sustainable defence effort might well avert a war altogether. Chamberlain did not regard these points as debatable. Baldwin had preferred to finesse the party; he was happy to allow things to blur at the edges. Chamberlain wanted to rule the party; he prized clarity.

Chamberlain had no intention of being first among equals in Cabinet. He was confident that he could dominate it. Among the older men he could rely on John Simon and Samuel Hoare. Still smarting from their humiliations, they were glad to be in senior positions once more. They hardly looked on Eden with a friendly eye. Eden and Cranborne had friends among the younger members of the Cabinet: Oliver Stanley, 'Shakes' Morrison, Duff Cooper and Ramsay MacDonald's son, Malcolm. These younger members of the Cabinet, however, were also their rivals. Eden had streaked ahead of them. If he were pulled back it was their gain. Neither could Eden look for much support among the middle-aged group. While Billy

Ormsby-Gore, Cranborne's brother-in-law, could be relied on to do his best in his pompous way, the professional 'pols' knew which side their bread was buttered. Indeed, a member of this group immediately threatened Cranborne's position. Edward Halifax had come a long way since he served as Macmillan's model 'ginger group' leader. Having inherited a viscounty and ruled India he was regarded by many as the perfect foreign secretary in waiting. In the meantime Chamberlain asked him to 'help out' at the Foreign Office. It was now Halifax rather than Cranborne who was entrusted with the role of 'caretaker' while Eden was away from the office.

The party apparatchiks of the Baldwin years were also happy to transfer their allegiance to a new chief. Chamberlain was pleased to accept their homage and to use their talents to further his own ends. He had four main groups working for him. The Whips Office, led by David Margesson and James Stuart, could be expected to enforce discipline. The prime minister's Press Office could be expected to spin news the prime minister's way. Their activities were supplemented by more shadowy figures such as Horace Wilson, an ambitious career civil servant who was attached to Downing Street as the prime minister's 'fixer'. Although Wilson was a former permanent under-secretary at the Ministry of Labour, he was determined to extend his empire into the conduct of foreign affairs. 'Sir Horace Wilson's power is very great,' observed the rising young Chamberlainite Rab Butler, 'he is the Burleigh of the present age.'[73] Even more sinister was the influence of Sir Joseph Ball. A 'tubby man with dark twinkling eyes, persistent but elusive', Ball had been recruited by the party from the Security Service in the 1920s.[74] His specialities were surveillance and black propaganda. He was Chamberlain's 'plumber'. The Edenites were one of his main targets. He kept a close watch on their activities and, at some point, started bugging their conversations. In 1936 Ball had obtained control of a failing magazine called *Truth*. *Truth* was of little importance of itself, but Ball used it as a vehicle for leaking news stories to the commercial press.[75] In February 1938 he boasted of having taken 'certain steps privately' to destroy 'the cases of Eden and Cranborne' in the Conservative press.[76]

It was thus that Jim Thomas walked through the doors of the

Foreign Office in July 1937. Thomas was Eden's new parliamentary private secretary. The 'sound' Roger Lumley had just accepted the chance to govern Bombay. Thomas was a different type altogether. Jim Thomas was most definitely not 'one of us'. He was a Rugbeian in a team of Etonians. Among a team of old soldiers, he was a man who had had three years at school to complete when the war ended. He had spent five years as PPS to his fellow Welshman, the disreputable Labour colonial secretary Jimmy Thomas, and had just finished mopping up the mess following the latter's enforced resignation as a result of corruption. Thomas thought Cranborne was stiff-necked and unwelcoming. Cranborne did not trust Thomas.[77] He was quite right not to do so, for Thomas's appointment was merely the opening gambit in a covert war against Eden's circle. Horace Wilson, David Margesson and Joseph Ball had sent him to Eden as a 'mole'. He was expected to spy on Eden and Cranborne and feed their private conversations back to his controllers. At the same time he was to feed information from them to Eden in an attempt to bend Eden to Chamberlain's point of view. The first priority of the Chamberlain team was to destroy the power of Robert Vansittart, who ran an intelligence and news management network to rival their own. Thomas was instructed, in particular, to fan the distrust with which Eden and Cranborne already regarded Van.

Thomas's mission began immediately. He received his marching orders from Joseph Ball. They purported to show that Ball had received from Signor Dingli, the legal adviser to the Italian embassy, private intelligence that the ambassador had orders from Rome to seek an accommodation with Britain.[78] If, Ball implied, Eden was to follow a conciliatory course rather than the 'unreasonable' attitude expounded by Cranborne, he would reap the glory. Thomas duly sought a private meeting with Eden to cast this bait, but Eden did not bite. He told Thomas to show the message to Cranborne and Vansittart. They both dismissed Ball's information. Thomas was told to warn off Ball from conducting private diplomacy.[79]

It was at this stage that the Chamberlainites' plan began to go awry. In July 1937 Thomas had carried out his orders, albeit unsuccessfully. He had been keen to express his enthusiasm for further missions. Soon thereafter Thomas underwent a Damascene conversion. Anthony Eden had an enchanting personality. He was an upright war hero rather than a man who plied his trade in the shadows. He had celebrated his fortieth birthday only a month before and had a long political career stretching before him. Thomas decided that he preferred his new boss to his old masters and switched sides. Thomas had ample evidence of Chamberlain's malevolence to reveal to his new friends.

For Cranborne the events of July 1937 had three main consequences. First, they alerted him to 'the fundamental difference of outlook' between the Edenites and the Chamberlainites. This being so, and looking to the example of his father, he had at hand a recipe for political conflict. Be obstructive, he advised Eden, just say 'no'. Threaten to resign; be prepared to carry out your threat. It was a long-term strategy suited to someone who, like the Cecils, did not mind incurring short-term political damage. It was not, on the other hand, a strategy that could, in the first instance, appeal to Eden, whose political career so far had been based on courting popularity. Cranborne was thus committed to a struggle for his friend's soul. Secondly, Thomas's change of sides had implications for Bobbety. He had never really been suited to acting as Eden's 'bagman'. He was both his senior in age and his social superior. Thomas was clearly Eden's junior. The young Welshman increasingly took on the role of Eden's eyes, ears and legs. Cranborne's bond with Eden was not thereby weakened, but it was subtly changed. He gained both distance and authority. Thirdly, Thomas's defection had one less positive outcome for the Edenites. They had defeated the plans of their enemies so easily, virtue had so obviously triumphed, that they were blinded to the fact that this was the forlorn hope rather than the main charge. As late as February 1938 Oliver Harvey, having noted that 'Fleet Street is full of rumours of the division in the Cabinet between the PM and AE' and having been told by Rex Leeper, the chief of the Foreign Office's News Department, that the leaks had come from Downing Street, still couldn't believe that Chamberlain had 'put them out'.[80]

Chamberlain and his men, for their part, were not to be treated with contumely: they would come again. Faced with Chamberlain's mastery of both the Cabinet and the party machine, the Edenites were in fact highly vulnerable. In the following months Chamberlain's men would whisper that they were unbalanced, burnt-out hair-splitters. The most damaging charge of all was that they were 'glamour boys': all style, no substance and out of their depth. As Joseph Ball knew as well as Josef Goebbels, the most effective black propaganda was based upon a grain of truth.

While Chamberlain's minions stabbed them in the back, Chamberlain repeatedly stabbed them in the front. There were two 'enormities' before the final confrontation. In September 1937 Chamberlain tried to stop Eden from demonstrating his popularity within the party by speaking at a large Conservative rally in Wales. Eden went anyway and enjoyed 'the greatest success, enormous crowds and great enthusiasm'.[81] Even more subversively, Chamberlain asked Edward Halifax to undertake a diplomatic mission to Hitler in November 1937. Cranborne protested vigorously but in vain. He had to telephone Eden, who was in Brussels, to tell him that the 'PM and Halifax are absolutely determined that the visit shall take place regardless of the fact that H. is forcing himself on Hitler, and of the impression it will produce on the Germans of our anxiety to run after them'.[82] It was at this moment that the Eden circle started to discuss seriously resignation as a weapon of last resort.[83] The prime minister had revealed to the world that not only did he have a shadow foreign policy he also had a shadow foreign secretary. Chamberlain 'was only waiting my opportunity to stir it up with a long pole'.[84] On 7 December 1937 Chamberlain took yet more decisive action and dismissed Vansittart from the Foreign Office.[85]

The last thing in the world Anthony Eden wanted to do was resign. On the other side, Chamberlain was playing a most clever game. He was not about to give his foreign secretary a clear-cut matter of principle on which to resign. Instead he ensured that Eden was bound by collective responsibility while being undermined by a whisper here, a slight there. For his part, Eden did all he could to avoid the final confrontation. If Cranborne had been willing to back him, he would have continued to buy time with a series of compromises on the calculation that Chamberlain's age would limit the length of his time in Downing Street. In particular he could have given way to Chamberlain over Italy – indeed, Cranborne himself had once suggested that this would be a wise tactical retreat.[86] With Chamberlain firmly ensconced in power, however, Cranborne was not willing to allow Eden such room for manoeuvre. It was on the *de jure* recognition of Italy's conquest of Abyssinia that Cranborne urged Eden to make his stand.[87] Given Chamberlain's attitude, Cranborne's intuition was undoubtedly sound.[88] But as the Edenites themselves came to realize, the stance taken by Cranborne had distinct disadvantages. They could with justice be labelled hair-splitters, given the fact that Mussolini was already master of Abyssinia. It was very hard to explain to MPs, even close acquaintances of many years' standing, what all the fuss was about. 'Shakes' Morrison, a friend and contemporary from Oxford who sat in the Cabinet as Minister of Agriculture, did not understand the issue when Cranborne tried to explain it to him in person. Even after Cranborne put it all down on paper, 'Shakes' was none the wiser.[89]

To make matters worse, the Edenites, including Cranborne, were caught flat-footed by the final breakdown of relations between Eden and Chamberlain. It had seemed to them as if the dispute about the *de jure* recognition of the Italian annexation of Abyssinia could be spun out for some time.[90] In the meantime, Eden longed to get away for a holiday. Cranborne later admitted that Eden's absence on the Riviera fatally weakened the position of his supporters.[91] While Eden was in France, Roosevelt made the direct approach to the British government that Cranborne had been hoping for since his meeting with Norman Davis in April 1937. Roosevelt's plan in itself was somewhat bizarre. He wanted to call a world disarmament conference to achieve a 'general settlement' of world problems. No one in the British government believed that such a conference could achieve anything worth while. It could, however, in Cranborne's view, have been the start of a long road towards an Anglo-American alliance. Chamberlain, on the other hand, had no time for a president whom he considered 'woolly and dangerous' and sent back a dusty answer. He consulted neither Eden nor his senior supporter in England,

Cranborne. When Cranborne heard about Roosevelt's approach, 'he said at once that we must accept outright'.[92] By then it was too late. The one route that Cranborne had seen out of the dead end in which Britain found itself was in the process of being thrown away. This was a crisis.[93]

Chamberlain's actions fully revealed a gulf 'of the most fundamental kind'. Eden, Cranborne said, 'couldn't stay in the Government if the PM refused to agree to Roosevelt's plan if it still proved to be open, and that he also should resign if it was found that the PM had killed it'.[94] He found a firm ally in Jim Thomas. Their initial relationship had been frosty. The 'Roosevelt crisis' 'brought us together,' Thomas later wrote. The younger man now 'realized to the full how valuable [Cranborne] was to Anthony Eden and to all of us. He saw so clearly the rights and wrongs of the position and showed . . . how clear to him was the principle involved; he was so completely untrammelled by worldly considerations of the average politician. At this time he was quite firmly convinced that the break was inevitable and it was just a question of how long the present state of affairs could continue.'[95]

There was now a united war party in Eden's entourage. They did their best to make the divide between Eden and Chamberlain as wide as possible. Jim Thomas was dispatched to see Horace Wilson with a threat. Cranborne and Thomas knew that Chamberlain knew that he had placed Eden in an awkward position. If Eden resigned, as they wanted, it would be a 'difficult wicket for him in view of the inability to publish the reasons without the permission of the President of the USA'. Thomas therefore made a declaration of hostilities. 'I said,' he recalled, 'that if Anthony Eden did resign it might well be that the whole of this American business might leak out from the American end and that the country would then know that the PM preferred to turn down the help of a democracy in order that he might pursue his flirtation with the Dictators untrammelled.' The glove had been thrown down and Wilson had no hesitation in picking it up. Wilson was famed as 'wise, calm, serene': now the mask slipped. In 'a towering rage – the first time I had seen him with the mask off (most unpleasant)', Thomas reported, he turned on his former agent. If 'America produced the facts', Wilson snarled, 'he would use the full power of the government machine in an attack on Anthony Eden's past record with regard to the Dictators and the shameful obstruction by the Foreign Office of the PM's attempts to save the peace of the world'.[96] Eden's friends had started a war to the knife on Eden's behalf while he was sunning himself in France.

Eden himself still wanted to compromise with the prime minister by finding some form of words that would keep Roosevelt talking. When Chamberlain agreed to this on 20 January, Eden was triumphant. Cranborne, on the other hand, was despondent.[97] He worried that Eden's will would break under the strain. In the Foreign Office he and the rest of the coterie could affirm Eden. But it was Eden who had to walk alone into the Cabinet. It was Eden who, on an almost daily basis, had to face the hostility or incomprehension of his colleagues. There was always the risk that Eden would be worn down and cave in.[98] Cranborne was now, more than ever, convinced that both he and Eden 'would be better outside the government'.[99]

Chamberlain agreed with Cranborne. He wished to delay Eden's demise only until he could trap him on an even stickier wicket. This did not take very long. On 25 January Eden reluctantly left England once more on a scheduled trip to Geneva for a League of Nations meeting. Cranborne delayed his own departure as long as possible, but a few days later had to follow him in order to conduct League business. Only the most junior member of the team, Jim Thomas, was left in London. Joseph Ball had built Chamberlain a shadow foreign-policy apparatus, complete with 'back channel' links to Italian fascists. While Eden and Cranborne were away, Chamberlain used this network to pave the way for a 'spectacular' – recognition of Mussolini's conquests and the return to Anglo-Italian amity.

On their return, Eden wobbled. Maybe he should, after all, concede some ground on Italy to Chamberlain. Cranborne was aghast. He once more set to work stiffening Eden's sinews. This was not about Italy, he reminded him, this was about the whole future of British foreign policy. 'The practical application of such a policy,' he wrote, 'depends not, as in totalitarian states, merely on the decision of a few political chiefs: it depends on a common sympathy and understanding linking the people of the two countries.'[100] Where would that sympathy between the democracies of Britain and America be if Britain went whoring after Mussolini, the man Eden himself had described as the 'anti-Christ'?[101]

If Cranborne was cramping Eden's room for manoeuvre in the Foreign Office, Chamberlain was doing the same in the Cabinet. Chamberlain was determined to have an alternative foreign secretary. It had been insulting enough when he used Lord Halifax as an emissary to Hitler; it was even worse when he used as an emissary to Mussolini his sister-in-law, Ivy Chamberlain – 'a rather stupid lady who had been spoon fed by two very clever and unscrupulous men' as Cranborne put it.[102] Having circumvented Eden, Chamberlain insisted that the two of them should meet Dino Grandi, Mussolini's ambassador to London, with a view to recognizing Italy's annexation of Abyssinia. To Grandi's amusement, the two Britons acted like 'two enemies confronting each other, like two cocks in true fighting posture.'

That evening Eden left London for a political engagement in his constituency. Meanwhile Cranborne prepared yet another brief, 'taking the line that this was not the time for opening any formal conversations with Muss' to further stiffen his resolve.[103] The next morning, and through luncheon, Eden's team sat with him, repeatedly going through his arguments. That afternoon Eden walked into a three-hour Cabinet meeting. Cranborne's 'hawks' had spent their time in preparation well. When he entered the Cabinet room Eden was placed under enormous pressure to give ground. Eden, however, had learnt Cranborne's brief by heart and repeated it as if by rote.[104] In the end he brought himself to offer his resignation. That Saturday evening he returned to the Foreign Office like a punch-drunk boxer to his corner.

The Cabinet was due to meet on Sunday to consider his proffered resignation. He had a dinner engagement that evening with Malcolm MacDonald, one of the younger members of the Cabinet who wanted to broker a compromise between Chamberlain and Eden. Cranborne and Jim Thomas made sure they joined him after dinner to ensure that he had not been 'got at'. At three o'clock on Sunday, Eden went back into Cabinet. The team at the Foreign Office waited tensely, afraid 'lest he should be giving way under the third degree'. Eden rang through at 6.30. He was 'quite exhausted': those friendly to him in Cabinet were putting him under enormous pressure to accept a compromise. Harvey, who took the call, 'begged' him to come back to the Foreign Office to think. Once more the beaten fighter returned to his corner men. Immediately Cabinet ministers started arriving to put pressure on him. Malcolm MacDonald told him that all his friends in the Cabinet thought he must agree to a compromise with the prime minister: 'they had moved far to meet him, he was putting his personal considerations before the National Government'.

Once more Cranborne played a crucial part in convincing Eden he must stick to his guns. He would, he assured him, stand shoulder to shoulder with him in the House of Commons: they would account for their actions together. When Edward Halifax called, he 'felt at once the atmosphere emanating, I thought mainly from Bobbety, was very much pro-resignation'.[105] At 7.30 Eden went back into the Cabinet room and resigned. He and Bobbety went home together, dined, and started preparing their resignation speeches. Eden was still like a cat on a hot tin roof, wondering whether 'they may still come after him'. At midnight, however, the die was cast. A letter arrived from Chamberlain accepting the resignation.[106]

Monday, 21 February 1938, saw Bobbety Cranborne's finest moment. Anthony Eden was in something approaching a state of shock. He had, in Oliver Stanley's phrase, 'been through Hell to make up his mind'. The morning after the night before was bound to be bleak. Eden had not wanted to resign. He could not quite bring himself to believe that Chamberlain was determined to crush him. He had hoped something would turn up. He had no desire to be the darling of the Labour party or the cynosure of half-crazed Tory mavericks like Winston Churchill. Churchill had been in the political wilderness for nine long years; Eden had no wish to join him for even nine months.

A resignation speech had to be a crisp statement of the high principles of the resigner and a crisp indictment of the low morals of those who had driven him to resign. When Eden walked into the House of Commons, he had every right to look 'very pale and a trifle nervous' because he knew he could not make such a speech. Over luncheon a message had come in that 'the Roosevelt story was known in Fleet Street'. Eden, however, had his hands tied behind his back: he could not tell the story without committing such a serious breach of diplomatic protocol as to make himself look both untrustworthy and incompetent. He was thrown back on a long-winded explanation of the Italian saga. In consequence his speech was a damp squib. 'He makes a speech,' noted his supporter Harold Nicolson, 'which was not really very good. There was just a sufficient note of recrimination to spoil the dignified effect and not enough to constitute an appeal.'[107] Standing up as Eden sat down, Cranborne had no such problem. He had no doubts about his resignation. He had no illusions about the implacable hostility of the Chamberlain coterie. He welcomed the act of self-immolation as a welcome escape.

They had walked in together 'shyly' and sat 'in the famous seat below the gangway'.[108] 'They were side by side on the upper back benches and nothing could have been more impressive,' wrote Harvey, 'than the way these two young men got up in turn and announced they had resigned for their principles.'[109] In fact, Cranborne had a lot of work to do to make it clear that they *had* resigned on principle. He began with charming self-deprecation, 'Clearly, in comparison with the resignation of a Foreign Secretary, the resignation of an Under-Secretary is a very small affair. It hardly ruffles the surface of politics.' 'No!' the encouraging cry went up around the House. Then Cranborne delivered an encomium on Eden. To say that he had resigned for pettifogging reasons was nonsense. 'I have,' he declared, 'felt myself [forced] to resign because I am in the fullest agreement with my right honourable Friend. I am bound to him not only by those natural ties of affection which will be felt by anybody who had the privilege of working with him, but also because I believe him to be absolutely right.' To draw a distinction between the fine details of diplomacy and points of principle was also non-sense. In diplomacy the devil was in the details. It was pointless to negotiate agreements with a regime which would flout them.

Mussolini had to prove that he did not lead such a regime before Britain could negotiate with it. The fascists could do this easily: 'they could stop anti-British propaganda in the Near East; they could bring back some of their troops from Libya, which can present a threat to nobody but ourselves; they could, finally, and most important, withdraw some of their forces from Spain. Any such evidence – not formulas, not promises, but concrete achievement,' he would welcome. But he did not believe that these things would happen. The matter was simple: if the British government negotiated with Italy it was 'a surrender to blackmail'.[110] It was a simple and effective phrase – as even those who disagreed realized.[111]

On that afternoon Bobbety Cranborne stood high in the estimation of both friend and foe. He had, however, not done enough. The debate dribbled away into a scratchy and confused affair. Eden and Cranborne were in the House again the next day sitting in the third row behind the government, but faced with a Labour motion of censure, the Conservative party rallied to its prime minister. Some of the problems that Eden faced were of his own making, some can be laid at Cranborne's door. Eden had no exit strategy because he had not intended, until the last moment, to make his exit. Cranborne, on the other hand, had been thinking seriously about going since November 1937. By January 1938 he was absolutely convinced that they would have to resign and sooner rather than later. He had allowed Jim Thomas to declare war on Horace Wilson. He had sent his own PPS Mark Patrick to stir up opinion in the party's Foreign Affairs Committee, but this initiative was quickly and easily snuffed out by the chief whip, David Margesson. It had merely served to show the Edenites' weakness.[112] Cranborne had a freer hand and a clearer vision than Eden, but he failed to rally effective support for his friend.[113] They had failed to mobilize their own generation. Or, to be more specific, they failed to mobilize sufficient enthusiasm in the *successful* members of their own generation. Wherever they looked they were met with embarrassed coughs and the shuffling of feet. The heads of their contemporaries had ruled their hearts.[114] 'Shakes' Morrison made a 'light bantering after dinner sort of speech' mocking them.[115] Oliver Stanley didn't resign – 'the Stanleys have been trimmers ever since Bosworth', sneered Betty Cranborne when she heard.[116] If Stanley had followed Eden out of the door, he might well have sparked the revolt of the *jeunesse dorée*. Yet Cranborne must have known that it was pointless to rely on his fellow aristocrat.

The 1890s generation had two figures to measure themselves against. One was Anthony Eden. In home affairs, however, it was his Etonian contemporary Oliver Stanley. Stanley had an easy if reticent charm. Like his friend Lyttelton, he made money in the City and moved easily between business and politics. His wife, Maureen, the daughter of Lord Londonderry, was an ambitious social live wire.[117] Having played the game of social conscience as well as Macmillan had played it badly, Stanley's rise was rapid. If the betting was on Eden to be his cohort's prime minister, Oliver Stanley was a short-odds second favourite.

It had come as a shock therefore in 1935 when Stanley self-destructed. Unable to master the complexities of Unemployment Assistance, he had had a 'nervous collapse'.[118] Given that Unemployment Assistance had been regarded as an issue of major importance to the party in an election year, Stanley's seniors were not sympathetic. In Baldwin's brutal phrase, 'Oliver Stanley had failed because he had "no guts".'[119] Oliver Stanley's breakdown was the talk of Westminster. Yet whatever its leaders thought in private, the party did a good job of covering up the incapacity of one of their stars. He was moved to the Board of Education. No one in the party ever quite trusted Stanley again,: his new nickname became 'Snow White'.[120] His performance and the way in which it was hushed up compromised him as a figure of any independence or integrity. Stanley's humiliation suggested to the party leadership that 'the failure of the younger men to develop' would mean their own continuing dominance into the foreseeable future.

Chamberlain might talk unkindly about a 'Boys' Brigade' in his Cabinet, but he did not fear them. He could see that there was no generational solidarity between them. When Cuthbert Headlam went to stay with Oliver and Maureen Stanley towards the end of January 1938, Stanley was dismissive of his own generation. 'He tells me,' recorded Headlam after the two of them had braved a winter walk, 'that none of the young men in the House of Commons is displaying much promise.' The only one he rated in the Cabinet was 'Shakes' Morrison, 'whom he considers very clever'. Eden did not even win a mention. Of course Stanley had his own ambitions. Given his weakness when acting unsupervised, his best chance lay in being tightly bound into the party hierarchy so that 'every string will be pulled for him when the time comes'.[121] Stanley might flirt with rebellion, but he would never carry it through.

Stanley's position also had important consequences for Harry Crookshank. Like Stanley, Crookshank was another who could not bring himself to throw away four years' hard toil on the throw of the dice. In 1935 Baldwin had appointed Crookshank as Minister of Mines. The job was a bruising one. The Minister of Mines presided over the internecine conflicts of 'die-hard' mine owners, often led by Lord Salisbury, and the militant miners' unions. Quite often they turned their ire on him.[122] It was to his intense chagrin therefore that, after two years' hard work, Chamberlain made Oliver Stanley president of the Board of Trade, and in consequence his boss, in May 1937. Stanley's appointment in May 1937 played a large part in shaping Crookshank's actions in February 1938.

Fate had kept Crookshank away from foreign affairs, but he was exceptionally well informed about the real political struggle that underlay them. His close friend Paul Emrys-Evans was the most energetic Edenite on the Tory backbenches.[123] Crookshank kept up with old friends who had stayed in the Foreign Office. Charles Peake, the deputy head of the Foreign Office News Department, used Crookshank's 51 Pont Street home as his London *pied à terre*. It was the News Department that was most aware of the machinations of Horace Wilson and Joseph Ball as they tried to spin the newspapers in the opposite direction.[124] Neither his own observations in Parliament nor the gossip he picked up from Peake filled Crookshank with confidence about the government's commitment to rearmament.[125]

When rumours of Eden's resignation began to filter out on the morning of Sunday, 20 February 1938, Crookshank telephoned Stanley to tell him 'that if there was a Cabinet show down about Foreign Affairs some of the juniors might have views'. Stanley, however, played his cards very close to his chest. He refused to fill Crookshank in about what was happening or to transmit his views to other members of the Cabinet. It was only that evening that Crookshank heard, along with everyone else in the political world, that Eden had resigned. When Eden and Cranborne made their resignation speeches the next day, Crookshank was in an agony of indecision. He rang round some of the other under-secretaries but could find none who was willing to oppose the government. Nevertheless he sought out the chief whip and warned him that he himself was 'very wobbly'.[126] He offered Oliver Harvey dinner to find out the latest news. Harvey described him as 'very troubled indeed, but having been completely ignorant, and as his chief Oliver Stanley has not resigned, feels it very difficult for him to do so alone'.[127]

Crookshank went to bed on the evening of 21 February 1938, having decided not to resign. The next morning he ran into an acquaintance, Rob Bernays, the thirty-six-year-old under-secretary at the Ministry of Health. Falling into conversation on the topic of the hour, they discovered they were both equally unhappy with Chamberlain.[128] Nevertheless, after a 'long talk', they 'concluded we should support the government. It was quixotic of the two of us who were in things to go out when Ministers in the Cabinet who might hold our view did not. So we left it.' With these thoughts buzzing in his head, Crookshank went into the Chamber to hear Chamberlain speak. Freed of the Eden incubus, the prime minister was almost playful. The League of Nations, he declared, was a thing to be laid aside until better days. Some were overjoyed. 'Neville,' wrote the former Tory minister Leo Amery, 'delighted me by having the courage to declare that collective security was dead and only a dangerous sham ... Neville's speech is the first breath of fresh air on the Government bench for many long years.' 'But he couldn't have delivered it while Eden was in the Government,' Amery observed, and Eden 'couldn't have stayed in the Government after that speech, even if there had been no other issue. The speech went down very well and greatly heartened the Party.'[129]

Crookshank was appalled. He felt that if the prime minister had really meant what he had said, then he must resign. Then, once again, he was paralysed by loneliness. It seemed so unfair that he should sacrifice his career while others continued to prosper. His salvation was Bernays. They had agreed to act together, and Bernays hadn't heard the speech. With relief he concluded 'we had better wait for Hansard and see the text'. What Chamberlain had stated quite clearly, Crookshank had succeeded in making unclear to himself. With some relief he passed through the government division lobbies.

The next morning he and Bernays met to pore over Hansard. There in black and white were exactly the words Crookshank had thought he had heard. Having ducked the issue the previous evening, he felt he must do *something*. All day he and Bernays worked on letters to the prime minister, asking for an assurance that he had not meant what he had said: that he still believed in collective security. Draft followed draft as they tried to put these sentiments in the least confrontational manner possible. At last it was done and the letters were irrevocably in the post.

The next morning, promptly, Chamberlain's reply arrived. He was 'very cordial: it had been put to him that one's was a friendly enquiry'. He invited Crookshank and Bernays to call on him that very day. When they were ushered into his presence, Chamberlain was emollient charm itself. Of course there had been no change of policy, he assured them. If he was asked in public, he would make it clear that he was not contradicting any of his previous statements about the importance of collective security. Crookshank heaved a sigh of relief: 'this, as the PM's words *must* count'. When Crookshank emerged from the prime minister's study he was a much relieved man. He had done the right thing. He had acted honourably. But he did not have to sacrifice his career. The prime minister was not even angry with him.[130] For Chamberlain, by contrast, their interview was merely one more proof that the young were weak and predictable and that he would always triumph over them.

The last gasp of the Eden resignation crisis was played out the next day. Eden was due to make a speech in his constituency explaining his resignation. Some wondered whether he would make the fighting speech on Friday which he had so signally failed to deliver in the

House of Commons on Monday. Crookshank was worried enough to write to Eden to tell him 'to go no further than his House of Commons speech in what he said to his constituents'. If Eden tried to rally support in the country, the crisis would re-ignite and his sympathizers would once more have to look to themselves. He and Eden talked about the speech on the telephone. Charles Peake reported to Eden's friends in the Foreign Office that Crookshank had 'been in close contact with AE and helping with speech'.[131] Chamberlain's men were less worried. They had the measure of the foe. 'Anthony Eden makes a big speech tomorrow at Leamington,' noted Chips Channon, who was about to slip into Jim Thomas's shoes at the Foreign Office. 'There is some apprehension lest he be too bitter: but I believe not: firstly because he is a gentleman, and secondly because he is too shrewd a statesman to burn his boats irretrievably.'[132] And so it proved.[133] Crookshank was safe from difficult decisions for the time being. Each of the younger generation of Conservative ministers chose to 'keep a tight hold of the old gentleman's coattails'.[134] Lord Halifax moved into Eden's place, Rab Butler into Cranborne's and Chips Channon into Jim Thomas's with hardly a ripple.[135]

If the resignation of Eden and Cranborne created uncomfortable turbulence for many of their contemporaries, it was a godsend for Harold Macmillan. Crookshank had frequently consulted his friend Macmillan as he wrestled with his conscience. But he had placed more credence on the views of acquaintances like Bernays because they were in the same boat as himself: they had something to lose. Macmillan had no pros and cons to weigh up. He was unambivalent about the possibility of a bonfire of his contemporaries' careers. The resignations of Eden and Cranborne were his political salvation. For over the previous four years his political career had gone from bad to worse. From 1934 his ginger grouping had become more and more desperate. In the 1920s the YMCA had not been liked but they had been regarded as talented. With his contemporaries achieving advancement, Macmillan had been thrown back on his own resources: the Macmillan publishing empire that continued to churn out his tracts and his personal political journal, *New Outlook*; his business contacts; and the dregs of parliamentary talent whom he could drag along to his expensive lunches in the grand hotels of London.

Macmillan's Tory confidants were one-parliament wonders in their early thirties such as had no future in politics. Even those politicians who thought he was 'on the right lines' doubted 'whether he is the man to run a campaign: he simply does not possess the vim and persuasive appeal that is necessary'.[136] He forced himself upon the attention of party leaders, but they dismissed him as a proponent of 'naked socialism'.[137] It was as if he spoke a special language, 'the idiom and the jargon of the economists ... vague and unpractical' that other politicians were too obtuse to understand.[138] A sympathetic fellow MP thought he was 'really getting more and more *exalté* and futile – he is becoming a perfect monomaniac about himself and his policy and a colossal bore – a pity.'[139] After the 1935 election Macmillan was even more isolated, his small band of sympathizers and acolytes having suffered electoral oblivion. He had nothing to lose in voicing in public what some of his contemporaries said about Baldwin's foreign policy in private. Disenchanted with the party at all levels, he even described Baldwin himself as 'ludicrous'. He was one of only two Conservative MPs who voted against lifting sanctions on Italy. To 'frigid' indifference, he resigned the Conservative party whip to give himself a 'free hand'. To equally crushing indifference, he slunk back into the party once Baldwin had resigned.

When he ran out of Conservatives who would give him the time of day, Macmillan increasingly mixed with leftists campaigning for a 'Popular Front' government.[140] As so often, the Left was more fratricidal than fraternal. Many populists suspected Macmillan's interest in the Popular Front was little more than a search for a political base after he left the Tories.[141] 'If,' he wrote to Lloyd George, the figurehead of the movement, after months of futile plots and caucuses, 'the Popular Front proves impossible – if the progressive groups will not come together – then the only thing for people like myself to do is to revert back to the old policy of trying to influence the present government.'[142]

Macmillan was thus delighted to find some like-minded souls in the party, even if they were almost as unpopular as himself. In May 1936 he joined the December Club, a group of pro-rearmament MPs chaired by Louis Spears, an able and energetic friend of Churchill of whom Duff Cooper said, 'If he had the word SHIT written on his forehead in letters of fire it wouldn't be more apparent than it is now.'[143] The club was to be based on the model that Macmillan had been unsuccessfully trying to emulate for years, Edward Halifax's 'Group'.[144] Unfortunately, as with Macmillan's previous ginger groups, the December Club made little impact. Although the December Club was still meeting in 1938, Macmillan was delighted to abandon it for the greener Edenite pastures. At last he could associate himself with a serious politician. Until that point Eden had barely ever noticed Macmillan. Now Eden was willing to entertain Macmillan's courtship. Observing them at dinner, a Tory peer who disliked them both noted, 'Macmillan MP kept pumping sedition into his ear. This seemed to be agreeable to Eden and every now and then one could see a wicked, vindictive gleam in his eye.'[145]

5

Glamour Boys

In February 1938 Cranborne's aristocratic *élan* seemed more heroic than Crookshank's bourgeois caution. Yet it was Crookshank who was to prove the more representative figure. Cranborne had screwed Anthony Eden's courage to the sticking place once but could not bring himself to do it again. Eden had resigned to further his career, not to end it. Although the resignation itself was a political fiasco, Cranborne and Eden calculated they would get a second chance. Left to himself, they believed, Chamberlain would prove such a disaster in foreign affairs that they could get a second bite at the cherry.[1]

If Cranborne's confidence that Chamberlain's embrace of Mussolini would soon prove to be untenable was justified, then it was vital for the Edenites to retain popularity within the Conservative party. It would be damaging to be seen plotting against the party, 'fatal to be seen plotting with the Socialists'.[2] Harry Crookshank warned an audience in Lincoln that 'highly as we continue to respect and admire Mr Eden, we cannot accept at its face value all the Socialists are now saying about him ... the Socialists try and bring party politics into high affairs of international policy.'[3] In any case, although Eden hinted at the need for *a* National Government rather than *the* National Government in the speech he gave in Leamington after his resignation, the creation of a new national government was not, he realized, 'a practical proposition at the moment'. Eden was reviled by the Labour party for his policy of non-intervention in the Spanish Civil War. Cranborne, who had once expressed scepticism as to whether a Republican victory in Spain might lead merely to a 'dictatorship of the Left' and who, as a result, had fought hard to prevent the arming of Republican troops and for civil relations with Franco, was even less trusted.[4] 'To agree on a foreign policy,' lamented Mark Patrick, Cranborne's former private secretary, 'would not be difficult if it were not for the cursed question of Spain which, even now, plainly obsesses them to the exclusion of anything else.' If there was a move towards a National Government, the Edenites would seek to benefit from it. They would not, however, try to precipitate it.[5] The Edenites agreed that it was best to let sleeping dogs lie. Eden and Cranborne would both take a holiday and lie low for a while.

The drum of international politics failed to beat in time with the Edenites' needs. In January 1938, when Roosevelt had suggested a disarmament conference, Anthony Eden had been on holiday in the Riviera. In March 1938, when Hitler seized Austria, Eden was once again on holiday in the south of France. Cranborne and Eden had hoped for a breathing space of six months without any comment or intervention from themselves while Chamberlain's diplomacy unravelled. They had based this hope on an accurate assessment of Mussolini's duplicity. They were, of course, right to believe that Chamberlain would be a disastrously incompetent international leader. They were, as usual, wrong to underestimate his ability to manage domestic politics. They were also wrong to assume that the expected demonstration that Mussolini was untrustworthy would dominate the international agenda. As Hitler started to assert himself, Mussolini seemed like a mere pygmy.

Nevertheless the German invasion of Austria on 12 March 1938, less than a month after Eden and Cranborne had resigned, was potentially a golden opportunity to parade their foresight and damn Chamberlain. The true depths of his incompetence had been obscured by the details of the Italian negotiations; now everyone could see the rottenness at the heart of government. As so often before, however, it was the perceived demands of British politics that took precedence. Eden and Cranborne had agreed on their strategy and decided to stick to it: there would be no campaigning, no attempts to disrupt the smooth running of diplomacy. The Edenites would move in step with and attempt to capitalize on public opinion, they would not get too far in front of it. On 5 March 1938 Cranborne attended a luncheon with another of his grandee diplomat acquaintances. Would England, Count Colleredo Mansfield asked him, support Austria? Cranborne's answer was unequivocal. England would consider military action only if France or Belgium were threatened directly. 'This very naturally seemed to him,' Cranborne conceded, 'a most unsatisfactory attitude, but it is no use to give the Austrians further hopes.'[6]

Given their political strategy, the Edenites could make little of the *Anschluss*. Sir Timothy Eden, Eden's elder brother and Bobbety's old friend, begged Cranborne to get Anthony back from France and to accompany him to London so that that they both might denounce Chamberlain in clarion terms.[7] But Timothy Eden, although a much-loved intimate, was held not to understand 'politics'. In fact, with Eden, Cranborne and Jim Thomas all absent from the capital, the role of point man and political rapporteur devolved on Mark Patrick. Patrick too was a trusted friend but, as even he admitted, he was not much of a politician. He started one of his reports with the words, 'I have never really managed to like politics.' 'I wish I could give you a definite account of opinion here,' he wrote to Cranborne, 'but the outlines are still too blurred.'[8] 'The attitude of our side,' he wrote to Eden, 'is very hard to sum up.' Patrick dithered over whether to summon his mentors back to London and in desperation turned to Winston Churchill for advice. 'His advice,' he wrote in apology, 'may be anything but sound.' 'At any rate,' he concluded, 'everyone whom I consulted was agreed that you would do well not to come back for a little. The general opinion was that events were arguing your case more forcefully even than you could do.' Patrick, on his own initiative, linked up with another Tory backbencher, Victor Cazalet, to demand a government statement that Britain would fight over Czechoslovakia. 'We shall not save our necks by doing nothing,' Patrick concluded.

> That will mean that we shall have to face not merely Germany and Italy, but *Mitteleuropa*, with all its resources – Hungarian grain, Rumanian oil and the rest – at the disposal of Germany's

organizing power. We just succeeded last time in choking Germany by sea power because even her and Austria's pre-War frontiers together were not a wide enough base for a long war; but with *Mitteleuropa*, conceivably with the Ukraine thrown in, is another matter. Our one great asset, sea power, would not avail against such a mass of raw material. *Mitteleuropa* seems in the process of construction before our eyes. To back the Czechs seems the only chance of arresting the process before it's too late. It may be only one chance in a hundred, but it is a chance, and there seems no other.

Having reached this conclusion Patrick spent a day in the House 'propagating this doctrine to anyone I could get to listen'.[9]

It was inevitable that Patrick should be regarded as Cranborne's mouthpiece. 'The H. of C.,' observed Chips Channon, 'is humming with intrigue today, and the so-called "Insurgents" are rushing about, very over-excited. They want to bring back Anthony Eden.'[10] Yet as Bobbety's conversation with Count Mansfield had shown, Patrick was far in advance of Cranborne's own position. If Cazalet and Patrick had succeeded in whipping up a sensation he might have been forced to act. As it was the move soon petered out.[11] Although Patrick 'got a far more favourable response than I had expected', this was merely 'due to a "hang over"' from the shock of the *Anschluss* itself'. 'I daresay nothing will be done,' he reassured Cranborne, and he was right.[12] Cazalet was pacified by pro-Czech noises made by Chamberlain.[13]

On 16 April 1938 the Anglo-Italian Easter Agreement was signed after a month of negotiations. It was a wide-ranging attempt to remove points of tension between the two countries. The excitements of the *Anschluss* notwithstanding, Cranborne had not changed his view that it was Chamberlain's dealings with Mussolini that would expose him as a fool. The Edenites should give him enough rope to hang himself. 'If you can be silent, it would be far wiser,' Cranborne adjured Eden sternly.[14] Once again he could offer no succour to his supporters on the backbenches. 'The Italian Debate,' he warned Paul Emrys-Evans, 'I shall avoid.' The agreement was loathsome in spirit and detail. It was merely 'a repetition of undertakings which have already been given and already broken'. 'As far as Spain is concerned,' he noted, 'we seem to give Muss a free hand to finish the war as and when he likes, with the certainty that he will get an agreement with us at the end – all this makes me very humiliated and ashamed.' But that humiliation altered nothing. 'I do not think to say so at the present moment would do much good. The Government must have a full opportunity to try their policy. To try and put spokes in the wheel would be merely to get the worst of both worlds – so I shall stay away.'[15] 'I am more and more relieved,' he wrote to his uncle Robert a few days later, 'that Anthony and I are out of this Italian agreement.'[16]

But even Cranborne did not stick to his resolution entirely. The rapid pace of international events once more upset his calculations. On 2 May Hitler arrived in Italy to meet Mussolini and the dictators were publicly bound together in a fascist-Nazi embrace. In wake of the formation of the Axis Cranborne did go to the House of Commons to listen to the debate on Italy. It shook him. Their own tactics, he concluded, were still correct. 'I am glad that you were not there,' he wrote to Eden. 'You could have hardly sat through the PM's speech in silence and you would only have been bracketed in the public eye with Lloyd George and the Socialists – that was no doubt why Winston, who had meant to speak, did not do so.' Their strategy of 'wait and see' was, however, daily riskier. 'I am afraid,' he explained, '[that Chamberlain] will only tend to consolidate the Liberal and Socialist oppositions. For this reason, I expect that you may soon have to define your position however embarrassing that may be. Obviously you do not want to identify yourself with the Opposition; but it seems that there is a possible middle line.' 'We can't be silent forever,' he exhorted his friend.[17]

There was a risk that Chamberlain would pick them off individually. On 16 May Billy Ormsby-Gore was removed from the Cabinet, 'pushed out by PM who hates him and the whole Cecil connection'.[18] Even Nazi observers saw Ormsby-Gore's sacking as a deliberate insult to the Cecils.[19] The Cecils certainly understood it in this way themselves. Cranborne was willing to put up with slanders against his friend and indeed himself. It was Chamberlain's attack on his family above all else that convinced him they should move into open opposition.[20] Lord Salisbury told Eden he should speak out.[21] Eden's friends in the Foreign Office were also urging him to define an anti-Chamberlain position. Eden was convinced: 'I really believe the time has come.'[22] Yet Eden's call to arms was not as stirring as it should have been. Cranborne had talked of a 'middle line'. Eden's idea was to slip round the irrevocable step of castigating Chamberlain's foreign policy by speaking on 'broad national issues'.[23] He was going to 'hit out, taking as his text that the Tory Party must be progressive or succumb'.[24] This was hardly what the moment called for.

Once more the moment passed them by. The international situation moved quicker than their political calculations. By the third week in May the Sudeten crisis – Germany's claim to western Czechoslovakia with its large German-speaking population – had begun to boil in earnest. By August Cranborne was seriously alarmed. 'I don't like the look of things at all,' he said in a letter to Eden. 'Not that I can believe Hitler really wants an European war – but he seems to be playing the sort of game of bluff that is only too likely to land him in a situation out of which he cannot extricate himself without loss of prestige except by some military adventure.'[25] Yet Cranborne still did not advocate action. He believed that press leaks had already, in all probability, sold the pass by telling the Germans that Britain would not make a stand on behalf of the Czechs.[26] In any case, he had a skewed view of the leadership of the Sudeten Germans. In reality this leadership had been deeply penetrated by Nazism.[27] When he had been at the Foreign Office, Cranborne's relationship with Dr Rutha, the representative of the Sudeten Germans in London, was most cordial. When the 'direct and honest' Rutha told him of the sufferings of the Sudetens Cranborne regarded his information as 'a most powerful and distressing indictment of the Czech government'.[28] In September 1938 he had still not altered this view. 'I have never been an extremist over the Czech problem,' he told Walter Monckton. 'Anyone who has had much to do with it must recognize that if things have come to this pass, the Czech government must bear their full share of the blame – it is their past mismanagement which has made the Sudeten *Deutsch* so fruitful a ground for German propaganda, and if, as a result, these have finally made up their minds they want to join Germany, sooner or later they will have to be allowed to do so.'[29]

If Austria had not been the issue for a public break with Chamberlain, neither it seemed would be the fate of Czechoslovakia. When Chamberlain announced his intention of flying to Germany to negotiate face to face with Hitler, it was not the fate of Czechoslovakia that perturbed Cranborne, but the fact that Britain should sully its hands with that fate. It was little more than a 'cynical farce'. In the wake of the dismissal of Billy Ormsby-Gore, Cranborne had started to stir his family to oppose Chamberlain, but when Lord Robert offered him the chance to deliver a personal broadside against Chamberlain he declined. His uncle was trying to organize a LNU rally at the Albert Hall in support of Czechoslovakia and urged Cranborne to speak at it. 'I cannot accept,' his nephew replied. 'The moment seems to me much too serious to take part in what amounts to a protest meeting, which can only tend to split the country at a moment when, above all, it should be united.'

Thus three days before Chamberlain flew to Munich to meet Hitler, Cranborne reassured his uncle that 'whatever may be said of the Government's past misdeeds, they will now have to take a firm line and resist German pretensions. No other course is open to them.' It was Sunday, 25 September. Lord Robert's rally was planned for Friday, 30 September. 'When that moment comes,' Cranborne continued, 'and presumably it will come before Friday, we shall want to give them support in as dangerous a situation as the country has ever had to face. In the circumstances I could not say a single word or take part in any demonstration that might tend to impair the unity that is essential if we are to get through.'[30] Cranborne was right about the timetable of diplomacy. He was entirely wrong about the line Chamberlain would take at Munich. Eden followed his lead. He refused to join Churchill in signing a telegram to Chamberlain begging him not to betray the Czechs.[31]

Given the lack of pressure from outside the government, it was hard for those inside to know what to do for the best. When Anthony

Eden had admitted that he was confident that he would succeed Chamberlain as prime minister, Oliver Harvey told him that he would not get into No. 10 without actively accumulating support: he needed 'to see some of his younger colleagues and MPs, especially Crookshank'. If, Harvey argued, Eden had cultivated Crookshank, then perhaps he would not have funked his resignation in February 1938.[32] Crookshank's Foreign Office contacts were already working on him, telling him that he should not believe the assurances that were being so liberally spread around by the prime minister's allies: rearmament was 'hopelessly behind and daily worse: the inner Cabinet is completely defeatist'.[33]

Eden's friends tried their best to recruit Crookshank as an out-and-out Edenite.[34] Yet as Eden's silence lengthened into months, Crookshank was one of those who began to doubt whether Eden really had it in him to seize the leadership.[35] On the other hand, he realized that he had been duped by Chamberlain. Chamberlain had been willing to see him and make a fuss of him in February, but had no real interest in him, his actions or his career.[36] Despite the soft words of five months previously, he had no interest whatsoever about Crookshank's views on foreign affairs.[37] Crookshank was as surprised as anyone else when Chamberlain 'threw in the Guard' and flew to Germany to see Hitler.[38]

Crookshank's demands that junior ministers should be informed about what was going on resulted only in a fruitless meeting with Edward Halifax. Crookshank certainly did not need that to grasp that the result of Chamberlain's diplomacy would be 'peace at expense of Czechs (with dishonour)'.[39] Like Cranborne, he was convinced that after Chamberlain's mission to Germany even the prime minister would be unable and unwilling to compromise further. After a long talk with Macmillan, he approached Oliver Stanley to suggest that the possibility that Mussolini might oppose Hitler's ambitions in Czechoslovakia should be explored. Stanley vaguely promised to pass it on. Sitting behind Chamberlain the next evening, Crookshank witnessed the theatrical moment when, as the prime minister was speaking, Hitler's invitation to a further summit in Munich was brought to him on the floor of the House. His main feeling was one of satisfaction: Mussolini too was to be at Munich. Perhaps someone in the government was listening to him at last. 'I wonder if it was *my* suggestion,' he mused.[40] This satisfaction was rudely shattered a few days later when the deal that Chamberlain had struck with Hitler began to filter out.

In February Crookshank had not sensed great outrage at Eden's removal. Now many of his acquaintances seemed 'very bitter'. 'One wonders how far this has spread? Was the balloon about to go up for the Government?' He talked once more with Bernays. 'I think he and I will leave the government,' he concluded, 'but this will be very difficult for us personally when the world thinks Neville so great.' When Chamberlain's pact with Hitler was announced to MPs, Crookshank's view was that 'the man is crazy . . . and hypnotized by a loony'.[41] The next day Duff Cooper announced his resignation as First Lord of the Admiralty. This 'means I must send in mine,' Crookshank decided. 'I don't feel I can honestly go about saying all is well.'[42] Crookshank was consumed with worry. As he put it to Cooper, 'I have no responsibility for Foreign Affairs . . . [you] decided by knowledge whereas I can only do it by deduction and intuition.'[43]

At the beginning of October 1938 Duff Cooper made his resignation speech. Crookshank, who had spent the day composing his own letter of resignation, sped down to the House to hear it. Cooper's words confirmed Crookshank in his view that 'we were never either clear enough or firm enough'. Chamberlain's response was 'not very good'.[44] Eden spoke in Cooper's support, but was widely perceived as trying to keep the door ajar for his own re-entry to office. His friends 'were disappointed, not to say shocked'.[45]

If Crookshank was worried by his misreading of Chamberlain, Cranborne was angry at his. After months of avoiding confrontation, he finally walked into the House of Commons with the intention of bearding the prime minister in his lair. Over the past few months he had come to see the battle against Chamberlain as a family affair. It thus seemed entirely appropriate that he should ask Sir Sidney Herbert, an old family friend, to act as his seconder. Unlike Eden, Cranborne did not pull his punches. Chamberlain supposed himself to have secured 'peace with honour'. 'But where is the honour?'

Cranborne asked the House of Commons. 'I have looked and looked and I cannot see it.' The Munich agreement was no more than a 'wicked mockery'.[46] Setting aside his private views on Czechoslovakia, he declared: 'The peace of Europe has in fact been saved – and we had better face it – only by throwing to the wolves a little country whose courage and dignity in face of almost intolerable provocation had been a revelation and an inspiration to us all.' Chamberlain's diplomacy was an 'abiding source of shame'. The Munich agreement was 'one of the most humiliating episodes in our history'. 'That there should be,' he conceded, 'wider appeasement is the honest and sincere desire of us all, to whatever party we belong'. Cooper's resignation had meanwhile revealed the sinister underbelly of Chamberlainite appeasement. It was the appeasement of weakness not of strength. Chamberlain had done nothing to demonstrate British strength: 'If we had mobilized the Fleet earlier and had shown that we meant business, the last agonizing days would not have been experienced.' 'Is it surprising,' he asked, 'that the advisers of the German Chancellor concluded that they might leave England entirely out of account and that our policy was the policy of peace at any price?' His peroration contained a stark warning. 'Appeasement is no alternative to rearmament, and conciliation is no alternative to firmness.' 'If we do not learn that lesson, I am afraid that we shall only have paved the way to disaster, and that last disaster when it comes will be complete and, I am afraid, very richly deserved.' He sat down. It was 'quite a good little speech' but hardly one to shake the foundations of a government.

Herbert's speech, on the other hand, was much more sensational because he did not bother to conceal the true situation as the other Edenites thought they must. Sidney Herbert was a very ill man, badly affected by his war wounds. He rarely attended the House. Within six months he would be dead. He had, however, been Baldwin's private secretary in the 1920s and knew well the realities of politics and what hid underneath the stones. He himself was beyond political ambition. He stated two truths. First, something very nasty lurked within the Chamberlainite woodpile. Chamberlain was the head of a 'tiny Tammany Hall ring' who had bullied and manipulated their way into power. Having derided the sinister manipulators who surrounded Chamberlain, Sidney went on to deride the government's attempts to pretend they were taking rearmament seriously. Churchill's son-in-law, Duncan Sandys, had been threatened with military discipline for speaking openly about the parlous state of Britain's defences. Sir Sidney did not need a serving officer to point out the lack of vigour with which Chamberlain was pursuing rearmament. 'Of course it is known to Herr Hitler. It is known to the children in my village.' From his windows at Boyton Manor overlooking Salisbury Plain he could see that the army was ill-equipped – 'what is the good of having the men if we are to send them like sheep to the slaughter without armaments?' With scathing contempt he damned the government: 'We have talked long enough about "the years the locusts have eaten". I was led to suppose that the locusts had stopped nibbling about two years ago, but I can hear their little jowls creaking yet under the Front Bench.' As a shocked government supporter well understood, 'My honourable and gallant friend and the Noble Lord have questioned our support of the Government's policy on a moral basis.'[47]

Eden had refused to lead the charge, so Cranborne and Herbert conducted the attack for him. Nevertheless Cranborne had every sympathy with Eden's position. Chamberlain's 'Tammany Hall ring' were formidable opponents who would turn on any open critic. 'The party machine is being screwed up. Of course the PM will resist widening the Government to the uttermost as it will spell the end of his own dictatorship,' commented Cranborne's ally, Oliver Harvey. Within days constituency executives who previously had been delighted to have distinguished and talented young gentlemen as their MPs turned on them with a vengeance.[48] By pulling his punches, Eden averted the worst of their wrath. 'How wise you were to be more moderate,' Cranborne conceded to Eden himself.[49] 'It shows,' he wrote, somewhat inelegantly, to Jim Thomas, 'that Anthony was wise to be moderate in the House, for what he says matters far more than what I do.' Returning to Cranborne, he himself was brusquely summoned before his constituency executive. 'All my prominent supporters are rampant,' he reported to Thomas, 'breathing fire and slaughter, and I am quite expecting to be stoned next week.'[50]

Some of Eden's supporters, who, like Eden himself, were not independently wealthy but had refused to vote for the government in the Munich debate, were driven almost to despair. Paul Emrys-Evans was pushed to the verge of resigning from his seat in Derbyshire.[51] Even Churchill and Boothby were forced by threats of rebellion in their constituencies, stirred up by the *apparat*, to abandon the one 'glamour girl', Katharine, Duchess of Atholl, who, faced with deselection, had the courage of her convictions and forced a protest by-election.[52] Bereft of support from within the party, she was crushed. Only one man bucked the trend: Harold Macmillan thumbed his nose at the threats issued by his brother-in-law, James Stuart, and campaigned against the Conservative candidate in the Oxford by-election. 'They could,' he told an anti-Conservative election rally, 'always appease lions by throwing Christians to them, but the Christians had another word for it.'[53] He could afford to be offensive, for, as the Stockton constituency chairman reported to his executive, Macmillan owned them: 'if it were not for the generosity of Mr Macmillan, it would be impossible for the organization to carry on'.[54] Cranborne was nowhere near as confrontational, but he too could afford to be sanguine and face down his 'local Blimps' with aristocratic disdain. 'I have,' he reported to Uncle Bob, 'extorted from them, after a long wrangle, a free hand to say what I like about the Government's foreign policy. They think all the same that I am: (a) a Socialist, (b) a war monger and (c) a poison pen against the Prime Minister.'[55]

Not all the efforts of Cranborne and Herbert could fully disguise the fact that Eden had once again funked his opportunity.[56] On the evening after Eden, but before Cranborne had spoken in the Munich debate, Macmillan lured Hugh Dalton, a Labour party leader who had been under-secretary at the Foreign Office during the last Labour government, to a meeting with Eden and Churchill. This conclave achieved little. Although many of Eden's political plans continued to be based on the notion of a National Government including Labour, he was unwilling to dirty his hands conniving too obviously to achieve it.[57]

A caution similar to Eden's was also apparent elsewhere. The day Cranborne spoke out, Crookshank was closeted with Oliver Stanley. Although Stanley couldn't 'see how you can ask people to rearm and yet say it is peace', he had no intention of resigning. According to his logic, 'a Cabinet minister can really only resign on a decision he doesn't approve and there has been none: he having swallowed' the visits Chamberlain made to Germany before he struck a deal with Hitler at Munich. Crookshank told him he was going to resign. 'I envy you,' were Stanley's parting words. Thus committed, Crookshank sent his letter of resignation to Chamberlain and informed the Speaker that he wished to make a resignation speech.

For recidivists, Chamberlain believed in the big stick or the stiletto between the ribs. He was more than happy, however, to stroke waverers. As Crookshank sat down to dinner that evening, the chief whip delivered a summons from the PM. It was only polite, Margesson implied, that he should wait upon Chamberlain one more time. This was Crookshank's downfall. He resented the fact that he had resigned whereas Stanley had not. In this state of mind, he was once again easy meat for the prime minister's blandishments. First came Chamberlain's 'more in sorrow' than in anger act. He thought Crookshank had been doing so well – this sudden throwing over the traces came as a 'frightful shock'. Then Chamberlain let Crookshank lecture him. The prime minister *must* 'take back his words about peace with honour in our time', *must* press on with rearmament, *must* endorse collective arrangements including Russia 'not for material but for moral reasons'. But of course, Chamberlain averred, he could meet all these points. Indeed, he would do so when he wound up the debate in the House of Commons. He most certainly would not allow Harry to throw away his career until he had heard him speak. Crookshank called all this 'comic opera', but regrettably the joke was on him.[58] Knowing Chamberlain had stroked him in February and then ignored him, he nevertheless let him repeat the act. Chamberlain can hardly have been surprised when, two days later, he received a note asking him to burn Crookshank's letter of resignation.[59]

While his resignation threat was still active, Crookshank had run off to tell Anthony Eden of his stand.[60] He was talked of in the same breath as Cranborne as one of the men whom Eden would bring with him when he re-entered the Cabinet in triumph.[61] He was keen to shout Eden's praises. Eden 'was always urging the Cabinet to go ahead, full speed at rearmament – but they wouldn't – Anthony, therefore is the coming man.'[62] What he had meant to say in his resignation speech was this: 'real negotiations never took place at Munich or at the other meetings'. Problems were not 'tackled soon enough nor with sufficient vigour and foresight'. There was no 'saving thread of consecutive policy'. He had a ringing passage about his own sacrifices: 'no one can speak lightly of the possibility of War, least of all those of us who like myself will suffer in our bodies till our dying day from the results of the last'.[63] It was noble material, but he did not use it. Instead he praised the 'persistency and courage of the Prime Minister' and limited himself to the observation that 'we have escaped a great calamity but we do not know whether we have escaped it for good and all'.[64] Although he did not know, he had missed forever his chance to be a Glamour Boy.

Thus Crookshank was not among the disgruntled and dispossessed who gathered for a 'hush-hush' meeting in Jim Thomas's house in Great College Street. There was a ferment of excitement that they might actually *do* something. The Glamour Boys were joined by their former enemy, Leo Amery, Churchill's maverick Harrovian contemporary, who turned decisively against Chamberlain over Munich.[65] The meeting revealed, however, that they had no clear view of the way forward. Although they were all 'deeply disturbed by the fact that Chamberlain does not seem to recognize the gravity of the situation', caution prevailed. 'We decided that we should not advertise ourselves as a group or even call ourselves a group,' recorded Harold Nicholson. 'We should merely meet together from time to time, exchange views, and organize ourselves for a revolt if needed.'[66] It was the 'less heroic course'. For the Edenite core the dilemma was this: 'Should he break away from the Party and lead a crusade in the country? Or should he stay just inside the Party pressing rearmament?' 'Too firm a stand now,' they feared, 'might force the PM to have an immediate election which he might win. There must be an election within a year – a policy of attrition from within, damaging speeches from the backbenches, may be more effective in breaking the hold of the Party machine and securing a more easy change-over from the PM's regime to a wider Government.' A 'Gladstonian crusade' would be 'very dangerous'. 'It might not come off and AE would have shot his bolt in vain.'[67] 'The general upshot [was,]' Amery wrote, 'that Eden should make a speech laying stress on social reform and general national regeneration.' Thus Eden continued on his cautious path. When he rose to speak in the House on 10 November, his message was so coded as to be gnomic. It created 'much speculation', but 'nobody quite knew what he was talking about'.[68] By the end of the year waverers such as Crookshank had come to the conclusion that there was 'no alternative King to crown'.[69]

Eden favoured, and Cranborne had acquiesced in, a struggle of attrition rather than a *coup de main*. Yet they were peculiarly ill-suited to a war of attrition. Sidney Herbert, who had made their most effective rallying call and whose presence at the Great College Street meeting filled them with confidence, took no further part in their proceedings, retiring to France to die. Whatever Eden's virtues, stamina was not among them. His longing for sun-dappled holidays was becoming a pattern. The constant struggle was breaking Cranborne's health also. Never robust, infections seemed to fly towards him. He needed a rest-cure. His doctors advised an extended break somewhere warm. Preparations were put in train to depart for North Africa.

A war of attrition thus rather suited Chamberlain. He had a behind-the-scenes organization. It corralled and identified the opposition. Their meetings were supposed to be 'hush-hush', but Joseph Ball had soon organized a surveillance operation to watch their next moves. Chamberlain also had powers of patronage, which he was happy to use to prevent disaffection spreading. He did not, for instance, make the mistake of ignoring Crookshank again. At the beginning of November Crookshank was offered the deputy speakership, with the presumption that Chamberlain would back him for the chair.[70] He was sorely tempted, but it was too obvious a bribe to rely on and he feared his 'majority is not sufficiently safe'.[71] He now had every hope, moreover, that he would get a plum job within the government.[72]

The fact that Crookshank did emerge as an open critic of the government was more by accident than design. Crookshank had, since his interview with the prime minister, come to see himself as something of a truth speaker, with a licence to criticise the government from within, especially over rearmament. When Rob Hudson, the Minister for Overseas Trade, whom he had known since they were both in the Diplomatic Service, started running down the Secretary of State for War, Leslie Hore-Belisha, it was too good an opportunity to miss.[73] Crookshank had long been jealous of his contemporary, Hore-Belisha, a socially awkward, self-publicizing Jewish Liberal. Belisha was an easy target, as he was reviled by most of his contemporaries. Cranborne thought a conversation between Lord Mansfield and Dr Johnson best summed him up. 'Mansfield: "Suppose we believe one HALF of what he tells." Johnson: "Aye; but we don't know WHICH half to believe. By his lying we lose not only our reverence for him, but all comfort in his conversation." '[74] Hudson had rounded up some office-holding peers and complained to Halifax about Hore-Belisha.[75] Although Crookshank had enjoyed denouncing Hore-Belisha in their company, he had not banked on Hudson telling Halifax that up to eight under-secretaries, including Crookshank, might resign if Belisha was not sacked.[76] Matters became even more embarrassing when Chamberlain called Crookshank in to tell him 'he had submitted me for a Privy Councillorship in the New Year's List'. This was 'gratifying but awkward', for 'everyone will think it is the price of silence'.[77] He was not too worried, though, as such gossip was confined to the Palace of Westminster.[78] Then, to his dismay, the story was leaked to the press.[79] His name was in public print as a rebel, one of the 'revolting under-secretaries'.[80] One by one they all, including Crookshank, had to write to Chamberlain dissociating themselves from the attack on Hore-Belisha, leaving Hudson to carry the can.[81] It was not a glorious episode. As Crookshank understood, they had probably retarded the cause of rearmament by making Chamberlain even more reluctant to get rid of under-performing ministers lest he appear to have had his hand forced.[82] Yet another demonstration of the pusillanimity of the young was hardly going to make Chamberlain or Halifax take any more notice of them.

By Christmas 1938 the Glamour Boys had serious problems. By dint of an excellent publicity machine, cajoling, bribery, threats and dirty tricks, Chamberlain was more firmly in control of the party than he had been the year before. Far from taking over the party, the best Eden could hope for was a future for himself in a government led by Lord Halifax.[83] Despite Cranborne's disquiet, Eden had the bit between his teeth about reconciliation.[84] Halifax and Stanley had both approached him about rejoining the Cabinet, 'with a view to a future combination by AE and H, the latter as PM and the former as Leader of the House of Commons'. 'AE,' recorded Oliver Harvey after dining with Eden, 'would like to work with H in such circumstances, and as preliminary and in order to ensure H's succession he would like to return soon after [the recognition of Franco's rule in] Spain has been cleared up.'

As all the Edenites except Eden seemed to realize, the real enemy was Chamberlain, who had no intention of letting Eden rejoin the government.[85] Eden continued to believe that Halifax's growing influence would overcome the prime minister's objections and pave the way for his own rehabilitation with honour intact.[86] Cranborne, on the eve of his departure for North Africa, tried to get Eden to face reality. It was very unlikely, he assured him, that they would be approached to re-enter the government. If they were, 'it would be most essential, first of all, to make sure that not only Edward and the younger members of the Cabinet but the PM himself had become "sound" as to the attitude both towards Italy and Germany'. His definition of 'sound' was much the same as the one he had used in his Munich speech: 'Appeasement must no longer be regarded as an alternative to Rearmament–Rearmament must be regarded as the preliminary – and the essential preliminary – to Appeasement.' He did not believe that the government was 'sound'. There were missions being dispatched to Berlin to explore 'economic appeasement'; there were hints 'of how nice it would be if we could reach some agreement which would make Rearmament unnecessary'. To him government policy still seemed 'on the face of it insane'. Eden must not even flirt with the idea of a compromise unless it was clear that Chamberlain had adopted Edenite foreign policy. This he just could not see happening.[87]

With this wise exhortation, Cranborne dragged his weak body on board ship for Morocco. Eden would not, however, leave the matter alone. Friends noticed that 'he kept referring to Cranborne, and he obviously relies on him a good deal'.[88] Letters awaited Cranborne's arrival in Marrakesh. Much as he admired and liked Eden, Cranborne was starting to become irritated with his importuning. Instead of his usual exhortations, he decided to engage in a little moral blackmail. Of course Eden must rejoin Chamberlain's government if he was perfectly happy with its policy. That was entirely his decision. Cranborne himself would 'personally find it very difficult to serve under him again'. Even if a new crisis in Czechoslovakia forced Chamberlain to adopt a more bellicose attitude towards Germany, that did not mean they could trust him. 'I should feel,' he warned Eden, 'all the time as if I were washing on a volcano.' 'In any decision which you have to take,' Cranborne sighed nobly, 'don't bother about me – if you feel that you can honestly and confidently go back go – Please don't think that any consideration of personal friendship should influence you in your decision.' Why should Eden accept his judgement anyway? 'You may think this all very high faluting and absurd . . . I am probably wrong, and, in any case, I am perfectly happy on the backbenches, which are indeed my proper sphere.' He had become a liability. 'I should think that you would find it very difficult to get them to accept so unrepentant and impertinent a sinner.'

It was grand stuff, heartfelt but putting subtle pressure on Eden's weak points. Cranborne had thrown away his career for him, stood by him, spoken up for him, but no, he should go ahead and seize the prize.[89] Since on the day Cranborne wrote this all the English papers carried stories, subsequently traced back to a briefing by Chamberlain, in which he had sought to uphold the triumph of Munich, it was good advice.[90] Eden could do little other than accept: 'Let me reassure you,' he wrote straight back, 'I have no intention of making any move of course.'[91]

Cranborne's advice was good, Eden was wise to accept it; but within a day it was out of date. By the time Cranborne had moved on to Tangier, Hitler had invaded Czechoslovakia. Since Chamberlain had claimed the Munich agreement as his personal triumph, its destruction weakened his position within the government. It seemed to Chamberlain's colleagues – in particular Edward Halifax – that they must do something. They feared that Hitler would move on from Czechoslovakia to seize Poland and oil-rich Romania. The result was security guarantees to the two threatened countries. These guarantees were to be given some credibility by the introduction of conscription in Britain. Thus in March and April 1939 British foreign policy lurched towards a confrontation with Germany.

Reading the reports of debates in the House, Cranborne came to the conclusion that Halifax was taking over the government. 'One can only hope that we have not left things too long and that Hitler may still be amenable to some counsels of reason and prudence. That seems now the only chance of avoiding a cataclysm and it is not judging by past experience a very large one.' Accordingly he released Eden from his moral bondage. 'I need not say that all I wrote to you from Marrakesh is now washed out – I have still very little confidence in Neville – but events have forced his hand with a vengeance and by the latest reports the Government is doing what we should wish ... I wanted you to know that the events of last week have completely altered my outlook as expressed in my last letter to you and that I now have a completely open mind as to the attitude which you or any of us should adopt.'[92]

Stuck in sickly exile in Tangier, Cranborne could hardly be expected to be the best informed or most acute observer of the political scene. His second thoughts let Eden off the hook. Eden's game was still to play footsie with Chamberlain and Halifax so as to get back into the Cabinet. He did not raise a fuss about the government's half-hearted attitude to introducing conscription. With Cranborne acquiescent, he was hardly about to take much note of Harold Macmillan's despair. Macmillan was 'enraged that Chamberlain should remain on'. 'He thinks,' Harold Nicolson recorded in his diary, 'that all we Edenites have been too soft and gentlemanlike. That we should have clamoured for Chamberlain's removal. That no man in history has made such persistent and bone-headed mistakes, and we shall go on pretending all is well.'[93]

By the time Cranborne had got back to Britain, the moment had been lost once more. Chamberlain had finally conceded that it was logical to have a Ministry of Supply to coordinate rearmament. Harry Crookshank hoped he would enter the Cabinet as minister of supply. If he had, even the most radical Edenites such as Macmillan would have been satisfied. The thought seems never to have crossed Chamberlain's mind. Crookshank was shunted off to become financial secretary to the Treasury.[94] In peace this would have been a plum job. Now it was an exquisitely calculated insult. He could hardly refuse such an appointment.[95] It brought him to the centre of government, but it was made just at the moment when the Treasury ceased to be central to planning for war.[96] To the vital job of minister of supply Chamberlain appointed Leslie Burgin, an Irish Liberal MP. The almost universal response was Leslie who? Cranborne took his appointment as evidence that Chamberlain was still determined to have yes-men in every position of influence in the government. His Tangerine optimism had been misplaced. There were 'all sorts of little indicators that Appeasement is in the air again'. Crookshank's old *bête noire*, the hopelessly pro-Nazi Nevile Henderson, had been dispatched back to the embassy in Berlin with warm words from Halifax. King George VI had sent birthday greetings to Hitler. Despite Italy's invasion of Albania, there was talk once more of recognizing her conquest of Abyssinia. 'If the PM rats again,' Cranborne warned, 'I am afraid he must be written off as hopeless.'[97]

Frustrated by his own helplessness, Cranborne began to lose faith in Eden's willpower.[98] Surveying the papers from his sickbed, 'he was a little sorry to see so little mention of Anthony in the various articles and letters in the various papers. It is Winston, Winston, Winston all the time.' 'Actually,' he consoled himself, 'if they took Winston, I suppose, they would have to take Anthony too.' But it was a slender consolation, for, 'my fear is that if Winston occupies so much the centre of the stage now, he will, should Edward ever succeed to the Premiership, have the reversion of the Leadership of the House of Commons; and much as I like and admire him, I cannot help feeling that for that job Anthony would be safer and better.' 'If only,' he lamented, 'Anthony had been a little more definite in what he said in the last few months, how much better it would be now.' Eden should have been a candidate for the premiership himself. A year previously he had told his friends that, although he was 'almost at one with Winston', he could not 'think in terms of having Winston in the Cabinet'. 'He would be overshadowed he feared.'[99] Now even the second place in the government was slipping from Eden's grasp. 'I really do feel,' Macmillan wrote to Cranborne, 'that if it comes to war, or even to another acute crisis, there will have to be a change ... It seems to me that, in spite of many difficulties, a Halifax government with Winston leading the Commons would be the way out.'[100] Joseph Ball's black propaganda machine was being turned ever more against Churchill. *Truth* even claimed that 'the glamour boys' were merely *Churchill's* 'courtiers'.[101]

Such was Cranborne's mounting sense of hopelessness that he even considered turning to his own father as a potential saviour.[102] Jim Salisbury was seventy-eight and nearly as ill as his son. He seemed to have lost much of the die-hard abrasiveness of former years, talking in 'calm and sedate fashion which contrasts with the staccato and abrupt conversations of old days'.[103] Indeed, his family worried that his self-abnegation had gone too far. Always prey to spiritual doubt, in 1935 he had become entangled with a guru, Frank Buchman, the leader of a cult known as the Oxford Group. The cult was based around house parties at which members told each other of their sins. By this means they claimed to establish direct contact with God, dispensing with the services of Jesus Christ as only mediator and advocate. Christ's presumptive replacement, Dr Buchman, was rumoured to be 'on the closest terms with Himmler in Germany'. In August 1936 he had publicly thanked heaven 'for a man like Adolf Hitler who built a front-line against the anti-Christ of Communism'.

The Oxford Group cultists sedulously used Salisbury as a cover for their activities. He even invited them to Hatfield to meet the 'great and the good'. Like most cults, the group sucked in adherents with kind words and then tried to break their will by the ruthless exploitation of their feelings of guilt and unworthiness, so ill-advisedly confided in the privacy of a religious meeting. By the

beginning of 1939, the cultists were taunting Salisbury for his supposed lack of commitment. Why, they demanded, was he not ensuring their access to influential politicians? Their supposed purpose
was world peace, although as Cranborne was to repeatedly observe,
their real desires were more worldly, such as passports for Dr Buchman's dubious friends or exemption from military service. It says
something for Cranborne's desperation that he was willing to turn
to an elderly man beset by this swarm of crypto-Nazi parasites.[104]
Even as he did so, he concluded it was a forlorn hope. 'I think he
is very unlikely to fall in with it.' 'For him to do so,' he explained
to Jim Thomas, 'would be to take a leading part in pressing the
Government. He could not well do this unless he was ready to go
much further in the matter, and his health is not good enough for
this.'[105] Cranborne sensed that the Edenites had missed their moment.
They could only act successfully if they brought in older men to give
'bottom' to their faction. It was a tacit admission by an ill man that
they had been too lightweight to make a difference. He was so dispirited that he even talked of leaving the House of Commons rather than
playing out the game that Chamberlain was so obviously winning.[106]

The irritation with Eden that he had felt in North Africa kept
flaring up. Eden was talking about 'going on the offensive'. Yet Eden
did not seem like a man in fine fighting fettle, but looked 'thin and
scraggy'.[107] What exactly, Cranborne asked, were the Edenites to be
offensive about now? They could have made an issue out of rearmament. But they had not. They could have made an issue of Chamberlain's personal fitness to lead. But they had not. Now, Cranborne
told Eden, 'I don't personally quite see what, at the present moment,
would be the grounds of your attack.' Hitler was threatening to seize
Danzig. Edward Halifax had reaffirmed Britain's commitment to
Poland in a speech at Chatham House. Chamberlain had done the
same in the House. They might suspect that Chamberlain would
'rat', but 'so far as the words go' both statements were 'entirely
satisfactory'. 'You could not even if you wished,' Cranborne wrote,
striking at the nub of the issue, 'attack them merely because they
have not put you in the government.' The best Eden could achieve,
'dangerous though it might be', was to steel himself mentally to

strike. 'The opportunity for you to speak out may come sooner than we think.'[108]

Having tried to ginger up Eden for so long, Cranborne was frankly incredulous when Eden suddenly panicked and swung from excessive caution to wild talk about creating another 'New Party'. All his attention was suddenly focused by a premonition that Chamberlain would call an election on the anniversary of Baldwin's victory in 1935.[109] Cranborne's response verged on the contemptuous. Eden had his priorities hideously wrong. There was going to be a war not a political campaign – 'talk of a General Election seems slightly academic'. In any case, he wearily pointed out, 'I am afraid that we have left things rather too late for this.' 'Had we meant to do this,' he observed quite correctly, 'we should have decided either before Munich, or directly after, between October and April – during the whole of that time we really did disagree with the line they were taking – but since then government policy has changed – guarantee to Poland and Conscription.' He continued his forensic dissection of their political failure. In his last speech, Cranborne reminded him, Eden had 'started by paying a tribute to the forthright nature of the PM's remarks'. 'How are we,' he inquired, 'now going to switch round and say that we do not trust the Cabinet and never have?' 'Nor have we,' he concluded, 'the make up for a new Party. It is true that we have a different outlook on things from that of the old gentlemen who now lead us, both abroad and at home. But we have not formulated this difference – we could not define it.'[110] A display of naked ambition on the eve of war was hardly a recipe for political success.

And thus matters rested on 3 September 1939. As Britain stumbled into the war its politicians had fought so long to avoid, the three political members of the quartet found themselves completely stymied. Cranborne was 'still in the doctor's hands and he will not allow me to do anything'.[111] In December 1939 he started, cautiously, to come to London.[112] He even managed to attend a meeting of the Eden group.[113] In the New Year, however, he suffered a relapse, struck down with an influenza-jaundice combination. His mind was sound but his body simply would not function. The contrast with Harold

Macmillan was striking. Ever since he had joined the Edenites, Macmillan had positively fizzed with energy. 'It was rather sad,' Macmillan commiserated with Alice Salisbury after a visit to Hatfield, 'to see poor Bobbety in such discomfort, but I felt that, in himself, he was better, with great mental grasp of affairs and was morally on top of his illness. This is so often more important than the day to day symptoms, I do hope that he will soon make a real recovery.' It had come to something when one's best chance of political gossip occurred when Harold Macmillan managed to 'scrape an evening off somehow'.[114]

When war was declared, Chamberlain was concerned to neutralize any possible challenges to his leadership. Winston Churchill was thus brought into the Cabinet as First Lord of the Admiralty. Anthony Eden also accepted ministerial office as dominions secretary. The difference was telling. Churchill was catapulted to the heart of the war effort, Eden was put in a job where he could have little influence. That he was willing to accept this says much for his patriotism. The return to government was something he had longed for almost from the moment he resigned. His friends found this mixture of self-abnegation and ambition hard to accept.[115] His small band of parliamentary supporters appointed Leo Amery to lead them. The Amery group was merely the Edenites sailing under a flag of convenience. Yet when the Amery group met with their erstwhile leader, they found him too 'discreet'.[116] 'Office changes one's attitude,' wrote one of their number, Dick Law, the son of the former Tory prime minister Bonar Law. 'I don't mean that his personal attitude is changed or that he thinks that everything is perfect, but obviously he doesn't take so gloomy a view of the situation as some of us do. And he takes what I would call a defeatist attitude not about the war but about the old men. I fancy he thinks that death will provide the only release.'[117] 'The Group dinner was rather flat,' another member, Jubie Lancaster, reported directly to Cranborne. 'Somehow or other Anthony is so fair-minded (or senselessly loyal) about his colleagues that his presence seems to deaden any constructive criticism.' What he said to his loyal and devoted followers who had risked their careers for him 'didn't differ unduly from what he might have told the 1922 Committee'. 'We miss you,' Lancaster concluded. 'Everyone asked after you and you'd have blushed if you'd heard all the nice things Harold said about you.'[118] His friends thought Eden was shamefully and unwisely neglecting Bobbety.[119] They begged Cranborne to come to the meeting to stiffen his backbone once more. 'Alas and Alack,' was all he could say in return. 'I am not yet fit enough for the House of Commons. Indeed the doctors will not hear of me going back for another two months as I am still very jaundiced and as well have managed to acquire other infections.'[120]

Crookshank was equally impotent. His diary entries either side of the declaration of war told the story: 'didn't go to the Treasury as not wanted. I daresay I am the only minister who has nothing to do'; 'Absolutely no work! I seem to have got the sinecure office'; 'Another dull, stupid and pointless day. In the Office morning and afternoon. This is just a sinecure with £2,000 a year and I feel ashamed.'[121] He found the Chancellor, Sir John Simon, 'almost as difficult a chief to work for as Oliver Stanley'. Simon never consulted him. '[Crookshank] never knows,' observed Cuthbert Headlam, 'until the last minute what he is expected to do and when he has to make a speech.'[122] He spent most of his energies on hating Leslie Hore-Belisha and wishing he could have his job as secretary of war.[123] Belisha was dismissed when he challenged the authority of 'Fat Boy' Gort, the Grenadier general who commanded the British Expeditionary Force to Europe. When Hore-Belisha ran foul of the Grenadiers, Crookshank did not hesitate to spread bile about him. He could, however, claim little credit for the fall engineered by his former comrades-in-arms.[124] It was, perhaps, poetic justice that, when Belisha was sacked in January 1940, the job should go to, of all people, Oliver Stanley.[125] Crookshank realized too late that he had sold his birthright for a mess of potage.[126] Before the war broke out, he had been seen as a key figure in any reconstruction of the government along Edenite lines. Now he was only seen as important by blowhards.[127]

The only one of the Guardsmen for whom the outbreak of war brought a firm sense of mission was Oliver Lyttelton. As soon as British rearmament started to take its first stuttering steps, industrialists had sought to remind officials of the lessons that had been learnt about the supply of raw materials during the Great War.[128] 'Had adequate arrangements been in existence in 1914,' a delegation told the Board of Trade, 'millions of pounds would have been saved if immediate action had been taken and [the] system of buying by tender abrogated.' By 1936 Lyttelton was making the running on this issue. In the summer of that year he tried to broker a cartel in zinc. In order to force the Canadians into the cartel he approached the Minister for Defence Coordination and persuaded him that a minimum British production of zinc was vital for national security. This manoeuvre caused great controversy in the industry. Many accused Lyttelton of using the national security argument to further the interests of the companies of which he was a director.[129] Unabashed, he continued his campaign. In the spring of 1937 his position as the government's chief adviser on non-ferrous metals was formalized.[130]

The government, he said, would be criminally negligent to ignore the lessons of the past. Speculation in copper had caused its price to more than double between September 1915 and February 1916. Even then, attempts to control dealing had been largely ineffectual until state control was imposed in January 1917. 'State purchase and ownership from the outset of the emergency,' he urged, 'would be the most effective way of preventing a repetition of this exercise.' He had a plan to avoid this problem. In the event of war BMC would transform itself into an arm of the state and control the non-ferrous metals trade on the government's behalf. This was a play to become the czar of the industry and was recognized as such. The Board of Trade acknowledged that the idea had practical merit but refused to act on it immediately.[131] Civil servants were equally suspicious of his plan for the government to buy up the entire tin-smelter output of Malaya, in which he had a substantial financial interest.[132] Lyttelton's behind-the-scenes dealings with the government were potential political dynamite in two ways. First, they invited accusations of profiteering by the government's official adviser. Secondly, they revealed potential profiteering by the commercial interests Lyttelton was linked with in the Empire.[133]

Even after Munich all Lyttelton was empowered to do, and then somewhat vaguely, by the Board of Trade and the Colonial Office was 'to make some routine soundings' about the purchase of Australian lead and zinc and North Rhodesian copper in wartime.[134] He, of course, regarded these cautious officials as pettifogging bureaucrats. Accordingly he resolved to make an end run around them. The creation of the Ministry of Supply offered the opportunity he needed. Leslie Burgin seemed to be a weak man whom he could bully. In July 1939, both he and Burgin were invited to lunch at the home of Lord Horne, the former chancellor of the exchequer and banker in front of whom Lyttelton had first made his corporate mark in 1920. 'I went to luncheon unprepared for [a] cross-examination,' reported a somewhat shell-shocked Burgin. Mr Lyttelton 'proceeded unblushingly to use the luncheon interval for a detailed technical discussion of each of the substances in which he or his organizations were primarily interested. These were Copper, Lead, Zink [sic], Tin with a few cursory references to Wolfram, Tungsten and Vanadium.' Dutifully Burgin attempted to summarize the torrent of information and opinion that had cascaded over him for his civil servants. Lyttelton had suggested 'definite contracts now with South Africa and Canada for Copper, Australia for Zinc, and Malaya and Burma for Tin. He quoted the ruling prices of these metals and thought in each case the producers would in return for contracts to take the entire output be prepared to sell at existing (today's) prices.' Lyttelton was 'very scathing of War Office methods of buying, which he described as an approach to marine store dealers for taking small quantities off the shelf'.[135]

Lyttelton was taking a risk in throwing his weight around so much. It was not just politicians who felt the lash of his tongue. He made quite clear to others in the business that when war came he would be in charge, so they had better start doing what he said now. As a result a 'stop Lyttelton' campaign started to gain momentum on the eve of conflict. It was only nipped in the bud by war's very proximity. By being so active in the two years before the war, Lyttelton had made himself indispensable. Although his plan to put BMC in control of all non-ferrous metals had met with little initial enthusiasm, it was the only practical scheme anyone had put forward.[136] From their dealings with him, civil servants had little doubt that he would wreak his revenge if balked. 'It may be safely assumed,' concluded a last-minute review, 'that if Captain Lyttelton was now told that it was proposed to find some other and more suitable candidate for the post of Controller-designate he would at once cancel the arrangement for BMC as the nucleus of control ... it would then be necessary to build up an *ad hoc* organization which in any case would not be entirely satisfactory unless it could draw on the experience and staff of the Corporation ... not only would the progress of preparation ... be seriously retarded but much of the ground already travelled would have to be traversed.'

Lyttelton had them over a barrel. The Ministry of Supply did not believe he would take the line of patriotic self-abnegation. Since they had already issued an edict for the control of non-ferrous metals, they needed a controller.[137] The most they could do was utter 'a word in season to Captain Lyttelton from the Minister who might stress the desirability of using more tact'. Lyttelton had to be given the freedom to sew up the mineral resources of the Empire with bulk contracts.[138] Lyttelton led most of BMC down to Rugby, where he established the Control for Non-ferrous Metals.[139] Entertaining the Minister of Transport, Euan Wallace, to a slap-up lunch at the Savoy, he made no secret of his satisfaction that, in the end, the government had needed him more than he had needed the government. They had had to agree to all his terms. His staff got a free weekend rail ticket on one weekend in three, whereas the regular civil servants who had got in his way only got two a year.[140] A petty triumph but a sweet one.

While Lyttelton rose through his own efforts, his friends struggled to find patrons to advance their careers. Paradoxically, Macmillan and Cranborne's prospects were actually improved by Anthony Eden's humiliating entry into the government. Their best chance came when they served under older leaders with more strength of purpose and grasp of political tactics.[141] Indeed, it was Leo Amery who gave Harold Macmillan his first big break. Amery was put in charge of a government committee on aid to Finland, invaded by the Russians in November 1939. He asked Macmillan to accompany a Liberal peer, Lord Davies, on a fact-finding mission. Finland was a hot political issue. As Cranborne remarked, 'I am quite sure that if we pluck up our courage and say what we really think about this disreputable Finnish business we shall never regret it.'[142] Macmillan was determined to make his mark. He did so in two ways. First he kept a diary, a very funny and moving diary. A great deal of time was spent on comic 'business' at the expense of Davies, who was guyed as a bumbling idiot, always delaying the party by losing his false teeth. The diary darkly evoked also the frozen awfulness of the Winter War, the courage of the Finns, fighting 'not one Thermopylae, but Thermopylae every day', and the pusillanimity of those in Britain who had let them down. Macmillan had spent the 1930s writing boring books, vanity publications that few people read and even fewer understood. Now he found his *métier*. His diary achieved a studied spontaneity that always escaped him in his published writing. In person his wit was elephantine.[143] In his diary, however, he achieved a bleak but entertaining humour. Macmillan kept his Finnish diary to get himself noticed. As soon as he returned to England he was distributing copies. The success of this manoeuvre could be measured by the irritation it caused among those who were made to look ill-informed and incompetent. Oliver Stanley wrote to Macmillan in high dudgeon, having had the shortcomings of his War Office pointed out in Cabinet by Lord Halifax with quotations from Macmillan's diary.[144]

The second string to Macmillan's bow was more conventional: a speech in the House as a man with 'hands-on' experience castigating the stay-at-home do-nothings in the government. He was sorry, he said, that he had to speak at all. 'I should have preferred,' he told the House, 'that this discussion had been held in private.' He did not mention that thanks to his diary he was having his cake and eating it. Chamberlain had assured the House and the public that Britain had supplied the Finns with all the *matériel* for which they had asked. This was untrue. He had been there. He had seen their pitiful lack of weapons. The prime minister, he implied, was lying through his teeth. Stung, Chamberlain himself tried to intervene, but Macmillan swept on. The Finns had certainly asked, just as certainly they had not received. Government backbenchers called out points of order: he was giving away military secrets. Undeterred he pushed on to his peroration. The Finnish débâcle had thrown a 'piercing light on the present machinery and method of government. The delay, the vacillation, changes of front, standing on one foot one day and on the other the other before a decision is given.' The government was feeble.[145]

It was a good speech. 'Harold made a devastating attack,' Crookshank wrote admiringly of his friend.[146] Amery was pleased with the result. Macmillan had stated the case 'skilfully and moderately'.[147] A 'fine attacking speech,' echoed another of the group's members, Harold Nicolson.[148] Dick Law was even more in raptures: 'I still don't understand why Harold didn't bring down the government. Perhaps he has done so and we shall become aware of it soon.' Macmillan was a great example to them all. Even if he had not struck the killer blow, Law was 'sure we ought to continue. The more we weaken the government the more, I honestly believe, we strengthen England.'[149] This was heady stuff from the firebrand son of a former Conservative prime minister. Although government supporters dismissed Macmillan as 'irritable and irritating', he had made the kind of impression that had eluded him in the 1930s.[150] Macmillan now had allies to cheer him on. People were beginning to back Macmillan for office in the first time for a decade.[151]

Macmillan was rising in the Amery group's estimation. The Amery group was, however, diminishing in Cranborne's estimation. A futile meeting with Anthony Eden on 3 April 1940 was the final straw. In the brief weeks in December 1939 and January 1940 when he was well enough to come to London to attend the group's meetings, he adumbrated the way forward. 'A very small committee should be created of very respectable Conservatives.' Amery would represent the group's interests on the committee. It was that 'respectable' committee that would 'exercise pressure on the Cabinet'.[152] This was a Cecil plan rather than an Edenite plan. Although Cranborne's own health collapsed once more, and he was forced to return to the country, his father took over responsibility.

The organization that Salisbury created, which became known as the Watching Committee, was run entirely on Cecil lines.[153] It had three models: the Unionist Business Committee that had plotted to dethrone Asquith in 1916, Salisbury's Unionist War Committee that had kept up a torrent of criticism of Lloyd George between 1916 and 1918, and the organization Salisbury had created to oppose the India Bill between 1931 and 1935. The last of these campaigns had the inestimable advantage of forming a bond between Salisbury and Winston Churchill.[154] These three models had one thing in common. Each was designed to fight a war of attrition. The drip, drip of criticism would wear down the opponent, or at least keep him up to the mark in performing his duties. The fact that the Chamberlain government was destroyed within six weeks gives a misleading impression in retrospect. In April 1940 the Cecils were digging in for a long struggle. The Watching Committee was entirely their creation. It was based at their house, 21 Arlington Street. It was the antithesis of the 'glamour boys'. Men did not choose to join, they were invited to join. Cranborne's cousin Top Wolmer was charged with selecting men from the House of Commons. A number of Edenites were invited on to the committee, but by no means all. The few who were chosen, in particular Harold Macmillan and Paul Evans, were already close to the Cecils as well as having energy and useful organizational skills.

The committee was in fact run by its older members. Membership was made up of both Houses of Parliament, with the House of Lords dominating. In a further inversion, Cranborne, unable to attend meetings, acted as his father's confidential adviser rather than vice versa. The committee was not a pro-Eden body. Eden was not consulted about its formation, was kept in ignorance of its operation and was irrelevant to its plans. Cranborne had lost none of his affection for Eden. His family, on the other hand, was convinced that it was he who had made Eden tick. 'People didn't absolutely realize,' his sister fretted, 'he wouldn't have been half the man he was if you hadn't been there to counsel and to advise.'[155] The committee met for the first time on 4 April 1940. Within a week Hitler had launched his campaign to seize Scandinavia.

The Watching Committee was committed to the destruction of Neville Chamberlain. Salisbury went to see Chamberlain on 10 April to demand the formation of a War Cabinet made up of sound men and the more vigorous prosecution of the war. Chamberlain fobbed him off, seeming 'not in the least minded to consider the idea of a real War Cabinet or indeed that things wanted conducting with greater vigour and sense of time'.[156] When Salisbury raised the idea of 'unleashing' Bomber Command on Germany, 'he of course', Salisbury briefed his son, 'gave himself away: he showed that his conception was, as it were, limited to the question whose fault it was, whereas the real question, of course, is what their reaction is, especially upon the Credit and prestige of this country and the confidence we inspire elsewhere. Birmingham politics, in fact.'[157] Chamberlain might be contemptible, but his overthrow was regarded as a long-term goal. In Salisbury and Cranborne's conception the Watching Committee was a 'pretty formidable body', but as Cranborne wrote to its secretary, 'I am afraid it will have to exert itself to the utmost if it is to [affect] the PM, who seems quite convinced that, like the Pope, he is infallible.' 'The only thing that is likely to shake him,' Cranborne thought, 'is signs of rumbling within his own Cabinet, and he has, alas!, got rid of most of the potential rumblers – however, the burden he is putting on members of the Cabinet who have departments is now so terrific that they may crack under the strain, and this would force his hand.'[158]

If the committee could show it had better ways of fighting the war, it could expose Chamberlain as an unworthy national leader. Once this was achieved, it could put forward an alternative leader. They were all agreed on the need for a War Cabinet. Cranborne urged that they should lay aside their scruples and endorse a plan drawn up by 'the father of the RAF', 'Boom' Trenchard, for an all-out air offensive against Germany.[159] 'There,' he encouraged his father, 'we can act against Germany directly: and no doubt a formidable air offensive against German military targets would have a profound effect in neutral countries, who now are only influenced by determined and successful use of military force.'[160] The two possible alternative prime ministers were Halifax or Churchill, neither of whom the Cecils regarded with wild enthusiasm.[161] On the evening of 19 April, Salisbury hobbled along to see Churchill at the Admiralty.

His mission was to persuade him to give up the Royal Navy in order to become minister of defence coordination.[162] It was not a successful interview. Not only did Churchill not want to give up his beloved Admiralty, but Salisbury could not even get him to focus on the issue. 'The fact was,' he reported back to Cranborne, 'that whether by temperamental idiosyncrasy or by design nearly the whole of an hour's conversation was taken up with elaborate statistical details.' 'Frankly,' he complained, 'I was disappointed. No doubt had I been a little less tired I should have pressed him more closely, but he seemed to me rather to have lost his grip on the broad aspects of the War.'[163] Churchill did not want to entertain the Watching Committee's ideas, lest by giving up the Admiralty he became a 'mere busybody'. Nevertheless, once Salisbury had recited the names of the Watching Committee, Churchill immediately saw that he could turn their support to his advantage.[164] He certainly latched on to Salisbury's suggestion that he should be put in charge of the Chiefs of Staff, immediately marching in to Chamberlain to demand that very power, citing Salisbury and 'fifty people' who were backing him.[165]

The Watching Committee had initially assumed that Edward Halifax would be a more suitable premier than Churchill. As the days passed many of them began to have doubts. It was Halifax's attempts to keep Italy out of the war that turned Cranborne against him. His decisions were 'idiotic', appeasement 'in its most vicious form'.[166] Salisbury led a delegation to a 'tired and distressed' Halifax on 29 April and they all came away with an even worse impression of him than Salisbury had had of Churchill. 'He understands the dangers of the position,' Paul Evans informed Cranborne, 'but does not seem to have any ideas for dealing with it. Harold Macmillan said afterwards it all reminded him of a dinner at All Souls.'[167] The committee decided 'that a strong demand should be made for a really National Government in the hope that any attempt to form one will mean the elimination of the Prime Minister and his immediate advisers'.

In the wake of this meeting, support for Churchill grew strongly among committee members.[168] Lord Salisbury, however, continued to have qualms about Churchill. 'An interim government under Halifax,' Emrys-Evans reported, 'would allow a possible leader to come to the fore . . . as he is not vindictive and probably realizes his own limitations. The war could not be won by him, but he may find the man.' Since the 'man' self-evidently could not be found in the present leadership, this passage has been read to suggest that Salisbury was attracted by the possibility of grooming his own son for the leadership. It seems unlikely, given not only Cranborne's present infirmity but his history of breakdowns. Cranborne himself continued to deprecate the idea of Halifax as a leader.[169]

Indeed, having set up the Watching Committee as an organization predicated on Fabian tactics, Salisbury and Cranborne were as thrown off balance as the government by the defeat of the British Expeditionary Force sent to oppose the German invasion of Norway.[170] Cranborne was not even able keep fully apprised of the latest developments, relying as he did on the press and the reports sent down by his father and Emrys-Evans. 'I feel, down here, so remote and out of touch with events,' he confessed.[171] But a crisis was most obviously at hand. Lord Salisbury left his report to his son for 2 May uncompleted, instead writing in his own hand, 'I broke off here because the truth is things are so very bad I hardly like to dictate any more. We have come across some very grave scandals.' In particular it looked as if Oliver Stanley's War Office and Leslie Burgin's Ministry of Supply had messed up the provision of tanks to the army. Salisbury gave the task of investigating further to Harold Macmillan. 'The whole look is of a tottering government,' he told his son. 'My spot . . . is that Neville . . . will not survive further information.' Cranborne's friends urged him to come to London to be in at the kill.[172] A full-scale debate on the Norwegian disaster was scheduled. Although Cranborne knew only too well the vital importance of the debate, he simply could not drag himself to town.[173] He was stuck, unable to influence events any further.[174]

Cranborne was out of it and Crookshank a passive observer as these events moved rapidly to a conclusion.[175] Chamberlain failed to put up a convincing case for British failure in Norway. Leo Amery thundered out his devastating Cromwellian injunction: 'In the Name of God, go!' The Watching Committee was overtaken by the developing situation. At eleven o'clock on the morning of 8 May 1940 they convened at Arlington Street. Salisbury was still obsessed with the view that Churchill should not combine the roles of First Lord of the Admiralty and defence supremo.[176] He was due to thunder out a philippic on the subject in the House of Lords that afternoon. In the meantime he tried to restrain his Young Turks. If a division was called, they should abstain, not vote against the government. Sure and steady, he argued, would get the job done. This was unrealistic. When members of the Watching Committee reached Parliament they found it in ferment.[177] Chamberlain was destroyed not in the West End but in the fjords of Norway. Disgust that artillery had not fired a shot due to lack of ammunition, and that the wounded had not been treated due to lack of medical supplies, was the final straw.[178] Those Conservative MPs who were also serving officers in the armed forces were now out for his blood.[179] Their discontent infected and emboldened all the other malcontents.[180] Chamberlain won the vote but his position was untenable. As Crookshank, who had trooped loyally into Chamberlain's lobby, remarked, 'it was foolish to have a division forced by Labour, the vote was 281 to 200. One is always sorry for the chap when it happens, but it is a very good thing.'[181]

One man who could not conceal his joy was Harold Macmillan. As Cranborne lay on his sick-bed in Dorset and Crookshank sat sulkily in Pont Street, Macmillan rushed to and fro with tireless energy, stirring up opposition to Chamberlain. As the tellers announced the result of the vote, his excitement burst out in a failed attempt to rally the House in a chorus of 'Rule Britannia'. 'I felt quite unable to go into the Lobby afterwards,' wrote the loyal Chamberlainite Euan Wallace, who twenty years before had been another of Devonshire's ADCs in Canada, 'as I felt certain that I should have struck Harold Macmillan.'[182] Macmillan was still an ass, but he was, at last, an ass on the winning side.

As the implications of the vote of 8 May began to sink in, for all the participants the game was far from over. Chamberlain tried every trick he knew to stay on. At 9.30 on Friday morning, 9 May, the Watching Committee convened once more in Arlington Street.

They were all agreed that Chamberlain had to go. They had no firm line on whether Halifax or Churchill was to replace him.[183] Unbeknown to them, they were already too late. As a 'moderate and distressed' Salisbury shuffled off to tell Halifax of their conclusions, Halifax had made up his own mind.[184] At 10.15 he saw Chamberlain and told him he did not think he was the right man for the job. He repeated his conviction when he and Churchill saw Chamberlain together at 4.30.[185]

The next day they all awoke to the news that Germany had invaded Holland and Belgium. In the bizarre atmosphere of Westminster, this news seemed rather a remote problem. Crookshank wins the prize for the most parochial diary entry on this momentous day. 'I never liked him,' he wrote of Chamberlain, 'I find it hard to forgive his never mentioning coal to me in two years.'[186] It was more pressing to get Chamberlain out and the 'right people' in than to think about the war. This latter issue of the 'right people' was so pressing that even Cranborne reappeared on the scene. On Saturday morning, 10 May, the Watchers convened once again. They agreed that Chamberlain should be expelled from the Cabinet. Salisbury was to tell Churchill this.[187] Unfortunately they were once again behind events. Churchill had already agreed with Chamberlain that he *could* remain in the Cabinet.

All the rebels were terrified lest Churchill agreed to a 'Whips' Government'. He would take the premiership with the support of the existing *apparat*, leaving them out in the cold. That night Salisbury did not return to Hatfield, but went in the opposite direction to stay with his son at Cranborne.[188] They both knew that Salisbury was the stop-gap Cecil. All his life he had been an effective spoiler, but he would never be asked to join the Cabinet. If a Cecil was to emerge under the new regime, it had to be Cranborne. On Sunday morning Macmillan started ringing round other members of the committee with the news that Churchill and Chamberlain had done a deal. The Secretary of the Committee telephoned down these concerns to Cranborne.[189] Bobbety got on the telephone to Leo Amery to find out what was happening. Amery told him that his father had to get to Churchill. Salisbury phoned Churchill at the Admiralty:

'Chamberlain must go ... No Whips' Government,' he urged him.

Churchill never had any intention of selling out to the *apparat*. He knew they regarded him, in Rab Butler's words, as a 'half-breed American', 'the greatest adventurer of modern political history', and his followers as a 'rabble'.[190] To throw his lot in entirely with such hate-filled and treacherous allies would have been political suicide and he was too wily a bird for that. Instead he negotiated with the Labour party to join his government.[191] By Sunday evening Macmillan was telling his friends that 'after a hard day of negotiation it looked as if a satisfactory government would emerge'.[192] Churchill had requited his promise to Chamberlain to keep him in the Cabinet, but had ensured he would have no power. This was not clear to the Cecils at the time. Salisbury insisted on having lunch with Churchill the next day and bringing Cranborne with him.

Cranborne had his father urge his case on Churchill. Macmillan had no such patron. He desperately needed someone with access to Churchill to make sure his name was not forgotten, having no pull with the latter himself. It says something for their lack of intimacy that, at the beginning of the war, he had unsuccessfully tapped him for a job in the Ministry of Economic Warfare through the unappealing medium of Bob Boothby.[193] Now he turned to Leo Amery, flattering him and telling him he should be Churchill's defence supremo.[194] Amery was not the perfect patron. Although he and Churchill were friends, they had a prickly relationship stretching back to their schooldays at Harrow: rumour was unsure whether Amery had thrashed Churchill or vice versa. Churchill had no intention of giving Amery a central role. He was, however, the only entrée Macmillan had. Luckily it was enough. Two days after Salisbury and Cranborne were granted an audience, Amery got in to see Churchill. He spent much of his interview 'urging the claims of Macmillan and others of my young men'. They were in: Churchill was going to make Cranborne Paymaster General and find something for Macmillan.[195]

They were in, but it wasn't much. Of necessity Cranborne's job was a sinecure, since he was not well enough to do any work. 'Thank you,' his note of gratitude to Churchill read, 'for your great thoughtfulness in finding for me a job suited to my present decrepit state.'[196]

Macmillan was parliamentary secretary to the Ministry of Supply, a junior post but sensible in the light of his reputation for being able to grind through detail. Crookshank had no patron. He simply had to sweat it out.[197] It was two days later that Crookshank was sent for with the other dregs and brusquely told he would keep his job at the Treasury.[198] Macmillan had some cause to be satisfied; he was in government at long last. Cranborne and Crookshank were grimly relieved. They had played for high stakes and lost. They would have been among the leaders of an Eden government. As it turned out, they had sneaked into the new Churchillian regime by the skin of their teeth.

6

Churchillians

The events of May 1940 turned the political world turned upside down. No Tory politician in his forties had made career decisions on the basis that Churchill would become prime minister. As a result very few had a well-defined relationship with him. No serious pre-war politician was a Churchillian. Churchill's praetorian guard was therefore a rag-tag and bobtail of outsiders and amateurs: the Canadian press baron Max Beaverbrook, who had been Andrew Bonar Law's political fixer in the Great War but had tried to encompass Stanley Baldwin's overthrow, the Irishman Brendan Bracken, a former schoolmaster-turned-successful City press lord, Duncan Sandys, a young diplomat-turned-soldier who was Churchill's son-in-law, the German Frederick Lindemann, 'the Prof', an Oxford science don whose political career had comprised a failure to be elected for one of the university seats in 1937. With such exiguous support Churchill had been unable to make much headway before the war.

In May 1940, however, not only did he become prime minister but the prime minister's powers were greatly enhanced. Churchill created for himself the post of Minister of Defence. Churchill was forever quoting Napoleon's maxim that constitutions should be short and obscure. The powers wielded by the prime minister were an accretion of custom, those by the Minister of Defence, Churchill's invention. Their exact limits were indeed obscure, but their meaning could with ease have been written on the back of a postage stamp: 'I'm in charge.' Thus Churchill could augment his tiny personal following with the large and expanding personnel of the state: civil servants, professional and temporary; military officers, professional and temporary.

Churchill's power was extensive, but at first fragile. The bulk of his own party had only reluctantly accepted him as premier, he had not even been the leader of most of the outspoken anti-Chamberlainites. The key aspect of his political position was that he was one of the few Tory politicians acceptable to the Labour party and through them to organized labour. Yet for the Labourites too he was in office only because all other candidates were even worse. They had had great hopes of the cancelled 1940 election. Until the summer of 1942, many at Westminster doubted whether Churchill could hold his coalition together until the end of the war. Britain, after all, suffered defeat after defeat under his leadership in France, the Balkans, the Far East and in North Africa. His dominance seemed to rest upon negative rather than positive factors. There were no other credible leaders. Halifax had already sold the pass. Eden had the right anti-appeasement credentials, but he had managed to convince many that he was a weakling. The Labour alternative was hobbled by the fact that all their leaders, Ernest Bevin, Herbert Morrison, Hugh Dalton, thought that they could do a better job than the actual leader, Clement Attlee. In 1941 and 1942 the star of 'non-party' leaders rose briefly: Beaverbrook and Sir Stafford Cripps, the communist sympathizer who had been expelled from the Labour party in 1939. The fact that such 'cranks' could ever be thought of as national leaders was as good a testimony as any to the dearth of talent available.

Because he had been at the game so long, Churchill's knowledge of politics and politicians was virtually unrivalled. As a result his cynicism about politics and politicians was also unrivalled. He trusted neither their loyalty nor their competence. He had no intention of diffusing his own power. He had every intention of dividing and ruling. The circumstances of wartime coalition government gave him ceaseless opportunities for doing so. Ministers went in fear of him. He could dismiss them and they could never complain or create an effective cabal against him: to do so could all too easily be portrayed as unpatriotic. Voices of outright opposition in the House of Commons were in a tiny majority. In war potential rabble-rousers, of left or right, could be gagged or even imprisoned in the interests of national security. Others could be bought off. Churchill could combine ministers of all parties and none. Industrialists, shop-owners and civil servants were as likely to become ministers as politicians. Nearly everyone beyond his tiny political circle was dispensable. Churchill distrusted both the Chamberlainites and the Edenites: he wanted to ballast his Cabinet with technocrats. Indeed, one of the chief beneficiaries of this policy was Oliver Lyttelton. Almost by definition most technocrats were grey figures. When Lyttelton had bullied his way into a controllership, bruised civil servants had taken some comfort in the fact that many industrialists were well in front of him in the queue for preferment. But Lyttelton was a technocrat who was far from grey, and he was an old friend and comrade-in-arms of Churchill to boot.

Conservatives could not rely on Churchill's support. The lot of the individual Tory of ambition was fear of the purge. The lot of the Conservative party as a corporate body was prime ministerial indifference. Churchill could find interest in any aspect of warmaking. He could find interest in few aspects of party policy beyond those that acted on the stability of the governing coalition. For Conservative politicians there was thus little to be gained by politicking. They either played Churchill's game and submitted themselves to becoming cogs in the imperial war machine or they were ignored. Reluctantly or not, most Conservatives followed Churchill's lead and gave themselves over to the war effort. The vacuum thus created was sedulously filled by members of the Labour party fired by the belief that winning the peace was as important as winning the war. One hundred and fifty-four Conservative MPs served in the armed forces during the war, one third of the parliamentary party; fourteen Labour MPs joined up, a mere one tenth of its parliamentary party.[1] Churchill was a great warlord; he was also an appalling party leader. In March 1941 he frankly told the party's activists that, 'National unity requires sacrifices from all parties, and no party sacrificed more than the Conservative Party with its huge parliamentary majority. Many eminent men have had their careers interrupted, many ministers of promise their prospects obscured'.[2]

Whether any Tory politician had a 'good war' or a 'bad war' depended almost entirely on his personal relationship with Churchill and his entourage. This was most certainly the case as far as Cranborne, Crookshank, Lyttelton and Macmillan were concerned. There was a direct correlation between their relationship with Churchill and how far their careers prospered. Cranborne and Crookshank, potentially major political figures in 1939 and 1940, were doomed to a bad war. The story of the war is the story of the meteoric rise of Macmillan and Lyttelton. They were nowhere in 1940 – Lyttelton was not even an MP – but they were two of the most important figures in the party by 1945. In fact their lack of any independent political position became a recommendation rather than a disqualification. They were Churchill's men entirely.

As a result of a sharp Churchillian lesson that almost ended his career, it was Macmillan who was the first to understand how profoundly politics had changed. In the weeks following Churchill's elevation, Macmillan was 'rather excited and convinced that we ought to have an immediate revolution from below to sweep away the whole old governing powers'. He believed that if the new junior ministers acted in concert, Churchill would take them seriously. In other words he wanted to form a 'ginger group'. On 17 June 1940 he and his then patron, Leo Amery, drew up a three-point programme to be presented to Churchill. The organization of the government, they believed, was weak. The make-up of the War Cabinet was wrong. Churchill should appoint some 'strong men' not ciphers to run things. These War Cabinet 'strong men' should no longer coordinate other ministers, they should command them as of right. Ministers themselves should have a free hand to hire and fire whomsoever they wanted in their departments; they should not have to accept the civil servants they were given. Macmillan rounded up four other young radicals to meet with their 'elders', first at Amery's house, then at White's, and finally in Lloyd George's office. It was rather like one of Macmillan's Popular Front meetings: Macmillan and Boothby were joined by the Liberals, Arthur Salter, Clem Davies and Thomas Horabin.

At White's Jim Salisbury warned them that they were deluding themselves. When Duff Cooper was invited to join them, he gave the matter thirty seconds' thought and ran away lest he be tarred with the brush of disloyalty.[3] Many of those at the meeting suspected that he had been so worried at the thought of being labelled a plotter that he purloined a copy of the Amery–Macmillan memorandum and delivered it straight to Churchill. Churchill certainly knew something was going on when he interviewed Amery the next day. Churchill could not have been more brutally clear. Junior ministers should hold their tongues: 'their business was to stick to the job that he had given them. If anyone in the Government wished to criticize its working or its composition they should resign and criticize from the outside.' He needed the Labour party's leaders much more than them. For that matter, he still needed the Conservative party's old leaders more than them. They had hit, as Crookshank was subsequently able to tell Macmillan, on a particularly sore point. Lord Beaverbrook too was pressing Churchill to form a Cabinet of 'strong men'.[4] Given that Marshal Pétain had taken over the French government and was in the process of surrendering it to the Germans, Churchill had rather more pressing problems than a few has-beens and never-had-beens chewing the seditious cud at White's. He most certainly did not wish to spook the leaders of his fragile coalition at such a difficult moment by seeming to take seriously the ideas of hotheads. 'They had better all resign themselves for the time being to doing their work,' a chastened Amery told his young men.[5]

It was a message that Macmillan took to heart and learnt well. A few weeks before, Churchill had been little more than the equal of Leo Amery and Jim Salisbury. Now they were nothing and he was everything. Churchill was the only patron worth having. To put your head down and work your way into his good books was the only way forward. In future Macmillan confined his rants to chit-chat around the dining table. He told his acquaintances at the Turf that his boss, the Labour heavyweight Herbert Morrison, was 'timid'.[6] He told them at the Guards that Morrison was 'no good'.[7] He told them at the Beefsteak that Morrison 'cuts very little ice – except of course for having told other people to "go to it"'.[8] For years afterwards he dined out on the opinion that Morrison was 'the meanest man I

know'; that Admiral Sir Harold Brown, the director-general of supply, 'could hardly stomach him at all, for all his [Brown's] courtesy
and generosity of mind'; that Morrison's physical cowardice 'used
to send him down to the deep dug-out at the Ministry as soon as it
was dark', not to re-emerge 'till morning'; that Morrison was the
'kind of man who would never take the blame for what went wrong
– only credit for what went right'; that Morrison 'thought more about
publicity than armaments'; indeed, that Morrison's motto should not
be, 'Go to It!' or 'Keep at It!' but, 'Get Away with It!'[9] Yet if Churchill
saw the need to cultivate Morrison in a way that many of his intimates
found stomach-turning, then Macmillan would put all his contempt
aside, follow his lead and make no serious protest against Morrison's
role at the heart of the government.[10]

Macmillan's salutary lesson served him better than Cranborne's
more measured approach. The Cecils had intended to secure their
position by a slow ratcheting-up of pressure rather than any decisive
action. Chamberlain's rapid demise and Churchill's rise had come
as a surprise, but it did not seem to invalidate their strategy. Lord
Salisbury and his old guard in the House of Lords would maintain
a watching brief outside the government as Cranborne established
an influential place within it. They did not tread in awe of Churchill.
They 'were agreed that it must lie with some executive officer to
carry into effect the strategical decision of the Cabinet – that is to
say Winston'. They were 'terrified', however, by the thought that he
should be in charge both of grand strategy and its implementation.[11]
They thought that the 'White's cabal's' 'bull in a china shop' tactics
of Macmillan were foolish, but they nevertheless agreed with his
views. Cranborne found Lord Salisbury's interviews with government
ministers 'very depressing – whether they are all tired out, or what,
I don't know, but Ministers seem to have lost all grip of the situation
and to be sitting still wondering gloomily what [is] going to be hit
next. Even the PM, who is reported to be more active than the
others, had just that attitude.' Churchill, it seemed to him as to
Macmillan, was leaning too heavily on the 'old gang'.[12]

Churchill may not have thought much of his juniors' political
judgement. He knew that he was stuck with his Labour ministers.

He had every intention, however, of easing out Chamberlainites, or at least those who did not undergo a Damascene conversion, and bringing in his own men. At the beginning of October 1940 he was offered the biggest prize of all. Chamberlain himself, dying of cancer, offered his resignation. Churchill seized the opportunity to become leader of the Conservative party. Chamberlain's departure allowed for a clear-out of some of his confederates. Churchill signalled his view on 'supermen' by appointing one such, John Anderson, to the War Cabinet. Anderson was the perfect candidate for Churchill, an enormously capable former civil servant who sat as Independent MP for the Scottish universities; he was about the most apolitical politician it would have been possible to find. He had exhibited his lack of political skill at the Home Office by allowing Herbert Morrison to steal all the credit for building air-raid shelters. Anderson was exactly what Churchill wanted: someone who could be trusted to take on important tasks without for one moment being regarded as an alternative leader.

This Cabinet reshuffle also gave Churchill the opportunity to bring on others not tarred with the Chamberlainite brush. The 'most novel feature' of the reshuffle was Oliver Lyttelton's appointment as President of the Board of Trade. John Anderson's appointment as Lord President had been the second-best solution for Churchill. He had wanted to make a much more thoroughgoing change. He would, he had hoped, get his once and, potentially, future rival Lord Halifax out of the Foreign Office and replace him with Anthony Eden. Lyttelton had been summoned from Rugby to Chequers to be told that he would replace Anthony Eden at the War Office. The plan foundered on Halifax's refusal to move. To others, Lyttelton's appointment to the Board of Trade seemed like a spectacular promotion.[13] For him it was a profound disappointment. He would be dealing with spoons when he had thought he would be dealing with tanks.

If Churchill created a political career for Oliver Lyttelton, it was Cranborne who offered him the most immediate practical help. To go with his new eminence as a minister of the crown Lyttelton needed a seat in Parliament. The man charged with arranging this, Lord Windlesham, unaffectionately known by prospective candidates as

'Swindle'em', was a holdover from the previous regime. After a disastrous interview in which Lyttelton, dressed in blazer, flannels, Monte Carlo strollers and Zingari tie, confronted the noble lord, who was sporting a steel helmet, gas mask and rattle, in his Sunningdale villa, he was offered the opportunity of appearing on a short-list for an undesirable constituency somewhere in Wales.[14] Between them, Churchill and Cranborne soon sorted this out. Cranborne's cousin Top Wolmer agreed to take up one of his father's many baronies and move to the House of Lords. Lyttelton was installed as his replacement as MP for Aldershot, a safe seat with long-standing links to the military in general and the Guards in particular.[15] 'It is amusing,' wrote Cuthbert Headlam, one of a small band of MPs who already knew Lyttelton well, 'after all the contempt he had poured on the House of Commons to see him entering it – but of course he enters it easily and as a Cabinet minister, and can say quite fairly that he is forced in owing to being one of the "supermen".' 'I think he is likely to be very successful in the House,' Headlam further concluded. 'He has a sense of humour, great ability and plenty of self-assurance – indeed he may be the man to lead the Party – who knows?'[16]

Cranborne himself also benefited directly from the reshuffle. Now that he was well enough to do some real work, he was promoted to Cabinet status as Dominions Secretary.[17] 'I feel I have again been passed over,' an envious Crookshank confided to his diary. 'I don't see why I couldn't have been offered the Dominions just as suitably as Bobbety.'[18] Cranborne and Lyttelton kissed hands as Privy Counsellors at the same ceremony. By a 'strange conjuncture' not only had they joined the Grenadiers together but now they were entering the Cabinet together.[19] Yet whereas Lyttelton, out of ambition tempered by loyalty, buckled down to the Churchillian scheme of things, running unglamorous parts of the war economy, Cranborne was less sanguine. Less than a month after entering the Dominions Office he was involved in an unseemly spat with Churchill and his *équipe*. The High Commissioner in Ottawa, Sir Gerald Campbell, had dared to put on paper what everyone else thought: Churchill's confidant Max Beaverbrook was a rogue – an 'evil genius who exercised the very worst of influence over Winston'.[20] Unfortunately Campbell's opinion reached the ears of Beaverbrook himself. Beaverbrook did not take kindly to criticism from his home country. Beaverbrook went to Churchill and demanded the High Commissioner's dismissal. Churchill told Cranborne to get rid of him. Cranborne refused. Churchill was furious. It was 'rather a grubby business'. Beaverbrook was a 'bad and vindictive man'. It was 'a bore to have made such a bad start with one's Prime Minister'. In the end Cranborne had formally to rebuke his official. He had made a bad enemy in Beaverbrook. Even worse, he revealed to Churchill that he was likely to be 'pernickety' and stand on his honour. Cranborne had cavilled on what were, as he himself admitted, 'all very small matters compared with the general situation'.[21] Cranborne was his own Cecil and Churchill resented him for it.

The difference in Churchill's attitude to Lyttelton is striking. When Lyttelton stood up to him on a 'big matter' he won golden opinions. Lyttlelton's fear that the Board of Trade in wartime would throw up issues which combined complexity with a kind of comic dullness was amply borne out. The political hot potato that was thrust into his hands as he crossed the threshold was clothes rationing. Under his predecessor, Andrew Duncan, 'smoking too many large cigars and pale from too many *crêpes suzette*', in Macmillan's words, the board had seen rationing of household goods as something to be avoided at all costs.[22] There had been a general sense of satisfaction that such rationing was something for the Germans, choked by the power of the British naval blockade. Unfortunately war was too good for business. As the war industry soaked up unemployment, wages rose and affluence increased. Demand rose for domestic goods. If such goods were made available it would distract from *matériel* production. If civilian goods were not made available, there was a grave threat of inflation. In November 1940 Lyttelton decided that he needed to introduce rationing. If Lyttelton was to address this problem he had to get it right. Rationing was hardly likely to be popular. Even worse, if the scheme went off at half-cock there were the makings of a first-class political crisis, with panic buying and accusations of profiteering likely to ensue. Even less to be publicized was the decision by the Board of Trade that the best way forward was to import the German rationing system.

When, after seven months work, Lyttelton finally presented his ideas to the War Cabinet, Churchill was outraged.[23] Oliver was threatening civilian morale. He would destroy the government. He had turned into a pettifogging bureaucrat who wanted to dress Britain in rags and tatters. Why, Churchill demanded, couldn't everyone dress in boiler suits like him? Lyttelton bit back the remark that Churchill's boiler suits were made of the finest vicuna wool whose mass production would have 'taken up most of the Australian wool clip'. He did, however, point out that he was trying to avoid a class war. If there were clothing shortages, the 'well-to-do' would buy the clothes. Did the prime minister really want chaps in Monte Carlo strollers lording it over ragamuffin plebs? Churchill was just being difficult. He soon lost interest in the argument and went off to hunt the *Bismarck*. Lyttelton got permission for rationing, albeit only four days before he had to broadcast to the nation on Whit Sunday 1941.[24] His success in springing the necessary surprise was attested to by the Financial Secretary to the Treasury. 'First I heard of it!' complained an irritated Crookshank. 'It certainly seems that I am kept away from all news.'[25] The scheme would function for the next eight years. More importantly, Churchill noted that Lyttelton had handled a difficult matter competently and that he had stood up to a prime ministerial barracking. 'My unusual choice had been vindicated by results,' he noted with satisfaction.[26]

These opening shots between new ministers and Churchill were of great importance because the prime minister was far from happy with his team. He had made a start in October but was still looking for a chance to make more radical changes. Once more the angel of death gave Churchill a helping hand. Philip Lothian, the Christian Scientist British ambassador to Washington, hastened his own end by failing to seek medical attention. Lord Halifax could not resist the appeal made to his patriotism to replace him. Thwarted in October Churchill got rid of Halifax for good in December. He moved Anthony Eden from the War Office to the Foreign Office. He wanted Cranborne to follow the example of Top Wolmer and to take one of his father's baronies in the House of Lords. There he could take over Halifax's dual role of leading the House and answering for the Foreign Office. Churchill's scheme was delayed for a few weeks by the choleric response of his old friend George Lloyd, once so nearly Macmillan's first patron, who objected to serving under such a junior peer.[27] In January 1941, however, following Lloyd's death, Cranborne was raised to the peerage for his father's barony of Essendon in order to act as leader.[28] Although grand, the job was a good place to corral a difficult minister; providing much detailed work but little opportunity to influence the government's stance on central strategic issues.[29]

Cranborne's role at Dominions and his responsibility for Foreign Office affairs in the House of Lords did nevertheless push him back towards a political alliance with Anthony Eden. Although their personal friendship had never wavered, their political association had lain dormant since 1939. Churchill had wanted Cranborne in his government for what he represented as a Cecil rather than as an Edenite. The Watching Committee, though still in existence, was unlikely to provide Cranborne with further political capital, however. Churchill's rehabilitation of Eden made him once more a desirable ally.

Eden's friends meanwhile worried that Eden himself was losing touch with his important allies. Churchill's dominant personality was engulfing him. If only he would talk to Cranborne and Lyttelton on a regular basis, the three of them, wrote Oliver Harvey, would be able to have an impact on Churchill. Cranborne would rally the 'right-thinking' Conservatives to him while Lyttelton could do the same with the business-orientated. 'As it is,' Harvey observed, 'the PM is apt to go into a huddle with AE ... the others are left out in the cold and there is risk of AE becoming himself isolated from his own age group of colleagues.'[30] Churchill himself was not above dividing and ruling his younger friends. He told a dinner at Chequers, for instance, that 'Eden now had a serious competitor: Oliver Lyttelton who was *persona grata* with the Conservative Party and who had an opportunity of establishing his reputation'. 'Eden,' according to Churchill, 'was not supported in the House or in the

Party though personally he, Churchill, admired his great moral and physical courage. "He would equally well charge a battery or go to the stake for his principles – even though the principles might be wrongly conceived and he might charge the battery from the wrong angle." Oliver Lyttelton was "tough and stuffy" – and ready to take responsibility.[31]

Cranborne was held back from having much impact on affairs, not only by Eden's hauteur but also by yet another bout of illness which sent him back to the country in the summer of 1941. Like Harvey he feared that Eden was isolated: 'really, his colleagues are a miserable lot. They haven't got the nerve to say boo to a goose, much less to a lion.' Wartime conditions left him feeling even more isolated than he had during 1939. 'Alas!' he confided to Paul Evans, 'letters have become the only means by which I can hear anything – the telephone is quite impossible – the operator listens to every word, which in itself is death to any confidential conversation, and using his own judgement as to what is important and what is not cuts one off.' 'It is all very shocking,' he complained. 'I only wish that Shakes [Morrison] could keep some control over his department [the Post Office], and not allow it to become a sort of Gestapo.' Churchill's dominance, he feared, was storing up trouble for the future, 'it is like a tree which looks sound from the outside, but gradually becomes rotten at the core. Then one day it becomes subjected to a tremendous strain and it crumbles away – that is what happened to Neville – Winston should be very careful it does not happen to him.'[32]

Bobbety Cranborne was not the only one thinking of the Eden succession. Feeling himself utterly neglected by Churchill, Crookshank too began to turn his eyes towards Eden. He found his job at the Treasury an utter waste of time. 'Found no work at all today. I sometimes wonder what I ought to do in my sinecure office,' ran a typical diary entry.[33] It was made worse by the fact that one boss, the arch-Chamberlainite Sir John Simon, gave way to another former-arch-Chamberlainite, Kingsley Wood.[34] Crookshank sublimated his energies into other activities. He commanded the Whitehall Home Guard.[35] He spent many nights fire-watching at the Palace of

Westminster. Apart from considerable discomfort and danger – the House of Commons was destroyed by bombing in May 1941 – all he had to show for his efforts was a nasty attack of impetigo picked up from sleeping under dirty blankets. His Masonic activities proved more wholesome: 'Gulls eggs, pea soup, saddle of lamb, ice cream with strawberries and Kippers on toast. Pol Roger 1926 and brandy. Is there a war on?' he inquired after one lodge dinner.[36]

It says something for Crookshank's gilded inactivity that he even formed a ginger group, a political tactic that he had long eschewed. Unsurprisingly the idea came from Harold Macmillan.[37] It also says something about the different directions in which they were moving that, although Macmillan was a member of Crookshank's 'Café Royal' group, he stayed very much in the background. The main purpose of this group of eight junior ministers, all contemporaries, was to meet regularly, gripe bitterly and, as the name would suggest, lunch and dine indulgently.[38] In so far as the group had a programme, apart from promotions all round, it was similar to the one Macmillan had imprudently championed in 1940: a new administration with a War Cabinet that actually had some say over strategy. They also demanded monthly meetings of Conservative ministers so that the party could hold Churchill to account for the conduct of the war.[39]

Meeting regularly with prominent Edenites at the Café Royal, Crookshank also attempted to lobby Eden directly. Rather archly he chose to express his views in the persona of 'Mr Smith': 'the typical man in the street. I have met him in London, in my clubs, and among my friends, in my constituency, in the trains and in all the places where people get into conversation.' Mr Smith was 'getting very puzzled by the War'. Mr Smith was a champion of a 'Second Front Now'. He hadn't 'forgotten the Great War, and he cannot get it out of his head that the real help you give to a land war in the East is some form of land war in the West. And so he asks, why don't we make some landings on the Western European mainland even if they are only of the tip and run variety?' Mr Smith feared that the British government was becoming 'Maginot minded'.[40] Mr Smith was also an advocate of the unrestricted bombing of German cities. He could 'make neither head nor tail of our bombing policy', governed as it was 'by laws as rigid as those of the Medes and Persians'. From his fire-watching vantage he could see that 'German policy was a quite different one – an attack on morale'. He knew that the Germans had failed, but he was 'not sure that if similar attempts were not made *now* on German targets they might not reap a very big harvest'.[41]

Cranborne too, having read with interest the papers prepared by Trenchard for the Watching Committee, had drawn the conclusion that 'our situation is a desperate one, and can only be retrieved by a policy of indiscriminate bombing designed to destroy German morale'. He had one caveat: 'It is likely to be regarded both in Germany and the United States as counsel of desperation, and will to that extent encourage just those elements who are now going about the world saying we cannot win – it may well be the policy which we ought to put into operation, but it is not, I think, the policy we ought to publicize.'[42] Like Mr Smith, he too lobbied Eden to adopt Trenchard's ideas: he agreed with them 'whole heartedly'. Also like Mr Smith he believed 'there is no time to be lost'.[43] Cranborne and Crookshank were thus part of the culture which saw new, and subsequently controversial, expedients in British strategy. Lord Salisbury was tortured by the thought that, by adopting the ideas that his own committee had sponsored, 'we are losing moral superiority to the Germans'.[44] In February 1942 Churchill appointed Sir Arthur Harris to Bomber Command and equipped him with the 'St Valentine's Day directive,' which instructed him to wage unrestricted war against the civilian population of Germany. Yet the blame or the credit for strategic bombing can hardly be laid at the door of Cranborne or 'Smith'. These were decisions taken by Churchill on the advice of his closest advisers for what seemed the best reasons of grand strategy. Cranborne and Crookshank did not feel they were making any personal difference.

When it came to the possibility of falling from office, of course, Crookshank tended to lose his nerve. In April 1941 he had worked himself up into a snit about instructions to ministers to vote for the Sunday opening of theatres in a supposedly free vote. Although he told Kingsley Wood that he might well resign because of this assault on the rights of MPs, he had, as usual, second thoughts.[45] Also as usual, Cranborne was more feisty. Although he was interested in the imperial issues that crossed his desk, the Dominions Office quite often felt like a backwater. Dealing with the affairs of the Governor-General of Australia, another of their Eton contemporaries, Ronnie Cross, just did not feel like a major contribution to the war effort. 'I really don't know what has happened to Ronnie,' he confided to Paul Evans, 'apart from telegraphing every day to say that he must have a new car or two new bathrooms "on public grounds", he has now taken to lecturing Australian ministers as if they were small and rather dirty boys.'[46] Cranborne took his complaints straight to Churchill. He held a great office of state and was leader of the House of Lords, but he was not even in the real Cabinet. To have any real influence one had to be a member of the War Cabinet and sit on its committees. Since he was not a member of these bodies, he complained 'I do not myself know what is going on' even in matters that related directly to his office. 'Most of the important telegrams,' he castigated Churchill, 'are exchanged by you personally either with Heads of State or with Dominions Prime Ministers.'[47] Churchill's reply to these complaints was brutal. If Lord Cranborne did not find the role allotted to him to his taste, he could leave the government altogether.[48]

Churchill may have felt lofty contempt for his discontented underlings, but he had, at some level, to give them attention. It was a given fact of coalition management that no youngish contender of any political charisma should be allowed to emerge on the back-benches to rally the opposition to the government that, as Mr Smith had observed, was bubbling fierce and bilious under the surface.[49] Churchill was criticized not only in the smoking rooms but also in the press: he was, it was said, carrying too great a burden of work, his War Cabinet could neither stand up to him nor take any of the burden off his shoulders. Macmillan thought that 'the House of Commons is as badly disturbed as it was at the time of Norway'.[50] Although a formal vote of no confidence in the government ended in farce when only one MP, the Red Clydesider, James Maxton, voted against Churchill, it did little to remove the underlying disquiet.

It was clear that Churchill had to do something to reconstruct his government.

Cranborne hoped that Churchill would be forced to divest himself of the role of minister of defence and hand it over to Eden.[51] He might as well have hoped for the moon. There was never any chance that Churchill, as long as he remained prime minister, would relinquish his power over the war effort. Eden had seen himself as minister of defence, Cranborne as foreign secretary and Crookshank as a replacement for Churchill's henchman, Archie Sinclair, at the Air Ministry.[52] They were all to be disappointed. Churchill believed that his most dangerous adversary was Sir Stafford Cripps, the maverick Labour politician who had won great popular acclaim as the champion of the Soviet interest in British politics. On the principle that it was better to have him inside the tent pissing out than outside the tent pissing in, Churchill made Cripps a member of the War Cabinet. Cripps's real role, in Churchill's mind, was to lead the House of Commons, acting as Churchill's shield as he, at the Admiralty, had once acted as Chamberlain's. There was fury among the Edenites gathered at the Foreign Office at this news. Cranborne urged Eden to demand that he should be Leader of the House of Commons. This would signal to the political class that he, not Cripps, was Churchill's anointed successor.[53] As Churchill had guessed, however, Eden was unwilling to push the issue. 'This shows that Winston is not fit to be PM and that AE is not fit to be PM,' a furious and frustrated Dick Law was heard to say.[54] Worse was to come. Cranborne had been griping as dominions secretary. Now he found himself unceremoniously deprived of the office. Cripps was felt to need the further dignity of an ancient Cabinet rank. He thus replaced Clement Attlee as Lord Privy Seal. The leader of the Labour party, now deputy prime minister and still a War Cabinet member, needed a new job, so he took Cranborne's. On the Friday night of the reshuffle it even appeared that Bobbety was 'the only person out of a job among the present Ministry'.[55] It was only over the weekend that Churchill appointed him colonial secretary. Cranborne arrived at the Colonial Office to find Harold Macmillan already installed as his under-secretary. Macmillan had been appointed two weeks previously in the early stages of the reshuffle. Unlike Cranborne, he was happy enough with his new job. As an under-secretary to a peer he would get plenty of exposure to the House of Commons. Churchill had, however, made Cranborne sweat in order to teach him not to be so peremptory in his complaints. 'It is indeed a melancholy tale to tell,' Bobbety admitted ruefully to Eden, 'and a disappointing one.'[56]

Harry Crookshank too was caught up in the fag-end of these manoeuvres. Crookshank was lunching at the Turf. To his surprise a message was brought to the table that the prime minister was on the telephone. Hurrying to the club's telephone, he heard Churchill's distinctive growl on the line from Chequers. He wanted Crookshank to become Minister of Works and start thinking about post-war reconstruction. He would go to the House of Lords with a peerage. Crookshank was flabbergasted. On one level, Churchill's offer could be seen as a proof that the Café Royal group's efforts were bearing fruit. They had demanded a reconstruction of the government; and now Crookshank was being offered a Cabinet post. Crookshank, however, regarded the whole proposal as a sick joke. He indignantly refused Churchill's offer.[57] 'I know,' he told Churchill, 'that I would not be any good at, or in present circumstances, even interested in planning the post-war world.'[58] He despised the 'great theories and vast conceptions' of the 'new super race of super planners'.[59] He thought it was 'opera comic' that business should be transacted over a public telephone in a club to which neither he nor Churchill belonged. What really angered him, though, was the thought that Churchill was making a joke at his expense.

If a man wanted *gloire* for himself, he would stay in the House of Commons. If he desired *gloire* for his family, he would go to the House of Lords. But a hereditary peerage was of very little use to a castrato. He could have no son to whom the title might be passed.[60] As soon as he left the Turf, Crookshank sought out Macmillan. They had a boozy late night talking over Crookshank's wounded pride. Macmillan confirmed that, while Crookshank had only ever confided in a few close friends about his castration, the chief whip, Macmillan's brother-in-law James Stuart, was indeed aware of it. It was known of quite widely at Westminster.[61] 'I have been passed over twelve times,' Crookshank wrote in fury to Stuart, 'and then on the thirteenth vacancy was offered a post with conditions which anyone who had ever heard of me – let alone known me – must have realised was absolutely certain to be refused out of hand. One naturally wonders if the offer was made just to get a refusal.'[62]

There is no independent evidence to say whether the peerage offer was a cruel joke or the result of poor staff work. Churchill did have other things to think of – most pressingly the fall of Singapore and the collapse of the British Empire in the Far East. There was at least an argument that Crookshank was intelligent enough, and had shown himself to be pro-labour enough during the coal disputes of the late 1930s, to act as a credible Tory post-war planner. The episode did nothing to raise Crookshank in Churchill's estimation.[63]

If Cranborne and Crookshank emerged bruised from Churchill's machinations, then one of the main beneficiaries was Oliver Lyttelton. In the summer of 1941 the main theatre of land operations for Britain was the Middle East. British performance in that theatre was decidedly patchy. In April the British had been thrown out of Greece, in May they had lost Crete and Erwin Rommel had driven them out of Libya and back to the borders of Egypt itself. Churchill had lost confidence in his generals. He believed they had lost their nerve. He came back from lunch with Lyttelton one day proclaiming, 'The poor Chiefs of Staff will get very much out of breath in their desire to run away.'[64] The generals themselves believed that many of their problems were the result of Churchill's military incompetence. By forcing the commander in the Middle East, Sir Archibald Wavell, to invade Greece, Iraq and Syria as well as fighting in Libya and Abyssinia, he had spread British forces too thinly, ensuring their defeat in detail.[65] Churchill, for his part, was determined to assert even firmer control over the Middle East. He thought it was men not his measures that were the problem. Accordingly he looked for unconventional appointments to shake things up. He sacked Wavell and replaced him with an Indian Army general, Claude Auchinleck. This was not enough. He also wanted someone he could trust on the ground to ensure that his wishes were acted on. Days after he appointed 'the Auk' he appointed Oliver Lyttelton as his political commissar. Lyttelton was to go out to Cairo to perform a dual task. He would be there to keep an eye on the generals. He would also be there to take various organizational, political and diplomatic tasks out of their hands so that they could concentrate on the job of fighting.

Churchill was determined not to let the generals run the war. Lyttelton was his chosen instrument. It was a spectacular promotion. As Minister Resident in Cairo, Lyttelton would become part of the War Cabinet – the key body that Cranborne, despite holding major departments of state, would never achieve. Having passed his first test at the Board of Trade, Lyttelton, according to Churchill, 'had an opportunity of establishing his reputation in Egypt'.[66] Yet, for all the honour, the job contained many potential pitfalls. What Churchill wanted was clear enough, but he gave little guidance as to how it might be achieved. Lyttelton did not have command of anything. He started with a staff of three, and one of those, Henry Hopkinson, was a Foreign Office 'minder', there as much to keep an eye on him as to serve him.[67]

Lyttelton had nothing but Churchill's vague imprimatur and his own personality to rely on. He also had an incubus to bear. The idea of the Minister Resident had originated with Randolph Churchill, the prime minister's son. Those who criticized Winston nearly always acknowledged that his energy, imagination and drive were irreplaceable. No one had a good word for Randolph: drunk, dilettante, blowhard, plotter, parasite was the widely held view. Sponsored by such a creature, Lyttelton had almost endless possibilities for alienating those with whom his responsibilities now overlapped; the military, the Foreign Office and indeed Churchill himself.

Lyttelton had little choice but to face the political realities of his position. Whatever power he had stemmed from his relationship with Churchill. The younger Churchill was in uniform but was self-evidently no ordinary junior soldier under military discipline. One of Lyttelton's first acts was to appoint Randolph as his 'liaison officer' with his father. This was a war very different from the one Lyttelton had gone to fight in 1915. He and his friends had used their influence to get into the Guards, but they had nevertheless served in a front-line infantry unit in the main theatre of operations. The then prime minister's son, Raymond Asquith, had fought and died as a subaltern in Lyttelton's battalion. Many young men took the same course in the Second World War. Both Lyttelton's second son, Julian, and Cranborne's eldest son, Robert, served also in the Grenadier Guards.[68] Many educated and well-connected men, on the other hand, with the example of the Great War before them, decided that service in front-line infantry, artillery or tank units was a mug's game. There was an enormous proliferation of 'specialists' in intelligence, political warfare, economic warfare, logistics, propaganda, special forces. Quite often, as Lyttelton discovered, they expended more energy fighting each other than they ever did the Germans.[69] In Cairo there was 'inefficiency, extravagance, and even corruption'.[70] Randolph Churchill used his position as his father's son to politick at the highest level. Leo Amery's son, and Harold Macmillan's future son-in-law, Julian, was allowed to swan around the Middle East solely because he was the son of a Cabinet Minister.[71] Many mini-Randolphs and mini-Julians were busy politicking away at a lower level. Lyttelton subsequently attempted to cleanse these Augean stables.[72] Yet 'the atmosphere of jealousy, suspicion and intrigue' continued for the next two years.[73] Mr Smith, for one, himself a Cairene by birth, was 'puzzled about the Middle East: he has lots of his friends out there, but he cannot make out what they are doing or going to do. He asks if they are just sitting there waiting to be attacked?'[74] This was the viper's nest into which Lyttelton's flying boat descended at dawn on 5 July 1941.

Standing erect in the gleaming embassy launch coming out to meet him was the formidably tall and massive figure of Sir Miles Lampson, the British High Commissioner. Lampson was a long-serving orientalist whose job was to manipulate Egyptian politics in the British interest. Although he greeted Lyttelton affably enough, he was hardly pleased to see him. Lampson believed that many of the practical problems had been created by Wavell's 'secretiveness'. The Auk, on the other hand, was 'a grand man, most responsive and easy'.[75] Lampson maintained that, with Auchinleck in charge, many of the existing problems would have been solved without a 'super-man'. He worried that Lyttelton would merely become the centre of yet more political intrigue in a city already awash with it. Indeed, Lyttelton's office at 10 Sharia Tolumbat was inevitably christened simply 'No. 10'. Lampson's nose was put out of joint by the implica-tion that Lyttelton rather than he was now the British government's senior representative in Egypt, although he was willing to put the spats over 'silly details as the flying of flags, provision of escorts and similar stuff' down to Lyttelton's 'overzealous' private secretary. He was even more worried when 'after a singularly restless night having been kept up till all hours owing to OL and Randolph having gone into a huddle . . . it was made clear to me that OL took instructions from no-one but the Prime Minister'. Lampson felt like a 'poor white' in his own house.[76]

In those first hectic days Lyttelton had to use the force of his own personality to establish himself. One of his first jobs was to sort out the appalling logistics mess which resulted in military supplies, acquired at huge political and financial cost from the United States, rusting away on Egyptian docks, unused for want of a proper supply system to get them to the fighting troops. Immediately on arrival he established a Middle Eastern War Council with its own defence committee. His aim was to get the three services to start coordinating their activities. With Auchinleck now in charge and prepared to be cooperative, this stood some chance of working.[77] The fly in the ointment was Sir Robert Haining, the so-called Intendant-General, in charge of the badly run supply operation. Haining was, in the view of one of his own colleagues, 'quite useless . . . he understands nothing about military matters and messes everything up'.[78] He balked at having a junior Indian Army officer like Auchinleck pro-moted over his head and quickly made it known that he wasn't about to let Lyttelton lay down the law either. Nevertheless even Lampson was willing to admit that 'OL has got into his stride remarkably quickly and already the wheels seem to be going round smoothly and well [he] has evidently got the knack of . . . steering skilfully through shoal water'. 'There is no doubt,' Lampson added, 'that from the angle of efficiency in our war organization there has been an immediate stride forward. Indeed one wonders why such an organization did not exist before.'[79] Lyttelton insisted that when he met with the military commanders and Lampson it should be a meeting of principals, able to get things done, not a talking shop. The only official present was his own *chef de cabinet*, Arthur Rucker, to keep the minutes. He gave himself an ambitious set of targets. The three services had to be persuaded to work together. The port system had to be made to work properly with proper facilities constructed at the southern end of the Suez Canal. The local economy of the Middle East, particularly the supply of food, so disrupted by the the war raging around it, had to be put on a proper footing. Supplies had to flow freely to and from India, East Africa and South Africa, not only to keep the armies fighting but also to ensure that civilian populations in the occupied territories remained, at the very least, acquiescent. Since Lyttelton arrived in the middle of a joint British–Free French operation to wrest Syria and Lebanon from Vichy control, such issues of pacification were most pressing.[80]

The Levant campaign presented Lyttelton with his first great test. It also provided him with a formidable ally in the shape of Edward Spears. Spears was, like Lyttelton, a personal friend of Churchill. Brought up in France, and with a colourful career as a liaison officer in the Great War, he was now serving as the prime minister's link man with the Free French leader Charles de Gaulle. His initial admiration for de Gaulle was rapidly turning to deep distrust. Although he believed that the general had taken a brave stand in publicly branding the Pétainist Vichy regime as illegitimate, he was beginning to suspect that de Gaulle was an anglophobe quite willing to disrupt the war effort to further his own interests, which he egotistically equated with those of France. Lyttelton and Spears had barely been acquainted before July 1941, but they took an instant liking to each other. Indeed, Lyttelton immediately intervened on Spears's behalf. In London a committee under the chairmanship of Dick Law had come to the conclusion that the most efficient way of governing the Levant was to hand it over to the Free French. Lyttelton was having none of this. He insisted that an expanded Spears mission should be 'the pivot of the administration of Syria'.[81] Lyttelton was, in fact, merely confirming Churchill's firm instructions that in no circumstances should French control of the Levant be allowed to affect the conduct of the war by stirring up Arab populations against Britain. Nevertheless this intervention cemented his relationship with Spears. It also paved the way for a conflict with de Gaulle.

The commander of the British invasion of Syria, General 'Jumbo' Wilson, accepted the surrender of the Vichy forces on 11 July 1941. There was little that Lyttelton, sitting in his dressing gown in the chancery of the Cairo embassy, his only useful link with Wilson an army telephone in Jerusalem, could do to influence events. Unencumbered by political interference, Wilson took the line of least resistance and signed a mutually agreeable armistice with his Vichy counterpart. Since the Free French were an obstacle to the successful conclusion of his operation, Vichy officers regarding them 'as traitors to France', Wilson simply treated the Free French representative, George Catroux, as one of his subordinates rather than the emissary of a foreign power.[82] When the armistice was formally signed on 14 July 1941, it included a protocol preventing Free French agents contacting Vichy troops in an effort to win them over to the Allied cause. The Vichyites were to return to France 'with honour'. Wilson's actions were in line with Churchill's intentions.[83] Lyttelton, however, regarded them as foolish. When he learnt of the protocol, he was 'incensed' by Wilson's stupidity.[84]

What Lyttelton regarded as crass insensitivity towards an ally, de Gaulle saw in a much more sinister light. It was little more than a plot by perfidious Albion to seize French colonies for its own empire. Boiling with indignation, de Gaulle himself dashed to Cairo. At eleven o'clock on 21 July 1941, a very hot Cairene day, de Gaulle stalked into 'No. 10', 'white with suppressed passion'. 'There was nothing for it but what women call "a scene",' Lyttelton recalled, 'and a scene we certainly had.'[85] Churchill had instructed him 'to let de Gaulle know where he gets off'.[86] Lyttelton was free to use the fact that the entire Free French operation, military, political and diplomatic, was financed by the British. Without British aid, de Gaulle was merely a jumped-up junior general with no claim to represent anyone. Lyttelton, even so, had every sympathy with de Gaulle, even if he knew accusations of an 'English plot' to be nonsense. Even before de Gaulle arrived in Cairo, Lyttelton had asked Spears to fly to Beirut to start work on a compromise with Wilson and Catroux. After four days of haggling he got de Gaulle to agree to it: the armistice would stand but the rights of the Free French, in particular that to recruit in the Levant, would be recognized. On signing the Lyttelton–de Gaulle accord, Lyttelton was most satisfied with his work.[87] 'He has every reason to be pleased,' Lampson confirmed, 'as he seems to have satisfied both de Gaulle and our military! No mean achievement.'[88] Auchinleck told Churchill that Lyttelton had handled de Gaulle most impressively, given that the Frenchman was 'mad and consumed with personal ambition'.[89] He had pulled off a *coup*. He had defied the prime minister, worked hard to put his own solution in place and resolved a dangerous situation. Churchill chose as his friends 'real men' who would stand up to him on important issues. He had expected Lyttelton to be 'stuffy', and he was being 'stuffy'. Churchill's friends had to show, however, that they were not simply self-aggrandizing. It was a fine line to tread and Lyttelton was treading it well.

He was doing less well on the substance of the matter. Lyttelton believed he had cut a deal with de Gaulle to nullify specific complaints made by the Frenchman. De Gaulle then maintained that Lyttelton had conceded to the Free French 'an arrangement . . . recognizing our entire sovereignty over the Levant states'. Almost on a weekly basis thereafter, de Gaulle would claim that Britain was failing to live up to the accords. In August Lyttelton himself went to Syria to mediate the first round of these disputes. His conversations with de Gaulle lessened not one whit the French leader's belief in the English plot, nor his belief that he could get his way by bullying anyone who stood in his path. The last week in July was a turning-point for Spears. Watching de Gaulle berate Lyttelton, his growing distrust of the French leader turned into hatred. As Britain's representative in the Levant, Spears did indeed start to plot the very thing, the complete exclusion of French influence from Syria and Lebanon, of which de Gaulle had falsely accused Lyttelton.[90]

Lyttelton had prevented the Levant crisis from diverting too many military resources from the main theatre of operations to the west, against the Germans in Libya. That was probably all that could be achieved. As de Gaulle's foreign policy adviser, Maurice Dejean, admitted, 'unfortunately, the Levant was the least favourable territory possible for military and political cooperation between France and England'.[91] This was not the fault of Lyttelton, or even Spears. It was simply that the two powers had been bickering distrustfully about the area since 1916 if not before. That Lyttelton had applied little more than a sticking plaster to the problem was clearly demonstrated by the fact that Harold Macmillan was to be tested by a rerun of the crisis with many of the same players only two years later.

The Levant crisis was a good blooding. Lyttelton had every reason to think he had done well. He and Lady Moira were settling in true proconsular style. He had acquired a suitable residence in the form of the Blue House, lent to him by the American-born metals magnate Chester Beatty, a world-famous collector of oriental art. Since he was also supposed to be keeping 'the glorious East in fee,' he set out from Cairo to tour his vast domain: Lebanon, Syria, Transjordan, Persia. Yet unless there was a specific problem to deal with, such as the fall-out from the Lyttelton–de Gaulle agreement, these could be little more than 'flying visits'. Indeed, it became increasingly clear to Lyttelton that no one in London really had any interest in setting him up as the political lord of the Middle East.[92] Although he was a member of the War Cabinet, this seemed little more than a titular honour. No one felt 'personally responsible' for consulting him.[93] 'I am very much displeased,' he confided to his mother, 'with the lack of information on matters outside my vast territory from London . . . you can hardly imagine how out of touch one feels: send me all the gossip, especially political you hear.'[94]

His main job remained to get the War Council working on the logistics problem and to start to prod Auchinleck towards launching an offensive against Rommel with the *matériel* thus assembled. He himself was satisfied with his performance in this role: 'the three commanders-in-chief don't move far without my advice,' he noted with satisfaction. 'Of course this adds to the responsibilities of this job but in a way which I love.'[95] 'OL himself is a pillar of strength,' Lampson confirmed. 'My admiration for the way he takes things grows from day to day. He has the great knack of keeping the discussion to the point.'[96] When he returned to London to brief the War Cabinet in October 1941, Lyttelton was brimming with confidence and talking of an 'advance to Tripoli or even further.'[97] Enjoying an excellent luncheon with Cranborne at a restaurant in Leicester Square, he was 'delighted with himself'.[98]

By mid August, however, Churchill was starting to demand action rather than promises. Lyttelton was the man in the middle trying to reconcile political demands for instant action with military demands for proper preparation. He could see the justice of both points of view. 'Much has had to be improvised and that must leave muddle and mess behind,' he informed his mother. 'Many of these improvisations have been brilliant successes, the original Cyrenaican campaign, the deadly blow at Italian prestige, Iraq, Syria. But one cannot make war by a series of gambles. Islands of order have to made in the morass: troops equipped, the coils of the spring bent back in readiness for release ... but the sands in the hour glass are the most precious of all the atoms that make the British empire ... they must not be let run out into the dust.'[99] Once again he then took the risk of irritating Churchill by supporting Auchinleck's view that the offensive could not begin until mid November 1941. Churchill, he believed, had misinterpreted his own maxims, 'his doctrine of *toujours de l'audace, toujours de l'audace* was never intended to mean the use of unprepared troops in improvised formations, it was meant to say that when battle is joined, the campaign in full swing ... commanders should keep the initiative and take the risks.'[100]

Lyttelton had to some extent backed the wrong horse. Auchinleck's great 'Crusader' offensive, which began in mid November 1941, was indeed well-planned and well-supplied. Yet, despite the British superiority in *matériel* over Rommel's Italo-German forces, and the initial success it produced, the offensive brought no stunning victory. What seemed to be lacking was that very audacity in the tactical handling of British troops that Lyttelton believed was vital. With Lyttelton's support, Auchinleck sacked his senior field commander during the campaign for having lost his nerve. Lyttelton was 'infuri-ated' by the lack of drive shown by the army's commanders. 'You can't make blitz without straw,' as he put it. He was left wondering 'why we can't breed some junior generals who are any good'. 'I think,' he told his daughter, 'avoidable mistakes have been made and that we have paid a high price for a lack of middle-aged generals – most of the good ones got killed in the last war.'[101] It was in this aspect of Lyttelton's conduct that Churchill found most to criticize. He had, exclaimed the prime minister in frustration, 'failed badly' in not looking after the generals more. Lyttelton had been 'taking too much interest in local politics and foreign affairs, and not enough in what he was intended to do'.[102]

Lyttelton did indeed have his fingers in a great many pies, in-cluding negotiations with the King of Saudi Arabia, the Shah of Iran and the King of the Hellenes.[103] His part in the most spectacular showdown with royalty of the war was, as it happened, more a loyal attempt to support a colleague than an example of self-aggrandizement. Sir Miles Lampson was convinced that King Farouk of Egypt 'would be a willing and dangerous tool' of the Nazis if he ever got the chance. In his view, Egyptian politicians ranged from 'dangerous' to 'potential Quislings' to, at best, 'non-belligerents'.[104] As news of Rommel's military successes filtered back to Cairo, student demonstrators took to the streets with cries of, 'We are Rommel's soldiers.' On the morning of 4 February 1942 Lampson told the king that he would appoint the government of Lampson's choice or he would be deposed at six o'clock, by military force if necessary. Lyttel-ton backed up Lampson. At a crucial moment, however, he did intervene to rein in the ambassador. Although the king had not capitulated by the six o'clock deadline, Lyttelton convinced Lampson that if he did agree to all the High Commissioner's demands when Lampson and his military escort confronted him later in the evening, he should not be deposed as Lampson intended. 'I personally,' the High Commissioner wired Eden the next day, 'was never so sorry as when, at the very last second, the Monarch yielded. I had discussed at dinner here with OL just before I left for the Palace what I should do if he did so yield. And I agreed with Oliver's increasingly strong view that we should have a greatly weakened case before the public if we kicked the boy out on a matter of three hours' delay, even though that wasn't the *real* point.' Having acted without reference to London, Lyttelton insisted that he rather than Lampson should carry the can if their actions met with disapproval.[105] It was a brave offer. Churchill was worried enough about the situation to consider flying to Cairo, although all thoughts of Cairo were soon swept away by the disaster in Singapore.[106]

Lyttelton may have shaken the thrones of kings, but he had failed to act as the political commissar Churchill had wanted. 'I am subsequently rather *dégonflé*,' he admitted.[107] Whether Churchill's choice of fighting generals would have been any more successful than Auchinleck's is open to serious doubt. Lyttelton had decided that he had to back the man on the spot rather than his master in London. His efforts had not been crowned with success and he had to take the flak.

The narrowly averted overthrow of Farouk proved to be Lyttelton's last act in Egypt. Within a few days he was recalled to London. He was relieved to find on his return that Churchill's irritation with him was only a passing phase. He had been rated a still promising alpha-minus. Once again he had shown himself to be 'stuffy'. What was striking was how he had got on so well with abrasive personalities like Spears and Lampson. In contrast to the doubts about him Lampson felt on his arrival, he was positively gushing in admiration on his departure. 'So the blow has fallen!' he wrote to Eden, 'and Oliver is torn from us. This is going to be a *very* great loss. He has shown the requisite firmness and at the same time the consummate tact.' Cairo had not been quite the sparkling success Churchill had hoped it would be for him, but that was hardly Lyttelton's fault. 'Operation Crusader' had been lost on the battlefield not in Cairo – victory would have cast an entirely different light on his activities. The very nature of those activities meant that while those he worked with admired him greatly, it was impossible to broadcast them to a wider audience: logistics foul-ups, secret services running amok, pro-Nazi politicians, under-performing tanks and fallible generals were hardly things to be openly addressed before the press during wartime. Little wonder that the correspondent for Beaverbrook's *Daily Express* in Egypt, Alan Moorehead, should conclude that Lyttelton was hard-working and respected, but 'his press conferences were so appallingly dull, his words so banal and evasive that it was impossible to put him before the public as a leader'.[108] In less public circumstances – addressing MPs in private, for instance – Lyttelton was on better ground. Reviewing his tenure as Minister of State at an all-party gathering of MPs, he 'made an excellent speech and a profound impression on the meeting'.[109]

Churchill had called Lyttelton home not because of his performance in Egypt but because he wanted someone he could trust to balance the political nominations, such as Cripps, he had had to take into the War Cabinet.[110] Churchill wanted the man rather than the minister. His initial idea was that Lyttelton would replace the Chamberlainite David Margesson at the War Office.[111] Within days a different job, which Churchill thought suited his particular skills more, opened up for him. Faced with continued rumblings that he himself was trying to do too much and that he should give up the Ministry of Defence, Churchill affected to concede to his critics that there should, at least, be one 'czar' in charge of munitions production. That 'czar', many learnt to their horror, was to be his own close ally, Lord Beaverbrook. Yet this gesture was, in some ways, a sham. Churchill needed a Minister of Production because he wanted someone to negotiate as an equal with President Roosevelt's recently created Director of War Production. He had no intention of creating a Ministry of Munitions. It had been Lloyd George's tenure of that office that enabled him to overthrow Asquith in 1916. It took Beaverbrook fourteen days to work this out. Once he did so, he resigned. His immediate replacement by Oliver Lyttelton nipped any potential political storm in the bud.

Churchill was trusting Lyttelton with a hot seat. The Ministry of Production did not yet exist. Three large production ministries did: the Ministry of Supply for the army, the production side of the Admiralty for the Royal Navy and the Ministry of Aircraft Production for the RAF. Lurking behind them all, and touching all their activities, was the Ministry of Labour under the unassailable organized labour leader Ernest Bevin. In January 1942 Churchill had told Harold Macmillan to draw up a blueprint for a Ministry of Production. Macmillan concluded that the rational way forward, and most certainly the way forward his boss Beaverbrook wanted for himself, was to put the supply of military equipment, aircraft, ships and the direction of labour under a single ministry. Britain would then have had a true production 'czar', an English Albert Speer. Bevin, however, said no and that was the end of it. The Labour party's leading trade unionist was not willing to have his control of the labour force challenged by a Tory businessman. The Ministry of Production, as it emerged in February 1942, was little more than a committee structure sitting uneasily on the top of the existing British war effort. Churchill was quite aware that this put any minister in an invidious position. In 1940 he himself had resisted a move from the Admiralty to a coordination role because he believed it was akin to political castration. The creation of the Ministry of Production did, however, serve Churchill's own political purposes. Since taking over in May 1940, he himself had dominated the setting of production priorities through the Defence Committee of the War Cabinet.[112] With an increasingly vocal campaign among MPs and the press damning this system as a failure, he needed to divert blame from himself. Lyttelton would act as his shield.

In February 1942 the British war effort was a failure. The twin handicaps of patriotism and lack of detailed information, however, made it most difficult for anybody outside Churchill's immediate circle to offer coherent and well-informed criticisms of British strategy and military operations. Ill-informed criticism could not be made to stick. On the other hand, MPs had a surfeit of information about the problems of war production. It was going on in their constituencies. Factory owners and trade unionists came to them with their complaints. Deprived of most of their other functions, MPs could claim that it was their patriotic duty to excoriate any perceived failure in military supply.[113] There were many such failures to choose from, the most popular being the inadequacy of British tanks – 'death traps', in the harsh words of one MP who had served in North Africa.[114] Every day for the next three years Lyttelton would face critical questions about military production. Since the Ministry of Production was not, in fact, directly in charge of producing anything, these questions were often hard to answer. He was condemned to making a never-ending diet of banal, evasive and appallingly dull public statements.

Churchill continued to look upon Lyttelton with a fond eye. He enjoyed his company. He had every faith in his loyalty. He had every faith too in his ability to do his job. Lyttelton likewise had every faith in his own ability to do the job. He had taken a long time to get the political bug, but now had been bitten hard enough to choose to further his ambitions at home rather than become Viceroy of India when the possibility was mooted.[115] Talk of a great political future started to leach away none the less. On his return from Cairo, Lyttelton enjoyed a honeymoon period. 'I have heard several members suggest that Oliver Lyttelton might be a possible future leader of the Conservative Party,' George Harvie-Watt, Churchill's political spotter in the House of Commons, reported to his master in March 1942.[116] Cranborne believed Lyttelton would be a formidable political ally for Eden.[117] When it came to the crunch, however, his public performances were found wanting. At the end of June 1942 British arms suffered yet another humiliating blow when Rommel took Tobruk with seeming ease. This disaster and the risk that Egypt might fall precipitated another vote of confidence in the government. The government could hardly afford not to make a good case for itself.

Lyttelton seemed the perfect person to speak for the government: he could cover both the supply and the Middle East problem with authority. The ground was prepared perfectly for him when the Tory backbencher proposing the vote made the bizarre suggestion that the Duke of Gloucester, a royal field marshal of no appreciable talent whatsoever, should be placed in command of British forces. The whole House burst 'into ribald laughter at this quite unexpected solution of the problem of a better central control of our war effort'.[118] Lyttelton in his reply, however, made a 'proper balls of it'.[119] He managed to lose the House entirely by treating MPs as ill-behaved children while trying to read a prepared statement demonstrating that the government knew best. Many Conservative MPs enjoyed his discomfiture. 'So far things have been too easy for him,' was a widely held view.[120] He was cocky and condescending and in only two years had leapt to a political eminence that his contemporaries had been striving towards for over two decades. As Lyttelton himself ruefully acknowledged, that one speech hung round his neck like an albatross for the rest of his career. Since he put in good performances in the House in both the major debate before the vote of confidence and the major debate after it, the judgement was desperately unfair.[121] Nevertheless it meant that party managers could not be absolutely sure that 'he might not be capable of going off the deep end one of these days'.[122]

He was caught treating the House with contempt again in January 1943, when he was denounced for having tampered with Hansard, having told a lie to get off the hook in a debate.[123] All this came to Churchill's attention. *L'Affaire Lyttelton* of June 1944 required Churchill himself to apologize to President Roosevelt for Lyttelton's inadvertent interference in American politics.[124] In off-the-cuff remarks to the American Chamber of Commerce at the Savoy, he had claimed, first, that 'Japan was provoked into attacking the Americans at Pearl Harbor', and secondly, that 'it is a travesty to say America was forced into the war. Everyone knows where American sympathies were. It is incorrect to say that America was ever truly neutral even before America came into the war.' In the boozy Allied bonhomie of the Savoy, it had played well and he was cheered to the rafters. Unfortunately he had by implication just confirmed what Roosevelt's opponents had always claimed, that the president had conned Americans into fighting. The remarks were soon leaked and became grist to the mill of the forthcoming US presidential elections.[125] Churchill uttered the 'old prayer that we were to be spared from our friends'.[126]

These small incidents tarred Lyttelton with a reputation for bad political judgement. Churchill believed Lyttelton had strayed too much into areas that did not concern him in Cairo: he now kept him on a tight lead. Lord Halifax noticed that, far from becoming a power in the War Cabinet, Lyttelton put on a 'poor display'.[127] The Chief of the Imperial General Staff, Alan Brooke, liked him personally but dismissed him as one of Churchill's 'chorus of "Yes" men' and an 'amateur strategist'.[128] The senior air force leader, Sir Arthur Tedder, also thought Lyttelton was a 'yes-man' in front of Churchill.[129] Lyttelton did win plaudits for his conduct of supply talks in the United States in June and November 1942. Halifax, who had been so unimpressed with his performance in Cabinet, now reported to Churchill that 'Oliver has been handling his job with perfect combination of push and patience'.[130] Still, when Roosevelt engaged Lyttelton in conversation about the post-war peace settlement, Churchill tugged the lead. 'You must keep within the limits . . . You should stick to production,' he instructed down a transatlantic telephone line. 'I think entirely of production,' Lyttelton replied facetiously. 'That's right. Keep to your proper sphere,' Churchill reiterated, 'you keep to your job.'[131]

It remained true that Lyttelton was undoubtedly at the heart of affairs. His contemporaries, such as Cranborne and Crookshank, would have counted themselves fortunate indeed to have been negotiating their role between presidents and prime ministers. Churchill regarded them both as irritants who, because able, had the potential to become troublemakers. For many Conservative MPs Cranborne seemed to be that attractive creature, a sound liberal.[132] Churchill liked him well enough socially.[133] When it came to political discussion, however, there was something about Cranborne's unwillingness to admit that the prime minister was in the best position to judge – his willingness to suggest, in so many words, that Churchill was merely an equal with a temporary advantage – that enraged Winston. It was, Churchill assured his circle, 'less tiring to decide than to have to argue, as I might have to do with Cranborne, who might easily be ill for one fortnight and very obstinate the next'.[134] Cranborne's friends despaired of his inability or unwillingness to 'manage' the great man's moods.[135] It did him little good to feature in scheme after Edenite scheme for a 'strengthened' ministry. The point of each was that Eden should take on the role of co-ruler, viceregent and acknowledged successor to Churchill. Yet there was no reason why any of these schemes should appeal to Churchill. He had Eden's fealty, in any case; he did not need to give him any more power. Only a political crisis or illness might have forced his hand. As Cranborne knew all too well, Eden was much too unsure of his own mind to force such a crisis. Any change was most unlikely. 'The real truth, I think,' he confided in his father, 'is that Anthony cannot make up his mind.'[136]

Churchill wanted Crookshank even more out of the way. Lyttelton had pioneered the role of Minister Resident. Churchill regarded the experiment as a qualified success. In Lyttelton's wake other appointments were made: Duff Cooper to Singapore, the Australian politician, Dick Casey, to replace Lyttelton in Cairo, Louis Spears in the Levant. Churchill had something similar in mind for Crookshank. In mid May 1942 James Stuart invited Crookshank to dinner at the Carlton Club to meet the prime minister. After the Minister of Works fiasco, they wanted to make sure that he was properly stroked. Stuart hoped the general air of mystery and bonhomie would help to persuade Crookshank to move on, though Stuart's tactics were somewhat spoilt by Macmillan, who 'gave me the dope so that I wasn't caught unawares'.

Churchill wanted Crookshank to fly out to West Africa to become Minister Resident there. Despite the excellent dinner and two bottles of champagne the prime minister poured down his throat, Crookshank was most unimpressed. The idea of leaving England and living in Africa for an unspecified period did not attract him in the least. It was easy enough to provide himself with a doctor's note declaring him unfit for tropical service. The one man who thought he was making a big mistake was Harold Macmillan. He could see the potentialities in the job to have a 'good war'. Indeed, the eventual incumbent, Philip Swinton, did just that. Crookshank for his part was adamant – he was not leaving England. Once again Crookshank had shown himself to Churchill as a curmudgeon.[137] He had now turned down a planning and a front-line job. His political prospects remained bleak.

The Café Royal group continued to meet, but there was little to be done. The 'boys' could see no advantage in making waves over the Tobruk disaster.[138] Someone else, on the other hand, did see how to make political hay. Oliver Stanley had been side-lined by Churchill.

Not only had he stuck to Chamberlain, but his track record did not suggest he would be an asset as a wartime minister. Stanley, never willing to accept demotion meekly, began to stir up Conservative backbenchers against the way in which their views were being ignored. On 18 November 1942 he assembled 150 Tories to draw up a petition on the subject to be presented to Churchill. Four days later, Churchill made him Colonial Secretary. Stanley's manoeuvre set in motion a chain of events that was to involve Cranborne and Crookshank closely and transform Macmillan's political career.

Stanley took Cranborne's job. Cranborne was shifted to the sinecure office of Lord Privy Seal. Bobbety's health was still giving concern. 'He looks quite deplorably sick and emaciated,' Cuthbert Headlam noticed at the end of September.[139] It was the second time in eight months that he had lost a great office of state because Churchill needed it for someone with greater political pull. His brother-in-law, Billy Ormsby-Gore, was in little doubt that this was a mark of Churchill's disfavour. 'Thus to demote one of the best men in the Government is really lamentable. Why Winston has got a down on him no one can understand.'[140] The person who felt Cranborne's removal most grievously was another brother-in-law. Macmillan and Cranborne had worked together harmoniously. More importantly, Macmillan had had the opportunity to lead for the Colonial Office in the House of Commons. He had been building a good name for himself.[141] Now he was to play second fiddle to Stanley. Stanley had always played the game better than he. In 1940 the tables had been turned. Now, it seemed, as soon as Stanley exerted himself, they had been turned back.

Macmillan was furious. He had put his nose to the grindstone, caused no trouble, yet had been treated with contumely. There no longer seemed much point in being a good boy. Crookshank's accustomed bitterness and Macmillan's newly minted irritation played off against each other. Crookshank stormed off to James Stuart to tell him that if he and Macmillan were not promoted they would resign from the government. Stuart was hardly frightened by the threat. In the middle of a major reshuffle, the most important element of which was the extrusion of Stafford Cripps from the War Cabinet, the concerns of one habitual moaner and a relapsed troublemaker, even if it was his own brother-in-law, were not near the top of his list of priorities.[142] All he had to offer Crookshank was a reheated version of the Ministry of Works idea.[143] Crookshank and Macmillan were both on very dangerous ground. Neither had a large political following. Their presence in the government was marginal to its success. If they created too many waves, there was a risk they would be exiled to the backbenches with no hope of recall. This was exactly the warning that Brendan Bracken gave Macmillan when he took his woes to him.[144] When Crookshank persisted with his complaints to Stuart, stories began to appear in the press about an 'under-secretaries revolt'. The ground was being laid to purge them.[145]

Reprieve emerged for Macmillan when, by chance, another Minister Resident job hove into view at that very moment. Since Oliver Lyttelton had left Cairo there had been a revolution in affairs in North Africa. In November 1942 Churchill's attention was not fixed on the political ambitions of his junior ministers. Instead he could regard the success of his own policy. Having sacked Auchinleck, he saw the hitherto untried combination of Harold Alexander, Lyttelton's companion in the forlorn hope at the Somme, and Bernard Montgomery triumph over Rommel at the second battle of Alamein. Days later a joint Anglo-American invasion force landed in French North Africa.

The invasion, 'Operation Torch', in fact created a messy political situation. The main issue in Anglo-American relations during Lyttelton's last days in Cairo was whether the American ambassador to Egypt would sleep with Diana Cooper. Now the Americans demanded that their voice should be heard in the politics of the Middle East. Roosevelt's personal representative, Robert Murphy, was already there, stirring up the region with money and treason. The same problem that had faced Lyttelton in the Levant, of which Frenchmen Britain should back, was made doubly difficult by the need to act in concert with the Americans. In the Levant 'Jumbo' Wilson had slipped temporarily from the control of Cairo, but at least he was a British general. In Morocco and Algeria command was vested in an American general, Dwight D. Eisenhower. If Churchill had doubts about de Gaulle's suitability as the leader of France, this was as nothing to those held by the Americans. In short order they turned up not one but two potential rivals to de Gaulle. General Henri Giraud, by the lucky accident of having been taken prisoner by the Germans and then daringly escaped, was in hock neither to Vichy nor the Free French. Regrettably he had as yet no great following in North Africa. Admiral François Darlan was a deep-dyed Pétainist, but he could command many of the French officers in the recently invaded territories. He was willing to collaborate with the British and the Americans. For the moment, Darlan was the Americans' favourite.

With Murphy politicking furiously, to what ends no one was quite sure, with Eisenhower seemingly politically unsure, with many in the House of Commons queasy if not openly critical of the Darlan deal, Churchill wanted his own man on the spot.[146] If he was to do any good, he had to get there quickly, so options were limited. Lying together on Churchill's desk were the Darlan papers and the Crookshank–Macmillan complaints. Both had been in a group of Conservatives organized by Charles Peake to meet de Gaulle a few months before. The meeting had gone well. Over a convivial dinner at the Travellers, de Gaulle had gone so far as to declare that England would become France's favourite ally, '*car les Américains deviendront trop fatigants et les Russes trop inquiétants*'.[147] Churchill could kill two birds with one stone. It was Crookshank who was offered the job first, though it is to be doubted whether this was a serious offer. Crookshank had made it quite clear that he did not want to go to Africa and Churchill had seen his extensive medical file. It was not what one would look for, for such a strenuous task. In any case, Crookshank had already been offered, and decided to accept, the job of Postmaster General, on condition that Macmillan should replace him as Financial Secretary to the Treasury.[148] No one can have been very surprised when he rejected the post of Minister Resident out of hand.[149] Offering the job to Macmillan would therefore clear up any loose ends. The previous month Churchill had described Macmillan as 'unstable'. He had even so had his eye on him for some position of responsibility.[150] He wanted his man in place. He had placed his trust in Oliver Lyttelton because he knew him to be a friend. He placed his trust in Harold Macmillan because he knew him to be a political dependant.[151]

Macmillan had urged his friend Harry Crookshank to take the jobs he was offered, whether as Minister Resident in West Africa or as Minister of Planning. It did not matter what the job was, Macmillan maintained, it was what one made of it that mattered. It was a chance to prove one's mettle. By refusing offer after offer, Crookshank had condemned himself to a post of utter unimportance. He now had the Cabinet status he had wanted for so long, but with it came the task of scrutinizing the designs of post offices that would never be built. It was symbolic that the GPO's most important wartime task was organizing secure communications for the Enigma code breakers at Bletchley Park. Yet although he was one of the few ministers who knew exactly what Bletchley was, Crookshank would never see any of her product.[152]

Unlike his friend, Macmillan accepted the Algiers job without cavil. It was not because it was the perfect billet. He fretted that he was being sent to political Siberia, and the terms of the job itself kept changing as Roosevelt attempted to persuade Churchill that Macmillan should merely be a member of Eisenhower's staff. Yet Roosevelt's attempt to emasculate the post merely made Churchill the more determined to defend Macmillan.[153] Through no action of his own, Macmillan's position had become a symbol of British honour. This was fortunate indeed for Macmillan, for on Christmas Eve 1942, even before he had left London, the putative need for his presence was done away with. Admiral Darlan was murdered by a group of ultra-right monarchists with suspiciously Gaullist connections. The almost universally held view was 'good riddance'. Churchill nevertheless 'attached great importance to getting Macmillan out to Algiers as soon as possible, as we were quite unrepresented and yet our fortunes were being committed by events there'.[154] Two days later Roosevelt agreed 'without enthusiasm' to Macmillan's appointment.[155]

Having arrived in Algiers on 2 January 1943, the highlight of Macmillan's first month in office was the opportunity to attend one of the great Churchill–Roosevelt summits in which the most important aspects of the Anglo-American alliance were hammered out. From the mundanity of the Colonial Office, where he had sat at Cranborne's right hand, to the exoticism of Casablanca, where he sat, if not at the right hand of Churchill, at least in close proximity, was a spectacular leap. Yet Macmillan's opportunity was over almost as soon as it had begun. Not because of any political *faux pas* but because of the bane of politicians fighting a global war: an air crash. Such crashes killed a number of Macmillan's contemporaries, most notably Victor Cazalet and John Whiteley, who were with the Polish leader General Sikorski when his aeroplane went down off Gibraltar. Rob Bernays, Crookshank's sometime confederate, was killed in an air crash later in the war. Macmillan's accident happened on 22 February 1943 as his twin-engine Lockheed Hudson bomber was crashed by 'its rather casual gum-chewing Australian pilot' during a night take-off from Algiers. As the aeroplane burst into flames, Macmillan was in the worst possible place, the cockpit. With flames licking around him, he managed to pull himself from the wreckage, landing on the ground with a thump. His private secretary, John Wyndham, who had clambered shaken but unharmed from the fuselage of the Hudson, had watched in horror Macmillan 'struggling to get out of the pilot's side window, his moustache burning with a bright blue flame'.[156] Macmillan was lucky. Although painfully burnt, he did not suffer the horribly twisted flesh that would have required long care by an Archibald McIndoe. This, however, was not immediately clear. Barely conscious, he was rushed to a nearby military hospital for treatment. According to Macmillan's own account, he was hallucinating. He cried out for his mother. He thought it was 1916 once more.[157]

Something profound happened to Harold Macmillan in the early months of 1943. The temporarily pink-skinned and white-bearded figure that emerged from its swathes of bandages was a man made anew. It is a romantic notion that near-death experience changes a man. But Macmillan himself felt that he was on the cusp of a change. As he lay in his hospital bed, his mind reviewed his career to that point. He had struggled through years of failure, he pointedly told his wife, but 'ambition, patriotism, pride' had, at last, brought him 'within the hallowed precincts of the Privy Council and the Cabinet'. He might be a middle-aged and rather portly publisher 'encumbered by the weight of his own dignity', but he was determined not to give up his new life lightly. Exactly one week later, though still in great pain, Macmillan boarded another aircraft and flew to Cairo to continue with his mission to help negotiate the surrender of the Vichy navy berthed in Alexandria harbour. He showed admirable courage and an insouciance which did not go unnoticed by Churchill.

Though Macmillan's joust with fate had not brought about an instantaneous change in personality, by the time of the crash another side of his personality was beginning to manifest itself. He had always been clever. He could be good company. Yet until the middle of the war there was always something that turned his own peers against him. He was self-obsessed, he was a bore, he appeared weak, even pathetic. His political tactics up until that point had suggested his insecurity. He had always wanted to be part of a group, the YMCA, the defeated members, the Next Five Years, the December Club, the Glamour Boys, the Watching Committee, the Café Royal boys. As his self-belief increased, he now took more control of his own destiny. He struck out for himself. From then on the coterie with which he surrounded himself were younger men rather than contemporaries. Like Lyttelton, he had arrived in North Africa with a very small team. These young men were beholden to him not vice versa. He no longer sought a political coterie.

This new independence of spirit did not mark any immediate political independence. Macmillan had seen that he did not need allies, he needed patrons. Given the circumstances of the war, there was never any doubt as to who those patrons would be. He was Churchill's man when he arrived in North Africa and he had no intention of being anything else. He knew Churchill well enough to realize that he did not like a doormat, but he was absolutely determined that every action he took would increase his standing in Churchill's eyes. Then, on arriving in Algiers, he acquired another boss in Dwight Eisenhower. He had to work hard to get himself into Eisenhower's good books. Their first meeting was inauspicious. Eisenhower did not know who he was or what he was for. The

Americans would have preferred him to be little more than a functionary on Eisenhower's staff. Churchill had fought hard to give him an independent status. Within days Macmillan had recognized that he could best prosper by acting as if he *was* a member of Eisenhower's staff, standing on his dignity as a minister of the Crown as little as possible. He would get on good terms with Bob Murphy and they would act as a team sorting out knotty political problems for Ike. 'It isn't this operation that's wearing me down,' the supreme commander had moaned before Macmillan's arrival, 'it's the petty intrigue and the necessity of dealing with little, selfish, conceited worms that call themselves men.'[158] Macmillan, on the other hand, heartily enjoyed dealing with the worms. 'I feel so happy,' he wrote, tongue partly in cheek, to London, 'to be out here. The purely Balkan politics we have here are more to my liking. If you don't like a chap, you don't deprive him of the whip or turn him out of the Party. You just say he is a Monarchist or has plotted to kill Murphy and you shoot him off into prison or a Saharan concentration camp. Then a week or two later, you let him out and make him Minister for something or other. It's really very exhilarating.'[159]

For anyone with eyes to see, Casablanca had been a salutary experience. On one level Churchill and Roosevelt had met as equals. Britain was carrying as great a proportion of the overall war effort as was the United States. At another level it was clear this equality would not last much longer. Roosevelt's once ill-substantiated promises that the United States would act as the 'arsenal of democracy' were indeed close to realization. As each month passed, although the alliance prospered, the Americans became more assertive. Macmillan had with luck ended up on the winning team in domestic politics. He was determined, by good judgement, to end up in good odour with the winning team in international politics. He had spent two years biting his tongue in the office even if letting its barbs show in private. It was good training for what was to come. So Macmillan became an enthusiastic member of Eisenhower's team. This position explains the oft-noted asymmetry between Macmillan's self-portrait of himself as Eisenhower's close, cordial and key adviser and his relative lack of impact in American reports. Macmillan was working for Eisenhower. He was working diligently and intelligently on important tasks, but there was neither the friction nor intimacy between them which would cause a superior to take extensive note of a subordinate.[160] Macmillan's reward was not words but outward signs of favour. As Macmillan realized, he had the inestimable advantage of acting within the context of victory. Lyttelton did not win as many laurels in the Middle East as Churchill had initially hoped for him because he presided over a defeat. The laurels were now in Eisenhower's gift. When the Allies celebrated their victory in North Africa with great military parades, Eisenhower invited Macmillan on to the victory podiums at both Algiers and Tunis to share in the glory.

Of course there was a difficulty in serving two masters if their interests clashed. 'It is a great mistake,' Churchill chided, 'to be shy about defending with the Americans "vital British interests in the Mediterranean". I do not like your expression "old empire stuff" which also seems to argue an apologetic outlook.'[161] Macmillan himself believed that he could keep both his patrons happy if he was clever enough: there were 'fashions in phrases as in costume which it might be politic to follow'.[162]

It was not only the emergence of a major new regional power in the shape of America that had changed things. One and a half years before, Lyttelton had arrived as a pioneer Minister Resident. Macmillan was merely one such minister among many. In Cairo sat Lyttelton's successor, Dick Casey. As a member of the War Cabinet, Casey was senior to Macmillan. In Beirut lurked Louis Spears, where Lyttelton had helped establish him. Macmillan's diplomacy was as much about liquidating their political influence as anything else. To make a success of his mission, it was he who had to emerge as Churchill's representative. He always had a bad word for his fellow ministers resident. The Cairo operation was a 'racket' with ambitions to muscle in on Algiers.[163] Casey was 'very pleasant', but, according to Macmillan, 'ill-educated', 'weak', 'inexperienced' and 'not very clever.' Spears was 'a clever man' but a rogue elephant. 'I cannot help thinking that being a popular hero in the Levant has rather gone to his head,' Macmillan wrote.[164]

Having picked his patrons, Churchill and Eisenhower, Macmillan was quite prepared to be rude to anyone who got in their or his way. Bad relations with Casey and Spears were inevitable. Conflict with Charles de Gaulle was inevitable also. Even the francophile Lyttelton had been unable to pacify the general. Now de Gaulle was locked in a desperate political struggle to translate his dominance of the Free French movement into dominance of the more broadly based French Committee of National Liberation and then to turn the FCNL into a government in waiting with himself at its head. Indeed, his ambitions ran even further than this: he wanted nothing less than to be treated as the leader of a great power equal in every way to Churchill and Roosevelt. Macmillan regarded himself as a friend to de Gaulle, but he had no time for Gaullism. He described de Gaulle as standing 'head and shoulders above all his colleagues' not only as a day-to-day politician but 'in the breadth of his conceptions for the long term'.[165] He also described de Gaulle as a 'fundamentally reactionary' mystic. He mocked the Gaullists' 'pathetic belief that by insisting verbally upon France's greatness they make her in fact great again'.[166] He told officials to have 'the courage to deal firmly with de Gaulle if he behaved in an absurd way'.[167] He was always more comfortable with more pragmatic Frenchmen, such as Jean Monnet. In return, de Gaulle regarded Macmillan as little more than the mouthpiece of an Anglo-American plot to do down France. Macmillan was always to be found plotting with Murphy. He was too glib, de Gaulle complained, in his protestations of friendship.[168] Nevertheless de Gaulle rubbed along with Macmillan as well as he did with any other Anglo-Saxon politician. At one meeting the Frenchman even looked on unconcerned as the naked Minister Resident bathed himself in the Mediterranean.

When the simmering tensions in Anglo-French relations came to a head in the Lebanese crisis of November 1943, Macmillan was in a good position to profit from them. Ever since Lyttelton had intervened to broker a settlement in the Levant, the answer to the fundamental question, who were the true masters of Syria and Lebanon, the British or the French, had remained unresolved. While Macmillan was away in Italy, the bibulous senior French representative in the Levant, Jean Helleu, made a clumsy attempt to resolve the question in France's favour. He arrested the entire Lebanese government. In doing so he played straight into the hands of Louis Spears. Spears's loathing of de Gaulle by now knew no bounds. He was praying that a clash between 'this megalomaniac and popular leaders' would destroy him.[169] Helleu's incompetence gave Spears his chance to act. He proposed that the British military should impose martial law, thus publicly breaking French power and humiliating de Gaulle. Spears quickly won Dick Casey over to his view. Churchill too was attracted to it when he and Spears talked 'whisky and soda treason'.

Macmillan, however, was able to get at Churchill directly, since the prime minister was on his way to the Teheran summit via the Mediterranean. They met on board HMS *Renown*. Macmillan argued that the crisis could be contained. The Lebanese ministers would be released, Helleu would be dismissed, but there would be no breakdown in relations with the FCNL. Macmillan denounced Spears as the main cause of the trouble. It was a dangerous political manoeuvre. He was contradicting the policy Churchill's heart, if not his head, wanted. He was making a vicious personal attack on Churchill's friend. Churchill was not pleased.[170] Yet Macmillan was acting from sound political calculation. He had had three days to talk to French leaders. He was confident that he could engineer a face-saving deal. He also knew that Churchill was about the only man in the British government who had not become disillusioned with the violence of Spears's conduct.

Macmillan's political calculations were correct. When Casey delivered an ultimatum to the French on 19 November 1943, to back down or face martial law, de Gaulle's colleagues overrode him and insisted on backing down. In one sense Spears had triumphed. He had shown the French that the British were in charge.[171] Yet, as Macmillan had calculated, a Fashoda showdown had been avoided, albeit narrowly. More importantly, his denunciation of Spears, in retrospect, seemed timely. Even Churchill was reluctantly coming to the conclusion that Spears was a liability.[172] Spears's loss was Macmillan's gain. The contrast was plain: Spears was a stiff-necked loner.

THE GUARDSMEN

Macmillan was a flexible, intelligent team player. Macmillan was the coming man while Spears was the fading force. Macmillan realized that Anglo-French relations were a quagmire. Even before he brokered the November 1943 deal he was taking steps to divest himself of any responsibility for them. 'I have seen so much of these Frenchmen in their Balkan period that I feel it would be better to fade out gracefully . . . there will always be a source of awkwardness one has towards a chap when one has nursed him through an attack of DT,' he advised London.[173] He saw much brighter opportunities elsewhere once the Allies had invaded Sicily in July, and Italy itself at the beginning of September 1943.

The first six months of 1944 were some of the most important in Macmillan's career. It was then that Churchill placed the mark of favour openly on his brow. In September 1943 Macmillan had been in a difficult situation. With the Allied invasion of Italy, North Africa became little more than a backwater. Macmillan had to move on or be left behind. He was determined to establish himself in Italy and beyond. In July 1943 the Italians themselves had overthrown Mussolini. The Allies were unsure in their own minds whether Italy was thus a defeated enemy or a potential ally. It seemed to Eden and Dick Law at the Foreign Office that the best thing to do was to tie the Italians down with detailed and restrictive peace terms. Churchill was less sure. He thought that it might be possible to cut a deal with the Italian government, even one that retained quasi-fascist elements. The Americans were even less happy with Eden's legalistic approach. They wanted Italy turned over to Eisenhower as military governor. He could make whatever political deal he liked in order to keep military operations to the minimum. As a result, conflicting orders and suggestions poured into Algiers. A crescendo was reached on 29 July 1943. Eisenhower was due to broadcast to the Italian nation. A text had to be agreed. Macmillan was in his element, shuttling from meeting to meeting, drafting and redrafting.[174]

When Eisenhower's voice floated over the airwaves, he spoke from an American text agreed by Macmillan. He commended 'the Italian people and the House of Savoy', he offered 'peace under honourable conditions', a 'mild and beneficent occupation' and the restoration of 'the ancient liberties and traditions of your country'.[175] This was a long way from 'unconditional surrender'.[176] It was also a long way from good judgement.[177] It was based upon the surmise that the Italians had some value as co-belligerents. As it was, Marshal Badoglio's government did nothing to prevent the Germans taking over those parts of the country not invaded by the Allies. The British and Americans were condemned to a bitter and long-drawn-out campaign in Italy just as the Italians were condemned to a bitter and long-drawn-out occupation.

The Eisenhower broadcast was the first shot in Macmillan's campaign to transfer his empire from North Africa to Italy and the Balkans. Once again he had potential competitors. Eden sent out a professional diplomat, Sir Noel Charles, to challenge him for the role.[178] His most obvious rival, however was Sir Frank Mason-MacFarlane, the governor of Gibraltar who was appointed head of the British Military Mission to Italy. There were thus three conduits for Anglo-Italian relations in play: the diplomatic, the military and the political. As long as he had Churchill's support, Macmillan could dominate Charles.[179] It also soon became clear that Italy presented problems more of politics than of military administration. This favoured Macmillan in his rivalry with Mason-MacFarlane. Nevertheless it was Mason-MacFarlane who was dispatched to negotiate with Badoglio and the king. Macmillan merely served as his 'adviser'.

It was, however, Macmillan who emerged with all the credit from the surrender negotiations. He portrayed himself as the 'putative father' of Italian democracy, with Mason-MacFarlane and Charles dancing to his tune as the 'the midwives'.[180] When Mason-MacFarlane complained that his work was not being recognized, Macmillan told him that he was 'ridiculous'.[181] Yet the reason Mason-MacFarlane was doing the work but getting none of the credit was close at hand. Macmillan was following Churchill's line that the fascist-tainted king should abdicate in favour of his son Umberto while the competent quasi-fascist Badoglio should continue to lead the Italian government. It was Macmillan's reports that Churchill was reading and it was Macmillan who was getting the credit. 'You have evidently handled the situation with remarkable skill,' cabled an approving prime minister.[182] In trying to escape from Macmillan's dominance, Mason-MacFarlane and Charles played into his hands. Mason-MacFarlane wanted to accompany Prince Umberto and Bad-oglio to Rome as soon as the Eternal City fell into Allied hands. Macmillan warned that they would be entering a snake-pit of Italian politics.[183] Mason-MacFarlane was determined to have his hour of glory, so Macmillan distanced himself from the whole exercise and retired to North Africa, 'rather amused', to watch the fiasco unfold.

The Italian politicians in Rome acted just as Macmillan predicted. They accepted Prince Umberto but refused to serve under Badoglio. The prince was forced to appoint one of their number, the septuagen-arian former liberal premier, Ivanoe Bonomi, as his prime minister.[184] As Macmillan admitted, Mason-MacFarlane was 'intrinsically right' to have agreed to this change in government.[185] 'Badoglio was [after all] a bad man, a war criminal, a man who had worked with Fascism and a general. Now at least we have a return to parliamentarians who, though old, are anti-Fascist.'[186] Churchill, however, was 'livid' to read of this major change of policy in his morning newspaper. Mason-MacFarlane was soon thereafter removed from office. Chur-chill was heard to say that, 'If Macmillan had been there this would not have happened.'[187] Churchill wanted Macmillan fully in charge. 'I feel the great need of a competent politician and Minister there, like Macmillan, rather than a General,' he told Roosevelt.[188] Mac-millan felt confident enough to dictate the terms on which he would accept the job.[189]

Having spent twenty years amassing a reputation for poor politi-cal judgement, Macmillan had now built a reputation for sound political judgement, at least with the one man who mattered, in just two.[190] He basked in Churchill's favour. He made little secret of the fact and hinted widely that he should be brought back to Britain in a very senior role indeed.[191] It was a mark of his rising fortunes that he was making powerful enemies. He had become a threatening figure. Anthony Eden wasted no opportunity to denigrate Macmillan. He flew into a fury when Macmillan came home in October 1943 to press his campaign for widened responsibilities in the Mediter-ranean.[192] Eden believed that Macmillan should be acting as little more than an events organizer for the foreign secretary's own visit to the Middle East, yet Macmillan was telling the prime minister that the Foreign Office was 'very tired and very unimaginative'.[193] Eden wanted a factotum, but got instead a rival for Churchill's favour. Friends could not altogether understand why Eden was so 'fantastically jealous' of Macmillan. Surely, they said, he presented no threat to Eden. Eden was merely being paranoid. Yet they did not understand the Eden–Churchill relationship. It was not quite as fond as some imagined. Churchill was certainly not above taunting Eden by setting up potential rivals. He had done it with Lyttelton earlier in the war, although that effort had petered out into nothing. Now he was doing it with Macmillan. Macmillan was on his way to becoming the dominant voice in the Mediterranean, quite eclipsing Eden.

Before the war ended all three were brought together when prime minister, foreign secretary and minister resident all flew into Athens to sort out a civil war in Greece. In October 1944 Churchill had ordered British troops to invade Greece to prevent a take-over by the communists. Macmillan quietly arrogated responsibility for Greek politics to himself.[194] Yet the Greek situation was a case of the ineffable in pursuit of the unacceptable. For years ministers had been telling Churchill that the Greek monarchists, most of all George, King of the Hellenes himself, in whom he was placing his trust, were a shower. As early as September 1941 Lyttelton had observed the unpopularity and political incompetence of the monarchy through his interviews with Greek exiles. George had 'only made half-hearted and totally inadequate efforts to conciliate Greek public opinion'. If things went on as they were, he had warned, 'we should be faced with the invidious alternatives of abandoning the King or imposing his return by force.'[195] Since in the intervening four years the monarchists had neither forgotten nor learned anything, Lyttelton's prediction had indeed come to pass. Nearly everyone – Macmillan, Eden, diplomats, military advisers and Greek politicians – agreed that if a stable anti-communist Greece was to be created, British military intervention had to stand for something more than placing King George back on his throne. Churchill did not appear to agree. They were all rather taken aback when, on his way to Moscow, he stopped off in Italy to deliver a homily 'in praise of monarchy in general and King George of Greece in particular.'[196] When Macmillan went ashore with the invasion forces on 18 October 1944, he was walking into a very hazy political future.

On Sunday, 3 December 1944, the shooting started. It was a difficult moment for Macmillan. During November he had returned to London in an attempt to manoeuvre himself into another role – a major mission to the United States to discuss machinery for the supply of liberated Europe. He did not believe there was much more political capital to be made out of the war in the Mediterranean. Churchill, however, turned on him for 'deserting his post'. 'He almost hinted,' noted a worried Macmillan, 'that my absence from Rome and Athens was poltroonery.'[197] If he wanted to continue to enjoy the prime minister's favour, there was nothing for it but to get back to the Mediterranean as soon as possible.[198] But Macmillan was walking a tightrope. Although he was Churchill's man, he thought that Churchill's views on Greece were antediluvian in principle and unworkable in practice.

He was in for a difficult few weeks. There was considerable feeling in both press and Parliament that Churchill was backing an unpleasant group of reactionaries against the people who had actually fought the Germans. Macmillan himself had some sympathy with this view. He had to ensure that he was neither tarred with the reactionary brush nor blamed for a bloody débâcle, while at the same time retaining Churchill's favour. It was a tall order. As Macmillan found on arrival, even the British military position was fragile. 'We have underestimated the military skill, determination and power of the insurgent forces,' he recorded on 11 December, 'the British forces (and the Embassy) are besieged and beleaguered in the small area of central Athens. Our airfield at Kalamaki is very insecure and the communications between it and the main body in Athens all under fire. We do not hold a port at all. In other words, we have no secure base anywhere from which to operate.' To get from the embassy, where Macmillan holed up, to Army HQ, one had to go by armoured vehicle or drive very fast in a soft skin.

The only good news was that Rex Leeper, now ambassador to

Greece, had thought up a plan. Archbishop Damaskinos, a respected cleric, should be appointed regent. The forces of anti-communism could then be rallied around a monarchical establishment shriven of its unacceptable right-wing elements. It was the only practicable idea on the table. Macmillan had to run with it.[199] King George himself had no intention of handing his power over to His Beatitude. Neither had any of the Greek politicians. It was a frustrated Macmillan who sent cable after cable to the relentless rattle of rifle fire. The king was a nasty little autocrat, not worth one drop of British blood, the Greek politicians were treacherous weasels, determined to 'fight to the last British soldier', yet Churchill was accusing him of being 'rattled'.[200] Damaskinos was a Quisling and Macmillan was a 'fussy-wuzzy', Churchill declared.[201] It was most unfair. Worse news was to follow. At eleven o'clock on Christmas Day, 'Alex' arrived with an explanation of why communications with London had been so gnomic for days. Churchill was flying in himself within a few hours to sort out the mess. Macmillan was not the only one who expected a 'difficult time'. Anthony Eden had no intention of letting Churchill cook up a Greek solution with Macmillan. He insisted that if the prime minister was determined to spend Christmas in Athens, then so would he.

So, on a bitterly cold airfield among the opening shots of the Cold War, Macmillan waited for Churchill and Eden to arrive. It really was a fool's errand – they were like 'a couple of housemaids answering every bell'.[202] As even Churchill himself admitted, there were more pressing issues to deal with back in London, such as responding to the German Ardennes offensive or the political back-wash from Churchill's decision to sacrifice Poland to Stalin.[203] To make matters worse, as Macmillan sat gratefully out of the cold in Churchill's brand-new toy, a 'beautifully appointed' Douglas C-54 Skytrain, a gift from the US Air Force, he soon realized that the prime minister did not actually have any alternative policy to offer on Greece.[204] After two hours of hard talking, they set off for the Piraeus in a convoy of armoured cars, the crews cheerfully assuring them that if they poked their heads out they would be shot off. With Churchill settled on the cruiser HMS *Ajax*, Damaskinos was ferried out to meet him. Having been convinced that the archbishop was the only horse in the race, Churchill decided he liked the look of him after all, placing everyone in the 'curious topsy-turvy position of the Prime Minister feeling strongly pro-Damaskinos'.[205]

Everything had thus turned out well for Macmillan. Instead of receiving a rocket, his reputation for political sagacity and good judgement of men had been confirmed. There was no doubting his dynamism. 'I have found Harold the greatest help here,' Rex Leeper, the author of the Damaskinos plan, wrote home to Bobbety Cranborne. 'He has always come over when I have telegraphed to him and I find him a joy to work with, with his very constructive mind.'[206] It was Eden's rather than Macmillan's nose that was put out of joint by Churchill's volte-face. Churchill's visit was big news. Even if most of the press was dubious about British policy in Greece, it did the party proud with the extent of its coverage. Macmillan was plastered over front pages, standing a heartbeat away from the prime minister. If anything it did him even more good with Tories outside his natural hinterland, right-wingers who were glad to see 'Reds', at home and abroad, confounded. It ensured that Macmillan's war in the Mediterranean ended on a dramatic high long after the theatre had ceased to be of primary military importance. 'Macmillan,' wrote an infuriated Alan Brooke, 'is donning the coat of the Supreme Commander of the Mediterranean and submitting wild schemes for employing further forces in Greece, quite forgetting that we are fighting Germany!!!'[207]

Many years later, it was to be claimed that he actually ended his war in an act of infamy. In May 1945 he made a 'truly wonderful' transalpine flight to Klagenfurt in Austria to meet 'killer Keightley', the general commanding British troops in the area. Among those surrendering to the British were 'about 40,000 Cossacks and "White" Russians, with their wives and children. To hand them over to the Russians is condemning them to slavery, torture and probably death,' Macmillan wrote. 'To refuse,' he continued, 'is deeply to offend the Russians ... We have decided to hand them over.' It was a brutal decision, but not one that gave Macmillan much pause.[208] His mind was already turning urgently towards English politics. 'The work entailed [in continuing as minister resident], however important at times, would be so small that ... it should prove intolerable to any honest man.'[209]

Called home to discuss the problem on the borders of Austria, Italy and Yugoslavia, he was immediately swept up by Churchill into British politics.[210] The slaughter of the Cossacks was barely a blip on the horizon which did not return to haunt him until eight months before his death.[211] It was Athens, not Klagenfurt, that Churchill and the Conservative party remembered him for. His cold-bloodedness was indeed a recommendation rather than a black mark. The longer the war went on, the bigger Macmillan's reputation seemed to get. A vote of confidence certainly came from the Cecils with the arrival of Cranborne's only surviving son to act as his ADC. 'He is, I think,' wrote Cranborne, 'extraordinarily lucky to be with Harold, who has ... a first-rate brain and a very wide interest. It is just the training I should have wished for Robert.'[212]

As Macmillan went from strength to strength, his contemporaries seemed tired and diminished.[213] In 1944 both Bobbety Cranborne and Oliver Lyttelton lost sons. Julian Lyttelton, a Grenadier officer, was killed in combat in Italy. Dicky Cecil, a sergeant in the RAF, was killed in a motor-cycle accident while on his way home to visit his parents. Cranborne and Lyttelton were tight-lipped at the deaths of their sons, but the necessity of going on regardless was taking its own toll.

As for politics, Cranborne admitted that he 'sometimes felt at my wit's end' at the Dominions Office.[214] He managed to fit in one more bitter argument with Churchill before hostilities ended. When news had reached London in June 1941 that Hitler had attacked the Soviet Union, Cranborne had taken the 'Tory standpoint' that Russia could be no more than a military ally of convenience, 'politically Russia was as bad as Germany'.[215] He had seen or heard nothing in the intervening years to make him change his mind. He was thus most uncomfortable with Churchill's 'appeasement' of the Russians at Yalta. He aligned himself with those who attacked Churchill's Polish policy. Stalin's actions in Poland made a mockery of the liberty for which Britain had supposedly gone to war. If Britain continued to turn a blind eye to Soviet behaviour, 'we shall only make ourselves party to a vast fraud – and a fraud which will very soon be exposed'.

In such circumstances, Cranborne maintained, there was little point in carrying on with the inauguration of the United Nations planned to take place in San Francisco. A UN Security Council in which Russia wielded a veto was not a vehicle for world peace but merely 'an umbrella of respectability for her misdeeds'. He himself could not defend the plan for the UN agreed at Yalta.[216] Churchill's reply was scathing. He was going ahead with the San Francisco Conference. The creation of the UN was at the centre of the balance of power he had agreed with Roosevelt and Stalin. Churchill accused Cranborne of putting his visceral dislike of the Russians before any rational understanding of international politics. 'You say you can "only trust to your own instinct",' Churchill admonished: 'I have offered you reasons at the end of a long day.'[217] Lord Cranborne could either be on the aeroplane to San Francisco or he could clear his desk now. Forced into a corner, Cranborne could not bring himself to resign.[218]

Having departed for San Francisco on such a sour note, Cranborne found himself thrown into a round of thankless negotiations.[219] The iniquities of British imperialism provided the butt of complaints from not only the Soviets but also many of the smaller powers present. Even some representatives of the British Empire itself, most notably the egregious Australian foreign minister Dr Evatt, saw the opportunity to establish themselves as world statesmen by following an independent line. Britain was to be 'stigmatized as a reactionary'.[220] The United States was happy to court popularity by aligning itself with 'anti-imperialism'.[221] Cranborne seemed at first faced with an uphill struggle. Accordingly he worked hard at getting on good terms with his American opposite number, Harold Stassen, an ambitious young Republican with his sights on the Presidency.[222] He was helped by the perceptible waning during the conference of American interest in anti-imperialism. With Japan on its last legs, and with a super-weapon on the verge of completion, winning the trust of Asian nationalist movements within the Japanese empire seemed less important. Men like Stassen could see that Russia rather than Japan was the enemy in the East.[223] Cranborne averted a serious attack on British colonialism, albeit narrowly.

'You never saw anything more beautiful,' Cranborne said of San Francisco itself. He and Betty lived in the 'greatest luxury'. Even to the owner of Hatfield the wealth of the Americans came as a surprise. Despite these compensations, the conference itself was hardly to his taste. This was not the gentlemanly diplomacy of the pre-war years. Instead he felt himself drowning 'in a babel of tongues and pressmen – I never saw so many. They jump out from behind every pillar, and one can hardly hear the speeches in the clicking of cameras.' This circus, he predicted, would take too long, 'all the chief delegates will have to leave and the small fry will be left to squabble over details, which will be a most unedifying start for the new world order'.[224] Indeed, the main feature of the new world order seemed to be 'incessant and interminable cocktail parties'.[225]

He was right in his prediction. Within days of the British party arriving on the West Coast, Germany surrendered. The Labour party refused to countenance maintaining the coalition for any longer. Macmillan was already in London discussing tactics. Lyttelton too, having duly celebrated victory in a bibulous night at the Mayflower Hotel in Washington, flew back to London.[226] Churchill showed his true view of the importance of the UN by ordering his team back to London to prepare for the coming struggle.[227] The fact that Cranborne was left in San Francisco indicated that he carried little political weight. He himself had little desire to rush back. The outward flight via Gander, Montreal and Denver had played havoc with his lungs. He had every intention of making a leisurely and recuperative sea voyage home.

Perhaps Cranborne, in his reluctance to hurry home, was as good a judge of electoral politics as any. Churchill, together with many of his associates, overestimated his own popularity. Churchill's subordinates had each spent the later years of the war enmeshed in their ministerial responsibilities. Macmillan had been out of the country. Much of Lyttelton's responsibility had made him cast his eyes across the Atlantic. They thought that they might win an early general election.[228] They were sadly out of touch. Yet the experience of his own family should have given Macmillan a clue to the future. At the beginning of 1944, Eddie Devonshire had unceremoniously sacked another brother-in-law, Henry Hunloke, from the Devonshire family seat of West Derbyshire for cheating on his sister. Hunloke's misdemeanours were an opportunity to launch Andrew Hartington, Devonshire's son and Macmillan's, and indeed Cranborne's, nephew, on his political career. Things did not go as planned. An 'independent' with support from the Labour party turned a 5,000 Tory majority into a socialist majority almost as large.[229] The West Derbyshire by-election was as strong an indication as any that politics could not be seen to go on in the old ways. Yet the next year Lyttelton made a point of boasting to Dick Law's Hull constituents of the 'continuity of our politics'. Law's father, he reminded them, had been prime minister, Lord Cranborne's grandfather had been prime minister. In his enthusiasm for this spectacle, he even claimed that Churchill's father had been prime minister.[230] Needless to say, Law lost his seat. Only Crookshank, excluded from Churchill's magic circle, saw things differently. The 'beastly man' had not even recognized him in his caretaker government. When Macmillan suggested that his friend should be minister of labour, Churchill replied, 'I know nothing of Crookshank.'[231] Crookshank in turn, having spent the previous two years with very little to do, was pretty pessimistic about Churchill's electoral appeal.[232] For once, Crookshank was the best political judge.

7

Tories

The Tory electoral débâcle of July 1945 was not entirely bad news for Macmillan, Lytteltton, Cranborne and Crookshank. More than anything, it made them the standard bearers of their generation. Electoral demographics meant that the 1945 general election amounted to a mass cull of their contemporaries. Most lost their seats; others, such as Victor Cazalet, had been casualties of war. Younger men who established themselves before and during the war, such as Dick Law, Brendan Bracken and Duncan Sandys, also lost their seats. Some would return, others never. A number of aristocrats, including John Loder and Roger Lumley, drifted out of politics to become ornaments of imperial governance.

In the place of these discarded Conservatives came a slew of Labour MPs in their early fifties. These men were contemporaries of the Conservative subalterns, but they had nothing else in common with them socially or politically. They made as little impact on their Tory peers as they did on broader politics. Much more important was the influx of younger men. 'What a House of Commons it is going to be,' observed Cuthbert Headlam, whose own nephew was elected, 'filled with young, half-baked, young men – mainly from the RAF so far as I can make out.'[1] Most of these young sprigs sat in the Labour interest, but a similar breed of newcomers was also entering the Conservative party organization – from 1945 Ted Heath, Reginald Maudling, Enoch Powell and Iain Macleod all worked for the party while nursing the constituencies they would win in 1950. Many of these 'thirtysomethings' had had interesting wars; the up and coming Labourites, Dick Crossman and Kenneth Younger, for instance, had both worked with Macmillan in the Mediterranean in the intelligence services. To men in their early fifties it seemed as if the ground below and around their feet had suddenly been cut away. For the first time, time seemed short.[2]

The prick of anxiety felt by the Great War generation was symbolized by an odd rumour that started doing the rounds. Harry Crookshank was heard to say in the tea rooms and bars of the Palace of Westminster that Guards officers used the phrase 'as brave as Mr Macmillan' when they wanted to denote a special act of coolness under fire.[3] This was plainly nonsense. This was not Grenadier language. The claim had much more to do with the reality of 1940s than of 1916. There was a need to assert the specialness of the Great War now that it had been superseded by the much fresher memories of the Second World War.[4]

Beyond this collective change in self-image, Macmillan, Crookshank and Lyttelton's individual responses to the new order were also determined by their parliamentary constituencies. Cranborne had given up South Dorset for the House of Lords during the war. This relieved him of the need to worry too much about the specifics of the election. Constituency affairs worked very much in Crookshank's favour. He won Gainsborough with the narrow but sufficient majority of 1,645 over the Labour candidate. Although the formerly strong Liberal interest in the constituency was now fading, it had still played some part in splitting the anti-Tory vote. If Gainsborough could survive the 1945 disaster it was a safe seat. The 1945 election saved Crookshank's political career. If Churchill had won he would have been unchallenged in the party. He had already shown that he had no interest in advancing Crookshank. The electoral defeat, however, cleared away many of Crookshank's front-bench rivals. It also played to his skills. He was first and foremost a House of Commons performer and the Tories badly needed such talents in opposition, 'quick at the up-take – always knows his subject and puts his stuff across good naturedly and effectively'.[5] He made a number of high-profile attacks on left-wing ministers such as Nye Bevan, John Strachey and Emanuel Shinwell in the House. He succeeded in getting under the skin of the Labour party. In a vituperative article, Michael Foot described him as a man without principle, a tetchy pedant and a lightweight.[6] His reputation as 'sniper-in-chief' did, of course, do him immeasurable good in the Conservative party.

The position for Macmillan and Lyttelton was more complex. One of the great plusses for Macmillan was that he lost his seat. He had long wished to be freed of the incubus of Stockton. It was too precarious a base from which to launch himself into high office. At each election he risked having his career terminated by local political fluctuations.[7] As usual Stockton was one of the first results to be announced. As in 1929, Macmillan's defeat was a harbinger of the overall result. Macmillan, however, was one of the few among those caught up in the bonfire of the ambitions to remain sanguine. His *sang froid* was a tribute to the immense confidence his war work had given him. The previous year he had explored the possibility of taking over Duff Cooper's seat, Westminster. He had not gone to Westminster, because he refused to supplicate a constituency association for a safe seat.[8] He believed that the war had made him a prize catch for any constituency.[9]

With so many former ministers losing their seats, however, it was necessary to be confident to remain cool. The number who could be brought back through by-elections was strictly limited. Some older MPs, notable for their safe seats rather than their talent, could be persuaded to relinquish them in return for peerages or sinecures. Many others approached had little intention of budging. They were happy with the honour and dignity of their position and had no wish to give it up. The party could not, in any case, draw from the well of its electors' loyalty too often. One of the first orders of business in the humiliated party was therefore a bitter little civil war about who was to be resurrected.[10] It was a tribute to Macmillan's position that he sailed through these troubles so briskly when others, much closer to Churchill personally, had to wait. The first seat to become available was Bromley in Kent. The constituency was a plum; a safe Tory seat in a pleasant suburb close to London. Indeed, the sitting MP had been returned at the head of the poll despite having died before the votes were counted. Churchill's first thought was to grasp the candidature for his son Randolph.[11] Instead Bromley was handed to Macmillan: a triumph of political rationality over dynastic sentiment. The award of Bromley to Macmillan was a public acknowledgement that he was a man the party could not afford to do without.

The complications in Oliver Lyttelton's political future lay elsewhere. He sat for the safe seat of Aldershot. He was faced not even by a Labour candidate but by a representative of Richard Acland's Common Wealth Party. Acland, one of Harold Macmillan's pre-war Liberal associates, had formed and led a political movement which had a brief but powerful political efflorescence during the wartime electoral truce. Common Wealth stood for common ownership; the wealthy baronet Acland divesting himself of his own estates. These romantic guild socialists found Lyttelton a tempting target as the representative of global monopoly capitalism. They dug up information about his cartel activities at BMC which could be made to look most sinister. In the event, Common Wealth's taunts held little interest for the burghers of Aldershot.

Lyttelton for his part had to give serious consideration to how to balance his political and business activities. He had been bitten by the political bug. Like the professional politicians, he had steered clear of the Viceroyalty of India in mid war, knowing that for all its glamour and importance it was a political dead end. Two and a half gruelling years at the Ministry of Production had whetted rather than diminished his appetite. At the end of the war he made no secret of his ambition to have a 'great career'.[12] On the other hand, he had no intention of embracing poverty. Lacking capital, he needed a salary to maintain himself as a gentleman. Thus, when the board of AMC asked him to return as their chairman, he equivocated. The salary on offer was only £1,500 a year.[13] As Common Wealth's campaign in Aldershot demonstrated, AMC was not a good berth for a politician. Lyttelton told the AMC board that 'I should very likely be damaging the company, as I cannot avoid being a controversial figure, and I am afraid that a great deal of unnecessary criticism would be fixed upon the metal group if I were there.'[14] The opposite was true also; the company could damage the politician. Lyttelton now regarded AMC as his fallback position if he couldn't do any better.[15] Happily for him he could. In February 1945 Sir Felix Pole, the chairman of Associated Electrical Industries, one of Britain's blue-chip companies, fell ill. By July 1945 it had become clear to the AEI board that they had to seek a replacement. AEI picked up the feelers Lyttelton had put out in the City.[16] He leapt at the chance of becoming chairman and chief executive of the company.[17] It was a good deal for him. Instead of the £1,500 salary offered by AMC, he would receive £12,000 a year with a company house in Eaton Square thrown in.[18] Lyttelton could ride the political and business horses at the same time.

The party of which Macmillan, Lyttelton, Cranborne and Crookshank were now leading parliamentary figures was not a happy ship. Churchill was much diminished by his electoral defeat. Stripped of the wartime state apparatus that had made him all-powerful, he could no longer pick up and discard politicians as if they were military equipment. He needed the Tories as much as they needed him. He was by no means fatally wounded though. Although his lieutenants started to take on individual political identities separate from his own, they could never entirely escape his orbit. They remained occluded by the great man. One thing that had not been diminished by defeat was Churchill's will to power. He had no intention of fading from the scene. He was as keen to divide and rule his subordinates as ever. Instead of forming the traditional 'shadow cabinet', for instance, he created a leader's consultative committee.[19] Its meetings degenerated, as Churchill intended, into gargantuan drunken lunches at the Savoy. He was determined that senior members of the party would continue to be defined by their relationship to him rather than as a corporate body in which he was merely first among equals. Churchill had no hesitation in favouring loyal technocrats over more competent politicians.[20] 'All this,' Cranborne complained, 'seems to bear the stamp of our old friend Palace Government. Winston wants to run the opposition himself, in his own way, and does not intend to allow anyone to interfere or oppose him.'[21] How one felt about this new dispensation depended powerfully on wartime experience.

Oliver Lyttelton's position was straightforward. He was a Churchillian. His personal relations with Churchill were exceptionally warm. They maintained an easy banter over such matters as Julius Caesar's bawdy sense of humour.[22] Having decided to be a politician, Lyttelton worked hard to make himself a professional. Yet he and others were quite aware that any future promotion would come through Churchill's patronage.[23] He made a number of able speeches in Parliament, but could never quite catch the mood of the House.[24] To be thought a lecturer when one was a powerful minister running the war effort was bad enough, to come across in the same way as a mere opposition spokesman was quite dangerous. It was generally agreed that he was 'getting more the hang of things', but slowly.[25] Lyttelton's problem in establishing an independent role was exacerbated by his relationship with Oliver Stanley. They were friends of long standing.[26] They worked closely together on the trade, industry and finance side of the party. But in reality there was only room for one major figure in the berth they both jointly filled. Stanley was no Churchillian, but that was no longer such a disadvantage. Most tellingly, his light style of oratory was well suited to a party in opposition. Like Crookshank, his star was increasingly in the ascendant. In the event it was bad health that brought Stanley down, leading to his early death in 1950. For four years before that Lyttelton had had to play second fiddle. For a man who had started his political career so late, it was time he could ill afford to lose.

If Lyttelton was a Churchillian by nature, then Macmillan was determined to maintain the position as a Churchillian for which he had worked so hard. Indeed, the Chief Whip lumped him and Lyttelton together as those who managed Churchill best, because they 'would amuse him with their conversational wit'.[27] Macmillan would have been pleased by this assessment. He 'entirely disagreed' with those who believed Churchill was 'now very difficult to deal with'. 'On the contrary,' he was heard to say, 'he had mellowed. One always had to be patient with Winston and wait for one's chance to speak. It rarely produced an immediate effect, but eventually he would come back to one's point and show that he appreciated it ... He implied rather smugly that he knew how to manage Winston.'[28]

Macmillan threw himself with enthusiasm into Churchill's pet schemes, such as changing the name of the party and fusing with the Liberals.

More substantively, Macmillan took a prominent part in the United Europe Committee launched by Churchill in the wake of a headline-grabbing speech in Zurich. Organized by Duncan Sandys and financed by the CIA, the European Movement was a means of fighting the Cold War. As a member of Churchill's inner sanctum, Macmillan took a particular interest in the 'rollback' of communism.[29] Many other Tories regarded Churchill's private Cold War enterprise with grave suspicion. It was, wrote Cranborne, a 'pantomime', a 'talking shop for cranks', a monument to Churchill's vanity.[30] Cranborne told Macmillan that he would not speak in public about the organization, for if he did he would denounce it.[31] The European Movement even so enabled Conservatives such as Macmillan to have a role in foreign policy despite their exclusion from government. Macmillan's role in the movement reached a climax in 1949 when he led the Conservative delegation to the Council of Europe in Strasburg. The European stage appealed to him because he could flaunt his acquaintance with French, Italian and Greek politicians stretching back to the war.[32]

Macmillan had more strings to his bow than his relationship with Churchill. He was an asset to the party in the House of Commons.[33] Anthony Eden had a visceral dislike for him that, 'like a woman', he could not conceal.[34] Eden's supporters nevertheless saw in Macmillan a man with whom they could work. They might find him a bore, but they recognized his ability.[35] 'Harold,' Cranborne told them, 'seems to have done very well and to have greatly improved his position in the House. I am very glad of this, as he is a man with ideas, and the more he gets the ear of the House the better it will be.'[36] Their chief concern was not Macmillan but 'the Rabbit', Rab Butler.[37]

Butler was the one senior Conservative who had escaped Churchill's spell. Too young to have fought in the First World War, an intellectual and a cripple, he had side-stepped the macho posturing that Churchill had imposed on all his other subordinates in the

Second. His decision to spend his political exile at the Board of Education was a rejection of Churchill's conception of the Tory party in arms. It proved to be an act of political genius. The 1944 Education Act was the one piece of progressive legislation that the Conservatives could boast of in the 1940s. Butler's name was emblazoned upon it. Macmillan had gained immeasurably through his relationship with Churchill, but he had to cede the leadership of liberal Toryism to Butler. Although he worked in harness with the younger man, he never saw him as anything other than a rival. Macmillan was pro-Churchill but anti-Rabbit, which gave him plenty of common ground with the Edenites. They had a mutual interest in preventing the day 'the Rabbit will come into his predestined kingdom'.[38]

The autumn of 1945 saw the re-emergence of the Edenite faction within the Conservative party. Those who, unlike Macmillan or Lyttelton, had not felt the warmth of Churchill's favour were convinced that he should, ere long, resign from the leadership of the party. He had been a hostilities-only expedient and the hostilities were now over. This was the view taken by Crookshank and Cranborne.[39] Cranborne set about organizing a 'cry' against the 'really quite mad' Winstonian leadership of the party.[40] Yet the Edenites were even less well equipped to take on Churchill than they had been to take on Chamberlain. The already small faction of 1938 had been decimated by death and political defeat. Of the old guard only Cranborne, leading the Opposition in the House of Lords, Jim Thomas, now vice-chairman of the party, and Dick Law remained. Eden himself was a diminished figure. He had failed badly in 1940. He was exhausted after five years at the Foreign Office, his son had been killed in the last days of the war, his marriage was breaking up. His friends could see a clear distinction between him and Churchill, but others were less clear as to the difference. Eden's personality seemed almost to have been subsumed into Churchill's during the war. Churchill made much of this absorption. He never stinted in his praise of Eden while making it clear that the younger man was and always would be the junior caesar. Paradoxically, Eden had become the ultimate Churchillian. This above everything else was the weakness of Churchill's enemies in the party. Eden had never shown any capacity for seizing the moment and striking down an enemy. It was even less likely that he would mount a *coup* against the father of the nation. Churchill himself was confident that his foes would not have the strength of will or purpose to combine against him. He had the measure of his men.[41] In the spring of 1946 Eden asked Churchill to step aside for him. Churchill refused and Eden did not have either the will or the means to push him out.[42] Also par for the course was the fact that Cranborne, Churchill's most articulate critic, was rendered *hors de combat* by his chronic liver problems.[43]

Despite Cranborne's self-imposed exile in Portugal, both sides in the dispute turned their eyes to him. The chief whip, James Stuart, appealed to him to act as a peacemaker. Stuart's contention was that most of the blame for the poisonous atmosphere in the party was the fault of the Edenites. Churchill had been prepared 'to delegate full leadership of the opposition in the House to Anthony – while retaining himself the Leadership of the Party in the country'. Stuart claimed that he himself had been in favour of this arrangement, 'and even went to the Treasury on his instructions to find out if – and how – he could hand over the salary of the Leader of the Opposition to another'. 'We had,' Stuart claimed, 'everything in order and the Treasury squared.' 'At this point,' the chief whip maintained, 'I can only imagine that Anthony was primed by some of his more bogus admirers to go for everything – i.e. Party leadership as well. Anyway Anthony subjected us to some temperamental tantrums and WSC recoiled: relations were not, in fact, too happy for a little.' Stuart proposed a truce. If Cranborne called off the Edenite dogs, 'I think that the matter could be worked out amicably and that our affairs could be managed efficiently. As you say, the solution may not be "ideal" – and even if any solution were, it won't work so long as some of our young gentlemen are worked up to revolt against it all the time. There must always be a wish to make any system work – and this desire is necessary among the "rank and file" as well as those responsible at the top.' Stuart would try and reconstruct the deal that would give Eden the leadership of the Opposition if Churchill retained the leadership of the party.

Eden was not, as Stuart disingenuously maintained, being egged on by young 'bogus admirers', but by his oldest friends, with Cranborne at their head. Cranborne advised Eden 'that it was in fact so difficult for two men, both with definite and often divergent views as to the course which the Party should pursue, to run in double harness as Leader of the Conservative Party in the country and Leader of the Party in the Commons that the experiment was not even worth trying, and rather than attempt it, I should prefer to stand down and follow my own line in Parliament.'[44] He would have preferred Eden to strike the blow for himself, but understood why he was reluctant to do so: 'Either he would invite a bitter quarrel with Winston or the latter would adopt a pained and grieved attitude which would make Anthony feel an utter cad. In either case he would have to give way.' If Churchill was to be felled, Eden's friends would have to do the job for him: 'there should', Cranborne suggested to Jim Thomas, 'be a joint approach by a number of his colleagues to Winston. He would probably never forgive the colleagues and they might very naturally be reluctant to take part in such an approach. I do not at present see any alternative step.' As 'leaders of the Party' they had to 'take their courage in both hands'.[45]

Cranborne was prepared to lead a cabal against Churchill.[46] But there was little point in striking down the 'imperious Caesar' if Hamlet would not seize the throne. 'Time and time again' upon his return from Portugal, Cranborne told Eden that there was no point speaking fair words to Churchill, for 'nothing will budge him but a massed demonstration by his colleagues'. He stood ready to organize such a demonstration, but Eden would never give the word. Without Eden's active connivance, it would be impossible to convince any other party leader to act. If he would not put his head above the parapet, then neither most certainly would they.

All the old doubts that Cranborne had had about his friend in 1939 and 1940 began to resurface. As spring turned to summer, autumn and winter, Cranborne's frustration grew. Even Dick Law, 'who is certainly not by nature a wobbler,' was reluctant to adopt his plan.[47] Finally Cranborne let it be known that he did not 'propose to take any further part in the controversy'. 'Until Anthony,' he explained to Jim Thomas, 'makes up his mind to do what he knows in his heart to be the right thing, he will never get anywhere and these constant complaints to his friends are merely futile and exasperating.' 'You know,' he confided in Paul Emrys-Evans, 'how devoted I am to him, so you will not misunderstand this frank expression of my views. But if he wants to be regarded as a leader, he must act like one. At present, I am afraid, he is rapidly losing ground. He can only regain it by some resolute step, such as he took when he resigned in 1938. That got him the reputation of a strong man, but he cannot live on this one incident in his career for ever.'[48] Coming from Cranborne, this was savage criticism. He was too fond of Eden to draw out the full implications of his own remarks, but they amounted to this: Eden had not made a worthwhile political act since 1938. He was a weak man living on an unwarranted reputation.

As it was, Cranborne had no political options open to him. He himself had no political following in the House of Commons; without Eden he was impotent. When Eden had proven a broken reed in the 1930s, Cranborne had looked to his own family for assistance. Now this was no longer an option. His father and Lord Robert were ailing men.[49] On the death of Lord Salisbury in the summer of 1947, Cranborne was further distracted from national affairs by those of Hatfield, which he found in poor order.[50] Billy Ormsby-Gore and Top Wolmer were grazing happily on the red benches of the House of Lords. His grandfather had put his three sons in the House of Commons as a Cecil phalanx. In happier circumstances, Bobbety might have done the same. Now he only had one son left, and although he was interested in politics, he was not yet in a position to help his father. Robert Cecil had stood, unsuccessfully, for Parliament in July 1945. He was chiefly known to the public from a court case that resulted from him hitting a reporter who had infiltrated his wedding. The Cecils were a much-reduced political dynasty. The leader of the greatest political family in England found himself 'pottering round the garden, doing odd jobs that would be far better done by the gardeners', 'becoming lazier and lazier and less inclined to leave the country'. As he wryly admitted, 'perhaps, for this very reason, I should not criticize Anthony'.[51]

In the event it was Crookshank who took up a pale imitation of Cranborne's plan. In February 1947 he reconvened the Café Royal Group. Of the old members, Crookshank, Macmillan, Dick Law, Osbert Peake and Ralph Assheton were still MPs. To make up the numbers, they recruited two Scottish lawyers as new members, James Reid and, more importantly, a rising figure in the party, David Maxwell-Fyfe. A contemporary of Boothby at Balliol, an MP since 1935, a 'terrible appeaser', Fyfe began to make a mark after 1945, most famously as a prosecutor at the Nuremberg Trials. Macmillan and Fyfe were allies in the European Movement.[52] Eden too had cultivated Fyfe.[53] Eden's representative in the group, Dick Law, had felt 'doubtful' about Cranborne's plan for 'definite action' to get Churchill to budge. The Café Royal Group could, however, act as an effective stalking-horse. The members were not self-evidently Edenites. If they precipitated Churchill's resignation, Eden could not be accused of regicide. The most outspoken advocate of 'dishing' Churchill was Crookshank himself.[54]

This was Macmillan's last brush with one of those 'ginger groups' that had done such damage to his career. He came to the meeting that decided to push for Churchill's retirement late since he had just returned from a business trip to India. The removal of Churchill was most definitely not in his political interests. Ensuring that Eden did not lose ground to Rab Butler was, on the other hand. He is not recorded as expressing a view at the Café Royal Group about Churchill's removal. In December 1945 he, Cranborne, Crookshank and Stuart had discussed the succession over dinner. They had agreed then that Churchill could not be 'shoved' but must go of his own accord.[55] Cranborne and Crookshank had moved on since then, but it is most likely that Macmillan continued to adhere to this position, as Stuart most certainly did.

A reluctant James Stuart was invited to a 'clandestine meeting' with the group. The purpose of the meeting was to convey to Churchill the opinion that he had 'had it' and that 'it was in the better interests of the Party that he should seek peace in retirement'. The plotters convened for luncheon in an upstairs drawing room of 51 Pont Street. Stuart subsequently declined to name the eight people present, beyond himself and Crookshank, though there were indeed seven members of the Café Royal Group. There were, he noted, 'others not present because of other engagements that day – I was reminded of the parable of the supper guests'. Stuart was not impressed by the calibre of the group: 'we had among us those deep thinkers whose mental processes will not follow the normal sensible course of other people, lest that should relegate them to the level of the ordinary and let others forget how clever they are. Such people I find are almost always wrong.' Stuart can hardly, however, have been surprised at what they had to say. He had heard it all before, not least from Cranborne months previously. The chief whip had to concede that Churchill was a poor leader of the Opposition. He agreed to convey the group's view to Churchill.

'Winston,' in Stuart's later recollection, 'received me alone in his room at the House. He reacted violently, banging the floor with his stick and implying that I too had joined those who were plotting to displace him.' In fact Churchill was relieved by the weakness of the dissenters. He and Stuart had been seeing off the Café Royal Group for years. Unless either Eden or Butler or a coalition of the two conspired directly against him, he was safe. The message Stuart conveyed back to Pont Street was that Churchill had no intention of resigning. With a whimper rather than a bang, the agitation against him died away. 'No more was heard of his retirement for several years,' wrote Stuart 'and none of the others present at our private meeting repeated to him the views which they had so kindly invited me to convey.'[56] The fact that no one had the courage to face Churchill directly meant that he could sail on. Giving up a lost cause, the leaders of the party just had to get on with running an Opposition on the assumption of his leadership.

Having settled, or rather failed to settle, the question of the leadership, Churchill's would-be successors needed perforce to turn their attention to defeating the Labour party. Here they had more luck than in their internal party squabbles. It had soon become clear that the social revolution promised by the 1945 landslide would either fail to materialize or would have most uncomfortable side-effects. Power had shifted into the hands of a group of middle-class men who, if not actually Oxford dons, were most certainly donnish. Of the Labour leaders with impeccable working-class credentials, Ernest Bevin proved so enthusiastic about the British Empire that he won as many plaudits from Bobbety Cranborne as he did brickbats from his own backbenchers; Nye Bevan, the party's most effective orator, never seemed fully part of the team and indeed broke with Attlee in 1950. The Labour leadership could never quite conceal how much they hated each other. At the same time as senior Tories were plotting to overthrow Churchill, Labour leaders rallied by Herbert Morrison were planning to dish Attlee. As little came of the latter plot as of the former. Compared to the Labour party, however, the Tory plotters, with their paranoid meetings behind Crookshank's frosted windows, were masters of discretion.

Such discord might not have mattered if the Labour government's competence had matched their parliamentary majority. It did not. There were major financial crises in 1947 and 1949. With some justice the government could argue that they were a legacy of wartime expenditure. Their case was hardly strengthened, however, by the fact that the chancellor of the exchequer, 'the dirty doctor', Hugh Dalton, had been forced to resign a few months after the first currency crisis for burbling out budget secrets to a journalist. Life in Britain under Labour was, if anything, bleaker than it had been during the war.

Harry Crookshank enjoyed his greatest success in exposing the government's incompetence in securing food supplies. The search for meat had driven the Labour ministers into the arms of the Argentine dictator Juan Perón and his lovely wife Evita. The Labour government had paid up front for Argentine beef, but the Peróns pocketed the money and failed to deliver. Observing Britain's desperation for food, they saw endless opportunities for the sort of criminal extortion they practised in their own country to be translated on to an international scale. In a series of masterly parliamentary performances, 'powerful in attack, well phrased and witty', Crookshank was able to unfold the scale of the government's gullibility.[57] His mastery of detail was such that government ministers started contradicting and blaming each other for the fiasco.[58] Opinion polls showed that problems in food supplies translated directly into government unpopularity.[59]

Not only did the government seem unable to alleviate the people's suffering, but it revealed, under pressure, a rather nasty authoritarian turn of mind, a sense that anyone who complained that the road to New Jerusalem was too hard was a Tory running dog. The Conservatives had fertile ground in which to recover. The apocalyptic view that they would be out of office for a generation was, within a year, replaced by a sense that, although the road back was difficult, it was possible to traverse it. There were various things the Tories could do to augment their position. They could launch a powerful parliamentary opposition to Labour, they could reinvigorate the constituency organizations that had fallen into desuetude during the war, they could improve the quality of their candidates, they could, as Churchill wanted, make grand set-piece gestures that would see them still striding the world stage. All the key players, Eden, Butler, Macmillan, Stanley, Cranborne, Crookshank and Lyttelton, were themselves convinced they had to do one thing above all others. They had in some way to convince the electorate that the party was 'progressive' rather than 'reactionary'.[60] They had to find something new to offer. 'People don't want to go back to the old days,' Cranborne acknowledged, 'we must give them an alternative line of advance.'[61]

The 'pinkish portion' of the party, led by Butler and Macmillan, were later to be seen as the main begetters of this new line.[62] But the right of the party were in the field just as quickly. Cranborne was one of the first to encourage new thinking. He suggested that the way forward was 'co-partnership'. The 'small man' must be made into a 'stakeholder'. 'Anyone who wants to own a house of his own should be encouraged and where possible given assistance to buy one,' he wrote, 'anyone who works in industry should be encouraged to become a shareholder.'[63] Eden disinterred an old piece of YMCA phraseology from the 1920s and launched the great new theme of a 'property-owning democracy' in the autumn of 1946.[64]

Whatever the personal rivalries in the party, there was only limited ideological friction. What there was was mainly stirred up by Dick Law, who chose to stress the other side of the Cecilian credo, that 'the right and power to make and preserve a private fortune must be jealously guarded as the key incentive for men to sacrifice leisure to industry'.[65] Cranborne wrote this in 1941, but nothing in the interim had changed his mind. 'Of course,' he acknowledged in 1946, 'a good deal of what we should have to say would be most unpopular with a great many people. We should have to make it clear that we don't believe in complete egalitarianism, that we don't believe that high wages are themselves the cure for all ills, that we don't hold with confiscatory taxation of any class of income.'[66] The main opponent of 'stakeholders', Oliver Lyttelton, in fact based his opposition on much the same arguments.[67] Where Lyttelton and Cranborne parted company was over Cranborne's insistence that the 'low tax' message had to leavened by some innovative thinking aimed at the 'small man'. This was why Cranborne championed Macmillan. Macmillan had the fertile imagination and the attention to detail that would make such a programme credible.

Yet if Cranborne and Macmillan had much in common, then so too did Macmillan and Lyttelton. Lyttelton cried with Macmillan that 'the bankruptcy of Conservative economic policy between the wars must not be repeated'. Like Macmillan, he laid down a marker as someone who had criticized the economic policy of the party in the 1930s.[68] The kind of 'corporatist' policies that had appealed to Macmillan were also championed by Lyttelton.[69] 'In the field of public ownership,' Oliver had declared in 1944, 'I am a great believer in insulating the Government by means of corporations run on commercial lines from negotiations and from the haggling of the market.'[70] In endorsing the view that the government should try and create full employment, he accepted that 'we must certainly be prepared to see the state exercising some influence and direction over the timing and magnitude of new capital construction by local authorities, public utilities and large companies'.[71] He published a pamphlet arguing that free enterprise 'does not mean that we are bound to oppose State or public ownership of anything at all times'.[72] Neither was Lyttelton a foe of large-scale public works. As early as 1942 he was telling his fellow Tories that 'the central fact of post-war economy is ... that the modern world has not yet realized its own capacity to re-create its wealth. If we fix our minds on the immense capacity to re-create wealth, we shall not [follow] a niggardly and deflationary financial policy. It is not difficult to create by good simple financial measures a very large construction fund.'[73] In the early months of the next Conservative government, he was as good as his word and supported Macmillan 'on the absurdity of the whole conception of the rigid capital ceiling'.[74] Although he carped, Lyttelton did sign the centrepiece of the Conservative 'New Look', the 1947 *Industrial Charter*. His criticism of the document was that it was rhetoric rather than a definite plan of action.[75] Yet he went on to defend this 'ingenious' document against the attacks of right-wing Tory backbenchers. He was as convinced as anyone about the need for the Conservatives to persuade the electorate that they were not 'fat cats'.[76]

Lyttelton's main problem was one of perception. He had been one of the first into the lists after the election defeat, rallying the Conservatives in Parliament and in the press. Cranborne had seen at the time that this was 'not so wise'.[77] Lyttelton had admirers on the backbenches, but he also had an image problem. In 1948 he and Louis Spears, disgusted at what they saw as the 'wayside violet mentality – the feeling that if industry keeps quiet, does not engage in any political activity or political propaganda, that it will be allowed to blush unseen and that the wayside violet will escape the sickle of nationalization', had revived a moribund organization called the Institute of Directors. As chairman of the new institute's executive committee, Lyttelton made it his first priority to organize propaganda for free enterprise.[78] This was, in fact, part of a wider campaign coordinated by Lord Woolton from Conservative Central Office to encourage industrialists to condemn nationalization. Its best-known manifestation was Tate & Lyle's 'Mr Cube' campaign, against the nationalization of the sugar industry. The free-enterprise campaigns were little more than sensible self-defence. They were portrayed by socialists, of course, as somehow being sinister.[79] Lyttelton himself was vilified as the leader of a group of capitalist illuminati. 'To many on the Labour benches,' a journalist later wrote, 'he was a symbol of privilege, the arrogance, and the formidable determination, of Toryism. There was always something in his manner – the elegant correctness of his clothes, the uncompromising edge of instinctive authority in his voice – which rankled with the working-class rank and file in the Labour Party, and provoked its intellectuals to paroxysms of fascinated hatred.[80]

Lyttelton's finest moment in opposition was leading in the House of Commons against the nationalization of iron and steel. This was a deliberate act of class war launched by the socialists for political rather than economic reasons. According to Hugh Dalton, the government's aim was to break 'the power of a most dangerous body of capitalists'.[81] 'If we cannot get Nationalization of steel by legal means,' Sir Stafford Cripps declared, 'we must resort to violent methods.'[82] The British steel industry was, unlike coal, profitable and relatively efficient. The leader of the ironmasters, Andrew Duncan, Lyttelton's colleague and Macmillan's boss during the war, was quite willing to reach a compromise settlement with the government.[83] Lyttelton was thus able to launch a most effective attack on Labour authoritarianism. He thoroughly enjoyed the 'pretty hot parliamentary debate, as hot as you've seen'. The campaign against steel nationalization was the one that most galvanized the party.[84] Yet in the *Industrial Charter* atmosphere of the late 1940s, Lyttelton did not seem able to reap the full benefit from his efforts. 'They tell me,' observed Cuthbert Headlam, 'that his ambition is to be made Chancellor of the Exchequer, but I fancy Oliver Stanley is the more likely man to get the job if and when we get back.'[85]

Steel nationalization had a rather ambivalent effect on Cranborne's reputation too. His own accession to the House of Lords, coupled with the depletion of his contemporaries at the 1945 election, had weakened his links with the House of Commons. To any Conservative elected after 1941, he was an Olympian figure going about the business of the 'other place'. Harold Macmillan was constantly reminding younger MPs about his own anti-appeasement record. As Churchill and his team of writers churned out a multi-volume Churchillian history of the Second World War in the post-war years, such a past was most valuable.[86] In this context, Cranborne's contribution seemed little more than ancient history, his Commons role forgotten by all but the *cognoscenti*. His recurring illnesses kept him away from London at Hatfield or abroad for months at a time. He had been one of the early advocates of a 'progressive' party, but without the energy to follow up his initial contributions, which in any case had mainly been made in private, this memory too soon faded. It was the steel debates that brought him once more to the forefront of the party's attention.

Whatever successes Lyttelton might have in the Commons, the parliamentary arithmetic of Labour's huge majority meant that they could push steel nationalization through without trouble. It was then up to the Conservatives to decide whether they would veto it by using their own majority in the House of Lords. The decision lay with Cranborne on whether to unleash his followers upon the measure. Although the 'Independent Unionist Peers' were not always an easy group to direct, Cranborne was both the titular and real leader of the Tory peers.[87] Newcomers, whatever their position in the Tory hierarchy, such as Swinton, Cherwell or Woolton, had no real sway in the House without his backing. Cranborne's position nevertheless placed him in a difficult situation. Lord Salisbury's death had laid a number of heavy charges on his son: unravelling his financial affairs, maintaining Hatfield, leading the family. The weightiest of all was the future of the House of Lords itself. The fourth Marquess had been haunted by the Parliament Act of 1911. If the Lords could be stripped of their power once, it could happen again. From the 1920s onwards, he had thrown himself into schemes for reform of the Lords which would cement their position within the constitution. By the time he was incapacitated by illness in 1944, Lords reform had become his overriding political interest.

The election of the Labour government in 1945 presented the single largest threat to the Lords since 1911. The socialists and the peers glowered at each other in a posture of mutual deterrence. The government knew that half-way through their term the delaying powers that had been left to the Lords under the 1911 Act would become effective. Legislation moved after that point could be delayed until the eve of or beyond a general election. Cranborne, on the other hand, knew that if he allowed the House to become 'Mr Churchill's poodle', an instrument in an all-out political offensive against the socialists, he would be handing the Labour government the perfect excuse to emasculate or even abolish the second chamber.[88] He was thus the very model of a 'hedger'. He opened up a friendly dialogue with Christopher Addison, the former Liberal who was now leader of the Labour party in the Lords, promising to keep his own 'backwoodsmen' in check. 'It is fair to say that at present we get on very well indeed,' Addison assured his colleagues.[89] The House of Lords, Cranborne reassured his father, was more important to him than the Conservative party.[90]

Although by his studied moderation Cranborne managed to win Addison over to the view that the Lords should be left alone, the rest of the socialist Cabinet were not convinced. Steel nationalization was the crunch issue. The decision to deal with the less controversial nationalization of the utilities first meant that it was pushed back later in the government's programme. The delaying power of the House of Lords thus became germane. Steel nationalization was meant to be a double body blow to the Conservatives. Not only would a key group of capitalists be crushed, but so too would the peers. They would be emasculated by a pre-emptive strike. A new Parliament Act would cut the Lords' delaying powers by half. Instead of becoming an effective restraint on the government at the half-way point of a Parliament, the Lords would only be allowed to pick off the fag-end of its legislation. With their powers reduced the Lords would be unable to cripple steel nationalization.[91]

Lord Salisbury had left his son a drawer full of reform schemes. He had latterly come to the conclusion that if the Lords was to be preserved life peers would be the 'principal feature' of the reformed House.[92] For Salisbury this had been a reluctant conversion. Cranborne was willing to go one step further. He believed that 'a choice had to be made between the hereditary system and a strong Second Chamber. We cannot any longer have both.' He would 'abolish the hereditary principle so far as the House of Lords is concerned'. As each existing peer died, the monarch, on the advice of the prime minister of the day, would create a life peer to take his place.[93] There was no talk of female peers since George VI had already told Cranborne that he was 'especially concerned' that women should be excluded.[94] In order to avert the new Parliament Act, Cranborne needed to make a deal with the Labour party. He would agree to a progressively radical reform of the composition of the House of Lords if its delaying powers were left untouched.

He was stymied by three factors. Cranborne wanted to compromise with Labour over steel nationalization. If the Labour party would abandon their determination to force through reform of the Lords, he would ensure that the Lords passed a steel bill voluntarily. His own colleagues were, however, unwilling to allow him to do this. Steel was supposed to be a great rallying-point for the party. They were unwilling to allow the House of Lords to sell the pass.[95] Secondly, Cranborne had wanted to ditch the hereditary principle. To this the 'backwoodsmen' would not agree. They would, reluctantly, accept life peers, but not as replacements for their own sons.[96] The most serious problem remained that the Labour party had the scent of blood in its nostrils. Addison believed that a statesmanlike constitutional settlement was on offer. He was told firmly that this was not what the party wanted. Labour MPs delighted in peer bashing; their leaders were pleased to let them have their head on an issue that cost no money and diverted attention from their own failures.[97]

In the spring of 1948 there was a series of meetings between a government team, led by Attlee, and a Tory team, led by Cranborne. Although weighty constitutional issues were discussed in a polite and thorough manner, there was little chance of a compromise. Attlee had no interest in talking about composition. The only point on which he was willing to have a genuine discussion was over the three months' difference created by choosing different starting-points for the 'one year' delaying power the new Parliament Act would grant the House of Lords. As Cranborne said as they broke up, 'there was a fundamental difference of view between the two Parties as to the function of the Second Chamber'.[98]

Having failed as a 'hedger' Cranborne immediately reinvented himself as a 'ditcher'. He rallied their Lordships to oppose both the Parliament Bill and the Iron and Steel Bill with all might and main.[99] He realized he had put himself in a difficult position and insisted there should be no full disclosure of what had been said in the inter-party meeting, since 'in putting forward some suggestions, and in tentatively accepting others, he had recognized that he would be taking his supporters further than they would wish to go'.[100] Yet the meetings had, in fact, leaked like a sieve; the details of the discussion were widely known.[101] Conservative MPs were well aware of Cranborne's activities. Many could not see 'what use there is in a Second Chamber like the House of Lords nowadays'.[102] Whereas no one doubted Lyttelton's passion when he assaulted the steel legislation as a constitutional outrage, Cranborne's arguments had to be taken with a pinch of salt. He himself never doubted for a moment the importance of reforming the House of Lords. For him the 1948 constitutional talks were an important stepping-stone to 'comprehensive reform' under the next Conservative administration.[103] Yet this adherence to a deeply felt constitutional principle had a cost. At the beginning of the opposition Cranborne had had the opportunity to carve out for himself a powerful position in the party as a 'sound' man who was also a 'progressive'. This opportunity had dribbled away. At the end of the opposition he was primarily associated with the 'reactionary' cause of the House of Lords. He remained an important symbolic figure in the party, but the very nature of his political interests meant his constituency was limited and shrinking. He was out of tune with those dynamic elements of the party he had been so keen to encourage.

The new political mood that Cranborne had helped to create was, on the other hand, greatly to the benefit of Harold Macmillan and Rab Butler. It was Butler, with his control of the party's internal think-tank, the Conservative Research Department, which did most of the detailed work on new policy documents, who seemed in the best position to benefit from a commitment to progressive Conservatism. Macmillan then managed to trump him by getting the press to pick up the line that the *Industrial Charter* was the second volume of his 1938 book *The Middle Way*. The leader of the younger progressives, Quintin Hogg, against whom Macmillan campaigned in the 1938 Oxford by-election, declared, 'Conservatives have always sought progress along the *Middle Way*.'[104] Macmillan had succeeded in drawing a clever contrast between their pre-war activities. Butler had been a loyal Chamberlainite while he, Macmillan, had been ploughing a lone furrow. It mattered little that the *Middle Way* had not been the starting-point for the *Industrial Charter*. Indeed, meetings tended to run into the sand when Macmillan insisted on reading out chunks of his book. If anything the starting-point for the new approach was to be found in the pragmatic policies followed by Harry Crookshank at the Ministry of Mines in the late 1930s: 'support of cartelization and market-sharing within a protectionist framework'.

The *Industrial Charter* was a signal of intent rather than a practical policy. It was, of course, much harder to make real decisions. As Cranborne recognized early on in the debate, 'there is far too much general principles about our arguments and far too little detailed programme'.[105] Yet there was no doubt that Macmillan and Butler had seized the high ground within the party.[106] Eden liked to portray himself as a progressive, but he did not have the staying power to convince anyone that he was making a significant contribution to domestic policy. As even his best friend acknowledged, he was 'going to get us nowhere'.[107] It was in fact Eden who publicly launched the *Industrial Charter* at a large rally held at Cardiff castle, but few people were fooled. As one political correspondent wrote, 'The really solid work of plotting the Party's future course has been largely done by two men – Mr Butler and Mr Macmillan. While the immediate succession would fall automatically to Mr Eden, the influence of Mr Butler and Mr Macmillan will remain a highly important factor.'[108]

None of the 'fiftysomethings' would claim to have enjoyed the period in opposition. They had started it physically more worn down than any Opposition during the century. Their task in Parliament had often been thankless. 'I found the House of Commons uncongenial,' Lyttelton recalled, 'the manners of our opponents made life harsh and disagreeable.'[109] They had each, however, managed to consolidate the position they had achieved by 1945. Macmillan and Crookshank had made great strides forward.[110] Few doubted their right to inhabit the upper reaches of the party.[111] They were, as the *Daily Mirror* put it, 'the men who think they will rule Britain'.[112] Indeed, they had been part of a great political achievement. An electorate that had rejected the past so decisively in 1945 was by 1951 willing to entrust, grudgingly, the governance of the country once more to an ageing social élite. In the February 1950 general election, the Labour majority of 146 seats had been reduced to a mere 5. Such a slender majority was simply too small to carry on for long. In September 1951, Attlee announced he was going to the country again. The Conservatives won the October general election with an overall majority of seventeen seats.

8

Ministers

One issue that the Tory election victory failed to resolve was the future leadership of the Conservative party. For Cranborne and Crookshank in particular, tyrannicide was merely a duty postponed.[1] Macmillan was more subtle. He had modelled himself as a loyal Churchillian. On the other hand, he was rapidly coming to the conclusion that Churchill had served his purpose and was turning into a liability.[2] Because his own claims on the purple were as yet tenuous, it served him to play the waiting game. Max Beaverbrook whispered to him, 'There will be an Eden section, there will be a Butler section. You may easily slip in.' It was a 'stimulating medicine'. Yet he knew he had to proceed with caution and not risk becoming reviled by both camps.[3] Because of their personal antipathy and because they were fighting over the same political territory, an alliance of convenience with Butler was unlikely.[4] If anything, Eden and Macmillan disliked each other more than did Butler and Macmillan. In political terms, however, they had something to offer each other: Macmillan's support for Eden's candidature for the prime ministership in return for a promise of the Foreign Office in any Eden government.[5] Eden was even willing, he assured Macmillan, to ignore Salisbury's claim to the office.[6] The road to advancement seemed open. Eden was gathering allies around him to try and prise Churchill out of Downing Street.[7] Macmillan was drawn into the conspiracy.[8]

Churchill had no intention of giving up his throne to anyone. His opening gambit was to wrong-foot his potentially fractious ministers. None of them got quite what they wanted or expected. The biggest shock was Lyttelton's. He had confidently expected to be made chancellor of the exchequer, but Rab Butler was appointed in his place.[9] The very centrality of the Treasury and the difficult circumstances of 1951 militated against Lyttelton's ambitions. He was unswervingly loyal to Churchill. Churchill returned his loyalty with affection. Lyttelton had worked hard to make himself a professional politician. Yet he was too much of a risk. The very success of his hard work in opposition had done him harm. Unlike Lords Cherwell, Leathers, Ismay and subsequently Alexander, all included in the Cabinet, or indeed his own younger self, he could no longer be presented as a non-party man, a vaguely rightish technocrat. His manner, his chairmanship of AEI, his activities at the Institute of Directors made it all too easy for detractors to portray him as the personification of uncaring big-business interests, a member of the 'forty thieves', a 'merchant of death'. Perhaps more importantly, Churchill could not rely on him in the Commons. If the chancellor managed to turn the House against the government, it would be in serious trouble. Comparing Butler, whom he took every chance to denigrate, and Lyttelton, whom he liked and admired, during the budget debates a few months later, Macmillan admitted that the former 'made a fine speech' while the latter 'made a poor one'. Lyttelton's fatal flaw was apparent: 'he has no real sense of the House of Commons'.[10] Churchill's choice was entirely rational: Butler was his most intelligent candidate.

Lyttelton had learnt to his cost not to put one's trust in princes. Nevertheless Churchill was willing to offer him consolation in the form of a shop-soiled offer of the Colonial Office. Brendan Bracken had turned it down on the grounds of ill-health. Bobbety Salisbury too had turned it down, on the grounds that it promised more hard knocks than he felt able to endure.[11] The offer appealed to both Churchill and Lyttelton's sentimental side: Alfred Lyttelton had become colonial secretary the year in which Churchill had defected from the Conservative party. Neither of them was under any illusions, however, that they were talking about the end of Lyttelton's political career. In the changed circumstances of the empire in the post-1945 world, the Colonial Office offered precious few opportunities for glory. Lyttelton agreed to give the job a chance for two years before returning to the chair of AEI.[12]

Perhaps because he went to the Colonial Office as a last posting rather than as a stepping stone to something better, Lyttelton made his mark within weeks. Days before he took up his office, the British Empire received a sickening blow: on 7 October 1951 the High Commissioner for Malaya, Sir Henry Gurney, was murdered, gunned down in an ambush by communist terrorists. Britain had been fighting the communist guerrillas since 1948. Gurney's bullet-riddled vehicle bore witness to her failure to come to grips with her enemies. In retrospect there was a case to be made that the military and civilian leaders had already found the key to defeating the communists. By a policy of enforced resettlement of so-called 'squatters', the Chinese who had moved on to rural land from the towns, mainly during the Japanese occupation, they could cut the guerrillas off from their people. Without their support the communists would no longer be a spectral force of terror capable of seeming to appear from nowhere and murder with impunity before melting back into an anonymous mass of Chinese collaborators. Instead they would be forced into the role of a guerrilla army living off the land. Although still hard to find in the jungle, they would be susceptible to more conventional military operations designed to seek out and destroy them.[13] Yet the population control plan, though already being pursued, would not be worth the paper on which it was written if the men supposed to implement it were too confused and demoralized to be able to do so. The prospect of victory in the long-run was of no earthly use if defeat loomed in the short-term.

The disarray Lyttelton found was potentially terminal. The architect of population control, General Harold Briggs, was in neither good health nor good spirits. Having already extended his tour of duty he wanted to leave Malaya within weeks. William Jenkin, the director of intelligence, mortified by Gurney's murder, was 'not far off a nervous breakdown' and had offered his resignation. The commissioner of police, Colonel W. N. Gray, had not only failed in his task of creating an efficient police service but was engaged in a vicious turf war with Jenkin.[14] The man who had bravely stepped into Gurney's shoes, his deputy, M. V. del Tufo, commanded no one's confidence.[15]

Within days Lyttelton had understood the depth of the crisis. It was no good waiting for things to shake themselves down. When he demanded details of who was responsible for what in Malaya, he found the Colonial Office cupboard was bare. His predecessors had not bothered to ask, so London only had the vaguest idea of what was going on.[16] He realized that if any shaking was to be done he would have to do it himself.[17]

A decade previously, when he had flown into a Cairo faced with the prospect of military defeat, he had descended on to a peaceful Nile to be greeted by Miles Lampson's well-appointed launch. His arrival in Malaya was much less serene. The pressurization of Lyttelton's aeroplane failed *en route*, making for an extremely uncomfortable flight. He was met at the aerodrome by Malcolm MacDonald, the former colonial secretary who had tried so hard to persuade Anthony Eden and Bobbety Cranborne not to resign in 1938, but who was now Commissioner-General in South-East Asia, with a convoy of armoured cars. Having lost a High Commissioner, the military and police authorities were determined not to lose a colonial secretary. As the aeroplane came to a halt it was surrounded by a human wall of uniformed policemen. A crumpled colonial secretary said what he believed were a few well-chosen words about the primacy of security, which he was irritated to find sent the Malay political classes into a clucking fit.[18]

The tour of Malaya, the meetings with officials, planters and local politicians, merely confirmed what Lyttelton already suspected: that there had to be a complete clear-out. As one planter wrote to a clerical friend of Neville Talbot, the quartet's Grenadier chaplain in the war, 'I think most of us in this country were very impressed by Lyttelton and he has certainly done a grand job. If he can carry out all he proposes I feel we will be seeing the beginning of the end soon.'[19] Lyttelton did carry through all his proposals and it was the beginning of the end.[20] As in Cairo in 1941, he needed to get outsiders in to sort out the mess in the police and intelligence services. While in Malaya he visited Chinese schools, sniffing out subversion. In one school a group of small boys was learning English. 'What's that?' he had asked a 'smiling Chinese child of about four or five, pointing to a picture in his primer'. 'Peeeg,' the little boy squealed with delight. Lyttelton, however, glared at the children's books with disfavour: 'they can be useful or dangerous political instruments', he minuted as a result of his visit.[21] The Secretary of State could not, of course, devote himself personally to such campaigns. He persuaded Colonel Arthur Young, the chief of the City of London's police force, to go out for a year. 'The importance of intelligence in the Malayan campaign cannot be exaggerated,' Lyttelton declared in a seminal Cabinet paper. 'Every police operation is in large measure an intelligence task and the Malayan campaign is in essence a police operation . . . [yet] in Malaya little or no deep penetration of the enemy has been achieved.'[22] He knew nevertheless that, however much he cajoled, encouraged and monitored intelligence operations, – and he instructed that all intelligence reports from Malaya were to be brought straight to his desk in London – the real drive had to come from a man on the ground.[23]

In retrospect the choice he made seemed so brilliantly successful as to have been obvious. In fact it was a tribute to Lyttelton's own acumen. He knew that he wanted a 'first eleven' general.[24] The army establishment recommended the commandant of Berlin, Geoff Bourne.[25] Lyttelton interviewed Bourne but chose instead another candidate: Gerald Templer. As in the past, strong men were drawn to Lyttelton and he to them. Templer, he realized after their first meeting, had 'very good brains, is quick and decisive and is interested in all political aspects of problem'.[26] Lyttelton made an equally outstanding choice in backing his own conviction that the Malaya job would break one man. He chose a brilliant colonial service officer with no experience of Malaya, Donald MacGillivray, as Templer's deputy.[27] MacGillivray was almost as great a success as Templer and Lyttelton subsequently appointed him to succeed the general.[28] Malcolm MacDonald protested that all the men that Lyttelton had installed 'directing operations and the political campaign against Communism are all completely new to Malaya with its complex racial and other problems.'[29] That was precisely the point: Lyttelton believed that the 'sinuous diplomatists', including MacDonald him-self, who understood the sensitivities of all sides, had made a complete mess of things.[30] 'It is though a breath of fresh air has blown through all the offices and also all our minds here,' confirmed del Tufo's former private secretary, 'and the effect can only be described as dynamic. His Excellency has gone down incredibly well, and every-body on all sides pays tribute to the perspicacity shown in selecting him for the post.'[31]

In contrast to Lyttelton, Salisbury had an easier and much less exciting entry into office. His position as leader of the Conservative party in the House of Lords was unassailable. Whatever his formal title, he was always going to have an important voice in imperial affairs. What Salisbury wanted was influence rather than administrat-ive power. The government's slender majority, won with a lower share of the popular vote than the Labour party had garnered, preyed upon his mind. He would stand as a bulwark against the adoption 'of a violent party line' lest 'the whole conception of a Council of State will go by the board'.[32] He was keeping half an eye on the possibility of forming a National Government. As the Cabinet gath-ered for its first few meetings, Salisbury's was one of the most power-ful presences in the room.[33] He may not have been a great electoral asset, but he had the reputation of being right on the major issues. He had been right about appeasement, he had been right about the Russians in 1945, when Churchill had been wrong, he had been one of the first to see the need for a new 'progressive' identity for the party. He was known to be close to Eden and Eden stood only a heartbeat away from the premiership. Rising stars of the party treated him with respect.[34]

The passage of Macmillan and Crookshank into office was more protracted. Their names were not on the first list of Cabinet ministers read out on the six o'clock news. As soon as the wireless announcer had stopped speaking, they were on the telephone to one another. Surely there had been a mistake. Perhaps, they worried, Churchill was about to double-cross them and operate with a small inner Cabinet. Macmillan was calmer than Crookshank; Churchill would ditch Crookshank without a second thought, but Macmillan was confident that he had built up both his relationship with the grand old man and his position in the party to such an extent that it would be impossible to pass him over.[35] Indeed, there was little cause for concern. The next day they received their summons to Chartwell. Macmillan arrived first. His ambition was to become Minister of Defence. Churchill gave this idea short shrift: he was to be his own Minister of Defence. In any case, Eden was quite determined to extrude Macmillan from having any say in international affairs.[36] Instead Macmillan was to 'build the houses for the people' as Minister of Housing. Crookshank arrived not long afterwards to be told that he was to care for the health of the people as Minister of Health. They were thus each given half of what had, in their early days in politics, been one ministry. Neither was particularly delighted. Neither 'rabbit hutches' nor false teeth held any intrinsic interest for them.

In its own way, however, this was a Churchillian vote of confidence. Health was one of the hottest of political potatoes, having split the Labour party over the issue of prescription charges.[37] Housing was even more in the front line. Churchill was clear in his own mind that it was an issue that could make or break the government. The 1950 Party Conference, which Macmillan had not bothered to attend, had in a moment of excessive enthusiasm agreed to a proposal to build 300,000 houses a year. No practical thought had been given as to how this might be done. It had, however, proved a useful campaigning tool with which to beat Labour. Now someone needed to deliver. The advantage of the job for Macmillan was that he was now in charge of one of the few projects that it was necessary to pursue with vigour. He had direct access to the prime minister.[38] The disadvantage was that there was no proof that the election promise could be requited. Yet within months Macmillan had turned this into an advantage. The government had so few positive policies to offer that he could threaten Churchill with the 'terrible political implication of cutting the Housing programme'.[39]

Macmillan's appointment as Minister of Housing created tension between him and Salisbury. Salisbury's demands that he should get on with creating the property-owning democracy were met with bland indifference by the Minister of Housing.[40] His promises to limit council-house building always came to nought.[41] Macmillan presided over a massive increase in council housing. Local-authority building offered the quickest, if far from the best, fix to the problem of requiting manifesto promises.[42] Macmillan gave permission for as many 'subsidized local authority houses' to be built as there were applications.[43] When Salisbury attacked Macmillan's plans as a betrayal of progressive Toryism, he found that Churchill 'and others of my colleagues felt that I pressed the point unduly strongly'.[44]

Macmillan's appointment had guaranteed that he and Butler had also to be at each other's throats. Butler was trying to restore financial stability. Macmillan, to succeed, had to claim a disproportionate share of national funds. In opposition they had circled each other warily. Both had a claim to the progressive crown. Now only one could prevail.[45] Butler became vulnerable when he failed to convince the Cabinet to adopt his 'big idea', the convertibility of sterling, 'whoring after the nineteenth century stuff' as Macmillan described it. Macmillan taunted the wounded chancellor, mocking his weakness, challenging him to trials of strength.[46]

If Churchill's appointments had implications for the power struggle in the party, it also marked a parting of ways for the old friends Crookshank and Macmillan. Not that their friendship itself was in the least affected. Theirs was one of the most striking intimacies in modern British politics, based on strong affection rather than habit and interest. In October 1951 they were equals. Now they took quite different paths.

Macmillan plunged into his new office determined to make it work for him. One of his first acts was to appoint a 'fixer', the industrialist Percy Mills, whom he had got to know at the Ministry of Supply in the war. Everyone was to be infused with a 'can do' attitude. His battle-cry was 'standardization, simplification and pre-fabrication'.[47] The only thing that mattered was making the target: it didn't matter how good the houses were or who built them as long as there were over 300,000 a year put up.[48] He described his approach as 'Beaverbrookism', despite the fact that he himself had once defined 'Beaverbrookism as running "round talking but never doing anything effective and beating up much dust and making a great deal of noise"'.[49] Crookshank, on the other hand, dragged himself into the Ministry of Health with the look of a man about to be hanged. He hated every day he was there and made little secret of the fact.[50] It was true that his job of retrenchment was trickier than Macmillan's of expansion, for the National Health Service was already well on its way to becoming a national obsession. The minister was guaranteed a high political profile. Iain Macleod, the young 'One Nation' Tory from the class of 1950 who eventually succeeded to the job, chided Crookshank for having missed a prime political opportunity.[51] It was a sad abnegation for a man who still prided himself upon having taken the Ministry of Mines by the scruff of its neck in the rough-and-tumble of the 1930s.

What enthused Crookshank was his other role in the government. Churchill made him deputy leader of the House of Commons. In normal circumstances helping to run the 'usual channels' in the parliament would have been a useful but middling task. In such an evenly balanced house the job became vital. To Crookshank's chagrin, although he did most of the work, he was not given the honour of the title. Anthony Eden insisted, to the despair of his friends, that *he* should be Leader of the House as well as Foreign Secretary. 'I can't help thinking that Anthony is rather an ass in having Leadership of the House of Commons as well as the Foreign Office,' wrote Salisbury. 'He won't,' Salisbury judged, 'be able to do both properly, and will probably end by not giving enough time to either, and killing himself in the bargain: ambition is a funny thing.'[52] Salisbury was spot on about his old friend. Eden couldn't manage the leadership and had to turn it over to Crookshank in 1952. Crookshank himself leapt at the chance to escape the vile durance of the Health Ministry and take on the leadership of the House full-time. Yet in doing so he stepped away from the populism where real political power lay and took a step back into the old politics, recognizable from his youth.[53] Macmillan was greeted as the darling of the 1952 Party Conference, whereas Crookshank 'was not asked to speak a single word'.[54]

Crookshank was even tripped up in the sphere in which he had confidence. He suffered the humiliation of having the Steel

Renationalization Bill counted out because not enough MPs were in the chamber.[55] He was, as Macmillan observed, 'being made the target for vicious attack by the Opposition. Some of our more foolish members are falling into the trap and are indulging in similar criticism.'[56] Crookshank's choice did have important implications for Macmillan's success. As chair of the government's legislation committee, he controlled the progress of proposed Acts of Parliament. The passage of government bills gave individual Cabinet ministers the chance to appear dynamic.[57] Crookshank made it his business to see off threats to Macmillan's legislative programme.[58]

By surprising his subordinates with new jobs and by setting them up in competition with one another, Churchill bought himself time. He well knew that he also needed some positive achievement to set alongside this political manoeuvring. He was in need of a theme, a crusade that could focus his waning energies, something which no ordinary politician could carry through; something that would make him once more irreplaceable. In March 1953 the Soviet dictator Joseph Stalin died. This was Churchill's opportunity. He would, he declared, meet with Stalin's successors. He would go to Moscow on a 'solitary pilgrimage'. 'I am very anxious to know these men and talk to them as I think I can frankly and on the dead level,' he informed a newly elected and, in Churchill's view, 'weak and stupid' President Eisenhower.[59] 'My hope is that it is their self-interest which will bring about an easier state of affairs.'[60] His projected mission turned into a projected crusade when, while he was lying ill at Chartwell, the Soviet Union detonated its first H-bomb. 'I can,' he said, 'imagine that a few simple words, spoken in the awe which may at once oppress and inspire the speakers, might lift this nuclear monster from our world.'[61] Having won the Second World War, he would crown his career by ending the Cold War.[62]

Churchill's peace crusade stimulated in his Cabinet one thought. They had to get rid of this mad old man. He was no use in domestic politics and now he seemed to be planning a 'super-Munich'.[63] His personal crusade, his 'big game,' would submerge any plans for winning the next election. This was the substance of a discussion Salisbury and Macmillan had while watching the Derby.[64]

In 1953 the limitations of mortality transformed Churchill's situation. The plans of his enemies were thrown into confusion when, in April, Anthony Eden was cruelly prostrated by a botched cut of the surgeon's knife. Barely had these changed circumstances sunk in before Churchill himself was felled by a severe stroke. Within months the government had been decapitated. Yet with Eden fighting for his own life, the obvious successor was Butler. Edenites of conviction, like Salisbury, and Edenites of convenience, like Macmillan, were in a dilemma. If they mounted a Cabinet *coup* against Churchill they would let in Butler.

Churchill's incapacitation created a series of unexpected temporary alliances. Salisbury and Butler cooperated to prevent the government collapsing. When Churchill regained the power of thought and speech, an alliance also came into existence between Churchill and Salisbury.[65] The Edenites were praying that Churchill would survive long enough for Eden to convalesce sufficiently.[66] Hostilities could resume if and when they both recovered their health. If either Churchill or Eden were too weak, incoherent or visibly ailing to attend the Conservative Party Conference in October 1953, then they were finished.[67] There thus followed an elaborate charade, staged to convince politicians and the press that Churchill was unwell rather than non-functioning.[68] Crookshank lamented 'that history will accuse us all – Rab, Bobbety, and the politicians in the Cabinet – of weakness and cowardice'.[69] Nevertheless some of the conspirators were 'positively gay'. 'It was the kind of conspiracy we were all in,' Macmillan recorded, 'and it was rather fun to have such respectable people as Salisbury, Butler and Co. as fellow conspirators.'[70]

If he was to keep the whole package together, Salisbury had to agree to become acting foreign secretary.[71] He knew that he was accepting a poisoned chalice. He would immediately have to fly to Washington for an important meeting with his American and French opposite numbers.[72] His colleagues thought his exposition of foreign policy was 'masterly'.[73] Yet the Americans knew little of him and were highly suspicious of Churchill's Russian policy.[74] Both the Opposition, who were in the dark about the true position, and Max Beaverbrook, who knew every detail, believed that they could damage

Salisbury by portraying him as 'the warmonger' in contrast to Churchill 'the peacemaker'.[75] Salisbury was thus in an invidious position. He had to raise and defend the issue of a 'world leaders' summit' when he himself did not think it was a good idea. He suspected that Churchill was willing to do any damage to relations with the United States, sacrifice any trust the nations of NATO had in Britain, for his own personal aggrandizement.[76] Yet he could hardly say to John Foster Dulles, the American Secretary of State, that he thought his own prime minister was a menace.[77]

Although Salisbury himself made an able defence in the House of Lords of his conduct in Washington, Butler's failure to do the same in the House of Commons opened him to a pillorying.[78] 'He is now being attacked,' lamented the diplomat Evelyn Shuckburgh, 'by the Opposition and all the optimists for having whittled [Churchill's] glorious initiative . . . down to a mundane and routine meeting of Foreign Ministers confined to the topic of Germany.'[79] Salisbury's position was exacerbated by the fact that Churchill was quite happy to collude with Beaverbrook, letting it be known that Salisbury did not have his support.[80] Any lingering possibility that Salisbury might become foreign secretary was extinguished at the same time as any lingering desire he might have had for the post.[81]

In the end both Churchill and Eden made it to the Conservative Party Conference in Margate. To all outward appearance they appeared as men reborn. For those who had covered and covered up for them, it was as if that awful summer had never happened. Everyone nevertheless emerged hardened in their previous positions. Churchill was determined to hang on, to open up more and more fronts of international diplomacy. His mind turned to government reshuffles that would, like all such plans since 1945, appease Eden's dignity without yielding to him the ultimate prize. Eden longed for the old man to pack his bags. Salisbury and Crookshank were thinking hard as to how they might bring this about. In the light of his experiences over the summer, Salisbury was quite willing to use the 'Samson option'. He would sacrifice his own career if only he could bring Churchill down with him. He was finding 'a steadily growing distaste for political life'.[82] 'The time has come,' he informed Churchill directly, 'when you ought to retire from the leadership ... if you continue to lead, the Party will move forward loyally but despairingly to what they know will be a certain disaster at the next election.'[83] Macmillan agreed with Salisbury that 'we will drift on to disaster unless we can get a faith to inspire more than material gain ... that unless Churchill goes, we shall continue to drift'; 'younger men are getting bitter, and feel their careers are sacrificed to one old man's vanity'.[84] Even Lyttelton told Churchill he must make way for Eden.[85]

The events of the summer confirmed in Oliver Lyttelton's mind the conclusion that he should tarry no longer in politics. Despite the fact that he was in London watching the England–Australia test match, no attempt was made to call him in during the discussions that took place in the hours after Churchill's stroke. Lunching with him at the Turf a few days later, Macmillan found him 'incensed'.[86] The initial two years of service he had promised Churchill were up as Eden and Churchill basked in the adulation of the Conservative faithful at Margate.[87] If he lingered much longer, the reversion of the chairmanship of AEI would slip from his hands. His enemies on the AEI board were within an ace of ousting him. Churchill's appeals for him to stay on could hold him for a few months but not more.[88] 'The plain fact is,' he admitted, 'that when I had a very big income (and no thought of politics) I charged it up with all I could ... So when my income shrinks by fifteen or twenty thousand a year all this has to come out of capital ... My accountants say it has cost me £75,000 being a Minister and my free savings are pretty well exhausted.'[89]

The year 1953 had seemed endless. They had found no means of cutting the Gordian knot. Yet 1954 seemed to promise more of the same. Both Crookshank and Salisbury openly told Churchill that he was not fit to remain prime minister and should resign immediately.[90] Macmillan passed on the same message, though initially through Brendan Bracken rather than directly.[91] In the end he too told Churchill to go.[92] Churchill responded with all his usual wiles. To Salisbury he was hurt and sorrowful.[93] He recommended Crookshank for the Companionship of Honour.[94]

But Churchill had an even more devastating set of cards to play. As he and Eden sailed for Britain after a visit to the United States, he wired the unrepentantly Stalinist Soviet leader Vyacheslav Molotov to propose an Anglo-Soviet summit.[95] Churchill had browbeaten Eden to such an extent that he agreed that the telegram should be sent. This really was the final straw. Salisbury's angry threat to resign if things went any further was not token posturing. Churchill's 'second bombshell' was an almost casual announcement to the Cabinet that Britain would build the H-bomb. Crookshank got up and left the Cabinet room in protest and the rest of the Cabinet dribbled out after him.[96]

Churchill was far from finished. The next day he turned on Crookshank. Crookshank was obliged to admit that he had no objections to building the bomb: he objected to a few ministers taking the decision and then delivering it to the Cabinet as a *fait accompli*. Crookshank had funked the task of standing up to Churchill.[97] Salisbury did no such thing. He delivered a stinging lecture on Churchill's constitutional impropriety. Churchill's face went white, then puce. Ministers feared that 'he was going to have another stroke'. When Salisbury finished no one else uttered a word. Finally Churchill choked out his usual line, 'I should greatly regret a severance. But I hope our private friendship would survive.' In private he said he didn't 'give a damn' if Salisbury resigned.[98] Eden, however, was horrified at the possibility of Salisbury leaving the government. On their voyage Churchill had promised Eden that he would resign on 20 September 1954. The summit was to be his last hurrah. The last thing Eden wanted was for Salisbury, in trying to right Eden's failure to stand up to Churchill, to rip the government apart. Macmillan agreed. On behalf of Eden and himself, Macmillan set off for Hatfield that Friday evening to 'beg' Bobbety to stay his hand.[99] Salisbury was barely persuaded. He did, at least, agree not to act precipitately.[100] When Macmillan met him for a pre-arranged luncheon the next Wednesday, he was still determined to go. This was difficult because, as Macmillan was forced to admit, he too believed that Churchill was mentally unbalanced.[101] Feeling the need for reinforcements, Macmillan rounded up Oliver Lyttelton. The two of them once again begged Salisbury to delay his resignation until he could have a full discussion with Eden, who had, in the interim, departed for Geneva.[102]

Afterwards Lyttelton and Macmillan met up again to drown their sorrows with champagne cocktails. All they could do with 'two very obstinate men', they agreed, was to gain time. The next day Macmillan warned Clemmie Churchill that, if Salisbury went, Crookshank would follow and the government would crumble. Mrs Churchill agreed to try and talk Winston round over luncheon. It was not a happy experience. Churchill shouted at his wife. He raved against Salisbury that his resignation would be as fruitless as Lord Randolph's, that Salisbury was as guilty as he for concealing the H-bomb decision, that he, Churchill, would never apologize to Salisbury or anyone else for his actions. Macmillan could only think that this confirmed the view that his stroke had mentally deranged the prime minister.[103] Towards the end of the meal, Churchill began to calm down and consider whether Salisbury's departure really would wreck the government.[104]

On 23 July 1954 the Cabinet convened again. Churchill stated that he intended to meet Molotov in Berne, Stockholm or Vienna in early September. Salisbury replied at once. White and tense, he spoke from notes. The prime minister had deliberately flouted the conventions of Cabinet government. He had done so in pursuit of a foolish goal. A meeting with Molotov would achieve nothing except damage to Anglo-American relations. Salisbury was wrong, Churchill retorted. He had been careful not only to consult Eisenhower but he had also acted after the fullest consultation with Eden. Eden burst out in turn that that was not true: the prime minister was twisting the truth. If he was twisting the truth, he was not the only one, Churchill shot back. Salisbury had kept information about the British hydrogen bomb from his colleagues because he thought it was in the national interest to do so. Churchill was doing no more and no less. Eden intervened again. This was getting them nowhere. Whether they liked it or not, they were now in negotiation with the Soviet Union about a summit. They had to take some decisions about what to do next. Very well, Churchill replied, let us ask the other members of the Cabinet what they think. There was silence.

Finally Macmillan spoke. He agreed with Eden: there was no point in dwelling on the past, to do so would endanger the very survival of the government. They needed some kind of diplomatic manoeuvre that would make them look like neither appeasers nor reactionaries. Lyttelton spoke up. He looked at Churchill and said, 'I am one who was not at all happy about the past.' But Macmillan was right: they had to go forward with some kind of imaginative policy. Crookshank spoke up: he had no trouble with what Eden, Macmillan and Lyttelton had said, 'but in saying that, I must make it clear that I support the Lord President's protest'. He paused for effect. 'I would not like him to think he was alone.' It sounded like a threat; Churchill bridled, the puce colour rising once more in his face. Macmillan broke in, 'I must in loyalty to Lord Salisbury say that I think his protest justified.' Lyttelton spoke again. Everyone, especially Churchill, knew that he was loyal.[105] Within days he was to leave the Cabinet of his own volition, 'the really strong and splendid figure we can ill spare', as Macmillan put it. He had no axe to grind.[106] When he said, 'I must tell the Prime Minister that I share Lord Salisbury's view about the past' it was a crushing blow.

One by one, in sorrow or in anger, each of them had denounced Churchill. It was a 'terrible day'.[107] 'All of us,' thought Macmillan, 'are being slowly driven into something like hatred.'[108] For Lyttelton his political duty was done. He retired with Churchill to Chequers for a stag party. 'Here was much laughter, many anecdotes, and prodigious feats of repetition of verse.' 'But the air of crisis permeated all,' observed Jock Colville.[109] The terrible day presaged a 'terrible week' for everyone. The only ray of light was a violently hostile Soviet message that made it impossible for Churchill to damn his colleagues with an immediate public announcement of a summit.[110] Yet, denied his triumph, Churchill was most certainly not going to resign on 20 September as he had promised.[111] He would double-cross them all if he could, Macmillan and Crookshank agreed.[112]

They may have thwarted Churchill's will, but now they were faced with a beast at bay. Churchill could, in the phrase they all used, 'turn rogue elephant'. Even if they could finish him off, he might do awful damage to them. Churchill knew that the united front they had formed against him was fragile. He intended to appeal to their own ambition so as to split one from the other.[113] Macmillan, in any case, had no intention of risking his own career for Eden's benefit: 'I told him that one cannot really resign because one is not made Prime Minister.' The most they could agree on was a demand for a major reconstruction of the government, even if Churchill remained in office.[114] This presented a major problem for Macmillan. In any such reconstruction Churchill was keen to finish off Harry Crookshank: he wanted 'to throw him overboard quite ruthlessly'. Macmillan balked at sacrificing Crookshank. 'Nothing,' he told Eden and Butler, 'would induce me to turn out Harry Crookshank, my oldest personal friend for over fifty years, from the Leadership of the House.'[115]

Churchill was going to make it as difficult as possible. They had demanded a reconstruction of the Cabinet – very well, he would reconstruct the Cabinet. Eden would become deputy prime minister and Leader of the House of Commons. Macmillan would become foreign secretary. If Macmillan would not abandon Crookshank, Churchill would buy Crookshank off with the Home Office. He hoped to bind Macmillan once again to him. It was Macmillan he drew aside to tell him of his plans, it was Macmillan he used as his emissary to the others.[116] Eden too saw that Macmillan was the pivotal figure: couldn't Harold tell Winston he had to go?[117] Churchill understood Macmillan rather better than Eden did. He would go about the 'tiresome' business of mediation in the way that suited him.[118] 'It's all "settled",' he wrote a few days later, 'Churchill has won on every point and Eden capitulated completely. Churchill remains Prime Minister without any commitment, written or verbal, as to date . . . He has played off one against the other – and he has come out triumphant.'[119] 'I am very sorry for Anthony,' Salisbury concurred with disgust, 'but I am afraid that he is more responsible for the present situation than anyone else. No one could take the lead for him: he had to do it for himself; and he wouldn't.'[120]

Churchill had bested Eden again. Macmillan had played his own game and was not displeased. On 10 October 1954 there was every likelihood that Churchill would lead the Conservative party into the next election and press ahead with his crusade for peace. He was, however, to be tripped up by the obstinacy of Harry Crookshank and Bobbety Salisbury. When Macmillan went to see Crookshank, he refused to budge from the leadership of the House. 'I said at once this settled it,' Macmillan recorded. 'I said (on the telephone to Churchill) that Harry refused to be home secretary. If Churchill wanted him to resign, he was ready to go. I could not possibly agree, in these circumstances, to take his place.'

Macmillan himself turned over Housing to Duncan Sandys, believing that he had sucked its political pith dry, and moved over to the Ministry of Defence. Eden, Salisbury and Crookshank stayed exactly where they were. Yet Crookshank had been within a whisker of being sacked. He had been saved only by Macmillan's protection. Like Eden, Crookshank had always suffered a failure of nerve in trying to seize political power. He was, however, so incensed by his treatment on this occasion that he could not be anything other than disruptive.[121] He took to avoiding Churchill if he could – 'whisked away by the Crookshank escape apparatus', as an amused subordinate put it.[122]

Churchill had won a Pyrrhic victory. He had faced down Eden but he had not driven a deep enough wedge into the 'sixtysomething' bloc.[123] Macmillan would not help Eden, neither would he betray Crookshank. It was a measure of Churchill's impotence that he could not crush Crookshank, the weakest of his foes. With Harry and Bobbety immovable and glowering malevolently across the Cabinet table, there was little chance that Churchill would be allowed to rush into the arms of the Soviets.[124] The game was over. In the New Year Churchill agreed to go.[125] He could feel his own powers waning and the plain truth was that no one wanted him to stay. He viewed them all with 'cold hatred,' but neither the chill nor the charm altered the situation.[126] With a great dinner at Downing Street for the Queen, the man of destiny bowed out. He forgave Salisbury and Macmillan enough to invite them.[127]

For all Crookshank's 'tuggish little whimpers and ways,' they had finally done it. They had pushed Eden, the champion of their generation, over the finishing line. It was a time of celebration only

Lyttelton and Anthony Eden look on as Churchill talks with Vyacheslav Molotov and Ivan Maisky in the garden of No. 10 Downing Street, May 1942.

Doffing a hat to the Empire: Cranborne inspects troops from Newfoundland, January 1941. As Dominions Secretary Cranborne felt that, whilst he worked hard to make imperial relations run smoothly, it was Churchill who made high policy in direct dealings with the Dominions' prime ministers.

The Home Front: Crookshank inspects ATS auxiliaries (wearing 'teddybear' smocks) crewing London's AA defences, December 1943. As Postmaster-General, Crookshank was allocated many such duties. He himself commanded the Whitehall Home Guard and acted as a firewatcher.

Smoking statesmen: Cranborne and Clement Attlee take the opportunity for a smoke whilst waiting on Westminster pier for a boat to take them to dinner at the Royal Naval College, Greenwich, May 1944. Cranborne is talking to Jan Christian Smuts, the Prime Minister of South Africa.

Left On Ike's team: Macmillan, Walter Bedell Smith, Eisenhower's chief of staff, and Sir Arthur Tedder, the senior RAF officer in the Middle East, wait to brief Eisenhower, 1943.

Below On Churchill's team: Eden, Churchill and Macmillan hold a press conference in front of Macmillan's house in Algiers, June 1943.

Bottom On the winning team: Macmillan on the podium at the allied victory parade in Tunis, May 1943. Robert Murphy, Macmillan's American opposite number, talks to Sir Arthur Tedder. Sir Andrew Cunningham (with stick), the British naval commander in the Mediterranean, and 'Mary' Coningham, leader of the Desert Air Force, survey the scene.

Right *Inglese Italianato,*
è un diavolo incarnato:
Macmillan in front of an
Italian war memorial, 1944.

Below The Liberators:
Lieutenant-General Scobie and
Macmillan on the bridge of
HMS *Orion* en route to save
Greece from Communism,
October 1944.

The Victors: Oliver Lyttelton, Ernest Bevin, Churchill, Sir John Anderson, Lord Woolton and Herbert Morrison. The War Cabinet accepts the applause of the crowds on VE Day, 8 May 1945.

The Tory team: Macmillan, Salisbury and Crookshank, alongside Woolton, David Maxwell-Fyfe, Anthony Eden and Rab Butler, November 1950.

LYTTELTON   SALISBURY   CROOKSHANK   MACMILLAN

'The men who think they will rule Britain': Lyttelton, Salisbury, Crookshank and Macmillan caricatured by a hostile *Daily Mirror*, September 1951.

Right Butler, Crookshank and Salisbury put on an insouciant air, July 1953. In reality they were working feverishly to cover up Churchill's stroke. 'It was the kind of conspiracy we were all in,' Macmillan recorded the day after this cartoon was published, 'and it was rather fun to have such respectable people as Salisbury, Butler and Co. as fellow conspirators.' The only member of the Cabinet actually at the Test match against Australia, alluded to in Low's cartoon for the *Manchester Guardian*, was Oliver Lyttelton – and he was 'incensed' not to be within the inner core of conspirators.

THREE OF 'EM! CAD, SIR, NOW WE SHALL SEE SOME *REAL* CRICKET

HOPE OF THEIR SIDE

A different type of guardsman: Macmillan as Foreign Secretary, 1955.

The Tory front bench in the House of Commons, July 1953: Crookshank, Butler, Maxwell-Fyfe, Lyttelton, Florence Horsbrough and Sir David Eccles as seen by Michael Cummings in *Punch*. The older members created an atmosphere that was a cross between an officers' mess and a pupil room. Outsiders were unwelcome. Florence Horsbrough, the only female member of the Cabinet, was known as the 'old grey mare'. David Eccles was derided as 'Smarty-Boots'.

'No signs of life', December 1955: Salisbury's passionate commitment to the modernisation of the House of Lords earned him mockery within Eden's Cabinet and, as Vicky's cartoon in the *New Statesman* demonstrates, beyond. In the month this cartoon was published Salisbury told Eden that he would remain in the government until 1958 in order to pursue his House of Lords campaign.

Above Big cigars: Reginald Maudling, one of the post-Second World War generation of Tory politicians rising most rapidly towards high office, Sir Henry Self, Lyttelton's former Permanent Secretary at the Ministry of Production, Macmillan and Lyttelton enjoy a good dinner, April 1956. 'You can't imagine Reggie,' Lyttelton once remarked of Maudling, 'going to the stake for anything unless it was well covered with Béarnaise sauce.'

Left The Winner: Macmillan returns to Downing Street as Prime Minister, January 1957. His first important appointment was a meeting with Salisbury.

Right The last Guardsman considers resignation, as seen by Vicky in the *Evening Standard*, April 1963.

"ME, WALK OUT? NEVER!"

for Macmillan. He finally entered the portals of the Foreign Office as its master. Salisbury and Crookshank had expended much of their political capital in the struggle against Churchill. Lyttelton had not lasted the course.[128] 'I only wish that you were still in the team. You will know how much I wish that,' Eden lamented.[129] Many said that Eden had had to wait too long for high responsibility. Churchill said of Eden, 'I don't believe Anthony can do it.'[130] He could have said the same of any of them.

9

Successors

Each for his own reason, Salisbury, Crookshank and Macmillan had worked hard to put Anthony Eden into No. 10. Their efforts were crowned by a decisive general election victory for the Conservatives under their charismatic new leader. Instead of their paltry majority of seventeen in October 1951, from May 1955 the Tories enjoyed a comfortable sixty-seat majority in the House of Commons. Yet it was never going to be easy for men older than the prime minister to thrive. Too many elder statesmen in the Cabinet were bound to be a problem. Beneath the now 'sixtysomethings' was a whole new generation of ambitious Conservatives who had come to the fore since 1945. Eden had to make some room for them if the party was to prosper. This instability of prospects was a political fact of life. It was rendered even more uncertain by Eden's mercurial personality. Convinced that the office he now held was his by right, setting his sights on greatness, yet seeing disappointment around every corner, gratitude for past support did not rank high in his list of priorities.

The first man to feel the chill of the new regime was Harry Crookshank. Since the 1930s he and Eden had been allies of a kind but that alliance had never been truly consummated. Now Crookshank was superfluous to requirements. He was not an electoral asset. His skill in parliamentary sniping was not much use to a party that would not be in opposition again before his retirement. His management of the House of Commons had not been without its problems. With no need any longer to fret about a wafer-thin majority, parliamentary management was itself of much reduced importance.[1] Although Crookshank himself continued to protest that he had had experience of the key economic and social issues, his colleagues took this with a pinch of salt.[2] It was over fifteen years since he had been a serious departmental minister. Under Churchill he had manoeuvred himself out of a departmental berth.

Crookshank had little to offer Eden and so Eden ignored him. Crookshank got most of his news of what was going on in the government from Macmillan.[3] By the end of 1955 he had run out of political options. Eden wanted to make Rab Butler leader of the House of Commons so Harry was told that he had to resign. He would not even be allowed to keep his sinecure office of Lord Privy Seal.[4] In compensation, he was offered a peerage and the opportunity to keep his seat in the Cabinet if he agreed to act as Salisbury's deputy in the House of Lords.[5] Throughout his career, Crookshank had shown a pathological fear of resignation. Even he, however, could not take this: on offer was no power and precious little prestige. The defeat was so complete that he could not even work up his accustomed bile. It was merely the ' "slings and arrows" of the game'.[6] After discussing the whole thing with Macmillan and Salisbury, he slipped gracefully into the House of Lords and retirement.[7] He had, at least, the compensation of throwing himself into Masonic leadership. The Masons installed him as a Provincial Grand Master at an off-season ceremony at Butlin's Holiday Camp, Skegness.[8]

Despite outward appearances, Salisbury was not in much better shape. Eden was careful to show that he was consulting his old friend and valued his opinion. His advice was readily accepted on points of detail, but he seemed unable to make much impact on the great scheme of things.[9] The excuse of a small majority could no longer be made in objection to his two favoured legislative programmes: reform of the House of Lords and the control of coloured immigration. Eden was encouraging, yet these issues remained mired in a round of endless discussions.[10] Cabinet deliberations showed 'no signs of life'.[11] Quite often the greatest procrastinator was Harold Macmillan: he believed that these were subjects for 'cranks'.[12] Younger members of the Cabinet followed Macmillan's lead in standing up to Salisbury, often in provocative fashion.[13] 'I was, as usual, in a minority of one,' he wrote despairingly when he was, once again, contradicted.[14] Even young officials noticed his 'bitterness' that his influence was fading.[15] Salisbury's plans were disappearing into an indeterminate future. At one and the same time, frustration both turned his mind to retirement and gave him an excuse to stay on. He talked of giving House of Lords reform until 1958 to reach fruition.[16]

Long before then, he was brought up short by his own lack of pull. The many and various objections that Anthony Eden and Harold Macmillan had found to a summit with the Russians when Churchill was at the helm miraculously dropped away once they themselves were in control of foreign policy. Within weeks of the election, they were in Geneva trying to create a spirit of *détente* to replace the Cold War. Churchill could have been forgiven a wry smile when Macmillan informed him that, 'I do not despair of making progress, if we have patience. I get the impression that the Russian position does not quite present the monolithic strength it used to do.'[17]

Salisbury also found this about-face hard to take. He found it even harder to stomach when, in the 'spirit of Geneva', Eden invited the Soviet leaders, Nikita Khrushchev and Nikolai Bulganin, to make a state visit to Britain in 1956. He grumbled about this through the winter of 1955 and 1956. By the spring he had concluded that Eden had misled him. The visit was not, as Eden maintained, a 'possibility' contingent on Soviet good behaviour and American approval, but a cast-iron certainty. Knowing the Soviets were abusing Britain in their propaganda and thumbing their noses at diplomatic protocol, 'We can't afford,' he bewailed, 'to let the visit break down: we have to accept whatever the Russians impose on us. That seems to me a hopelessly weak position from which to start negotiations.' Having agonized over this, he told Eden, he had decided to resign: 'You will, I know, see that I have no option, any more than you had in 1938.'[18] Eden, as it happened, did not see that at all. He immediately had Salisbury round to luncheon to convince him to stay. Other ministers were rallied to tell Salisbury he was a pivotal member of the government.[19] Salisbury allowed himself to be persuaded, though he had few illusions. He even confided his disenchantment to an acquaintance of relatively recent vintage, the head of the Atomic Energy Authority,

Sir Edwin Plowden. Plowden was so struck by Salisbury's sense of despair that he presumed to try and pep him up. 'After I left you last night, I dined with Sir Norman Brook,' Plowden wrote. 'He thought I was right in saying that your views had great influence on the opinions and decisions of your colleagues.' 'With respect,' Sir Edwin continued, 'this is one thing on which outsiders are best able to judge. You will, I know, forgive me for referring, for the last time, to something which is not my business, but about which I feel deeply.'[20] Since Brook, the deputy Cabinet secretary, had only a few months before written a report for the prime minister outlining Salisbury's failure to garner support for his legislative schemes, he was merely being polite. Plowden's encouragement, heartfelt though it obviously was, came from someone who was not in a position to know what went on at the heart of government. It was with some sense of relief therefore that Salisbury found himself, for what turned out to be the last time, in harness with Harold Macmillan.

By the summer of 1956 Macmillan was a good man with whom to be in harness. When he achieved a lifetime's ambition and walked into the Foreign Office as its master in April 1955, some observers believed he had placed himself in an invidious position. Brendan Bracken, for instance, warned him that 'Eden would keep a grip on foreign policy as strong as a vice'.[21] Macmillan in fact entered the great office brimming with confidence. The party chairman, Fred Woolton, could only applaud his chutzpah on his first day as foreign secretary as he 'posed in the middle of the roadway' waiting for photographers to get him in focus for a flattering shot. 'Eden does it in a very gentlemanly way,' Woolton wrote in his diary, 'bringing his hand up to the semi-salute. But there is nothing semi about Harold; he sort of says "Give me a cheer", and waves to them although they are not waving to him.'[22]

Macmillan himself had no illusions about the likely problems of working with Eden. He had, after all, seen Eden and Churchill in action at close quarters. He did not have to pretend irritation when Eden started, within a fortnight of the election, to intervene in the details of Foreign Office business; the irritation was genuine enough.[23] Macmillan was determined to fight his corner, with personal rudeness if need be.[24] For, he believed, he had learnt something from the previous twelve months. If Eden and Butler were pushed hard enough, they would give way. Their courtesy, intelligence and sensitivity could be exploited. The faulty political tactics he had pursued early in his career had, in all likelihood, denied him a chance at the premiership. He would be sixty-four by the time the next general election was due: the same age as Churchill when he became prime minister, to be sure, but it was unlikely that anything as dramatic as a war would open the way as it had done for Churchill. Within his grasp, however, was the next best thing. If he could extend his sphere of influence from the field of foreign affairs into that of economic policy, he would build for himself an unassailable position in the government from which he could dominate Eden and Butler. Butler, recently widowed, was visibly tiring after four years at the Treasury. 'How you stood four years of it, without going crazy, I don't know,' Macmillan crowed.[25] Eden, as those close to him bewailed, was 'not interested in economics'.[26] It had been done before by Neville Chamberlain, another late developer.

Barely two months after the election Macmillan started to make his play. His way in was through the means of his old bailiwick of defence. 'Pray forgive these rather general ideas which I have not had time to think out,' he wrote to Butler, 'but I really believe that economy cannot stand defence expenditure on the present scale indefinitely, and that we ought to consider abandoning those parts of it which are really useless.'[27] Macmillan's critique of the state of Britain's defences was cogent enough.[28] A defence review of the size and scope that he was proposing would have the advantage of inserting him into all major economic decisions. It was, however, merely the opening shot of his campaign. A fortnight after his *démarche* on defence he was pressing Butler and Eden on the whole range of government economic policy. The economy, he chided, was overheating. It was time to cut back on government-induced demand. Defence was a good place to start. There were plenty of other areas that could be cut, however – the bloated housing programme for one. On mature consideration, Butler had probably been right. More fiscal discipline and a radical currency reform had been the way to go.[29] What he had once dismissed as a mad plan cooked up by a cabal of Treasury officials now appeared to him as little more than common sense. Macmillan himself could point out that the economic conditions of 1955 were quite different from those of 1951. Once again, the advantage of a big idea requiring a major review of government policy would catapult the foreign secretary into the heart of domestic as well as international policy.

Macmillan was following a rational strategy aimed at maximizing his power. He could never have calculated that it would succeed so spectacularly. Eden soon found Macmillan's presence at the Foreign Office unbearable. If he moved Macmillan out of the Foreign Office, Eden could insert his 'bell-hop' Selwyn Lloyd.[30] The prime minister would then be able to reassert himself as a leading world statesman. Macmillan, Eden conceded, seemed to be talking sense as far as the economy was concerned. He was coming off better in his arguments with Butler.[31] Macmillan had a taste for technicalities; he could deal with the knotty economic problems facing the government. Butler could be shifted to the second-line job of leader of the House of Commons, displacing Crookshank, who was a dead-weight.[32]

This reshuffle was a disastrous miscalculation on Eden's part. Macmillan had planned to increase his grip step by step as review followed review. Eden was so obviously in the wrong in removing him from the Foreign Office, however, that he could play the pained martyr and drive a very hard bargain indeed. He told everybody, domestic and foreign, that he was 'deeply distressed at leaving the FO', he had 'so many projects'.[33] He insisted on complete autonomy at the Treasury. He could be a 'revolutionary' if he so pleased. He vetoed Eden's intention of making Butler deputy prime minister. Macmillan was to be the 'undisputed head of the Home Front'.[34] He soon made plain in practice that this was not an empty title. He did not want to hear Cabinet discussion of his plans because 'my mind is quite made up'. If Eden did not give him *carte blanche* he would resign.[35] As those two cynical observers, Brendan Bracken and Max Beaverbrook, observed to one another, 'Unfortunately for Eden he has given this man a job which puts him plumb at the centre of the political stage.'[36] Eden had replaced Butler who was often disloyal in word but rarely in deed, with a man who was disloyal to his core. Macmillan intended to dominate the Eden government.

In the event Macmillan's plans were quickened by a major international crisis. In the summer of 1956 Gamal Abdel Nasser, the leader of Egypt, nationalized the Suez Canal, the great international waterway owned and run by an Anglo-French company. Nasser's bold move diverted the tolls from the canal into his own fighting fund, humiliated the British and the French, and dared them to respond. There is no evidence to suggest that the Suez crisis was any more than contingently part of Macmillan's master plan. Macmillan did not lead Anthony Eden on to Nasser's guns. Both Eden and Macmillan wanted Nasser crushed. Macmillan pursued a policy with regard to Egypt in which he genuinely believed. Yet, as soon as that strategy started to rack up unacceptable costs, he abandoned it without a second thought. He followed the lesson he had learnt in the war: try to pick the victor and stick with them; if in doubt, assume the Americans will win. In an inspired series of short-term manoeuvres, he managed to lay the blame for the Suez crisis on Eden and Butler rather than himself. As a political adventurer it was his finest moment.

Macmillan's manoeuvres were not entirely extemporaneous. If he used smoke and mirrors, he had the mirrors in place and the smoke bombs ready. Both as foreign secretary and chancellor he sedulously insisted that he, personally, had a 'special relationship' with the Eisenhower administration. Exploiting his wartime acquaintances, he was able to establish himself as the primary conduit of high-level communication between Washington and London. Eden, who had equal claims on the acquaintance of key Americans, was at a disadvantage since many of them, especially the Secretary of State, John Foster Dulles, disliked and distrusted him. The foreign secretary, Selwyn Lloyd, and his deputy, Anthony Nutting, whose all too open search for solace from his 'marital difficulties' in New York embarrassed the British and Americans alike, were never in the game. When Nasser nationalized the Suez Canal in July 1956, it was Macmillan who leapt into conclave with his old opposite number from Algiers, Bob Murphy, Dulles's assistant at the State Department.[37] It was

Macmillan who conducted the main talks with Dulles himself when he followed Murphy to London.[38] As luck would have it Macmillan undertook a pre-planned visit to the United States in the autumn of 1956 to celebrate his American mother. Eisenhower found it impossible not to see him.[39] Through the Macmillan prism the British obtained rather too rosy a view of American approval for their actions, whereas the Americans received rather too secure an opinion of British willingness to follow their lead. This carefully crafted image of Macmillan as the irreplaceable interlocutor was to be his trump card in the winter of 1956.[40]

For most of 1956, it seemed that developments in the Middle East were more likely to bind the old anti-appeasement alliance of Macmillan, Eden and Salisbury back together rather than drive them apart. Macmillan described their Tory critics as 'sons of "Munichites"'.[41] At the Foreign Office he was a champion of schemes for removing or neutralizing the charismatic Nasser. Since the Second World War, Macmillan had been a sceptic about formal colonies but an enthusiast second to none for informal empire. The 'hidden hand' and 'fancy footwork' exercised an enduring fascination for him. It was these very networks of influence that Nasser was in a prime position to disrupt. His Arab nationalist message subverted the respectability of cooperation with Britain. Britain's Hashemite allies in Jordan and Iraq shifted uneasily on their thrones. Nasser's burgeoning relationship with the Soviet Union meant that, unlike other anti-Western despots, he increasingly had the means to subvert the physical control of advanced weaponry by which Britain, France and America had rendered the Arab powers militarily impotent. When Nasser nationalized the Suez Canal, he was deliberately humiliating Britain. The only question for the British was whether they needed a 'quick fix', to hasten Nasser's defeat by direct military action.

Much has been made of Eden's visceral hatred for the Egyptian leader. Eden certainly needed no encouragement to 'get' Nasser. He had a solid bloc of support for doing so, led by his lieutenants Macmillan and Salisbury. It was Macmillan who described Nasser as an 'Asiatic Mussolini'.[42] It was Macmillan and Salisbury who went to see the chairman of the BBC to ensure that the corporation avoided 'speculation' on British military action. It was Macmillan and Salisbury who championed what proved to be the most controversial and damaging part of the ensuing operation: the agreement signed in October 1956 by Eden and Selwyn Lloyd with the French and the Israelis that provided for an Israeli attack on Egypt followed by an Anglo-French invasion with the supposed aim of restoring peace between the combatants.[43] As Macmillan observed, 'the Jews have character'.[44] It was Macmillan who was most enthusiastic to find some treacherous army officers who would overthrow Nasser.[45] During their hand-in-glove cooperation, Macmillan thought Salisbury 'particularly good' as they cast around for a 'popular "casus belli"'.[46] They worried away at this problem together repeatedly.[47]

'My dear Harold,' Salisbury wrote, 'I have been through the Charter of the United Nations, and I am bound to say that I have found very little that would seem to justify the use of forceful methods by a member state ... all this is, I am afraid, rather depressing. If we take forceful action we should, I feel myself, be sailing pretty near the wind: we might well be charged, in future, with having destroyed' – at this point Salisbury crossed out what he had written and substituted – 'struck a mortal blow at the United Nations.'[48] It was the Macmillan and Salisbury double-act who once again whisked Dulles off to Hatfield to lobby him, in the right surroundings, to see the British point of view. 'Bobbety and I both got the impression that Foster was getting rather "sticky". He won't help us any more with economic sanctions, etc.,' Macmillan recorded accurately. 'I cannot help feeling that he really wants us to "go it alone",' he added with a leap of faith, 'and has been trying to help us by creating the right atmosphere.'[49] It was Macmillan and Salisbury who combined to marginalize those in the Cabinet who doubted both the legality and practicality of a war against Egypt.[50]

Their alliance was disrupted not by any difference of view but by Salisbury's old bugbear, his health. As he prepared to leave for Llandudno to help rally the Conservative troops at the party conference, he had a mild heart attack.[51] A reluctant Anthony Nutting was ordered to deliver Salisbury's text. 'One look at the notes,' Nutting later recalled, 'confirmed my fear that Salisbury had intended to deliver a very belligerent speech indeed. Not only was Nasser to be accused, once again, of "an act of seizure and plunder in flagrant breach of the fundamental principle of international conduct", but he was to be threatened with the use of force if the UN failed to induce him to satisfy our demands.' According to Nutting's account, 'Before I reached Llandudno, I had managed to tone down some of the more menacing phrases and make a bow or two to the UN, by expanding Salisbury's somewhat cursory rehearsal of the respect which we had so far shown to our obligations under the UN Charter. But without vitiating the whole speech, I could not make any further changes, and what remained for me to read out was undoubtedly a very combative piece of prose.'[52] Nutting endured an unwanted and undeserved ovation as the party conference rose to his delivery of Salisbury's message.

Although Salisbury managed to make it back to London within a fortnight of his heart attack, his ability to conduct business was much reduced. 'It was while he was in bed at Hatfield, with more time than usual to read Intelligence Reports, that the magnitude of the Soviet aid to Egypt and Syria had become clear to him.' In his own mind he had at last found a watertight justification for their actions.[53] He could do little more than acquiesce to Macmillan's spectacular volte-face at the beginning of November, however. When the Anglo-French-Israeli invasion of Egypt they had both championed began, stark reality struck home: the Eisenhower administration was willing neither to support the pound nor to provide Britain with the quantity of oil that Middle Eastern nations immediately choked off. Macmillan had spent months of heroic Micawberism. He had talked boldly of Britain going down with all guns blazing if the Americans let them down. He had told his colleagues of Britain's economic vulnerability and had then assured them that it would be all right: something was bound to turn up from the other side of the Atlantic. Unfortunately, John Foster Dulles was not such a mug as Macmillan had assumed. He had observed Macmillan's *modus operandi* at the Foreign Office, months before Suez.[54] Thus forewarned, Dulles had no intention of being played for a fool. He was an Anglophile compared to some of his subordinates. When he was taken ill in at the very height of the crisis in November 1956, only his injunction not to trust the British remained.[55]

The Americans did not trust Harold Macmillan, but they liked the depths of his self-abnegation. In order to recoup his disastrous error of judgement, Macmillan was willing to go a very long way to meet them. As chancellor of the exchequer he was in the pivotal position for a government begging for financial and economic aid. Once again he was helped by the incapacity of colleagues. Eden's health broke under the stress of Suez: as in the 1930s, he sought recuperation in the sunshine, flying off to Ian Fleming's home, Goldeneye, in Jamaica. Salisbury was unwell. The Foreign Office was in disarray. Anthony Nutting had resigned in protest at the collusion with the Israelis. Poor Selwyn Lloyd was borne down by the humiliating negotiations, which took place in the glare of the spotlight of the United Nations, for British forces to withdraw from Egypt.

The two senior politicians still operating were Butler and Macmillan. Butler had been sent to lead the House of Commons as a rest cure from the rigours of the Treasury. Instead of the steady routine of a leader with a comfortable majority, however, he found himself faced on all sides by barely disguised malevolence. The Labour party saw the opportunity for destroying the government. Many in the Conservative party wanted to hunt down and execute the guilty men who had bungled so badly. Macmillan brilliantly 'kippered' Butler on 29 November when they both addressed an angry meeting of the 1922 Committee. Butler addressed the MPs in a downbeat and matter-of-fact manner. Macmillan was due to add a few words in support. Instead he delivered a thirty-five-minute speech dwelling on the future greatness of Britain and the Conservative party. One member present, Enoch Powell, recalled it as 'one of the most horrible things that I remember in politics ... the way in which Harold Macmillan ... succeeded in false footing Rab. The sheer devilry of it verged upon the disgusting.' A few days later that experienced Macmillan watcher, Brendan Bracken, observed, 'His real intentions are to push his boss out of No. 10 and he has a fair following in the Tory Party. The so-called Canal diehards think better of him than they do of Eden or Butler.'[56]

By the time Macmillan delivered this bravura performance his plans were well advanced. On 18 November 1956 he sought an interview with the American Ambassador to the Court of St James, Winthrop Aldrich. He wanted Aldrich to arrange an immediate invitation for Macmillan to fly to Washington as 'Eden's deputy'. He and Salisbury, Macmillan told the ambassador, were holding the line against hotheads in the Cabinet who wanted to begin military operations once more. Aldrich came away from their meeting with the distinct impression that this was the opening gambit in an attempt to displace Eden. To make sure that Aldrich was under no misapprehensions, Macmillan called on him again the next day to tell him that Eden 'will have to go on vacation immediately, first for one week and then for another, and this will lead to his retirement'. Macmillan 'was desperately anxious to see the President at the earliest possible opportunity', Aldrich reported. Eisenhower was happy to accommodate his former subordinate. Harold Macmillan was a man with whom he could do business.[57] As Oliver Lyttelton pointed out in the *Sunday Times*, all but the most rabidly anti-American Tories knew that a deal had to be struck with the US.[58] Macmillan was keen to tell his colleagues back in London that American disgust with Eden made the 'reconstruction of the business' both inevitable and necessary.[59]

In his eagerness to ensure that he was the man who would create a bridge with the Americans, Macmillan had made liberal use of Salisbury's name. He needed him as ballast. Any chance Macmillan might have of the succession would be likely to disappear if the government foundered before Christmas 1956. For his part, Salisbury was willing to keep things ticking over to see whether the stricken leader could make it back to the mark. Salisbury was well aware that many Tory MPs wanted Eden's head. Eden himself was lying in a high fever in Jamaica with his wife, for fear of publicity, telegraphing to London for medical advice rather than consulting local doctors. Salisbury's advice to him was 'complete your cure. You will then be better able to pilot the country through the difficult times which must lie ahead.'[60] Salisbury and Macmillan soldiered on in harness, one hoping that Eden would return, the other determined that he should not.

Their partnership was short. By the first week in January it became clear, as Salisbury explained, almost in tears, to the Cabinet, that Eden was broken in health and could no longer remain prime minister. In contrast to Salisbury's unconcealed grief, Macmillan left the Cabinet table glad that Eden's genuine illness obviated the need to invent an indisposition as cover for his removal.[61] If Eden had not gone voluntarily, Macmillan would have toppled him in a *coup*. In private, with Crookshank, Macmillan did not even bother to dissemble. 'Anthony had completely lost his nerve.'[62]

It was Salisbury who interviewed each member of the Cabinet, the chief whip and the chairman of the Conservative party, asking each in turn whether they preferred Macmillan or his rival Rab Butler.[63] The question he asked each, 'Well, which is it, Wab or Hawold?' soon entered political folklore.[64] It was Salisbury who had conveyed the news to Sir Michael Adeane, the Queen's private secretary, that with the exception of two ministers, Patrick Buchan-Hepburn, who had supported 'Wab', and the foreign secretary, Selwyn Lloyd, who had been unable to make up his mind, everyone wanted 'Hawold'.

The choice was a triumph for past record over present reality. Macmillan's outstanding record in two world wars made him seem 'sound', though the course he had pursued in the last few months had been notable for its tergiversation. Butler, whose line had been much more consistent, had no such leeway for error. He was too young to serve in the Great War and had deliberately avoided a job directly concerned with the war effort during the Second World War. Now Butler appeared to have been AWOL for a third war. The Tory party was looking round for someone to blame for the Suez disaster. They could hardly savage the incapacitated Anthony Eden. 'They had therefore,' said the party chairman, Oliver Poole, 'looked around for a scapegoat and had pitched on Rab.' Butler's sin was to have 'indiscreetly, during the previous Autumn, expressed, in private conversation, doubts as to the wisdom of the Suez policy, and his remarks had been widely repeated'. One of the reasons why Butler was so popular with the party's young intellectuals was his ability to make them feel as if they were running on the inside track by his confidences and indiscretions. In January 1957 he was undone by his own cunning. To the non-intellectuals in the Conservative party he seemed 'too clever by half'; and non-intellectuals outnumbered intellectuals by a considerable margin. Butler had 'acted silly' as Macmillan put it to Crookshank.[65]

Clever people did not like to believe it had been so straightforward. Norman Brook, the secretary to the Cabinet, for instance, convinced himself that it was not true that 'a straight vote between the two either in Cabinet or in the Party would have left Rab in a humiliating minority'. Neither did he accept that, if Butler had been chosen, 'there would have been some conspicuous and highly damaging resignations and the Parliamentary Party might well have disintegrated in public'.[66] It was nevertheless the case. As the chief whip, Ted Heath, explained to Salisbury, 'Hawold' was the overwhelming favourite in the House of Commons. The right-wing MPs would not follow 'Wab', 'who they regarded as having been weak-kneed throughout'. The left-wing MPs preferred Butler, but would follow Macmillan.[67]

Conspiracy theorists had a field day. Had not Macmillan and Salisbury been brothers-in-law through marriage into the Cavendish family, they whispered, were not their Cavendish wives cousins? Had not Salisbury, they asked, spent the New Year closeted with the Queen?[68] Macmillan's succession was, according to the rumour mill, a 'personal and private effort by the head of the Cecils'.[69] The gossip would have been even more intense if political correspondents had known that Macmillan's best friend, Harry Crookshank, had installed the man managing the succession at the Buckingham Palace end, Michael Adeane, in the Masonic Bard of Avon Lodge in 1939.[70] It did not hurt Macmillan to have such good contacts. Macmillan's sedulous exploitation of his image too was certainly a factor in his success – most Conservatives believed that he was an 'officer and a gentleman' and that Butler was neither. He became prime minister, however, for the simple reason that the overwhelming majority of Conservative leaders consulted believed he would do a better job than Butler of digging the party out of the ordure in which he had helped to bury it.

Salisbury was the first person of any importance whom Macmillan saw when he returned from the Palace. Yet whereas for Macmillan the day was one of triumph, for Salisbury the meeting was uncomfortable. Since they had been children, Bobbety had had an advantage over Macmillan. At school, Bobbety was treated as the heir of the greatest political family in England. At Oxford, Viscount Cranborne had been the centre of attention. In the 1930s he had risen rapidly to be one of the most important politicians in England. In the 1940s he had been Secretary of State for the Colonies while 'Hawold' was his parliamentary under-secretary. In 1951, when the Conservatives returned to office, Lord Salisbury was one of the most powerful members of the government while Macmillan filled the unglamorous post of Minister of Housing. Yet now their roles were quite reversed.

Macmillan and Salisbury had been bound to each other for so long that they could not but be aware of the change in their fortunes. They did not need to talk of this directly. Instead they concentrated on details. Macmillan asked Salisbury to serve under him. Salisbury agreed with reluctance. They talked about who should be the government's ministers in the House of Lords. Salisbury asked Macmillan if he would see through Salisbury's most cherished political project, the reform of Parliament. Macmillan replied that in the present circumstances this was an unimportant distraction.[71] Macmillan requested that Salisbury should give up his direction of Britain's atomic energy programme to Macmillan's confidant, Percy Mills. This was hard to accept. Salisbury had been one of the architects of the Atomic Energy Authority and had proudly supervised it from its beginning.[72] He said he would need time to think about it.[73]

Despite the difficulty of their meeting, Salisbury was left in his room hoping that, although Macmillan was now first among equals, he himself would retain a position of power, honour and influence.[74] Only Macmillan knew that Salisbury would soon be powerless. The prime minister would erect an insuperable barrier, 'a sort of Iron Curtain', between them. He would, for the moment, accede to Salisbury's request that the Atomic Energy Authority and its director, Salisbury's sincere admirer, Sir Edwin Plowden, should not become merely a cog in the Ministry of Power.[75] On Saturday evening Macmillan telephoned Salisbury to confirm their agreed appointments in the House of Lords. They chatted amicably.[76] Yet Salisbury would never again be consulted on an issue of political importance. Macmillan instructed his civil servants to brief the press about Salisbury's loss of influence.[77] Salisbury's advice on constructing the new government was ignored. When they met on 10 January Macmillan had already decided to sack Salisbury's protégé in the House of Commons, the minister of defence, Brigadier Antony Head.[78] The first Salisbury knew of Head's ouster was when he read the news in his morning paper.[79]

Macmillan had no intention of creating a Cabinet of equals. He removed his brother-in-law, James Stuart, from the Cabinet and had sacked the home secretary, Gil Lloyd George. Salisbury was the only contemporary of Macmillan who remained in the government. The next most senior figure was David Maxwell-Fyfe, born in 1900 but an MP only since 1935. Fyfe had only reached a training battalion of the Scots Guards before the Great War ended. Although Macmillan complained that his government contained 'no tough guys ... [like] Oliver Lyttelton', if this was so, then it was his own fault: he created a firebreak between himself and his own generation.[80] In the early part of his career, Macmillan had tried again and again to form alliances with his contemporaries. These efforts had each ended in failure. Since 1940 he had come to the conclusion that it was impossible to have friends in politics. A prime minister could have only clients.

Macmillan came to power at a desperate moment. Suez had been a national humiliation. The only thing he had on his side was time. The Conservatives had won the 1955 election by a comfortable margin. There was no need to hold another election until the spring of 1960. There was time to rebuild. All that would be wasted, however, if the internal divisions revealed by Suez suppurated and spread. Macmillan repeated like a mantra: if we can survive until Parliament disperses over the summer, we can go on to win. For his first six months as prime minister, all his energies were bent towards survival. 'All through my life,' he angrily admonished his chancellor of the exchequer, Peter Thorneycroft, who dared that to suggest that fiscal probity might enter their calculations, 'I have heard people talk about the long-term problems. This is an excuse to avoid short-term ones.'[81] He would give people what they wanted, bread and circuses: the centrepiece of Thorneycroft's budget in April 1957 was the abolition of entertainment tax. Macmillan expected all to submit themselves to the greater good of short-term survival; there was no room for 'principle', to rock the boat was little better than treachery. 'I have,' he reminded Bobbety, 'taken on a very difficult job, in circumstances almost unparalleled in political history.'[82] 'His policy could not incur the stigma of opportunism,' wrote Oliver Lyttelton, implying that it could. 'It had form, courage and enlightenment, and when history looks back upon his Administration, though it will, perhaps, not be counted one of the very highest, it will be judged as one of remarkable achievement in the face of pressing dangers and perplexities.'[83]

Whatever the primacy of electoral politics, Macmillan knew from his first day in office that his government could not afford to drift. His policy truly needed 'form and courage'. To survive he had to appease America. He needed Dwight Eisenhower to smile upon Britain once more, to say in public that Suez had been no more than a caesura in Anglo-American relations caused, it could be implied, by the madness of one man, Anthony Eden. Macmillan and Eisenhower, old friends and comrades-in-arms, would heal what he had rent asunder. It was not only fine words that Macmillan needed. Eisenhower's men had their feet firmly placed on Britain's economic windpipe. Without their say-so, no one would lend Britain any money. Without their permission, no oil would flow into Britain's refineries. Britons could be subjected to a cold, poor, crippled and humiliating winter. No government could survive the return of short-ages and rationing when the sunlit uplands of a consumer society had been attained only five years before. Fuel rationing affected 'almost every man and woman whose willing and enthusiastic co-operation we need'.[84]

Eisenhower, for his part, had no wish to cause Macmillan's down-fall. All he had to do was come to heel, apologize and, more import-antly, give guarantees that Britain would never be in a position to cause Eisenhower – or any other American president – such trouble again. Well might Macmillan christen his trip to Bermuda to do obeisance for Britain's sins 'Operation Canossa'.[85] The trick would be to give in gracefully and hope that some people, especially anyone with a vote, would not notice Britain's reduction to clientage. Once more Macmillan felt that this sleight of hand would buy him time. Once American anger had been appeased, he could start to rebuild.

The delicate tightrope Macmillan chose to walk could be upset all too easily. Some American demands – that Britain should act as a base for their ballistic missiles – were relatively easy to accept. They could always be explained away in terms of Cold War solidarity. Indeed, when the hapless foreign secretary, Selwyn Lloyd, dared to suggest that Britain might be better off cooperating with the Europeans on nuclear weapons, he had been slapped down by Lord Salisbury. 'Our main aim at the present time,' Salisbury snapped, 'should be to repair the breach which had been made in Anglo-American relations by the Suez dispute.'[86] He said this on the day before Macmillan became prime minister. There was no dispute between them, in this matter at least. The problem was that the Americans had some rather more outrageous demands to make. It was not only Eisenhower whom Macmillan was expected to appease, it was Nasser too. Before Macmillan left for Bermuda Salisbury pleaded with Lew Douglas, the former American ambassador to the Court of St James, not to push him too hard. They had, Salisbury admitted, made terrible mistakes in the way they had handled Suez. They had committed the greatest sin of all: failure. They were nevertheless hurt that the Americans had turned their backs. But, Salisbury said, both nations could let bygones be bygones; relations could start afresh with little long-term damage, 'if we can get over the one really big hurdle which remains'. 'That is of course,' he told Douglas, 'the opening of the Suez canal and what happens then. I do feel that it is vital that we should stand together over that. Otherwise, a wound may be inflicted which it may take generations to heal. For on that Nasser is clearly in the wrong.'[87]

American leaders chose not to hear these anguished pleas. Eisenhower condemned the British for being unable to 'talk constructively' because of the 'blinding bitterness they felt towards Nasser'. They were 'obsessed with the possibilities of getting rid of Nasser'.[88] American officials briefed the press back home about British stupidity.[89] Macmillan might writhe in anguish, he might hope that given time he could talk the Americans round, but in March 1957 his marching orders were all too clear: the Suez Canal would be reopened and Britain would meekly pay its tolls over to Nasser. Although Salisbury, in charge of the Foreign Office while Lloyd accompanied Macmillan to Bermuda, had backed Harold in his mission to appease, this stuck in his throat. Had Macmillan, he wondered, talked tough but backed down too easily?

Before Egypt could become an issue between them, however, Macmillan rammed another bone down Salisbury's throat. Suez was not the only unappealing legacy from the previous regime. Eden had bequeathed them a nasty little war on the island of Cyprus. Greek terrorists were waging a brutal campaign to force Britain to hand the island over to Greece, thus achieving the dream of *Enosis*. The public face of the Cypriot Greek nationalist movement was Archbishop Makarios. Everyone on the British side, including Macmillan and Salisbury, agreed he was up to his neck in the blood of murdered British soldiers, Turkish Cypriots and pro-British Greeks. If he had not been so intransigent, they might have been able to cut a deal with the Greek government. In their frustration they had decided it was best to decapitate the uprising even if it meant making this turbulent priest a martyr.[90] Not that Makarios had been scourged by his martyrdom. He had been packed off into comfortable exile in the Seychelles. Oliver Lyttelton always maintained they had made a grave mistake: Makarios should have been dumped on the Greek mainland to fall out with his 'friends' in Athens.[91] Macmillan had no doubts that they had done the right thing. He had even fewer doubts about Makarios's character: he was a 'twister'.[92]

Almost exactly a year after they had all thought they had seen the back of the archbishop he burst into the headlines again. His reappearance came at a most unwelcome moment. Macmillan was preparing to leave London for his tryst with Eisenhower in Bermuda. Everyone knew he was going; even Cypriot terrorists. The Middle

East was on the agenda for the talks. Since the British were supposed to be cowed 'imperialist aggressors', what better moment to draw attention to their abuse of another charismatic Mediterranean leader? Leaflets started to appear on Cyprus. If Makarios was released, they announced, EOKA, the militant wing of the nationalist movement, would call a ceasefire. Macmillan was not impressed: if the terrorists were appealing to the United Nations, it suggested that British military action was working. On the other hand, the most important thing was 'to satisfy home and foreign opinion that we are dealing with the new situation in an "imaginative" way'. 'Imagination' was Macmillan's lodestar: there was little point in him going to Bermuda and claiming a new start if Britain was made to look like an imperialist dinosaur by Cypriot priests and murderers. He was all in favour of hanging terrorists, but unfortunately the United States had had the 'impudence' to complain about one strung up a few days previously. Cyprus would have to take its place in the great scheme of things. There was little point in being stiff-necked about Makarios. He must be released from the Seychelles in the interests of peace. He gave the colonial secretary, Alan Lennox-Boyd, instructions to this effect.[93]

When Macmillan decided on this course he was under no illusions that 'some of the Cabinet will jib at this'. He was right: Salisbury was aghast. Appeasing the United States was unpalatable but necessary, appeasing Nasser was unacceptable, appeasing Makarios was self-abnegation gone mad. There was a blazing row in the Colonial Policy Committee between Boyd and Salisbury. Both threatened to resign if their view did not prevail.[94]

There is a definite air of 'did he jump or was he pushed' about events as they unfolded over the next few days. Macmillan had taken care to isolate Salisbury over the previous two months. In Macmillan's view, he was useful in the Cabinet only as a figurehead, a sort of badge of authenticity that this was still a government of 'sound' men. He had made it quite clear that he had little use for his advice. Macmillan even had his doubts whether soundness was of much value. He doubted whether the 'middle classes' really cared about Tory principles.[95] What they wanted, he thought, was peace, 'nest eggs' and white goods.[96] He judged that even the most out-spoken suburban patriot, who saw Makarios as a hirsute monster, did not want his national serviceman nephew put at risk so that the archbishop could spend a few more months in an Indian Ocean paradise.

Salisbury, it seemed to Macmillan, had failed to understand not only reasons of state but even elementary politics. Macmillan had told him that reform of the House of Lords was simply not a high priority for a government in crisis, but he had wilfully refused to listen.[97] The very day that Macmillan left for Bermuda, Salisbury was still pestering him with demands for his support in a comprehensive reform of the House. He would be waiting for an answer, Salisbury assured him, the moment he stepped off the aeroplane back on English soil.[98] Macmillan had come to the conclusion that he could have the advantages of Lord Salisbury's brand of Conservatism with-out being bothered by the man himself. He had found his own Lord Salisbury in the Scottish peer, Alec Home. Home had the aristocratic lineage, he was respected by his peers, the peers, and he was right wing.[99] He had a slightly embarrassing pedigree – as Chamberlain's private secretary he had gone the extra mile to prevent Churchill becoming prime minister – but this could be forgiven as the mistake of a young man who had taken loyalty to an unfortunate extreme. Now that blind loyalty looked more of an asset. Home could always be trusted to proffer his views in a straightforward and manly fashion. Men respected his ability to argue his corner. But he would always give in to Macmillan. He was capable without being clever.[100] Salis-bury realized too late that Home was to Macmillan what Lord Halifax had been to Neville Chamberlain.[101]

When Macmillan's aeroplane took off for Bermuda on the evening of 19 March he was unwilling to see dissent at home as anything other than a 'stab in the back'. The calculations that made it unlikely that Macmillan would take a step back also made it unlikely that Salisbury would back down. He felt keenly his loss of power. Ever since January he had been in a fatalistic state of mind. His career had been littered with threats of resignation, threats that had often been effective because no one doubted he would carry them out. The drama was played out with thousands of Atlantic Ocean miles between them. Within days, with Macmillan deep in his discussions with Eisenhower, the matter came to a head. Macmillan returned from a hard day at the Mid-Ocean Club to find a sheaf of telegrams from members of the Cabinet. Boyd was sticking to his view that they had to release Makarios. Salisbury sought to remind Macmillan how much of a 'twister' they both thought the archbishop was. He repeated his threat to resign if Makarios was released.[102] In London the Cabinet favoured Boyd. In Bermuda the foreign secretary inclined to agree with Salisbury. If they had all been together round the Cabinet table, the issue might have been closer. But Macmillan had already made up his mind. He had kept Lloyd at the Foreign Office for occasions such as these. With a snap of the prime minister's fingers, Lloyd was brought into line.[103] The message from Bermuda was: 'get on with it'. This was the point of no return. When the Cabinet met the next day, Salisbury made a long and impassioned speech against releasing Makarios. Once again he threatened to resign. His colleagues listened politely to his harangue but ignored him. Nobody bothered to contradict him, they just got on with discussing the actual details of the release as Macmillan had decreed.[104] Salisbury was already irrelevant.

On Wednesday, 27 March 1957, Macmillan arrived back in England glowing with windswept triumph. What awaited him at home was tiresome but no more than a little local difficulty. He made a cosmetic attempt to convince Salisbury that he should accept the 'general view'.[105] Since Salisbury had told him on at least three occasions that he could not be bound by collective Cabinet responsibility, this was merely a polite formality. That evening Salisbury called on Macmillan for an after-dinner talk. He was 'very charming', but just as it was when they had sat together in January, the denouement was clear.[106] The last rites were performed the next day. It was a mark of how quickly events had moved on that Cyprus did not even have a day to itself. The Cabinet held three meetings that Friday. At the first, all the arguments about Makarios's release were rehearsed as if by rote.[107] Salisbury tendered his resignation, but this caused barely a hiccough. Ministers rolled on to two further meetings.

Lennox-Boyd was dispatched to the Commons to announce the decision about Makarios, but by that evening he was back leading the discussion about self-government for Singapore.[108] Macmillan wasted no time in drawing Salisbury's attention to his isolation. Boyd had met 120 backbenchers at the party Commonwealth Affairs Committee. He had a great success, there was no discord: 'our political situation is therefore good and gives no cause for disquiet'.[109]

Towards the end Macmillan was goading Salisbury to resign. It had come home to him that, if Salisbury was not going to accede to every twist of his new foreign policy, it was better to get him out of the way quickly. Macmillan had been unable to square the Americans on Nasser; he knew what was coming. On 15 April 1957 the Egyptians announced that the Suez Canal would reopen and that all tolls would pour into Nasser's coffers. The Americans were going to pay 'on the drumhead'. The British were going to have to swallow their pride and do the same. 'Our real problem,' in Macmillan's own words, 'is how to use the Canal with minimum short-term loss of face.' 'A hands-down victory for Nasser,' was the only conclusion that could be reached.[110] This was a dangerous moment. Cyprus was an irrelevance compared to Suez. It was Suez that could bring him down.[111] If the true story began to leak out, Macmillan's role, the collusion, the incompetence, then Macmillan's whole career would be wrecked. And Salisbury knew everything.

No wonder Macmillan was exultant when Salisbury resigned over Cyprus. 'It's much better,' he thought, as he surveyed the coverage in the Sunday newspapers, 'to have lost Salisbury over Cyprus than over the Canal.'[112] 'What a blessing he went over Makarios,' he reminded himself months later.[113] He was sick with nerves at the thought of facing the House of Commons over Cyprus the next day, but at least he was sure of his ground. In the event it was Hugh Gaitskell, the Labour leader, who 'faltered; wobbled; hedged'. If this had been a vote of confidence over Suez, Macmillan knew that his own MPs would have been as likely to turn on him as to cheer him to the echo. Of course it had never been likely that Salisbury would make a clean breast of the Suez affair. He himself was deeply implicated and Eden's reputation would have been damned beyond redemption. But if the whole sorry mess was kept in the forefront of the public gaze, there was always a chance that the worms would start crawling out of the dungheap.

One thing was certain; Salisbury's resignation ended any affection he and Macmillan might once have had for each other. 'One thing comforts me,' Macmillan wrote in farewell, 'you refer to my old friendship: that we can surely keep.'[114] He told the first Cabinet to meet without Salisbury that 'they would feel deeply the loss of his support and counsel'. For him personally, he continued, it was a great sorrow to be parted from a colleague and a friend with whom he had worked in harmony for so many years. These were certainly not Macmillan's true sentiments. 'All through history,' he wrote in his diary the weekend of Salisbury's departure, 'the Cecils, when any friend or colleague has been in real trouble, have stabbed him in the back – attributing the crime to qualms of conscience.'[115] Macmillan was delighted that his calculation that Salisbury would become politically irrelevant was correct. He was an 'inflamed tooth' of whom his colleagues were glad to be rid. His demise had 'left scarcely a ripple on the surface'.[116] Lunching with Max Beaverbrook, whose *Daily Express* was the chosen reading of every patriot, he was delighted to find him 'very scornful'. Knowing that Salisbury and Beaverbrook loathed one another, he took the opportunity to assure him what a 'very old and dear friend' Salisbury was before slipping the knife in: he still couldn't find 'any good grounds' for the resignation.[117]

Macmillan now regarded Salisbury as an implacable foe. There was no point, he told Alec Home, in listening to Salisbury's views. He was already plotting with right-wing MPs, 'who now regard him as their leader'.[118] In fact Salisbury had every sympathy for Macmillan's efforts in the foreign field. He realized that they were a deeply unpleasant necessity. It just seemed to him that Macmillan was overdoing the lengths to which the Conservatives had to go to survive. Not everything of worth should be thrown overboard. They didn't have to release Makarios when his statements still showed him supporting violence in Cyprus. They didn't have to submit to Nasser as soon as he shoved a collecting tin under their noses.[119] It all smacked of appeasement.[120] The old gang agreed with him. As

Churchill's fixer, Brendan Bracken, put it in his letter of condolence, 'who save fossils can object to constant capitulation to greedy aggressors abroad and at home'.[121] 'Of course,' ran Oliver Lyttelton's words of support, one had to teach the 'compromisers that national policy can't be just a series of retreats'.[122]

Nevertheless, Salisbury knew that the ground for his resignation in March 1957 was entirely barren. He had few illusions about his popularity among the generation of Conservative MPs elected since the war. Only two years before he had been booed, jeered and cat-called in a private meeting by MPs who did not like his views on commercial broadcasting. He could see as well as Macmillan the looming split between them over the Suez Canal. He knew the dangers this held and was as relieved as Macmillan that he had gone over Cyprus. 'Whatever happens,' he wrote to Eden, 'I am far happier out of the Government than in, especially with Suez blowing up, on which a row with my colleagues would have been far more embarrassing.'[123] He could now object to the appeasement of Nasser – 'using the Canal if Nasser will graciously allow us and will accept our money!' – as Macmillan himself put it, which he did in a letter to *The Times* on 15 April 1957, without the risk of undermining the government. Even Macmillan concluded that, 'I don't think it is really meant to be a bid for power.'[124]

There was a group of die-hard MPs who were willing to challenge the government over Suez. Charles Waterhouse, an old friend and contemporary of Crookshank who had been a regular presence at Pont Street in the 1930s; Sir Timothy Eden's son John, an MP in his early thirties; Lord Hinchingbrooke, 'Hinch', 'an eccentric Whig', the heir to an earldom who combined liberal social views with an unyielding commitment to the Empire and who sat for Salisbury's old seat in Dorset. Salisbury, and indeed Macmillan, knew them well. 'I think they will succeed,' predicted a gloomy Macmillan, 'in injuring, perhaps humiliating the government – without destroying it – not a very clever plan, but about their level of intelligence.'[125] Macmillan remained convinced that it was Salisbury, aided by Eden, who was pulling the strings.[126] His suspicions were fuelled by the unflattering letters written by Eden shown to him by those who wished to curry favour with the man in power.[127] But Hinch and his pals were not stalking-horses for Salisbury. Bobbety would later attempt to recruit them, but not in 1957. The government's most cogent critic was Angus Maude, a founder member, along with Iain Macleod and Enoch Powell, of the 'One Nation' group of liberal Tories whom neither Macmillan nor Salisbury knew well.[128]

In mid May, when the time came to announce the Suez capitulation, Macmillan had worked himself into a lather. Barracked by the Opposition and fearing the blow from behind, he 'fumbled' his speech. Eight Conservative MPs, led by Hinch and Maude, had already announced that they would abstain: Macmillan did not know how many would join them. He calculated anywhere between sixteen and thirty – 'the latter figure would be serious and make it difficult for me to go on'.[129] He turned to his chief whip for succour. Ted Heath bullied, cajoled, threatened and promised. He got the number down to fourteen. Macmillan was greatly relieved but utterly exhausted by the tension.[130] Macmillan would always see Salisbury lurking around the next corner ready to trip him up. This went beyond mere politics.

This fearsome figure was, in fact, to be found accompanying his wife to the Chelsea Flower Show and the National Portrait Gallery. 'In fact, I am enjoying myself.' Far from being the leader of a cabal, he felt 'very isolated'. 'The last thing I want to do,' he told Eden, 'is to embarrass the Government.'[131] 'I've got so detached from politics,' he wrote at the end of the parliamentary session, 'that it is beginning to seem like a dream that I was ever in them and I greatly doubt whether I shall ever go back.' He accepted that Macmillan probably had little choice over the Suez Canal: it was the relish and speed with which he appeased Third World dictators that appalled Salisbury.[132] And that was the nub of the matter. 'Oh dear! Oh dear!,' he lamented, 'I don't think I am meant for politics, especially Harold's kind. He is *too clever by half* for me.'[133] Macmillan regarded Salisbury as a traitor; Salisbury was beginning to suspect that Macmillan had fooled them over all these years. 'I cannot with the best will in the world get on with your successor,' he confided to Eden. 'It isn't that I don't think him a very able man. I do; and if I had to advise the

Queen again, I should give the same advice as before. But his mind and mine don't click; and he knows that as well as I do. So it is really better that he should go his own way; and run things his own way.'[134] Although they were sometimes forced into each other's company – their first meeting after Salisbury's resignation was at the Derby – Macmillan and Salisbury did their best thereafter never to meet.[135]

Macmillan's relationship with Salisbury was not the only one complicated by his accession to the premiership. In November 1958 Ian Harvey, the under-secretary at the Foreign Office, was discovered in an act of sodomy with a guardsman in St James's Park. Macmillan had first been introduced to Harvey by Ronnie Knox, as one of the monsignor's Anglo-Catholic acolytes. But Harvey had a secret life. Since the war he had been an enthusiastic 'cottager'. The parks of London offered a 'veritable parade' of members of Her Majesty's Horse and Foot Guards supplementing their income by having sex with gentlemen. For thirteen years Harvey had been an enthusiastic participant in this bacchanal. It was only a matter of time before he was caught.[136] Normally Macmillan would have treated such an upset with detached cynicism. 'He says,' reported Oliver Lyttelton, 'the Conservative policy to win the next election is not very appealing. It appears to be (a) to make homosexualism legal (b) to establish a Government betting shop in every street (c) a Government brothel in every town, and (d) to spend a million on the PM's house.'[137] In this case Macmillan, however, thought Harvey's fall 'a terrible thing' and was 'greatly distressed'.[138] He was right to be worried. Harvey's exposure 'greatly distressed' other homosexual Tories. Although the most prominent of these was Alan Lennox-Boyd, the closest to Macmillan personally was Harry Crookshank.[139]

After he retired from the Cabinet, Harry Crookshank began campaigning on behalf of Desmond Kilvington, a young man who wished to become the Conservative parliamentary candidate for Grimsby. Kilvington had first appeared in Crookshank's life in about 1950. Just past his thirtieth birthday at that time, he was a merchant seaman from Brighton. He was a familiar face in Gainsborough campaigning for Crookshank in the 1950, 1951 and 1955 general elections. After the death of Crookshank's mother in 1954, Kilvington moved into Pont Street. Crookshank bankrolled him to set up a company called Tipdex that manufactured filing cabinets. They told the world that they were 'cousins'. The Grimsby constituency association were delighted to adopt a candidate from such a distinguished stable. Crookshank was the most highly regarded Conservative in Lincolnshire. He was known to have the ear of the prime minister and that of the chief whip, Ted Heath.

The deaths of Crookshank's sister and his mother had destroyed his warm and loving family. Left lonely and bereft, he had turned to his lover for a more conventional 'married' life. Sadly any dreams of connubial domestic bliss Crookshank may have entertained were not to be. Like Harvey, Kilvington was a drunk. He made a complete mess of Tipdex, which rapidly headed towards bankruptcy, taking Crookshank's investment with it.[140] Harvey's fall came at a most dangerous time; Crookshank's relationship with Kilvington was on the rocks and the latter was showing most unnerving signs of instability. Kilvington had a paranoid fear that Crookshank was talking about his drinking behind his back. He was threatening to move out.[141] The moment of danger came when, increasingly dissatisfied with their erratic candidate, Grimsby Conservative Association decided to get rid of Kilvington. There was a scene and Kilvington went to the press to complain of his unjust treatment. It was no more than a 'weekend wonder', but all the press reports identified Kilvington as Crookshank's protégé.[142] Although Kilvington moved out of Pont Street, Crookshank remained sensitive to the possibility of publicity.[143] It was not until they met for the last time in January 1961, when Kilvington flounced into Pont Street to announce that he was leaving for Nigeria and '*never* coming back to England', that Crookshank could relax.[144]

Whatever relief Crookshank, or indeed Macmillan, might once have felt at this parting was now of little importance. By the time Kilvington left the scene for the last time Crookshank was dying of cancer. Crookshank had been rushed to hospital in June 1960 for a 'terrible operation'.[145] The prognosis was not good. In 1955 he had set up an annual lecture at the Royal College of Radiologists in memory of his mother and sister. Now the same disease that had killed them was killing him: he had liver cancer. His operation won him only a few months' remission. His condition worsened at the beginning of 1961.[146] Ill and in pain he took off for the United States and the West Indies in the hope of some recovery. By July 1961 he was in inexorable decline.[147]

In the difficult final years of his friend's life, Macmillan did all he could to buoy his spirits. Just before the illness was diagnosed, he secured the High Stewardship of Westminster, the senior lay position in the abbey hierarchy, for Crookshank. The two friends took great pleasure in indulging their joint interest in ecclesiastical politics. In July 1960 they combined to ensure that no memorial to Nye Bevan was installed in the abbey.[148] 1961 had looked like a good year for this pastime: there was the mouth-watering prospect of appointing a new Archbishop of Canterbury: they had every intention of tweaking the nose of the Anglican establishment by rejecting their preferred candidates.[149]

On 14 September 1961, the eve of the forty-fifth anniversary of the day they were both terribly wounded at the Somme, Macmillan and Crookshank dined together. 'We talked of old times mostly,' was Macmillan's wistful note. 'He is wonderfully brave, but I fear he is a dying man.'[150] A fortnight later Macmillan visited Pont Street again. He knew Crookshank could not live for much longer.[151] A week later he was in attendance once more. He sat by Crookshank's bedside for nearly an hour, holding his friend's hand. Full of morphine, Crookshank was barely able to talk. Looking down at his emaciated form, the image that kept forming in Macmillan's mind was of the chubby eight-year-old he had known at Summer Fields.[152] It was the last time they saw each other. Crookshank lapsed into unconsciousness and died a few days later. 'I shall miss him very much,' was Macmillan's simple response when the news was brought to him.[153] Crookshank had no heirs. It was left to Macmillan to organize the funeral. True to his 'Black Protestant' origins, Crookshank, it turned out to the considerable chagrin of the Dean and Chapter, had insisted that their ritualist pomp should be suppressed. The Collegiate Body of Westminster Abbey presided over Harry

Crookshank's funeral denuded of their copes, dressed in simple choir habits.[154] Once the ninetieth Psalm, 'we spend our years as a tale that is told', had been sung by the choir, he was sped northwards to Lincoln where his ashes were interred. A simple memorial plaque was inserted into the ambulatory of Lincoln cathedral near the High Altar and next to the monument he had erected to his sister thirteen years previously.[155] In Macmillan's carefully crafted epitaph to his friend, he maintained that his 'friendships and diverse interests' had 'in many ways' filled 'more of his real life than politics'. This was a polite lie. Crookshank had taken his frequent political set-backs with ill-grace. He died an unhappy, disappointed and lonely man.

10

Enemies

It was the African question that turned Salisbury and Macmillan's relationship from one of mutual distrust into one of open hatred. Salisbury had loved English-speaking southern Africa since he first went there with Billy Gore forty-five years previously. He had bought farms in Southern Rhodesia in the 1940s. In January 1956 he had received the freedom of its capital, Salisbury, which had been named in honour of his grandfather. He had described Rhodesia as a 'new pulsating civilization', its founders were the 'greatest men' of the 'modern world'. Rhodesia, he declared, was founded in the true ideals of freedom of thought, speech and action transplanted to 'primitive surroundings'. He told his all-white audience that Rhodesia was a beacon of racial partnership, 'which will serve as a pattern to which the whole African continent south of the Sahara may ultimately conform'.[1] In Rhodesia he detected 'extraordinary buoyancy', 'champagne in the air' and 'enormous opportunities for UK trade'.[2] As soon as he resigned from the government, Paul Emrys-Evans brought him on to the board of the British South Africa Company, Cecil Rhodes's chartered company that had once ruled Rhodesia and now dominated its economy. An African tour that Salisbury made at the beginning of 1959 to visit his farms and the company's copper mines merely confirmed his affection for the country.[3]

In 1953 Salisbury had been one of the architects of the Central African Federation, a union of Southern Rhodesia, Northern Rhodesia and Nyasaland. One consequence of the creation of the federation and Salisbury's continuing interest in its welfare was a burgeoning friendship with its prime minister, Roy Welensky. The friendship between the English aristocrat and the uncouth African politician was genuine.[4] Welensky and Salisbury were attracted by each other's wholehearted enthusiasm; they felt they could trust each other. In addition they shared a growing distaste for Harold Macmillan. 'Quietly, and for your ear,' Welensky wrote, Harold Macmillan made him feel a 'bit sick'.[5] 'I am so glad,' Salisbury replied, 'that you felt like I did.'[6]

Harold Macmillan and Bobbety Salisbury had first worked together on African affairs, amicably, at the Colonial Office in 1942.[7] Even then Macmillan had disputed the premiss that, 'on this analogy of American colonies, the claims to self-government of any substantial number of Englishmen who have settled permanently in a country cannot be resisted'. In contrast to Salisbury, his early observations of Kenyan and Rhodesian colonists had left him with a distaste for them and their pretensions. 'Gradually,' he argued in 1942, 'the white stock will become contaminated by the effect of the climate or by some inter-breeding.' This decadent white population 'surrounded by a native population', that, Macmillan maintained, would 'become increasingly crowded and land hungry', was bound to spark off a land and race war.[8] His wartime experiences with French colonists in North Africa had merely confirmed him in this view.[9]

Macmillan, no less than Salisbury, regarded the indigenous population of Africa as 'barbarians'. 'In places like Kenya and the Federation,' Salisbury urged, 'we should not be handing over Europeans and loyal Africans, who have the right to look to us for protection, to the tender mercies of men little removed from the primitive savages we found there when we first came to Central Africa less than a century ago.'[10] Yet for Macmillan the Africans were 'powerful, swift and elemental' barbarians even if they had the minds of 'children'.[11] 'The real truth,' he said of the leaders of Rhodesian black opinion, 'is that the Africans are vain and childish. Like children, they easily get excited.'[12] He parted company with Salisbury in refusing to accept 'trusteeship' as the logical corollary of 'childishness'.[13] Trusteeship 'is permeated', he stated, 'by the unimaginative spirit of colonial administration in decline'.[14] Proponents of 'trusteeship' such as

Salisbury believed that in 'a policy of partnership between black and white ... rests the only hope both for a peaceful and prosperous future for Africa'. That future would be destroyed by 'handing over the reins of government to militant African leaders'. The result would be 'not partnership and harmony but chaos and terrorism and cruelty and economic disaster'.[15] Macmillan did not necessarily disagree: what he found laughable was the idea that the white colonists could take a leading and productive part in that partnership. They were, to him, the rag-tag sweepings of the scum of Europe, with an unhealthy admixture of decayed British aristocrats. 'Happy Valley' was White Africa. It was decadent. British officials saw Roy Welensky as an impressive figure: energetic, capable of 'taking the Government machinery by the scruff of the neck and shaking it into shape'; reasonably enlightened on the race issue; and a realist.[16] To Macmillan, Welensky was no more than 'an emotional Lithuanian Jew'.[17] He had no intention of treating with Welensky, or any other settler leader, in good faith.[18]

Salisbury abhorred this approach.[19] He regarded the Rhodesian and Kenyan settlers as Britons, whatever their actual country of origin. If the British government made promises, they were making promises to countrymen whose leaders were close and trusted personal friends. You did not treat with friends like a shyster lawyer. The spirit of agreements was as important as their actual words. Britain needed to stand up for Britons even if this incurred criticism from foreigners.[20]

By the time Macmillan faced his first general election as prime minister, the race war he had predicted a decade and a half before was on the point of breaking out.[21] 'We may,' he lamented, 'find the natives quite out of hand.'[22] The native who got quite out of hand first was the unlikely leader of Nyasa nationalism, the fly-whisk-wielding elder of the Church of Scotland, Dr Hastings Banda. Fearing a plot to murder whites in Nyasaland, the governor declared a state of emergency and arrested Banda and his dissidents in the spring of 1959. The robust policing of Nyasaland provoked calls for a public inquiry. Macmillan thought that a long-drawn-out inquiry with some bland results would defuse the situation. It would conclude that there was confusion, that the men on the spot did their best, and that there were isolated examples of zealotry on all sides. Unfortunately for Macmillan, he chose the wrong judge to conduct this investigation. Patrick Devlin was able but, as Macmillan described him in a subsequent fit of bile, 'he is (a) Irish – no doubt with that Fenian blood that make Irishmen anti-Government on principle, (b) a *lapsed* Roman Catholic, (c) *Hunchback*, (d) bitterly disappointed at my not having made him Lord Chief Justice'.[23] In a 'dynamite' report, Devlin said in no uncertain terms that Nyasaland was not being robustly policed; it was a police state.

To Macmillan's chagrin, though not to his surprise, Nyasaland was part of a wider pattern. As colonial secretary Oliver Lyttelton had been faced with Mau Mau: a violent anti-European, anti-Christian and anti-government conspiracy based within the Kikuyu tribe of Kenya.[24] The Mau Mau uprising had been bad enough. To make matters worse, British officials suspected that there were settlers who would welcome a land war as much as the Kikuyu. Stung by the articulate criticisms of their greed and brutality put forward by educated Africans, not trusting the British government to give overriding priority to their interests, the settlers knew that their hold on the land would be strengthened by a show of force. Inferiority in numbers would be offset by superiority in firepower if one were not too fussy against whom the firepower was used.[25] 'Europeans with the low whisky prices and high-altitude pressures are irresponsible and hysterical,' Lyttelton had told Churchill.[26] 'Middle-class sluts,' Bobbie Erskine, the British military commander Lyttelton appointed, said of the people he was defending.[27]

To get a grip on this dangerous situation, Lyttelton had sacked an ineffectual governor and appointed in his stead an aristocratic colonial service officer, Evelyn Baring. Behind a charming façade, Baring had proved to be an even more Cromwellian figure than Lyttelton had hoped.[28] At the time Macmillan's view was that 'Oliver Lyttelton is . . . obviously handling the whole position in a masterly way'.[29] Yet the festering sore of Baring's regime was Lyttelton's legacy to Harold Macmillan's premiership.[30]

In the white-heat of Mau Mau, Baring had turned a blind eye

to acts of institutionalized brutality against Kikuyu tribesmen;
Lyttelton had turned a blind eye to his blind eye. The fruits of this
Nelsonian system were reaped in 1959 when it became clear that the
Kenyan government was murdering Mau Mau '"hard core" rebels
and fanatics' in concentration camps.[31] Macmillan was appalled. 'It
may well blow this government out of office,' he exclaimed melo-
dramatically.[32] He forced Alan Lennox-Boyd, who had succeeded
Lyttelton at the Colonial Office, to brazen it out.[33] Boyd was sent
into the Commons on two consecutive days to defend his conduct
over Kenya, then over Nyasaland. 'When you have ermine around
your neck,' wrote Lyttelton in a comforting if rather ill-chosen bibli-
cal note, 'you and I will go to Baiae, like Pontius Pilate.'[34] The report
on the concentration camp at Hola and Devlin's 'police state' report
on Nyasaland confirmed Macmillan in all his beliefs about Africa.
'The Africans,' he decreed, 'are not the problem in Africa, it is the
Europeans who are the problem.'[35]

At the end of 1959 Macmillan went to Africa in person. Some
journalists later assumed that Macmillan had been affected by what
he saw there. His grand tour of the continent south of the Sahara
did not, however, alter Macmillan's views. His entourage left Britain
with a speech condemning the whites in Africa 'already in our bag-
gage'.[36] It was simply a matter of getting the wording right. 'Do you
remember,' wrote one of his private secretaries to another, 'that the
first draft of the famous phrase ran on the lines of the following,
"No one can be long in this Continent without feeling the wind of
change on his cheek." It got altered in the drafting process that
started in early December 1959 and which was carried through Accra,
Lagos, Ibadan, Enugu, Kaduna, Salisbury, Lusaka, Zomba, Pretoria
and Cape Town.'[37] By the time Macmillan finally rose to address the
South African Houses of Parliament in Cape Town on 3 February
1960, he said: 'The most striking of all the impressions I have formed
since I left London a month ago is the strength of this African
national consciousness.' He had found his aphorism: 'The wind of
change is blowing through this Continent.'[38]

At the end of 1959, Macmillan decided on two key appointments
in colonial affairs. He nominated Iain Macleod to replace Alan

Lennox-Boyd at the Colonial Office. Macleod had identified Africa as the Achilles heel of the party's claim to be progressive.[39] Macmillan had no doubt, when he asked Macleod to take over the Colonial Office, that he would run it in a way which would appeal to progressive opinion in Britain and beyond. He also appointed his friend Walter Monckton as the chairman of the commission to review the future of the Central African Federation (CAF). He was confident that the commission would draw up a case for the termination of the federation. The members of the commission were assured that they could recommend the break-up of the federation. The Labour peer, Hartley Shawcross, let this out of the bag in a television interview. Monckton's adviser, the businessman Ronald Prain, a member of Macmillan and Monckton's Sussex cricket parties, was already courting the most radical Northern Rhodesian black leader, Kenneth Kaunda, and acting as a conduit between Kaunda and the Colonial Office as they pursued their common goal of destroying the federation.[40] Macleod promised the government of Northern Rhodesia that pro-federal constitutional reforms would never be introduced.[41]

The Monckton Commission had been launched like a torpedo into the flank of the CAF.[42] It wreaked the damage Macmillan had planned.[43] At the end of July 1960 Monckton began writing his report. It was to be submitted before a conference on the federal constitution assembled in London. Macmillan knew that Monckton's report would be the death knell of the federation. It would recommend that Northern Rhodesia and Nyasaland should be allowed to secede from the CAF. 'The Monckton Report,' he admitted, 'has done exactly what we all expected.' 'There will no doubt be allegations,' he admitted to his private office, 'that Sir Roy Welensky has been badly treated in this matter . . . it could be argued that my statements in the House of Commons, the terms of reference, and the private assurances which I gave from time to time in my messages to Sir Roy, made it clear that the recommendation for secession or the contemplation of the break-up of the Federation was not within the terms of reference.'[44]

Sir Roy Welensky had been suckered. He had not believed that Macmillan could squirm out of guarantees given over a seven-year period by a Conservative government which had been repeatedly reiterated by Macmillan himself.[45] A 'shocked' Bobbety Salisbury had every sympathy with Welensky. In the *Daily Telegraph*, in *The Times*, in the House of Lords he supported Welensky's accusation of bad faith.[46] To cement their alliance Welensky had taken the 'extraordinary step' of sending Salisbury the dossier of correspondence between Macmillan and himself.[47] Having read and burnt the dossier, Salisbury was more than ever convinced of Macmillan's bad faith. He had to admit Macmillan's verbal dexterity: 'At a first reading, I must confess, I still remain uncertain as to what meaning, exactly, was to be attached to Harold's assurances, with their reiterated mention of the terms of reference of the Commission – themselves, I thought, not altogether clear in their limitations.' As he read further, all his worst suspicions were confirmed. 'There is a passage in his second letter which,' he averred to Welensky, 'could only be read as giving you all the reassurances you wanted. It is that which begins with the words: "We have no intention of making an extension of the terms (of reference) to include secession," and ends with the words, "Every member of the Commission has after all accepted on that basis." That passage, I should have thought, could only have one meaning.'[48] Salisbury advised Welensky to release the letters Macmillan had written to him. This would show Macmillan up as a liar.[49]

The 'affair of the letters' was something of a Rubicon for Salisbury. His unhappiness with Macmillan had been growing for years. He had publicly attacked details of government policy in the House of Lords and in the press. Now he was urging the leader of a British colony to publish secret diplomatic correspondence from the prime minister of Great Britain. The ultimate Establishment figure, Salisbury had hitherto believed that such breaches of secrets were rarely in Britain's national interest.[50] Now he risked putting himself beyond the pale. Lord Egremont, who was not only Macmillan's long-serving private secretary but also Robert Cranborne's brother-in-law, observed: 'I am sure that the attitude which his Cecil conscience (the Cecil conscience is a rum one) has caused him to adopt has also caused him much heart-searching and unhappiness.'[51] Macmillan, less indulgent of the Cecil conscience, ordered MI5 to monitor Salisbury as a potential threat to national security.[52] 'From our sources of information,' Macmillan noted with satisfaction, 'we know that Welensky and his High Commissioner give every private document and all private discussions to Lord Salisbury.'[53]

Although Macmillan realized that the letters were potentially damning, he was confident Welensky and Salisbury were bluffing.[54] If Welensky published the letters, it would 'disrupt the system of confidential communication amongst Commonwealth Prime Ministers'.[55] This seemingly innocuous phrase was actually a veiled threat. Welensky was not technically a Commonwealth prime minister since the CAF was not an independent country. He was treated as one merely on sufferance. These privileges could be removed as easily as they were granted. Starting with secret intelligence, Welensky could be choked of the sustenance that gave his rule any credibility. Macmillan certainly did not want to take such a step – it would provoke a political crisis – but the consequences for Welensky would be even worse. In this game of bluff, as Macmillan had predicted, Welensky had to back down. Confident in the knowledge that his letters were safe under lock and key, Macmillan could claim that they would have vindicated him in any case.[56] Neither side had mentioned the letters in public. If anyone tried to controvert Macmillan's version of events, they would merely 'giving away the fact that he had been put in possession of confidential information'.[57]

When Salisbury resigned from the government, Macmillan had suspected him of plotting to unseat him. Salisbury had been doing no such thing. Having concluded an alliance with Welensky, however, he started to agitate for Macmillan's overthrow. In December 1960 Salisbury formed a Watching Committee. It was consciously modelled on his father's Watching Committee of 1940. That Watching Committee had been established to fight a war of attrition against Neville Chamberlain, and its own roots lay in the anti-India Bill agitation of the 1930s. As Salisbury remembered well, although the Indian campaign had ultimately failed, it did such deep damage to the Conservative party that the wounds took years to heal. In 1960 Salisbury was not confident of success, but he knew he could cause Macmillan considerable, perhaps fatal, political damage.

As one of the most enthusiastic and energetic members of the 1940 Committee, Macmillan himself had no illusions about the Watching Committee's ultimate goal, whatever the fair words spoken to disguise its purpose. As with the 1940 committee Salisbury planned to start with a few 'sound' men drawn from the House of Lords and the House of Commons. Their elderly Lordships would be in charge, develop a strategy and make sure the wild men were kept in check. The younger House of Commons men would do the legwork and act as shock troops in Parliament.[58]

At first sight the Watching Committee did not appear formidable, it even seemed a little comical.[59] One of the MPs Salisbury recruited, for instance, was Tony Lambton, heir to the earldom of Durham. Lambton's voracious sexual appetites and willingness to express his views in the most colourful terms made him an object of suspicion to most other members of the Conservative party: in Macmillan's view, he was 'hysterical', 'mad', 'vain' and 'dishonest'; to Salisbury he was 'both original-minded and brave' if 'rather strong meat'.[60] Salisbury decided he was worth the risk. Unfortunately the impeccably aristocratic, if 'hysterical' and 'mad' Lord Lambton thought the impeccably aristocratic Lord Hinchingbrooke, another of Salisbury's recruits, hysterical and mad himself. 'Hinch and his henchmen,' in Lambton's view, would damage the prestige of the committee. 'The trouble with them,' he warned Salisbury, 'is that they are so Right Wing and so anti-American in the House of Commons, that their influence has been quite considerably reduced . . . in effect this means that quite a lot of sensible middle-of-the-roaders who are intensely worried about Africa will be kept out.'[61] It was hardly helpful that Salisbury's two most energetic lieutenants in the House of Commons should self-evidently be barking scions of the nobility. It spoke volumes for his commitment that he persisted. The 1940 Watching Committee had, after all, found a use for energetic pariahs such as Harold Macmillan.

Despite his recruitment of borderline fanatics, Salisbury was convinced that the Watching Committee should not launch a frontal attack on Macmillan. This would be bound to fail. If the committee tried to whip up such an attack, it would 'cost us the help of many

Conservatives who are profoundly unhappy about Government policy in Africa but would not be prepared to go into opposition'.[62] The line they would take was 'that it is not colour or creed but merit and capacity which should govern the grant of a vote' and that this was indeed the message of Macmillan's Cape Town speech. 'It is for him and Iain Macleod to live up to what he said in that speech.' For tactical reasons alone, they should chip away at Macmillan by attacking Macleod first.[63] 'The real truth,' Salisbury wrote, expounding his strategy to Anthony Eden, 'is no one really counts in this government but Harold. He goes whatever way he wants and they have to follow.' But it was Macleod who was more vulnerable: 'Iain Macleod gets worse and worse. In the colonies he seems to be hated to a degree I never remember in any minister'. That was not of much political help, but Salisbury hoped and thought that 'even the Conservative Party in this country is getting more and more restless'.

Salisbury could, he believed, get to Macmillan through Macleod. Macmillan had backed Macleod so strongly that if the latter fell, Macmillan too would be damaged; if Macmillan held on to Macleod, he could be tarred with guilt by association. It would be hard to mobilize the party against them – 'the lead would have to be a pretty strong one' – but it might be possible.[64]

Salisbury added a new twist to his political tactics. By chance, just as he started to construct the Watching Committee, he received a letter from a young man called Paul Bristol. Bristol wanted to set up a campaigning 'think-tank' of right-wing young Conservatives to counter the 'pernicious' influence of the liberal Bow Group. He was particularly interested in condemning the government's African policy, and he was very hostile to Harold Macmillan personally.[65] Bristol's group of seven like-minded souls was firmly rooted in the lower middle class. Of the three most active members of the group, one, Bristol himself, worked in a ship-broking firm, one was the works director of a light engineering company and the third, the only member with formal party experience, having lost his job as Conservative agent in Stoke Newington, now worked as a freelance photographer. They were not Salisbury's kind of people, but he sprinkled them with the gold of Cecil glamour. In the hierarchical

Conservative party, it was easy to snub men with no contacts and unglamorous jobs, less easy to ignore them if they were welcome guests at Hatfield. Salisbury became the patron of the so-called Monday Club. Subsequently he arranged with Paul Emrys-Evans for the Chartered Company to fund their activities.[66] The Monday Club was, however, a side-show for Salisbury. The tried and trusted method of the Watching Committee was the main business.[67]

Before long Welensky asked Salisbury to launch his attack on Macleod.[68] The Monckton Report had burst the bubble of the federation. It was impossible to re-inflate it. To have given the federation any chance of survival, the anti-Macmillan campaign would have had to have taken place in 1958–9 not 1960–61. Macleod was intent on breaking up the federation and creating black majority rule in Northern Rhodesia. There was little, in Macmillan's view, that Welensky could do to prevent it.[69] This was, however, a dangerous game to play. Tempers were running high in Cabinet. Tempers were running high also in Africa. If the Central African Federation descended into civil war, setting British officials against white settlers, the political problem at home would be magnified many times over. Faced with resignations or violence or both: 'our Government and Party', Macmillan feared, 'will be split in two'.[70] Salisbury saw this possibility as clearly as Macmillan. He and the Watching Committee would try and stoke the fires of discontent. If, he calculated, the sympathizers of the federation, 'among them many most highly respected of the older generation of backbenchers', were angered enough to overcome their loyalty to the party, there were enough of them to bring Macmillan down.[71]

Neither Macmillan nor Salisbury, as it happened, thought it likely that the government could be destroyed by the Central African Federation alone. If Salisbury attempted a *coup de main*, he would only reinforce loyalty to Macmillan. Even as his father had decried any direct attack on Chamberlain, so Salisbury abjured any direct attack on Macmillan.[72] The Watching Committee would attempt to ratchet up the pressure on the government.[73] Yet, if they were to act as a focus for discontent, they had to be discreet and 'not too Right Wing'.[74] The first step would be the same as it had been for Salisbury's father: a delegation to the prime minister. Salisbury recognized that for some of the committee the aim was to unseat Macleod and reconstruct the government. They were not yet willing to follow him in an all-out attempt to destroy Macmillan.[75]

On 7 March 1961 the House of Lords held a debate on Africa. Salisbury rose to give the most effective speech he had delivered since his resignation from the Foreign Office twenty-three years previously. Ever since his second resignation four years to the month previously, he had spoken disparagingly of Harold Macmillan as being 'too clever by half'. Salisbury knew Macleod but slightly. He disliked him for his views. He did, however, pour the torrent of bile which, in other circumstances, might have been destined for Macmillan, upon Macleod's head. Years later he regretted that he had got such bold headlines for his attack on Macleod that, when he denounced Macmillan by name, the press took no notice.[76]

Unfortunately for Macleod the characterization Salisbury had designed for Macmillan fitted him rather too well for comfort. Macleod was famed for his fondness for cards. 'It is not,' Salisbury observed, 'immoral, or even bad form, to outwit one's opponents at bridge. On the contrary, the more you outwit them, within the rules of the game, the better player you are.' 'It almost seems to me,' he continued, 'that the Colonial Secretary, when he abandoned the sphere of bridge for the sphere of politics, brought his bridge tech-nique with him.' Macleod had set out to outwit the 'white people' of Africa and 'he had done it successfully'. 'He has been too clever by half.'[77] For the time and place it was a devastating attack. Harold Macmillan, after all, had routed Rab Butler by convincing the Con-servative party that the latter was 'unsound'.[78] Yet Salisbury's attack, however damaging to Macleod, had little impact on its real target, Macmillan himself.[79] It was Salisbury himself who emerged bruised and damaged.[80] Lord Hailsham accused him of an 'error of judge-ment'. Just as 'too clever by half' was code for 'liar and cheat', so the 'error of judgement' identified by Hailsham was Tory code for 'senile old fool'.

When Salisbury, at the head of a Watching Committee delegation, confronted Macmillan face to face, theirs was a dialogue of the deaf. Macmillan set the tone from the outset. He drew attention to Salisbury's performance in the House of Lords by mentioning he would not mention it. He merely uttered the code: 'Disraeli' – Disraeli had once described the great Lord Salisbury as 'a great master of jibes and flouts and jeers'. Once they had started on that track, things could hardly get better. Macmillan followed his Disraeli sneer by implying that the federation had been a crackpot idea in the first place.[81] So incensed was Salisbury that he nearly let the mask of politeness slip. For a moment it seemed as if the most distinguished peer of the realm, known for his exquisite manners, might bellow at the prime minister across the table. Collecting himself he said, tightly and bitterly, that 'our people were being abandoned: they had come and asked and gone away empty; anything that the Government could do to reassure them would be well done'.[82]

Salisbury left more than ever convinced that the softly-softly approach had to be abandoned in favour of an all-out effort to bring Macmillan to his knees. He cleared the decks for action. He resigned from the board of the British South Africa Company. He was not going to give anyone the chance to say that he was bought and sold for Rhodesian gold. Some of the MPs on the Watching Committee were not as scrupulous about receiving 'favours' from Rhodesia. When British intelligence provided Macmillan with evidence for this, he did not hesitate in letting that very accusation be put abroad. At least Salisbury had left his own hands clean.[83] Since the chartered company's business practices were not always entirely commendable, his association with them risked making 'everything I'd said about I[ain] M[acleod] ... horribly insincere'.[84] Business and politics did not mix and he had always preferred politics.

On the eve of Macmillan's departure for a tour of the West Indies, his secretary was surprised to see the limping figure of Bobbety Salisbury delivering his own mail to the prime minister's private office. It could only mean 'the maximum possible trouble'.[85] Salisbury's hand-delivered letter did not mince its words. He dispensed with 'Dear Harold', 'My dear Harold' long since having been abandoned. 'Dear Prime Minister,' he said of their meeting earlier in the day, 'I am afraid I must say quite frankly that we got little comfort from it.' The threat was not even veiled: 'We represented not only our own views but those of a very considerable body of Conservative opinion throughout the country – far more considerable, I must confess, than I had any idea of.'[86] Macmillan hardly needed any more explicit declaration of war. Even if he did, the next day Dick Law chipped in with a 'more in sorrow than in anger' letter. Think back to the old days, Law urged him. This was like the fight against appeasement. 'Of course Redmayne [the chief whip] will continue to command his majority in the House of Commons by a wide margin, just as David Margesson continued to command it until it was too late.' Unless Macmillan took notice of 'the point of view of very large numbers of Conservatives throughout the country', they would stir up 'so bad a period that everything that you have been trying to do ... will be brought in ruins to the ground'.[87]

Macmillan was willing to admit the seriousness of the situation. Rhodesia was a running sore for the party. The pressure was the worst he had endured 'since the days before Suez'. 'You know how much I worry about this Rhodesian affair,' he admitted to Burke Trend. 'We have not surmounted the crisis although we have postponed it.'[88] There was little point in Law appealing to his 'good side'. He regarded the Watching Committee with utter contempt: 'rather a ragamuffin lot, without much brains or authority'. This was a personal fight between himself and Salisbury: 'He is the centre and the only real figure in the revolt.'[89]

Macmillan feared that the Salisbury alliance might be capable of 'mobilizing a great attack on Macleod and me'.[90] He found that Salisbury's activities placed him under great strain.[91] He longed for some respite. He was suffering from 'squalid and petty' health problems. 'But when and how,' he wailed on receiving his doctor's advice to take it easy, 'can I rest. I am beginning (at last) to feel old and depressed.' The strain was tearing his government apart as it exposed all its petty jealousies and dislikes. Ministers were deliberately needling each other. 'Perhaps,' Macmillan prayed, 'if Central Africa can *really* be quiet for a bit and all the unpleasantness of these quarrels cease, I may be able to get back my zest.'

Instead of Macmillan's longed-for respite, events gave Salisbury valuable ammunition with which to return to the attack.[92] Even small events seemed to be blown up out of all proportion. In 1959 the Queen had been due to make a state visit to Ghana, the first African colony that Lyttelton had, reluctantly, pushed towards independence. Salisbury had been revolted by the thought of the Ghanaian leader Kwame Nkrumah putting his 'impertinent' words in the Queen's mouth. He had written to Macmillan to beg him to stop the trip, 'whatever excuse has to be made'.[93] In the event the visit was postponed because of the Queen's pregnancy. Elizabeth herself, however, as an enthusiastic proponent of a multi-racial Commonwealth, wanted to go to Ghana. She insisted that the plan be resurrected once she recovered from her confinement. Two years later she was raring to set off for West Africa.

Macmillan struggled to match his sovereign's enthusiasm. In private he agreed with much of Salisbury's analysis. The whole trip was 'ludicrous'. What was the point of playing up to a dictator for the sake of the Commonwealth if that dictator was more than likely to ditch membership of the Commonwealth as soon as he had enjoyed the publicity of a royal visit? It invited little more than a slap in the face to the Queen.[94] 'I am terribly worried about all this,' he complained. 'There is so much to lose and so little (except rather impalpable) to be gained.'[95] 'The Queen in Danger', whether of embarrassment or injury, was the perfect banner to march under for all those Conservatives who loathed Macmillan's policy in Africa but were too cowed by the party machine to complain of it. The whips could hardly castigate an MP who, for all his faults, loved his Queen.

There followed a few days of comic opera, with delegations of patriotic Conservatives leaping to the defence of their monarch. The 'instigators of this revolt in the Conservative ranks', Macmillan noted, 'were very good men'. She was so beloved, so delicate, the flower of English womanhood, they declared, how could the government think of placing her safety in the hands of the vile Nkrumah? The chief whip estimated that there were about 100 potential Francis Drakes on the Conservative benches. If the Labour party put down a motion deploring Macmillan's lack of concern for the Queen's safety, they could, in fact, whip up enough votes to defeat the government.

Macmillan shuttled to and from the Palace to lay the constitutional difficulties before his Sovereign. 'All this we discussed,' he recalled, 'at considerable length, during these anxious days, with a sort of mock seriousness. It all seemed too absurd to be true.' Of course it was a storm in a teacup. The Queen insisted that she was going. The Labour party did not organize any vote. Concerned Conservatives, on being told of their Sovereign's pleasure, yielded to her will.[96] Yet the whole saga suggested that Salisbury's claim that the party was restive at the thought of white womanhood being placed at the mercy of the uncivilized native – even if he had been educated at the London School of Economics – was rather closer to the mark than was comfortable.

Macmillan's real problem was in fact the Congo.[97] The huge former Belgian colony was breaking up in a bloody civil war. The Congo's spectacular descent into bestiality, assisted by the 'amateur, irresponsible, incompetent and totally disorganized' intervention of the UN would, if anything could, rouse the sleeping tiger of Toryism against its own leaders.[98] The Congo frightened Macmillan because it was so volatile. 'It is,' he said, 'more like the Crazy Gang than anything I can remember.'[99]

The Congo crisis threw up numberless factions but three notable leaders. Patrice Lumumba was a politician possessed of endless charisma, but he was a prima donna, in the pay of the Russians, and often high on drugs. One UN official described him as an 'utterly maniacal child'.[100] Joseph Mobutu was a quiet and unassuming but murderous army colonel. Macmillan was delighted when Mobutu's supporters captured Lumumba, though he feared lest the Baluba tribesmen should 'eat him'. This, he thought, would 'bring discredit on the Congo government'.[101] It was, however, the third member of this triumvirate Macmillan feared most. Moishe Tshombe had declared his Katanga province in south-east Congo an independent state. Katanga bordered Northern Rhodesia. Geologically they were the same country, sitting on top of the fabulously wealthy mineral deposits of the Copperbelt. For businessmen Katanga was the only part of the Congo that mattered – the rest of the country could descend into blood-soaked oblivion as long as the mines kept working. Mobutu handed Lumumba over to Tshombe, who murdered him.

Tshombe was a hero to the Europeans.[102] Tshombe was the black African leader opponents of African nationalism like Salisbury and Welensky could hail as an example of the way forward. 'It was true,' Roy Welensky admitted to Macmillan, 'that the Federation had allowed Mr Tschombe to send £800,000 in gold three-franc pieces through their territory to Switzerland which may have predisposed Mr Tschombe to them.' Yet, Sir Roy maintained, 'Mr Tschombe was a remarkable man . . . and unlike most other Africans in that he did not try to get something for nothing.'[103] Salisbury and Welensky regarded it as a disaster when the Congolese government tried to repeat Mobutu's success with Lumumba by kidnapping Tshombe. 'It only shows,' commented Salisbury, 'how close these eminent persons still are to the primitive man.'[104]

If Macmillan were to be seen conniving in Tshombe's destruction it could be enough to tip the balance against him in the party. Yet he had so to connive, because President Kennedy had decided that the Congo must be preserved from communism and this could only be done if it remained united. The Americans decreed that the UN should be unleashed in the Congo to create an anti-communist bulwark. Macmillan had always been sceptical about the threat of communism in Central Africa.[105] He was convinced, on the other hand, that he had to accommodate himself to Kennedy's view.[106]

Toeing the American line, however reluctantly, and condoning, let alone financing, however reluctantly, the behaviour of the UN, was sure to inflame the Tory party even further.[107] On 13 September 1961 the head of the UN Mission in Katanga, Conor Cruise O'Brien, launched a military *coup* to seize its capital, Elizabethville, from the secessionists. Even liberal members of the Cabinet were sickened by the UN's behaviour; 'a terrible blunder, worse still, such a terrible crime, and such an abuse of his power', was how Lord Hailsham put it.[108] Macmillan himself described the purpose of the UN's operation in Katanga as 'driving the remaining Europeans out and . . . disrupting the one area which so far had had an orderly administration'.[109] Not that he had any intention of doing a thing about it. His actions were directed at the 'main problem' of how to 'present this action publicly'.[110] The most he would do was insist that O'Brien's boss, Dag Hammarskjöld, the UN secretary-general, should meet a British minister, George Lansdowne, on the border between Katanga and Northern Rhodesia. This insistence was to have fatal consequences for Hammarskjöld when his aeroplane crashed in the bush.

As Hailsham had warned Macmillan, O'Brien was acting as a recruiting sergeant for the Watching Committee.[111] Salisbury himself believed that 'there is an increasing body of opinion which is being shaken by what has happened in the Congo'. Such people were 'open to conversion' to the federation's cause. If the Congo continued to boil, it was worth carrying on the uneven struggle with Macmillan.[112] Salisbury redoubled his efforts to recruit senior Conservatives to the Watching Committee. He wanted to balance off the 'more extreme people like Tony Lambton' with respected figures who would appeal to the 'anxious Conservatives'. His main target was Alan Lennox-Boyd.[113] Lennox-Boyd was desperate to avoid making any public statement on Africa. Active political campaigning would interfere with his hold on the company he headed, Guinness. Active political campaigning about Africa could provoke Macmillan to a counter-campaign showing just how dirty Lennox-Boyd's hands were. He was constantly reminded 'of the trouble we had over the Devlin Report and of how we all rallied to his support in relation to that'.[114]

Nevertheless even Lennox-Boyd felt he had to give Salisbury some support in private and join the Watching Committee.[115] Salisbury also rounded up Buck de la Warr, Macmillan's neighbour in Sussex, and Henry Hopkinson, Lyttelton's former deputy at the Colonial Office.[116] 'Katanga has stirred people up,' Salisbury reported as he watched the wind fill the sails of his campaign: 'Even the most loyal of Government supporters are horrified. It is, I think, one of the wickedest, most irresponsible things that have been done in my lifetime – and I've seen some pretty bad ones.'[117]

As Macmillan himself acknowledged, ill-disciplined UN troops seemed to provide an awful warning against destroying 'civilized' rule in Africa.[117] Welensky avidly supplied Salisbury with atrocity stories to tell his friends.[119] Ethiopian troops were by far the worst perpetrators. When Henry Hopkinson went on a fact-finding visit to Katanga on behalf of the Watching Committee in February 1962,

he found 'at least three deaths of British women who were murdered
or blown up in the fighting and there were, of course, dozens of other
cases of French, Belgian, Swiss and other foreigners as well as Katangese, who were murdered or massacred'. The International Red Cross
had demanded that the UN investigate the deaths of ythree ambulance workers who were kidnapped, murdered and buried in shallow
graves by the Ethiopians. Indian and Swedish troops had murdered
civilians and the Irish had turned to looting. Only the Malays had
acted properly. 'The atrocities and ruthlessness,' concluded Hopkinson, 'in the conduct of operations was far worse than anything I
saw perpetrated by the Germans in the Italian campaign.'[120]

The Watching Committee was *parti pris*, but these stories had
the required effect because they were being confirmed by independent
journalists.[121] Macmillan found dry amusement in reading through
the reports he was receiving from his own diplomats and SIS as
well as the press. 'The chances,' he noted on these reports, 'of being
a survivor if you are wounded in this war are said to be slender.
You are likely to be killed and eaten either by the backward races of
the Congo or the advance guard of civilization represented by the
UN army. Yesterday an Ethiopian soldier shot a Swiss banker in
Elizabethville with a bazooka. No one knows why, and no one
cares.'[122]

A week after the UN attack on Katanga, Salisbury was able to
send Macmillan a 'very tiresome' message boasting of the new wave
of support enjoyed by the Watching Committee.[123] Here he had
Macmillan on a sticky wicket. Salisbury had made big claims for his
support in the party over Rhodesia, yet he had been unable to translate sentiment into political action. His friends in the House of Lords,
however well respected, did not appear to ambitious MPs as the
wave of the future. His friends in the House of Commons appeared
to their fellow MPs as little more than a lunatic, and probably
corrupt, fringe. Now, on the Congo, not only was the bulk of the
party closer to Salisbury's than to Macmillan's opinion, but so was
the bulk of the Cabinet.[124]

Macmillan affected insouciance. He had seen off Salisbury over
Rhodesia. The Congo was no different. MPs might froth over their

club claret, but they were not going to risk their seats and emoluments over a very large country a long way away of which they knew little. 'I am sure,' he reassured his chief lieutenant, Ted Heath, 'we can hold the Party here in spite of the extremists if we present a calm, clear and consistent policy.' Behind the scenes he was actually taking desperate measures. The way out of the impasse was to get some kind of peace deal between the Katanganese and the Congolese. If the UN were removed from the situation, the British government would no longer have to make high-profile decisions – watched closely by America and Third World nations as well as by Conservatives at home. As long as the blacks only slaughtered each other and left the Europeans alone, the Congo would soon fade from the political radar.[125] Macmillan used intermediaries to tell Tshombe that, if he did not strike a deal with the Congolese government, then the UN would murder him and there was nothing Britain could or would do to prevent it.

Just as Macmillan was seeing a way out of the Congo imbroglio, the UN once again created difficulties for him. During its attack on Katanga in September 1961, the UN had been severely embarrassed by its inability to deal with the lone fighter aircraft of the Katangan air force. As the UN planned to crush Katanga once and for all, its officials assembled their own air force to deal with the problem: four fighters from Ethiopia, five fighters from Sweden and six British-made Canberra bombers from India. The UN then demanded that Britain should supply the Canberras with the bombs to attack the Katangese.

By early December, as UN troops restarted the war in Elizabethville, UN officials threatened to accuse the British in public of colluding with Katanga to thwart the will of the international community if they did not supply the bombs. Getting wind of the possibility that Britain would give in to UN demands, Salisbury warned Lord Home that the Watching Committee would have no compunction in stirring up the fiercest possible criticism. This presaged the most 'acute and dangerous' internal crisis in the Conservative party over Africa. A late-night meeting on Thursday, 7 December, showed that the Cabinet itself was dangerously divided on this issue. Home and

Hailsham argued that the government should tell the UN bluntly that if they wanted to slaughter the Katangese they could do so without Britain's help. Much as Macmillan agreed with their anti-UN sentiments, he was not willing to order a U-turn. They hammered out a compromise: the UN could have the bombs if they used them only in 'self-defence'.

A UN official in Stockholm then let the cat out of the bag. The UN team did not want the bombs for 'self-defence' but for 'smashing the military strength of the present leadership' of Katanga. By Monday, 11 December, reports were arriving from the Congo that UN officials were saying that, whatever form of words the British government might like to use, they were going to use the bombs as part of an operation '"imposing a political settlement" by conquering Katanga by force, even if this meant the collapse of any administration in Katanga'. The Palace of Westminster was thereupon in 'full cry'. Hurriedly Macmillan gathered together all the ministers he could find on a Monday morning for an impromptu Cabinet. Edward Heath was dispatched to make a 'dry' statement in the Commons that, 'in view of all the uncertainty, we would hold up the delivery of the bombs'. Heath had a hard time of it, with remorseless questioning both from the Conservatives and Labour. Macmillan reconvened his ministers. No one was keen on supplying bombs to the UN, but they all realized that it would be a huge victory for Salisbury if they did not. If Macmillan accepted in public that 'barbarism' was the inevitable concomitant of destroying European influence in the Congo, then it would become very hard for him to argue that 'civilization' could result from black majority rule in Central Africa.

The mood in the party on Monday night was 'very tense'. The real trouble, Macmillan wrote, was 'that in addition to the small group of people who hate me ... the anxiety about the UN's performance in the Congo had spread to the whole *centre* of the Party'. The Congo itself was not the real issue. Salisbury had always claimed that he, not Macmillan, represented the true views of the party. The Congo provided displacement for those MPs who hated the appeasement of blacks in Rhodesia but kept silent out of party loyalty. Now they could wallow in self-righteous indignation.[126]

Then, as quickly as it had arisen, the crisis fizzled out. The leader of the Congolese government, Adoula, and Tshombe agreed to meet. Macmillan never for one moment thought that 'the two negro gentlemen' would agree on anything.[127] That was not the point. The appearance of some kind of constructive diplomacy got the Americans, the UN and the Conservative party off his back. Parliament broke up for the Christmas recess. As Macmillan understood full well, once the House rose for Christmas it would be impossible to re-create the pressure-cooker atmosphere of November and December. Members could contemplate the dire consequences of a rebellion – the collapse of the government and an early general election – over their Christmas turkey. With relief, Macmillan flew off to meet President Kennedy in Bermuda.

As in the spring of 1961 over Rhodesia, however, Macmillan was taxed to his limits. He had felt the strain 'far more than I should have done, have worried and slept badly and so on'.[128] 'Parliament,' he moaned, 'meets for too long in the year. Ministers have no holidays. Although I have been away for a day or two to shoot or play golf I have not been away from the telegrams, the office, the boxes, for five years.'[129]

As it happened, Macmillan was not the only one who spent Christmas 1961 in a state of some exhaustion and depression. Salisbury too was beginning to have doubts about his course. Both he and Macmillan were, after all, now in their late sixties. It had been a tall order for a private individual, however eminent, to wage a personal vendetta against the prime minister of England with all the powers of the state and the party at his disposal. Macmillan accused Salisbury of pulling the strings of the diehards: MPs who opposed him were, he thought, Salisbury's 'agents' bought by Welensky's gold.[130] They were, Macmillan said, Salisbury's pawns without Salisbury's charm. Yet Salisbury himself deprecated the time he had to spend with 'extremists' who, although politically useful, were hardly congenial.[131] After his attack on Macleod, even friendly government ministers treated him with grave suspicion.[132] As his friend Dick Law warned him, he was in danger of becoming a 'one-man band'.[133] The Congo crisis had been his last best chance. After Christmas 1961

Salisbury did not have a realistic chance of bringing Macmillan down. The Central African Federation was already doomed.[134] Regretfully, Salisbury stood down his troops. No one would understand if the Watching Committee's MPs voted against the government.[135]

Salisbury's capitulation over the fate of the Central African Federation was a sweet moment for Macmillan.[136] When Macmillan ran into Salisbury at the unveiling of a statue of Arthur Balfour he could afford to be civil.[137] He was talking to a man whom he knew he had beaten. For his part Salisbury reluctantly came to the same conclusion. Macmillan was even worse than Neville Chamberlain; he was Lloyd George reincarnated, 'the man leading the Conservative Party but not really of it'. 'But,' he admitted to Anthony Eden, 'I don't see what is to be done about it, unless someone in the Government itself is willing to come out and say what so many leading Conservatives in the country are thinking.'[138]

If the Watching Committee was to continue, it had to be as a relatively constructive lobby group trying to persuade sympathetic ministers such as Home and Butler to grant independence to Southern Rhodesia. The goals of preserving the Federation and over-throwing Harold Macmillan had run in parallel for Salisbury and his radical followers. This was not true of the Southern Rhodesian agitation.[139] Salisbury and Macmillan even agreed to meet. 'I enjoyed our talk immensely,' Bobbety assured Harold, 'it was quite like old times.'[140] The sentiment fooled neither of them, but this new-found civility in personal relations reflected the new political reality. 'One feels,' Salisbury admitted – not, of course, to Macmillan – 'completely isolated, and I often feel inclined, now that I am nearly 70, to throw up politics altogether.'[141]

With defeat imminent in Africa, Salisbury allowed himself some desultory sniping against Macmillan over entry to the EEC but could not work up much enthusiasm.[142] Out of personal friendship, he reluctantly accepted Roy Welensky's invitation to visit the federation. This involved some sacrifice of principle. His doctors told him to go by sea. He had to break his vow never to sail through the Suez Canal again.[143] But there was no point in politicizing the visit.[144] 'I am afraid,' he admitted, 'that the Federation really is dead.'[145] Although

Harold made him 'slightly sick' he no longer led a cabal against Macmillan.[146]

For over a debilitating year, however, Macmillan had been obsessed with his dirty little war with Salisbury. He had always tried to think of Salisbury as the unacceptable face of 'old' politics, which he, as the representative of the 'new' politics, would sweep away. Salisbury was living proof that Macmillan had surpassed his generation in worldly success and understanding of the world. If only he could free himself of this incubus, Macmillan thought, he could take wings. Unfortunately, from Macmillan's point of view, the rest of the world did not see things in quite the same way. Macmillan had always argued that Salisbury and his allies were dinosaurs. Most observers agreed. But he had spent so much time with them that he himself was beginning to appear as just another species of dinosaur. The electorate rather rudely intruded into the duels of clubland on 14 March 1962 by turning a Conservative majority of 14,760 in the suburban heartland seat of Orpington into a Liberal majority of 7,855. It was revealing of Macmillan's turn of mind that the main conclusion he drew from a long-drawn-out Orpington post-mortem was that 'this must, in the long run, mean an attack on the leadership of the Party ... the enemies of the Leadership, already numerous, have undoubtedly been strengthened. And Lord Salisbury is working hard, with growing power.'[147] Faced with a Cecil and a suburban revolt Macmillan rather fancied himself as Elizabeth I. 'It was by,' it struck him, 'the vacillations, hesitations, and "middle of the road" course that she kept going. Had she yielded to Cecil ... she would (of course) have rallied the Protestants ... but she might have lost control of England.'[148] Accordingly, Macmillan did not hesitate from indulging in a little Renaissance tragedy of his own. In 1957 he had rid himself of all his contemporaries. In July 1962 he rid himself of many of the next generation. Seven Cabinet ministers, headed by Selwyn Lloyd and David Kilmuir, lost their jobs in his 'night of the long knives'. This bloodletting finally seemed to lay the ghost of Salisbury.[149]

When the married minister John Profumo got himself into a 'silly scrape' consorting with whores, Macmillan found a 'certain spice of humour to this degrading story'. After all, it was 'women this time, thank God, not boys', as it had been in the case of Ian Harvey.[150] Salisbury hoped that the Profumo scandal would bring Macmillan down, but he too found this bitter consolation.[151] It would have been one thing to have felled Macmillan for 'the liquidation of the Commonwealth', but to throw the 'Monarch of the Glen', as Salisbury referred to Macmillan, out 'because of the activities of a couple of sluts' could merely demonstrate that they lived in a world turned upside down.[152] Whatever the scandals, Salisbury could no longer believe anything short of an election defeat would remove Macmillan from the premiership.[153] All he could do was criticize him in the Tory press in the hope of making his life a little more difficult.[154] By lowering the standards of public and political morality by his behaviour, Salisbury suggested, Macmillan had created the conditions in which cads and liars like Profumo flourished. The Profumo scandal was the illegitimate stepchild of the Monckton Report, he argued. Even Salisbury's sister, Moucher, thought this was below the belt. 'Is there a danger,' she warned her brother, 'that your audience may think that you are hitting him when he has been let down over Profumo?'[155] If anything, Salisbury's hostility strengthened Macmillan's resolve to stay on as prime minister. He would not give Salisbury the satisfaction of having played any part in the end of his career. 'I would be seen to have yielded to the group of malcontents, who are swayed either by personal resentment or purely reactionary sentiment.'[156]

If defiance of Salisbury played some part in Macmillan's decision not to resign in the summer of 1963, the memory of another old friend influenced his decision to do so in October 1963. Much has been written about the incompetent medical advice Macmillan received when, having rallied his Cabinet, he was taken ill. An enlarged prostate became, in his mind, prostate cancer. Having seen Harry Crookshank killed by cancer, it had become a recurrent fear for Macmillan that he too would be struck down. What his doctors told him personal experience made him all too ready to believe.[157]

Some atavistic churning of his mind convinced him that he must also stop Lord Hailsham, whom he had previously favoured, from succeeding him. Hailsham reminded Macmillan of his younger self.[158] But Macmillan was no longer sure he wanted the 'old me'. He wanted the even 'older me', the kind of man he had aspired to be before he entered politics. On the morning of 15 October 1963, he dictated his 'political testament' from his hospital bed. Each candidate for the succession was damned with faint praise until he came to Alec Home. Of Lord Home he could not speak too highly. He was 'clearly a man who represents the old governing class at its best and those who take a reasonably impartial view of English history know how good that can be'. The succession really had to be seen as a struggle between generations. Home had 'exactly that quality that the class to which he belongs have at their best . . . they think about the question under discussion and not about themselves. It is thinking about themselves that is really the curse of the younger generation – they appear to have no other subject which interests them at all and all their books, poems, dramas, and all the rest of it are almost entirely confined to this curious introspective attitude towards life'. Home could stand above the unseemly solipsism of his juniors. Macmillan searched for the greatest compliment he could pay Home. 'Had he been of another generation,' he convinced himself, 'he would have been of the Grena-diers and the 1914 heroes.' It was ironic that Macmillan's encomium for Home and his requiem for his own generation rendered him rather more reactionary than the other Grenadiers. Salisbury sup-ported Hailsham, albeit with the caveat that he would be 'v. happy with Home'.[159] Lyttelton favoured Butler.[160] Macmillan's last political act was to anoint a successor who had much more in common with his contemporaries than with himself.[161]

11

Relics

Macmillan and Salisbury slipped into retirement. Macmillan's greatest challenge, so he claimed, was crossing Haymarket unaided by a phalanx of private secretaries, drivers and bodyguards. When Macmillan departed from the political scene, Lord Salisbury started 'to make his peace with the Government'.[1] With no Macmillan to bait he could think of little constructive to do.[2] When the Tories lost the October 1964 general election, the Watching Committee lost much of its *raison d'être*.[3] If a coalition of Tory grandees and right-wing Tory MPs had had but limited influence with a Conservative government, they were hardly likely to be embraced by the socialists.

Enraged by what he saw as Edward Heath's collusion with the Wilson government, Salisbury made his most public and populist intervention in politics. To considerable applause from the assembled ranks of Conservative activists at the 1965 Party Conference at Brighton, and to the considerable embarrassment of the Conservative leadership, he moved a motion against imposing sanctions on 'our friends and kinfolk' in Rhodesia. 'We have, I think,' he congratulated himself, 'stopped any bipartisan policy.' Yet, as he himself realized, it was a quixotic gesture.[4] The 'friends and kinfolk' did little to live up to Salisbury's billing. Days later Harold Wilson was greeted in Rhodesia by the Duke of Montrose performing a lewd dance with a coin clenched between his buttocks.[5] A few weeks later the 'kinfolk' launched an armed rebellion against Britain. In such circumstances Salisbury's continuing campaign on behalf of the whites of Southern Rhodesia seemed little more than an exercise in pure reaction leavened only a very little, as Lyttelton observed, by the '*douceur* of the Cecils'.[6]

Lyttelton himself seemed a man more at ease with his times. He was part of that 'magic circle' of Etonians which, a thwarted product of a minor Scottish public school bitterly claimed as late as 1964, ran the country.[7] Somerset Maugham declared that Lyttelton was the only man whose biography he would wish to write.[8] At a time of life when most men reach retirement age, Lyttelton still cut a fine figure. His head was bald, his shoulders were hunched, his frame was fleshy, but still he dominated any room he entered. There was a sense of bigness about him. A portrait in the style and society magazine *Harper's* showed him as a successful dynast. He was posed in front of his country pile in Wiltshire, Trafalgar House, once the home of the Nelson family. But the Lytteltons were not portrayed as mere National Trust heirlooms. Next to Lyttelton on the page was a brooding picture of his black-clad youngest son, Adrian, who had just won a prize fellowship to All Souls. Adrian, it was announced, had more progressive political views than his father. The family enterprise exuded success. Lyttelton was passing the baton on to sons whom he had prepared well for the new age.[9]

Lyttelton himself might face any formal occasion impeccably clad in morning dress, but he deliberately put himself in the most modern settings. He moved the annual conference of the Institute of Directors from that ultimate monument of Victoriana, the Royal Albert Hall, to the cool modernism of the Festival Hall. A fashionable young photographer, Tony Armstrong-Jones, was commissioned to memorialize Lyttelton and his directors in their symbolic new environment. Armstrong-Jones produced a portfolio heightening the angular contrasts between the dark-suited directors, the gleaming new concrete and glass of their surroundings and the equally gleaming and new plastic of their specially commissioned Tupperware lunch boxes. At the heart of this great modern extravaganza stood Lyttelton, resplendent in tails, surveying his work with satisfaction. Snowdon's pictures told a story. Lyttelton was confident that he could straddle the age of his father and the age of his sons. He was a pivotal figure, neither tarnished nor afraid.

In fact, things were less comfortable. Until 1959 everything Oliver Lyttelton touched had seemed to turn to gold. His tenure as colonial secretary was regarded as an outstanding success. As the years passed, it took on an added lustre. Many harked back to Lyttelton's 'golden age'. Once Lyttelton shifted from the Colonial Office to the Chairman's office at AEI, it too seemed to enjoy a golden age. Lyttelton, with his big personality, seemed to be moulding AEI in his image. He was, in the words of an executive director, Sir Joseph Latham, 'a genial tyrant definitely in charge'. In 1958 the company moved into opulent new purpose-built headquarters in Grosvenor Square. Lyttelton had been a 'face' in the City since 1920. His time in government made him the ultimate 'blue chip' chairman. He was able to raise huge sums to finance the company's ambitious expansion programme: £59 million between 1955 and 1958.[10]

In the 1930s Lyttelton had been one of the best cartel managers in the business. The same skills that made him so good at raising money made him a master at the deals and ego massaging necessary to keep perpetually suspicious businessmen cooperating to their mutual benefit. This way of doing business proved to be, however, Lyttelton's weakness. A wind of change was beginning to blow through British business. Just as Harold Macmillan was settling into Downing Street in February 1957, the Monopolies Commission denounced the 'ring' run by the big three electrical companies, AEI, GEC and English Electric, that suppressed competition and kept the price of electrical goods at deliberately inflated levels.

Regrettably AEI was in remarkably poor shape to meet this new challenge. As money poured into its coffers, it had got bigger but not more efficient. The two core businesses, BTH in Rugby and Metrovick in Manchester, loathed each other. Lyttelton knew this as well as anyone. Much of his energy was directed at creating an integrated company. Unfortunately he was in a poor position to achieve this. All the lines of command passed directly through him. He liked it this way. As a consequence he never appointed a managing director, much less a management team, to see through change. Every problem eventually arrived on his desk. He could dominate his colleagues when they were in the same room, but as soon as they returned to their own fiefdoms, plans unravelled and good intentions ran into the sand. 'I am in some despair,' he admonished the managing director of BTH, 'every move or change is blocked . . . you are not apparently ready to admit . . . that the best men should have the top jobs unless it can be done without any disturbance or inconvenience to anyone.'[11]

Lyttelton's problems were exacerbated by two other factors. He was perceived to have made a number of errors of judgement.[12] In 1957 he had overseen the building of the world's first privately owned nuclear reactor at Aldermaston.[13] It was hardly an auspicious year for nuclear power: a major nuclear accident at Windscale shook Macmillan's government in October of that year. In 1962 the reactor was closed down because no one wished to pay to use it for research. The Aldermaston research station itself, Lyttelton's pride and joy, only lasted until January 1963. In July 1963 he was forced to sack Robert Craig Wood, the marketing 'whizz-kid' he had personally installed as head of Hotpoint. It was one of Lyttelton's constant laments that the directors were too old. Yet Lyttelton's faith in youth backfired badly. Craig Wood did indeed prove a 'whizz-kid' at selling washing machines; he proved less of a 'whizz-kid' at making a profit while doing so. He also became a 'whizz-kid' at tampering with company accounts to conceal the fact he was selling units at below cost price.

The problems caused by the breakdown of the electrical goods cartel, exacerbated by the civil wars in AEI, resulted in a very public embarrassment for Lyttelton. In 1955, the first full year of Lyttelton's second term as chairman, AEI had a net capitalization of £58 million and had made profits of £15.3 million. In 1963, his last year as chairman, the company's net capitalization was £150 million and profits were £6.6 million. He had borrowed millions to slash profits. As the company secretary pointed out, 'we, AEI – the greatest of the electrical engineering companies – are regarded by the market as being as about as good an investment risk as a rubber plantation in the Far East'.[14] Shareholders felt the same. The air of hostility at the 1962 AGM towards Lyttelton was palpable. The only man in the room who rose in his defence owed him a very personal debt. The speech in Lyttelton's support by Richard Merton, the man he had saved from the Holocaust, was a touching testament to a friendship rather than a business relationship.[15] It was the end of the road. Lyttelton persuaded his colleagues to extend his term of office for a few months, but they insisted on his retirement soon after he passed his seventieth birthday.[16]

In the years before the collapse of his business reputation Lyttelton had, however, been able to deploy his amassed political capital to good effect in another area. In the 1960s he was on a quest which verged on obsession. He was determined to build a National Theatre. Lyttelton was not a man without culture. Indeed, his views on culture were as robust as all his other opinions. It was he who coined the *obiter dictum* that no man should do anything that bored him after the age of thirty-five: he had given up gambling and Wagner. Despite his preference for Mozart as an operatic composer, Lyttelton was no reactionary foe of twentieth-century artistic endeavour. He regarded Henry Moore as 'a friend and possibly the only saint, except Benjie Britten, that I still know.'[17] Henry James had been a neighbour in Rye and the characters in his novels became 'old friends'. His favourite author, in the same vein, was Proust, for whom he acquired a taste in the 1920s; Macmillan only tackled Proust in the 1950s, was bored by him, and never managed to finish *À la recherche du temps perdu*. Nevertheless it was not so much the smell of greasepaint that made Lyttelton pursue the dream of a National Theatre with such single-minded, indeed bloody-minded, determination, as an overriding desire to create a monument worthy of his parents.

The idea of a National Theatre had started as a typically turn-of-the-century campaign for national self-improvement and self-glorification. Two of the good and the great roped in to support the campaign were Alfred Lyttelton and his wife Didi. Unlike her son, Didi Lyttelton was in love with the theatre. Numbered among her closest friends was the actress Mrs Patrick Campbell, whose 'glorious beauty, black glossy hair, and a voice in the contralto range which stirred your blood' had made a great impact on the pubescent Oliver.[18]

Didi Lyttelton herself was a playwright and novelist of modest but not contemptible talent. The campaign for the National Theatre remained close to her heart. Didi Lyttelton passed on to her son something more corporeal than a dream: money. By 1937 the Shakespeare Memorial National Theatre Committee had raised a total of £150,000 and had bought land in Kensington opposite the Victoria & Albert Museum. After the war the Shakespeare Memorial National Theatre Committee, in effect the Lytteltons working out of Great College Street, formed a new joint council with the Old Vic Theatre to make a fresh start.

The idea of a National Theatre had some appeal to a governing party so much in favour of nationalization. Even as Lyttelton bitterly fought nationalization in the House of Commons, so he also lobbied for the nationalization of the theatre. The result was the 1949 National Theatre Act and a deal with London County Council to swap the Kensington site for one on the South Bank, soon to host the Festival of Britain. On 13 July 1951 Lyttelton conducted Her Majesty Queen Elizabeth, accompanied by her daughter Princess Elizabeth, to lay the foundation stone that read: 'To the living memory of William Shakespeare on a site provided by the London County Council in conformity with the National Theatre Act 1949 in the year of the Festival of Britain.' Yet, for all the pomp, Her Majesty might as well have been patting down a tombstone as a foundation stone. The Act gave the Treasury the power to contribute £1 million to the National Theatre. It was a power it had no intention of using. Even those who thought that a National Theatre was a good idea afforded it little priority. It was a concert hall rather than a theatre that rose on the South Bank as the centrepiece of the festival. The theatre was a sideshow, dwarfed by County Hall even on architects' models. Stone laid, queen and princess departed, the theatre drifted into a limbo of projects pending.

It was an inverted testimony to the importance of Lyttelton's personality that, in the years he was running the British Empire or leading AEI's dash for growth, the National Theatre project did not move forward. Only when he took up the reins again did things start to happen. In the spring of 1960 Lyttelton started to knock heads together. Civil servants had fondly believed that the joint council was moribund. The Old Vic was attempting 'to establish its claim to become the National Theatre', thus poaching one half of the National's *raison d'être*. The Stratford Memorial Theatre was doing its best to portray itself as the natural national custodian of Shakespeare's legacy, thus poaching the other half. The Old Vic and Stratford were clamouring for subsidies. They would, it seemed, trample the National dream and the Shakespeare Memorial National Theatre Committee into the dust in the rush towards a government handout. It thus came as a shock to Whitehall when it became clear that Lyttelton had 'succeeded in establishing agreement in principle that the three interests will cooperate in promoting a National Theatre'. Lyttelton had promised that, if the theatres reaffirmed their belief in the National, he would use his entrée into the highest levels of government to fight for higher levels of subsidy.[19]

His commitment to the National Theatre dream even affected his relationship with Salisbury and Macmillan, for Lyttelton could not afford to fall out with the prime minister. One of the main things that made Salisbury feel so 'isolated' was his failure to attract the wholehearted support of Oliver Lyttelton. When Macmillan and Salisbury fell out over Africa, Lyttelton was determined to remain friends with them both.[20] There was little doubt about Lyttelton's private sympathies. It hardly took an acute political journalist to realize this. 'British East and Central Africa,' recorded *Harper's* society columnist, 'owe Lord Salisbury and Lord Chandos similar debts of gratitude for their firm and faithful interest in the territories. There can be little risk in suggesting that Lord Chandos shares the feelings of his old friend Lord Salisbury about recent happenings between the Nile and the Limpopo.'[21]

There was indeed little risk of so suggesting. Lyttelton's view of the Monckton Commission was the same as Salisbury's: 'I never thought I would live to see a dozen or more educated men led by a successful ex-Minister put on paper that the best way of keeping a Federation together was by allowing the constituent states the right to secede.' His view on the Congo was the same as Salisbury's: 'One would have thought that the Congo offered a pretty clear warning of the dangers of handing over to African majorities the power to govern.'[22] His view of Iain Macleod was the same as Salisbury's: ' "Truth sometimes arises out of error but never from confusion." I am not sure that Mr Macleod should not have this written above his desk during the Central African talks ... The one thing to be avoided – which is not being avoided – is to alienate both sides.' His underlying sentiments were the same as Salisbury's: 'It may even be in the long run that we have to support our kith and kin ... I am reactionary enough to believe that if you have to alienate anybody, it is better to alienate the aliens, especially when they cannot be seen on a dark night.'[23] Yet, to Salisbury's abiding frustration, Lyttelton refused even to go as far as Alan Lennox-Boyd in opposing Macmillan's African policy. He did not speak in the House of Lords; he most certainly did not join the Watching Committee. Salisbury knew that he was fighting a losing battle without Lyttelton.

When Lyttelton did finally break his silence on Central Africa it was months, if not years, too late. He spoke out in December 1962 because he felt that Macmillan had gone so far in bending the facts about the origins of the Central African Federation that he was in danger of impugning Lyttelton's personal honour. He told the House of Lords that Welensky had a very good case for claiming that, in 1953, he and Salisbury had indeed pledged that no part of the federation would be allowed to secede. They had intended the federation to be a permanent union.[24] Yet having made that dramatic statement, he allowed himself to be persuaded by Macmillan's emissaries that these pledges were not as watertight as he had once thought.[25] There was no point, he told his friends, in making a fuss: 'All this raking through the past is very tiresome and takes time and does no good.'[26] 'Times change and we are changed with them,' Lyttelton maintained. Lyttelton was as aware as Salisbury of Macmillan's ability to be two-faced. He was amused rather than horrified by this trait. Macmillan was 'very amusing', Lyttelton later wrote, 'he should really have been a Cardinal Archbishop in the Middle Ages, where absolution from irregularity over the facts could always be obtained by a short visit to the Vatican'.[27] Both Lyttelton and Macmillan got what they wanted. Lyttelton's honour was satisfied, but his warm relations with Macmillan were undamaged. Lyttelton's intervention had diverted accusations of bad faith against Macmillan into a confused thicket of 'pure mumbo-jumbo'.[28]

Lyttelton used his bantering relationship with Macmillan to good effect. True to his word, he resurrected the National Theatre project in a personal meeting with the prime minister. Ministers, led by the chancellor of the exchequer, Selwyn Lloyd, and the minister of education, David Eccles, were horrified. Surely Macmillan knew that there was 'considerable feeling' that the 'Government should *not* do this'. Apart from the cost, they 'doubted whether the subsidization of a further theatrical venue in London would be in the best interests of national drama'. If the government was going to spend this money on the theatre, it would be much better off giving grants to provincial repertory theatres.[29] Lyttelton knew exactly how to play the system. He treated Macmillan's bland encouragement as if it was unambiguous support for his plans. Lyttelton announced to Selwyn Lloyd that he should stop shilly-shallying and act.[30] All of a sudden civil servants realized that 'we cannot hope to defer a decision much longer.'[31] Both senior officials and junior ministers came to dread Lyttelton's implacable footfall.[32]

The most eloquent opponent of the National Theatre in government was David Eccles. Eccles was a rich, intelligent, cultured man with an international reputation as an art collector. He was Macmillan's political ally, the two having worked together in the European Movement in the 1940s. Ten years younger than Macmillan and Lyttelton, he, like his contemporary Butler, could never quite escape the charge that he was too fly to be a true Conservative. In Eccles's case he was not helped by a *petit maître* dress sense. His nickname was 'Smarty-Boots'. Eccles dismissed 'the concept of the National Theatre' as 'a pre-war idea, springing from a time when culture was the monopoly of the upper middle class'. It had no relevance to modern conditions. 'The younger generation,' Eccles maintained, 'were developing in the Arts, and Drama, in particular, was flourishing. This was partly because television was doing for Drama what radio had done for Music.' Lyttelton and his cronies were the representatives of those people who were doing the most to destroy theatre. Theatre in big provincial cities was dying 'because it was run badly and without an eye on modern conditions'. For Eccles modern conditions meant 'where the public was provided with somewhere to eat, somewhere to park their cars'. His vision was for a national network of community centres where all the arts could gather. 'Good taste is not part of the curriculum,' as Churchill said when he first appointed Eccles education minister.[33] Eccles's logic, if not his sentiments, made an impact on Macmillan. Yes, he agreed, the National Theatre was an old-fashioned idea. Yes, he feared, his friend Lyttelton was tending to think of something rather too lavish.[34]

For the moment Eccles was in the ascendant. The government had intended to do nothing until Lyttelton had called on Macmillan and stirred them into action. In the belief that Lyttelton could count on the prime minister's support, the debate had hummed around Whitehall. As soon as Macmillan told Eccles that he had doubts about the whole endeavour, that activity ground to a halt. To the relief of many it seemed as if Lyttelton was about to be evicted from the inside track.[35] Whitehall did its best to ignore Oliver Lyttelton. Officials schemed to sideline him.[36] There would, they thought, be no purpose-built National Theatre. Instead, either the RSC or the Old Vic, or both, would be *designated* National Theatres.[37] The National Theatre, Lloyd warned Macmillan, 'would develop into a tremendous racket'. It seemed as if Lyttelton's efforts had been in vain. Many in government hoped that, ageing and tired, faced with the difficulties of his business career, he would lose heart and fade away.[38]

Nothing was further from Lyttelton's mind.[39] Instead he found a way of outflanking Lloyd. He persuaded the leader of the London County Council, Sir Isaac Hayward, to offer financial support to the theatre. If, Lyttelton pointed out to Hayward, the theatre was not built, Country Hall would be surrounded by urban squalor.[40] Lloyd had intended to shut the door firmly on the National Theatre; Lyttelton promptly kicked it ajar once more.[41] He had support from a number of sources: an all-party group of MPs, Sir Kenneth Clark, the recently retired head of the Arts Council, the Sadler's Wells Opera, which saw an opportunity to secure its own precarious future by coming in on the South Bank, and the *Sunday Times*. Just as importantly, Lyttleton's enemies did not push against him in unison: in Lloyd's scheme the Old Vic and the RSC were supposed to be the two 'limbs' of the National Theatre. Each made it publicly clear, however, that they wanted nothing to do with the other. The huge egos of Peter Hall at Stratford and Laurence Olivier at the Old Vic rebounded around the national press.

Lloyd's plan opened up the government to ridicule as its supposed beneficiaries engaged in unseemly verbal brawling. Within three months Lloyd was asking Lyttelton to stitch together a 'package deal', once more based on a merger of the Old Vic and the RSC.[42] It was thus with some satisfaction that Lyttelton gathered together all the competing parties and told them they could drop their pet schemes. Peter Hall could forget any idea of the RSC becoming *the* National Theatre. Larry Olivier should forget any idea of taking the government's money and merging the Old Vic with the Royal Court Theatre rather than the National Theatre. Although Lloyd had asked him to aim for peaceful 'fusion', this was not part of Lyttelton's agenda.[43] Lyttelton really did not care who staffed the building as long as there was a National Theatre. He was planning an organization in which any component parts would 'completely or virtually completely lose their identities'.[44] When Peter Hall rejected his ideas, he threw his support once more behind Laurence Olivier and the Old Vic.[45]

Lyttelton may have been playing both ends against the middle, but even the Treasury was beginning to concede that his original plans had been better than what they had ended up with.[46] By procrastinating, the government had built up such expectations that they could not get out of an expensive scheme.[47] It was these thoughts that landed on Macmillan's desk in the spring of 1962. It seemed as if his old friend was in the best position to solve his political problem with the 'chattering classes'. He was happy therefore to proceed with a National Theatre under Lyttelton's tutelage.[48]

Lyttelton had made himself a controversial, indeed disliked, figure. As he himself acknowledged, he could not head the South Bank Board that was to be created, at his suggestion, to build the National Theatre. The Treasury would not give him such power at any price.[49] He was quite satisfied to be appointed as chairman to the National Theatre Board. This gave him control of the aspects of the project about which he was concerned.[50] By bending with the wind over the South Bank Board, Lyttelton had secured the quid pro quo that he would have the National Theatre job. The prime minister supported him; the Cabinet supported him. He was the inevitable man. The plain fact was that 'it would be exceedingly difficult to supplant Lord Chandos at this stage by anyone – even though such a person were felt to be ideal for the job'.[51]

By agreeing to a duumvirate with the head of the Arts Council, John Cottesloe, who became the chairman of the South Bank Board, Lyttelton had seen off any possibility that he would be excluded from the National Theatre. He had originally envisaged himself as overall supremo, but it seemed a reasonable and necessary compromise to make. He had less success in his next manoeuvre. He convinced Cottlesloe that they should try to keep Larry Olivier off the National Theatre Board. Olivier, Lyttelton argued, was untrustworthy. He had whored after the gods of the avant-garde in his flirtation with the Royal Court. He complained about Lyttelton's treatment of the Old Vic. He had plotted to exclude Lyttelton himself from the National Theatre. Actors were, Lyttelton maintained, hardly the kind of people one would want for transacting serious business. In Olivier's stead, Lyttelton proposed the appointment of the Labour politician John Wilmot, who had been a junior minister at the Ministry of Supply during the war. He was Lyttelton's contemporary, he was a politician and he had spent the war doing some proper work rather than prancing around in front of the cameras in a pair of tights.[52] The kind of 'theatre chap' Lyttelton wanted was the epicene impresario, Binkie Beaumont, who would be 'extremely useful about bars, restaurants, scenery docks and other base details'.[53] Lyttelton's attempted *coup* was unsuccessful. He could hardly hope to replace Britain's greatest actor, indeed the man who for most people *was* the National Theatre. Just as Lyttelton was the inevitable man, then so, for quite other reasons, was Laurence Olivier. He could not be treated as if he were a stupid and wilful child.[54] When Olivier was named as director of the National Theatre in August 1961, he was also on its board. Most of the other National Theatre board members were personally chosen by Lyttelton.[55]

From March 1960 through to December 1962 Lyttelton had, as far as possible, played a lone hand. He 'had been determined to take all decisions himself' and had treated others 'as rubber stamps for endorsing his own views'.[56] In transforming the National Theatre from a lobby into a real organization, he had nevertheless had to accept some dilution of his control. Yet anyone who expected him to bed in as a member of a team was going to be rudely disappointed. Whitehall hoped that, with the South Bank and National Theatre boards coming into existence, a more regular chain of command could be established, running from the Treasury, through the Arts Council, to the South Bank Board and finally down to the National Theatre Board. Lyttelton was having none of it. He 'never willingly accepted that the South Bank has an independent role to play in the planning and building of the National Theatre, any more than he is willing to accept the Arts Council as having an effective concern with the policy of the National Theatre Board'.[57] As soon as it had been formally announced that a publicly funded National Theatre was to be built, with Lyttelton chairman of the board and Sir Laurence Olivier its director, Lyttelton was back in the Treasury threatening to resign. On no account would he 'be content with an arrangement under which the National Theatre would be required to have an annual argument with the Arts Council and the Treasury about their requirements for the following year'. He knew very well that the government was hardly going to allow a man known as the prime minister's friend to resign within days of a major public project being announced. He intended to have a guarantee of long-term funding to ensure that 'nobody would be able to claw back any of the money if they thought the National Theatre could manage with less or the needs of some other body was greater'.[58]

Lyttelton was thus the gatekeeper to any government funding.[59] The Treasury assessor on the board, who found himself in 'an excruciatingly difficult position', was there merely as a symbol of Lyttelton's 'special relationship with the Treasury'.[60] With his hands on all the money, Lyttelton could keep the 'theatrical types' in line. They would need to show due gratitude for what they were given.[61] The Treasury thought they could control Lyttelton. They were wrong. He had every intention of pushing up both the running and the capital budget of the National Theatre. He confidently expected that he could bully more out of the government whenever it was needed.[62] Civil servants found such sharp practice 'pretty shocking'.[63] The reality was that Lyttelton's use of the inside track had worked.

On 7 October 1963 the chief secretary to the Treasury, John Boyd-Carpenter, sat down to a luncheon to which Lyttelton had summoned him. Boyd-Carpenter was fully up to speed with the Treasury's plans for containing Lyttelton's spendthrift ways. He found, in the event, that this was little proof against Lyttelton's prandial bludgeoning. He was going to ask for more money, Lyttelton told him, and Boyd-Carpenter was going to hand it over. A somewhat dazed chief secretary staggered back into the Treasury to tell Sir Ronald Harris, the official in charge of the National Theatre project, to face facts: he 'emphasized to me', Harris informed his junior officials, that Lyttelton 'was a very powerful person and that, looking to the future, one had to be prepared to take account of the realities of the situation'.[64]

These 'realities' were overturned by the Labour victory in the October 1964 election. John Boyd-Carpenter was replaced as minister overseeing the National Theatre by the Labour icon Jennie Lee. Lee herself was in favour of building a National Theatre. Attitudes towards Lyttelton, however, changed overnight. Bureaucrats who had once trodden in fear of him now delighted in twisting his tail.[65] Quite suddenly he was no longer 'a very powerful person' but an old fogey to be twitted and contradicted at every turn. The Treasury leaked a report to the *Sunday Times* describing 'the National Theatre people' as untrustworthy and accusing Lyttelton of deliberately ramping up the theatre's costs on the 'cynical assumption that in the end the Exchequer would have to pay'.[66] With Labour's grip on power confirmed by the 1966 general election, the technocrats and the 'theatrical types' were in charge. They spared no opportunity to bait Lyttelton.[67]

At the same time as Lyttelton's foes in government were unleashed, he faced his most determined enemy within the theatre.

'It was generally thought,' Lyttelton had conceded when selecting a board for the National Theatre, 'that the Board ought to include a woman and a "rebel", but nobody was yet able to suggest any suitable names.' To his everlasting regret he tentatively suggested that the drama critic Kenneth Tynan might do as a 'rebel'.[68] Although Tynan did not make it on to the board, Lyttelton could hardly object when Olivier appointed him as the National's literary manager. It would be hard to imagine a more poisonous choice. Tynan knew Lyttelton was guilty: guilty of being old, guilty of being aristocratic, guilty of being a philistine. Lyttelton represented a whole generation that Tynan wanted to sweep away. Harold Macmillan had contributed 'wind of change' to the English language; Bobbety Salisbury had chipped in with 'too clever by half'; Tynan's enduring fame is that he was the first man to say 'fuck' on BBC television.

For Ken Tynan the fact that a man had fought on the Western Front was not merely irrelevant but just cause for mockery. As a student journalist he had condemned the ex-servicemen returning to Oxford after their war because they made the place so boring. By Tynan's own account, his life truly began on the day in 1945 when he went up to Oxford. He was thus of that fortunate generation too young to have been called up for, let alone to have served in, the Second World War. While 'the rest of the world wore their army greatcoats and uniforms with the insignia ripped off', Ken dazzled in a purple doeskin suit and gold satin shirts. He shirked peacetime National Service by presenting himself to the army medical board as a sexual fetishist. Lyttelton and Tynan had only one thing in common. They both believed in the National Theatre. In 1958 Tynan had staged an appropriately theatrical photo opportunity, standing next to the foundation stone laid by the Queen in 1951 and wearing undertaker's garb to protest at the lack of action. But even here their agreement was barely skin deep. Lyttelton saw the National Theatre as a flowering of Englishness. Tynan admired the state theatres he saw in East Berlin and Warsaw.[69]

Lyttelton and Tynan hated each other. It was loathing based on utter contempt. Olivier and Lyttelton disliked each other greatly too. But they recognized that they had a genuine goal in common. Those who liked Lyttelton admired his 'brutal wit', those who disliked Lyttelton admitted that that 'brutal wit' made him a powerful enemy. Tynan saw no wit at all. All he saw was a repulsive bully. He recoiled when Lyttelton's wattled face, flushed with fury, pressed too close to his own. Tynan was determined to show Lyttelton up for what he truly was. It was Tynan's hope that, if he found plays offensive enough, he could provoke Lyttelton to resign. Tynan even hoped that he might sweep away the National Theatre Board, which he regarded as little more than a group of reactionary social-climbing parasites leeching off and leaching away the theatrical genius of directors, actors and, his own name for himself, the 'dramaturge'.[70]

As soon as the Labour government was confirmed in power, Tynan turned up two dramatic vehicles that would demonstrate to Lyttelton that he was not fit to survive under the new order. Tynan's eye fell first on the work of a young German playwright, Rolf Hochhuth. Hochhuth was the perfect tool for Tynan. Burning with indignation about the holier-than-thou attitude of the British towards their behaviour in the war, Hochhuth fell under the spell of David Irving. He devoured Irving's book *The Destruction of Dresden*, for it showed the British to be war criminals every bit as bad as the Nazis. Dresden, in Irving and Hochhuth's view, was as much a mass murder of innocents as Auschwitz. Hochhuth was quite as taken with Irving's next project, which purported to show that Churchill had ordered the murder of the Polish leader General Sikorski because he would not keep quiet about Stalin's massacre of the Polish officer corps at Katyn.[71] By Christmas 1966 Hochhuth had spatchcocked together the two stories in his play *Soldiers*. It was a wholly incompetent piece of theatrical writing, dull and incomprehensible. Tynan did not care: the key thing was that the play was offensive to Lyttelton beyond measure. Not only was Churchill depicted as a war criminal, but so also was anyone who put on a British uniform: 'One picks up a noose and a medal by the same roadside' as one of the main characters is made to say.[72]

Tynan was insistent that the National Theatre should put on the play. Lyttelton was predictably apoplectic. Not only was he himself a decorated veteran, but his beloved son, Julian, had been killed serving in the army during the Second World War. Even better from Tynan's point of view was that he was putting Olivier in an excruciatingly difficult position. The ageing Olivier was forever striving to swing with the younger generation. The more they mocked him as a Tory, the more desperately he claimed to be a socialist. Here, Tynan claimed, was a cut-and-dried issue of artistic freedom. The *auteur* must be able to say the unsayable and the director must be allowed to stage it. Olivier the artist knew the play was theatrical poison. 'I remember saying to Larry one night,' Joan Plowright recalled, '"Well, what do you actually, honestly feel about the play?" ... And he said, "I don't like the bloody thing. But I expect it'll get near grounds for divorce if you think I'm frightened of doing new stuff. You'll despise me, won't you."'[73] 'The theatrical motto,' wrote a contemptuous Lyttelton, 'is if there is no thin ice let us refrigerate some water and put our feet in it.'[74] The stage was set for a titanic confrontation. Lyttelton was adamant that the National would have nothing to do with the play. Tynan was adamant that they must certainly produce it as a matter of principle. Olivier gyrated uncomfortably between them.

Lyttelton had two lines of attack. The archaic laws of theatrical censorship were on their last legs, but he sounded out the Lord Chamberlain, Lord Cobbold. He could probably get the play banned if necessary. This, however, would play into Tynan's hands. Lyttelton much preferred that the National Theatre Board should turn down the play. Driven by his own insecurities, Olivier would champion the play to the board, but Lyttelton was confident that this body, created in his image, would hold the line.

Rallied by Lyttelton's ally Kenneth Clark, the board did indeed refuse to produce the play. Tynan, who up to that point had played a brilliant game, was now revealed as having been 'too clever by half': he had implied that the Regius Professor of History at Oxford had seen some historical merit in *Soldiers*. The regius professor was Hugh Trevor-Roper, a Tory appointed by Macmillan and the mastermind behind Macmillan's own election as Chancellor of the University. At the time Trevor-Roper, a specialist on seventeenth-century England, was regarded as a leading expert on Germany, having investigated the Nazi leadership as an intelligence officer in the occupation forces. He was able to assure Lyttelton that he had indeed given Tynan his opinion: *Soldiers* was utter drivel. Infuriated by the humiliating exposure of his duplicity, Tynan nevertheless continued his campaign to get at Lyttelton. He flew to Germany for a press conference. Sitting next to Hochhuth and Irving, the publication of whose Sikorski book had been timed to coincide with the first night of *Soldiers* in Berlin, Tynan lauded the play as capturing the true spirit of Britain's wartime conduct. He organized a production of *Soldiers* in London which flopped. His attempts to get Richard Burton to play the lead were scuppered by Elizabeth Taylor, whose godfather, Victor Cazalet, had died in the Sikorski crash.

By then Tynan's eye had fallen on another theatrical property. Like Hochhuth, Conor Cruise O'Brien was determined to expose British villainy. As the UN's point man in Katanga, O'Brien's behaviour had provided Salisbury with brickbat after brickbat to throw at Macmillan. O'Brien himself was convinced that the British government had conspired to get him sacked. His play *Murderous Angels* was bizarrely similar to *Soldiers*. It too was incompetent as a piece of theatrical writing. Critics who saw it performed in New York, Berlin, Dublin and France variously labelled it 'a disaster', 'awful' and 'a nightmare.'[75] It too accused the British government of conspiring to kill a world leader, Dag Hammarskjöld, in a faked aeroplane crash. It too mixed historical and invented characters.

For the purposes of his polemic O'Brien needed a historical figure who would symbolize the villainy of British imperialism as it plotted to assassinate the Secretary-General of the United Nations. The actual colonial secretary in office at the time of Hammarskjöld's death, Iain Macleod, did not really fit the bill. But Oliver Lyttelton certainly did. So Lyttelton was thrown into O'Brien's *mélange* as one of the murderous characters, despite the fact he had retired from the Colonial Office seven years before the events the play purported to describe. O'Brien's accusation was obviously an actionable libel. Since O'Brien had no defence in truth for his defamation, a threat of legal action by Lyttelton forced him to bowdlerize his own play.[76] When the play was published in England the Oliver Lyttelton character had been replaced by the Duke of Tamworth, a ruthless businessman, but the disguise was gossamer thin. O'Brien did not have enough imagination for subtlety: Tamworth/Lyttelton's sidekick in the play is called Sir Henry Large-White.[77]

Tynan was in raptures. If a play that labelled Churchill a murderer had failed to remove Lyttelton, then surely a play that labelled him a murderer would. What a sweet irony. The company of the theatre that Lyttelton was building as monument to himself, his family and his caste would damn him. Unfortunately for Tynan *Murderous Angels* was, after the *Soldiers* débâcle, too libellous for the National Theatre Board to touch.[78] Lyttelton would most certainly have turned it into another *Soldiers*-style confrontation if necessary, but there was no need. He found it difficult to stomach, however, that the play had been dropped on lawyers' advice not 'on grounds of the absurdity of the charge'.[79]

The wrangles over *Soldiers* and *Murderous Angels* destroyed Kenneth Tynan's position at the National Theatre. Yet, as he had hoped, they also irreparably soured any working relationship between Lyttelton and Olivier. Olivier let it be known that, if Lyttelton was not removed as chairman of the National Theatre, he himself would have to resign. The Labour-dominated Arts Council of Lord Goodman and Jennie Lee had little compunction in telling Lyttelton that the National would be better off without him. Weakened by the serious kidney disease that would eventually kill him, Lyttelton had little energy left to fight. In the last public act of his life, he bade farewell to the National, acknowledging that he was an 'extinct volcano'.[80]

Lyttelton's ouster from the National Theatre was a personal tragedy. Yet the unkindest cut to his generation's reputation was delivered by a much better and more influential play than either *Soldiers* or *Murderous Angels*. In 1962 Lyttelton had written his memoirs. What he wrote fifty-eight years after he had joined the Grenadiers showed no diminution in his passionate pride in being a Guardsman. The Brigade of Guards was 'the best human organization, the most efficient and the most clearly knit'. Its members were 'all Guardsmen first, had the same standards of discipline, the same professional training, the same pride'.[81] He drew some memorable character sketches of the officers, like 'Ma' Jeffreys and 'Crawley' de Crespigny, whom he had admired. The years, on the other hand, had given him a certain critical distance. In particular he made no secret of the deep tensions that had run between the staff and the front-line soldiers. He had some harsh words about staff officers, safe in their *châteaux*, intriguing for medals and honours. He wrote of his embarrassment at having secured a place on Lord Cavan's staff and his fear of being regarded as *embusqué*.[82]

At the same time as Lyttelton was drafting his book, Macmillan was wondering, to the considerable embarrassment of his aides, whether his 'contempt for those "gentlemen of England now abed", whether in the First or the Second [World War], who voluntarily missed their chance or chose to avoid danger by seeking positions of security', could be harnessed to political advantage. He had used the trick against Rab Butler since the 1940s with great success. Now his eye fell on the Labour leader Hugh Gaitskell, that 'contemptible creature – a cold-blooded, Wykehamist intellectual and *embusqué*'.[83] 'Poor Mr Gaitskell,' he observed viciously as they waited at the Cenotaph on Armistice Day, 'always seems a little conscious on these occasions that he has no medals. However, he supported the War, from Dr Dalton's side, in the Ministry of Economic Warfare.'[84] Would it not be a good idea, he asked his press office, to draw attention to this in a speech? When the Opposition mocked him for his Edwardian unflappability, he could riposte that unflappability was a virtue rather than a vice: 'I learned that in early youth under fire on the battlefield. Unfortunately, for reasons which I wholly understand, this experience was not vouchsafed to Mr Gaitskell, Mr Wilson, Mr Brown, Mr Jay and the other leading members of the Labour front bench.'[85]

Harold Macmillan thought Lyttelton 'gave the best description of war from the regimental officer's point of view that has been written since Tolstoy'.[86] When he himself came to write about his own experiences three years later, he could almost have been using Lyttelton as a template. Lyttelton had portrayed himself as 'shy and scholarly ... an educated *flâneur*'.[87] Macmillan considered himself to have been a 'strange animal from another world, who read books and argued about philosophy with any of my fellow officers whom I could get to listen'. Lyttelton had become a 'case-hardened man' as he aped the professional soldiers whom he had admired. Under Crawley de Crespigny's watchful eye, Macmillan learnt 'the genuine pleasure in high standards of discipline'.[88] Lyttelton 'learnt that in war all front-line soldiers are of the same age, whether they are forty or twenty, because they are all the same distance away from death. This abolition of age is another thing which knits the fraternity of fighting regimental soldiers together and which seems to widen the cleavage between staff and troops.'[89] Macmillan also remembered that the 'First War was conducted by men of lesser quality from their *châteaux*. These feelings about the command were widespread throughout the Army, even before the Somme ... the spirit of animosity between the regimental officers and the staff was therefore strong.'[90]

Macmillan had thought that by labelling the leaders of the Labour party as cowards he could reap a political advantage. His press officer urged him to abandon the idea. Such thoughts no longer fitted into the political idiom of the age. If such things were to be said, it should be in memoirs rather than in speeches. Although Macmillan and Lyttelton were quite clear as to who had been the heroes – the warriors themselves – and who the villains – the *embusqués*, Gaitskell and Tynan and their ilk – others were less sure. They were in search of a different kind of hero. Lyttelton, even in memorializing the war, as he honestly thought, was doing little more than feeding the myth that was growing up around the 'rebel' war poets, most particularly Siegfried Sassoon and Wilfred Owen. They too had felt part of a 'band of brothers', they too had exhibited outstanding bravery, they too had experienced the pity of war, they too had observed the corruption of old men sending young men to their deaths while preserving their friends and relations. These outsiders – Sassoon because of his homosexuality, Owen because of his class – brought together at Craiglockart had much more resonance in the 1960s than anyone who persisted in seeing the war as the just defence of a just order.

Raymond Asquith's poems, for instance, had disappeared as if they had never been. John Buchan had known them by heart, but Buchan had been in his own grave for nearly thirty years.[91] Wilfred Owen's reputation flowered many decades after his death, whereas Asquith's reputation, so high when he died at the Somme, had withered to nothing with the years. Although Asquith had had ambivalent feelings about the young Lyttelton, the aged Lyttelton penned an unalloyed elegy to the man and what he represented: 'England lost one of its rarest men. Even a stranger could have seen that his good looks and noble profile disclosed a man of the finest character and powers. His astringent but kindly humour many times illuminated our darkness, but with all his brilliance he was simple and unselfish enough to make the sacrifice with men who were not his equals.'[92]

For Lyttelton, Asquith and his friends were 'shining figures in a golden age of young men'. Yet it was as if the funeral pyre for the glorious dead had been looted and used in a different ceremony. The 1960s' most successful memorial to the dead of the First World War was not the memoirs of those who had fought but *Oh! What a Lovely War*, a stage musical based on the script of a radio play by Charles Chilton, *The Long, Long Trial*, and developed in workshop by young radical actors.[93] It was a particular woe to Lyttelton that *Oh! What a Lovely War* was produced by another of his theatrical *bêtes noirs*, Joan Littlewood. Littlewood made Tynan look like a running dog of the ruling orders. A small, ugly, badly dressed woman with a pronounced regional accent, her work was the antithesis of the National Theatre dream, just as her words excoriated its realization. For Littlewood the future of the theatre was drama by the people for the people. *Lovely War*, written and performed by her collective company, saw the light of day at her Theatre Workshop, based deep in the East End of London at the Theatre Royal, Stratford East. Unlike the theatrical duds Tynan was to urge on the National, *Lovely War* was angry political theatre that also amused and entertained. It was relevant because it was successful. It soon moved from run-down Stratford to the West End. *Lovely War*'s originality was to take war memoirs and combine them with contemporary songs. The jaunty tone of the songs clashed shockingly with the underlying tale of millions slaughtered as the dupes in a class war.

One scene in particular of *Lovely War* transmogrified the story of the war from the story of personal virtue and vice, in which some had shirked but most had done their duty, that Macmillan and Lyttelton preferred to tell, into a condemnation of their class. Macmillan, Crookshank and Lyttelton had all seen action at the battle of Loos in 1915. Lyttelton had served as an ADC to their divisional commanding officer, Lord Cavan. In *Lovely War* an unnamed commanding officer visits a front-line unit during the battle.

CO: Now, you men, I've just come from having a powwow with the Colonel; we think you've done some damn fine work – we congratulate you.

Soldiers: Thank you, sir.

CO: I know you've had it pretty hard the last few days, bombs, shells and snipers; we haven't escaped scot free back at staff either, I can tell you. Anyway, we're all here – well, not all of us, of course; and that gas of ours was pretty nasty – damned wind changing.

Lieutenant: Indeed, sir.

CO: But these mishaps do happen in war, and gas can be a war-winning weapon. Anyway, so long as we can all keep smiling; you're white men all. Sector all tidy now Lieutenant?

Lieutenant: Well, we've buried most of the second Yorks and Lancs, sir; there's a few DLIs and the men from our own company left.

CO: I see, well, look, let the lads drum up some char – Ye Gods! What's that?

Lieutenant: Oh, it's a Jerry, sir.

CO: What?

Lieutenant: It's a leg, sir.

CO: Well, get rid of it, man. You can't have an obstruction sticking out of the parapet like that.

The butchery, the cowardice, the incompetence, the insensitivity were thus summed up in a few lines of mockery. Lyttelton's critique of some senior officers had become a condemnation of all officers: the commanders whom he had admired as much as the staff officers he had criticized. The disposal of dismembered corpses that he himself had described in graphic detail in letters to his mother had become a vehicle for black comedy.

Lyttelton's memoirs and Littlewood's play were coeval, but it was the producer rather than the witness whose views triumphed. Lyttelton's view of the past continued to lose ground. *Lovely War* was followed by the BBC documentary series *The Great War*, narrated by Michael Redgrave. His friend Kenneth Clark's son, Alan, had already given the bandwagon impetus with his popular history of the war, *The Donkeys*.[94] If an Old Etonian former Household Cavalry officer like Alan Clark agreed with Joan Littlewood, then it was clear which way the wind was blowing. *Lovely War* itself did not go away. The play was made into a film, directed by Richard Attenborough, and released in 1969.

Perturbed, Lyttelton attempted to right these perceived wrongs with a second volume of memoirs reproducing a large number of letters from his private archives. 'We, by which I mean both officers and men,' he wrote in justification of offering a second tome that covered the same ground as his first, 'did not feel so doom-laden, so utterly disenchanted. We thought we were fighting in a worthy cause, and had no idea that our efforts would one day appear to Miss Littlewood as merely absurd.'[95] The tone of this volume stressed even more his sense of belonging to a 'lost world'. The first half of the book concerned the courtship of his mother and father and evoked the world of the late Victorian aristocracy. The second half comprised many of the letters he had sent his mother from the trenches. Using these letters, he attempted to paint a picture of an army grappling with the almost insurmountable problems created by military technology. 'It is easy,' he castigated Clark junior, 'to write books like *The Donkeys*, and to deride British and French generals, many of whom were admittedly not stars in their profession, but the authors who air these criticisms must attempt to answer the question, "What would you have done?"' According to Lyttelton, the experiences of 1914 and 1915, discussed 'professionally for hours at a time', had 'early convinced me and others of my age and rank that it would be some years before the offensive initiative could be regained effectively by either side in the West'. Douglas Haig was an 'underrated commander', not only 'because to regain the initiative was virtually impossible when he succeeded to the command', but also because 'the subordinate generals, his instruments, were not, with few exceptions, of high professional calibre . . . [they] had little or no experience of handling large bodies of troops and had not, by their past or training, been able to replace experience by professional or theoretical knowledge of their art'. There was therefore some truth in the 'lions led by donkeys' case, but it did not justify the mockery meted out in *Lovely War*. An entirely different portrait could be drawn, from exactly the same material, of a commanding officer at Loos, taking Lyttelton's own CO, Cavan, as its model. Cavan may have 'never studied the profession of arms from a theoretical or historical standpoint'. His ambitions had, after all, never aspired to any post higher than commanding a battalion of Grenadier Guards rather than the brigade, division, corps or army which was his eventual lot, but he was not a fool, he was not callous, and he was most certainly not a coward. He merely 'exhibited one of the most outstanding virtues in a fighting soldier: he remained calm at all times and in all circumstances'.[96]

Lyttelton was too late. He was much too late. His book was admired by the usual suspects. Macmillan regarded it as 'marvellously objective'.[97] The Queen Mother let it be known that it was splendid.[98] The critical response was much more mixed. Philip Toynbee excoriated it in the *Observer*. Lyttelton had not understood the war in which he had fought. 'The experience of war failed to penetrate very deeply,' Toynbee charged. Lyttelton was not 'objective', he was merely dim. 'Can it be, perhaps,' Toynbee asked, 'that the qualities admired in the officers' mess, Tory Cabinet and boardroom are not of the kind which are needed by an acute self-examiner, a reflective writer or even an observant social annalist?' As an account of the Great War, Lyttelton's memories and letters were worthless, Toynbee concluded. All they did was expose the fact that: 'In war as in peace there is the same upper-class cliqueishness; the same hearty good fellowship. We read of "Porkie", "Fatty", "Boy" and the ubiquitous "Bobbety" – all good fellows and all from the top drawer.'[99]

If such cliqueishness was to be forgiven, less scathing reviewers argued, it was on the grounds that Macmillan had put forward in 1966. Macmillan claimed 'an obligation to make some decent use of the life that had been spared to us'. 'A certain bitterness began to eat at our hearts,' he recalled, 'at the easy way in which many of our elders seemed to take up again, and play with undiminished zest, the game of politics. "Old men lived; the young men died."' He had 'learnt for the first time to understand, talk with, and feel at home with a whole class of men'. In Macmillan's version, this sense of public service and sympathy for the plight of working men was a legacy of the war.[100] Lyttelton too remembered that many 'weedy and narrow-chested' recruits were 'swept into the Army by unemployment and starvation, the two press gangs of those days'. 'I have never forgotten this,' he wrote, 'have never criticized the "dole" for being too generous.'[101] 'Both Oliver Lyttelton and Harold Macmillan were permanently marked by the war,' remarked the historian F. S. L. Lyons. 'But for the public in Britain this was not all loss, for they carried with them into politics something of the truth which Owen thought must die untold – "the pity of war, the pity of war distilled".'[102] The phrases of professional reviewers upon reading Lyttelton revealed a great deal. The Guardsmen had been hoist with their own petard. Those who admired them, as well as those who execrated them, did so, not on their own terms, but by measuring them against Wilfred Owen, a lower-middle-class jobbing teacher who had fought and died in a provincial infantry regiment.

Lyttelton, Macmillan and Salisbury had been made to carry a burden of guilt that they did not feel. Macmillan was partly to blame for this. He wrote in his memoirs that, 'We almost began to feel a sense of guilt for not having shared the fate of our friends and comrades.'[103] It is impossible to know the emotions that welled in inner recesses of a man's heart. Yet it is equally hard to see how either a 'sense of guilt' or a distaste for the 'elders who played the game of politics with undiminished zest' shaped Macmillan's career. He himself played the game with zest. Guilt and anger seem to have been much more the products of his early personal and political failure than the war. Toynbee was nearer the mark when he accused

Lyttelton of being 'unreflective'. A degree of insensitivity helped one to survive. 'I can see your life in the trenches,' wrote Lady Waverley on reading *From Peace to War*, 'and realize why my brothers, Ronnie and Josselin, are victims to this day of shell shock from which they have never emerged. Your character is formed of "sterner stuff" and you have always been marvellous in every way.'[104]

Ava Waverley was a sad and silly woman. One could dismiss her observation on those grounds alone. It is worth pausing, however, to ask: is it wise to treat a group of disillusioned littérateurs, any more than a group of self-satisfied Etonian politicians, as representative of their generation? Just as the war was fought, in reality, not by a great mass but by many small groups of men, the legacy of the war was felt in those smaller groups rather than as a collective experience.[105] Most of those poets, later famous, who survived ended up as internal exiles, such as Sassoon, or actual exiles, like Graves. The pattern was repeated in those closer to the Guardsmen. Geoffrey Madan, the Colleger who shone the brightest in their Eton pupil room, was the most notable internal exile in their own circle.[106] Having served as an infantry officer, Madan withdrew into himself after the war. His friends tried to help. Macmillan put him up for Pratt's, Lyttelton gave him a job at BMC, but the 'most brilliant scholar of his generation' produced nothing except a commonplace book which he maintained with pathological care.[107] Madan would have achieved complete anonymity but for his appeal to a certain type of homosexual Oxford High Tory whom he encountered at high table.

Osbert Sitwell, having shone briefly as a cultural icon of 1920s London, subsequently found the relaxed ways and mores of Italy more to his taste. He discovered that his true subject was the baroque Velazquezian horror of his family. The quartet's Etonian and Grenadier contemporary wrote about the war but little, and then with studied dullness. The other famous Etonian writer of their generation, Aldous Huxley, was a non-combatant. Blessed with poor eyesight, he spent the war at Oxford rather than in Flanders. Perhaps he felt *embusqué*: his fictional *alter ego* in *Eyeless in Gaza*, Anthony Beavis, does join up but is kept out of the fighting because of an accident with a hand grenade in training. Having 'swung', like Sitwell, in

1920s London, Huxley too sought a more healthy physical and a more relaxed moral climate abroad. In 1937 he decamped to California, where he began his consciousness-expanding experiments with LSD and mescalin. Ken Tynan saw Huxley as a role model.

Madan, Sitwell and Huxley's trajectories suggest that becoming part of the 'lost generation' was more a matter of personality than of experience. With their less striking intellectual gifts, Macmillan, Salisbury, Lyttelton and Crookshank were always destined for the kind of careers they pursued. In the summer of 1918 Harold Macmillan had lain in a hospital bed with half the bullet that had nearly crippled him still inside his body. Then he had dreamed of exile, turning his back on the sordid world of public affairs, forgetting the trenches in a sun-drenched Tuscan idyll. Yet this was merely a passing phase. He and his friends were exactly the ambitious, hard-working, pragmatic, unimaginative types who, war or no war, became Conservative MPs. It was only fifty years after the event, with their partial collusion along the way, that it seemed sensible to measure it by the yardstick of the poet and the artist.

In the later part of his life, Macmillan always insisted that he was an Edwardian who had survived beyond his time. Oliver Lyttelton wryly reported in 1966, after lunching with Macmillan, 'Harold arrived in the character of senile, bland retired statesman puttering about with little steps. "After all one has had one's successes and one's failures. I am very old." After two glasses of Pol Roger he forgot to be so old and old Adam began to appear.'[108] Despite Macmillan's habitual gilding of the lily, it was nevertheless the case that by the 1960s his *équipe* were, in their own minds, and in the twilight of their life, the 'Great War generation'. The war had sundered the old world from the new. To the 1960s generation they appeared to be members of a homogeneous élite living in much the same way as each other: elegant houses in the best parts of London, country mansions, members of the same London clubs. To those who observed them, they seemed like characters from a novel in which the novelist had overstretched 'the possibilities of coincidence'.[109]

That the result was nearer farce than tragedy was illustrated by an incident at the beginning of the 1970s. In June 1970 Roy Strong, the youthful and fashionably hirsute director of the National Portrait Gallery, attended a rather odd luncheon party. It was thrown by Lady Diana Cooper. Lady Diana had been widowed for sixteen years since the death of her husband, Duff. It was as a young, recently decorated, officer in the Grenadier Guards that Duff Cooper had wooed and won her.[110] As she wrote to the sister of Patrick Shaw-Stewart, one of her many lovers: 'I feel that in marrying Duff that my life continues in the same loved channel. I think that no one, save one who knew, remembered and loved our dead friends, could have made me happy.'[111]

Fifty-two years after the end of the war, Strong admired her 'timeless magic which cuts across the generations and makes differences in age irrelevant'. Unfortunately, Lady Diana's timeless magic was not matched by organizational ability. She had booked her cook for the wrong day. Thus it was that Strong found himself sitting in the Maida Vale Steakhouse with Harold Macmillan, or 'Horse' as Lady Diana affectionately called him, 'bent double over a stick, deaf and complaining of a cataract', and Lord Salisbury 'wearing a straw hat engulfed in white net'.

It is to be doubted that Macmillan and Salisbury were delighted to find themselves seated with Strong in a restaurant whose manager claimed 'he was used to having all the pop stars but not the politicians'.[112] Macmillan certainly did not bother to hide his contempt for the young gallery director – thus finding himself placed upon Strong's list of 'the rudest men I have ever met'.[113] Macmillan and Salisbury seemed to Strong merely two crotchety old men out of touch with modern life. The young gallery director cared little for the saga that brought them to that Maida Vale Steakhouse or that they only spoke to each other at all because of a memory of 'how long ago all the nicest things were'.[114]

CONCLUSION

This book has unearthed the history of four boys who started on the same road together in 1906. They were lucky enough to live in tumultuous times. What they did made a difference both then and now. Yet their careers have been occluded for decades. Many people remember the elderly Harold Macmillan. He died in 1986, an ornament to national life. The older Macmillan bore only a passing resemblance to his younger self. His class and generation were deeply unfashionable in the 1960s and 1970s, dismissed as little more than 'blimps' or lauded for qualities of paternalistic compassion that they themselves did not rate highly. There has been a growing reluctance to accept a history of the Great War that concentrated on the scions of the élite. Just as the Guardsmen had more or less willingly become followers of Winston Churchill, so history was, and is, written in a Churchillian mould. Churchill has recently been voted the 'greatest Briton'. In his shadow the reputations of few others may flourish.

From an early age the Guardsmen recognised that first money and then power were the keys to advancement. Politics for them was a constant war of manoeuvre and attrition. In their age, as in every other, this struggle was projected in idealistic rhetoric, aimed at securing and buttressing power. The history of a political generation seen from within reveals the true working of their system. There is an inevitable disjunction between politics as it is projected to outsiders and the reality for insiders. Each generation has its own 'rules of the game'. The Guardsmen were players from the beginning. With the possible exception of Oliver Lyttelton – and he strove to rectify the fault – the Guardsmen were professional politicians. As individuals they were shaped by Eton and the Brigade of Guards, as public men they were moulded by an equally powerful institution – the Conservative party. Their belief that a man should be rich before he entered politics is no longer fashionable. It did, however, provide a bulwark against personal corruption that later generations have lacked. The manoeuvre and compromise of professional politicians is worldly and may seem disreputable. The English imagination seems to prefer gifted amateurs to committed professionals. The Guardsmen stand out, however, because they never lost sight of big issues. The honourable side of worldliness is realism. This group of men showed remarkable prescience when faced with great challenges. They were not taken in by the siren voices of either authoritarianism or appeasement. They were the first generation of British politicians who spent their careers wholly within the system of universal suffrage that operates to this day. They saw that fascism and Nazism were evil and had to be opposed. Bobbety Salisbury, in particular, had an uncanny knack of accurate prediction. Even the least successful of the quartet, Harry Crookshank, was perceptive, if not always daring enough to back his own judgement. Each of these men was intelligent and ambitious. Their political judgement was of a high order.

One of the enduring qualities of the myth of the 'lost generation' is that Britain might have enjoyed better leadership without the casualties of the First World War. At times the Guardsmen themselves paid lip service to this view. It is impossible to prove a negative. The study of politics as they unfolded after the war does nevertheless provide warning against a search for the lost leader. There are many examples of MPs with brilliant qualifications who did not have the qualities to flourish as politicians. There is, for instance, the striking case of Edward Marjoribanks, the long-forgotten older half-brother of Lord Hailsham, the heir to a barony, a star at Eton, president of the Union at Oxford, a considerable athlete, a double first, an MP before he was thirty, dead by his own hand in 1932. One can legitimately ask about those that survived: would there have been a better winner than Harold Macmillan? The answer is no. Macmillan reached the top because he was the best politician of his generation. No-one could match his mixture of political intelligence, determination to succeed and skill in manoeuvre. Macmillan was unusual amongst his contemporaries in his early and detailed work on economic policy. He was at one with them in seeing economics as the handmaiden of politics. He and his contemporaries were also entirely at one in believing that the great issue with which politicians had to deal was foreign affairs. Given the events through which they lived it would have been bizarre to have any other view. In his early and middle career Macmillan was right about most foreign-policy issues. The sheer devilry of his later adventures in foreign policy shocked some but he remained both the consummate professional and the hard-headed realist. In other words the system worked: from the talent pool available the best man emerged. Macmillan's victory was the result of decades of hard work, not luck.

NOTES AND REFERENCES

Chapter 1: Sons

1 Oliver Lyttelton, Memoir of Harold Macmillan for the *Daily Telegraph*, 18 April 1958, Chandos Papers, Churchill College, Cambridge, CHAN II, 4/18.

2 Jane Abdy and Charlotte Gere, *The Souls*, London, 1984, and Kenneth Rose, *Superior Person: A Portrait of Curzon and his Circle in Late Victorian England*, London, 1969. Oliver Lyttelton was one of Rose's sources.

3 Jane Brown, *Lutyens and the Edwardians: An English Architect and His Clients*, Harmondsworth, 1997, pp. 111–12.

4 Viscount Chandos, *From Peace to War: A Study in Contrast, 1857–1918*, London, 1968, p. 21; Harold Macmillan, *Winds of Change, 1914–1939*, London, 1966, p. 78.

5 Alfred Lyttelton to Oliver Lyttelton, 10 October 1905, CHAN I, 8/1.

6 John Vincent, ed., *The Crawford Papers: The Journals of David Lindsay, 27th Earl of Crawford and 10th Earl of Balcarres during the years 1892 to 1940*, (henceforth Crawford, *Journals*) Manchester, 1984, 22 February 1904.

7 Crawford, *Journals*, 18 July 1908.

8 Philip Williamson, ed., *The Modernization of Conservative Politics: The Diaries and Letters of William Bridgeman*, London, 1988, 20 December 1906.

9 Oliver Lyttelton to Didi Lyttelton, 2 December 1908, CHAN I, 8/1.

10 Crawford, *Journals*, 9 September 1909.

11 Oliver Lyttelton to Edith Lyttelton, 24 October 1909, CHAN I, 8/1.

12 Lord Salisbury to Sir Roy Welensky, 10 May 1957, Papers of 5th Marquess of Salisbury, Hatfield House. 'Bobbety' was a nursery name. On the death of his grandfather Bobbety was accorded the title of Cranborne, the honorific traditionally bestowed on the heir to the marquessate.

13 Kenneth Rose, *The Later Cecils*, London, 1975, pp. 48–110 (James), 127–84 (Robert).

14 Interview with Lord Salisbury, 15 December 1998.

15 Crawford, *Journals*, 13 March 1905.

16 Crawford, *Journals*, 3 February 1906; Bridgeman, *Diaries*, 20 December 1906.

17 Crawford, *Journals*, 16 September 1909.

18 Lord Midleton to Lord Selborne, 9 September 1908, quoted in Andrew Adonis, *Making Aristocracy Work: The Peerage and the Political System in Britain, 1884–1914*, Oxford, 1993, p. 142.

19 Crawford, *Journals*, 21 July 1911.

20 Crawford, *Journals*, 6 July 1911.

21 Lord Cromer, *Modern Egypt*, II, London, 1908, pp. 492–4.

22 Timothy Mitchell, *Colonizing Egypt*, Cambridge, 1988, p. 97.

23 Coles Pasha, *Recollections and Reflections*, London, 1918, pp. 96–8.

24 Cromer, *Egypt*, II, pp. 313–14.

25 Robert L. Tignor, *Modernization and British Colonial Rule in Egypt, 1882–1914*, Princeton, NJ, 1966, pp. 369–73.

26 Daniel Yergin, *The Prize: The Epic*

Quest for Oil, Money and Power, London, 1993, pp. 39–47.

27 John Pollock, *Kitchener*, London, 2001, p. 228.

28 Harry Crookshank to Aunt Harrie, December 1903, Crookshank Papers, Lincoln Record Office.

29 Nicholas Aldridge, *Time to Spare? A History of Summer Fields*, Oxford, 1989, p. 59.

30 Henry Willink, 'As I Remember', Willink Papers, Churchill College, Cambridge.

31 Tim Card, *Eton Renewed*, London, 1994.

32 Oliver Lyttelton, Lord Chandos, *Memoirs*, London, 1962, p. 7.

33 Harold Macmillan to Nellie Macmillan, 6 June 1916, Macmillan Diary, Bodleian Library, Oxford.

34 Oliver Lyttelton to Didi Lyttelton, 8 October 1911, CHAN I, 8/1.

35 Oliver Lyttelton to Didi Lyttelton, 10 October 1908, CHAN II, 4/1.

36 Lubbock to Alfred Lyttelton, 29 December 1911, CHAN II, 4/3.

37 Lubbock to Alfred Lyttelton, 3 April 1912, CHAN II, 4/3.

38 John Joliffe, ed., *Raymond Asquith: Life and Letters*, London, 1980, Raymond Asquith to Katharine Asquith, 29 November 1915.

39 Lord Kilmuir, *Political Adventure: The Memoirs of the Earl of Kilmuir*, London, 1964, p. 193.

40 Oliver Lyttelton to Didi Lyttelton, 3 July [1909], CHAN I, 8/1.

41 Oliver Lyttelton to Didi Lyttelton, 19 September 1910, CHAN I, 8/1.

42 Sir Osbert Sitwell to Lord Salisbury, 24 May 1957, Salisbury Papers.

43 Crookshank War Diary, 30 November 1917, ES3/036 Diary of H. F. C. Crookshank, Royal HQ, Grenadier Guards, Wellington Barracks, London.

44 Grades for Lent half, 1912, CHAN II, 4/3.

45 Programme for Speech Day, 4 June 1912, Crookshank Papers.

46 Macmillan, *Winds of Change*, p. 42.

47 Harold Macmillan to Lord Salisbury, 14 March 1963, PREM11/4300.

48 Macmillan Diary, 12 November 1957.

49 Harold Macmillan to Maurice Macmillan, 29 April 1916, Macmillan Diary.

50 G. H. Martin and J. R. L. Highfield, *A History of Merton College, Oxford*, Oxford, 1997, p. 313. I owe this reference to my wife, H. R. Ball.

51 Quoted in Penelope Fitzgerald (née Knox), *The Knox Brothers*, London, 1977, p. 120.

52 Oliver Lyttelton to Didi Lyttelton, 26 March 1913, CHAN I, 8/1.

53 Oliver Lyttelton to Didi Lyttelton, [1913], CHAN II, 4/1.

54 Oliver Lyttelton to Didi Lyttelton, [winter 1914], CHAN I, 8/1.

55 Serge Obolensky, *One Man in His Time*, London, 1960, pp. 98–108.

56 Charles Fisher to Lord Cranborne, February 1912, Salisbury Papers.

57 Harvey to Lord Cranborne, 22 June 1913, Salisbury Papers.

58 Douglas Jerrold, *Georgian Adventure*, London, 1938, p. 66.

59 Obolensky, *One Man*, p. 98.

60 Lord Salisbury to Anthony Eden, 21 May 1963, Avon Papers, University of Birmingham Library, AP23/60.

61 F. Fremantle (District Commissioner, Northern Provinces, Nigeria) to Lord Cranborne, 14 July 1914, Salisbury Papers.

62 Lord Harlech to Lord Cranborne, 29 May 1941, DO121/107.

63 Jock Balfour to Lord Cranborne, 1 July 1913, Salisbury Papers.

64 Frank Walters to Lord Cranborne, 29 September 1912, Salisbury Papers.

65 Tutor's Note, 7 April 1913, Crookshank Papers.

66 Macmillan, *Winds of Change*, p. 38.

67 Anne Powell, *Bim: A Tribute to the Hon. Edward Wyndham Tennant, Lieutenant, 4th Battalion, Grenadier Guards, 1897–1916*, Salisbury, 1990, Edward Tennant to Lady Glenconner, 19 September 1915.

68 John Ramsden, ed., *Real Old Tory*

NOTES AND REFERENCES

*Politics: The Political Diaries of Sir
Robert Sanders, Lord Bayford, 1910 to
1935*, London, 1984, 8 July 1913.

69 Oliver Lyttelton to Didi Lyttelton,
26 March 1913, CHAN 1, 8/1.

70 Stuart Ball, ed., *Parliament and
Politics in the Age of Churchill and
Attlee: The Headlam Diaries,
1935–1951*, Cambridge, 1999 (hereafter
Headlam, *Diaries*, 11), 23 October
1939.

71 James Stuart, *Within the Fringe*,
London, 1967, pp. 145–6; Robert Cary
to Patrick Buchan-Hepburn,
14 September 1954, Hailes Papers,
Churchill College, Cambridge,
HAILES4/13.

72 Oliver Lyttelton (Shire Hall, Chester
Castle) to Didi Lyttelton, [1914],
CHAN 1, 8/1.

73 Chandos, *Memoirs*, xvi.

74 Jeanne Mackenzie, *The Children of the
Souls*, London, 1986, p. 262.

Chapter 2: Grenadiers

1 Quoted in Paddy Griffith, *Battle
Tactics of the Western Front: The
British Army's Art of Attack, 1916–1918*,
New Haven, Conn., 1994, p. 80.

2 Stuart, *Within the Fringe*, p. 20.

3 Jay Winter, *The Great War and the
British People*, Basingstoke, 1985,
Table: University casualties by
matriculation year. Of those who
matriculated at Oxford between 1910
and 1914, 29.3 per cent were killed; the
figure for Cambridge was 26.1 per
cent.

4 Cranborne Record of Service,
12 August 1914, WO339/15553.

5 Chandos, *Memoirs*, pp. 31–4.

6 Chandos, *Memoirs*, p. 42.

7 Oliver Lyttelton to Didi Lyttelton,
[1914], CHAN 1, 8/2.

8 Oliver Lyttelton (Dovercourt) to Didi
Lyttelton, [1914], CHAN 1, 8/2.

9 Oliver Lyttelton to Didi Lyttelton,
21 October 1914, CHAN 1, 8/2.

10 Oliver Lyttelton to Didi Lyttelton,
12 November 1914, CHAN 1, 8/2.

11 Crookshank Record of Service,
1 September 1914, WO339/500794.

12 Crookshank War Diary (1915),
Introduction.

13 Macmillan, *Winds of Change*,
pp. 63–4.

14 Anthony Eden, *Another World:
1897–1917*, London, 1976, p. 62.

15 Frederick Ponsonby, *The Grenadier
Guards in the Great War of 1914 to
1918*, London, 1920, 3 vols., 1,
pp. 216–17.

16 Chandos, *Memoirs*, p. 50. 'Star,
Thistle and Grenade' were the
Coldstream, Scots and Grenadier
Guards.

17 E. R. M. Fryer, *Reminiscences of a
Grenadier 1914–1921*, London, 1921,
p. 41.

18 Chandos, *Peace to War*, p. 146;
Macmillan, *Winds of Change*, p. 79.

19 Chandos, *Memoirs*, p. 38.

20 Oliver Lyttelton to Didi Lyttelton,
1 June 1915, *Peace to War*, p. 125.

21 Chandos, *Memoirs*, p. 52.

22 Chandos, *Peace to War*, pp. 147–8.

23 Chandos, *Memoirs*, pp. 40–41.

24 Macmillan, *Winds of Change*, p. 79.

25 Oliver Lyttelton to Lady Salisbury,
[1915], CHAN 1, 8/3.

26 Ponsonby, *Grenadier Guards*, 1,
pp. 216–19.

27 Griffith, *Battle Tactics*, p. 72.

28 Niall Ferguson, *The Pity of War*,
London, 1998, pp. 375–7.

29 Ponsonby, *Grenadier Guards*, 1,
p. 222.

30 Oliver Lyttelton to Didi Lyttelton,
15 March 1915, CHAN 1, 8/3.

31 Oliver Lyttelton to Didi Lyttelton,
14 May 1915, CHAN 1, 8/3.

32 Oliver Lyttelton to Didi Lyttelton,
25 March 1915, CHAN 1, 8/3.

33 Oliver Lyttelton to Didi Lyttelton,
6 April 1915, CHAN 1, 8/3.

34 Oliver Lyttelton to Didi Lyttelton,
24 May 1915, *Peace to War*, p. 115.

35 Ponsonby, *Grenadier Guards*, 1,
pp. 256–9.

36 Oliver Lyttelton to Didi Lyttelton,
28 May 1915, *Peace to War*, p. 121.

37 Ponsonby, *Grenadier Guards*, 1, pp. 259–60.

38 Ponsonby, *Grenadier Guards*, 1, p. 260.

39 Medical Case Sheet, 26 May 1915, and Proceedings of Medical Board, 27 May 1915, WO339/15553.

40 Ponsonby, *Grenadier Guards*, 1, pp. 261–2.

41 Oliver Lyttelton to Didi Lyttelton, 21 June 1915, *Peace to War*, p. 127.

42 Ponsonby, *Grenadier Guards*, 1, p. 262.

43 Proceedings of Medical Board, 27 May 1915, WO339/15553.

44 John Murray (Christ Church) to Lord Cranborne, 11 June 1915, Salisbury Papers.

45 John Bevan (1st Hertfordshires) to Lord Cranborne, 2 June 1915, Salisbury Papers.

46 Oliver Lyttelton to Lord Cranborne, 9 June 1915, Salisbury Papers.

47 Philip Cary to Lord Cranborne, 13 June 1915, Salisbury Papers.

48 Crawford, *Journals*, 10 May 1908.

49 Lord Richard Cavendish to War Office, 22 November 1915, WO339/15553.

50 Raymond Asquith to K. Asquith, 19 January 1916, *Life and Letters*.

51 Reginald McKenna to C. P. Scott, Scott Diary, British Library, f. 74.

52 Duggy Balfour to Didi Lyttelton, 9 July 1915, CHAN 5/3.

53 Oldric Portal to Lord Cranborne, [1915], Salisbury Papers.

54 Lord Cavan, *Private Diary of the Formation of the 'Guards Division'*, WO79/71.

55 Crookshank War Diary (1915), 22 and 28 August 1915.

56 Ponsonby, *Grenadier Guards*, 1, pp. 275–6.

57 Ponsonby, *Grenadier Guards*, 1, p. 278.

58 Fryer, *Reminiscences*, p. 50.

59 Crookshank War Diary (1915), 6 August 1915 (later notes).

60 Macmillan, *Winds of Change*, p. 100.

61 Harold Macmillan to Nellie Macmillan, 10 September 1915, Macmillan Diary.

62 Edward Tennant to Lady Glenconner, 7 September 1915, *Bim*.

63 Oliver Lyttelton to Didi Lyttelton, 26 June 1916, *Peace to War*, p. 159.

64 Harold Macmillan to Nellie Macmillan, 26 August 1915, Macmillan Diary.

65 Edward Tennant to Lady Glenconner, 31 August 1915, *Bim*.

66 Crookshank War Diary (1915), 17–18 September.

67 Ponsonby, *Grenadier Guards*, 1, p. 294.

68 Ponsonby, *Grenadier Guards*, 1, p. 298.

69 Ponsonby, *Grenadier Guards*, 1, p. 307.

70 Ponsonby, *Grenadier Guards*, 1, pp. 308–9.

71 Harold Macmillan to Nellie Macmillan, 27 September 1915, Macmillan Diary.

72 Ponsonby, *Grenadier Guards*, 1, pp. 310–13.

73 Ponsonby, *Grenadier Guards*, 1, pp. 314–17.

74 Macmillan, *Winds of Change*, pp. 76–7.

75 Harold Macmillan to Nellie Macmillan, 2 October 1915, Macmillan Diary.

76 Oliver Lyttelton to Didi Lyttelton, 9 October 1915, CHAN 1, 8/3.

77 Griffith, *Battle Tactics*, p. 61.

78 Ponsonby, *Grenadier Guards*, 1, p. 335.

79 Crookshank War Diary (1915), 23 and 24 October 1915.

80 Chandos, *Memoirs*, p. 50.

81 Mary Soames, ed., *Speaking for Themselves: The Personal Letters of Winston and Clemmie Churchill*, London, 1998, Winston Churchill to Clemmie Churchill, 12 December 1915; Ponsonby, *Grenadier Guards*, 1, pp. 337–9.

82 Cuthbert Headlam, *The Guards Division in the Great War, 1915–1918*, 2 vols., London, 1924, 1, p. 89.

83 Chandos, *Memoirs*, p. 48.

84 Oliver Lyttelton to Didi Lyttelton, 4 September 1915, CHAN 1, 8/3.

85 Oliver Lyttelton to Didi Lyttelton, 27 October 1915, *Peace to War*, p. 138.

86 Oliver Lyttelton to Didi Lyttelton, 25 October 1915, *Peace to War*, p. 138.

87 Oliver Lyttelton to Didi Lyttelton, 15 November 1915, CHAN 1, 8/3.

88 Oliver Lyttelton to Didi Lyttelton, 27 October 1925, *Peace to War*, p. 139.

89 Personal Diary of Brigadier-General G. D. Jeffreys (1916), 15 January 1916, E3/028, Royal HQ, Grenadier Guards, Wellington Barracks, London.

90 Raymond Asquith to Katharine Asquith, 26 October 1915.

91 Diary of Colonel Corry (1915), E3/036, Royal HQ, Grenadier Guards, Wellington Barracks, London, is little more than incoherent jottings.

92 Fryer, *Reminiscences*, pp. 64–6.

93 Oliver Lyttelton to Didi Lyttelton, 27 October 1915, *Peace to War*, pp. 139–40.

94 Fryer, *Reminiscences*, pp. 71–2.

95 Oliver Lyttelton to Didi Lyttelton, 2 November 1915, *Peace to War*, pp. 140–44.

96 Oliver Lyttelton to Didi Lyttelton, 15 November 1915, CHAN 1, 8/3.

97 Oliver Lyttelton to Didi Lyttelton, 22 December 1915, CHAN 1, 8/3.

98 Oliver Lyttelton to Didi Lyttelton, 30 December 1915, CHAN 1, 8/3.

99 Raymond Asquith to Katharine Asquith, 29 November 1915, *Life and Letters*.

100 Raymond Asquith to Katharine Asquith, 10 December 1915, *Life and Letters*.

101 Jeffreys Diary, 5 January 1916.

102 Jeffreys Diary, 12 January 1916.

103 Jeffreys Diary, 14 and 15 January 1916.

104 Oliver Lyttelton to Didi Lyttelton, 27 January 1916, CHAN 11, 8/7.

105 Proceedings of Medical Board, 26 March 1916, WO339/15553.

106 Major-General L. G. Drummond, HQ Southern Command to GOC, London District, 8 March 1916, WO339/15553.

107 F. S. Robb to GOC Southern Command, April 1916, WO339/15553.

108 Griffith, *Battle Tactics*, pp. 130–31.

109 Crookshank War Diary (1916), 24 May 1916.

110 Crookshank War Diary (1916), 29 April 1916.

111 Crookshank War Diary (1916), 13 May 1916.

112 Crookshank War Diary (1916), 25 May 1916.

113 Crookshank War Diary (1916), 1 May 1916.

114 Harold Macmillan to Nellie Macmillan, 4 April 1916, Macmillan Diary.

115 Harold Macmillan to Nellie Macmillan, Good Friday 1916, Macmillan Diary.

116 Harold Macmillan to Nellie Macmillan, 13 May 1916, Macmillan Diary.

117 Harold Macmillan to Nellie Macmillan, 29 May 1916, Macmillan Diary.

118 Crookshank War Diary (1916), 31 May and 2 June 1916.

119 Harold Macmillan to Nellie Macmillan, 17 June 1916, Macmillan Diary.

120 Crookshank War Diary (1916), 16 June 1916.

121 Crookshank War Diary (1916), 29 June 1916.

122 Ponsonby, *Grenadier Guards*, 1, p. 374.

123 Raymond Asquith to K. Asquith, 23 June 1916, *Life and Letters*. Floris is a long-established floral perfumer in Jermyn Street, London.

124 Crookshank War Diary (1916), 13 July 1916.

125 Ponsonby, *Grenadier Guards*, 1, pp. 375–6.

126 Harold Macmillan to Nellie Macmillan, 19 July 1916, Macmillan Diary.

127 Crookshank War Diary (1916), 1 July 1916.

128 Harold Macmillan to Nellie Macmillan, 18 July 1916, Macmillan Diary.

129 Tim Travers, *The Killing Ground: The British Army, the Western Front and the Emergence of Modern Warfare, 1900–1918*, London, 1990, p. 173.

130 Crookshank War Diary (1916), 28 July 1916.

131 Crookshank War Diary (1916), 17 August 1916.

132 Crookshank War Diary (1916), 11 August 1916.

133 Griffith, *Battle Tactics*, pp. 59 and 65.

134 Griffith, *Battle Tactics*, p. 67.

135 Crookshank War Diary (1916), 4 August 1916.

136 Crookshank War Diary (1916), 5 September 1916.

137 Crookshank War Diary (1916), 1 September 1916.

138 Harry Crookshank to Emma Crookshank, September 1916, Crookshank War Diary (1916).

139 Ponsonby, *Grenadier Guards*, II, pp. 43–9.

140 Crookshank War Diary (1916), 11 September 1916.

141 Ponsonby, *Grenadier Guards*, II, pp. 86–96.

142 Ponsonby, *Grenadier Guards*, II, pp. 50–52.

143 Crookshank War Diary (1916), 13 September 1916.

144 Oliver Lyttelton to Didi Lyttelton, 21 September 1916, *Peace to War*, pp. 163–71.

145 Ponsonby, *Grenadier Guards*, II, p. 59.

146 Ponsonby, *Grenadier Guards*, II, p. 61.

147 Ponsonby, *Grenadier Guards*, II, pp. 63–4.

148 Crookshank War Diary (1916), 15 September 1916.

149 Crookshank War Diary, 15 September 1916 (later notes).

150 Oliver Lyttelton to Didi Lyttelton, 21 September 1916, CHAN 1, 8/4.

151 Ponsonby, *Grenadier Guards*, II, pp. 101–6.

152 Ponsonby, *Grenadier Guards*, II, p. 106.

153 Oliver Lyttelton to Didi Lyttelton, 21 September 1916, CHAN 1, 8/4.

154 Oliver Lyttelton to Didi Lyttelton,

21 March 1917, CHAN 1, 8/4 (this letter was later typed up and appears in *Peace to War* dated 3 May, p. 182).

155 Oliver Lyttelton to Didi Lyttelton, 6 October 1916, CHAN 1, 8/4.

156 Oliver Lyttelton to Didi Lyttelton, 19 November 1916, *Peace to War*, p. 172.

157 Travers, *Killing Ground*, p. 186.

158 Crookshank's Record of Service, 10 March 1917, WO339/500794.

159 Macmillan to Cranborne, October 1916, Salisbury Papers.

160 Michael Hardyman (Somerset Light Infantry) to Cranborne, 10 July 1918, Salisbury Papers.

161 Sidney Peel to Cranborne, 21 October 1916; Josiah Wedgwood to Cranborne, 23 October 1917, Salisbury Papers.

162 Oliver Lyttelton to Didi Lyttelton, 25 December 1916, *Peace to War*, p. 173.

163 Stuart, *Within the Fringe*, p. 26.

164 Oliver Lyttelton to Didi Lyttelton, 15 April 1915, *Peace to War*, p. 180.

165 Oliver Lyttelton to Didi Lyttelton, 30 May 1917, CHAN 1, 8/5.

166 Chandos, *Memoirs*, pp. 78–9.

167 Oliver Lyttelton to Didi Lyttelton, 15 April 1917, CHAN 1, 8/5.

168 Oliver Lyttelton to Didi Lyttelton, 9 January 1917, CHAN 1, 8/5.

169 Crookshank's Record of Service, 28 September 1917, WO339/500794.

170 Crookshank War Diary (1917–18), September 1917.

171 Crookshank War Diary, 15–18 October 1917 and 27 October 1917.

172 Crookshank War Diary, 11 November 1917.

173 Crookshank War Diary, 26 November 1917.

174 Crookshank War Diary, 14 November 1917.

175 Oliver Lyttelton to Didi Lyttelton, February 1918, CHAN 1, 8/6.

176 Headlam, *Guards*, II, p. 37.

177 Chandos, *Memoirs*, p. 81.

178 Charles Reid to J. Edmonds, 8 March 1928, and Lieutenant-Colonel Buchanan Dunlop to Edmonds,

11 June 1927, cited in Travers, *Killing Ground*, pp. 231–2.

179 Chandos, *Memoirs*, p. 82.

180 Travers, *Killing Ground*, p. 240.

181 Chandos, *Memoirs*, pp. 82–3.

182 Chandos, *Memoirs*, p. 84.

183 Headlam, *Guards*, 11, pp. 48–9.

184 Headlam, *Guards*, 11, pp. 58–9.

185 Chandos, *Memoirs*, pp. 85–9; Travers, *Killing Ground*, pp. 240–41.

186 Chandos, *Memoirs*, p. 91.

187 Chandos, *Memoirs*, pp. 96–7.

188 Headlam, *Guards*, 11, pp. 84–92.

189 Lyttelton's Record of Service, 22 April 1918, WO339/15551.

190 Chandos, *Memoirs*, p. 100.

191 Lyttelton's Record of Service, 11 June 1918, WO339/15551.

192 Cranborne's Record of Service, 1 May 1918, WO339/15553.

193 Brigadier Sandilands to J. E. Edmonds, 14 August 1923, reproduced in Travers, *Killing Ground*, Appendix 1.

194 Cranborne's Record of Service, 19 May 1918, WO339/15553.

195 Lord Salisbury to Cranborne, 25 May 1918, Salisbury Papers.

196 Macmillan to Cranborne, 4 August 1918, Salisbury Papers.

197 Alix Godley to Cranborne, 18 October 1918, Salisbury Papers.

198 Crookshank War Diary, 14 June 1918.

199 Lyttelton's Record of Service, 24 June 1918, WO339/15551.

200 Interview with Lord Salisbury, 15 December 1998.

Chapter 3: Bottle-washers

1 Oliver Lyttelton to Didi Lyttelton, 11 December 1917, *Peace to War*, p. 190.

2 Macmillan to Cranborne, 4 August 1918, Salisbury Papers.

3 Macmillan, *Winds of Change*, p. 105.

4 John Ponsonby to War Office, 4 February 1916, WO339/15551.

5 Regimental Adjutant, Grenadier Guards to Harry Crookshank, 9 October 1920, Crookshank Papers.

6 GOC London District to War Office, 3 February 1921, WO339/500794.

7 Oliver Lyttelton to Didi Lyttelton, 12 August [1919], CHAN 11, 4/1.

8 Chandos, *Memoirs*, pp. 115–23.

9 J. A. Gere and John Sparrow, eds., (Foreword by Harold Macmillan), *Geoffrey Madan's Notebooks: A Selection*, Oxford University Press, Oxford, 1981, p. 66.

10 'Cecil Budd' in David Jeremy, ed., *Dictionary of Business Biography*, 1, London, 1985.

11 The British Metal Corporation Limited. Report of the Proceedings at the Third Ordinary General Meeting, 16 March 1921, AMC Papers.

12 Chandos, *Memoirs*, p. 127: exchange of correspondence between P. Donald (Managing Director, Rownson, Drew & Clydesdale) and Sir Howard Frank (Chairman, Disposal Board), August 1923; Paul Bass to Messrs. Rownson, Drew & Clydesdale, August 1923, AMC Papers.

13 The British Metal Corporation Limited. Report of the Proceedings at the Third Ordinary General Meeting, 16 March 1921, AMC Papers.

14 BMC, Report of Ordinary General Meeting, 13 March 1924, AMC Papers.

15 'Richard Tilden Smith', *Dictionary of Business Biography*, v.

16 PSO (BT 15), Memorandum on Zinc, June 1928, SUPP3/69.

17 Chandos, *Memoirs*, p. 120.

18 Zara Steiner, *The Foreign Office and Foreign Policy, 1898–1914*, Cambridge, 1969, pp. 17–20.

19 Lord Cecil of Chelwood's Paris Diary, 23, 28 and 29 February 1919, CHE75, Hatfield House.

20 John Balfour, *Not Too Correct an Aureole: The Recollections of a Diplomat*, Salisbury, 1983, p. 15.

21 A. Lentin, *Guilt at Versailles: Lloyd George and the Pre-History of Appeasement*, London, 1985, p. 33.

22 Erik Goldstein, *Winning the Peace: British Diplomatic Strategy, Peace Planning and the Paris Peace*

Conference 1916–1920, Oxford, 1991, p. 110.

23 James Headlam-Morley, *A Memoir of the Paris Peace Conference 1919*, London, 1972, 25 January 1919.

24 Lord Riddell, *Intimate Diary of the Peace Conference and After 1918–1923*, London, 1933, 23 February 1919.

25 Headlam-Morley to Alfred Zimmern, 18 February 1919, *Paris Peace Conference 1919*.

26 Harold Macmillan to Lord Cranborne, 2 July 1919, Salisbury Papers.

27 Arno J. Mayer, *Politics and Diplomacy of Peacemaking: Containment and Counterrevolution at Versailles 1918–1919*, London, 1967, pp. 585–6.

28 Seth P. Tillman, *Anglo-American Relations at the Paris Peace Conference of 1919*, Princeton, NJ, 1961, p. 406.

29 Howard Elcock, *Portrait of a Decision: The Council of Four and the Treaty of Versailles*, London, 1972, pp. 280–82.

30 Mayer, *Politics and Diplomacy*, pp. 796–8.

31 Minutes of a Meeting of the British Empire Delegation at the Hôtel Majestic, Paris, on Friday, May 30, 1919, at 3 p.m. in Michael Dockrill, ed., *British Documents on Foreign Affairs*, Part II, Series I: *The Paris Peace Conference of 1919*, Frederick, Md, 1989.

32 Lentin, *Guilt*, p. 127.

33 Robert Skidelsky, *Oswald Mosley*, Macmillan, London, 1990, p. 96.

34 Sir Frank Walters to Cranborne, 29 December 1924, Salisbury Papers.

35 Cranborne to Cecil, 22 April 1922, Cecil of Chelwood Papers, British Library; Lady Moyra Cavendish to Cranborne, [1922], Salisbury Papers.

36 Lord Salisbury to Lord Cranborne, 12 September 1919, Salisbury Papers.

37 Balfour, *Aureole*, pp. 16–17.

38 Crookshank War Diary, 27 November 1917.

39 War Office to GOC, London District, 4 March 1921, Crookshank Papers.

40 Martin Gilbert, *Sir Horace Rumbold: Portrait of a Diplomat 1869–1941*, Heinemann, London, 1973, pp. 219–98.

41 Crookshank to Paul Emrys-Evans, 2 September 1922, Emrys-Evans Papers, British Library.

42 Peter Neville, *Appeasing Hitler: The Diplomacy of Sir Nevile Henderson 1937–39*, Basingstoke, 2000, pp. 1–10.

43 Rumbold on 4 January 1921 and 14 February 1922, cited in Gilbert, *Rumbold*.

44 Neville, *Henderson*, pp. 1–10.

45 Crookshank to Paul Evans, 26 September 1922, Emrys-Evans Papers.

46 Crookshank to Paul Evans, 3 October 1922, Emrys-Evans Papers.

47 Conference of Ministers: Minutes, 11 a.m. and 4 p.m., 28 September 1922, in Martin Gilbert, *Winston S. Churchill*, IV, Companion, Part III, Documents, *April 1921 to November 1922*, London, 1977.

48 Curzon to Rumbold, Tel. 441, 28 September 1922, in W. N. Medlicott, Douglas Dakin and M. E. Lambert, eds., *Documents on British Foreign Policy 1919–1939*, First Series, Volume XVIII: *Greece and Turkey, September 3, 1922 to July 24, 1923*, HMSO, London, 1972.

49 Crookshank to Paul Evans, 3 October 1922, Emrys-Evans Papers.

50 R. J. Q. Adams, *Bonar Law*, London, 1999, p. 318.

51 Crookshank to Paul Evans, 7 November 1922, Emrys-Evans Papers.

52 *The Nation*, 14 October 1922, reprinted in J. Ramsay MacDonald, *Wanderings and Excursions*, London, 1925, pp. 152–8.

53 David Marquand, *Ramsay MacDonald*, London, 1977, pp. 272–5.

54 Crookshank Diary, 14 July 1934, Bodleian Library, Oxford.

55 Crookshank to Paul Evans, 7 November 1922, Emrys-Evans Papers.

56 Crookshank to Paul Evans, 13 June 1923, Emrys-Evans Papers.

57 Crookshank to Paul Evans, 24 October 1923, Emrys-Evans Papers.

58 Jan Christian Smuts, 'South Africa Club Speech', 23 October 1923, in Jean Van der Poel, ed., *Selections from the Smuts Papers*, V: *September 1919 to November 1934*, Cambridge, 1973.

59 Crookshank to Paul Evans, 24 October 1923, Emrys-Evans Papers.

60 Macmillan, *Winds of Change*, p. 109.

61 Diary of 9th Duke of Devonshire, Chatsworth, Derbyshire, 29 January 1919. Subsequently referred to as Devonshire Diary.

62 Devonshire Diary, 6 February 1919.

63 Devonshire Diary, 18 April 1919.

64 Devonshire Diary, 26 July 1919.

65 Devonshire Diary, 2 January 1920.

66 Devonshire Diary, 7 December 1919.

67 Devonshire Diary, 26 December 1919.

68 Devonshire Diary, 6 January 1920.

69 Crawford, *Journals*, 19 June 1908.

70 Macmillan, *Winds of Change*, p. 113.

71 Devonshire Diary, 24 October 1922, 6 November 1922 and 6 March 1923.

72 Macmillan, *Winds of Change*, p. 129.

73 Ronald Hyam, *The Failure of South African Expansion 1908–1948*, London, 1972, pp. 47–71.

74 Robert Blake, *A History of Rhodesia*, London, 1977, pp. 189–91.

75 Devonshire Diary, 2 February 1923.

76 C. J. D. Duder, 'The Settler Response to the Indian Crisis of 1923 in Kenya: Brigadier General Philip Wheatley and "Direct Action"', *Journal of Imperial and Commonwealth History*, 17 (1989), pp. 349–73.

77 Elspeth Huxley, *White Man's Country: Lord Delamere and the Making of Kenya*, London, 1953, II, pp. 140–66.

78 Devonshire Diary, 16 November 1922.

79 Devonshire Diary, 24 April 1923.

80 Devonshire Diary, 30 October 1924.

81 Balfour, *Aureole*, p. 29.

82 Crookshank to Paul Evans, 28 March 1924, Emrys-Evans Papers.

83 Chris Cook, *The Age of Alignment: Electoral Politics in Britain, 1922–1929*, London, 1975, pp. 310–11.

84 Crookshank to Evans, 25 December 1924, Emrys-Evans Papers.

85 Simon Moore, 'The Agrarian Conservative Party in Parliament, 1920–29', *Parliamentary History*, 10 (1991), pp. 342–62.

86 Devonshire Diary, 29 October 1924.

87 Cook, *Age of Alignment*, pp. 310–11.

88 Crookshank to Paul Evans, 15 November 1924, Emrys-Evans Papers.

89 Crookshank to Paul Evans, 25 December 1924, Emrys-Evans Papers.

90 Duff Cooper to Diana Cooper, 16 December 1924, in Artemis Cooper, ed., *A Durable Fire: The Letters of Duff and Diana Cooper 1913–1950*, Collins, London, 1983.

91 Duff Cooper to Diana Cooper, 11 December 1924, Cooper, *Durable Fire*.

92 Parliamentary Debates, Commons, 15 December 1924.

93 Crookshank to Paul Evans, 25 December 1924, Emrys-Evans Papers.

94 Stuart Ball, ed., *Parliament and Politics in the Age of Baldwin and MacDonald: The Headlam Diaries, 1923 to 1935* (hereafter, Headlam, *Diaries*, 1), London, 15 December 1924.

95 Duff Cooper to Diana Cooper, 16 December 1924, *Durable Fire*.

96 Bridgeman, *Diaries*, July 1929, p. 225.

97 Parliamentary Debates, Commons, 11 March 1925.

98 Cook, *Age of Alignment*, pp. 310–11.

99 Headlam, *Diaries*, 1, 19 December 1927.

100 Quoted in John Stubbs, 'The Impact of the Great War on the Conservative Party', in Gillian Peele and Chris Cook, eds., *The Politics of Reappraisal 1918–1939*, London, 1975, p. 27.

101 Stuart Ball, 'The 1922 Committee: The Formative Years, 1922–1945',

Parliamentary History, 9 (1990), pp. 129–57.

102 Sanders, *Diaries*, 5 November 1917.

103 Andrew Roberts, '*The Holy Fox*': *A Biography of Lord Halifax*,London, 1991, pp. 12–13.

104 Macmillan–Butler correspondence, 1933, Butler Papers, Trinity College, Cambridge.

105 Headlam, *Diaries*, I, 16 December 1924.

106 Headlam, *Diaries*, I, 15 July 1925.

107 Parliamentary Debates, Commons, 6 March 1925.

108 Headlam, *Diaries*, I, 8 December 1925.

109 Robert Rhodes James, *Bob Boothby: A Portrait*, London, 1991, pp. 64–8.

110 John Ramsden, *An Appetite for Power: A History of the Conservative Party since 1830*, London, 1998, pp. 264–5.

111 Macmillan, *Winds of Change*, p. 223.

112 Macmillan to C. W. G. Eady, 28 January 1927, Macmillan Constituency Correspondence, Bodleian Libray, Oxford.

113 Headlam, *Diaries*, I, 7 December 1926.

114 Bridgeman to Baldwin, 10 January 1927, quoted in Bridgeman, *Diaries*, p. 202.

115 Martin Gilbert, ed., *Winston S. Churchill*, v *Companion*, Part 1, *Documents: The Exchequer Years, 1922–1929*, London, 1979, Cabinet Memorandum by Winston Churchill, 12 December 1927.

116 Neville Chamberlain to Lord Irwin, 25 December 1927, *Exchequer Years*.

117 Churchill to P. J. Grigg, 21 December 1927, *Exchequer Years*.

118 Macmillan to Churchill, 1 January 1928, *Exchequer Years*.

119 Churchill to Baldwin, 5 January 1928, *Exchequer Years*.

120 Churchill to Macmillan, 15 January 1928, *Exchequer Years*.

121 Grigg to Churchill, 6 March 1928, *Exchequer Years*.

122 Baldwin to King George VI, 24 April 1928, *Exchequer Years*.

123 Macmillan to Lord Cecil, 8 November 1928, Cecil of Chelwood Papers.

124 Macmillan to Cranborne, 27 January 1928, Macmillan Constituency Correspondence; Macmillan to Cranborne, 30 January 1928, Salisbury Papers.

125 Crookshank to Paul Evans, 25 December 1924, Emrys-Evans Papers.

126 Mary Herbert to Cranborne, n.d., Salisbury Papers.

127 Raymond Greene to Cranborne, 23 July 1924, Salisbury Papers.

128 Cranborne to Foa, 10 June 1924, Salisbury Papers.

129 Edward H. King to Cranborne, 11 January 1927, Salisbury Papers.

130 BMC, Report of Ordinary General Meeting, 12 March 1925, AMC Papers.

131 BMC, Report of Ordinary General Meeting, 11 March 1926; BMC, Report of Ordinary General Meeting, 10 March 1927, AMC Papers; Chandos, *Memoirs*, pp. 129–30.

132 BMC, Report of Ordinary General Meeting, 13 March 1930, AMC Papers.

133 Chandos, *Memoirs*, p. 132; PSO (BT) 147, June 1932, SUPP3/76; Francis L. Coleman, *The Northern Rhodesia Copperbelt: Technological Development up to the End of the Central African Federation*, Manchester, 1971, pp. 27–77.

134 Board of Trade *v.* Henry Gardner, Extract of Judgement of Lord Chief Justice, 30 May 1919, AMC Papers.

135 Agreement in Principle, 23 July 1929, AMC Papers; AMC, 3rd Meeting of Directors, 31 December 1929, AMC Papers; AMC, Meeting of Directors, 11 March 1931, AMC Papers; Review of AMC activities in 1934, AMC Papers; Henry Gardner's evidence to Zinc Committee, SUPP3/7.

136 *Manchester Guardian Commercial*, 16 October 1930.

137 John Hillman, 'Malaya and the International Tin Cartel', *Modern Asian Studies*, 22 (1988), p. 256; Agreement for appointment of Captain Lyttelton as Managing Director of British Tin Investment

Corporation Ltd., 31 August 1932, AMC Papers.

138 Clauson minute, 15 May 1938, CO852/139, quoted in Hillman, 'Malaya', fn. 76.

139 COS 158, 11 June 1929, SUPP3/69; PSO (BT) 218, March 1934, PSO (BT) 219, March 1934, SUPP3/79; PSO (BT) 272, July 1935, SUPP3/31; PSO (BT) 318, [1936], SUPP3/84.

140 *The Economist*, 27 May 1933.

141 *Joint Stock Companies Journal*, 25 April 1934.

142 George Herbert to Cranborne, 27 May 1927, and Lord Sackville to Cranborne, 7 October 1927, Salisbury Papers.

143 Crawford, *Journals*, 1 August 1928.

144 Lady Salisbury to Macmillan, 31 May 1929, Macmillan Constituency Correspondence.

145 Crookshank to Macmillan, [1929], Macmillan Constituency Correspondence.

146 Macmillan to Terence O'Connor, 13 July 1929, Macmillan Constituency Correspondence.

147 Terence O'Connor to Macmillan, 15 July 1929, Macmillan Constituency Correspondence and Headlam, *Diaries*, 1, 18 July 1929.

148 Meeting of ex-MPs, 19 July 1929, Macmillan Constituency Correspondence.

149 Moore-Brabazon to Baldwin, 23 July 1929, Macmillan Constituency Correspondence.

150 Baldwin to Moore-Brabazon, 26 July 1929, Macmillan Constituency Correspondence.

151 Macmillan to Colin Coote, 9 August 1929, Macmillan Constituency Correspondence.

152 Headlam, *Diaries*, 1, 5 December 1929.

153 Martin Gilbert, ed., *Winston S. Churchill*, v *Companion*, Part II *Documents: The Wilderness Years*, London, 1981, Churchill to Salisbury, 13 May 1933.

154 Stanley Baldwin to Lady Lytton, 7 December 1929, quoted in Lord

Lytton, *Antony: A Record of Youth*, London, 1935, pp. 307–8.

155 Macmillan to Sir Charles Heaton-Ellis, 2 December 1929, Macmillan Constituency Correspondence.

156 Macmillan to Sir Albert Bennett, 9 December 1929, Macmillan Constituency Correspondence.

157 Bridgeman, *Diaries*, July 1929.

158 Rhodes James, *Boothby*, p. 114.

159 David Gilmour, *Curzon*, 1994, pp. 104–5; Oliver Lyttelton to Didi Lyttelton, [Winter 1914], CHAN 1, 8/1.

160 Duff to Diana Cooper, 1 and 17 February 1926, *Durable Fire*.

161 Stephen Ward, 'Great Britain: Land Fit for Heroes Lost', in S. R. Ward, *The War Generation: Veterans of the First World War*, Port Washington, 1975, pp. 10–37.

162 Oswald Mosley, 'What I Am Fighting For', *Sunday Express*, 25 May 1930, quoted in Skidelsky, *Mosley*, pp. 225–6.

163 Skidelsky, *Mosley*, p. 224.

164 Philip Williamson, *National Crisis and National Government: British Politics, the Economy and Empire*, Cambridge, 1992, pp. 147–8.

165 Lady Moyra Cavendish to Lord Cranborne, 31 May 1930, Salisbury Papers.

166 Macmillan to Cecil of Chelwood, 8 November 1929, Cecil Papers.

167 Harold Nicolson, *Diaries and Letters, 1930–1964*, London, 1996, 2 July 1930.

168 Nicolson, *Diaries*, 15 February 1931.

169 Bridgeman to Davidson, 2 November 1930, Robert Rhodes James, ed., *Memoirs of a Conservative: J. C. C. Davidson's Memoirs and Papers, 1910–1937*, London, 1969.

170 Nicolson, *Diaries*, 30 November 1930.

171 Williamson, *National Crisis*, pp. 147–8.

172 Nicolson, *Diaries*, 30 May 1931.

173 Headlam, *Diaries*, 1, 22 May 1930.

174 Headlam, *Diaries*, 1, 3 January 1931.

175 Macmillan to Sir Charles

Heaton-Ellis, 2 April 1931, Macmillan Constituency Correspondence, c. 141.

176 Lord Cranborne, 'The Future of Democracy', in *Quarterly Review*, 511 (January 1932), p. 169.

177 Gilbert Murray to Macmillan, 2 June 1929, Macmillan Constituency Correspondence, c. 65.

178 H. Crookshank, 'The Jamborees Compared', article for the *National Review*, 1 September 1929, Crookshank MSS., Bodleian Library, Oxford.

179 Profile of Crookshank in the *Yorkshire Post*, 13 October 1930.

180 Headlam, *Diaries*, 1, 22 May 1930.

181 Rally at Aisthorpe Hall, 6 June 1931, Crookshank Papers.

182 Robert C. Self, ed., *The Austen Chamberlain Diary Letters: The Correspondence of Austen Chamberlain with his Sisters Hilda and Ida, 1916–1937*, London, 1995, pp. 377–83.

183 Headlam, *Diaries*, 1, 18 April 1932.

184 Headlam, *Diaries*, 1, 10 December 1929.

185 Gillian Peele, 'Revolt over India', in Peele and Cook, *Reappraisal*, pp. 114–45.

186 Stanley Baldwin to J. C. C. Davidson, 15 December 1930, Davidson, *Memoirs and Papers*.

187 Winston Churchill to Clemmie Churchill, 13 April 1935, *Wilderness Years*.

188 Cranborne to J. C. C. Davidson, [1932], Salisbury Papers.

189 John Murray to Cranborne, 14 December 1931, Salisbury Papers.

190 Lord Cranborne, 'Conservatism and the National Government', in *Quarterly Review*, 513 (July 1932), pp. 160–77.

191 Cranborne, 'Democracy', pp. 167–85.

192 Philip Goodhart and Ursula Branston, *The 1922: The Story of the Conservative Backbenchers' Parliamentary Committee*, London, 1973, pp. 47–62.

193 Stuart Ball, 'The 1922 Committee: The Formative Years, 1922–1945', *Parliamentary History*, 9 (1990), pp. 129–57.

194 Parliamentary Debates, Commons, 13 December 1933.

195 Sir John Simon to Cranborne, 1 November 1933, Salisbury Papers.

196 Austen Chamberlain to Ida Chamberlain, 28 February 1932, Chamberlain, *Diary Letters*.

197 Austen Chamberlain to Hilda Chamberlain, 17 July 1932, Chamberlain, *Diary Letters*.

198 Donald S. Birn, *The League of Nations Union 1918–1945*, Oxford, 1981, pp. 142–54.

199 Gilbert Murray to Austen Chamberlain, 21 July 1934, Austen Chamberlain Papers, Birmingham University Library, AC40/6.

200 Cranborne to Cecil, 19 July 1934, Cecil Papers.

201 Cranborne to Austen Chamberlain, 19 July 1934, AC40/6.

202 Cranborne to Cecil, November 1934, Salisbury Papers.

203 Headlam, *Diaries*, 1, 1 June 1933.

204 Headlam, *Diaries*, 1, 9–10 April 1932.

205 Williamson, *National Crisis*, pp. 469–78.

206 Daniel Ritschel, *The Politics of Planning: The Debate on Economic Planning in Britain in the 1930s*, Oxford, 1997, pp. 193–4, 204–7.

207 Headlam, *Diaries*, 1, 1 March 1934.

208 Headlam, *Diaries*, 1, 11 March 1934.

209 Cranborne–Macmillan, miscellaneous correspondence, Salisbury Papers.

210 Devonshire Diary, 17 August 1924.

211 Chandos, *Memoirs*, p. 291.

212 Devonshire Diary, 21 November 1924.

213 'Pratt's' in Charles Graves (foreword by P. G. Wodehouse), *Leather Armchairs: The Chivas Regal Book of London Clubs*, London, 1963.

214 Crookshank Diary, 20 March 1940.

215 Eddie Hartington to Harold Macmillan, 1 June 1929, Macmillan Constituency Correspondence, c. 65.

216 Macmillan, 'Foreword', Madan, *Notebooks*; Geoffrey Madan to Harold Macmillan, 5 January 1927, Macmillan Constituency Correspondence, c. 53.

217 Jonathan Ruffer, *The Big Shots: Edwardian Shooting Parties*, London, 1998 edn, pp. 144–5.

Chapter 4: Anti-fascists

1 Richard Griffiths, *Patriotism Perverted: Captain Ramsay, the Right Club and British Anti-Semitism, 1939–40*, Constable, London, 1998.

2 Crookshank Diary, 10 July 1934.

3 Crawford, *Journals*, 13 February 1935.

4 Ian Harvey, *To Fall Like Lucifer*, Sidgwick & Jackson, London, 1971, p. 61.

5 Cranborne minute on a note by Roger Makins, 22 April 1936, quoted in A. J. Sherman, *Island Refuge: Britain and Refugees from the Third Reich 1933–1939*, London, 1994, p. 71.

6 Sherman, *Refuge*, pp. 55–6 and 81.

7 Cranborne to Eden, 29 October 1939 [this date seems dubious], AP14/1.

8 Henry Gardner, *A Statement* (For Private Circulation Only), 1917, p. 2, AMC Papers.

9 *The Globe*, 21 October 1915.

10 'Metals for Munitions – Some Facts', Supplement to the *Metal Bulletin*, 11 December 1917.

11 *The Globe*, 21 October 1915.

12 Exchange of Merton Shares held by Germans against German Shares and other Securities held by British Subjects: Conference held at The Hague, 7 and 8 February 1916, AMC Papers.

13 Report of the Imperial Resources Board Committee, 30 July 1917, SUPP3/56.

14 *Morning Post*, 4 December 1917; *The Ironmonger*, 8 December 1917.

15 Sir Woodburn Kirby to Merton's Shareholders, 9 March 1920, AMC Papers.

16 PSO (BT 11), April 1928, SUPP3/69.

17 BMC, Report of Ordinary General Meeting, 10 March 1927, AMC Papers.

18 BMC, Report of Ordinary General Meeting, 15 March 1928, AMC Papers.

19 *The Statist*, 18 February 1928.

20 AMC, Meetings of Directors, 12 March 1930, 9 April 1930, 9 July 1930, AMC Papers.

21 AMC, Meeting of Directors, 16 May 1930, AMC Papers.

22 Extract from Protocol of Exchange of Shares Agreement between AMC and Metallgesellschaft dated 21 May 1930, AMC Papers.

23 AMC, Meetings of Directors, 13 August 1930 and 12 November 1930, AMC Papers.

24 *Manchester Guardian Commercial*, 16 October 1930.

25 *Berliner Tageblatt*, 29 May 1930.

26 Chandos, *Memoirs*, p. 133.

27 Minutes of AMC Board, 13 April 1938, AMC Papers.

28 Address at West London Synagogue, 10 June 1963, CHAN 11, 4/17.

29 Based on the reports of the British Consul-General in Frankfurt, A. F. Dowden, quoted in Anthony Read and David Fisher, *Kristallnacht: Unleashing the Holocaust*, London, 1989, pp. 101–4.

30 Sherman, *Island Refuge*, pp. 173–7.

31 Oliver Lyttelton to Isaiah Berlin, 4 July 1950, quoted in Michael Ignatieff, *Isaiah Berlin: A Life*, London, 1998, p. 176. I owe this reference to my father, E. R. Ball.

32 Address at West London Synagogue, 10 June 1963, CHAN 11, 4/17.

33 Cranborne to Emrys-Evans, 24 February 1938, Emrys-Evans Papers.

34 Obolensky, *One Man*, p. 98.

35 Lord Salisbury to Anthony Eden, 21 May 1963, AP23/60.

36 Crawford, *Journals*, 2 November 1938.

37 Andrew Best and John Sandwich, eds., *Hinch: A Celebration of Viscount Hinchingbrooke, MP, 1906–1995*, Beaminster, 1997, Hinchingbrooke, *Journal*, 19 June 1938.

38 Cranborne to Sir Samuel Hoare, 23 November 1935, Salisbury Papers.

39 Sir Samuel Hoare to Lord Cranborne, 29 November 1935, Salisbury Papers.

40 Cranborne Diary, 24 March 1935, Salisbury Papers.

41 Cranborne Diary, 25 and 26 March 1935, Salisbury Papers; David Dutton, *Anthony Eden: A Life and Reputation*, London 1997, p. 41.

42 Quoted in Robert Rhodes James, *Anthony Eden*, London, 1986, p. 144.

43 Cranborne Diary, 1 April 1935, Salisbury Papers.

44 Cranborne to Lord Cecil of Chelwood, 16 September 1935, Salisbury Papers.

45 The phrase 'two Kings of Brentford' was coined by Winston Churchill in a parliamentary debate, 11 July 1935.

46 Headlam, *Diaries*, 1, 30 April, 2 May and 9 May 1935; Austen Chamberlain to Ida Chamberlain, 11 May 1935, *Diary Letters*.

47 Hoare to Neville Chamberlain, 18 August 1935, quoted in Dutton, *Eden*, p. 49.

48 Cranborne Diary, 10 September 1935, Salisbury Papers.

49 John Barnes and David Nicholson, eds., *The Empire at Bay: The Leo Amery Diaries, 1929–1945*, London, 1988, 24 September 1935.

50 Hoare to Eden, 16 October 1935, quoted in David Carlton, *Anthony Eden*, London, 1981, pp. 67–8.

51 Eden minute, 26 November 1935, quoted in Richard Lamb, *The Drift to War, 1922–1939*, London, 1989, p. 152.

52 Churchill to Cranborne, 8 April 1936, and Cranborne to Churchill, 17 April 1936, in Martin Gilbert, ed., *Winston S. Churchill*, v Companion: *1936–39*, London, 1981.

53 *The Times*, 18 December 1935.

54 Corbin to Flandin, 6 March 1936, quoted in Martin Thomas, *Britain, France and Appeasement: Anglo-French Relations in the Popular Front Era*, Oxford, 1996.

55 Vansittart to Eden, 14 October 1935, quoted in Michael Roi, *Alternative to Appeasement: Sir Robert Vansittart and Alliance Diplomacy, 1934–1937*, New York, 1997, p. 101.

56 Cranborne Diary, 7 and 8 September 1935, Salisbury Papers.

57 Hinchingbrooke, *Journal*, 8 December 1938.

58 Cranborne minute, 27 January 1936, quoted in Lamb, *Drift to War*, pp. 166–7.

59 Nicolson, *Diaries*, 13 February 1936.

60 Lamb, *Drift to War*, p. 170.

61 Cranborne memorandum, March 1936, FO800/296.

62 Chamberlain to Flandin, 29 January 1936, quoted in Gustav Schmidt, *The Politics and Economics of Appeasement: British Foreign Policy in the 1930s*, Leamington Spa, 1986, p. 201.

63 Nicolson, *Diaries*, 9 March 1936.

64 Cranborne to Eden, 16 June 1936, quoted in Dutton, *Eden*, p. 103.

65 Robert Rhodes James, *Victor Cazalet: A Portrait*, Hamish Hamilton, London, 1976, Cazalet Journal, 17 March 1936.

66 Nicholas Crowson, ed., *Fleet Street, Press Barons and Politics: The Journals of Collin Brooks, 1932–1940*, Cambridge, 1998, 5 June 1936.

67 Lamb, *Drift to War*, p. 192.

68 Cazalet Journal, 21 June 1936.

69 Cranborne to Eden, 16 September 1936, FO954/8.

70 Cranborne Diary, 6 March 1938, Salisbury Papers.

71 Interview with Norman Davis, 20 April 1937, FO800/296.

72 Neville Chamberlain to Benito Mussolini, 27 July 1937, quoted in Lamb, *Drift to War*, pp. 205–6.

73 Quoted in John Lukacs, *Five Days in London: May 1940*, New Haven, Conn., 1999, p. 58.

74 Ian Colvin, *Vansittart in Office*, London, 1965, p. 191.

75 Richard Cockett, *Twilight of Truth: Chamberlain, Appeasement and the Manipulation of the Press*, London, 1989, pp. 9–12.

76 Joseph Ball to Neville Chamberlain, 21 February 1938, quoted in Cockett, *Twilight*, p. 51.

77 J. P. L. Thomas to Cranborne, 3 June 1943, Salisbury Papers.

78 William C. Mills, 'Sir Joseph Ball, Adrian Dingli and Neville Chamberlain's "Secret Channel" to Italy, 1937–1940', *International History Review*, 24 (2002), pp. 278–317.

79 Jim Thomas to Joseph Ball, 26 July 1937, Cilcennin Papers, Carmarthen Record Office.

80 John Harvey, ed., *The Diplomatic Diaries of Oliver Harvey, 1937–1940*, London, 1970 (hereafter, Harvey, *Diaries*, I), 12 February 1938.

81 Harvey, *Diaries*, I, 17 October 1937.

82 Harvey, *Diaries*, I, 11 November 1937.

83 Harvey, *Diaries*, I, 7 November 1937.

84 Neville Chamberlain to Hilda Chamberlain, 24 October 1937, quoted in Carlton, *Eden*, pp. 111–12.

85 Roi, *Vansittart*, p. 158.

86 Cranborne to Eden, 12 November 1936, FO800/296.

87 Cranborne to Eden, 30 August 1937, FO800/296.

88 J. P. L. Thomas to Cranborne, 3 February 1943, Salisbury Papers.

89 Cranborne to W. S. Morrison, 23 February 1938, Salisbury Papers.

90 Harvey, *Diaries*, I, 7 November 1937.

91 Colvin, *Vansittart*, p. 183.

92 Harvey, *Diaries*, I, 15 January 1938.

93 Memorandum of events leading up to Anthony Eden's resignation by Lord Cranborne, in circulation by 1943 but written some time previously, Salisbury Papers.

94 Harvey, *Diaries*, I, 17 January 1938.

95 J. P. L. Thomas to Cranborne, Salisbury Papers, 3 June 1943.

96 J. P. L. Thomas to Cranborne, 3 June 1943, Salisbury Papers.

97 J. P. L. Thomas to Cranborne, 3 June 1943, Salisbury Papers.

98 Harvey, *Diaries*, I, 24 January 1938.

99 Harvey, *Diaries*, I, 20 January 1938.

100 Cranborne to Eden, 4 February 1938, Salisbury Papers.

101 Harvey, *Diaries*, I, 19–23 December 1937.

102 Cranborne to W. S. Morrison, 23 February 1938, Salisbury Papers.

103 Harvey, *Diaries*, I, 19 February 1938.

104 Nicolson, *Diaries*, 21 February 1938.

105 Halifax account quoted in Dutton, *Eden*, p. 106.

106 Harvey, *Diaries*, I, 20 February 1938.

107 Nicolson, *Diaries*, 21 February 1938.

108 Nicolson, *Diaries*, 21 February 1938.

109 Harvey, *Diaries*, I, 21 February 1938.

110 House of Commons, Debates, Personal Explanation by Lord Cranborne, 21 February 1938.

111 Amery, *Diaries*, 21 February 1938.

112 Paul Emrys-Evans, Memo for Anthony Eden [1961], Emrys-Evans Papers.

113 Cranborne to Emrys-Evans, 7 February 1938, Emrys-Evans Papers.

114 Walter Elliot to Baffy Dugdale, 22 February 1938, quoted in Colin Coote, *A Companion of Honour: The Story of Walter Elliot*, London, 1965, p. 156.

115 Harvey, *Diaries*, I, 22 February 1938; Cranborne to W. S. Morrison, 23 February 1938, Salisbury Papers.

116 Harvey, *Diaries*, I, 27 February 1938.

117 Headlam, *Diaries*, II, 14 July 1942 and Duff to Diana Cooper, 14 September 1938, *Durable Fire*.

118 Headlam, *Diaries*, I, 6 February 1935.

119 Austen Chamberlain to Hilda Chamberlain, 22 December 1935, *Diary Letters*.

120 Robert Rhodes James, ed., *Chips: The Diaries of Sir Henry Channon*, London, 1967, 16 September 1939.

121 Headlam, *Diaries*, II, 22 and 23 January 1938.

122 Barry Supple, *The History of the British Coal Industry*, IV: *1913–1946: The Political Economy of Decline*, Clarendon Press, Oxford, 1987, pp. 271–358.

123 Crookshank Diary, 10 November 1937.

124 Cockett, *Twilight*, pp. 91–3.

125 Crookshank Diary, 14 March 1936; Address to Gainsborough Annual Meeting, 1937, Crookshank MSS.

126 Crookshank Diary, 21 February 1938.

127 Harvey, *Diaries*, I, 21 February 1938.
128 N. Smart, ed., *The Diaries and Letters of Robert Bernays, 1932–1939: An Insider's Account of the House of Commons*, Lampeter: NY, 1996.
129 Amery, *Diaries*, 22 February 1938.
130 Crookshank Diary, 24 February 1938.
131 Harvey, *Diaries*, I, 25 February 1938.
132 Channon, *Diaries*, 24 February 1938.
133 Harvey, *Diaries*, I, 26 February 1938.
134 Cranborne to W. S. Morrison, 23 February 1938, Salisbury Papers.
135 Cranborne to R. A. Butler, 25 February 1938, RAB B11.
136 Headlam, *Diaries*, I, 1 August 1934.
137 Record of Proceedings of Meeting of Committee on Relations between Industry and the State, 25 October 1934, quoted in Ritschel, *Politics of Planning*.
138 Headlam, *Diaries*, II, 31 May 1936.
139 Headlam, *Diaries*, I, 1 August 1935.
140 *New Outlook*, February 1937, quoted in Ritschel, *Politics of Planning*.
141 Clifford Allen to R. C. Davidson, 6 February 1937, quoted in Ritschel, *Politics of Planning*.
142 Macmillan to Lloyd George, 16 January 1937, quoted in Ritschel, *Politics of Planning*.
143 Quoted in Max Egremont, *Under Two Flags: The Life of Major-General Sir Edward Spears*, London, 1997, p. 137.
144 Minutes of December Club, 19 May 1936, Macmillan Constituency Correspondence.
145 Crawford, *Journals*, 2 November 1938.

Chapter 5: Glamour Boys

1 House of Commons, Debates, Personal Explanation by Lord Cranborne, 21 February 1938; Patrick to Eden, 15 March 1938, Salisbury Papers.
2 Cazalet to Baldwin, 24 February 1938, Rhodes James, *Cazalet*; Amery, *Diaries*, 24 February 1938; Nicolson, *Diaries*, 25 February 1938.
3 Harry Crookshank, Notes for Speech in Lincoln, April 1938, Crookshank MSS.
4 Minutes of a meeting between Lord Cranborne and the Spanish Ambassador, 9 November 1936, quoted in Douglas Little, *Malevolent Neutrality: The United States, Great Britain and the Origins of the Spanish Civil War*, Ithaca, NY, 1985, pp. 254–5; Gerald Howson, *Arms for Spain: The Untold Story of the Spanish Civil War*, London, 1998, p. 231; Jill Edwards, *The British Government and the Spanish Civil War, 1936–1939*, London, 1979, pp. 95–6.
5 Patrick to Cranborne, 16 March 1938, Cilcennin Papers.
6 Lord Cranborne's Diary, 4–11 March 1938, 5 March 1938, Salisbury Papers.
7 Sir Timothy Eden to Cranborne, 6 March 1938, Salisbury Papers.
8 Mark Patrick to Cranborne, 16 March 1938, Cilcennin Papers.
9 Mark Patrick to Eden (copy to Cranborne), 15 March 1938, Salisbury Papers.
10 Channon, *Diaries*, 17 March 1938.
11 Channon, *Diaries*, 21 March 1938.
12 Patrick to Cranborne, 16 March 1938, Cilcennin Papers.
13 Rhodes James, *Cazalet*, p. 201.
14 Cranborne to Eden, 13 April 1938, AP14/1.
15 Cranborne to Paul Emrys-Evans, 21 April 1938, Emrys-Evans Papers.
16 Cranborne to Lord Cecil, 23 April 1938, Cecil Papers.
17 Cranborne to Eden, 3 May 1938, AP14/1.
18 Harvey, *Diaries*, I, 19 May 1938.
19 Karl-Heinz Abshagen, *King, Lords and Gentlemen: Influence and Power of the English Upper Classes*, London, translation of German edition published in Stuttgart in 1938, 1939.
20 Harvey, *Diaries*, I, 7 June 1938.
21 Harvey, *Diaries*, I, 20 June 1938.
22 Eden to Cranborne, 8 June 1938, AP14/1.
23 Hinchingbrooke, *Journal*, 19 June 1938.

24 Harvey, *Diaries*, I, 7 June 1938.
25 Cranborne to Anthony Eden, 15 August 1938, AP14/1.
26 Duff to Diana Cooper, 9 September 1938, *Durable Fire*.
27 Donald Cameron Watt, *How War Came*, London, 1989, pp. 26–8.
28 Cranborne to Eden, 27 September 1936, FO800/296.
29 Cranborne to Walter Monckton, 21 September 1938, Salisbury Papers.
30 Cranborne to Cecil, 25 September 1938, Cecil Papers.
31 Nicolson, *Diaries*, 29 September 1938.
32 Harvey, *Diaries*, I, 22 April 1938.
33 Crookshank Diary, 10 April 1938.
34 Crookshank Diary, 20 June 1938.
35 Crookshank Diary, 19 July 1938.
36 Crookshank Diary, 28 July 1938.
37 Harvey, *Diaries*, I, 19 June 1938.
38 Crookshank Diary, 15 September 1938.
39 Crookshank Diary, 16 September 1938.
40 Crookshank Diary, 28 September 1938.
41 Crookshank Diary, 30 September 1938.
42 Crookshank Diary, 1 October 1938.
43 Crookshank Diary, 1 October 1938.
44 Crookshank Diary, 3 October 1938.
45 Harvey, *Diaries*, I, 11 October 1938.
46 House of Commons, Debates, 4 October 1938.
47 House of Commons, Debates, 4 October 1938.
48 Harvey, *Diaries*, I, 11 October 1938.
49 Cranborne to Eden, 9 October 1938, AP14/1. The manuscript has 9 September and is often quoted as being of this date (see, for example, Dutton, *Eden*, p. 125). The similarity in wording with a letter sent to Jim Thomas on 8 October and the context strongly suggest an emendation to 9 October.
50 Cranborne to Thomas, 8 October 1938, Cilcennin Papers.
51 Crookshank to Emrys-Evans, 21 October 1938, Emrys-Evans Papers.
52 Rhodes James, *Boothby*, pp. 187–8.
53 Quoted in Geoffrey Lewis, *Lord Hailsham: A Life*, London, 1997, p. 56.
54 Quoted in N. J. Crowson, 'Much Ado about Nothing: Macmillan and Appeasement', in Richard Aldous and Sabine Lee, eds., *Harold Macmillan: Aspects of a Political Life*, Basingstoke, 1999, p. 69.
55 Cranborne to Cecil, 16 October 1938, Cecil Papers.
56 Cranborne to Thomas, 30 October 1938, Salisbury Papers.
57 Macmillan, *Winds of Change*, pp. 568–9; Hugh Dalton, *The Fateful Years*, London, 1957, pp. 199–210.
58 Crookshank Diary, 4 October 1938.
59 Crookshank Diary, 6 October 1938.
60 Crookshank Diary, 5 October 1938.
61 Harvey, *Diaries*, I, 16 October and 25 December 1938; Hinchingbrooke, *Journal*, 8 December 1938.
62 Headlam, *Diaries*, II, 30 November 1938.
63 Harry Crookshank, Draft Resignation Speech, October 1938, Crookshank MSS.
64 Harry Crookshank, Constituency Speech, October 1938, Crookshank MSS.
65 Amery, *Diaries*, 8 November 1938.
66 Harold Nicolson to Vita Sackville-West, 9 November 1938, *Diaries*.
67 Harvey, *Diaries*, 8 October 1938.
68 Harold Nicolson to Vita Sackville-West, 11 November 1938, *Diaries*.
69 Crookshank Diary, 14 December 1938.
70 Crookshank Diary, 2 November 1938.
71 Crookshank Diary, 3 November 1938.
72 Crookshank Diary, 28 January 1938.
73 J. C. C. Davidson to Hamar Greenwood, 19 December 1938, Davidson, *Memoirs and Papers*.
74 Cranborne to Jim Thomas, n.d. [1938], Cilcennin Papers.
75 Crookshank Diary, 12 December 1938.
76 Hore Belisha's Account of Junior Ministers' Revolt, 19 December 1938, Hore Belisha Papers, Churchill College, Cambridge, HOBE5/42.
77 Crookshank Diary, 13 December 1938.
78 Crookshank Diary, 14 December 1938.
79 Headlam, *Diaries*, II, 20 December 1938.

80 *Evening Standard*, 19 December 1938.
81 Hore Belisha's Account of Junior Ministers' Revolt, 21 December 1938, HOBE5/42.
82 Crookshank Diary, 14 December 1938.
83 Harvey, *Diaries*, 1, 14 and 20 January 1939.
84 Cranborne to Emrys-Evans, 27 January 1939, Emrys-Evans Papers.
85 Harvey, *Diaries*, 9 March 1939; Emrys-Evans, *Memoirs*, Emrys-Evans Papers.
86 Harvey, *Diaries*, 22 February 1939.
87 Cranborne to Eden, 21 February 1939, AP14/2.
88 Hinchingbrooke, *Journal*, 8 December 1938.
89 Cranborne to Eden, 10 March 1939, AP14/2.
90 Harvey, *Diaries*, 1, 10 March 1939.
91 Eden to Cranborne, 13 March 1939, AP14/2.
92 Cranborne to Eden, 22 March 1939, AP14/2.
93 Nicolson, *Diaries*, 11 April 1939.
94 Crookshank Diary, 20 April 1939.
95 Crookshank Diary, 24 April 1939.
96 G. C. Peden, *British Rearmament and the Treasury, 1932–1939*, Edinburgh, 1979, p. 50.
97 Cranborne to Eden, 21 April 1939, AP14/2.
98 Cranborne to Emrys-Evans, 27 June 1939, Emrys-Evans Papers.
99 Hinchingbrooke, *Journal*, 19 June 1938.
100 Macmillan to Cranborne, 13 August 1939, Salisbury Papers.
101 Cockett, *Twilight*, p. 115; Cranborne to Jim Thomas, 8 August 1939, Cilcennin Papers.
102 Cranborne to Eden, 26 June 1939, AP14/2.
103 Crawford, *Journals*, 18 April 1939.
104 Rose, *Later Cecils*, pp. 48–110.
105 Cranborne to Jim Thomas, 5 July 1939, Cilcennin Papers.
106 Cranborne to Eden, 13 July 1939, AP14/2.
107 Cranborne to Jim Thomas, 8 August 1939, Cilcennin Papers.
108 Cranborne to Eden, 16 July 1939, AP14/2.
109 Eden to Cranborne, 12 August 1939, AP14/2.
110 Cranborne to Eden, 17 August 1939, AP14/2.
111 Cranborne to R. A. Butler, 20 October 1939, Salisbury Papers.
112 Cranborne to Jim Thomas, 9 December 1939, Cilcennin Papers.
113 Jim Thomas to Paul Emrys-Evans, 22 December 1939, Emrys-Evans Papers.
114 Harold Macmillan to Lady Salisbury, 29 March 1940, Macmillan Constituency Correspondence.
115 Anthony Eden to Paul Evans, 21 March 1940, Emrys-Evans Papers.
116 Nicolson, *Diaries*, 3 April 1940.
117 Dick Law to Paul Evans, 1 April 1940, Emrys-Evans Papers.
118 Jubie Lancaster to Cranborne, 4 April 1940, Salisbury Papers.
119 Harvey, *Diaries*, 1, 30 March 1940.
120 Cranborne to Emrys-Evans, 2 April 1940, Emrys-Evans Papers.
121 Crookshank Diary, 26 August, 20 October, 30 October 1939.
122 Headlam, *Diaries*, 11, 23 October 1939.
123 Crookshank Diary, 17 October 1939, 14 November 1939, 4 January 1940.
124 Crookshank Diary, 5 January 1940.
125 Crookshank Diary, 9 January 1940.
126 Harvey, *Diaries*, 1, 4 January 1939; Crookshank Diary, 4 April 1940.
127 Kenneth Young, ed., *The Diaries of Sir Robert Bruce Lockhart*, 2 vols., London, 1973 and 1980, 11, 2 May 1940.
128 PSO 407, 19 December 1933, SUPP3/79.
129 ZI 11. Report by CID Sub-committee on Zinc Exports, 6 December 1937, SUPP3/7.
130 Notes on the Appointment of the Controller-designate for Non-ferrous Metals and Aluminium, 19 September 1939, SUPP14/626.
131 PSO (BT) 377, December 1937, SUPP3/87.
132 PSO (BT) 388, December 1937, SUPP3/88.

133 Minute by C. J. Pyne (Industry and Manufactures Department), 17 May 1938, SUPP3/56.

134 Minute SO 314/59, 8 February 1939, SUPP3/56.

135 Leslie Burgin to Sir Arthur Robinson, 21 July 1939, SUPP14/624.

136 Minutes of AMC Board, 22 November 1939, and Minutes of AMC Board, 1 April 1940, AMC Papers.

137 Statutory Rules and Orders 1939, No. 997, 1 September 1939.

138 Notes on the Appointment of the Controller-designate for Non-ferrous Metals and Aluminium, 19 September 1939, SUPP14/626.

139 Minutes of AMC Board, 22 November 1940, AMC Papers.

140 Euan Wallace Diary, Bodleian Library, Oxford, 21 December 1939.

141 Cranborne to Thomas, 29 September 1939, Cilcennin Papers.

142 Cranborne to Thomas, 9 December 1939, Cilcennin Papers.

143 Nicolson, *Diaries*, 3 April 1940.

144 Oliver Stanley to Harold Macmillan, n.d. [March 1940], Macmillan Constituency Correspondence.

145 House of Commons, Debates, 19 March 1940.

146 Crookshank Diary, 19 March 1940.

147 Amery, *Diaries*, 19 March 1940.

148 Nicolson, *Diaries*, 19 March 1940.

149 Dick Law to Paul Emrys-Evans, 1 April 1940, Emrys-Evans Papers.

150 Channon, *Diaries*, 19 March 1940.

151 Paul Emrys-Evans to Anthony Eden, 17 March 1940, Emrys-Evans Papers; Harvey, *Diaries*, I, 11 September 1939.

152 Nicolson, *Diaries*, 17 January 1940.

153 Larry Witherell, 'Lord Salisbury's "Watching Committee" and the Fall of Neville Chamberlain, May 1940', *English Historical Review*, cxvi (2001), pp. 1134–66.

154 Martin Gilbert, ed., *Churchill War Papers*, Volume I: *At the Admiralty, September 1939 to May 1940*, London, 1993, Churchill to Salisbury, 19 December 1939.

155 Mima Harlech to Cranborne, n.d. [c. 3 October 1940], Salisbury Papers.

156 Amery, *Diaries*, 10 April 1940.

157 Salisbury to Cranborne, 13 April 1940, Salisbury Papers.

158 Cranborne to Emrys-Evans, 15 April 1940, Emrys-Evans Papers.

159 Amery, *Diaries*, 17 April 1940.

160 Cranborne to Salisbury, 18 April 1940, Salisbury Papers.

161 Salisbury to Cranborne, 17 April 1940, Salisbury Papers.

162 Amery, *Diaries*, 23 April 1940.

163 Salisbury to Cranborne, 20 April 1940, Salisbury Papers.

164 Lord Salisbury's Report on his Meeting with Winston Churchill, 20 April 1940, Salisbury Papers.

165 Lord Camrose, *Diary*, 3 May 1940, *Churchill War Papers*.

166 Cranborne to Emrys-Evans, 30 April 1940, with postscript dated 1 May, Emrys-Evans Papers.

167 Emrys-Evans to Cranborne, 5 May 1940, Salisbury Papers.

168 Paul Emrys-Evans (Secretary, Watching Committee) Diary, 23 April to 14 May, 1 May 1940, Emrys-Evans Papers.

169 Cranborne to Salisbury, 3 May 1940, Salisbury Papers.

170 Cranborne to Salisbury, 3 May 1940, Salisbury Papers.

171 Cranborne to Emrys-Evans, 30 April 1940, Emrys-Evans Papers.

172 Ronnie Tree to Cranborne, 2 May 1940, Salisbury Papers.

173 Cranborne to Salisbury, 3 May 1940, Salisbury Papers.

174 Cranborne to Emrys-Evans, 6 November 1947, Emrys-Evans Papers.

175 Crookshank Diary, 7 May 1940.

176 Nicolson, *Diaries*, 8 May 1940.

177 Amery, *Diaries*, 8 May 1940.

178 Cazalet Diary, 9 May 1940, Rhodes James, *Cazalet*.

179 Cazalet Diary, 7 and 8 May 1940, Rhodes James, *Cazalet*.

180 Emrys-Evans Diary, 8 May 1940.

181 Crookshank Diary, 8 May 1940.

182 Wallace Diary, 8 May 1940.
183 Amery, *Diaries*, 9 May 1940.
184 Nicolson, *Diaries*, 9 May 1940.
185 Graham Stewart, *Burying Caesar: Chamberlain, Churchill and the Battle for the Tory Party*, London, 1999, pp. 414–19.
186 Crookshank Diary, 10 May 1940.
187 Amery, *Diaries*, 10 May 1940.
188 Amery, *Diaries*, 11 May 1940.
189 Emrys-Evans Diary, 11 May 1940.
190 John Colville Diary, 10 May 1940, *Churchill War Papers*.
191 Amery, *Diaries*, 11 May 1940.
192 Emrys-Evans Diary, 11 May 1940.
193 Boothby to Churchill, 7 September 1939, *Churchill War Papers*.
194 Amery, *Diaries*, 12 May 1940.
195 Amery, *Diaries*, 13 May 1940.
196 Cranborne to Churchill, 14 May 1940, Churchill Papers, Churchill College, Cambridge, CHAR20/11.
197 Crookshank Diary, 14 May 1940.
198 Crookshank Diary, 15 May 1940.

Chapter 6: Churchillians

1 John Ramsden, *The Age of Churchill and Eden, 1940–1957*, London, 1995, p. 49.
2 Central Council Minutes, 27 March 1941, quoted in Ramsden, *Age of Churchill*, pp. 38–9.
3 Amery, *Diaries*, 17 June 1940.
4 Crookshank Diary, 3 July 1940.
5 Amery, *Diaries*, 18 June 1940.
6 Wallace Diary, 4 October 1940.
7 Crookshank Diary, 8 October 1940.
8 Headlam, *Diaries*, 11, 24 June 1940.
9 Macmillan Diary, 24 October 1951.
10 John Colville, *The Fringes of Power: Downing Street Diaries, 1939–1955*, 2 vols., London, 1985, 30 October 1940.
11 Lord Salisbury to Lord Cecil, 3 July 1940, Cecil Papers.
12 Cranborne to Evans, 17 May 1940, Emrys-Evans Papers.
13 Crookshank Diary, 3 October 1940.
14 Chandos, *Memoirs*, pp. 194–5.
15 Cranborne to Salisbury, Papers of 4th Marquess of Salisbury, Hatfield House, 9 October 1940.
16 Headlam, *Diaries*, 11, 4 October 1940.
17 Amery, *Diaries*, 3 October 1940; Wallace Diary, 3 October 1940.
18 Crookshank Diary, 4 October 1940.
19 Chandos, *Memoirs*, pp. 191–4.
20 Alex Danchev and Daniel Todman, eds., *Field Marshal Lord Alanbrooke: War Diaries, 1939–45*, London, 2001, note on Diary, 17 August 1940.
21 Cranborne to Salisbury, 27 October 1940, Salisbury Papers.
22 Crookshank Diary, 14 February 1941.
23 E. L. Hargreaves and M. M. Gowing, *Civil Industry and Trade*, London, 1952, pp. 303–14.
24 Chandos, *Memoirs*, pp. 204–5.
25 Crookshank Diary, 1 June 1941.
26 Winston S. Churchill, *The Second World War*, 111: *The Grand Alliance*, London, 1950, p. 312.
27 Lord Lloyd to Churchill, 4 January 1941, CHAR20/34.
28 Lord Cranborne's Opening Address, 28 January 1941, House of Lords Record Office, LH/D/7.
29 Cranborne to Churchill, 21 December 1940, CHAR20/11.
30 John Harvey, ed., *The War Diaries of Oliver Harvey, 1941–1945*, London, 1978 (hereafter Harvey, *Diaries*, 11), 24 July 1941.
31 Colville, *Diaries*, 1, 9 July 1941.
32 Cranborne to Evans, 31 July 1941, Emrys-Evans Papers.
33 Crookshank Diary, 3 June 1941.
34 Crookshank Diary, 8 August 1940.
35 Headlam, *Diaries*, 11, 3 May 1942.
36 Crookshank Diary, 13 June 1941.
37 Crookshank Diary, 14 February 1941.
38 Crookshank Diary, 1 July 1941. Apart from Crookshank and Macmillan the group comprised Paul Emrys-Evans, Tommy Dugdale, Charles Waterhouse, Osbert Peake, Harold Balfour and Dick Law. They were later joined by Ralph Assheton.
39 Crookshank Diary, 3 December 1941 and 21 January 1942.

40 Crookshank to Eden, 22 August 1941, FO954/31.

41 Crookshank to Eden, 3 January 1942, FO954/31.

42 Cranborne to Trenchard, 23 May 1941, Salisbury Papers.

43 Cranborne to Emrys-Evans, 31 August 1941, Emrys-Evans Papers.

44 Salisbury to Sir Archibald Sinclair (Secretary of State for Air), 26 November 1943 and Sinclair to Salisbury, 29 November 1943, quoted in Max Hastings, Bomber Command, London, 1981, pp. 204–5.

45 Crookshank Diary, 1 April 1941.

46 Cranborne to Evans, 31 August 1941, Emrys-Evans Papers.

47 Cranborne to Churchill, 18 November 1941, DO121/10A.

48 Churchill to Cranborne, 20 February 1942, in Winston S. Churchill, The Second World War, IV: The Hinge of Fate, London, 1951, pp. 76–7.

49 Headlam, Diaries, II, 21 November 1942.

50 Amery, Diaries, 16 January 1942.

51 Cranborne to Emrys-Evans, 13 February 1942, Emrys-Evans Papers, and Harvey, Diaries, II, 16 February 1941.

52 Anthony Eden's thoughts on the Cabinet, 16 February 1942, AP20/39.

53 Harvey, Diaries, II, 18 February 1942.

54 Harvey, Diaries, II, 19 February 1942.

55 Kevin Jeffery, ed., Labour and the Wartime Coalition: From the Diaries of James Chuter Ede, London, 1987, 20 February 1942.

56 Cranborne to Eden, 5 April 1942, AP20/39.

57 Crookshank Diary, 22 February 1942.

58 Crookshank to Churchill, 22 February 1942, in Diary.

59 Crookshank Speech, Oxford, May 1943, Crookshank MSS.

60 Crookshank Diary, 22 February 1942.

61 Crookshank Diary, 22 February 1942.

62 Crookshank to Stuart, 24 February 1942, in Diary.

63 Crookshank Diary, 28 February 1942.

64 Colville, Diaries, 5 March 1941.

65 Brooke, Diaries, 17 June 1941.

66 Colville Diaries, 9 July 1941.

67 David Dilks, ed., The Diaries of Sir Alexander Cadogan, 1938–1945, London, 1971, 27 June 1941; Lampson to Eden, 15 January 1942, FO954/5.

68 Robert Cecil was known to his family as Peter. His father, however, usually referred him as Robert when writing to third parties.

69 WP (42) 2nd Revise, April 1942 (Lyttelton's official report to Churchill on his tenure as Minister of State), PREM 11/305/7.

70 Lyttelton to Dalton, 10 July 1942, FO954/24.

71 Dossier for Lyttelton handed to Rucker by Colonel Thornhill, 28 July 1941, HS3/192; Alan Brooke, Diaries, 3 July 1942.

72 Report by Sir Frank Nelson on his visit to the Middle East, 30 July to 20 August 1941, HS3/193, and MEWC (S) (41) 1st Concs., 13 August 1941, HS3/193.

73 Artemis Cooper, Cairo in the War, 1939–1945, London, 1995, p. 260.

74 Crookshank to Eden, 22 August 1941, FO954/31.

75 Oliver Lyttelton to Julian Lyttelton, July 1941, CHAN 1, 8/9.

76 Lampson to Eden, 12 July 1941, FO954/5.

77 Oliver Lyttelton to Julian Lyttelton, July 1941, CHAN 1, 8/9.

78 Alan Brooke, Diaries, 13 February 1941 and 27 March 1942.

79 Lampson to Eden, 12 July 1941, FO954/5.

80 Oliver Lyttelton to Didi Lyttelton, 16 July 1941, CHAN 1, 8/9.

81 Martin Thomas, The French Empire at War, 1940–1945, Manchester, 1998, pp. 107–8.

82 Wilson to War Office, 16 July 1941, quoted in G. E. Maguire, Anglo-American Policy towards the Free French, Basingstoke, 1995, p. 37.

83 Lyttelton to Foreign Office, 29 July 1941, quoted in A. B. Gaunson, The Anglo-French Clash in Lebanon and

Syria, 1940–1945, Basingstoke, 1987, p. 55.

84 Lyttelton to Churchill, 15 August 1941, quoted in Gaunson, *Lebanon and Syria*, p. 57.

85 Chandos, *Memoirs*, pp. 247–8.

86 Lyttelton to Foreign Office, 17 August 1941, quoted in Gaunson, *Lebanon and Syria*, p. 59.

87 Lyttelton to Churchill, 24 July 1941, quoted in Gaunson, *Lebanon and Syria*, pp. 61–2.

88 Lampson to Eden, 15 August 1941, FO954/5.

89 Colville, *Diaries*, 30 July 1941.

90 Egremont, *Under Two Flags*, pp. 228–35; Jean Lacouture, *De Gaulle: The Rebel, 1890–1944*, London, 1990, pp. 303–4.

91 Quoted in Jean-Louis Crémieux-Brilhac, *La France libre: De l'appel du 18 juin à la Libération*, Paris, 1996, p. 165.

92 Bruce Lockhart, *Diaries*, 12 August 1941.

93 Information for Minister of State, [August 1941], CAB21/798.

94 Oliver Lyttelton to Didi Lyttelton, 21 August 1941, CHAN 1, 8/9.

95 Oliver Lyttelton to Didi Lyttelton, 22 October 1941, CHAN 1, 8/9.

96 Lampson to Eden, 15 August 1941, FO954/5.

97 Amery, *Diaries*, 2 October 1941.

98 Headlam, *Diaries*, 11, 2 October 1941.

99 Oliver Lyttelton to Didi Lyttelton, 21 August 1941, CHAN 1, 8/9.

100 Oliver Lyttelton to Didi Lyttelton, 22 October 1941, CHAN 1, 8/9.

101 Oliver Lyttelton to Rosemary Lyttelton, 5 February 1942, CHAN 1, 8/9.

102 Harvey, *Diaries*, 11, 9 February 1942; Amery, *Diaries*, 24 September 1941.

103 WP (42) 2nd Revise, April 1942 (Lyttelton's official report to Churchill on his tenure as Minister of State), PREM3/305/7.

104 Lampson to Eden, 24 June 1942, FO921/34.

105 Lyttelton to Eden, 5 February 1942, FO954/5.

106 Harvey, *Diaries*, 11, 9 and 11 February 1942.

107 Oliver Lyttelton to Rosemary Lyttelton, 5 February 1942, CHAN 1, 8/9.

108 Quoted in Cooper, *Cairo*, p. 128.

109 Harvie-Watt to Churchill, 24 April 1942, Harvie-Watt Papers, Churchill College, Cambridge, HARV2/1.

110 Chuter Ede, *Diaries*, 20 February 1942.

111 Harvey, *Diaries*, 11, 16 February 1942.

112 J. D. Scott and Richard Hughes, *The Administration of War Production*, London, 1955.

113 Address to the 1922 Committee, 8 February 1944, CHAN4/17.

114 Harvie-Watt to Churchill, 24 March 1944, HARV4/1.

115 Amery, *Diaries*, 7 May 1943 and 5 June 1943; Harvey, *Diaries*, 11, 6 May and 11 May 1943.

116 Harvie-Watt to Churchill, 27 March 1942, HARV2/1; Chüter Ede, *Diaries*, 24 March 1942.

117 Cranborne to Eden, 5 April 1942, AP20/39.

118 Headlam, *Diaries*, 11, 1 July 1942.

119 Channon, *Diaries*, 1 July 1942.

120 Headlam, *Diaries*, 11, 1 July 1942.

121 Harvie-Watt to Prime Minister, 25 June and 17 July 1942, HARV2/1.

122 Amery, *Diaries*, 7 May 1943.

123 Harvie-Watt to Churchill, 22 January 1943, HARV3/1.

124 Churchill to Roosevelt, 23 June 1944, in Warren Kimball, ed., *Churchill and Roosevelt: The Complete Correspondence*, 111, *Alliance Declining*, Princeton, N.J., London, 1984.

125 *Time*, 3 July 1944.

126 Churchill to Roosevelt, 26 June 1944, Kimball, *Correspondence*, 111.

127 Harvey, *Diaries*, 11, 18 July 1942.

128 Brooke, *Diaries*, 19 July 1943 and 6 March 1944.

129 Bruce Lockhart, *Diaries*, 6 May 1944.

130 Halifax to Churchill, Tel. 5741, 23 November 1942, BT87/15.

131 Note of telephone conversation

between Oliver Lyttelton and Winston Churchill, 22.34 to 22.39 hrs, 10 November 1942, BT87/12.

132 Harvie-Watt to Churchill, 25 May 1943, HARV3/1.

133 Colville, *Diaries*, 22 June 1941.

134 Churchill to Randolph Churchill, 18 April 1944, CHAR1/381; Colville, *Diaries*, 20 April 1944.

135 Law to Cranborne, 5 November 1943, Salisbury Papers.

136 Cranborne to Salisbury, 20 March 1944, Salisbury Papers.

137 Crookshank Diary, 19 and 20 May 1942.

138 Crookshank Diary, 24 June and 2 July 1942.

139 Headlam, *Diaries*, 11, 24 September 1942.

140 Harlech to Emrys-Evans, 24 November 1942, Emrys-Evans Papers.

141 Harvie-Watt to Churchill, 7 May 1942, HARV2/1; Crookshank Diary, 24 June 1942.

142 Crookshank Diary, 23 November 1942.

143 Crookshank Diary, 25 November 1942.

144 Crookshank Diary, 9 December 1942.

145 Crookshank Diary, 13 December 1942.

146 Harvey, *Diaries*, 11, 20 November 1942.

147 Crookshank Diary, 3 July 1942, and Harvey, *Diaries*, 11, 3 July 1942.

148 Crookshank Diary, 3 December 1942.

149 Crookshank Diary, 8 December 1942.

150 Amery, *Diaries*, 26 November 1942.

151 Churchill to Roosevelt, 12 December 1942, FO954/16.

152 Churchill to Crookshank, 16 October 1943, CHAR20/94B/201.

153 Strang to Eden, 21 December 1942, FO954/16.

154 Harvey, *Diaries*, 11, 28 December 1942.

155 Harvey, *Diaries*, 11, 30 December 1942.

156 Lord Egremont, *Wyndham and Children First*, London, 1968, p. 84.

157 Harold Macmillan, *The Blast of War, 1939–1945*, London, 1967, p. 272.

158 Eisenhower to Bedell Smith, 9 November 1942, quoted in Maguire, *Free French*, p. 64.

159 Macmillan to Eden, 27 February 1943, FO954/16.

160 Churchill to Macmillan, Tel. 1490, 2 August 1943, FO954/13.

161 Churchill to Macmillan, 5 March 1943, FO954/16.

162 Macmillan to Churchill, 13 March 1943, FO954/16

163 Macmillan to Eden, 27 February 1943, FO954/16.

164 Harold Macmillan, *War Diaries: The Mediterranean, 1943–1945*, London, 1984, 3 March 1943, 25 November 1943 and 23 March 1944.

165 Macmillan, *War Diaries*, 13 November 1943.

166 Macmillan to Churchill, 3 January 1944, PREM3/182/6.

167 Macmillan's notes of a paper by Kenneth Younger, [1943], FO660/15.

168 Charles de Gaulle, *Mémoires de Guerre*, 3 vols., Paris, 1954–9, 11, p. 93.

169 Sir Edward Spears, 'Memorandum on Anglo-French Relations in Syria and the Lebanon', 5 July 1943, quoted in Gaunson, *Lebanon and Syria*, p. 117.

170 Macmillan, *War Diaries*, 16 November 1943.

171 Maguire, *Free French*, p. 51.

172 Gaunson, *Lebanon and Syria*, pp. 147–9.

173 Macmillan to Eden, Tel. 1376, 3 August 1943, FO954/8.

174 Macmillan, *War Diaries*, 29 July 1943.

175 Elena Agarossi, *A Nation Collapses: The Italian Surrender of September 1943*, Cambridge, 2000, p. 69.

176 Harold Macmillan, 'An Armistice Quiz', 10 August 1943, quoted in Agarossi, *A Nation Collapses*.

177 Harvey, *Diaries*, 11, 1 September 1943.

178 Harvey, *Diaries*, 11, 25 September 1943 and 8 October 1943.

179 Macmillan to Eden, Tel. 413, 11 March 1944, FO954/14.

180 Macmillan, *War Diaries*, 20 April 1944.

181 Macmillan, *War Diaries*, 22 April 1944.

182 Macmillan, *War Diaries*, 8 April 1944.

183 Macmillan, *War Diaries*, 28 May 1944.

184 Macmillan, *War Diaries*, 9 June 1944.

185 Macmillan, *War Diaries*, 12 June 1944.

186 Harvey, *Diaries*, 11, 12 June 1944.

187 Bruce Lockhart, *Diaries*, 22 June 1944.

188 Churchill to Roosevelt, 12 September 1944, Kimball, *Correspondence*, III, p. 321.

189 Macmillan to Churchill, Tel. 353, 19 September 1944, FO954/14.

190 Duff Cooper to Eden, Tel. 54, 17 September 1944, FO954/14.

191 Bruce Lockhart, *Diaries*, 22 June 1944; Amery, *Diaries*, 6 September 1944.

192 Harvey, *Diaries*, 11, 8 October 1943.

193 Macmillan, *War Diaries*, 8 October 1943.

194 Macmillan, *War Diaries*, 4 October 1944 and 28 October 1944.

195 WP (42) 2nd Revise, April 1942, PREM3/305/7.

196 Macmillan, *War Diaries*, 8 October 1944.

197 Macmillan, *War Diaries*, 8 December 1944.

198 Churchill to Macmillan, 9 December 1944, FO954/14.

199 Macmillan, *War Diaries*, 11 December 1944.

200 Macmillan to Eden, 21 December 1944, FO954/11.

201 Harvey, *Diaries*, 11, 21 December 1944.

202 Jim Thomas to Emrys-Evans, Emrys-Evans Papers, 28 December 1944.

203 Colville, *Diaries*, 23 December 1944.

204 Colville, *Diaries*, 25 December 1944.

205 Colville to Martin, 26 December 1944, in *Diaries*.

206 Leeper to Cranborne, 23 March 1945, Salisbury Papers.

207 Brooke, *Diaries*, 5 February 1945.

208 Macmillan, *War Diaries*, 13 May 1945.

209 Sir Desmond Morton to Churchill, 13 June 1945, FO954/14.

210 Colville, *Diaries*, 20 May 1945.

211 Ian Mitchell, *The Cost of a Reputation*, Islay, 1998, pp. 144–5. Nikolai Tolstoy's book, *The Minister and the Massacres*, was published in April 1986, Macmillan died in December 1986.

212 Cranborne to Leeper, 19 April 1945, Salisbury Papers. Misidentified in the published *War Diaries* (p. 713), see Colville, *Diaries*, 19 May 1945.

213 Cranborne to Cecil of Chelwood, 15 April 1945, Cecil Papers.

214 Cranborne to Emrys-Evans, July 1945, Salisbury Papers.

215 Colville, *Diaries*, 22 June 1941.

216 Cranborne to Churchill, 3 April 1945, PREM4/31/7.

217 Churchill to Cranborne, 3 April 1945, PREM4/31/7.

218 Cranborne to Cecil of Chelwood, 15 April 1945, Cecil Papers.

219 Cadogan, *Diaries*, 24 May 1945.

220 BCM (45) 2 'Territorial trusteeship': Minutes of the 2nd Meeting of the British Commonwealth, 5 April 1945, in S. R. Ashton and S. E. Stockwell, eds., *British Documents on the End of Empire: Imperial Policy and Colonial Practice, 1925–1945*, London, 1996, I, Document 41.

221 Cranborne to Oliver Stanley, Tel. 300, 14 May 1945, PREM4/31/7.

222 Halifax to Churchill, Tel. 461, 27 May 1945, PREM4/31/7, and Cranborne to Emrys-Evans, 29 May 1945, Emrys-Evans Papers.

223 Paul Gore-Booth (San Francisco) to Michael Wright (Washington), 4 June 1945, FO371/50723.

224 Cranborne to Emrys-Evans, 29 April 1945, Emrys-Evans Papers.

225 Cranborne to Emrys-Evans, 29 May 1945, Emrys-Evans Papers.

226 George Blaker to Roger Stevens, 4 May 1945, BT87/22.

227 Churchill to Eden, 10 May 1945, PREM4/31/7.

228 Macmillan, *War Diaries*, 21 and 26 May 1945; Cadogan, *Diaries*, 6 July 1945.

229 Kevin Jefferys, *The Churchill Coalition and Wartime Politics, 1940–1945*, Manchester, 1990, pp. 156–8.

230 Speech in Hull, 2 July 1945, CHAN 11, 4/17.

231 Macmillan, *War Diaries*, 22 May

1945, and Crookshank Diary, 28 May 1945.

232 Crookshank Diary, 10 May 1945.

Chapter 7: Tories

1 Headlam, *Diaries*, 11, 26 July 1945.
2 Cranborne to Emrys-Evans, 19 January 1946, Emrys-Evans Papers.
3 Ramsden, *Appetite for Power*, p. 361.
4 Headlam, *Diaries*, 11, 2 August 1947.
5 Headlam, *Diaries*, 11, 28 January 1947.
6 *Evening Standard*, 29 June 1948.
7 Macmillan, *War Diaries*, 5 October 1944.
8 Macmillan, *War Diaries*, 28 November 1944.
9 Crookshank Diary, 27 August 1945.
10 Cranborne to Emrys-Evans, 26 August 1945, Emrys-Evans Papers.
11 Jim Thomas to Emrys-Evans, 18 August 1945, Emrys-Evans Papers.
12 Bob Brand to Didi Lyttelton, 12 May 1945, CHAN 1, 5/3.
13 AMC Board Minutes, 22 August 1945, AMC Papers.
14 Oliver Lyttelton to Walter Gardner, 25 August 1945, AMC Papers.
15 AMC Board Minutes, 21 November 1945, AMC Papers.
16 AEI Board Minutes, 13 September 1945, GEC Archives, Chelmsford.
17 AEI Board Minutes, 8 November 1945, GEC Archives.
18 AEI Board Minute 8727, 29 March 1951, GEC Archives.
19 Crookshank Diary, 9 October 1945.
20 Cranborne to Salisbury, 30 August 1945, Salisbury Papers.
21 Cranborne to Emrys-Evans, 17 September 1945, Emrys-Evans Papers.
22 Lyttelton to Churchill, [1946], CHAN 11, 4/5.
23 Headlam, *Diaries*, 11, 6 July 1948.
24 Headlam, *Diaries*, 11, 10 March 1947.
25 Headlam, *Diaries*, 11, 2 August 1947.
26 Oliver Lyttelton to Didi Lyttelton, 13 July [1913], CHAN 11, 4/1.
27 Stuart, *Within the Fringe*, p. 105.

28 Bruce Lockhart, *Diaries*, 4 September 1947.
29 Macmillan to Dorothy Macmillan, 26 August 1949, Macmillan Diary.
30 Salisbury to Emrys-Evans, 12 May 1948, Emrys-Evans Papers.
31 Salisbury to Macmillan (letter not sent), 30 October 1950, Salisbury Papers.
32 Macmillan to Dorothy Macmillan, 22 August 1949, Macmillan Diary.
33 Crookshank Diary, 20 January 1946.
34 Bruce Lockhart, *Diaries*, 30/31 March 1946.
35 Dick Law to Emrys-Evans, 30 October 1945, Emrys-Evans Papers.
36 Cranborne to Emrys-Evans, 12 December 1945, Emrys-Evans Papers.
37 Dick Law to Emrys-Evans, 25 August 1945, Emrys-Evans Papers.
38 Dick Law to Emrys-Evans, [1946], Emrys-Evans Papers.
39 Emrys-Evans to Cranborne, 10 February 1946, Salisbury Papers.
40 Cranborne to Emrys-Evans, 17 September 1945, Emrys-Evans Papers.
41 Crookshank Diary, 19 December 1945.
42 Cranborne to Emrys-Evans, 1 April 1946 and 5 April 1946, Emrys-Evans Papers.
43 Cranborne to Woolton, 25 February 1946; Cranborne to Salisbury, [1946], Cranborne to Emrys-Evans, 27 March 1946, Salisbury Papers.
44 Cranborne to Eden, 21 August 1946, AP20/14.
45 Cranborne to Thomas, 26 April 1946, Cilcennin Papers.
46 Cranborne to Salisbury, 7 May 1946, Salisbury Papers.
47 Cranborne to Emrys-Evans, 17 January 1947, Emrys-Evans Papers.
48 Cranborne to Emrys-Evans, 9 January 1947, Emrys-Evans Papers.
49 Cranborne to Rab Butler, 7 November 1952, RAB B19.
50 Salisbury to Lord Rankeillour, 18 June 1947, Salisbury Papers; Salisbury to Thomas, 16 September 1947, Cilcennin

Papers. On the death of his father Cranborne became 5th Marquess of Salisbury.

51 Cranborne to Emrys-Evans, 16 September 1946, Emrys-Evans Papers.

52 Macmillan to Dorothy Macmillan, 24 August and 2 September 1949, Macmillan Diary.

53 Bruce Lockhart, *Diaries*, 30/31 March 1946.

54 Crookshank Diary, 25 February 1947.

55 Ramsden, *Age of Churchill*, p. 102.

56 Stuart, *Within the Fringe*, pp. 145–7. Luke 14:16–24.

57 Headlam, *Diaries*, II, 8 February 1951.

58 House of Commons, Debates, 5 July 1951.

59 Ina Zweiniger-Bargielowska, 'Consensus and Consumption: Rationing, Austerity and Controls after the War', in Harriet Jones and Michael Kandiah, eds., *The Myth of Consensus: New Views on British History, 1945–1964*, Basingstoke, 1996, pp. 79–96.

60 Cranborne to Thomas, 26 April 1946, Cilcennin Papers.

61 Cranborne to Eden, 9 August 1946, AP20/14.

62 Headlam, *Diaries*, II, 28 October 1947.

63 Cranborne to Eden, 9 August 1946, AP20/14.

64 Cranborne to Emrys-Evans, 16 September 1946, Emrys-Evans Papers.

65 Harriet Jones, 'A Bloodless Counter-revolution: The Conservative Party and the Defence of Inequality, 1945–51,' in Jones and Kandiah, *The Myth of Consensus*, pp. 1–16.

66 Cranborne to Thomas, 14 June 1946, Cilcennin Papers.

67 Oliver Lyttelton, Speech to Trade and Industry and Finance Committee, 15 November 1945, CHAN II, 4/17.

68 Speech to 1922 Committee, 7 October 1942, CHAN II, 4/17.

69 Helen Mercer, 'Industrial Organization and Ownership and a new Definition of the Post-war "Consensus" ', in Jones and Kandiah, *The Myth of Consensus*, pp. 139–56.

70 Speech to London Conservative Association, 2 March 1944, CHAN II, 4/17.

71 Speech to Federation of University Conservative Associations, 26 November 1943, CHAN II, 4/17.

72 John Singleton, 'Labour, the Conservatives and Nationalisation', in Robert Millward and John Singleton, *The Political Economy of Nationalization in Britain, 1920–1950*, Cambridge, 1995, pp. 13–36.

73 Speech to 1922 Committee, 7 October 1942, CHAN II, 4/17.

74 Macmillan Diary, 17 July 1952.

75 Lyttelton to Butler, 26 September 1947, RAB G/19.

76 Oliver Lyttelton, Address to Conservative Members Committee, House of Commons, 18 March 1948, CHAN II, 4/17.

77 Cranborne to Emrys-Evans, 26 August 1945, Emrys-Evans Papers.

78 Institute of Directors, *Annual Reports*, 1949 and 1951.

79 Michael Kandiah, 'Conservative Leaders, Consensus and Strategy, 1945–1964', in Jones and Kandiah, *The Myth of Consensus*, pp. 58–78.

80 Geoffrey Hodgson, 'The Steel Debates: The Tory Recovery', in Michael Sissons and Philip French, *The Age of Austerity*, London, 1963, pp. 295–316.

81 Singleton, 'Labour, the Conservatives and Nationalisation', in Singleton and Millward, *Nationalization*, p. 23.

82 Channon, *Diaries*, 16 November 1948.

83 Ruggo Ranieri, 'Partners and Enemies: the Government's Decision to Nationalize Steel, 1944–1948', in Singleton and Millward, *Nationalization*, pp. 275–308.

84 Crookshank Diary, 17 November 1948.

85 Headlam, *Diaries*, II, 9 May 1949.

86 David Reynolds, 'Churchill's Writing of History: Appeasement, Autobiography and *The Gathering*

Storm', *TRHS*, XI (2001), pp. 221–47.

87 Cranborne to Woolton, 25 February 1946, Salisbury Papers.

88 Cranborne to Lord Fairfax, 3 July 1946, Salisbury Papers.

89 CP (46) 382, Note by Leader of the House of Lords, 15 October 1946, PREM8/1059.

90 Cranborne to Salisbury, 27 February 1946, Salisbury Papers.

91 Attlee to Addison, 15 October 1947, PREM8/1059.

92 Salisbury to Cranborne, 18 December 1942, Salisbury Papers.

93 Memorandum by Lord Cranborne, undated [1947], Salisbury Papers.

94 Tommy Lascelles to Cranborne, 17 January 1946, Salisbury Papers.

95 Ramsden, *Age of Churchill*, p. 192.

96 Lord Salisbury's notes on House of Lords Reform: Note on Committee of Opposition Peers to prepare for the Parliament Act when it reached the House of Lords, December 1947, Salisbury Papers.

97 C. J. Harris to C. A. C. J. Hendriks, 13 January 1947, LH/B/5.

98 Fifth Meeting of Party Leaders, 18 March 1948, PREM8/1059.

99 Cranborne to Emrys-Evans, 12 May 1948, Emrys-Evans Papers.

100 Sixth Meeting of Party Leaders, 20 April 1948, PREM8/1059.

101 Norman Brook to Attlee, 17 March 1948, PREM8/1059.

102 Headlam, *Diaries*, II, 24 July 1947.

103 Cranborne to Cecil of Chelwood, 28 June 1948, Salisbury Papers.

104 Ritschel, *The Politics of Planning*, pp. 343–4.

105 Cranborne to Thomas, 14 June 1946, Cilcennin Papers.

106 Cranborne to Cecil of Chelwood, 28 March 1951, Salisbury Papers.

107 Cranborne to Thomas, 14 June 1946, Cilcennin Papers.

108 Ramsden, *Age of Churchill*, pp. 153–5.

109 Chandos, *Memoirs*, p. 334.

110 Crookshank Diary, 8 February 1951.

111 Crookshank Diary, 13 February 1951.

112 *Daily Mirror*, 27 September 1951.

Chapter 8: Ministers

1 Crookshank Diary, 11 June 1952.

2 Macmillan Diary, 21 June 1952 and 24 June 1952.

3 Macmillan Diary, 23 April 1953 and 27 April 1953.

4 Macmillan Diary, 6 May 1953.

5 Macmillan Diary, 12 January 1953.

6 Macmillan Diary, 17 January 1953.

7 Crookshank Diary, 23 January 1953.

8 Macmillan Diary, 22 March 1953.

9 Macmillan Diary, 27 October 1951.

10 Macmillan Diary, 18 March 1952.

11 Salisbury to Emrys-Evans, 29 October 1951, Emrys-Evans Papers.

12 Lyttelton to Churchill, 27 July 1954, CHAN II, 4/5.

13 Karl Hack, 'British Intelligence and Counter-Insurgency in the Era of Decolonisation: The Example of Malaya', *Intelligence and National Security*, 14 (1999), pp. 124–55.

14 W. A. Muller to Hugh Fraser, 22 December 1951, CO1022/165.

15 Richard Stubbs, *Hearts and Minds in Guerrilla Warfare: The Malayan Emergency*, Oxford, 1989, pp. 136–9.

16 J. D. Higham to Acting High Commissioner, Tel. 1263, 19 November 1951, CO1022/7.

17 Churchill to Lyttelton, 5 November 1951, PREM11/152.

18 Security Arrangements for Oliver Lyttelton's visit to Malaya in 1951, CO1022/81.

19 E. R. G. Larwill (Jemina Estate, Siliau, Negri Sembilan) to Revd. 'Tubby' Clayton (All Hallows, Byward Street), 20 December 1951, CO967/241.

20 Lyttelton to MacDonald, Tel. 66, 1 February 1952, CO1022/51.

21 Chandos, *Memoirs*, p. 371.

22 Appendix IX of C (51) 59, 21 December 1951, CO1022/51.

23 Lyttelton to Churchill, Tel. 1214, 8 December 1951, PREM11/639; Minute by Lyttelton, 13 May 1952, and J. D. Higham to J. P. Morton (Security Service/Director of

Intelligence-designate), 22 May 1952, CO1022/51.

24 PM (51) 10, Lyttelton to Churchill, CO1022/101.

25 Lyttelton to MacDonald, Tel. 588, 30 December 1951, CO1022/101.

26 Lyttelton to Churchill, Tel. 29, 4 January 1952, CO1022/101.

27 Lyttelton to Churchill, Tel. 1214, 8 December 1951, PREM11/639; Sir Thomas Lloyd to J. D. Paskin, 29 January 1952, CO1022/101.

28 Lyttelton to Churchill, 16 November 1953, A. J. Stockwell, ed., *British Documents on the End of Empire: Malaya*, III, London, 1995, Document 308.

29 MacDonald to Lyttelton, Tel. 736, 31 January 1952, CO1022/101.

30 Lyttelton to MacDonald, Tel. 65, 1 February 1952, CO1022/101.

31 J. C. Bottoms to Angus Mackintosh, February 1952, CO1022/101.

32 Salisbury to Emrys-Evans, 29 October 1951, Emrys-Evans Papers.

33 Macmillan Diary, 25 January 1952.

34 Iain Macleod to Salisbury, 22 May 1952, MH80/60.

35 Macmillan Diary, 27 October 1951; Crookshank Diary, 27 October 1951.

36 Macmillan Diary, 7 December 1951; Evelyn Shuckburgh to David Pitblado, 10 December 1951, PREM11/162.

37 Notes for Lobby Conference, 1 February 1952, MH80/59.

38 Churchill to Macmillan, 8 June 1952, PREM11/689.

39 Macmillan Diary, 15 July 1952.

40 CC (52) 66, 8 July 1952.

41 Marples to Brown, 24 June 1953, HLG101/473.

42 H/POL/66, Memorandum by Sir Percy Mills, September 1952, HLG101/506.

43 J. G. Owen, Notes on C (53) 230, 20 August 1953, T227/806.

44 Salisbury to Churchill, 10 September 1952, Salisbury Papers; Macmillan Diary, 16 September 1953.

45 Macmillan Diary, 30 December 1951.

46 Macmillan Diary, 11 July 1952;

Macmillan Diary, 1 to 5 September 1952; Note by R. A. Butler on Macmillan's 'Grand Design', 23 January 1953, T227/805.

47 Wilkinson to Hickinbotham, 15 May 1952, HLG101/505.

48 Minutes of Meeting between Harold Macmillan, Ernest Marples, Sir John Wrigley and S. F. Wilkinson, 14 November 1951, HLG101/504.

49 Macmillan Diary, 13 March 1952; Emrys-Evans to Cranborne, 29 July 1941, Emrys-Evans Papers.

50 Crookshank Diary, 27 March and 3 April 1952.

51 Iain Macleod to Harry Crookshank, 31 March 1952, MH80/60.

52 Salisbury to Emrys-Evans, 29 October 1951, Emrys-Evans Papers.

53 Crookshank Diary, 17 September 1952 and Macmillan Diary, 11–12 September 1952.

54 Macmillan Diary, 10 October 1952, and Crookshank Diary, 9–11 October 1952.

55 Memorandum by the Lord Privy Seal, 26 June 1952, PREM11/235; Crookshank Diary, 25–27 November 1952 and 30 November 1952.

56 Macmillan Diary, 12 December 1952.

57 See file PREM11/724.

58 GEN 423/4th meeting, 22 April 1953, CAB130/83.

59 Colville, *Diaries*, 24 July 1953.

60 Peter Boyle, ed., *The Churchill–Eisenhower Correspondence, 1953–1955*, Chapel Hill, N. C., 1990, Churchill to Eisenhower, 7 May 1953.

61 Churchill to Eisenhower, 9 March 1954, *Churchill–Eisenhower Correspondence*.

62 Colville, *Diaries*, 19 July 1953.

63 Macmillan Diary, 12 May 1953.

64 Macmillan Diary, 1–7 June 1953; Macmillan to Churchill, 9 June 1953, and Salisbury to Churchill, 11 June 1953, PREM11/428.

65 Macmillan Diary, 2 and 4 July 1953.

66 Macmillan Diary, 4 July 1953.

67 Colville, *Diaries*, October 1953.

68 Macmillan Diary, 20 December 1953.

69 Macmillan Diary, 1 September 1953.
70 Macmillan Diary, 2 July 1953.
71 Macmillan Diary, 30 June 1953.
72 Salisbury to Emrys-Evans, 3 July 1953, Emrys-Evans Papers.
73 Macmillan Diary, 6 July 1953.
74 Eisenhower to Churchill, 6 July 1953, *Churchill–Eisenhower Correspondence*; Salisbury to Butler, 11 July 1953, PREM11/425; Evelyn Shuckburgh, *Descent to Suez: Diaries, 1951–1956*, London, 1986, 24 July 1953.
75 Colville, *Diaries*, 11, 31 July to 4 August 1953.
76 Salisbury to Churchill, 11 June 1953, PREM11/428.
77 Minutes of 2nd Bipartite Meeting between Salisbury and Dulles, 14 July 1953, PREM11/425.
78 Colville, *Diaries*, 21 July 1953, and Macmillan Diary, 31 July 1953 and 2 August 1953.
79 Shuckburgh, *Diaries*, 21 July 1953.
80 Macmillan Diary, 10 August 1953, and Colville, *Diaries*, 31 July to 4 August 1953.
81 Jim Thomas to Emrys-Evans, 1 August 1953, Emrys-Evans Papers; Shuckburgh, *Diaries*, 26/27 August 1953; Macmillan Diary, 1 September 1953.
82 Salisbury to Emrys-Evans, 23 December 1953, Emrys-Evans Papers.
83 Salisbury to Churchill, 27 September 1953 and Salisbury to Churchill, n.d. [September 1953], Salisbury Papers.
84 Macmillan Diary, 13 December 1953 and 20 December 1953.
85 Macmillan Diary, 6 June 1953.
86 Macmillan Diary, 6 July 1953.
87 Lyttelton to Churchill, 3 December 1953, CHAN 11, 4/5.
88 Macmillan Diary, 30 August 1953 and 28 April 1954.
89 Lyttelton to Eden, [May] 1954, AP23.
90 Crookshank Diary, 13 April 1954 and Macmillan Diary, 15 April 1954.
91 Macmillan Diary, 28 April 1954.
92 Macmillan to Churchill, 18 June 1954, in Macmillan Diary.
93 Churchill to Salisbury, 22 April 1954, Salisbury Papers.
94 Crookshank Diary, 7 November 1954.
95 Macmillan Diary, 6 July 1954.
96 Macmillan Diary, 7 July 1954.
97 Macmillan Diary, 8 July 1954.
98 Colville, *Diaries*, 16 July 1954.
99 Macmillan Diary, 9 July 1954.
100 Shuckburgh, *Diaries*, 12 July 1954; Salisbury to Churchill, draft letter of resignation, July 1954, Salisbury Papers.
101 Macmillan Diary, 10 July 1954.
102 Macmillan Diary, 14 July 1954.
103 Macmillan Diary, 16 July 1954.
104 Colville, *Diaries*, 16 July 1954.
105 Lyttelton to Churchill, 27 July 1954, CHAN 11, 4/5.
106 Lyttelton to Churchill, 31 July 1954, CHAN 11, 4/5.
107 Macmillan Diary, 23 July 1954, and Crookshank Diary, 23 July 1954.
108 Macmillan Diary, 31 July 1954.
109 Colville, *Diaries*, August 1954.
110 Crookshank Diary, 26 July 1954; Shuckburgh, *Diaries*, 28 July 1954.
111 Macmillan Diary, 24 August 1954; Colville, *Diaries*, August 1954.
112 Crookshank Diary, 8 September 1954.
113 Macmillan Diary, 24 August 1954.
114 Macmillan Diary, 25 August 1954.
115 Macmillan Diary, 27 August 1954.
116 Crookshank Diary, 11 October 1954.
117 Macmillan Diary, 2 October 1954.
118 Macmillan Diary, 5 October 1954.
119 Macmillan Diary, 10 October 1954.
120 Salisbury to Emrys-Evans, 28 November 1954, Emrys-Evans Papers.
121 Crookshank to Eden, 12 October 1954 (misdated 1955 in manuscript), Salisbury Papers.
122 Robert Cary to Patrick Buchan Hepburn, 18 December 1954, HAILES 4/13.
123 Macmillan Diary, 22 December 1954.
124 Crookshank Diary, 17 January 1955.
125 Macmillan Diary, 17 February 1955; Macmillan Diary, 12 and 14 March 1955, and Crookshank Diary, 14 March 1955.

126 Colville, *Diaries*, 29 March 1955.
127 Robert Cary to Patrick Buchan Hepburn, 11 April 1955, HAILES 4/13.
128 Lyttelton to Eden, 14 April 1955, PREM11/883.
129 Eden to Lyttelton, 17 April 1955, PREM11/883.
130 Colville, *Diaries*, April 1955.

Chapter 9: Successors

1 Robert Cary to Patrick Buchan-Hepburn, 14 December 1955, HAILES 4/13.
2 Patrick Buchan-Hepburn to Eden, 19 July 1955, PREM 11/820.
3 Crookshank Diary, 6 October 1955.
4 Crookshank Diary, 15 December 1955.
5 Crookshank Diary, 19 December 1955.
6 Robert Cary to Patrick Buchan-Hepburn, 20 December 1955, HAILES 4/13.
7 Crookshank Diary, 20 December 1955.
8 Programme of Installation by the Grand Master, Lord Scarborough (Roger Lumley), 16 September 1954, Crookshank Papers.
9 Salisbury to Eden, 10 August 1955, PREM11/874.
10 Eden to Lloyd George, 9 April 1955, PREM11/824; Eden note on Woolton to Eden, 31 October 1955, PREM11/2029.
11 Norman Brook to Eden, 14 November 1955 (Lords), PREM11/2029, and Norman Brook to Eden, 10 November 1955 (Immigration), PREM11/2920.
12 Macmillan to Eden and Crookshank, 14 January 1955, PREM11/824; Freddie Bishop to Eden, 4 October 1956, PREM11/2030.
13 Duncan Sandys to Eden, 18 May 1956, and David Eccles to Salisbury, 10 October 1956, PREM11/2029.
14 Salisbury to Eden, 31 December 1956, PREM11/2121.
15 Freddie Bishop to Macmillan, 29 January 1957, PREM11/2121.
16 Lord Salisbury to Eden, 3 December 1955, PREM11/2029.
17 Macmillan to Churchill, 2 November 1955, FO800/679.
18 Salisbury to Eden, 5 April 1956, Salisbury Papers.
19 Alec Home to Salisbury, 10 April 1956, Salisbury Papers.
20 Sir Edwin Plowden to Salisbury, 11 April 1956, Salisbury Papers.
21 Brendan Bracken to W. S. Robinson, 28 January 1955, quoted in Charles Lysaght, 'Dear Brendan and Master Harold', in Richard Aldous and Sabine Lee, eds., *Harold Macmillan: Aspects of a Political Life*, pp. 67–96.
22 Woolton Diary, 5 April 1955, quoted in Ramsden, *Age of Churchill and Eden*, p. 288.
23 Macmillan to Eden, 8 June 1955, Eden to Macmillan, 10 June 1955, Macmillan to Eden, 11 June 1955, FO800/666.
24 Handwritten note by Harold Macmillan, 10 November 1955, FO800/686.
25 Macmillan to Butler, April 1956, RAB G/30.
26 Oliver Harvey to Paul Emrys-Evans, 20 October 1956, Emrys-Evans Papers.
27 Macmillan to Butler, 10 August 1955, FO800/668.
28 S. J. Ball, 'Macmillan and British Defence Policy', in Richard Aldous and Sabine Lee, eds., *Harold Macmillan and Britain's World Role*, Basingstoke, 1996, p. 153.
29 Macmillan to Butler and Eden, 'Dizzy with Success', 23 August 1955, FO800/679.
30 Oliver Harvey to Paul Emrys-Evans, 20 October 1956, Emrys-Evans Papers.
31 Macmillan to Eden, 29 August 1955, PREM11/886; Dutton, *Eden*, pp. 272–3.
32 Crookshank Diary, 6 October 1955.
33 Macmillan to John Foster Dulles, Tel. 6136, 21 December 1955, FO800/689; Shuckburgh, *Diaries*, 21 December 1955.
34 Lewis Johnman, 'Opportunity Knocks: Macmillan at the Treasury, 1955–1957', in Aldous and Lee, *Harold Macmillan: Aspects of a Political Life*, p. 34.
35 Macmillan to Eden, 11 February 1956; Note for the Record of a Meeting between Macmillan and Eden;

Macmillan to Eden, 13 February 1956, T172/2127.

36 Richard Cockett, ed., *My Dear Max*, London, 1990, pp. 189–90.

37 Macmillan Diary, 30 July 1956.

38 Macmillan Diary, 1 August 1956.

39 Macmillan Diary, 22–30 September 1956.

40 Scott Lucas, 'The Cost of Myth: Macmillan and the Illusion of the "Special Relationship"', in Aldous and Lee, *Macmillan: Aspects of a Political Life*, pp. 16–31; Nigel Ashton, 'Managing Transition: Macmillan and the Utility of Anglo-American Relations', in Aldous and Lee, *Macmillan: Aspects of a Political Life*, pp. 242–54; Nigel Ashton, 'Macmillan and the Middle East', in Aldous and Lee, *Harold Macmillan and Britain's World Role*, pp. 37–66.

41 Macmillan Diary, 12 September 1956.

42 Macmillan Diary, 27 July 1956.

43 Macmillan Diary, 3 August 1956.

44 Keith Kyle, *Suez*, London, 1991, pp. 170–73.

45 Macmillan to Eden, 27 August 1956, T172/2135; Scott Lucas and Alistair Morey, '"The Hidden Alliance": The CIA and MI6 before Suez', *Intelligence and National Security*, 15 (2000), pp. 95–120.

46 Macmillan Diary, 9 August 1956.

47 Macmillan Diary, 20 August 1956; Salisbury to Eden, 22 August 1956, PREM11/1113; Salisbury to Eden, 13 September 1956, CAB124/1210.

48 Salisbury to Macmillan, August 1956, CAB124/1210.

49 Macmillan Diary, 19 August 1956; Macmillan Diary, 18 September 1956.

50 Macmillan Diary, 24 August and 28 August 1956.

51 Salisbury to Eden, 16 October 1956, PREM11/2029.

52 Anthony Nutting, *No End of a Lesson: The Story of Suez*, London, 1967, pp. 81–3.

53 Colville, *Diaries*, p. 393.

54 Unpublished interview with John Foster Dulles for *US News and World Report*, 21 April 1956, quoted in Charles G. Cogan, 'From the Politics of Lying to the Farce at Suez: What the US Knew', *Intelligence and National Security*, 13 (1998), pp. 100–101.

55 Scott Lucas, *Divided We Stand: Britain, the US and the Suez Crisis*, London, 1991, p. 282.

56 Bracken to Beaverbrook, 7 December 1956, *Dear Max*, p. 199.

57 Kyle, *Suez*, pp. 504–50.

58 *Sunday Times*, 30 December 1956.

59 Macmillan to Butler (meeting with Dulles), 13 December 1956; Macmillan to Butler (meeting with Humphrey), 13 December 1956, T172/2137.

60 Salisbury to Eden, Tel. 75, 4 December 1956, PREM11/1548.

61 Macmillan Diary, 3 February 1957.

62 Crookshank Diary, 3 March 1957.

63 A. H. K. Slater to Salisbury (with Salisbury's annotations), 15 January 1957, Salisbury Papers.

64 Kilmuir, *Political Adventure*, p. 285.

65 Crookshank Diary, 6 March 1957.

66 Sir Burke Trend to Sir Timothy Bligh, 12 December 1963, PREM11/4115.

67 Lord Salisbury's account of Anthony Eden's resignation and subsequent events, Salisbury Papers.

68 Colville, *Diaries*, pp. 393–4.

69 Macmillan Diary, 3 February 1957.

70 Crookshank Diary, 2 December 1934 and 26 July 1939.

71 Macmillan to Salisbury, 11 January 1957, PREM11/2029.

72 Salisbury to Churchill, 5 November 1952, PREM11/779; Lorna Arnold, 'The Birth of the UK Atomic Energy Authority', *Atom*, 225 (1975), pp. 94–9.

73 Salisbury to Macmillan, 11 January 1957, PREM11/2551.

74 Salisbury to Macmillan, 10 January 1957, PREM11/2029.

75 Sir Norman Brook to Macmillan, 11 January 1957, PREM11/2551.

76 Harry Slater to Salisbury, 15 January 1957, Salisbury Papers.

77 Harry Slater to Freddie Bishop (and

reply), 16 January 1957, CAB124/1114.

78 Macmillan Diary, 3 February 1957;
    Slater to Salisbury, 15 January 1957,
    Salisbury Papers.
79 Salisbury's account, Salisbury Papers.
80 Note by R. A. Butler, 22 October 1957,
    RAB/G31.
81 Macmillan to Chancellor of the
    Exchequer, 22 January 1957, T172/2152.
82 Macmillan to Salisbury, 29 March
    1957, Salisbury Papers.
83 Oliver Lyttelton, Memoir of Harold
    Macmillan for the *Daily Telegraph*,
    18 April 1958, CHAN 11, 4/18.
84 Harold Watkinson (Minister of
    Transport) to Macmillan, 11 January
    1957, PREM11/1816.
85 Macmillan Diary, 9 February 1957.
86 Scott Lucas, 'The Cost of Myth:
    Macmillan and the Illusion of the
    "Special Relationship"', in Aldous
    and Lee, *Macmillan*, p. 25.
87 Salisbury to Lew Douglas, 11 March
    1957, Salisbury Papers.
88 Ashton, 'Middle East', *World Role*,
    p. 47.
89 Ashton, 'Managing Transition', in
    Aldous and Lee, *Macmillan*, p. 244.
90 Sir John Harding to Secretary of State
    for the Colonies, Tel. 506, 6 March
    1956, PREM11/1248.
91 Chandos to Salisbury, 2 April 1957,
    Salisbury Papers.
92 Macmillan to George Bell, Bishop of
    Chichester, 20 March 1956, T172/2127.
93 Macmillan Diary, 15 March 1957; CC
    (57) 21st, 18 March 1957.
94 Macmillan Diary, 19 March 1957.
95 Macmillan to Michael Fraser,
    17 February 1957, PREM11/1816.
96 Macmillan to Chancellor of the
    Exchequer, 2 March 1957, PREM11/
    1816.
97 F. A. Bishop to John Hunt,
    12 February 1957, PREM11/2029.
98 Salisbury to Macmillan, 19 March
    1957, PREM11/2029.
99 Lord Home to Macmillan, 5 April
    1957, PREM11/2029.
100 Memorandum dictated by Macmillan,
    15 October 1963, PREM11/5008.

101 Salisbury to Emrys-Evans, 8 January
    1962, Emrys-Evans Papers.
102 Salisbury to Macmillan, 23 March
    1957, Salisbury Papers.
103 Macmillan Diary, 24 March 1957.
104 CC (57) 23rd, 25 March 1957.
105 Macmillan to Salisbury, n.d.
    [24 March 1957], Salisbury Papers.
106 Macmillan Diary, 27 March 1957.
107 CC (57) 25th, 28 March 1957.
108 S. J. Ball, 'Selkirk in Singapore',
    Twentieth Century British History, 10
    (1999), p. 167.
109 Harry Slater to Salisbury (message
    from PM via Lord Privy Seal),
    28 March 1957, Salisbury Papers.
110 Richard Lamb, *The Macmillan Years:
    The Emerging Truth*, London, 1995,
    pp. 28–9.
111 Macmillan Diary, 1 April 1957.
112 Macmillan Diary, 31 March 1957.
113 Macmillan Diary, 14 May 1957.
114 Macmillan to Salisbury, 29 March
    1957, Salisbury Papers.
115 Macmillan Diary, 31 March 1957.
116 Macmillan Diary, 4 April 1957.
117 Macmillan Diary, 8 April 1957.
118 Macmillan's marginal note on Home
    to Macmillan, 17 April 1957, PREM11/
    1791.
119 Home to Macmillan (reporting a
    conversation with Salisbury the
    previous day), 17 April 1957, PREM11/
    1791.
120 Salisbury to Coleraine, 20 May 1957,
    Salisbury Papers.
121 Bracken to Salisbury, 16 April 1957,
    Salisbury Papers.
122 Chandos to Salisbury, 2 April 1957,
    Salisbury Papers.
123 Salisbury to Eden, 14 April 1957,
    AP23/60.
124 Macmillan Diary, 18 April 1957.
125 Macmillan Diary, 22 April 1957.
126 Macmillan Diary, 14 May 1957.
127 Macmillan Diary, 4 May 1957.
128 Macmillan Diary, 13 May 1957.
129 Macmillan Diary, 15 May 1957.
130 Macmillan Diary, 17 May 1957.
131 Salisbury to Eden, 21 May 1957, AP23/
    60.

132 Salisbury to Coleraine, 20 May 1957,
Salisbury Papers.

133 Salisbury to Eden, 21 May 1957, AP23/
60.

134 Salisbury to Eden, 23 July 1957, AP23/
60.

135 Salisbury to Eden, 6 June 1957, AP23/
60.

136 Ian Harvey, *To Fall Like Lucifer*,
London, 1971.

137 Lyttelton to Eden, 9 September 1957,
AP23/17.

138 Macmillan Diary, 21 November 1958.

139 Philip Murphy, *Alan Lennox-Boyd*,
Tauris, London, 1999, pp. 81–2.

140 Crookshank Diary, 30 September 1957.

141 Crookshank Diary, 24 September 1958;
Crookshank Diary, 27 March 1959.

142 Crookshank Diary, 3 May 1959.

143 Crookshank Diary, 6 July 1959;
Crookshank Diary, 30 July 1959;
Crookshank Diary, 22 October 1959.

144 Crookshank Diary, 8 January 1961.

145 Macmillan Diary, 4 June 1960.

146 Crookshank Diary, 5 January 1961.

147 Crookshank Diary, 27 July 1961 (the
last entry).

148 Crookshank Diary, 11 July 1960.

149 Macmillan Diary, 20 December 1960.

150 Macmillan Diary, 15 September 1961.

151 Macmillan Diary, 30 September 1961.

152 Macmillan Diary, 8 October 1961.

153 Macmillan Diary, 19 October 1961.

154 DS to Macmillan, 17 October 1961,
PREM11/3694.

155 Tribute to Harry Crookshank,
19 October 1961, PREM11/3694.

Chapter 10: Enemies

1 Freedom of Salisbury speech,
24 January 1956, CAB124/2602.

2 Impressions of the Federation
(written in Palazzo Morosini),
CAB124/2602; A. H. K. Slater to H.
Smedley (CRO), 28 February 1956,
DO35/4668.

3 Salisbury to Eden, 8 March 1959,
AP23/60.

4 Salisbury to Welensky, 4 May 1957,
Welensky Papers, Rhodes House

Library, Oxford, 665/1; Norman
Brook to PM, 3 July 1958, PREM11/
3239.

5 Welensky to Salisbury, 22 May 1957,
Salisbury Papers.

6 Salisbury to Welensky, 27 May 1957,
Salisbury Papers.

7 Notes of a Meeting between
Cranborne, Macmillan and Sir Henry
Moore, 25 August 1942, CO967/57.

8 Harold Macmillan to Sir George
Gater, 15 August 1942, CO967/57.

9 S. J. Ball, 'Macmillan, the Second
World War and the Empire', in
Aldous and Lee, *Macmillan*,
pp. 167–72.

10 Salisbury to Macmillan, 4 February
1961, PREM11/3414.

11 Philip E. Hemming, 'Macmillan and
the End of the British Empire in
Africa', in Aldous and Lee, *Macmillan*,
pp. 99–100; Macmillan Diary,
10 November 1959; Macmillan to Iain
Macleod, 6 August 1960, PREM11/
3077; Macmillan to Welensky,
16 December 1960, PREM11/3485.

12 Macmillan Diary, 12 December 1960.

13 Harvie-Watt to Churchill, 7 May 1942,
HARV2/1; Ronald Hyam,
'Bureaucracy and "Trusteeship" in the
Colonial Empire', in Judith Brown
and William Roger Louis, eds., *The
Oxford History of the British Empire*,
IV: *The Twentieth Century*, Oxford,
1999, pp. 255–79.

14 Minute by Macmillan, 3 July 1959,
based upon De Zulueta to Bligh,
1 July 1959, PREM11/2587.

15 Salisbury to Macmillan, 4 February
1961, PREM11/3414.

16 Burke Trend to Norman Brook,
13 October 1959, PREM11/2784;
Macmillan's notes on Burke Trend to
Norman Brook, 13 October 1959,
PREM11/2784.

17 Macmillan Diary, 25 February 1962.

18 Home to Macmillan, 18 April 1957,
PREM11/2477; C. O. I. Ramsden to
Macmillan, 22 April 1957, PREM11/
2477; Home to Macmillan,
5 September 1958, PREM11/2477; Alan

Lennox-Boyd to Macmillan, 10 September 1958, PREM11/2477.

19 Salisbury to Eden, 8 March 1959, AP23/60.

20 Salisbury to Eden, 23 September 1959, AP23/60; Philip de Zulueta to Tim Bligh, 1 July 1959, PREM11/2587.

21 Extract from Records of Conversations between the Prime Minister and the Foreign Secretary in Paris, 9 and 10 March 1959, CO936/562.

22 Macmillan Diary, 24 May 1959.

23 Macmillan Diary, 13 July 1959.

24 CID C.52/166, Kenya CID: Memorandum on Mau Mau intimidation, 12 September 1952, CO822/438.

25 Note of a Meeting between Lyttelton and Sir Philip Mitchell, 19 February 1952, CO822/543; Lyttelton to Churchill, 9 September 1952, PREM11/472; Lyttelton to OAG, Kenya (Henry Potter), Tel. 574, 16 September 1952; Willy Teeling to Lyttelton, 22 October 1952, CO822/438; Verbatim Report: Meeting between Lyttelton and European Elected Members held at Government House, 30 October 1952, CO822/460; Meeting between Lyttelton and Nominated Official Members, 30 October 1952, CO822/460.

26 Lyttelton to Churchill, Tel. 218, 7 March 1954, PREM11/696.

27 Randall Heather, 'Intelligence and Counter-Insurgency in Kenya, 1952–1956', *Intelligence and National Security*, 5 (1990), pp. 57–83.

28 Interview with Lord Chandos by Max Beloff, 27 February 1970, CHAN 11, 4/16; Charles Douglas-Home, *Evelyn Baring: The Last Proconsul*, Collins, London, 1978, pp. 216–76; David Percox, 'British Counter-Insurgency in Kenya, 1952–1956: Extension of Internal Security Policy or Prelude to Decolonization?', *Small Wars and Insurgencies*, 9 (1998), pp. 46–101.

29 Macmillan Diary, 4 March 1954.

30 Baring to Lyttelton, Tel. 616, 10 October 1952, PREM11/472; Baring to Lyttelton, 24 November 1952, CO822/450; Baring to Lyttelton, Tel. 773, 23 November 1952, CO822/450; Baring to Lyttelton, 24 November 1952, CO822/450; Sir Thomas Lloyd to Baring, Tel. 826, 26 November 1952, CO822/454; Lyttelton to Baring, Tel. 870, 4 December 1952; Lyttelton to Baring, Tel. 141, 12 February 1953, CO822/471; Baring to Lyttelton, Tel. 282, 9 March 1953, CO822/471; Baring to Lyttelton, Tel. 457, 19 April 1953, CO822/440; Baring to Lyttelton, 13 October 1953, CO822/441; Baring to Sir Frederick Crawford, Tel. 1150, 5 December 1953, CO822/499.

31 Macmillan Diary, 4 June 1959.

32 Macmillan Diary, 13 July 1959.

33 Macmillan Diary, 22 June 1959.

34 Chandos to Lennox-Boyd, 29 July 1959, quoted in Murphy, *Lennox-Boyd*.

35 Macmillan to Norman Brook, 28 December 1959, PREM11/3075.

36 John Wyndham to Tim Bligh, 8 April 1964, PREM11/4937.

37 Tim Bligh to John Wyndham, 26 May 1964, PREM11/4937.

38 Sir John Maud to Macmillan, 3 February 1960, PREM11/3073.

39 Iain Macleod to Macmillan, 25 May 1959, PREM11/2583.

40 Ronald Prain, *Reflections on an Era: Fifty Years of Mining in Changing Africa*, Metal Bulletin Books, London, 1981, pp. 144–5.

41 David Hunt to Macmillan, 15 January 1960, PREM11/3065.

42 Note of a Meeting of Ministers held at Salisbury, 19 January 1960, PREM11/3065; Welensky to Macmillan (Cape Town), Track 14, 3 Feb 1960, PREM11/3075; Sir Humphrey Gibbs to Lord Home, 6 February 1960, PREM11/3085; Macmillan Diary, 7 February 1960; Macmillan to Home, Tel. 198, 12 February 1960, PREM11/3075; Tim Bligh to Macmillan, 31 March 1960, PREM11/3076; Salisbury to Welensky, 4 April 1960, Salisbury Papers.

43 Tim Bligh to Macmillan, 3 August 1960, PREM11/3077.

44 Macmillan to Tim Bligh, 22 September 1960, PREM11/3078.

45 Roy Welensky to Salisbury, 21 September 1960, Salisbury Papers.

46 Monckton Commission, Note by Tim Bligh, 20 October 1960, PREM11/3941.

47 Welensky to Salisbury, 10 November 1960, WP665/2.

48 Salisbury to Welensky, 21 November 1960, Salisbury Papers. Welensky preserved a large number of letters Macmillan sent him in the autumn/winter of 1959. Presumably, the 'second letter' in Salisbury's burnt dossier was Macmillan to Welensky, 26 November 1959.

49 Salisbury to Welensky, 27 September 1960, WP665/2.

50 Salisbury to Churchill, 24 August 1953, PREM11/5209.

51 Wyndham to Macmillan, 14 March 1961, PREM11/4608.

52 Note for the Record of a Meeting between the Prime Minister, the Commonwealth Relations Secretary and the Colonial Secretary, 16 June 1961, PREM11/3492.

53 Macmillan Diary, 26 February 1962.

54 Lord Lambton's interview with the PM, 3 August 1961, WP665/9.

55 Macmillan Diary, 2 November 1960.

56 Macmillan Diary, 7 November 1960.

57 Tim Bligh to Macmillan, 14 March 1961, PREM11/3495.

58 Milverton to Salisbury, January 1961, Salisbury Papers.

59 Salisbury to Emrys-Evans, 24 December 1960, Emrys-Evans Papers.

60 Macmillan Diary, 11 December 1960.

61 Lambton to Salisbury, 18 February 1961, Salisbury Papers.

62 Salisbury to Emrys-Evans, 24 December 1960, Emrys-Evans Papers.

63 Salisbury to Welensky, 31 December 1960, Salisbury Papers.

64 Salisbury to Eden, 7 January 1961, AP23/60.

65 P. L. H. Bristol to Salisbury, 2 January 1961, Salisbury Papers.

66 Salisbury to Emrys-Evans, 19 February 1962, Emrys-Evans Papers. The party's file on the Monday Club is cited in Murphy, *Party Politics*.

67 Macmillan Diary, 4 February 1963.

68 Welensky to Salisbury, 27 January 1961, Salisbury Papers.

69 Macmillan Diary, 27 January 1961; Note for the Record of a Meeting between the Prime Minister, the Commonwealth Relations Secretary and the Colonial Secretary, 8 February 1961, PREM11/3486; Iain Macleod to Macmillan, 13 February 1961, PREM11/3486; Macmillan Diary, 26 February 1961.

70 Macmillan Diary, 4 February 1961.

71 Salisbury to John Biggs-Davison, 11 February 1960, Salisbury Papers.

72 Salisbury to Macmillan, 18 February 1961, PREM11/4608.

73 Minutes of Watching Committee, 16 February 1961, Salisbury Papers.

74 Minutes of Watching Committee, 23 February 1961, Salisbury Papers.

75 Richard Law to Paul Emrys-Evans, 25 February 1961, Emrys-Evans Papers.

76 Salisbury to Welensky, 21 July 1963, WP665/5.

77 Robert Shepherd, *Iain Macleod*, London, 1994, pp. 224–7.

78 Lambton to Welensky, [1961], WP635/9.

79 Redmayne (Chief Whip) to Macmillan, 17 March 1961, PREM11/3495; Macmillan Diary, 24 March 1961; Macmillan to Burke Trend, 30 March 1961, PREM11/3489; Coleraine to Salisbury, 10 May 1961, Emrys-Evans Papers; Lord Lambton's interview with Prime Minister, 3 August 1961, WP635/9.

80 Hailsham to Salisbury, 10 March 1961; Salisbury to Hailsham, 10 March 1961, Salisbury Papers.

81 Coleraine to Macmillan, 23 March 1961, PREM11/4608.

82 Note for the Record: Africa – Lord Salisbury's 'Watching' Committee,

22 March 1961, PREM11/4608. The delegation comprised four peers, Salisbury, Dick Law (Coleraine), Godfrey Huggins (Milverton), Lloyd, and six MPs, Biggs-Davison, Turton, Hinch, Grimston, John Barlow and John Eden.

83 Macmillan Diary, 22 June 1961.

84 Salisbury to Emrys-Evans, [March 1961], Emrys-Evans Papers; Letter of Resignation from Board of BSAC, 31 March 1961, Salisbury Papers.

85 Philip de Zulueta to Sir Charles Harris, 24 March 1961, PREM11/4608.

86 Salisbury to Macmillan, 22 March 1961, PREM11/4608.

87 Coleraine to Macmillan, 23 March 1961, PREM11/4608.

88 Macmillan to Burke Trend, 30 March 1961, PREM11/3489.

89 Macmillan Diary, 24 March 1961 and 25 March 1961.

90 Minutes of Watching Committee, 26 April 1961, Salisbury Papers; Macmillan Diary, 2 May 1961; Macmillan Diary, 4 May 1961; Macmillan Diary, 5 May 1961; Coleraine to Salisbury, 10 May 1961, Salisbury Papers; Iain Macleod to Macmillan, 10 May 1961, PREM11/3490; Note on Iain Macleod to Macmillan, 10 May 1961, PREM11/3490.

91 Macmillan Diary, 17 May 1961; Macmillan Diary, 3 June 1961; Macmillan Diary 11 June 1961.

92 Macmillan Diary, 9 September 1961.

93 Salisbury to Eden, 13 January 1959, AP23/60.

94 Macmillan Diary, 2 November 1961.

95 Macmillan Diary, 5 November 1961.

96 Macmillan Diary, 13 November 1961.

97 Alan James, Britain and the Congo Crisis, 1960–1963, Macmillan, Basingstoke, 1996.

98 Macmillan Diary, 6 August 1960.

99 Macmillan Diary, 16 September 1960.

100 Ralph Bunche to Dag Hammarskjöld, 16 July 1960, quoted in James, Britain and the Congo.

101 Macmillan Diary, 3 December 1960.

102 Keith Kyle, The UN in the Congo, Coleraine, 1995.

103 Summary of a Meeting between Macmillan and Sir Roy Welensky, 7 November 1961, PREM11/3192.

104 Salisbury to Welensky, 1 June 1961, WP665/3.

105 Macmillan to Welensky, 28 June 1958, PREM11/3239; Note for Macmillan by Burke Trend, 17 November 1958, PREM11/2477; Report of an SIS officer on a tour of Africa 'South of the Sudan', Norman Brook to Macmillan, 16 December 1959, PREM11/2585.

106 Macmillan to Home, 1 November 1961, PREM11/3192.

107 Macmillan to Welensky, Tel. 879, 9 May 1961, PREM11/3090.

108 Hailsham to Macmillan, 14 September 1961, PREM11/3091.

109 Macmillan to Home, PREM11/3091.

110 Account of Meeting between Macmillan, Edward Heath, George Lansdowne and Roger Stevens, Lord Privy Seal (Edward Heath) to Lord Home (New York), Tel. 3741, 13 September 1961, PREM11/3091.

111 Hailsham to Macmillan, 14 September 1961, PREM11/3091.

112 Salisbury to Welensky, 1 June 1961, WP665/3.

113 Salisbury to Boyd of Merton, 14 September 1961, Salisbury Papers.

114 Dilhorne to Macmillan, 11 February 1963, PREM11/4419.

115 Boyd of Merton to Salisbury, 10 July 1962, Salisbury Papers.

116 Minutes of Watching Committee, 14 November 1961, Salisbury Papers.

117 Salisbury to Welensky, 16 September 1961, WP665/3.

118 Home to Rusk, 29 November 1961, and Macmillan's comments on Home to Rusk, 29 November 1961, PREM11/3192.

119 Welensky to Salisbury, 17 September 1961, WP665/3.

120 Colyton to Salisbury, 12 February 1961, WP602/1.

121 Kyle, UN in the Congo.

122 Macmillan Diary, 19 December 1961.
123 Minutes of Watching Committee, 21 September 1961, Salisbury Papers; Salisbury to Macmillan, 21 September 1961, PREM11/4608.
124 Home (New York) to Macmillan, Tel. 1481, 23 September, PREM11/3091.
125 Macmillan to Home, 1 November 1961, PREM11/3192; Macmillan to Heath, 25 September 1961, PREM11/3091; Heath to Macmillan, 28 September 1961, PREM11/3091.
126 Macmillan Diary, 18 December 1961.
127 Macmillan Diary, 19 December 1961.
128 Macmillan Diary, 18 December 1961.
129 Macmillan Diary, 3 February 1962.
130 Macmillan Diary, 22 June 1961.
131 Salisbury to Paul Williams, 3 June 1961, Salisbury Papers.
132 Salisbury to Boyd of Merton, 14 September 1961, Salisbury Papers.
133 Salisbury to Coleraine, 15 December 1961, Salisbury Papers.
134 Macmillan Diary, 2 January 1962; Macmillan Diary, 19 January 1962; Sandys to Garner, 24 February 1962, PREM11/3943; Macmillan Diary, 28 February 1962; Minutes of Watching Committee, 1 March 1962, Salisbury Papers; Hinchingbrooke to Salisbury, 2 March 1962, Salisbury Papers.
135 Minutes of Watching Committee, 1 March 1962, Salisbury Papers.
136 Knox Cunningham to Bligh, 28 February 1962, PREM11/3943; Macmillan Diary, 28 February 1962; Note of a Meeting between Macmillan, Sandys, Maudling and Welensky, 1 March 1962, PREM11/3943; Macmillan Diary, 8 March 1962; Welensky to A. E. P. 'Robbie' Robinson (CAF High Commissioner in London), 16 March 1962, WP229/3.
137 Macmillan Diary, 14 May 1962.
138 Salisbury to Eden, 18 March 1963, AP23/60; Welensky to Salisbury, 6 April 1962, Salisbury Papers; Salisbury to Eden, 27 April 1963, AP23/60.
139 Minutes of Watching Committee,

8 May 1962, Salisbury Papers; Bligh to Wyndham, 15 May 1963, PREM11/4426.
140 Salisbury to Macmillan, 24 May 1963, PREM11/4426.
141 Salisbury to Welensky, 17 June 1962, Salisbury Papers.
142 Salisbury to Turton, 19 November 1962, Salisbury Papers.
143 Salisbury ('the middle of the Suez Canal') to Eden, 18 March 1963, AP23/60.
144 Salisbury to Turton, 6 February 1963, Salisbury Papers.
145 Salisbury to Emrys-Evans, 9 February 1963, Emrys-Evans Papers.
146 Salisbury to Butler, 21 April 1963, RAB E18/16; Salisbury to Eden, 27 April 1963, AP23/60.
147 Macmillan Diary, 24 March 1962.
148 Macmillan Diary, 31 March 1962.
149 Macmillan Diary, 26 December 1962 and 28 January 1963.
150 Macmillan Diary, 15 March 1963.
151 Salisbury to Welensky, 16 June 1963, WP665/5.
152 Welensky to Salisbury, 27 July 1963, Salisbury Papers; Salisbury to Welensky, 7 August 1963, WP665/5.
153 Salisbury to Welensky, 24 June 1963, Salisbury Papers.
154 Salisbury to Welensky, 7 September 1963, WP665/5.
155 Moucher Devonshire to Salisbury, n.d. [1963], Salisbury Papers.
156 Macmillan Diary, 7 October 1963.
157 Macmillan to Home, 9 October 1963, PREM11/5008.
158 Macmillan Diary, 14 October 1963.
159 Lord Aldwyn's notes of preferences of the House of Lords, 17 October 1963, PREM11/5008.
160 Lyttelton to Butler, 11 October 1963, RAB E18/3.
161 Macmillan Diary, 17, 18 and 19 October 1963.

Chapter 11: Relics

1 Martin Redmayne to Sir Alec Douglas-Home, 23 April 1964,

PREM11/4608. (On becoming prime minister, Home had renounced his hereditary title of Earl of Home to serve in the House of Commons as Sir Alec Douglas-Home.)

2 Salisbury to Welensky, 7 July 1964, WP770/3; Minutes of Watching Committee, 16 July 1964, Salisbury Papers.

3 Dick Coleraine to Salisbury, 30 October 1964, Salisbury Papers.

4 Salisbury to Welensky, 23 October 1965, WP770/4.

5 Alan Megahey, *Humphrey Gibbs, Beleaguered Governor: Southern Rhodesia, 1929–1969*, Basingstoke, 1998, pp. 103–4.

6 Lyttelton to Eden, 1966, AP23.

7 Iain Macleod, 'The Tory Leadership', *Spectator*, 17 January 1964.

8 *Forward*, 13 June 1958.

9 *Harper's*, 17 August 1961.

10 Robert Jones and Oliver Marriott, *Anatomy of a Merger: A History of GEC, AEI and English Electric*, London, 1970, pp. 226–55.

11 Chandos to Eric Ball, March 1960, quoted in Jones and Marriott, *Anatomy*.

12 Meeting between Oliver Lyttelton and Christopher Hinton, 18 July 1963, GEC63/140; Oliver Marriott to Arnold Weinstock, 14 November 1967, GEC Archives; Weinstock to Marriott, 16 November 1967, GEC Archives; Weinstock to Marriott, 4 December 1967, GEC Archives.

13 A. M. Allen to A. H. K. Slater, 16 February 1956, AB16/1783.

14 George Walker, draft of speech for Lord Chandos, October 1961, quoted in Jones and Marriott, *Anatomy*.

15 Minutes of AEI 1962 AGM, GEC Archives.

16 Extension of Lord Chandos's term of office, 15 November 1962, GEC62/198.

17 Chandos to Salisbury, 28 January 1970, CHAN 11, 4/16.

18 Chandos, *Peace to War*, pp. 67–75.

19 Support for the National Theatre, Memorandum by Burke Trend, 11 May 1960, T227/2130.

20 Oliver Lyttelton, Speech to Authors' Club Dinner, 9 March 1960, CHAN 11, 4/17.

21 *Harper's*, 17 August 1961.

22 Lyttelton to Eden, 20 February 1961, AP23/17.

23 Lyttelton to Eden, 20 February 1961, AP23/17; Lyttelton to Charles Lyttelton (Governor-General of New Zealand), 7 March 1961, CHAN 11, 4/7.

24 Lyttelton to Welensky, 2 January 1963, WP597/9; Welensky to Lyttelton, 21 December 1962, WP597/9.

25 Butler to Macmillan (Nassau), CODEL 50, 20 December 1962, PREM11/4418; Macmillan to Butler, 14 December 1962 and Macmillan to Butler, CODEL 51, 22 December 1962; Butler to Macmillan (letter from Swinton), 1 January 1963, PREM11/4418; Dilhorne to Macmillan, 11 February 1963, PREM11/4419; Macmillan's notes on Dilhorne to Macmillan, 11 February 1963, PREM11/4419; Dilhorne to Butler, 22 February 1963, PREM11/4419.

26 Lyttelton to Eden, 14 February 1963, AP23/17; Colyton to Welensky, 21 February 1963, WP602/2; Welensky to Salisbury, 22 February 1963, Salisbury Papers.

27 Lyttelton to Eden, 14 October 1971, AP23/17.

28 Colyton to Welensky, 21 February 1963, WP602/2.

29 Meeting with Lord Chandos, Briefing Minute for Macmillan, 17 March 1960, PREM11/3820; Lord Chancellor to Macmillan, 21 March 1960, PREM11/3820.

30 Chandos to Lloyd, 22 June 1960, T227/2130.

31 Support for the National Theatre, Memorandum by Burke Trend, 11 May 1960, T227/2130.

32 Trend to Thomas Padmore, 28 June 1960, T227/2130.

33 Colville, *Diaries*, 18 August 1953.

34 Note for the Record of a Meeting between Macmillan and the Minister of Education, 16 November 1960, PREM11/3820.

35 R. C. Griffiths to Sir Ronald Harris, 22 November 1960, T227/2130.

36 Harris to Couzens, 30 January 1961, T227/2138.

37 Norman Brook to Macmillan, 27 February 1961, PREM11/3820.

38 Harris to Couzens, 30 January 1961, T227/2138.

39 Chancellor of the Exchequer to Macmillan, 14 December 1960, PREM11/3820; Griffiths to Harris, 28 March 1961, T227/2132; Note to Chancellor of the Exchequer, T227/2132.

40 Note for the Record of a meeting between Lord Chandos and the Chancellor of the Exchequer, 30 March 1961, T227/2132.

41 Chandos to Lloyd, 12 June 1961, T227/2133.

42 Michael Cary to Macmillan, 3 April 1962, PREM11/3820; Note for the Record of Chancellor's meeting with Lords Chandos and Cottesloe, 23 June 1961, T227/2133

43 Chandos to Lloyd, 30 June 1961, T227/2133; Griffiths to Harris, 10 July 1961, T227/2133.

44 Padmore to Harris, 13 October 1961, T227/2133; Note for the Record of Lord Cottesloe's report on his talk with Lord Chandos, 11 October 1961, T227/2134.

45 Note for the Record of a meeting between the Chief Secretary to the Treasury and Lord Chandos, 21 December 1961, T227/2134.

46 Griffiths to Harris, 12 February 1962, T227/2134.

47 Norman Brook to Macmillan, 14 May 1962, PREM11/3820.

48 Michael Cary to Macmillan, PREM11/3820.

49 Note for the Record of a meeting between the Chief Secretary to the Treasury and Sir Thomas Padmore, 13 April 1962, T227/2134.

50 Draft letter to Lord Cottesloe, T227/2135; Harris to Hubback (record of a conversation with Sir Douglas Logan), 8 May 1962, T227/2135.

51 Harris to Hubback, 8 May 1962, T227/2135.

52 Note for the Record of Lord Chandos's suggestions, 18 June 1962, T227/2136.

53 Cottesloe to Harris, 15 May 1962, T227/2135.

54 Chandos to Brooke, 5 July 1962, T227/2136.

55 Cottesloe to Harris, 15 May 1962, T227/2135.

56 Henry Brooke to Ronald Harris, 12 July 1962, T227/2136.

57 Harris to Burrett, 6 March 1964, T227/2138.

58 Harris to John Boyd-Carpenter, 15 August 1962, T227/2137.

59 K. E. Couzens to Harris, 29 July 1963, T227/2138.

60 Couzens to Harris, 20 January 1964, T227/2138.

61 Harris to Padmore, 19 October 1962, T227/2137.

62 Couzens to Caulcott, 14 October 1963, T227/2138; Couzens to Harris, 20 January 1964, T227/2138.

63 Mary Loughnane to Couzens, 2 December 1963, T227/2138.

64 Harris to Couzens, 11 October 1963, T227/2138.

65 Couzens to Chandos, 9 March 1965, T227/2140.

66 Mary Loughnane to J. Rampton, 23 September 1965, T227/2140.

67 Brief for a meeting between Miss Lee, Lord Chandos, Lord Cottesloe and Lord Goodman, 20 December 1966, ED245/12.

68 Note for the Record of Lord Chandos's suggestions, 18 June 1962, T227/2136.

69 Kathleen Tynan, *The Life of Kenneth Tynan*, London, 1987, pp. 1–248.

70 Peter Lewis, *The National: A Dream Made Concrete*, London, 1991, pp. 31–46; John Elsom and Nicholas Tomalin, *The History of the National*

Theatre, London, 1978, pp. 189–205.

71 Margaret Ward, *Rolf Hochhuth*, Boston, 1977, pp. 48–70.

72 Rolf Hochhuth, *Soldiers: An Obituary for Geneva*, New York, 1968.

73 Quoted in Tynan, *Tynan*, p. 253.

74 Chandos to Eden, n.d. [1967], AP23/17.

75 Donald Akenson, *Conor: A Biography of Conor Cruise O'Brien*, Cornell University Press, Ithaca, 1994, pp. 211–14.

76 Chandos to Eden, 14 February 1969, AP23/17.

77 Conor Cruise O'Brien, *Murderous Angels: A Political Tragedy in Black and White*, Hutchinson, London, 1969.

78 Conor Cruise O'Brien, *Memoir: My Life and Times*, London, 1998, pp. 258–64.

79 Chandos to Eden, 14 February 1969, AP23.

80 Lewis, *The National*, p. 48.

81 Chandos, *Memoirs*, p. 35.

82 *Embusqué* was the term for those who deliberately avoided front-line service.

83 Macmillan Diary, 4 May 1959.

84 Macmillan Diary, 13 November 1960.

85 Macmillan to George Christ, 30 July 1961, PREM11/3479.

86 Macmillan to Chandos, 11 November 1968, CHAN II, 4/12.

87 Chandos, *Memoirs*, p. xvi.

88 Macmillan, *Winds of Change*, pp. 79–80.

89 Chandos, *Memoirs*, pp. 44–5.

90 Macmillan, *Winds of Change*, pp. 92–3.

91 Macmillan Diary, 27 January 1959.

92 Chandos, *Memoirs*, p. 66.

93 Theatre Workshop, *Oh! What a Lovely War*, London, 1965. First Performance 19 March 1963.

94 Alan Clark, *The Donkeys*, London, 1961.

95 Chandos, *From Peace to War*, pp. 83–4.

96 Chandos, *From Peace to War*, pp. 130–35.

97 Macmillan to Chandos, 11 November 1968, CHAN II, 4/12.

98 Ava Waverley to Chandos, 29 October 1968, CHAN II, 4/12.

99 Philip Toynbee, 'Review of *From Peace to War*', *Observer*, 27 October 1968.

100 Macmillan, *Winds of Change*, pp. 98–100.

101 Chandos, *Memoirs*, pp. 35–6.

102 F. S. L. Lyons, 'Review of *From Peace to War*', *Irish Times*, 9 November 1968.

103 Macmillan, *Winds of Change*, p. 98.

104 Ava Waverley to Chandos, 29 October 1968, CHAN II, 4/12.

105 David Lloyd, *Battlefield Tourism: Pilgrimage and the Commemoration of the Great War in Britain, Australia and Canada, 1919–1939*, Oxford, 1998, pp. 148–50.

106 Beatrice Brocklebank, ed., *Geoffrey Madan: A Memoir*, privately printed, 1984.

107 Madan, *Notebook*.

108 Oliver Lyttelton to Anthony Eden, 1966, AP23/17.

109 *Harper's*, 17 August 1961.

110 Diana Cooper to Duff Cooper, 30 March 1924, in *A Durable Fire*.

111 Jeanne MacKenzie, *The Children of the Souls*, London, 1986, p. 262.

112 Roy Strong, *The Roy Strong Diaries, 1967–1987*, London, 1997, 16 June 1970.

113 Strong, *Diaries*, 30 January 1973.

114 Macmillan to Salisbury, 9 March 1965, Salisbury Papers.

INDEX